Economics and Political Implications of International Financial Reporting Standards

Efobi Uchenna
Covenant University, Nigeria

Matthias Nnadi
Rivers State University of Science and Technology, Nigeria

Sailesh Tanna
Coventry University, UK

Francis Iyoha
Covenant University, Nigeria

A volume in the Advances in Finance, Accounting, and Economics (AFAE) Book Series

BUSINESS SCIENCE Reference
An Imprint of IGI Global

Published in the United States of America by
Business Science Reference (an imprint of IGI Global)
701 E. Chocolate Avenue
Hershey PA, USA 17033
Tel: 717-533-8845
Fax: 717-533-8661
E-mail: cust@igi-global.com
Web site: http://www.igi-global.com

Library of Congress Cataloging-in-Publication Data

Names: Uchenna, Efobi, 1984- editor.
Title: Economics and political implications of international financial reporting standards / Efobi Uchenna, Matthias Nnadi, Sailesh Tanna, and Francis Iyoha, editors.
Description: Hershey : Business Science Reference, 2016. | Includes bibliographical references and index.
Identifiers: LCCN 2015046858| ISBN 9781466698765 (hardcover : alk. paper) | ISBN 9781466698772 (ebook)
Subjects: LCSH: Financial statements--Standards. | Accounting--Standards.
Classification: LCC HF5681.B2 E296 2016 | DDC 657/.30218--dc23 LC record available at http://lccn.loc.gov/2015046858

This book is published in the IGI Global book series Advances in Finance, Accounting, and Economics (AFAE) (ISSN: 2327-5677; eISSN: 2327-5685)

British Cataloguing in Publication Data
A Cataloguing in Publication record for this book is available from the British Library.

For electronic access to this publication, please contact: eresources@igi-global.com.

Advances in Finance, Accounting, and Economics (AFAE) Book Series

Ahmed Driouchi
Al Akhawayn University, Morocco

ISSN: 2327-5677
EISSN: 2327-5685

Mission

In our changing economic and business environment, it is important to consider the financial changes occurring internationally as well as within individual organizations and business environments. Understanding these changes as well as the factors that influence them is crucial in preparing for our financial future and ensuring economic sustainability and growth.

The **Advances in Finance, Accounting, and Economics (AFAE)** book series aims to publish comprehensive and informative titles in all areas of economics and economic theory, finance, and accounting to assist in advancing the available knowledge and providing for further research development in these dynamic fields.

Coverage

- Corporate Finance
- Stock Market
- Internet Banking
- Economics of Risks, Uncertainty, Ambiguity, and Insurance
- Microeconomics
- E-finance
- Comparative Accounting Systems
- Borrowing and Lending
- Development Economics
- Health Economics

IGI Global is currently accepting manuscripts for publication within this series. To submit a proposal for a volume in this series, please contact our Acquisition Editors at Acquisitions@igi-global.com or visit: http://www.igi-global.com/publish/.

The Advances in Finance, Accounting, and Economics (AFAE) Book Series (ISSN 2327-5677) is published by IGI Global, 701 E. Chocolate Avenue, Hershey, PA 17033-1240, USA, www.igi-global.com. This series is composed of titles available for purchase individually; each title is edited to be contextually exclusive from any other title within the series. For pricing and ordering information please visit http://www.igi-global.com/book-series/advances-finance-accounting-economics/73685. Postmaster: Send all address changes to above address.

Titles in this Series

For a list of additional titles in this series, please visit: www.igi-global.com

Handbook of Research on Impacts of International Business and Political Affairs on the Global Economy
Norhayati Zakaria (Universiti Utara Malaysia, Malaysia) Asmat-Nizam Abdul-Talib (Universiti Utara Malaysia, Malaysia) and Nazariah Osman (Universiti Utara Malaysia, Malaysia)
Business Science Reference • copyright 2016 • 450pp • H/C (ISBN: 9781466698062) • US $235.00 (our price)

Relational Methodologies and Epistemology in Economics and Management Sciences
Lucio Biggiero (Università dell' Aquila, Italy) Pier Paolo Angelini (Interuniversity Research Centre for Sustainable Development (CIRPS), Italy) Mario Basevi (Italian National Institute of Statistics, Italy) Nunzia Carbonara (Politecnico di Bari, Italy) Antonio Mastrogiorgio (Interuniversity Research Centre for Sustainable Development (CIRPS), Italy) Eliano Pessa (University of Pavia, Italy) Enrico Sevi (Università dell' Aquila, Italy) and Marco Valente (Università dell' Aquila, Italy)
Information Science Reference • copyright 2016 • 485pp • H/C (ISBN: 9781466697706) • US $200.00 (our price)

Global Perspectives on Risk Management and Accounting in the Public Sector
Augusta da Conceição Santos Ferreira (University of Aveiro, Portugal) Graça Maria do Carmo Azevedo (University of Aveiro, Portugal) Jonas da Silva Oliveira (Instituto Universitário de Lisboa (ISCTE-IUL), Portugal) and Rui Pedro Figueiredo Marques (University of Aveiro, Portugal)
Information Science Reference • copyright 2016 • 510pp • H/C (ISBN: 9781466698031) • US $225.00 (our price)

Handbook of Research on Comparative Economic Development Perspectives on Europe and the MENA Region
M. Mustafa Erdoğdu (Marmara University, Turkey) and Bryan Christiansen (PryMarke, LLC, USA)
Business Science Reference • copyright 2016 • 568pp • H/C (ISBN: 9781466695481) • US $440.00 (our price)

Handbook of Research on Financial and Banking Crisis Prediction through Early Warning Systems
Qaiser Munir (Universiti Malaysia Sabah, Malaysia)
Business Science Reference • copyright 2016 • 514pp • H/C (ISBN: 9781466694842) • US $265.00 (our price)

Comparative Economics and Regional Development in Turkey
Bryan Christiansen (PryMarke, LLC, USA) and M. Mustafa Erdoğdu (Marmara University, Turkey)
Business Science Reference • copyright 2016 • 451pp • H/C (ISBN: 9781466687295) • US $205.00 (our price)

Analyzing the Economics of Financial Market Infrastructures
Martin Diehl (Deutsche Bundesbank, Germany) Biliana Alexandrova-Kabadjova (Banco de México, Mexico) Richard Heuver (De Nederlandsche Bank, The Netherlands) and Serafín Martínez-Jaramillo (Banco de México, Mexico)
Business Science Reference • copyright 2016 • 410pp • H/C (ISBN: 9781466687455) • US $220.00 (our price)

IGI GLOBAL
DISSEMINATOR OF KNOWLEDGE
www.igi-global.com

701 E. Chocolate Ave., Hershey, PA 17033
Order online at www.igi-global.com or call 717-533-8845 x100
To place a standing order for titles released in this series, contact: cust@igi-global.com
Mon-Fri 8:00 am - 5:00 pm (est) or fax 24 hours a day 717-533-8661

Table of Contents

Detailed Table of Contents

The purpose of this chapter is to review the consequences of IFRS adoption by reviewing circumstances under which the benefits and costs accrue to firms, countries and the world. Notwithstanding, all issues raised about the consequences, IFRS adoption has had positive consequences and no wonder nearly 120 countries around the world and significant markets have adopted it. The chapter contributes to our understanding of the importance of IFRS and its effects and it is important to regulators and parties involved with world economic stability.

This chapter investigates the determinants of and obstacles to the adoption of International Financial Reporting Standards (IFRSs) in Africa. Specifically we investigate whether English as an official language, educational levels, existence of a capital market, economic openness and economic growth are associated with the probability of a country adopting IFRSs with a sample of 46 African countries. Binary logistics regression was used to analyze the data. The results suggest that only English as one of the official languages was associated with the likelihood of a country adopting IFRSs. Through an examination of the Reports on the Observance of Standards and Codes of the World Bank, we document that the major obstacles to adopting IFRSs are the lack of enabling legislation for its adoption and a lack of capacity in all aspects of the accounting supply chain. The chapter concludes that more research is needed at a continent level given that most of the determinants we investigated are not associated with the likelihood of a country adopting IFRSs.

We revisit the effectiveness of IFRS adoption for FDI attractiveness by considering the adopting country's institutional structure. Attention was on the extent of corruption control (as a measure of institutional structure). Data was tested on 42 African countries for the period 2001-2012. Using the Panel Corrected Standard Error (PSCE) estimation technique, our result suggest that the effect of IFRS adoption on foreign investment differs based on the level of corruption control instituted in the sample countries. When the variable – IFRS adoption, was tested for the sample with corruption control below the median value, the coefficient was either negative or insignificant. However, the opposite was seen for the category of countries with corruption control above the median value. This result was robust to the inclusion of alternative measures of corruption, foreign investment, and control of global financial crisis and legal origin of the country.

This chapter analyses the political and economic impact of IFRS adoption in the Czech Republic. It contributes to the current understanding of IFRS adoption from the perspective of a small European transitional market, where local accounting standards were previously well developed and still play a major role in financial reporting mainly, however for local taxation purposes. Although there has been an observable increase in the country's exports, FDI and international trade since the beginning of the 1990s, the direct impact of IFRS is difficult to discern, because of many political and institutional changes that have taken place concurrently. However, it is clear that adoption of IFRS has contributed to greater cultivation of the economic environment and facilitated international operations. IFRS adoption is not highly prevalent but is gradually increasing. This is apparent mainly in Czech companies with foreign parents that are in any event required to report in IFRS.

Since the adoption of International Financial Reporting Standards (IFRS) and the subsequent directive by the European Union (EU), all companies operating in the EU are required to report their consolidated financial statements in line with the IFRS. This study examines the consolidated financial statements of the top 170 listed companies in three major EU stock exchanges (UK, France and Germany) and uncovered a disparity in the use of common nomenclatures. The findings reveal that the inconsistencies in the application of terminologies such as statement of financial position instead of balance sheet and sequence of arrangement of assets in order of liquidity constitute the main differences for entities operating in the three countries. Such differences pose an imminent challenge in the comparability and interpretation of financial results.

The aim of this chapter is to present Polish experience of the IFRS adoption process. The first part characterizes a cultural background of the Polish society. Using Hofstede and Inglehart cultural dimensions Poland is compared to other European countries. The impact of time on national culture is taken into consideration as well as its influence on financial reporting. The authors believe that the culture has a profound impact on the accounting practice and, therefore it can impede or ease the process of the IFRS adoption. In the second part the history of Polish accounting is presented as well as the evolution of an accounting regulatory framework. A special emphasis is put on the scope of the IFRS application in Poland and the issue of IFRS vs. Polish GAAP comparability. The last and the most extensive part is devoted to the positive and negative consequences of the IFRS application in Poland from the perspective of empirical research.

This chapter is aimed at examining the impact of IFRS convergence and revisions on the financial statements of companies listed in East Africa. This was achieved by determining whether firms report losses (LNEG) when they occur (timely loss recognition) or report small positive income (SPOS) or whether incomes reported exhibit variability in net income (NI) over time. Simultaneously, the chapter tests whether there is any influence of corporate governance on these three measures which are considered indicators of financial reporting quality. Four models applying GLS random effects are applied on 520 firm year observations for firms listed in Nairobi Securities Exchange (NSE) between 2005 and 2014. The result shows that a positive coefficient on frequency of large losses reported in the finding interpreted as firms with converged and revised IFRS recognize large losses (LNEG) as they occur. The findings also show a negative coefficient on small positive income (SPOS) interpreted as firms applying non-converged and revised standards manage earnings towards small positive amounts more than firms applying converged standards. The post convergence\revisions are significant for Chi, R2 and the residual which suggest that variability in net income (NI) improved in the post convergence period while corporate governance show insignificant mixed coefficient with the three indicators.

This chapter reports on the impact of the adoption of IFRS in Ghana. It first traced the history of accounting standards in Ghana and the reason for the adoption of IFRS in 2007. One of the key issues that IFRS talk about is the disclosure of financial and non financial information in corporate financial reports. Hence this chapter provides evidence on the extent of disclosures, the quality of the disclosures and the determinants of the disclosures. The disclosure of financial ratios, forward-looking information and internal control information in corporate annual reports were extensively studied and findings reported in this chapter. The results of the quality of financial information disclosure mean of 76.80% (pre adoption) and 87.09% (post adoption) for the two years indicate that the quality of financial reports has improved significantly after adopting IFRSs. The findings thus confirms that the implementation of IFRSs generally reinforce accounting disclosure quality. However, the low levels of other disclosures (accounting ratio disclosure quality 6.64%, level of disclosure 60%; forward looking information 35%; internal control information 42%) by listed firms in Ghana do not support signaling theory which suggests that firms with good performance will wish to signal their quality to investors, hence are more likely to disclose their performance by disclosing more voluntary information. It is therefore important for the SEC and The Ghana Stock Exchange to do more by enforcing adherence to the corporate code of corporate governance.

This chapter aims, to highlight a review of IAS history, followed by approaches of accounting regulations. The development of accounting regulation within developing countries is also highlighted and discussed in the context of cultural diversity. It also aims to shed light into the motives that drive the adoption and implementation of IASs/IFRS. The political nature of lobbying and accounting standards setting process is also discussed in this chapter. In addition, the chapter discusses those factors that may be perceived as challenges which may delay or even block the convergence into the IASs/IFRS. Finally the authors provide key remarks about the IASs and venues for future research.

The IFRS is a useful international financial reporting framework that ensures comparable and quality financial information disclosure. IFRS perceived benefits compare to local and regional accounting standards has led to its adoption and implementation by several countries around the globe. However, IFRS is argued to benefit the developed countries the most due to their strong market and institutional settings (He, Wong & Young, 2009). This paper critically explores the question of whether IFRS adoption benefits in a developing country such as Nigeria is time-lag. The paper is a library research thus inferences were drawn deductively base on previous works conducted in Nigeria and elsewhere on IFRS adoption. This approach was further complimented by the conduct of interview with three professional accountants in practice and two economics analysts. It was revealed and concluded that due to their weak market, institutional settings and other factors, a time-lag is necessary for Nigeria and indeed all other developing countries to fully maximise the benefits of IFRS adoption and implementation. Notwithstanding, the paper recommends that to fast track IFRS benefits, developing countries and Nigeria in particular, should overhaul capital market infrastructure and ensure a strong ethical and good corporate governance environment as well as strict compliance with IFRS requirements through increase monitoring and use of sanctions by regulators.

The chapter is aimed at analyzing the collective perception of the accounting community of Vietnam towards the adoption of International Financial Reporting Standards (IFRS). This perception is premised on the twin issues of legitimacy and isomorphism. A broad sample survey of 728 persons out of 3000 accountants, auditors and academics was undertaken with a detailed questionnaire sent to each. With a net response rate of 24 per cent from this community, there emerged a definite influence of coercive, mimetic and normative isomorphisms as well as legitimacy motives. The study provides practical implications for the policymakers of Vietnam for the transformation of the accounting profession in the country and the strategic planning towards full mandatory IFRS adoption by 2020.

A recent publication by the World Bank on Millennium Development Goals (MDGs) has established that extreme poverty has been decreasing in all regions of the world with the exception of sub-Saharan Africa (SSA), in spite of over two decades of growth resurgence. This chapter explores the role of transfer mispricing in SSA's extreme poverty tragedy. The analytical structure entails: (1) emphasis of rational asymmetric development as the dark side of transfer pricing; (2) linkages between financial reporting, international financial reporting standards (IFRS), transfer pricing and poverty; (3) evidence that the recent growth resurgence in African countries has been driven substantially by resource-rich countries which are experiencing high levels of exclusive growth and extreme poverty; (4) the practice of transfer mispricing by multinationals operating in resource-rich countries of SSA and (5) a Zambian case study of extreme poverty and transfer mispricing schemes by Glencore in the copper industry. While transfer mispricing is contributing to diminishing African growth, available evidence shows that the component of growth that is not captured by transfer mispricing does not trickle down to the poor because the African elite is also animated by practices of rational asymmetric development. Policy implications for the fight against extreme poverty are discussed.

This chapter contains a brief history of accounting practices in Brazil, the Brazilian convergence process that resulted in using the IFRS, and new perspectives about the IFRS after implementation. In order to highlight the issues, it includes some empirical evidence and cases. The USGAAP served as the major influence on Brazilian accounting from 1978 to 2007. In 2008, the process of the IFRS convergence started in Brazil, resulting in an important culture change. For the local standardization, the Brazilian Accounting Pronouncements Committee, known as the CPC, was created, issuing its norms in compliance with IFRS with no modifications. Brazil has a history of tax legislation influencing its accounting practices, but the process of Brazilian convergence to the IFRS has incurred a detachment of accounting from tax policies for corporate purposes. The chapter concludes with a description of the current activities associated with the IFRS and financial reports, such as the development of the XBRL (eXtensible Business Reporting Language) reporting standard.

The chapter examines the determinants and financial statement effect s of IFRS adoption in Nigeria. It also investigate into the impact of effect of the adoption of IFRS on accounting figures and ratios in the financial statements of 50 companies quoted in the Nigerian Stock Exchange. The determinants considered include firm's characteristics (firm size, operating cash flow, leverage, turnover, growth in turnover, profitability, liquidity and earnings quality) and corporate governance variables (board size, board independence and audit type). The data were obtained from the annual reports of companies listed in the Nigerian Stock

Preface

This book is an expansion to the debate on the globalisation of accounting information vis-à-vis its merits and challenges that have remained an issue of great concern in accounting literature. More intriguing is the budding argument that developing countries need not succumb to this move due to the weakness of their institutions, low capacity development and the suspicion of neo-colonialism. These issues and beyond have motivated the need to harness original research papers that have focused on both country and regional case studies, and has applied different statistical and econometric techniques to arrive at their conclusions.

This book aims at understanding the economic and political implication of the globalisation of accounting standards. The topics are structured such that they provide empirical discourse on the issues surrounding the adoption of IFRS, promote the understanding of the determinants and consequences of IFRS adoption and then elaborate on discussions relating to country cases that pertains to IFRS adoption that are not prominently featured in scientific journals. The country cases cover three continents of the world and provides a rich information that expands our understanding of financial reporting globalisation.

Since financial report is embedded in a broader concept of institutional structure that shapes and guide the behaviour of providers and users of accounting reports, I devoted a chapter in the book that emphasises on a peculiar institutional structure that may affect the benefit from accounting globalisation. The remaining topics are rich and concise, and they focus on other issues that relates with the mainstream financial reporting framework and its globalisation component.

Acknowledgment

I want to express my deep gratitude to my PhD supervisors for reacting with such encouraging and stimulating response to the original idea on linking accounting issues with macro-economic outcomes. Many who had the opportunity of listening or reading the idea have enriched the discussion with illustrations and comments, and I have incorporated some of them in the editing of this volume. In innumerable ways, my Mentor (Dr. Osabuohien) has been a constant source of help and encouragement while working on the realisation of this volume. The publishers have given me unending encouragement and cooperation from the time I contacted them about the manuscript. For this, I am very thankful.

Chapter 1
Adoption of International Financial Reporting Standards and the Changing Accounting Environment in Nigeria

Abdulkadir Madawaki
Katsina University, Nigeria

ABSTRACT

The purpose of this chapter is to examine the major differences between Nigerian financial reporting rules and International Financial Reporting Standards (IFRS) following Nigeria's accounting reporting convergence to IFRS. The chapter documented evidence of differences between Nigerian Statement of Accounting Standards (NSAS), Companies and Allied Matters Act, 1990, Nigerian tax rules and IFRS requirements. It also discusses the IFRS adoption process in Nigeria and the benefits Nigeria stand to gain in adopting IFRS. The chapter discusses the challenges that might be encountered in the process of adoption of IFRS in Nigeria. Finally, the chapter provides recommendations through which these challenges can be addressed and suggest ways for further IFRS adoption research in Nigeria.

INTRODUCTION

The introduction of International Accounting Standards (IAS/IFRS) for listed companies in many countries around the world is one of the most significant regulatory changes in accounting history (Daske *et al*, 2008). This regulatory change is anticipated to enhance the comparability of financial reporting, improve corporate transparency and increase the quality of financial reporting. Internationalization of accounting regulations has witnessed great boost by which more than 160 countries had either mandated or permitted the use of IFRS by publicly-traded entities (Jacob & Madu, 2009). International accounting literature provides evidence that accounting quality has economic consequences such as lower costs of capital, increased diversification, improved investment opportunities and returns, reduced information asymmetry; enhanced market liquidity and international capital mobility (Young & Guenther, 2002; Sun,

DOI: 10.4018/978-1-4666-9876-5.ch001

2006; Bushman *et al,* 2006; Hail & Leuz 2006; Christensen *et al,* 2008; Harris & Muller, 1999; Luez & Verrecchia, 2000; Bartov *et al,* 2005; Hung & Subramanyan, 2007). These studies provide evidence that the qualities of accounting information after mandatory IFRS adoption were mixed worldwide over the last two decades.

Recent demand for greater international harmonization of financial reporting has become a major challenge for accountants, auditors, capital market operators and standards setters. Increased globalization and demands by capital markets for relevant and comparable information internationally have necessitated the decision by Nigeria to adopt the International Accounting Standards for all listed entities from 1st January 2012. Harmonization of the Nigerian Statement of Accounting Standards (NSAS) and the International Accounting Standards (IAS/IFRS) will directly or indirectly affect the regulatory changes in Nigeria. International accounting systems provide an interesting setting to examine changes in the accounting environment following the change from national standards to IAS/IFRS.

The chapter highlights the implications of this major shift in financial reporting regime from Nigerian financial reporting rules to International Financial Reporting Standards (IAS/IFRS). The benefits that Nigeria stands to gain as well as the challenges to be encountered in the process of harmonization are also discussed. Recommendations for a smooth transition process to IFRS adoption and suggestions on future research for assessing the impact of the regulatory change on financial reporting at firm and country level are also presented.

LITERATURE REVIEW

The impact of financial reporting is commonly debated in relation to economic consequence: a notion introduced by (Zeff, 1978) as the impact of accounting information on decision making behavior of investors, creditors, government and businesses. Similarly, Leftwitch (1983), viewed accounting as having economic repercussion if changes in the accounting standards have any effect on firm's values and on wealth of those who make decisions based on accounting information. The constituent of these definitions is that accounting information can influence the decisions made by investors, creditors, government and businesses. However, the economic consequence may be intended and unintended if they can or cannot reconcile with the International Accounting Standards stated objectives (Bruggemann, *et al.,* 2013). Mandatory adoption of IFRS around the world has stimulated research that investigates the financial reporting effects; capital market effects; macroeconomic effects and tax reporting effects associated with an accounting regime change. These studies differ in their analysis, jurisdictional setting and research design and they report varying findings. In this section, a review of such studies is provided

Studies on the financial reporting effects of IFRS adoption include a focus on the properties of accounting numbers, particularly properties that proxy for earnings management such as earnings conservatism and earnings smoothing. An advocated benefit of mandatory IFRS adoption is that financial reporting becomes more transparent and comparable because IFRS provides users additional disclosure requirements and specifies measurement and recognition rules that directly impact the quality of accounting figures (Daske *et al.*, 2006). Beuselinek *et al.* (2007), examined the comparability of accounting earnings in14 European Union (E.U) member countries using accruals cash flows as proxy for earnings comparability. The results indicated that earnings comparability does not improve after mandatory IFRS adoption across Europe. Similarly, Paananen (2008), in a study of Swedish listed firms examined whether financial reporting quality has increased after mandatory IFRS adoption using value relevance, timely loss recognition and earnings smoothing as proxies for financial reporting quality. The result shows that financial reporting quality has decreased after mandatory IFRS adoption.

Further, Jeanjean and Stolay (2008) examined the effect of mandatory adoption of IFRS on earnings management using firms from Australia, France and United Kingdom. Finding of the study showed that earnings management in these countries did not decline after mandatory IFRS adoption they even increased in France. Barth, *et al.* (2008), indicated that firms that adopted IFRS engages in less earnings management and display more timely loss recognition and present more value relevance of earnings, which are the qualities, interpreted as evidence of higher financial reporting quality. Callao and Jarne (2010), analyzed the effect of mandatory IFRS adoption in the E.U on earnings management practices by comparing discretionary accruals in the period before and after mandatory adoption of IFRS. The result indicated evidence of an increase in discretionary accruals post- IFRS adoption. Chen *et al.* (2010), examined discretionary accruals for a sample of firms from 15 E.U member countries; the study found that discretionary accruals significantly decrease post-IFRS adoption. In a related study, Latridis (2010), investigates whether mandatory adoption of IFRS in the U.K reduces earnings management, the result indicated evidence of reduction in earnings management.

Using voluntary adoption setting VanTendeloo and Vanstraelen, (2005), examined whether voluntary IFRS adoption is associated with lower earning management using German firms. The result of the study indicated that voluntary IFRS adoption firms had more discretionary accruals and lower negative correlation between accruals and cash flow from operations than firms reporting under German GAAP. Barth *et al,* (2008), investigated whether voluntary adoption of IFRS improves accounting quality around the world. Their findings show that firms adopting IFRS exhibit lower frequency of small positive earnings, less earnings smoothing, more timely loss recognition and higher value relevance. This indicated that studies of the level of earnings management before and after IFRS adoption at firms' level and between countries adopting IFRS have generated mixed results.

Furthermore, studies from developing economies provide evidence that IFRS reporting impact on financial reporting quality see for example Outa, (2011), study the impact of IFRS reporting on accounting quality of Kenyan listed firms between 1995-2004 using four earnings management metrics, one timely loss recognition and three value relevance metrics. The findings showed a mixed result with the three out of eight metrics indicating the quality of accounting information has improved whereas the other five indicated the quality of accounting information has declined which he finally interpreted as accounting quality has almost remained the same. Similarly, Ames, (2013), study the impact of IFRS usage on accounting quality measured as accounting quality and value relevance using South African listed firms. The result indicated that earnings quality does not significantly improved among the sample firms post IFRS adoption. Finally, Alali and Foote, (2012), examined the value relevance of accounting information reported under IFRS regime in the United Arab Emirates financial market using a sample of firms traded on the Abu Dhabi Exchange. The result documented evidence of positive association between accounting information and market value among sample firms.

Studies on economic consequences of IFRS adoption and capital market effects are highly relevant given that IFRS are increasingly globally accepted, among such studies Daske, *et al,* (2008), who examined the capital market effects around the mandatory IFRS reporting using a variety of proxies. The study found increase market liquidity after mandatory IFRS reporting, as well as a decrease in firm cost of capital and a corresponding increase in equity valuation. However, Clarkson *et al,* (2011), analyzed the value relevance of book value and earnings for a period of pre and post IFRS adoption for 15 countries. The results showed no convincing evidence that IFRS improves the value relevance of book value of equity and earnings. Similarly, Subramanyan, (2007), examined German firms changing from German GAAP to IFRS for the period 1998-2002, the study found that the value relevance of book value of equity is not significantly different between the pre and post IFRS adoption periods.

Using voluntary adoption settings Leuz and Verrecchia, (2000), found that firms voluntarily adopting IAS have lower bid-ask spread and higher stock turnover ratios. Similarly, Ashbaugh and Pincus, (2001), in a study whether analyst forecast error decreases after firms adopt IAS, reported that IAS adoption reduces analysts cost of information acquisition and improves forecast accuracy. Jermakowikz *et al,* (2007), also reported an increase in the earnings and book value of equity after voluntary adoption of IFRS for a sample of DAX 30 firms from 1995-2004. Using a sample of firms listed on the Helsinki Stock Exchange between 1984 and 1992. (Kinnunen *et al,* 2000), reported a significant decrease in the correlation between accounting information and share price after voluntary adoption of IFRS.

In contrast using implied cost of capital estimates, Cuijpers and Buijink, (2005) do not find significant differences across local GAAP and IFRS in the European Union. Similarly, Leuz, (2003), examines bid-ask spread and stock turnover ratios for firms in Germanys New Market, where US GAAP and IAS are the allowed financial reporting standards the result did not show any significant differences in bid-ask spread and turnover ratios across the two standards. Numerous cross-country studies of how mandatory adoption of IAS/IFRS reported evidence of increasing or decreasing and no change in the value relevance of earnings associated with mandatory and voluntary IFRS adoption (Harris Muller, 1999; Bartov, *et al,* 2005; Daske, (2006) Hung and Subramanyam, 2007 Ismail, *et al,* 2010; Devalle *et al,* 2010; Chalmers *et al,* 2011; Abotino *et al,* 2011).

On studies related to developing markets, Afego, (2011), examined stock price response to earnings announcement in the Nigerian stock market. The result showed significant abnormal price reactions around earnings announcement which was interpreted that earnings announcement contain value relevant information. Similarly, Ajao and Wemambu, (2012), study the volatility estimation and stock price prediction of four major companies quoted on the floor of the Nigerian Stock Exchange. The study found the presence of volatility in all the four stock prices. However, when the volatility was regressed against stock price to determine their predictability the study showed evidence that out of four companies only two stock prices were predicted by volatility in their stock prices. Finally, Okoye *et al,* (2014), assesses the impact of IFRS on stock market movement and extend at which it can improve the position of corporate organization in Nigeria. The result indicated that IFRS adoption enhances the credibility of financial statements and provide basis for the strength of corporate entity in Nigerian capital market.

Differences in accounting standards are also viewed as hindrance to cross- border investments (Bradshow *et al* 2004). The global shift towards mandatory IFRS reporting may remove barriers to cross-border investment and integration of capital markets and making it easier for foreign investors to invest in a country (Covering *et al,* 2007). This in turn enlarges firm's investment portfolio and improves risk sharing and lower cost of capital. Study by Beneish *et al,* (2012), on macroeconomic effect of mandatory IFRS adoption provides evidence that IFRS adoption increases foreign debt investment. Additionally, Amiran (2009), examines the impact of a country-level mandatory IFRS adoption on aggregate foreign equity portfolio investment and indicated that countries that adopted IFRS experience higher level of foreign investment. Various studies conducted on the mandatory adoption of IFRS at country level have indicated that countries that have adopted IFRS experienced huge increases in direct foreign investment (Irvine and Lucas, 2006). Taken together, this evidence generally supports the notion that mandatory IFRS adoption yields macroeconomic benefits.

Okpala (2012), study the relationship between IFRS adoption and Foreign Direct Investment (FDI) effect as basis for economic growth in Nigeria. The result revealed that there is significant relationship between IFRS adoption and FDI in the country. The result further showed that this process poses difficulties which can be overcome by concerted efforts in training and employment of appropriate manpower and improving the existing accounting infrastructure in the country. Kanthapanit, (2011), investigated the influence of IFRS reporting in Thailand on impairment of assets (IAS 36) on the investment decision by individual shareholder in the Stock Exchange of Thailand (SET). The result indicated that sources of information that individual shareholder rated as most relevant when making investment decision post IFRS reporting are ranked as follows: financial statements; relevance and reliability of accounting information; reputation and financial opinions.

Tax values can be relevant for various economic decisions; they can serve as additional information in financial statements analyses and the evaluation of companies (Kager *et al,* 2011). Tax figures could be taken as a yardstick for evaluating earnings in financial statements and they can enhance the predictability of firm's future earnings. Kager *et al,* (2011), reported that analysts of German and Austrian GAAP use tax figures to calculate corporate taxable income to get information about earnings expectations. Calculation of corporate taxable income allows researches on the relation between earnings announce to shareholders and the returns reported to the fiscal authority. Several studies have examined the relation between IFRS and tax rules Gee, *et al,* (2010), examine the potential tax difference on IFRS consolidated financial statements of German and UK firms. The results shows that German IFRS practices are likely to be free from tax influence mainly because tax practices are based on Handelsgesetzbuch (HGB, i.e. Commercial Code) and is so clearly different from IFRS.

In contrast, to UK firms which were found to have no tax-relevant differences between IFRS and UK GAAP, Kager *et al,* (2011), analyzed whether tax balance sheet figures can be reconstructed using tax information provided by consolidated IFRS accounts. The findings indicated that for DAX 30 German Firm's differences exists between IFRS and tax reporting for intangibles and provisions while for Australian ATX Listed Companies divergence exists between IFRS and tax rules relating to fixed assets and provisions. Finally evidences were found that book values reported in IFRS balance sheet are generally higher than tax values. Gavana *et al,* (2013), analyzed the relationship between tax and financial reporting after mandatory IFRS adoption to assess the degree and the direction of the book-tax linkages. The results indicated that IFRS and tax reporting has a high degree of disconnection. Companies which use IFRS face a high degree of disconnection when converting financial to fiscal figures. Karampinis and Havas, (2013), investigated whether the mandatory IFRS adoption in Greece have affected tax-induced incentives for financial earnings management. The result supports the opinion that IFRS reduced book-tax conformity and thereby releasing financial income from tax implication.

FACTORS AFFECTING THE ADOPTION OF IFRS

Differences in accounting systems have significant economic effects on the interpretation of financial reporting at an international level (Choi & Levich, 1991; Bushman and Smith, 2001). As a result, international accounting and securities organizations introduced a process to advance the harmonization of accounting standards as a way of improving financial transparency and comparability. Shima and Yang (2012) reported that efforts by the International Accounting Standards Committee (IASC), predecessor of the International Accounting Standards Board (IASB), the International Organization of Securities

Commissions (IOSCO) and other worldwide accounting regulatory bodies have led to the development of International Accounting Standards now described as the International Financial Reporting Standards (IFRS).

Several factors influencing international accounting systems have been investigated by accounting researchers since the 1960's (Mueller, 1967). These factors include: political systems; level of economic development; country's legal systems; taxation; forms of business ownership; capital market and equity financing; foreign debt financing; colonialism; trade alliances; inflation; level of accounting education; cultural values and religious beliefs. The spread of IFRS adoption has also been achieved through the efforts of many international organizations such as: The World Bank; International Monetary Fund; International Federation of Accountants; International Organization of Securities Commissions and the World Trade Organization. Others are Multinational Corporations and Professional Accounting Firms. It is important to understand how these factors shape accounting reporting and disclosure practices in order to predict the progress towards harmonization efforts because the adoption of IFRS provides avenues for these factors to be linked with accounting development.

Political System

Archambant and Atchambant in (2009), examined countries that have decided to permit the use of IFRS for their listed firms. Their model included factors related to economic systems, political systems and cultural values. Their resulst showed that political systems do not influence a country's decision to permit the use of IFRS. On the contrary, Assenso-Okofo *et al* (2011) indicated that political systems have significant influence on financial reporting and disclosure practices of Ghanaian listed firms.

Nigeria has had experience with various political and military regimes due to coup d'états and a civil war that affected its political stability (Madawaki, 2014). Since independence in 1960, Nigeria has had 14 different governments; eight of them military eras and six civilian administrations. It can be testified that the rowdy political systems after independence have failed to improve accounting information disclosure. However, the stable democratic political system put in place since 1999 had shown some improvement in the country's accounting environment through the enactment of the Nigerian Accounting Standards Board Act, 2003; now replaced with Financial Reporting Council Act (No.6) of 2011 which mandated the adoption of IFRS. A repeal of Investment and Securities Act (ISA) 1991 with ISA 2007 in an effort to ensure effective regulation, protection of investment and maintenance of fair, efficient and transparent market. A repeal of Central Bank of Nigeria (CBN) Act 1991 with CBN Act 2007 provides for the establishment of a financial service regulatory coordinating committee to co-ordinate the supervision of financial institutions.

Capital Market and Equity Financing

A well-developed capital market promotes good accounting reporting and most likely leads to quality accounting reporting practices. On the other hand, equity financing is an important component in the development of accounting systems. Nobes (1998) posited that strong equity financing are mostly provided by outsiders who do not have opportunistic contact with the firm. Thus, creates an avenue for agency theory which implies that as the relationship between businesses and fund providers becomes far away, information asymmetry between managers and fund providers increases which creates the need for more financial disclosure requirements.

In countries where equity financing is prevalent, accounting takes on a more capital market inclination and higher levels of disclosures is observed (Salter, 1998). Countries with well-developed capital markets such as the United States usually have accounting standards considered to be superior and may not be willing to adopt alternative standards if the new standards are not as rigorous as their own (Ramanna *et al,* 2009) whereas countries with less-developed capital markets may be more willing to adopt internationally acknowledged standards in an attempt to attract foreign investment.

The Nigerian capital market classified as emerging market required all companies trading on its floor to adopt IFRS by January, 2012. The Nigerian Capital Market came into being in 1960 but stated operation with less than 10 stocks in 1961, the exchange now boasted about 254 stocks quite remarkable growth rate considering the number at the initial stage. Table 1 present indicators of capital market development in the Nigerian Stock Exchange. The market has experienced formidable growth in recent years, this growth being attributable to Securities and Exchange Commission (SEC) reforms aimed at enhancing investor confidence in the Nigerian. The SEC is in collaboration with two renowned global news media outlets namely: Thomson Reuters and Bloomberg for dissemination of real-time market data to the global investment community to complement that provided by the official website and local data center. Other areas of reforms were SEC's approval of a new code of corporate governance (2011) for public companies in order to entrench transparency and accountability in the Nigerian Capital Market and the putting in place of a strong regulatory environment with strict enforcement of rules and regulations on financial reports in order to improve the efficiency and depth of the market and to reduce transaction costs..

Table 1. Indicators of capital market development in NSE

Years	Number of Listed Securities	Volume of Stocks Traded (Turnover Volume) Billion	Value of Stocks Traded (Turnover Value) N'Billion	Value of Stock as % of GDP	Total Mkt Cap N'Billion	Total Mkt Cap as % of GDP
2002	258	6.6	59.4	0.7	747.6	9.4
2003	265	13.3	120.4	1.2	1324.9	13.1
2004	277	19.2	225.8	1.9	1925.9	16.5
2005	288	26.7	262.9	1.8	2900.I	19.5
2006	288	36.5	470.3	2.6	5120.9	28.1
2007	310	138.1	2,100.0	9.2	13294.6	56.0
2008	301	193.1	2,400.0	10.0	9535.8	39.7
2009	266	102.9	685.7	10.0	7032.1	28.5
2010	264	93.3	797.6	0.3	9918.2	33.6
2011	250	90.7	638.9	1.7	10273.3	27.5
2012	256	104.2	809.0	2.0	14800.9	36.5
2013	254	267.3	2,350.9	2.9	19077.4	23.5

Sources: Madawaki (2014) and CBN Annual Report (2013).

Legal System

Bogdon *et al* (2010) examined the link between IFRS adoption and a country's legal system. The result indicated that countries which are characterized by principles and practice-based systems are more likely to adopt IFRS. Furthermore, the result showed that full IFRS adoption is more likely to occur for countries with mono-system of common law than otherwise. It was further stated that IFRS adoption may translate into market benefits only where there are greater incentives for better disclosure (Daske *et al,* 2008). In common law countries, information asymmetry are likely to be overcome by timely disclosure whereas disclosure in code law countries is more likely to be privately done. Nigeria is classified as a common law country with strong rule of law, and an effective mechanism for property rights which may make the adoption of IFRS easier and more enforceable. Company financing has largely been through the capital market and the Nigerian code of corporate governance 2003 (revised 2011) provides strongly for basic shareholders rights to participate and vote at Annual General Meetings. The code further provides for protection of the rights of shareholders, board of directors and audit committee responsibilities.

Nature of Business Ownership

The level of economic development of a country is likely to influence the type of business ownership that exists in a country (Saudagaran, 2004). Developing economies are characterized by small, simple and less complex business entities. In contrast, developed countries are characterized by large and complex multinationals. The ownership structure of companies listed on NSE exhibit widespread ownership of private and institutional shareholders. Widespread ownership produces more transparent disclosure practices (Chau & Gray, 2002; Nobes & Parker, 2010). Private and institutional investors have been on the increase since the time Nigeria embarked on privatization programs in the 1980s the time when the Nigerian government withdrew its ownership in all privatized companies. Boutchkava and Megginson (2000) stated that privatization increases the number of shareholders in privatizing countries. It was therefore expected that changes in ownership structure brought about by the Nigerian privatization program would increase the need for greater and elaborate disclosure to the public.

Trade Alliances

International organizations whose principal aims are to bring about economic benefits through shared trade and investments have risen with the formation of such bodies as the World Bank; International Monetary Fund; World Trade Organization; African Union; African Development Bank and so on, of which Nigeria is a member. Membership of these bodies brings about benefits to minimize differences among members and to facilitate cross border trade and investment. For instance, extending credit across borders involves financial analysis which is more easily done if accounting standards are the same among countries. Regional trade organizations also foster compliance with international standards (Ramama, *et al,* 2009). Thus, the fact that trading organizations have adopted IFRS may prompt a country to adopt similar standards.

Educational Level

The quality of accounting education plays an important role in the development of accounting profession. Highly sophisticated accounting standards are meaningless if they are misunderstood (Choi & Meek, 2009). Professional accounting education is difficult to achieve where general educational level is low. ROSC (2011), observed that accounting curricula are not harmonized in Nigerian universities and generally not current with International Education Standards (IES). Furthermore within the structure of professional examinations in Nigeria there is no distinction between accounting qualification and auditing qualification and the professional examinations are not designed to adequately achieve IES8 competency requirements for audit professionals. There is also no uniform guidance in the organization and delivery of continuing professional education and development among professional accountants.

A major issue surrounding the adoption of IFRS is whether it is possible to bring the accounting educators and accounting professionals and other stakeholders up in a timely manner so as to have a smooth transition to IFRS. The major international and local accounting firms in Nigeria have however, already started on IFRS awareness campaign. The campaigns suggest that many accounting firms are being proactive in their preparation for IFRS adoption by Nigeria. Finally, IFRS education and training efforts apply mainly to accounting professionals and less to university accounting educators which indicate that more need to be done in this area in order to achieve complete and smooth transition to IFRS in Nigeria.

Level of Economic Development

As business deals become large and sophisticated, the stages of recording and reporting these deals will necessarily become more complex (Choi and Meek, 2008). However, prior studies have provided evidence on the relationship between economic development and accounting rules. Cooke and Wallace (1990) have provided evidence of a positive relationship between Gross National Product (GNP) growth and disclosure requirements. Similarly, Rajan and Zingales (1998) indicated that the growth rate of industries with heavy dependence on external financing was significantly higher in countries with higher public disclosure. On the other hand, Larson and Kenny (1995) in a study of developing countries reported a relatively small negative relation between economic growth and IFRS adoption.

At independence, the Nigerian economy was heavily reliant on the non-oil sector with agriculture contributing over 60 percent of GDP and 90 percent of export earnings with manufacturing sector contributing less than 3 percent of GDP and 1 percent of export (UNCTAD, 2009). This is referred to as stage 1 of economic development and at this stage the accounting records mainly concern recording of double entry and book-keeping systems. Like many African countries Nigeria's early independence years have seen an industrial strategy that relied heavily on import substitution. This appeared to work relatively well with the share of manufacturing to GDP increasing from 2 percent in 1957 to 7 percent in 1967 (Utomi, 1998). This is referred to as stage 2 of economic development; at this stage accounting records extend to financial reporting and auditing harmonization of standards and practices and environmental reporting.

The massive oil revenue in 1970's witnessed large investments in state-owned enterprises and the government privatization policy which resulted to boom in Nigeria's capital market. This implied rapid expansion of the industrial sector with subsequent returns on investments. Industrialization brings an increase in the volume of trade and commerce and thus a need for generally-accepted accounting standards and practices and improved transparency. This stage is seen as transcendental which includes the requirement for green reporting, money laundering reports and sophisticated accounting regulations. Figure 1 presents these stages.

APPLICATION OF IFRS IN NIGERIA

Nigerian accounting system is based on Anglo-Saxon model of accounting, it emphasized fair presentation, transparency and full disclosure and a separation between financial and tax accounting. It stress on shareholders right and offer stronger investor protection. Growing competition and globalization in recent times pushed a number of Nigerian companies to raise capital from international stock markets; others have established significant presence in other jurisdictions. Also, a good number of Nigerian entities hold securities of non-Nigerian issuers. However, international stock markets did not accept financial statements prepared on the basis of NSAS. Consequently, many multinational companies operating in Nigeria were required voluntarily to prepare a second set of financial statements in accordance with IAS/IFRS reporting benchmark.

In Nigeria, adoption of IFRS was launched in September 2010, by the Honorable Minister, Federal Ministry of Commerce and Industry, Senator Jubril Martins-kuye OFR. The adoption was organized such that all stakeholders use the IFRS by January 2014. The adoption was scheduled to start with Public Listed Entities and Significant Public Interest Entities who were expected to adopt the IFRS by January 2012. All Other Public Interest Entities were expected to mandatorily adopt the IFRS for statutory purposes by January 2013, and Small and Medium-sized Entities were mandatorily to adopt IFRS by January 2014. The transition should be phased so that the objectives were achieved within the time-frame. The phases were explained as follows:

Figure 1. Economic development and accounting

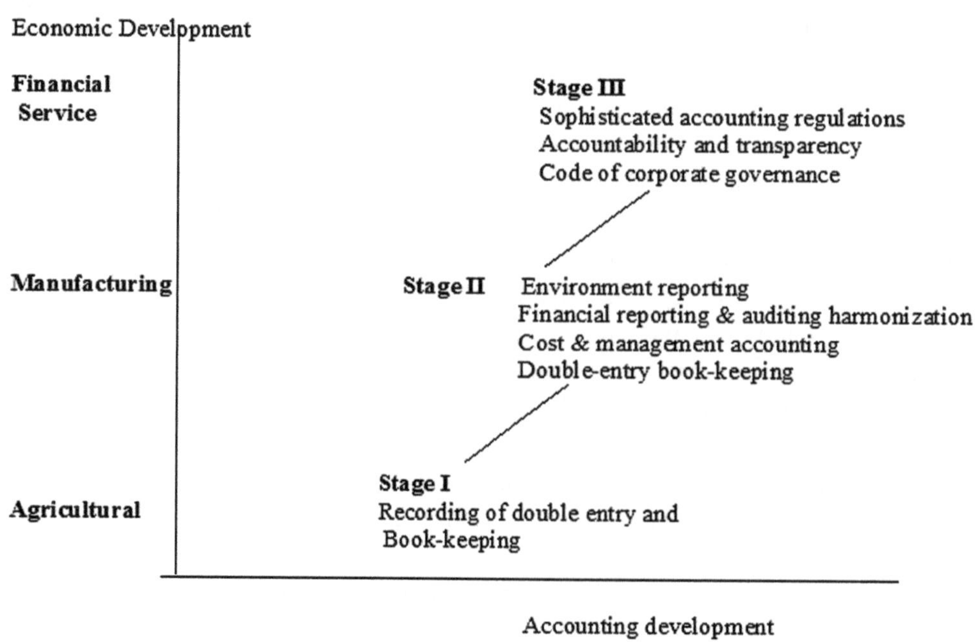

Phase 1: Publicly listed Entities and Significant Public Interest Entities were to prepare their financial, statements using applicable IFRS by January 1, 2012. The choice of January 1, 2012 was anchored on the need to effectively transit to IFRS over a three year period. Any entity that starts preparation for transiting would need to convert its closing balances at December 2010 to IFRS-based figures which then became the opening balance as at January 1, 2011 for IFRS based financial statements as at December 31, 2011. This provides opening balances for January 1, 2012 which were the first IFRS full financial statements as at December 31, 2012 (with 2011 as comparative year).

Phase 2: All other public interest entities were expected to mandatorily adopt IFRS, for statutory purposes, by January 1, 2013. This means that all other public interest entities in Nigeria were statutorily be required to issue IFRS based financial statements for the year ended December 31, 2013.

Phase 3: IFRS for SMEs were mandatorily adopted as at January 1, 2014. This means that all Small and Medium-sized Entities in Nigeria were statutorily required to issue IFRS based financial statements for the year ended December 31, 2014. Entities that do not meet the IFRS for SME's criteria were to report using Small and Medium-sized Entities Guidelines on Accounting (SMEGA).

Implementation of the IAS/IFRS regulation required all Nigerian listed entities to prepare their financial statements in conformity with IFRS. Adoption of IFRS should lead to greater harmonization with respect to the consolidated accounts of listed entities. Additionally, eliminating different methods of accounting for the same transaction led to improved comparability of financial statements which in turn made accounting information more decision useful to financial information users.

Issues in Practical Implementation of IFRS

The introduction of IAS/IFRS required major changes to the financial reporting framework. In Nigeria, accounting practices are governed by the Companies and Allied Matters Act (CAMA) 1990, and the Statement of Accounting Standards (SAS) issued by the Nigerian Accounting Standards Board (NASB). CAMA prescribes the format and content of companies' financial statements. The government of Nigeria in September 2010, approved conversion to IFRS, the CAMA requirements are not in line with IFRS. For example, the CAMA requires that the historical cost accounting rules be applied and the financial statements comply in form and content with requirements of Schedule 2 of the Act and with the accounting standards laid down in the NASB-issued SAS, provided such accounting standards do not conflict with the provision or Schedule 2 of CAMA. These CAMA requirements conflict with IFRS requirements. These provisions of CAMA need to be amended in order to facilitate implementation of IFRS.

Other existing laws such as Investment and Securities Act, 2007, the Central Bank Act, 2007 and Banks and Other Financial Institution Act, 1991, National Insurance Commission Act, 2003, Companies Income Tax Act 2004, Federal Inland Revenue Services Act 2007, all these prescribed some guidelines on preparation of financial statements in Nigeria; IFRS does not recognize the presence of these laws, as such some provisions of these laws need to be amended to comply with IFRS requirements.

Accounting Differences between NSAS and IFRS

The various differences between NSAS and IFRS have been documented in prior literature (Oyedele, 2011; Madawaki, 2012). A summary of some of the key differences between NSAS and IFRS is presented in Table 2. The differences in financial reporting may be relevant as they might affect the capacity of

Table 2. Key differences between NSAS and IAS/IFRS

Topic	Nigeria Statement of Accounting Standards	International Financial Reporting Standards
Financial statement presentation	• Income statement • Balance sheet • Cash flow statement • Value added statement • Accounting policies • Notes	• Statement of comprehensive income • Statement of financial position • Statement of changes in equity • Statement of cash flows • Accounting policies • Notes • Significant management estimates
Property plant and equipment	Measured using cost model	Measured using cost model with detailed guidance regarding: • Componentization • Useful lives • Residual values • Impairment calculation
Related parties transactions	Limited disclosure but expected	Detailed guidance on identification of related parties and detailed disclosure of related parties transactions
Segment reporting	More of geography	• Operating segment base on management view • Threshold for reportable segments is results or assets of an individual segment, should be 10% or more of all segments • If the aggregate revenue of all reported segments on this basis is 75% of total then more segments required until 75% threshold is reached
IFRS 1-First time adoption	Not applicable	Provides guidance and requirements on the transition to IFRS. Also provides relief for certain item in the preparation of the opening balance sheet
Financial guarantees	Disclosed as contingent liabilities	Requires financial guarantees to be recognized at their fair value
Scope of consolidation	General principles	Investments under control are consolidated. SPEs are potentially also consolidated
Employee benefits	General expense and disclosure on pensions	• Complex criteria of accounting • Recognized the undiscounted amount of short-term employee benefits
Risk management disclosures	Limited disclosure of foreign exchange and credit risk	Disclosures required for: • Credit risk • Liquidity risk • Price risk • Capital risk management • Risk management
Leases	Based on general guidelines –Operating and Finance leases	• Currently similar but updates to IFRS e.g IFRIC 4 will lead to only finance leases hence more items coming to balance sheet • Fair value and amortized costs used in valuations • Certain transactions containing hidden leases which needed to be accounted for
Impairments	No specific standard	• Carryout impairment test based on trigger vent • IFRS 36-Impairement on Non-financial assets • IAS 39-Impairement on financial assets
Financial asset classification and valuation	Classification include: • Cost • Amortized cost	Classification include: • Amortized cost • Fair value

Sources: Oyedele 2011 and Madawaki 2012

Nigerian public listed entities to prepare IFRS statements. For instance, with such areas as change in equity, income statement and significant management estimates and judgments are concepts that are not addressed in the local standards. There are also significant differences in property, plant and equipment, related parties, segment reporting, leases, impairment and risk management disclosure. Finally, significant differences are also found in other areas such as financial guarantees, scope of consolidation and employee benefits).

Principal Differences between NSAS 19 and IAS/IFRS12

The introduction of International Financial Reporting Standards (IFRS) in Nigerian by the Federal Inland Revenue Services (FIRS) has resulted in consequent treatment of various tax transactions in Nigeria. Section 55(1) of the Companies Income Tax Act Cap (21), LFN 2004 requires a company filling a return to submit its audited account to the FIRS while Section 8, 52 and 53 of the Financial Reporting Council of Nigeria Act 2011 gave effect to the adoption of IFRS. This implies that the audited accounts to be submitted to the FIRS shall be prepared in compliance with standards issued by International Accounting Standards Board (IASB). Certain differences exist between Nigeria Standards and IASB Standards with regard to tax issues as a result of conversion to IFRS more specifically on SAS19 (accounting for taxes) and IAS/IFRS 12 (on income and taxes). Nigerian businesses will converge from local SAS 19 to IAS/IFRS 12 with the attendant similarities and differences. Table 3 present the area of major differences.

In Nigeria, as in Anglo-Saxon countries, accounting is not influenced by tax rules, the measurements used in financial reporting are generally not binding for tax purposes. Tax regime in Nigeria is governed by various legislations with the Companies Income Tax Act (CITA) of 1979 as amended by Finance (Miscellaneous Provision) Decree 1993 and also amended in 2007 and 2011. Income Tax Management Act (ITMA) of 1961 repealed and replaced by Personal Income Tax Act No. 104 of 1993 and as amended in 2011, Sales Tax Decree of 1986 replaced with Value Added Tax Decree (VAT) No. 102 of 1993 and Petroleum Profit Tax Act (PPTA) of 1959 re-enacted as Chapter P13 of the Laws of the Federation of Nigeria (LFN) 2004. Taxation was much more of concern to tax payers and how the move to IFRS reporting would affect the computation of company's tax.

Economic Consequences of IFRS Adoption in Nigeria

Corporate reporting can have many economic consequences and better reporting and disclosure practices have the ability to change business cost of capital (Hail *et al,* 2010). It is observed that better reporting and disclosure practices improves corporate-decision making; for instance, the effectiveness of business investment decision (Lambert *et al*, 2007). The notion is that high quality reporting reduces information asymmetries that could have otherwise given rise to hostility in raising foreign financing. Improved corporate reporting and disclosure practices can lower estimation risk which directly lowers the required rate of returns of an individual equity as well as market uncertainty surcharge of the entire economy (Easley & O'Hira, 2004). Additionally, better disclosure has the ability to improve risk sharing in the economy by making investors to be aware of certain equities or by making them more inclined to hold them which reduces the cost of capital (Diamond & Verrecchia, 1991).

Prior studies uphold the existence of a statistically and economically significant relationship between corporate reporting quality and businesses cost of capital (Hail, 2002; Hail & Leuz, 2006). Umoren and Enang (2015) examined the value relevance of financial statement for twelve Nigerian banks for the

Table 3. Key Differences between NSAS 19 and IAS/IFRS 12

Topic	Nigeria Statement of Accounting Standards 19	International Financial Reporting Standards 12
Presentation	Deferred tax to be presented between long term and current liabilities (in case of liabilities) and between fixed and current assets (in case of assets).	Deferred tax liability to be classified as non-current on the balance sheet, attaching supplementary notes concerning the components of the temporary difference and what will be recovered within 12 months, and more than 12 months.
Applicable tax rate	Current tax rate is used as a reasonable estimate of the future tax rates, unless changes in tax rate are in advance.	Requires the use of tax rates and laws that are enacted or substantially enacted.
Computation of deferred tax	Tilts towards the income statement method which focuses on timing differences.	Requires balance sheet liability method, which focuses on temporary differences.
Temporary/timing differences to be accounted for.	Full provision for all timing differences.	Full provision for all taxable temporary differences, with limited exemption.
Extra ordinary items	Deferred taxes relating to ordinary items to be shown as part of the extra ordinary items.	Extra ordinary items are not permitted.
Investment in subsidiaries, Joint venture, and associates, re-treatment of undistributed profit.	Not required	Deferred tax is recognized except where the parent/ investor is able to control the distribution of profit and it is probable that the temporary difference will not reverse in the foreseeable future.
Disclosures	Not required	Any entities need to reconcile its effective tax rate to statutory rate and analyze the components of deferred tax assets/liabilities.
Fair value adjustment	The tax effect relating to the in the carrying value of a revalued asset should be determined and charged or credited directly to equity.	The revaluation of an asset does not always affect taxable profit/loss in the period of the revaluation and the tax base of the asset may not be adjusted as a result of the revaluation. If the future recovery of the carrying amount will be taxable any difference between the carrying amount of the revalued asset and its tax base is a temporary difference and will give rise to a deferred tax liability or asset.

pre-and-post IFRS adoption period. The results indicated that the equity value of earnings of banks is relatively value-relevant to share prices under IFRS than under NSAS. Furthermore, the results showed that earnings per share are incrementally less relevant in post-IFRS adoption; which they interpreted to mean that earnings reported by Nigerian banks have become more informative to equity investors.

Another aspect of corporate reporting is its comparability across businesses, businesses are deemed to have comparable reporting for a given set of economic events making it easier and less costly for investors and other interested parties to compare across businesses (De-Franco *et al* 2009). For example, more comparable corporate reporting may make it easier to distinguish between less and more profitable businesses or low-risk and high-risk businesses. Furthermore, comparable corporate reporting across businesses from various countries promote cross border investment and harmonization of capital markets making it easier for foreign investors to invest in a country (Aggarwal *et al,* 2005), thereby improving liquidity of the capital market and expanding businesses and investor bases with possibly better risk-sharing and reduction of cost of capital.

Additionally, improved comparability may also have salutary consequences on corporate decisions and in particular benefits from trade (Hail *et al,* 2010). Comparability reporting allows businesses to make better informed investment decisions due to better understanding of competing businesses both within and across countries. Abata (2015) examined the effects of comparability of financial statements prepared under IFRS and NSAS of fourteen Nigerian commercial banks and the findings of the study revealed that qualitative differences in the financial reports prepared under NSAS and IFRS are statistically significant. The study therefore concluded that IFRS has impacted on financial reporting of the sample banks.

Despite the numerous benefits of better and more comparable corporate disclosure and reporting practices, there are also direct and indirect costs of changing corporate reporting. The direct reporting and disclosure cost may arise in many forms and include the preparation, certification and dissemination of accounting reports (Hail *et al,* 2010). Moreover, these costs are likely to have fixed components and making certain reports burdensome particularly for smaller firms. There are also indirect reporting and disclosure practices costs to firms because other parties such as regulators, competitors, tax authorities, trade unions, etc; can use information provided for respective interests. For instance, detailed information about profitability and line-of-business may reveal important information to competitors (Leuz, 2004; Verricchia, 1983). Making firms to provide certain disclosures can have net cost to firms, particularly smaller firms (Bushee & Leuz, 2005). Standards setters and regulators therefore need to carefully measure the costs and benefits of the innovation to firms, investors and other parties in the economy.

Political Consequences of IFRS Adoption in Nigeria

A potential political benefit for Nigeria from IFRS adoption is that it signals an additional willingness on the part of Nigerian policy makers to cooperate with other major countries and world financial institutions on important global issues. However, there are also political risks for Nigeria, which are discussed below.

Under the former system, Nigerian government handed delegated the oversight function of public securities offering and the capital markets to the Securities and Exchange Commission (SEC), which in turn looked up to the Nigerian Accounting Standards Board (NASB), now Financial Reporting Council (FRC), an agency of the government for issuance and improving accounting standards. SEC supervises and maintains monopoly with respect to the use of standards by Nigerian listed firms and gives implementation guide while overseeing compliance with financial reporting practices by publicly-listed firms with standards. In addition, SEC issues additional disclosure requirements as required in the SEC code of corporate governance for publicly-listed firms that are registered with SEC.

The switch to IFRS reporting in Nigeria would certainly affect the structure of these institutions as well as create an additional player with a formal standard-setting role. IFRS are set by the International Accounting Standards Board (IASB) which is an independent-standard setting body appointed and overseen by the Trustee of International Accounting Standards Committee (IASC). Although IASB has promised in collaboration with national standards-setters to achieve convergence in accounting around the world (Hail, *et al* 2010), there is little left for national standards-setting bodies in a given country with regard to the standards themselves, except perhaps to act as local agents of IASB. In practice, this would apply to NASB (now FRC) and SEC and hence transfer the authority to set standards on presentation, disclosure and format of financial statements, measurement and recognition, to IASB. Such a delegation of standard- setting power to IASB presents many political challenges.

Another widely recognized concern was that adoption of IFRS requires major changes to financial reporting framework in Nigeria. For example, Companies and Allied Matters Act, (CAMA) 1990 and 2007; Securities and Exchange Commission Act, 2007; Central Bank of Nigeria Act, 2007; Bank and Other Financial Institution Act, 1991; National Insurance Commission Act, 2003; Companies Income

Tax Act, 2004; and Federal Inland Revenue Service Act, 2007. All these enactments prescribed some guidelines on the preparation, reporting and disclosure of financial statements in Nigeria. IFRS does not recognize the presence of these laws; as such some provisions of these laws need to be amended to comply with IFRS requirements. Furthermore, another concern of IFRS adoption from the Nigerian perspective is that foreign governments and interest groups may exercise an excessive influence on IASB and consequently the formulation of IFRS; and it may not be clear whether these countries have the same goals as Nigeria in defining the role of accounting. Nigerian standards tend to be capital market and investor oriented as in other Anglo-Saxon countries. In other words, many foreign governments may push for accounting standards that focus on creditor protection.

Finally, the infrastructure supporting Nigeria's corporate financial reporting includes financial and information intermediaries such as: auditors, consultants, accountants, investment bankers, financial analyst's etc. Much of these professionals have developed around the Nigerian Statement of Accounting Standards (NSAS) reporting paradigm and this expertise has been in higher demand by private and public sector organizations. For example, there are about 827,000 private limited companies and about 42,500 public limited companies in Nigeria with Institute of Chartered Accountant of Nigeria (ICAN) membership at 31,500 and Association of National Accountant (ANAN) membership at 15,720 (ROSC, 2011). Thus, a significant gap exists between the demand and supply of qualified professional accountants in Nigeria. Therefore, if Nigerian professionals' accountants are perceived as lacking IFRS-specific capabilities they will lose business to foreign counter parts because large multinational auditors are seen in a better position than small domestic auditors which lack IFRS expertise and international network to capitalize on IFRS services.

Benefits and Challenges of IFRS Conversion

It is advocated that adoption of IFRS implementation will lead to: greater transparency and comparability of result, lower cost of capital, reduced national standard-setting costs, facilitate easier international mobility of capital (Armstrong, *et al,* 2007, Covrig, *et al,* 2007, Daske *et al* 2008). On the other hand, the challenges in IFRS implementation include: interpretation of standards, continuous amendment to IFRS, accounting knowledge and expertise possessed by financial statement users, the complexity of certain IFRSs and tax orientation of most nations, enforcement mechanisms of IFRS especially in jurisdictions with weak institutions., (Ball, *et al,* 2000, Cairns, 2001, Larson & Street,2004). Table 4 lists the main benefits and challenges of IFRS conversion.

Changing accounting standards would fundamentally change the way businesses are run, the method that success is measured and the record and information that companies need to maintain (Eichhorst,

Table 4. Benefits and challenges of IFRS conversion

Benefits	Challenges
• Harmonization of internal and external reporting • Easier access to external capital for local companies • Better comparability with other businesses • Reduced national standards setting cost • Greater reporting transparency	• Enforcement and compliance mechanism • Accounting education and training • Amendments to the existing laws • High cost of implementing IFRS • Complex nature of IFRS • Lack of IFRS implementation guidance • Tax-driven nature of national standards

2002). Jermakowicz (2011), indicated that implementation of IFRS have a significant impact on financial reporting as well as on internal organization of Bel-20 companies in Belgium. His results further showed that convergence and streamlining of external and internal reporting by creating globalized accounting standards across businesses was often listed among the most important benefit of IFRS adoption. Okere, (2009), opined that IFRS adoption will enhance comparability of financial statements with other listed companies since it results in a movement towards similarity in the choice between alternative accounting treatments. Mike, (2002), reported that implementing IFRS should result in better reporting transparency. It is also believe that IFRS implementation would reduce the cost of doing business across borders by eliminating the need for supplementary information and ensure easier access to external capital for local companies.

However, the principal impending factor in the implementation of IFRS in Nigeria is accounting education and training UNCTAD, (2007) and Obazee, (2009), indicated that shortage of professional accountants who are adequately trained in IFRS was identified as a national issue. The lack of coordination between accounting education institutions may also serve as a bottleneck towards IFRS implementation. Similarly, Obazee, (2009), states that task of implementing IFRS is complex and costly; it requires a double workload during the transition period for accounting and finance staff because of the complex nature of some of the IFRS and the complexity of the task of implementing IFRS is further complicated by the fact that the body of IFRS has not been finalized

Additionally, Schipper, (2005), reported that the lack of adequate IFRS implementation guidance is also seen as a challenge. This lack of guidance creates risks for different local interpretations of IFRS and thus, increases the risk for 'manipulation of financial statements. Larson and Street, (2004), reported that tax-driven nature of national standards is also seen as a major challenge to IFRS implementation because tax considerations associated with the conversion to IFRS, like other aspects of a conversion, are complex. IFRS conversion calls for a detailed review of tax laws and tax administration. Specific taxation rules would have to be redefined to accommodate these adjustments. Accounting issues that may present significant tax burden on adoption of IFRS, include determination of Impairment, Loan loss provisioning and Investment in Securities/Financial Instruments. The great challenge faced by Nigeria is not its inability to adopt IFRS but rather to enforce the adoption of IFRS which will result in higher quality reporting. Obazee, (2009), reported that lack of preparedness of the enforcement agencies to facilitate IFRS implementation may hinder smooth transition. Embracing globalization and adopting IFRS requires reforms to a country's financial reporting rules (Obazee, 2009), indicated that there is lack of coherence between Nigeria's financial reporting rules and IFRS rules at entity level and country levels. Thus, there is the need to amend the existing rules to gain full benefits of IFRS adoption.

RECOMMENDATIONS

For Nigeria to gain full benefits of mandatory IFRS adoption, the following recommendations are hereby advanced. These recommendations may serve as useful inputs for adopting and implementing a country action plan for accounting regulatory changes in Nigeria.

Promote knowledge and awareness of professionals, regulators, preparers, and users on the importance of financial statements prepared under IFRS framework and the importance of compliance with accounting requirements through seminars and workshops.

Improve the statutory framework of accounting framework. This might necessitate the amendments of some sections of the Companies and Allied Matters Act, (1990); Investment and Securities Act, (2004), Companies Income Tax Act, (2004) and other laws and regulations that affect financial reporting in Nigeria. E.g. CAMA requires that historical cost accounting rules be applied and financial statements shall comply in form and content, with requirements of Schedule 2 of the Act, this section need to be redefined. The tax considerations associated with the conversion to IFRS for instance, tax laws which limit relief of tax losses to four year should be reviewed.

Strengthen professional and university accounting education and training. Students and trainee accountants should be provided with appropriate training and education in accordance with the International Education Standard (IES) issued by the International Accounting Education Standards Board (IAESB) of IFAC to ensure that they are sufficiently qualified to undertake accounting functions and assist them in implementing International Accounting Standards.

Fortify the powers of the regulatory agencies and review the adequacy of statutory enforcement provisions. Necessary steps should be taken to strengthen the capacity of regulators such as: Financial Reporting Council; Securities and Exchange Commission; Central Bank of Nigeria; Corporate Affairs Commission; Federal Inland Revenue Service that enable them to effectively deal financial reporting practices of the regulated entities.

FUTURE RESEARCH OPPORTUNITIES OF IFRS ADOPTION IN NIGERIA

The mandatory adoption of IFRS around the world has stimulated research to investigate the effects of IFRS adoption associated with an accounting regime change. This chapter has presented a review of the concept of IFRS which could set a stage for future research. Prior studies carried out in Nigeria focused on the prospects, and challenges of IFRS adoption (Iyoha & Jimoh, 2011; Okpala, 2012; Ayuba, 2012; Madawaki; 2012; Mary *et al*, 2013; Odia & Ogiedu, 2013; Bala, 2013; Demaki, 2013). It is thus, suggested that future studies could investigate the effects of IFRS on financial reporting quality using earnings properties metric. Further studies could also be staged in the area of capital market effects following mandatory IFRS adoption in Nigeria using value relevance; cost of capital and analyst forecast measures and the macro economic effects associated with IFRS adoption.

Further studies could be extended to the effects of IFRS adoption and compensation schemes. Compensation schemes typically include elements based on accounting-based performance metrics to align managers and shareholders' interests (Bruggemann, 2013). If performance metrics are based on GAAP in force at the date of calculation, changes in accounting rules such as mandatory IFRS adoption will affect compensation altering the efficiency of GAAP in resolving the agency conflict.

The mandatory adoption of IFRS potentially also affects firms income tax situation and the role of IFRS in determining accounting income. The adoption of IFRS by Nigeria's Federal Inland Revenue Service (FIRS) has resulted in consequent treatment of various tax transactions (see FIRS information circular March 2013). One obvious path for future research is to explore in details the IFRS and taxation link and identify cases where IFRS adoption directly affects taxation. Further research could also be on the association between corporate governance strength and the Nigeria's listed firms with respect to mandatory IFRS adoption. Corporate governance mechanisms are generally grouped into two: internal mechanisms and external mechanisms.

CONCLUSION

This chapter presents a study on the adoption of IFRS and changing accounting environment in Nigeria and identified major areas of differences between Nigeria Statement of Accounting Standards (NSAS) and International Financial Reporting Standards (IFRS/IAS). IFRS/IAS rules have significant implications not only for financial statements preparers, users, and regulators but also for the entire financial reporting institutions. Nigerian SAS and some provision of CAMA, 1990, ISA, 2004, and CITA, 2004, need to be amended in order to achieve the desired objectives of convergence with IFRS/ IAS and comparability of financial statements. Furthermore, the chapter highlighted factors relating to economic, political, capital market, nature of business ownership level of country accounting education and accounting system development. Finally, the chapter discusses the economic and political implication of IFRS adoption both at firm level and country level.

Harmonization of financial reporting under IFRS/IAS creates a single accounting language across the world and this was listed among the most important benefit of conversion. Other benefits include: easier access to external capital for local firms and enhanced knowledge of global financial reporting among others. Some key challenges in the adoption of IAS are: accounting education and training; amendment to the existing rules and the tax driven nature of Nigeria's NSAS which results in major differences in accounting requirements. Other key challenges in the process of adopting IAS include complex nature of some of the IAS and lack of adequate implementation guidance. It is believed that the change in accounting regime will have a positive impact on the competitiveness and growth of Nigerian companies. Based on this assumption recommendations were offered in order to ensure Nigeria's smooth transition to IFRS/IAS.

REFERENCES

Abata, M. A. (2015). The impact of IFRS adoption on financial reporting practices in the Nigerian banking sector. *Journal of Policy and Development Studies*, *9*(2), 169–184. doi:10.12816/0011215

Afego. (2011). *Stock price response to earnings announcement: evidence from the Nigeria stock market.* MPRA Paper No. 33931. University of Dundee.

Aggarwal, R., Klapper, L., & Wysocki, P. (2005). Portfolio preferences of foreign institutional investors. *Journal of Banking & Finance*, *29*(12), 2919–2946. doi:10.1016/j.jbankfin.2004.09.008

Agostino, M. D., Drago, D., & Silipo, D. B. (2011). The value relevance of IFRS in the European banking industry. *Review of Quantitative Finance and Accounting*, *36*(3), 437–457. doi:10.1007/s11156-010-0184-1

Ajao, M. G., & Wemambu, M. U. (2012). Volatility estimation and stock price prediction in the Nigerian stock market. *International Journal of Financial Research*, *3*(1).

Alali, F. A., & Foote, P. S. (2012). The value relevance of international financial reporting standards: Empirical evidence in an emerging market. *The International Journal of Accounting*, *47*(1), 85–108. doi:10.1016/j.intacc.2011.12.005

Ames, D. (2013). IFRS adoption and accounting quality: The case of South Africa. *Journal of Applied Economic and Business Research*, *3*(3), 154–165.

Amiram, D, (2009). Financial information globalization and foreign investment decisions. *Journal of International Accounting Research*, 41-70.

Archambault, J. J., & Archambault, M. E. (2009). An analysis of social factors influencing the adoption of International Financial Reporting Standards. *Journal of Global Business Advancement*, *2*(1), 38–53. doi:10.1504/JGBA.2009.023093

Armstrong, C., Barth, M. E., Jagolizer, A. D., & Riedl, E. J. (2007). Market reaction to the adoption of IFRS in Europe. *Accounting Review*, *85*(1), 31–61. doi:10.2308/accr.2010.85.1.31

Ashbaugh, H., & Pincus, M. (2001). Domestic accounting standards, International Accounting Standards, and the predictability of earnings. *Journal of Accounting Research*, *39*(3), 417–434. doi:10.1111/1475-679X.00020

Assenso-Okofo, O., Ali, M. J., & Ahmed, K. (2011). The development of accounting and reporting in Ghana. *The International Journal of Accounting*, *46*(4), 459–480. doi:10.1016/j.intacc.2011.09.010

Ayuba, A. (2012). A proposed rule-roadmap for the adoption of IFRS in Nigeria. Aresearch based perspective on FGN, NASB, & SEC. *American Journal of Economics*, 41–45. doi:10.5923/j.economics.20120001.10

Bala, M, (2013). Effects of IFRS adoption on financial reports of Nigerian listed entities: The case of oil and gas companies. *The Macrotheme Review: A Multidisciplinary Journal of Global Macro Trends, 2*(7), 9-26

Ball R., Robin, A & Wu, J. S, (2000). Accounting standards, the institutional environment and issuer incentives: Effect on timely loss recognition in China. *Asia-Pacific Journal of Accounting and Economics, 17*(2), 71-96.

Barth, E. M., Landsman, W. A., & Lang, M. H. (2008). International Accounting Standards and accounting quality. *Journal of Accounting Research*, *46*(3), 467–498. doi:10.1111/j.1475-679X.2008.00287.x

Bartov, E., Goldberg, S., & Kim, M. (2005). Comparative value relevance among German, U.S and International Accounting Standards: A German Stock Market perspective. *Journal of Accounting, Auditing & Finance*, *20*(2), 95–119.

Beuselinck, C., Joos, P., & Van der Meulen, S. (2007). *International earnings comparability*. Working Paper. Tilburg University.

Bogdan, D., Stefana, M., Marilen, D., & Gabriel, P. (2010). *National legislative systems and foreign standards and regulations: The case of International Financial Reporting Standards adoption*. Working Paper. University of Munich.

Boutchkova, M., & Meggison, W. (2000). Privatization and the rise of global capital market. *Financial Management*, *29*(4), 31–76. doi:10.2307/3666368

Bradshaw, M., Bushee, B., & Miller, G. (2004). Accounting choice, home bias, and U.S. investment in Non-U.S. firms. *Journal of Accounting Research*, *42*(5), 795–841. doi:10.1111/j.1475-679X.2004.00157.x

Bruggemann, U., Hitz, J. M., & Sellhon, T. (2013). Intended and unintended consequences of mandatory IFRS adoption: A review of extant evidence and suggestions for future research. *European Accounting Review*, *22*(1), 1–37. doi:10.1080/09638180.2012.718487

Bushee, B., & Leuz, C. (2005). Economic consequences of SEC disclosure regulation: Evidence from the OTC Bulletin Board. *Journal of Accounting and Economics*, *39*(2), 233–264. doi:10.1016/j.jacceco.2004.04.002

Bushman, R., Piotroski, J., & Smith, A. (2006). *Capital allocation and timely accounting recognition of economic losses*. Working Paper. University of North Carolina and University of Chicago.

Bushman, R., & Smith, A. (2001). Financial accounting information and corporate governance. *Journal of Accounting and Economics*, *32*(1-3), 237–333. doi:10.1016/S0165-4101(01)00027-1

Callao, S., & Jarne, J. I. (2010). Have IFRS affected earnings management in the European Union? *Accounting in Europe*, *7*(2), 159–189. doi:10.1080/17449480.2010.511896

Chalmers, K., Clinch, G., & Godfrey, J. M. (2011). Changes in value relevance of accounting information upon IFRS Adoption: Evidence from Australia. *Australian Journal of Management.*, *36*(2), 151–173. doi:10.1177/0312896211404571

Chau, G. K., & Gray, S. J. (2002). Ownership structure and corporate voluntary disclosure in Hong Kong and Singapore. *The Journal of International Accounting*, *37*(2), 247–265. doi:10.1016/S0020-7063(02)00153-X

Chen, H., Tang, Q., Jiang, Y., & Lin, Z. (2010). The role of International Financial Reporting Standards in accounting quality: Evidence from the European Union. *Journal of International Financial Management and Accounting*, *21*(3), 220–278. doi:10.1111/j.1467-646X.2010.01041.x

Choi, F., & Levich, R. (1991). Behavioral effects of international accounting diversity. *Accounting Horizons*, *5*(2), 1–13.

Choi, F., & Meek, G. (2008). *International Accounting* (6th ed.). Upper Saddle River, NJ: Pearson Education Inc.

Christensen, H., Lee, E., & Walker, M. (2008). *Incentives or standards: What determines accounting quality changes around IFRS adoption?* Working Paper. Manchester Accounting and Finance Group and Manchester Business School.

Clarkson, P., Hanna, J. D., Richardson, G. D., & Thompson, R. (2011). The impact of IFRS adoption on the value relevance of book value and earnings. *Journal of Contemporary Accounting and Economics*, *7*(1), 1–17. doi:10.1016/j.jcae.2011.03.001

Cooke, T., & Wallace, R. (1990). Financial disclosure regulation and its environment: A review and further analysis. *Journal of Accounting and Public Policy*, *9*(2), 79–110. doi:10.1016/0278-4254(90)90013-P

Covrig, V., Defond, M. M., & Hung, M. (2007). Home bias, foreign mutual fund holdings and the voluntary adoption of International Accounting Standards. *Journal of Accounting Research*, *45*(1), 41–70. doi:10.1111/j.1475-679X.2007.00226.x

Cuijpers, R., & Buijink, W. (2005). Voluntary adoption of non local GAAP in the European Union: A study of determinants and consequences. *European Accounting Review*, *14*(3), 487–524. doi:10.1080/0963818042000337132

Daske, H. (2006). Economic benefits of adopting IFRS or US-GAAP – have the expected cost of equity capital really decreased? *Journal of Business Finance & Accounting*, *33*(3), 329–373. doi:10.1111/j.1468-5957.2006.00611.x

Daske, H., Hail, L., Leuz, C., & Verdi, R. (2008). Mandatory IFRS reporting around the world: Early evidence on the economic consequences. *Journal of Accounting Research*, *46*(5), 1085–1142.

De Franco, G., Kothari, S., & Verdi, R. (2009). *The benefits of financial statement comparability*. Working Paper. MIT Sloan School of Management.

Demaki, G. O. (2013). Prospects and challenges of International Financial Reporting Standards to economic development in Nigeria. *Global Journal of Management and Business Research*, *13*(1), 69–74.

Devalle, A., Onali, E., & Magarini, R. (2010). Assessing the value relevance of accounting data after the introduction of IFRS in Europe. *Journal of International Financial Management and Accounting*, *21*(2), 85–119. doi:10.1111/j.1467-646X.2010.01037.x

Diamond, D., & Verrecchia, R. (1991). Disclosure, liquidity, and the cost of capital. *The Journal of Finance*, *46*(4), 1325–1359. doi:10.1111/j.1540-6261.1991.tb04620.x

Easley, D., & O'Hara, M. (2004). Information and the cost of capital. *The Journal of Finance*, *59*(4), 1553–1583. doi:10.1111/j.1540-6261.2004.00672.x

Eichhorst, P., Steens, B. Van der Tas, L. & Smits, M. (2002). *IAS 2005. preparing your enterprise for new International Financial Reporting Standards* (E&Y cap gemini).

Gavana, G, Guggiola, G & Marenzi, A, (2013). Evolving connection between tax and financial reporting in Italy. *Accounting in Europe, 10*(1), 43-70.

Gee, M, Haller, A & Nobes, C, (2010). The influence of tax on IFRS consolidated statements: The convergence of Germany and the UK. *Accounting in Europe, 7*(1), 97.

Guenther, D., & Young, D. (2000). The association between financial accounting measures and real economic activity: A multinational study. *Journal of Accounting and Economics*, *29*(1), 53–72. doi:10.1016/S0165-4101(00)00013-6

Hail, L. (2002). The impact of voluntary corporate disclosures on the ex-ante cost of capital for Swiss firms. *European Accounting Review*, *11*(4), 741–773. doi:10.1080/0963818022000001109

Hail, L., & Leuz, C. (2006). International differences in the cost of equity capital: Do legal institutions and securities regulation matter? *Journal of Accounting Research*, *44*(3), 485–531. doi:10.1111/j.1475-679X.2006.00209.x

Hail, L., Leuz, C., & Wysocki, P. (2010). Global accounting convergence and the potential adoption of IFRS by the U.S. (part 1): Conceptual underpinnings and economic analysis. *Accounting Horizons*, *24*(3), 355–394. doi:10.2308/acch.2010.24.3.355

Hail, L., Leuz, C., & Wysocki, P. (2010). Global accounting convergence and the potential adoption of IFRS by the U.S. (part 11): Political factors and future scenarios for U.S. accounting standards. *Accounting Horizons*, *24*(4), 567–588. doi:10.2308/acch.2010.24.4.567

Harris, T., & Muller, K. III. (1999). The market valuation of IAS versus US-GAAP accounting measures using Form 20-F reconciliations. *Journal of Accounting and Economics*, *26*(3), 285–312. doi:10.1016/S0165-4101(99)00003-8

Hung, M., & Subramanyam, K. R. (2007). Financial statement effects of adopting International Accounting Standards: The case of Germany. *Review of Accounting Studies*, *12*(4), 623–657. doi:10.1007/s11142-007-9049-9

Ismail, W. A., Van Zijl, T., & Dunstan, K. (2010). *Earnings quality and the adoption of IFRS-based accounting standards: Evidence from an emerging market*. Working Paper. University of Wellington and Bond University.

Iyoha, F. O., & Jimoh, J. (2011). *Institutional infrastructure and the adoption of International Financial Reporting Standards (IFRS) in Nigeria. School of doctoral studies (European Union)*. Journal.

Jacob, R. A., & Madu, C. N. (2009). International Financial Reporting Standards: An indicator of high quality. *International Journal of Quality & Reliability Management*, *25*(7), 712–722. doi:10.1108/02656710910975778

Jeanjean, T., & Stolowy, H. (2008). Do accounting standards matter? An exploratory analysis of earnings management: Before and after IFRS adoption. *Journal of Accounting and Public Policy*, *27*(6), 480–494. doi:10.1016/j.jaccpubpol.2008.09.008

Jermakowicz, E. K. (2004). Effects of adoption of International Financial Reporting Standards in Belgium: The evidence from BEL-20 companies. *Accounting in Europe*, *1*(1), 51–70. doi:10.1080/0963818042000270811

Jermakowicz, E. K., Prather-Kinsey, J., & Wulf, I. (2007). The value relevance of accounting income reported by DAX-30 German companies. *Journal of International Financial Management and Accounting*, *18*(3), 151–191. doi:10.1111/j.1467-646X.2007.01011.x

Kager, B., Schanz, D., & Niemann, R. (2011). Estimation of tax values based on IFRS information: An analysis of German DAX30 and Austrian ATX listed companies. *Accounting in Europe.*, *8*(1), 89–123. doi:10.1080/17449480.2011.574362

Kanthapanit, C., Sofocleous, S., & Clark, C. (2011). Adoption of international financial reporting standards in Thailand: Influence on decision making of individual shareholder. *Global Review of Accounting and Finance*, *2*(1), 18–28.

Karampinis, N. I., & Hevas, D. L. (2013). Effects of IFRS adoption on tax-induced incentives for financial earnings management: Evidence from Greece. *The International Journal of Accounting*, *48*(2), 218–247. doi:10.1016/j.intacc.2013.04.003

Kinnunen, J., Niskanen, J., & Kasanen, E. (2000). To whom are IAS earnings informative? Domestic versus foreign shareholders' perspectives. *European Accounting Review*, *9*(4), 499–517. doi:10.1080/09638180020025330

Lambert, R., Leuz, C., & Verrecchia, R. (2007). Accounting information, disclosure, and the cost of capital. *Journal of Accounting Research*, *45*(2), 385–420. doi:10.1111/j.1475-679X.2007.00238.x

Larson, R., & Kenny, S. (1995). An empirical analysis of international accounting standards, equity markets and economic growth in developing countries. *Journal of International Financial Management and Accounting*, *6*(2), 130–157. doi:10.1111/j.1467-646X.1995.tb00054.x

Larson, R. K., & Street, D. L. (2004). Convergence with IFRS in an expanding Europe: Progress and obstacles identified by large accounting firms' survey. *Journal of International Accounting, Auditing & Taxation*, *13*(2), 89–119. doi:10.1016/j.intaccaudtax.2004.09.002

Latridis, G. (2010). International Financial Reporting Standards and the quality of financial statements information. *International Review of Financial Analysis*, *19*(3), 193–204. doi:10.1016/j.irfa.2010.02.004

Leftwich, R. W. (1983). Accounting information in private markets: Evidence from private lending agreements. *Accounting Review*, *58*(1), 23–42.

Leuz, C. (2003). IAS versus US GAAP: Information-asymmetry based evidence from Germany's new market. *Journal of Accounting Research*, *41*(3), 445–472. doi:10.1111/j.1475-679X.2003.00111.x

Leuz, C. (2004). Proprietary versus non-proprietary disclosures: Evidence from Germany. In C. Leuz, D. Pfaff, & A. Hopwood (Eds.), *The Economics and Politics of Accounting* (pp. 164–197). Oxford, UK: Oxford University Press. doi:10.1093/0199260621.003.0007

Leuz, C., & Verrecchia, R. (2000). The Economic consequences of increased disclosure. *Journal of Accounting Research*, *38*(Supplement), 91–124. doi:10.2307/2672910

Madawaki, A. (2012). Adoption International Financial Reporting Standards in developing countries: The case of Nigeria. *International Journal of Business and Management*, *7*(3), 152–161. doi:10.5539/ijbm.v7n3p152

Madawaki, A. (2014). Impact of regulatory framework and environmental factors on accounting practices by firms in Nigeria. *Procedia: Social and Behavioral Sciences*, *164*, 282–290. doi:10.1016/j.sbspro.2014.11.078

Mary, J., Okoye, A. E., & Samson, A. O. (2013). Accounting standards in Nigeria: The journey so far. *Research Journal of Business and Accounting*, *2*(1), 1-10.

Mike, M. (2009). Seminar understanding IFRS. National GAAP vs IFRS, Lagos, Nigeria.

Nobes, C. (1998). Towards a general model of the reasons for international differences in financial reporting. *Abacus*, *34*(2), 162–187. doi:10.1111/1467-6281.00028

Nobes, C., & Parker, R. (2010). *Comparative International Accounting*. Pearson Education Limited.

Obazee, J. O. (2009). Practical challenges in implementing IFRS. *ABWA Journal*, *1*(3), 7–17.

Odia, J. O., & Ogiedu, K. O. (2013). IFRS adoption: Issues, challenges and lessons for Nigeria and other adopters. *Mediterranean Journal of Social Sciences*, *4*(3), 389–399.

Okoye, P. V. C., Okoye, J. F. N., & Ezejiofor, R. A. (2014). Impact of IFRS adoption on stock market movement in Nigerian corporate organization. *International Journal of Academic Research in Business and Social Sciences.*, *4*(9), 202–218. doi:10.6007/IJARBSS/v4-i9/1150

Okpala, K. E. (2012). Adoption of IFRS and financial statements effects: The perceived implications on FDI and Nigerian economy. *Australian Journal of Business and Management Research*, *2*(5), 76–83.

Olowo-Okere, E. (2009). *The International Financial Reporting and accounting issues: Imperatives of attainment of economic development of Nigeria*. Paper presented at 39th annual conference of the Institute of Chartered Accountants of Nigeria.

Outa, E. R. (2011). The impact of (IFRS) adoption on the accounting quality of listed companies in Kenya. *International Journal of Accounting and Financial Reporting*, *1*(1), 212–241. doi:10.5296/ijafr.v1i1.1096

Oyedele, T. (2011). *An overview of IFRS and challenges posed to professionals*. Paper presented at a seminar on IFRS adoption in Nigeria.

Paananen, M. (2008). *The IFRS adoption's effect on accounting quality in Sweden*. Working Paper. University of Hertfordshire.

Rajan, R., & Zingales, L. (1998). Financial dependence and growth. *The American Economic Review*, 559–586.

Ramanna, K., & Sletten, E. (2009). *Why do countries adopt international financial reporting standards?*. Harvard Business School Accounting and Management Unit Working Paper No. 09-102.

ROSC. (2011). *Report on the observance of standard and codes (Nigeria), accounting and auditing*. World Bank.

Salter, S. (1998). Corporate financial disclosure in emerging markets: Does economic development matter? *The International Journal of Accounting*, *33*(2), 211–234. doi:10.1016/S0020-7063(98)90027-9

Saudagaran, S. M. (2004). *International Accounting: A user perspective*. USA Globus Printing Inc.

Shima, K. M., & Yang, D. C. (2012). Factors affecting the adoption of IFRS. *International Journal of Business*, *17*(3), 276–298.

Sun, K. (2006). *Financial reporting quality, capital allocation efficiency, and financing structure: An international study*. Working Paper. University of Hawaii at Manoa.

Umoren, A. O., & Enang, E. R. (2015). IFRS adoption and value relevance of financial statements of Nigerian listed banks. *International Journal of Finance and Accounting.*, *4*(1), 1–7.

UNCTAD. (2009). *Nigerian investment policy*. Author.

United Nation Conference on Trade and Development (UNCTAD). (2008). *Conference proceedings held in New York and Geneva*. Author.

Utomi, P. (1998). *Managing uncertainty. Competition and strategy in emerging economies*. Ibadan, Nigeria: Spectrum Books LTD.

Van Tendeloo, B., & Vanstraelen, A. (2005). Earnings management under German GAAP versus IFRS. *European Accounting Review*, *14*(1), 155–180. doi:10.1080/0963818042000338988

Verrecchia, R. (1983). Discretionary disclosure. *Journal of Accounting and Economics*, *5*, 179–194. doi:10.1016/0165-4101(83)90011-3

Young, D., & Guenther, D. (2002). Financial reporting environments and international capital mobility. *Journal of Accounting Research*, *41*(3), 553–579. doi:10.1111/1475-679X.00116

Zeff, S. A. (1978). The rise of economic consequences. *Journal of Accountancy*, 56–63.

Chapter 2
Are Vietnamese Accounting Academics and Practitioners Ready for International Financial Reporting Standards (IFRS)?

Duc Hong Thi Phan
RMIT Vietnam, Vietnam

Mahesh Joshi
RMIT University, Australia

Bruno Mascitelli
Swinburne University, Australia

ABSTRACT

The purpose of this chapter is twofold. First, it reports the findings of a survey on the perception of Vietnamese accountants regarding the benefits and disadvantages of International Financial Reporting Standards (IFRS) as well as the potential costs and challenges of IFRS implementation. Second, it examines the differences in the perceptions of accounting academics and practitioners pertaining to IFRS adoption in Vietnam. Perceptions of Vietnamese accountants and academics were obtained and analysed from 3,000 mailing survey questionnaires across Vietnam in 2012. A total of 728 usable responses were received producing an effective response rate of 24 per cent. The respondents perceived that credibility and comparability are the most perceived benefits of IFRS reporting. Over-complexity and time-consumption are the most perceived disadvantages of IFRS reporting. Although IFRS reporting was perceived as being costly and challenging, surprisingly, the respondents were optimistic on the long-term benefits and two-thirds of the respondents showed their willingness to adopt IFRS.

DOI: 10.4018/978-1-4666-9876-5.ch002

INTRODUCTION

The motivation for this paper is in large part due to the recent debate among academics, accounting firms, professional bodies, government authorities on International Financial Reporting Standards (IFRS). More specifically on whether IFRS should be the global accounting standards and why and how developing countries should adopt IFRS to gain benefits from these quality accounting standards. Arguments in favour of IFRS adoption mostly focus on the effects of capital markets and investors. Scholars point out that IFRS are more capital market oriented and, hence, more relevant to investors as well as more comprehensive, especially with respect to disclosure, than most local accounting standards (Daske et al. 2013). The comparability, credibility, and positive capital market effects of IFRS adoption to capital market participants are not disputed, but the relevance of IFRS to different countries with different institutional and legal environments is less convincing. It is questionable if emerging economies can experience positive capital market effects as their capital markets are at an early stage of development and have not yet received effective enforcement mechanisms. The literature of factors that could influence the application of IFRS by emerging and transition economies is under researched. By way of example, recent studies by the Vietnam Association of Certified Public Accountants (VACPA) and the Confederation of Asian and Pacific Accountants (CAPA) call for more research in this area and specifically for Vietnam (VACPA & CAPA 2012). In the present paper, we address this research gap by providing the perception based evidence from the accounting academics and practitioners of Vietnam as an example of developing countries not yet adopted IFRS. More specifically, this study answers the following research questions:

RQ1: What are the perceived benefits of IFRS adoption in Vietnam?
RQ2: What are the perceived disadvantages of IFRS adoption in Vietnam?
RQ3: What are the challenges of IFRS adoption in Vietnam?
RQ4: How willing are Vietnamese accountants to adopt IFRS?
RQ5: Do accounting academics and practitioners have different perspectives regarding IFRS adoption?

The paper adds to the existing literature in several ways. Firstly, this study is one of a few, if not the first, comprehensive study to examine the perception of Vietnamese accountants on the advantages, disadvantages, costs and challenges of IFRS adoption in Vietnam. Recent trends in international accounting research seem to focus on key economies such as member states of the European Union. There are few studies about emerging economies and Vietnam has received limited scholarly coverage in these studies. The case of Vietnam, as a representative of developing countries, may be useful for the IASB in the process of improving global convergence of national accounting standards and IFRS.

The remainder of the paper is organised as follows. Section 2 describes the regulatory environment for financial reporting practices in Vietnam. Section 3 reviews the previous literature regarding IFRS adoption. Section 4 outlines the data collection and research methodology. Results of the study are discussed in Section 5. Finally, the conclusion and implication of the study are presented in Section 6.

THE FINANCIAL REPORTING ENVIRONMENT IN VIETNAM

Accounting has a long history in Vietnam but the accounting profession was only established in the early 1990s. In particular, the Ministry of Finance of Vietnam (MoF) founded the first two accounting and auditing firms (VACO and AASC) as late as 1991. In 1994, the MoF held the first exam for Vietnamese Certified Public Accountants certificates (Vietnamese CPA). In the same year, the Degree on Independent Auditing was approved by the government. However, over the past two decades, the accountancy profession has grown quickly. As of 31 December 2013, there were over 2,500 Vietnamese CPA members. In many ways, the accountancy profession in Vietnam has contributed to the economic development of Vietnam in general.

In the last decade, there has been much activity in Vietnamese accounting legislative systems with efforts from the Vietnamese government to reform the national accounting jurisdiction and thus boost the nation's economic development to attract foreign investment. In the context of international accounting convergence towards IFRS, Vietnamese accounting reform progressed to a new stage. In 2011, the MoF formed the Vietnamese Accounting Standards Board (VASB) and a project team of 44 members were organised to assist the VASB to revise the existing VAS and publish new standards to align with the current IFRS (VACPA & CAPA 2012). In 2013, the VASB proposed six new accounting standards for capital markets and amendments for eight existing accounting standards (CafeF 2013).

IFRS are not required or allowed in Vietnam as the financial reporting rules. All Vietnamese businesses are required to report under VAS. There are significant differences between the current VAS and IFRS. This is because VAS is generally based on the international accounting standards (IAS) issued prior to 2003 with adjustments for Vietnamese economic, finance and accounting conditions. According to Pham (2012), the overall *de jure* convergence (convergence by accounting regulation) of VAS and IFRS is about 66 per cent in which the measurement convergence is at a higher rate (75.8 per cent) and disclosure convergence is at the lower rate (61.9 per cent). The findings of Pham (2012) revealed that disclosure convergence between VAS and IFRS is significantly low because most of the IASB standards require additional disclosure relative to its equivalent VAS. This disparity leads to the concern that financial statements prepared under VAS may not fully meet the external users' needs for accounting information. Thus, it is not an uncommon practice in Vietnam that companies prepare two separate financial statements, one under mandatory VAS and the other voluntarily compliant with IFRS for overseas financing purposes.

Together with the introduction of new accounting system effectively in 1 January 2015, the Vietnamese Accounting Law 2003 is anticipated to be revised in late 2015 to establish the framework for the voluntary IFRS adoption by 2017 and eventual full IFRS implementation by 2020 in Vietnam (Vo, 2014). From 2017, IFRS shall be permitted and after 2020 required as part of the national accounting regulatory system for public interest entities (including publicly listed companies, financial, banking and insurance institutions); state owned joint-stock corporations, foreign-capital invested companies. Other non-public interest entities are recommended but not required to adopt IFRS. However, little is known or understood about the attitudes of key stakeholders in Vietnam towards this adoption announcement. Therefore, this study provides important perception based evidence from the Vietnamese accounting community to assist Vietnamese standard setters for insightful perception, this, in turn, could facilitate favourable accounting decisions affecting accounting practices in Vietnam.

LITERATURE REVIEW

Arguments Supporting IFRS Adoption

Most of the arguments in favour of IFRS adoption focus on the effects on capital markets and investors. One argument is that the adoption of IFRS improves financial reporting to outside investors. Scholars point out that IFRS are more capital market oriented and, hence, more relevant to investors as well as more comprehensive, especially with respect to disclosure, than most local accounting standards (Daske & Gebhardt 2006; Ding et al. 2007). Other scholars argue that if the switch to IFRS does, in fact, improve corporate reporting and disclosure, then, mandatory IFRS reporting should be associated with an increase in market liquidity as well as a decline in firms costs of capital (Hail & Leuz 2009; Al-Akra, Eddie & Ali 2010). This point of view assumes that firms were previously mandated to report under "lower-quality" standards that resulted in relatively poor reporting and disclosure outcomes (Cascino & Gassen 2010). The argument is, therefore, less applicable to countries in which their disclosure environments are already of high standard such as the United States (Hail, Leuz & Wysocki 2010a, b).

Reporting according to IFRS makes it less costly for investors to compare firms across markets and countries is another argument, which suggests favourable capital market effects of IFRS adoption (Armstrong et al. 2010). As previously discussed, greater comparability may make financial reports more useful to investors and other stakeholders, even if the quality of corporate reporting does not improve (Brochet, Jagolinzer & Riedl 2013). Moreover, using the same set of accounting standards across firms from different countries improves outsiders ability to detect earnings management and accounting manipulations (Capkun, Collins & Jeanjean 2013), as it limits the set of permissible accounting treatments, which in turn should improve firms reporting incentives (Hail & Leuz 2009). Thus, if the switch to IFRS does, in fact, improve the comparability of firm's reports, it has the potential to improve market liquidity and reduce cost of capital (Lambert, Leuz & Verrecchia 2012).

Differences in the accounting standards are also viewed as an impediment to cross-border investment (Aggarwal & Goodell 2010). Thus, the global movement toward IFRS reporting may facilitate cross-border investment and the integration of capital markets. Although the magnitude of the effects are unclear (Beneish & Yohn 2008), making it easier for foreigners to invest in a country s firms should in principle improve market liquidity and enlarge firms investor bases, which in turn should improve risk sharing and lower firms cost of capital (Hail & Leuz 2009).

Arguments Opposing IFRS Adoption

There are also arguments that make substantial capital market effects from IFRS adoption *per se* less likely or plausible. IFRS, like any other set of accounting standards, provide firms with substantial discretion and, hence, the reporting incentives argument applies. Firms that oppose the switch to IFRS or toward more transparency are unlikely to make material changes to their reporting policies (Daske et al. 2013). This concern applies not only to recognition and valuation rules, where firms are known to have substantial discretion (Jeanjean & Stolowy 2008), but also to footnote disclosures (Ashbaugh, Johnstone & Warfield 1999), in which firms can also provide additional information. Thus, even if the standards themselves mandate superior accounting practices and require more disclosures, it is not clear whether firms implement these requirements in ways that make the reported numbers more informative (Beuselinck et al. 2009). The same argument applies for comparability of financial reporting (DeFond et al. 2011).

The alternative argument is that the manager's incentives and institutional infrastructure overcome the accounting standards in creating the impact on the quality of the financial reporting (Lee, Walker & Christensen 2008). This incentives-based view suggests that countries institutional structures and changes therein play an important role for the capital market effects around IFRS adoption (Baker & Barbu 2009). Controlling all other factors, countries with stricter enforcement regimes and institutional structures that provide strong reporting incentives are more likely to exhibit noticeable capital market effects around the introduction of IFRS reporting, especially when there are substantial differences between IFRS and the local accounting standards (Peng & van der Laan Smith 2010).

Stricter enforcement and better reporting incentives imply that firms are less likely to get away with adopting IFRS merely as a label, without materially changing their reporting practices for related evidence (Daske et al. 2013). Conversely, one could argue that countries with better reporting practices before the introduction of IFRS should experience smaller capital market effects (Barth et al. 2013). However, there is an inconsistency with this argument. The argument rests on the presumption that changing the accounting standards alone improves firms reporting practices and ignores institutional reasons why firms in these countries have better reporting quality to begin with (Hail, Leuz & Wysocki 2010a). Conversely, Ahmed, Neel and Wang (2013) concluded that accounting quality declined after mandatory IFRS adoption in contrast with prior studies that document evidence suggesting an increase in accounting quality after IFRS adoption. However, the method of analysis of Ahmed, Neel and Wang (2013) has a number of limitations. Firstly, the conclusions draw a comparison over a shorter period. Secondly, Ahmed, Neel and Wang (2013) presumed that change in the accounting quality measures was driven by changes in managerial discretion or exercise of judgment rather than by changes in properties of accounting resulting from the new standards.

Studies of IFRS Adoption in Developing Countries

The potential benefits of IFRS in developing markets and the reasons why developing countries adopt IFRS are strongly argued by numerous scholars. Several studies point to the variation in IFRS benefits and adoption over a group of countries (Tarca, 2012; Brüggemann, Hitz, & Sellhorn, 2013). It is argued that IFRS benefits are related to factors such as extent and level of gaps between national GAAP and IFRS (Daske et al., 2008), and differences and extent of legal enforcement (Hope, Jin, & Kang, 2006). As explained above, it is expected that differences in the benefits at an individual country level will emerge. However, an emerging body of research is pointing to global benefits from the use of IFRS, mostly from the well-established capital markets (Soderstrom & Sun, 2007).

Similarly, there is strong evidence to suggest there is a strong relationship between IFRS adoption and trade as well as foreign direct investment. For instance, Chen, Ding, and Xu (2010) confirmed the positive association between FDI growth and degree of IFRS convergence, suggesting that IFRS adoption promotes cross-border investment. In contrast, Lasmin (2011) rejected the positive effects from IFRS adoption upon the trade and foreign direct investment inflows. Studies suggest capital market benefits following adoption of IFRS cautioned that the benefits occurred in countries with strong investor protection and so-called high quality financial reporting and enforcement (Frost, Gordon, & Pownall, 2008).

More recently, various studies document the process of adoption of IFRS in the former communist nations. For example, Vellam (2012) described the difficulties of conversion to IFRS and impact of adoption on financial statements in Poland. Similarly, Albu *et al.* (2011) described the complex nature of IFRS adoption process in Romania and Alon (2013) discussed the IFRS adoption experience of Russia. While some authors supported the claim that IFRS are beneficial for developing countries (Ismail, Kamarudin, Zijl, & Dunstan, 2013), others questioned whether real economic consequences achieve IFRS adoption (Elbannan, 2011). Some studies show that accounting quality improved post-IFRS adoption (Uddin & Tsamenyi, 2010). The other studies provided contrary evidence that accounting quality did not improve even after IFRS was mandated (Ashraf & Ghani, 2005).

Overall, despite the substantial number of IFRS adoption studies in the last two decades, scholars have not reached a consensus on the overall impact of IFRS adoption in developing countries. In comparison with research in developed countries, studies of developing countries are also under researched. Amongst the limited number of published studies in developing countries, several studies examined the former communist countries, particularly China, Romania, Poland, Hungary, and Russia. However, Vietnam has been neglected in the accounting literature. The next section reviews the current accounting literature related to Vietnam.

METHODOLOGY

The data collection methodology involved the distribution of 3,000 questionnaires in Vietnam to accounting professionals during 2012. The survey was segmented into three categories of accounting professionals and roughly apportioning 1,000 surveys per category. The first group included were auditors because of their specific task in applying accounting standards to their clients. The second group included accountants and accounting department heads because of the responsibility they have in reviewing or preparing financial statements for firms they represent. The third and final category related to the accounting educators selected because of their knowledge of accounting and because of their role in imbedding accounting understanding in the new generation of accountants. All three categories were well informed of the importance of this issue and as such the significance of the survey.

The questionnaire was reviewed during a pilot phase by 30 target participants (10 participants for each of the accounting groups). The pilot respondents were from different management levels (from junior to most senior). In addition, the pilot survey also received 5 responses from representatives of Ministry of Finance and accounting professional bodies. The survey content was revised upon the feedbacks of the pilot respondents. The questionnaire included both close-ended and open-ended format questions. A total of 728 usable responses were analysed producing an effective response rate of 24 per cent as shown in Table 1.

Table 1. Sample size and response rate per sub-group

Accountant groups	Questionnaires				Percentage	
	Sent	Returned	Unusable	Usable	Returned	Usable
Group 1: Auditors	1,000	250	71	203	27%	20%
Group 2:Accountants	1,000	435	101	371	47%	37%
Group 3: Academics	1,000	242	93	154	25%	15%
Total	**3,000**	**927**	**265**	**728**	**33%**	**24%**

Source: Authors

FINDINGS

Demographic Profiles of the Respondents

It was found that the accountant group represented the highest percentage of respondents (58 per cent) followed by the auditors (26 per cent) and the academics (16 per cent). On gender, the contribution from male respondents (57 per cent) is a little higher than the female (43 per cent). On the employment position, most of respondents were in senior or management levels and less than four per cent at a junior level. The majority of the respondents are also in their middle careers with the two most popular age groups from 31 to 40 (45 per cent) and 41 to 50 (19 per cent). This is consistent with the answers coming from those with work experience. The majority of respondents had between six to 15 years of work experience.

Two-thirds of the respondents are members of one or more professional accounting body. These include: (1) the Vietnam Association of Certified Public Accountants (VACPA at 32 per cent), (2) the Vietnam Accounting and Auditing Association (VAA at 28 per cent), the Association of Chartered Certified Accountants (ACCA at 13 per cent) and the CPA Australia at nine per cent. Over 16 per cent of the respondents were members of two professional bodies. One being local membership (VACPA or VAA) and one internationally recognized membership (ACCA or CPA Australia). The involvement of respondents in the professional bodies was also used as a control variable.

In terms of IFRS knowledge, 48 per cent of the respondents obtained this via self-study. The above-mentioned professional bodies also provided IFRS training to their members and students (33 per cent). The remaining respondents received training from in-house and/or on-the-job training sources. Amongst the professional bodies, the VAA is the dominant IFRS training provider (10.5 per cent), followed by the ACCA (9.5 per cent), the VACPA (4 per cent), and the CPA Australia (3 per cent).

RQ1: Perceptions on Benefits of IFRS Adoption

In answering RQ1, the respondents expressed their perceptions on the 14 benefits of IFRS adoption. The survey results show a strong positive view amongst the respondents with eleven of the 14 perceived benefits of IFRS (> 50 per cent agreement) listed in Table 2 were perceived as having a significant effect with regards to the IFRS adoption in Vietnam.

The survey results in Table 2 show that over 80 per cent of the respondents perceived that financial statements prepared under IFRS as “reliable”, “relevant”, and “comparable”. Perceptions of a “higher reporting quality than VAS” and “understandability” were also strongly supported at 62 per cent and 57 per cent respectively.

Moreover, IFRS adoption was perceived to create some positive effects for Vietnamese businesses such as:

- Easier access to global market than VAS (82 per cent);
- Improving the potential investors’ confidence (81 per cent);
- Increasing shareholder s trust (75 per cent);
- Obtaining external finance easier than VAS (69 per cent); and
- Improving creditor s relationship (54 per cent).

Table 2. Perceived benefits of IFRS adoption

Ranked Order	Items	Percentage (%) of Respondents "Agreeing"			
		Auditor	Accountant	Academic	Weighted Average
1	Reliable	84%	81%	83%	82%
2	Investor s confidence	79%	85%	74%	81%
3	Relevant	86%	78%	79%	80%
4	Comparable	86%	78%	78%	80%
5	Shareholder s confidence	60%	82%	77%	75%
6	Access global market	77%	86%	79%	75%
7	External finance	60%	74%	69%	69%
8	Reduced cost of parallel reporting	67%	63%	58%	63%
9	High quality	55%	65%	65%	62%
10	Understandable	59%	63%	42%	57%
11	Creditor s confidence	45%	56%	62%	54%
12	Reduced cost of analysing data	44%	53%	40%	48%
13	Reduced cost of raising capital	33%	37%	36%	36%
14	Reduced cost of issuing standards	15%	25%	23%	22%

Source: Authors

These descriptive results are further supported by the written comments made by the survey respondents. The theme of cross-category was the perceptions of reputable features of IFRS with typical comments such as "IFRS are more worldwide" (R65 2012)[1]; "IFRS help Vietnam enterprise join global trade better" (R208 2012); "IFRS help Vietnam to be known" (R24 2012); "IFRS has standardised framework and easy to understand in global view if other investors in other countries would like to invest into" (R31 2012).

The respondents also added some potential benefits when reporting according to IFRS. These additional benefits included the mobility of accountants and making the training of accountants easier (R12 2012), helping to evaluate the performance of subsidiaries within a group's global performance (R30 2012), helping with financial ratings (R368 2012), helping to increase enterprise and national reputation (R316 2012).

It should be pointed out that the words "easy", "easily" and "easier" are used by many respondents to express the perceived benefits of IFRS comparing with VAS. Table 3 includes extracts from the respondents' comments showing there is a marked recognition of this and this finding is in line with Naoum, Sykianakis and Tzovas (2011) who reported that half of the respondents perceived that companies applied IFRS would have easier access to foreign markets.

The written responses also reinforced transparency as an important desirable feature of financial statements prepared in accordance with IFRS. Two comments regarding this epitomize the comments: "Global standards will give a transparent view for investors to compare the enterprises at the same industry" (R203 2012), and "IFRS conversion increases the transparency of financial information assisting the management to make an informed decision" (R208 2012).

Table 3. Respondent comments on benefits of IFRS adoption

Respondent	Comment
Respondent 4	IFRS will help us *easily* access the global network of business (R4 2012)
Respondent 7	*easier* for multinational company consolidations (R7 2012)
Respondent 135	more worldwide acceptable, *easy* to approach to international capital market (R135 2012)
Respondent 257	*easy* to raise capital overseas (R257 2012)
Respondent 389	*easy* [international] integration (R389 2012)
Respondent 452	international financial institutions will *easily* lend funds (R452 2012
Respondent 657	Can *easily* follow and manage in the multinational corporation as sharing the common financial reporting system (R657 2012)
Respondent 729	*easier* for analyst (R729 2012)

Source: Authors

Moreover, the respondents viewed that IFRS adoption create the international opportunities which helped Vietnamese businesses to obtain access to international financial markets and create an image of a reliable market player. The respondents commented:

IFRS, in my opinion, attempts to bring all accounting and financial statements, in a more comparable platform, so as to derive more meaningful information for the management, promoters, employees and more importantly to investors and public at large. It will definitely help foreign investors to check the accounting, auditing and banking approach at other international locations and adopt international practices in the accounting system. (R829 2012)

The survey responses indicated that despite the difficulties and costs associated with conversion to IFRS, there appears to be a positive perception towards IFRS by Vietnamese accountants in general. Respondent 208, of the accountant group highlighted this:

My company is a publicly listed company in Vietnam. Though IFRS implementation brings us significant challenges, we really want to proceed in its implementation. The implementation of IFRS would increase the transparency of our financial statements, provide better cash-flow, equity and asset management, thus, increase the trust of our shareholders, especially international investors. (R208 2012)

Overall, the Vietnamese accountants, auditors, and academics are very optimistic on the potential benefits of IFRS adoption in Vietnam. Credibility and comparability of financial statements provided by the Vietnamese enterprises were perceived as the most desirable benefits from IFRS reporting. The respondents also perceived that IFRS adoption would provide opportunities for Vietnamese businesses to join the global capital market and in turn, enhance the national reputation of Vietnam.

RQ2: Perceptions on Disadvantages of IFRS Adoption

In answering RQ2, the respondents expressed their perceptions on the 14 disadvantages of IFRS adoption. Analysis of the results showed that four of the 14 items listed in Table 4 were perceived as having a significant effect with regards to the adoption of IFRS in Vietnam.

As shown in Table 4, the highest ranked disadvantage for IFRS implementation was the matter of its over-complexity. A majority of the respondents viewed both IFRS and IFRS for small and medium-sized enterprises are overly-complicated for Vietnamese businesses (at 65 and 68 per cent respectively). This view is reflected in the comment of one respondent from the accountant group:

Vietnam is a small country and in practice IFRS is very complicated for SMEs and it is hard to understand things that are so complicated comparing to the local standards which are very simple. (R41 2012)

In addition, 54 per cent of the respondents (mostly of the accountant sub-group) considered IFRS implementation a time-consuming procedure. The accountant group held the view that IFRS were "time consuming" (R250 2012) or "require doubling [amount of] work" (R718 2012). This is in contrast to the perceptions expressed by auditors who felt that "time" was a benefit in that they perceived that IFRS "saved time and labor" (R63 2012), "reduce[s] auditor s work" (R797 2012). Academics held a similar view in that IFRS "reduces labor cost of reporting in the global context" (R809 2012).

Table 4. Perceived disadvantages of IFRS adoption

Ranked Order	Items	Percentage (%) of Respondents "Agreeing"			
		Auditor	Accountant	Academic	Weighted Average
1	Too complicated for SME s	70%	67%	68%	68%
2	Complicated	75%	59%	67%	65%
3	Time consuming	64%	49%	54%	54%
4	In foreign language, hard to understand	53%	47%	51%	50%
5	Impossible to have single global standards	50%	48%	43%	48%
6	Not yet fully accepted globally	43%	40%	43%	41%
7	Influenced by political intervention	25%	25%	25%	25%
8	Subjective	34%	16%	25%	23%
9	Vietnam has no involvement	21%	24%	16%	22%
10	Cost outweigh benefit	15%	16%	28%	18%
11	Lack details, room for personal interpretation	21%	15%	15%	17%
12	Vietnam loses control	9%	18%	14%	15%
13	Increase risk of corporate fraud	9%	13%	17%	13%
14	Vietnam has no requirement	4%	4%	6%	5%

Source: Authors

The different orientation and focus between the two sets of standards were viewed as highly undesirable features of IFRS. It was believed that IFRS are more investor-oriented and the current Vietnamese accounting legislation was more tax-driven which could cause major differences in accounting recognition and disclosures requirements. This view is reflected in several comments made by respondents:

[IFRS could] conflict with the prevailing tax regime. (R65 2012)

Complicated finance and accounting regulations in Vietnam would require doubling the work if IFRS are applied. (R718 2012)

Enforcement of IFRS is a national issue, thus the quality of financial reports is likely to differ across jurisdictions. (R12 2012)

The principle-based concepts and professional judgments required for IFRS reporting were also perceived as difficulties for a majority of Vietnamese accountants. The matter of having to learn new skills, especially for those with no relevant prior experience, was perceived as important. Since Vietnamese accounting standards are more rule-based standards (as opposed to the IFRS are principled-based approaches), the conversion of financial statements from VAS to IFRS might change the financial results from favourable to unfavourable or vice versa. This was highlighted by Respondent 50 from the accountant group who commented that:

[IFRS] may create a significant impact to the owners of the enterprises in post-IFRS implementation, the financial results are significantly different and outside the expectation of the enterprises. Thus, IFRS implementation should be rejected. (R50 2012)

Overall, the respondents expressed concerns about the disadvantages and negative impact resulting from IFRS adoption. Over-complexity, time-consuming and less comprehensiveness were perceived as the most undesirable features of IFRS reporting. In addition, the respondents also concerned the negative impacts upon the conversion of financial statements from the current accounting legislation to complying with IFRS if IFRS adoption would occur in Vietnam.

RQ3: Perceptions on the Challenges of IFRS Adoption

In response to RQ3, the majority of the respondents (over 70 per cent) expressed their agreements with the ten challenging items listed in the questionnaire as shown in Table 5. Levels of agreement with challenges ranged from 73 per cent for the challenge relating to the lack of timely translations to as high as 90 per cent for the challenge of further educating staff. Table 5 also shows that on average, 75 per cent of the respondents list the lack of adequate IFRS implementation guidance as a challenge. This lack of guidance creates risks for different interpretations of IFRS and could increase the risks of manipulation in the interpretation of financial statements.

Table 5. Perceived challenges of IFRS implementation

Ranked Order	Challenges	Percentage (%) of Respondents "Agreeing"			
		Auditor	Accountant	Academic	Weighted Average
1	Educating financial personnel	90%	76%	81%	81%
2	Updating accounting processes	86%	77%	71%	79%
3	Educating managerial personnel	85%	74%	76%	78%
4	Limited coverage in the university curriculum	77%	81%	74%	78%
5	Updating software	85%	73%	75%	77%
6	Managing public perception	89%	70%	79%	77%
7	Managing transition workload	85%	69%	74%	75%
8	Insufficient guidance on first-time adoption	79%	74%	72%	75%
9	Updating auditing processes	76%	70%	68%	72%
10	Lack of timely translation into Vietnamese	73%	71%	71%	71%

Source: Authors

The list of perceived challenges can be categorised into four groups of challenges:

- **Process challenges** include:
  - Updating accounting process (79 per cent agreeing);
  - Updating auditing process (72 per cent); and
  - Updating software (77 per cent agreeing).
- **Educating challenges** include:
  - Educating financial personnel (81 per cent); and
  - Educating managerial personnel (78 per cent).
- **Transition challenges** include:
  - Managing transition workload (75 per cent); and
  - Managing public perception (77 per cent).
- **Guidance challenges** include:
  - Insufficient guidance (75 per cent);
  - Lack of timely translation (71 per cent); and
  - Limited coverage in the university curriculum (78 per cent).

As shown in Table 5, the majority of the respondents (over 70 per cent) expressed their concerns that the lack of IFRS guidance creates risks for different interpretations of IFRS and could increase the risks of manipulation in the interpretation of financial statements. Additional commentary showed that many respondents felt that IFRS-based financial reports were not recognized by most government authorities in Vietnam (R320 2012), and that current regulations are already too complicated and that the government does not want to undertake IFRS adoption and thereby undermine their control and power over Vietnamese businesses (R718 2012).

The majority of the respondents expressed their concerns on the educational and guidance challenges including the following responses:

Most of current high-level management in the enterprises have been trained with out-dated knowledge. They always find it difficult to apply new knowledge, especially international accounting standards. The new generation of the workforce has also been trained in the local universities, also with out-dated knowledge. Additionally, the academics are not likely to have knowledge on IFRS if they were not qualified from international training programs. In general, IFRS implementation process will face difficulties from the current problematic education system. (R715 2012)

The respondents also concerned that IFRS are not appropriate in Vietnam at this stage because it is the principle-based system. A typical comment was as follows:

VAS is somehow similar to rule-based while IAS [IFRS] was closer to principal-based. So if we want to adopt IAS [IFRS] and amend VAS, we should train the professional people who can understand IAS [IFRS] clearly and have the ability to teach what they understand to others. Hence, it will be better while we adopt IAS [IFRS] and not misunderstand what the standards say. (R27 2012)

Additional commentary showed that many respondents felt that IFRS-based financial reports were not recognised by most governmental authorities in Vietnam (R320 2012), that current regulations are already too complicated and that the government does not want to undertake IFRS adoption and thereby undermine their control and power over Vietnamese businesses (R718 2012).

Overall, the respondents perceived the greatest challenge of IFRS adoption is to educate financial personnel. This obstacle is more critical since there is lack of adequate IFRS implementation guidance in Vietnam, which increases the risk for a different interpretation of IFRS provisions and could create the inconsistency and non-compliance issues during the IFRS implementation process. The respondents also concerned the conversion from VAS to IFRS would not be happening because of lack of support for IFRS from the Vietnamese government.

RQ4: Willingness for IFRS Adoption

As shown in Table 6, two-thirds of the respondents of all three respondent groups indicated that they would consider adopting IFRS if the standards are permitted or required in Vietnam (hereinafter referred those respondents as voluntary adopters). It was anticipated that the voluntary adopters would work mainly in listed or foreign invested companies. (IFRS was perceived as over-complicated for small and medium companies and was mainly required in subsidiaries of the multinational corporations or companies raised capital overseas). As expected, a minority of voluntary adopters are from small businesses (5 per cent), the majority are from medium (50 per cent) and large size companies (45 per cent). Surprisingly, of those voluntary adopters, there are more respondents from private (34 per cent) and state-owned ownership (19 per cent) than from joint-venture (8 per cent), listed (15 per cent) or foreign invested companies (20 per cent). Furthermore, the willingness is consistent across the respondent groups (auditor 66 per cent, accountant 58 per cent, and academics 65 per cent).

The survey results indicate that except for small businesses, despite capital ownership, medium and large Vietnamese enterprises are willing to embrace IFRS. The result is further supported by the fact that close to half of the respondents (48 per cent) reported a dual reporting status in their companies consolidated financial reports, particularly VAS with IFRS reconciliation (23 per cent); IFRS and VAS

Tables 6. Willingness to voluntary IFRS adoption

Opinion	Auditor	Accountant	Academic	All Groups
Yes	17%	28%	16%	60%
No	8%	18%	8%	35%
Not sure	1%	3%	1%	5%
Total	26%	49%	25%	100%

Source: Authors

as two sets of reports (15 per cent); VAS with US GAAP reconciliation (2 per cent); VAS and US GAAP as two reports (2 per cent); VAS and other standards (10 per cent).

From the following comments of Vietnamese practitioners (public auditors and corporate accountants), it is reasonable to conclude that a part of Vietnamese businesses, mostly foreign invested and publicly listed companies, are well prepared or are ready for IFRS application. The typical comments of the respondents are "Our Company has been applying IFRS for 4 years" (R368 2012); "We use both!" (R34 2012); "We already applied it" (R223 2012).

Many other respondents show their excitement and willingness to prepare financial statements according to IFRS when the standards are permitted in Vietnam. About two-thirds of the respondents (448 over 775 respondents) provided a "Yes" answer when being asked if they would consider voluntarily adopting IFRS. Their typical remark was: "Yes. My company is a multinational company. It is good for our financial statements [being] and therefore comparable to other countries in the group" (R3 2012).

The literature indicates that the large size or foreign owned companies would more voluntarily adopt IFRS than the small sized or private owned companies (Goodwin & Ahmed 2006). However, this study found otherwise. Those respondents would not consider voluntary IFRS adoption was working for different company sizes and ownerships. Typical reasons for not considering IFRS voluntary adoption was related to cost effectiveness issues such as "cost > benefits" (R323 2012), "time consuming" (R250 2012); "complicated and not required in Vietnam" (R794 2012), "small size" (R888 2012), "no requirements on external financing" (R294 2012); "not ready" (R482 2012) and finally "family business"(R515 2012).

A reason that IFRS is not applicable or not mandated in Vietnam is referred to in the respondents' comments:

If not mandatory, we will not apply because of the complexity and irrelevance of IFRS to the management style of most Vietnamese businesses. (R562 2012)

IFRS based financial reports are not accepted by most government authorities in Vietnam. (R32 2012)

This opinion of a corporate accountant is also in line with opinions from the auditors and academics.

Time consuming and costly in training, no benefit if only operating in Vietnam and funded by local banks. (R73 2012)

While some of the above concerns are critical and require careful consideration, they reflect the insights from the current reporting practices and the desires of practitioners in Vietnam.

IFRS implementation requires advanced accounting personnel. However, the majority of Vietnamese enterprises are small and medium-sized. The competencies of accountants [of these companies] are not yet met in [the IFRS] requirements. Accounting education is not yet at a high-level standard in Vietnam. (R176 2012)

[IFRS] should apply to large company or multinational corporations. For small and medium size companies, it requires transition period and should let it be voluntary adoption. The mandatory adoption is unnecessary, over costly and time-consuming for small businesses. (R176 2012)

In summary, the survey results reflect the current reporting practices and the desires of practitioners in Vietnam. An implication of this is the possibility that IFRS should be permitted for voluntary adoption in Vietnam. IFRS adoption (or not) will be decided by the company upon the consideration of cost-benefit analysis, ownership, size and other organisational factors.

RQ5: Comparing Perceptions between Accountant Subgroups

The survey results indicate that, amongst the three subgroups of respondents, the corporate accountants have the most positive viewpoint on the IFRS, followed by the academics and then auditors in that order.

As summarized in Table 7, on average, the accountants (66 per cent) were more optimistic on the benefits of IFRS adoption than academics (62 per cent) followed by auditors (61 per cent). The accountants also had lesser concern of the disadvantages of IFRS (32 per cent), lower than the academics (34 per cent), and the auditors (35 per cent). Moreover, the accountants and academics (at 74 per cent) shared less concern on the challenges of IFRS implementation than the auditors (83 per cent). In addition, the favorable opinion of the corporate accountants on the net impact of IFRS adoption sets it apart from the two other groups. For example, 47 per cent of the accountants perceive a positive impact from IFRS conversion, which sets it apart from the auditors (41 per cent) and the academics (43 per cent). Despite concerns on the disadvantages and challenges of IFRS, the majority of the respondents (60 per cent) supported voluntary IFRS adoption in Vietnam with the highest support rate coming from the auditors (65 per cent), followed closely by the academics (64 per cent) and the least supported by the accountants (57 per cent).

Table 7. Summary results by accountant subgroups

Research Question	Description	Percentage (%) per Group			
		Auditor	Accountant	Academic	Weighted Average
1	Optimistic on benefits of IFRS adoption	61%	66%	62%	63%
2	Concerns on disadvantages of IFRS adoption	35%	32%	34%	34%
3	Concerns on challenges of IFRS implementation	83%	74%	74%	77%
4	Believing in positive net benefit of IFRS adoption in the long-term	41%	47%	43%	44%
5	Support for voluntary IFRS adoption in Vietnam	65%	57%	64%	60%

Source: Authors

SUMMARY AND CONCLUSION

The empirical evidence of this study illustrates the perception of IFRS adoption in an emerging economy like Vietnam. The respondents perceived that IFRS adoption would increase transparency, comparability for financial figures across firms and countries. The respondents also perceived that IFRS adoption would provide opportunities for Vietnamese businesses and Vietnam as a nation. In addition to the positive views on the potential benefits arising from IFRS adoption, the respondent also expressed concerns upon disadvantages and negative impact resulting from IFRS adoption. Over-complexity, time-consuming, and less comprehensiveness were listed amongst the most disadvantages of IFRS. The perceived cost impact of IFRS adoption was viewed as significant since majority of Vietnamese businesses are small to medium sizes. The respondents viewed re-training the financial staff from rule-based approach under VAS to principled-based approach under IFRS as one of the greatest challenges. Although IFRS reporting was viewed as being costly, time-consuming, and challenging, surprisingly, the respondents were optimistic on the long-term benefits. Avoiding cost of dual reporting was perceived as the greatest cost saving benefits. Despite several concerns of significant challenges resulting from IFRS implementation, two-third of the respondents showed their willingness to adopt IFRS to gain positive effects from IFRS reporting such as increasing trusts in shareholders, investors, thus, making access to global capital market and external financing easier than reporting under VAS. Overall, the survey results show the optimism by all three groups of accountants with more respondents agreed on the benefits and less respondents concerned on the disadvantages of IFRS. The enthusiasm of potential benefits of IFRS adoption outweighs the concerns of potential negative impact by the number of written responses received on both areas.

The survey results indicate that, amongst the three groups of respondents, the corporate accountants have the highest positive viewpoint of IFRS, followed by the academics, then the auditors. In particular, on average, the accountants are more optimistic than the academics and the auditors on the benefits of IFRS adoption. The accountants also have less concern on the disadvantages and challenges of IFRS implementation, set it apart from the auditors and the academic groups. In addition, the favourable opinion of the corporate accountant group on the net impact of IFRS adoption sets it apart from the two other groups. However, the survey results show that the corporate accountants, while favorable, are more reserved when it comes to willingness and readiness of IFRS adoption. The less willingness and readiness of the corporate accountants may be explained by the fact that they are more familiar with rules-based approach with a vast number of manuals, guidance and specific rules for each accounting transactions than the principles-based approach requiring professional judgment. Therefore, it is apparent that the auditors welcome IFRS adoption since the auditors make professional judgments on a regular basis. However, it is somewhat surprising that the academics are more willing and ready to adopt IFRS than the accountants. It may be that the academics are more open to underlying accounting concepts instead of specific rules because the educators can provide students with the ability to discover solutions on their own without having to learn every rule (Jackling, Howieson & Natoli 2012). This result implies a major challenge for the Vietnamese accounting profession to ensure the academics are fully prepared for teaching IFRS using a principle-based approach.

The result implies an urgent need for a rigorous IFRS capacity-building program to be embarked across the country in order to provide the needed resources for IFRS implementation. The program requires the cooperation and efforts by all professional bodies, regulatory bodies, firms and training institutions. The accounting professional bodies, in conjunction with the universities, should address both the needs of IFRS training for current practitioners and for future accountants. If IFRS adoption is to occur in

Vietnam, it requires substantive changes in accounting education and training. Most business schools and accounting programs lack experienced and qualified trainers to teach IFRS. Except for auditors working for the Big Four accounting firms, many auditors working for the local and private accounting firms are not yet fully equipped to perform the audit of IFRS compliant reports. Successfully addressing education and training deficiencies for practicing accounting professionals relies on the profession obtaining the support of the international organisations (such as the Big Four, the World Bank, the IFAC, the IASB) as well as government agencies and scholars nationwide. It is recommended that the professional bodies in conjunction with the Big Four focus on translating and modifying the training programs available at the IFAC s Education Committee to develop high quality IFRS training programs for the specific needs of Vietnam. Upon achieving sufficient international and national support, the Big Four and the professional bodies should participate in delivering these training programs to the public accountants, the financial and managerial personnel of all enterprises, including all size, industry, listed or non-listed companies.

This paper is subject to the limitation of a single survey questionnaire methodology. Given that information was collected from all key informants using a single questionnaire administered at a single point in time, the population surveyed may not be representative of the general population. To complement the findings of this thesis, future research could also be undertaken by exploring how IFRS are perceived and used by respondent groups other than accountants, such as investors, financial brokers, institutional lenders, regulators. Again, the uses of both quantitative and qualitative methods are appropriate and will lead to a better understanding of the relevance of IFRS in emerging economies like Vietnam.

REFERENCES

Aggarwal, R., & Goodell, J. W. (2010). Financial markets versus institutions in European countries: Influence of culture and other national characteristics. *International Business Review*, *19*(5), 502–520. doi:10.1016/j.ibusrev.2009.07.010

Ahmed, A. S., Neel, M., & Wang, D. (2013). Does Mandatory Adoption of IFRS Improve Accounting Quality? Preliminary Evidence. *Contemporary Accounting Research*, *30*(4), 1344–1372. doi:10.1111/j.1911-3846.2012.01193.x

Al-Akra, M., Eddie, I. A., & Ali, M. J. (2010). The influence of the introduction of accounting disclosure regulation on mandatory disclosure compliance: Evidence from Jordan. *The British Accounting Review*, *42*(3), 170–186. doi:10.1016/j.bar.2010.04.001

Albu, N., Caˇtaˇlin, N.A., Bunea, S., Calu, D.A., & Girbina, M.M. (2011). A story about IAS/IFRS implementation in Romania An institutional and structuration theory perspective. *Journal of Accounting in Emerging Economies, 1*(1), 76-100.

Alon, A. (2013). Complexity and Dual Institutionality: The Case of IFRS Adoption in Russia, *Corporate Governance. International Review (Steubenville, Ohio)*, *21*(1), 42–57.

Armstrong, C. S., Barth, M. E., Jagolinzer, A. D., & Riedl, E. J. (2010). Market Reaction to the Adoption of IFRS in Europe. *Accounting Review*, *85*(1), 31–61. doi:10.2308/accr.2010.85.1.31

Ashbaugh, H., Johnstone, K. M., & Warfield, T. D. (1999). Corporate reporting on the Internet. *Accounting Horizons*, *13*(3), 241–257. doi:10.2308/acch.1999.13.3.241

Ashraf, J., & Ghani, W. I. (2005). Accounting development in Pakistan. *The International Journal of Accounting*, *40*(2), 175–201. doi:10.1016/j.intacc.2005.01.010

Baker, R. C., & Barbu, E. M. (2009). *Institutions Involved in International Convergence of Accounting Standards: A Neo-Institutional and Historical Analysis*. CERAG.

Barth, M. E., Landsman, W. R., Lang, M. H., & Williams, C. D. (2013). *Effects on Comparability and Capital Market Benefits of Voluntary Adoption of IFRS by US Firms: Insights from Voluntary Adoption of IFRS by Non-US Firms (January 3, 2013)*. Rock Center for Corporate Governance at Stanford University Working Paper No 133.

Beneish, M. D., & Yohn, T. L. (2008). Information friction and investor home bias: A perspective on the effect of global IFRS adoption on the extent of equity home bias. *Journal of Accounting and Public Policy*, *27*(6), 433–443. doi:10.1016/j.jaccpubpol.2008.09.001

Beuselinck, C., Joos, P., Khurana, I., & Van der Meulen, S. (2009). *Mandatory IFRS Reporting and Stock Price Informativeness*. SSRN eLibrary.

Brochet, F., Jagolinzer, A. D., & Riedl, E. J. (2013). Mandatory IFRS Adoption and Financial Statement Comparability. *Contemporary Accounting Research*, *30*(4), 1373–1400. doi:10.1111/1911-3846.12002

Brüggemann, U., Hitz, J.-M., & Sellhorn, T. (2013, January 5). Intended and Unintended Consequences of Mandatory IFRS Adoption: A Review of Extant Evidence and Suggestions for Future Research. *European Accounting Review*, *22*(1), 1–37. doi:10.1080/09638180.2012.718487

Cafe, F. (2013). *Propose Vietnamese Accounting Standards for capital market (in Vietnamese)*. Retrieved from http://cafef.vn/pageprintnews.aspx?news_id=201307160018200179

Capkun, V., Collins, D. W., & Jeanjean, T. (2013). *The Effect of IAS/IFRS Adoption on Earnings Management (Smoothing): A Closer Look at Competing Explanations*. Retrieved from: http://ssrncom/abstract=1850228 or http://dxdoiorg/102139/ssrn1850228

Cascino, S & Gassen, J. (2010). *Mandatory IFRS adoption and accounting comparability*. SSRN eLibrary.

Chen, C.J., Ding, Y., & Xu, B. (2010). *Convergence of Accounting Standards and Foreign Direct Investment*. Finance and Corporate Governance Conference 2011 Paper.

Daske, H., & Gebhardt, G. (2006). International Financial Reporting Standards and Experts Perceptions of Disclosure Quality. *Abacus*, *42*(3).

Daske, H., Hail, L., Leuz, C., & Verdi, R. (2008). Mandatory IFRS Reporting around the World: Early Evidence on the Economic Consequences. *Journal of Accounting Research*, *46*(5), 1085–1142.

Daske, H., Hail, L., Leuz, C., & Verdi, R. (2013). Adopting a Label: Heterogeneity in the Economic Consequences Around IAS/IFRS Adoptions. *Journal of Accounting Research*, *51*(3), 495–547. doi:10.1111/1475-679X.12005

DeFond, M., Hu, X., Hung, M., & Li, S. (2011). The impact of mandatory IFRS adoption on foreign mutual fund ownership: The role of comparability. *Journal of Accounting and Economics*, *51*(3), 240–258. doi:10.1016/j.jacceco.2011.02.001

Ding, Y., Hope, O. K., Jeanjean, T., & Stolowy, H. (2007). Differences between domestic accounting standards and IAS: Measurement, determinants and implications. *Journal of Accounting and Public Policy*, *26*(1), 1–38. doi:10.1016/j.jaccpubpol.2006.11.001

Elbannan, M. A. (2011). Accounting and stock market effects of international accounting standards adoption in an emerging economy. *Review of Quantitative Finance and Accounting*, *36*(2), 207–245. doi:10.1007/s11156-010-0176-1

Frost, C.A., Gordon, E.A., & Pownall, G. (2008). *Financial Reporting and Disclosure Quality, and Emerging Market Companies Access to Capital in Global Markets.* SSRN eLibrary.

Hail, L., & Leuz, C. (2009). Cost of capital effects and changes in growth expectations around U.S. cross-listings. *Journal of Financial Economics*, *93*(3), 428–454. doi:10.1016/j.jfineco.2008.09.006

Hail, L., Leuz, C., & Wysocki, P. (2010a). Global Accounting Convergence and the Potential Adoption of IFRS by the U.S. (Part I): Conceptual Underpinnings and Economic Analysis. *Accounting Horizons*, *24*(3), 335–394. doi:10.2308/acch.2010.24.3.355

Hail, L., Leuz, C., & Wysocki, P. (2010b). Global Accounting Convergence and the Potential Adoption of IFRS by the U.S. (Part II): Political Factors and Future Scenarios for U.S. Accounting Standards. *Accounting Horizons*, *24*(4), 567–588. doi:10.2308/acch.2010.24.4.567

Hope, O.-K., Jin, J., & Kang, T. (2006). Empirical Evidence on Jurisdictions that Adopt IFRS. *Journal of International Accounting Research*, *5*(2), 1–20. doi:10.2308/jiar.2006.5.2.1

Ismail, W.A.W., Kamarudin, K.A., Zijl, T., & Dunstan, K. (2013). Earnings quality and the adoption of IFRS-based accounting standards: Evidence from an emerging market. *Asian Review of Accounting*, *21*(1), 53-73.

Jackling, B., Howieson, B., & Natoli, R. (2012). Some Implications of IFRS Adoption for Accounting Education. *Australian Accounting Review*, *22*(4), 331–340. doi:10.1111/j.1835-2561.2012.00197.x

Jeanjean, T., & Stolowy, H. (2008). Do accounting standards matter? An exploratory analysis of earnings management before and after IFRS adoption. *Journal of Accounting and Public Policy*, *27*(6), 480–494. doi:10.1016/j.jaccpubpol.2008.09.008

Lambert, R., Leuz, C., & Verrecchia, R. E. (2012). Information Asymmetry, Information Precision, and the Cost of Capital. *Review of Finance*, *16*(1), 1–29. doi:10.1093/rof/rfr014

Lasmin, R. (2011). The unwanted effects of the International Financial Reporting Standards (IFRS) adoption: evidence from developing countries. *Proceedings of the Allied Academies Internet Conference*, *13*(1).

Lee, E., Walker, M., & Christensen, H. (2008). Mandating IFRS: its Impact on the Cost of Equity Capital in Europe. *ACCA Research Report, 105*(1).

Peng, S., & van der Laan Smith, J. (2010). Chinese GAAP and IFRS: An analysis of the convergence process. *Journal of International Accounting, Auditing & Taxation*, *19*(1), 16–34. doi:10.1016/j.intaccaudtax.2009.12.002

Pham, H. H. (2012). *A Comparative Study of Vietnamese and International Accounting Standards*. (PhD Thesis). School of Accounting, Curtin University.

Soderstrom, N. S., & Sun, K. J. (2007, December 1). IFRS Adoption and Accounting Quality: A Review. *European Accounting Review*, *16*(4), 675–702. doi:10.1080/09638180701706732

Tarca, A. (2012). *The Case for Global Accounting Standards - Arguments and Evidence*. Academic Press.

Uddin, S., & Tsamenyi, M. (2010). *Research in Accounting in Emerging Economies*. Emerald Group Publishing Limited.

VACPA & CAPA. (2012). The Vital Role of Professional Accountancy Organisations. *The Vital Role of Professional Accountancy Organisations*. Vietnam Association of Certified Public Accountants (VACPA) and Confederation of Asian and Pacific Accountants (CAPA).

Vellam, I. (2012). *The adoption of IFRS in Poland: an institutional approach*. (PhD Thesis). University of Greenwich.

Vo, V. T. H. (2014). *Follow-up on the Accounting Development Tool (ADT) - Enhancing Vietnam's capacity for producing high-quality corporate reports*. Paper presented at the Intergovernmental Working Group of Experts on International Standards of Accounting and Reporting (ISAR), Palais des Nations, Geneva.

ENDNOTE

1 The use of character "R" followed by a number is to protect the anonymous nature of the survey comments made by the respondent. Respondent numbers were coding prior to data cleaning & excluding unusable response (missing data exceeding 10 per cent).

Chapter 3
Consequences of IFRS Adoption:
A Myth or a Reality -Selected Cases of Adoption Effects

Erick R. Outa
Strathmore University, Kenya

ABSTRACT

The purpose of this chapter is to review the consequences of IFRS adoption by reviewing circumstances under which the benefits and costs accrue to firms, countries and the world. Notwithstanding, all issues raised about the consequences, IFRS adoption has had positive consequences and no wonder nearly 120 countries around the world and significant markets have adopted it. The chapter contributes to our understanding of the importance of IFRS and its effects and it is important to regulators and parties involved with world economic stability.

INTRODUCTION

This chapter outlines the arguments for the claimed consequences of International Financial Reporting Standards (IFRS)[1] adoption and the extent to which research has vetted the consequences. IFRS or IAS are a set of standards stating how particular types of transactions and other events should be reflected in financial statements, issued by the International Accounting Standards Committee (IASC-IAS) and its successor the International Accounting Standards Board (IASB -IAS and IFRS).The goal of IFRS is to provide a global framework on how public companies prepare and disclose their financial statements. IFRS provides general guidance for the preparation of financial statements rather than set rules. This has led to the notion that IFRS has beneficial consequences in spite of the controversies, country differences, modes of adoption and the quality of the standards themselves. European Union (EU) Regulation No. 1606/2002 requires firms listed in the EU to prepare their consolidated accounts according to IFRS to help ensure a high degree of transparency and comparability of financial statements and, thus, improve the efficient functioning of the EU capital market. According to ICAEW[2] (2014), the regulation's objectives are to improve transparency and comparability, better functioning of the internal market, the efficient and cost-effective functioning of the capital market, the protection of investors and maintenance of

DOI: 10.4018/978-1-4666-9876-5.ch003

confidence in capital markets and help the EU companies compete on an equal footing for capital within the EU and on world capital markets. Nearly 120 countries around the world have also adopted IFRS or converged with IFRS or are in the process of doing so for the same reasons as the EU and also for other varied reasons. Other countries especially developing countries partly adopted IFRS as it was costly for them to produce their own standards. The widespread use of IFRS has seen academics, managers, regulators, policy makers and politicians wage in this murky debate of its consequences. Albrecht (2010) indicates that accounting theory are clear on three issues namely, accounting standards do not equally benefit all affected parties, they all have economic consequences and that they are not universal truth. Extant literature including Daske et al. (2008), Armstrong et al. (2010), Byard et al. (2011), regulators and many others alleges the consequences of IFRS as transparency, comparability, reduction in cost of capital and cost savings.

The purpose of this chapter is to review the debates about the consequences of adoption by applying descriptive analysis. The chapter starts off by looking at how we got to IFRS and why and from there on reviews the study approaches which have given rise to the consequences under analysis. It then looks at other IFRS consequences before analyzing country level consequences such as Tax, Foreign Direct Investment (FDI) and finally reviews IFRS adoption impacts on the environment.

Brüggemann et al. (2013) split the consequences into intended and unintended consequences. Intended consequences can be reconciled with the IFRS regulations which emphasize capital market as well as macroeconomic effects resulting from enhanced reporting transparency and cross-country comparability. On the other hand, unintended consequences are the effects absent from the IFRS regulation's explicitly stated objectives and relate to the contracting uses of IFRS such as compensation schemes, lending agreements, dividend payouts, taxation, and other regulatory restrictions and have received little research attention.

While a lot of research has taken place in various parts of the world, Herbert et al. (2013) in a Nigerian study found that despite the spate of research on IFRS, the question about the economic consequences of its adoption for developing countries has hardly been investigated and therefore remains a matter of empirical concern. They argue that developing countries joined the IFRS bandwagon in quest for global competitiveness and aspiration to mitigate the prevalence of poverty. The pressure of global bodies such as the World Trade Organization (WTO) and the World Bank (WB) may have also pushed them to adoption. This perhaps explains why the literature on the economic consequences of IFRS adoption is sparse, particularly in developing countries. Up to the end of 2014, studies in Africa attempting to look at the impact of IFRS adoption has been Elbanan (2011) Egypt and Outa (2011) Kenya. Efobi et al. (2014) based in Nigeria has also generated interesting findings on IFRS so the Africa situation is improving.

Overall, it appears from the studies that transparency (effects are market liquidity, cost of capital and value relevance), comparability, FDI and economic development, Tax and Environmental impact are associated with adoption of IFRS.

The next section reviews the background to IFRS and notes how we got there. It also looks at the approaches applied in IFRS studies and the impact of politics.

BACKGROUND TO IFRS

How Did We Get to IFRS?[3]

Camferman et al. (2007) reports that after the 2nd world war, each a country had its own national accounting standards, with crucial differences even among countries with active capital markets. In developing countries, financial disclosure was minimal. Both state that the 1950s saw a period of rapid growth of international trade and foreign direct investment, and companies began to expand their reach beyond their borders. The 1960s were marked by frequent international mergers and acquisitions, especially American corporations taking over European companies, and domestic companies began to redeploy their production operations as well as their management team internationally. This was also the beginning of the multi nationals. The duo concludes that this internationalist trend heightened the desire to compare financial statements prepared in different countries and so marked the beginning of internationalization of accounting and a quest to understand and compare financial reports produced in different countries.

In 1966, the president of the Institute of Chartered Accountants of England and Wales (ICAEW) George Benson, was invited by the accounting Institutes of Canada and the US to visit both countries. The agenda of the invitation was to dialogue on the gap between the accounting practiced between countries. From the deliberation of this meeting, Camferman et al. (2007) reports that an international study group was formed in 1967 to publish papers on accountancy topics leading to the development of a framework. These activities continued until 1973 when the group was renamed International Accounting Standards Committee (IASC) with additional membership from Australia, France, Germany, Japan, Mexico and the Netherlands. At its formation, the objective was to issue international standards to guide convergence of national standards over time. In 1981, a consultative group was formed together with representatives of the World Bank, the United Nations (UN), the Organization for Economic Co-operation and Development (OECD) with the UN setting up a commission and center on transnational reporting of multinational companies.

International Organization of Securities Commission (IOSCO) joined the group in 1987 together with the European commission and the US Financial Accounting Standards Board (FASB) joining in 1990. The finding of this larger group was that a number of developing countries were using the accounting standards voluntarily and recommended the revisions of the standards to cater for cross border listings from 2000 given the already wide usage. As these activities continued, the stakeholder base and usage diversified.

As a fast growing institution, IASC faced many challenges and its intention of creating uniformity in the preparation of financial reports hit by its failure to agree on a conceptual framework that met user needs. Governance was also problematic because of dominance by the accounting firms who contributed to the inadequate enforcement of standards. Political interference together with these governance issues made this institution bureaucratic and slow in responding to matters raised before them.

An attempt to resolve these hurdles especially independence and governance led to restructuring and the formation of a foundation registered in the US and creation of supervisory trustees whilst the IASC retained its headquarters in London. IASC was renamed International Accounting Standards Board (IASB) in 2001 to reflect the restructuring and the new standards renamed as IFRS with IFRS 1 issued in May 2002.In total IASC issued 41 standards and they are being withdrawn as revisions and new standards are issued as IFRS.

It can be seen from this story that right from the beginning, the objective of IFRS is to converge national standards into one global standard that could address the complexities of the growing global businesses. And that feat is still on.

Study Approaches

The reported consequences of IFRS are affected by the study approaches. IFRS studies approaches have taken either an accounting or a market approach, a distinction cited by Francis et al. (2004). Attributes such as accrual quality, persistence, predictability and smoothness are regarded as accounting based since they are typically measured using accounting information only. Attributes such as value relevance and timeliness use proxies for these constructs are typically based on the relation between market data and accounting data.

Accounting approaches such as discretionary accruals and earning persistence has been criticized as they do not provide direct evidence of the usefulness of accounting information to its end users in the capital market (Lee et al. 2013; Barth et al. 2011). Moreover, accounting approaches are conservative and IASB framework does not regard conservatism as a property of financial reporting. Market approaches such as value relevance and capital market consequences such as liquidity seem to be receiving justification. According to Leuz et al. (2014) market liquidity is regarded because economic theory predicts that transparency reduces information asymmetries between investors leading to increased liquidity which is well grounded in economics. Secondly, most capital regulators have stated their objective as building market confidence and market liquidity is closely related to market confidence and therefore researchers applying liquidity are focusing on what matters to regulators and policy makers.

Another issue in IFRS causal studies that has gained attention in recent literature is endogeneity. Recent critique of causal studies like the impact of IFRS, have made calls to pay attention to the correct estimation of non-experimental causal models with the major culprit being endogeneity. Endogeneity arises where for example; the effect of x on y cannot be interpreted because it includes omitted causes such as omitted selection, simultaneity, common-method variance, measurement error and others. Other reviews have also indicated that such studies need to distinguish correlationship which is not the same as causality.

The consequences for IFRS adoption reviewed in this chapter are assumed to have passed endogeneity and other measurement error tests. They are also based on accounting and market approaches.

Politics and IFRS

How has politics played into IFRS and why should it be involved? Politics is from the Greek word politikos meaning for citizens and its varied and practical meaning is the practice and theory of influencing other people on a global, civic or individual level. Since IFRS seeks to influence and determine how people live on the basis of their involvement in capital markets, politics cannot be ruled out. Politics is played through states where decisions and rules of governance are produced and where the government has a contract to protect and develop their people. Politics associated with IFRS has ranged from decisions to adopt and follow, to global financial crisis and the G20 meetings and recommendations to accounting standard setters. Regulations and adoptions are also regarded as political and this section will review these matters into detail.

The decision to adopt IFRS in the EU in 2005 was through an act of EU parliament so it is a political decision. The same applies to many jurisdictions where adoptions and rules are made from country laws enacted by political bodies in the interest of the country's population served by politicians.

The network theory by Ramanna et al. (2009), suggests that there are generally two factors to consider in adopting a network dependent product like IFRS. The intrinsic value (autarky) of the product (quality of IFRS) and the value of the products network (economies of scale and ability to leverage among many users). As a network dependent product, IFRS is a choice when the value of its adoption is higher than continuing with the domestic standard and these values can be economic and political. Political benefits associated with the political nature of accounting standard setting is about potential gain from being able to influence international standard setting to value lost from surrendering local authority over accounting standards. According to Veron (2007) the EU adopted IFRS as a block with conditions aimed at retaining sovereignty of the EU and keeping off American influence. And the arguments being that if the net political value of IFRS is high, then countries within a region can cede some authority over standard setting interest.

Another political issue is the decision by the world most powerful group, the G20 to back standard setting. The G20 meeting in London (IMF 2009) mandated IASB to continue with its independent and transparent standards setting process and develop a futuristic model on loan loss provisions is yet another indicator of what politics play in standard setting.

The effect of IAS 39 and fair value accounting has also been seen in politics. The requirement to mark to market in fair value accounting requires regular updates of financial statements and this can give rise to volatility in incomes. In July 2003, the then president of France, Jacques Chirac, wrote to the president of the European Commission protesting the adoption of that standard as it was felt that the adoption could affect the financial stability of European companies. His and other arguments that fair values have to be estimated, provides opportunities for earnings management and creative accounting. In response to this pressure, IASB carved out several paragraphs from the standards to accommodate the concerns raised by the president. The net effects are that EU financial statements are only partially compliant, thanks to the power of politics.

Based on the issues discussed here, it can therefore be concluded that, politics has major consequences on IFRS. Decisions to adopt and influence other institutions on functioning of IFRS are most of the time by political leaders. However, Albrecht (2010) has quoted influential personalities including former SEC and IASB chairs who have made public statements that the accounting standard setting process should and must be insulated from the lobbying of special interest groups and the meddling of government institutions.

After this background, the next section reviews the consequences including transparency, comparability and other consequences.

TRANSPARENCY EFFECTS

Different researchers define and explain transparency differently. Barth et al. (2008) define financial reporting transparency *as* the extent to which financial reports reveal an entity's underlying economics in a way that is readily understandable by those using the financial reports and says that it is not well defined in accounting literature. They argue that research supports the notion that transparency is a desirable characteristic of financial reports and suggests that it is associated with positive macroeconomic effects and reduced cost of capital. IFRS could increase transparency which leads to the quality of financial reporting and corporate disclosure with capital market consequences such as liquidity, accounting quality, value relevance, analysts forecast, default risk and predicting future cash flows. This should also improve capital allocation and portfolio decisions as well as facilitate monitoring and improvements in corporate decisions. However, Fox et al. (2013) have indicated disclosure has intangible costs such as concern with investors about the abilities or reputation of the reporting firms and disclosed information supplies other firms with competitive advantages.

Elbannan (2010) finds in a sample of Egyptian companies adopting IFRS that the incidence of earnings management does not decrease post adoption, even though these standards were adopted relatively early (in 1997), and subsequently revised. Elbannan attributes the lack of improvement to the lack of enforcement of these standards by regulators and inadequate training of practitioners. Agami (2007) listed 13 items of non-compliance with IFRS spite of the fact that Egypt officially adopted IFRS. The reasons for non-compliance are varied but not limited to lack of enforcement mechanism, auditor's independence, inadequate IFRS accountants and other cultural reasons. An empirical study of IFRS adoption in Egypt is therefore unlikely to conclude major consequences because of these noncompliance issues.

Outa (2011) applied earnings management, timely loss recognition and value relevance on Kenyan listed companies finds mixed results leading to the conclusion that IFRS adoption insignificantly improved accounting quality between post and pre adoption periods in the Kenyan context. He attributes the mixed results to Kenya Accounting Standards (KAS) as of the same frame work as IFRS and to some extent Kenya being a label adopter (not full compliance). Ames (2013) finds in a study of 3,950 firm-year global companies listed in South Africa between 2000 and 2011 that earnings quality is not significantly improved among firms in the sample post IFRS adoption. He also finds that specific components of the financial statements changed in value relevance post IFRS adoption. These results are consistent with the notion that IFRS standards improved the quality of some, but not all, financial reporting components in South Africa. He explains his findings as possibly due to lack of careful implementation, enforcement and probably data quality. In China, Lee et al. (2013) reported that both earnings and book values of 10,017 firm year Chinese companies were value relevant to some extent under Chinese Accounting Standards (CAS) which was determined to have converged with IFRS up to 74.97%.

Daske et al. (2008) in a 26 country worldwide study applying market liquidity, cost of capital and Tobin's Q with a large sample of 3,800 first time adopters find that market liquidity increases around the time of mandatory introduction of IFRS. The results for firms cost of capital are mixed but overall the results are consistent with the view that reporting quality is shaped by many factors in countries institutional environments, pointing to the importance of reporting incentives and enforcements.

Landsman et al. (2011) study on the impact of the use of IFRS on share prices and trading commonly known as abnormal return volatility and trading volume concluded that the information content of earnings announcements improved for IFRS reporters by reducing reporting lag, increasing analyst following and increasing foreign investment.

La Porta et al. (1997) in a 49 country study using data from 1994 show that countries with poorer investor protection have smaller and narrower capital markets. Subsequently, they found that common law countries have the strongest legal protection of investors while French civil law countries are the weakest with German and Scandinavian civil law are in the middle. Jackson et al. (2009) posit that public and private enforcement are important for development of markets, therefore IFRS adoption contribute immensely to the capital market development because of the confidence and disclosure associated with their requirements.

Daske, et al. (2013) look at the relationship between firms' different reporting incentives and the effects of IFRS adoption. The sample for mandatory adopters from 26 countries, and up to 7,252 firms shows that serious adopters experience a decrease in the cost of capital, whereas label adopters do not. Many other studies provided evidence on reductions in the cost of equity capital and in the cost of bonds, but that they were not experienced by all companies or in all countries and it is not clear they were all attributed to IFRS.

ICAEW (2014) reviewed over 170 research papers related to the EU and the world and on the question of transparency concluded that by and large, evidence suggests an improvement in transparency following IFRS adoption, although the evidence is far from clear. This is also supported by the work of Tarca (2012) where she states that transparency differ between firms and countries and the question of IFRS as the sole driver for the consequences is yet to be fully addressed.

COMPARABILITY EFFECTS

Comparability is one of the four 'enhancing' qualitative characteristics affecting the usefulness of information that is both relevant and faithfully represented even though it is not a well-defined concept or a directly measurable phenomenon. Comparability is explained as consistency and disclosure that occurs when similarities and differences can be discerned and evaluated. Accounting theory postulates that similarities and differences should happen over time and within industry (IFRS 2006). The biggest problem would arise when different enterprises use different accounting policies when for instances providing for depreciation, bad debts, stock valuations and so forth. Consistency as a problem is partially resolved by accounting standards, but the problem cannot be eliminated because of alternatives accounting permitted by standards which should have been eliminated by the convergence process. Zeff (2007) identifies 4 obstacles that affect comparability as the business and financial culture, accounting culture, auditing culture and the regulatory culture.

Leuz (2013) say that IFRS could make it easier and less costly to compare firms and hence evaluate investment opportunities. These effects can reduce information asymmetries among the investors while greater comparability could discipline firms reporting behavior and thereby improve reporting quality.

ICAEW (2014) explains several approaches to measure comparability including financial reporting information by looking at accounting policies, accruals, earnings and cash flows. Other methods include analysts forecast, stock market returns; methods based information transfers and opinion surveys.

Brochet et al. (2011) finds in a UK study of mandatory IFRS adoption and financial statement comparability that IFRS reduces private information by enhancing the comparability of financial statements. Specifically, abnormal returns to two proxies for private information (insider purchases and analyst recommendation upgrades) are reduced following IFRS adoption. Similarly David Cairns et al. (2005) in a study of IFRS fair value measurement and accounting policy choice in the United Kingdom and Australia find increased comparability within the UK in accounting for property (IAS 16, *Property, Plant and Equipment*), held-for-trading financial instruments, derivatives and share-based payments. They find decreased comparability in accounting for investment property and other financial assets and liabilities.

Callao et al. (2007) in a study of 35 Spanish firms compliant with EU regulation 1606 \2002 found that local comparability is adversely affected if both IFRS and local accounting standards are applied in the same country at the same time. Reforms to bring local rules in line with international standards are therefore, urgent to obtain better comparability.

Cascino, et al. (2012) in a comparability study between Germany and Italy using two comparability proxies found that the overall comparability effect of mandatory IFRS adoption is marginal at best and that only firms with high compliance incentives experience substantial increases in comparability.

Oduware (2012) indicates that some degree of comparability may not exist among the financial statements of Nigerian entities, even if they convert on the same date and are in the same industry, because IFRS are principle based and people differ in their judgments at the same time alternative policies exist. This is so in joint ventures, on controlling interest, and defined benefit accounting. He further explains that IFRS permits carry-over of matters from the predecessor standards depending on elections taken. There is also lack of guidance in industry specific matters such as mining, sustainability issues and so on. He also argues that at the time of conversion, firms may change the basis of certain transactions such as in financial instruments by redesigning their nature. Changes can also be made on measurement basis on plant, property and machinery by designation of fair value as the deemed cost or change investment properties from cost to fair value. Unexpensed deferral gains and losses arising from defined benefit pension plans may also be directly transferred to retained earnings. These alternatives or a combination of them or any other of the elections permitted in IFRS 1 or elsewhere in IFRS will definitely make comparability difficult hence diminish intended consequences of adoption.

So what were the consequences of IFRS adoption as far as comparability is concerned? There is evidence of comparability being achieved and some evidence that comparability is not achieved and this is explained by the alternative treatments allowed by IFRS but since this is being addressed by the standard setters, may be better results will be seen in the future. Differences in institutions and countries have also made it very difficult to achieve high level comparability.

OTHER CONSEQUENCES

As mentioned in the introduction, there are other unintended consequences of IFRS adoption which are scattered in literature. Tweedie (2009) mention facilitation of global education and training, integrated IT systems, easier consolidation, one set of books, understanding financial statements of overseers suppliers, customers and subsidiaries, reduced risk of insiders expropriating outsiders' investments, increased trade in goods and services within the EU, improved accounting-based assessment of executive performance, and reduced risk of share price crashes. These consequences perhaps flow from wider consequences of IFRS adoption and in view of the less available research in this areas, there is very little to discuss.

Brown (2013) has indicated other consequences as gain access to standard setting expertise not available in the home country as well as to share the costs of standard setting and of securing compliance with accounting standards. He also states that other consequences are to increase the mobility of supply in the labor market for accounting professionals and again these assertions are not tested in any study and because of lack of evidence cannot be discussed into any detail.

Cost consequences are regarded as negative to IFRS adoption and their impact has not been extensively studied. This section reviews some costs that firms incur in transition as well as continuing incremental preparation costs associated with IFRS. One of the arguments is that IFRS costs are incurred once for purposes of implementation and for learning the new requirements while the recurring costs such as audit and continuous improvements will almost be the same regardless of the standards in application. According to the report "EU implementation of IFRS and the fair value directive" (ICAEW 2007), the common costs of conversion to IFRS include IFRS project team, software and systems changes, additional external audit costs, external technical advice, training of staff, training other staff (such as IT staff, internal audit and management), communications with third parties, tax advice, additional external data costs and costs arising from changes such as renegotiating debt covenants. So the question is, does IFRS cause significant costs and where is the evidence?

In the United States where IFRS has not been implemented, questions have been raised as to whether the cost is worth it. The costs have been broadly defined and include confusion and market place in financial statements as low confidence can be costly to investors and the economy. The US culture is also litigation oriented and the costs associated with principle based accounting can be confounding since there is no direct evidence of judicial standard. Cost estimates by the Security Exchange Commission (SEC) indicate early adopters would each incur about $32 million (Johnson and Leone 2009) in filling their returns. It is also estimated that the transition costs would include disruptions and costs to capital market participants and other US entities that apply FASB standards (FASB 2008). Others conversion costs regarded in the US as huge include staff training, accounting and legal fees, staff costs to maintain two accounting systems and software costs.

In Vietnam, an emerging and transition economy in the process of IFRS convergence Phan et al. (2014) found that the Vietnamese accounting professionals are optimistic about potential benefits from IFRS adoption. She indicates expected costs and challenges in implementing IFRS and suggests strong support for a gradual switch from Viet Nam Accounting Standards (VAS) to IFRS, in a survey of 3000 people involved in accountancy in Vietnam. In Kenya, transition costs included, cultural changes, impact on taxation and size of entities applying the standards according to the local accounting Institute but it has not been possible to estimate their magnitude.

In South Africa, Ernst and Young (2006) reported greater complexity, high costs in some cases, poor understanding for the transition as well as the potential for confusion in transition from South Africa GAAP to IFRS in a study of 34 companies with R 5 billion and over.One-off costs of transition to IFRS was greater for larger companies and that costs increased as the ongoing costs of preparing financial statements under IFRS. They also found value relevance with 57% of respondents reported adverse impacts while 34% positive impacts on the bottom line with causes arising mainly from depreciation, financial instruments insurance contracts and some extent business combinations.

For recurring costs, Kim et al. (2012) look at the impact of mandatory IFRS adoption on audit fees in the EU using 2,860 firm-year observations over the period 2004-2008.They find that on average, the audit fee increase of 5.44 percent greater for the adopter firms, compared to that for the non-adopter firms in the control sample. They also find that the IFRS-related audit fee premium increases with the increase in audit complexity brought about by IFRS adoption, and decreases with the improvement in financial reporting quality arising from IFRS adoption. They also find some evidence that the IFRS-related audit fee premium is lower in countries with stronger legal regimes.

Voulgaris et al. (2014) on IFRS and the use of accounting-based performance measures in executive pay look at the effects of mandatory IFRS adoption on the use of earnings-based measures in management compensation contracts for 500 large UK companies for the period 2002-2009. They found that firms place a lower weight on EPS-based performance measures in management compensation contracts, post-IFRS. They argue that this may be because IFRS add "noise" to accounting numbers which makes reported earnings less useful.

UNCTAD (2005) reported that a survey of implementation of IFRS conducted by the accounting firm Mazars and involving 550 listed companies in 12 European countries, including Turkey, released in July 2005 showed only 45 per cent of the respondents considered the cost of conversion to IFRS as high, while 55 per cent believed that the benefits of conversion justified the costs. ICAEW (2007) also indicated recurring costs varies depending on the size of the firm and these costs can represent up to 24 per cent of turnover.

In conclusion, it can be said that whether costs are once off or recurrent, less research has been undertaken, it appears overall that these costs may not be significant because audit costs will always be incurred and changes will always be taking place and these operating costs will always be incurred.

The next section looks at IFRS consequences at country or regional levels as opposed to firms discussed above. It debates how IFRS impacts tax, foreign direct investments, environment and the global financial crisis.

COUNTRY ECONOMY LEVEL CONSEQUENCES

Tax Consequences

Tax accounting in many countries has not developed independently from financial accounting hence, the need to check the extent to which IFRS impacts tax base. There is scanty literature in this area but the few that exist in Europe are based on the fact that Europe has a multi tax regime. For listed companies in the EU, IFRS is required for consolidated financial statements. The rest of the companies in the EU have choices of US GAAP or national standards, implying there are up to three standards to choose from. The use of different accounting systems will therefore result in different tax bases. This section examines the impact of IFRS on tax to suggest whether IFRS makes economies competitive as a result of their adoption.

Haverals (2005) examined the impact of an IAS/IFRS- based tax accounting on the effective tax burden of Belgian companies for eleven different sectors. The results of using IAS/IFRS for tax purposes show that the tax burden of Belgian companies broadened by 3.8% to 14.6% depending on the sector's financial and accounting characteristics. These consequences are mainly attributable to the favorable regime of national standards which is not accepted by IAS/IFRS. From a European perspective, it appears that when the tax burden is determined by national GAAP then Belgium has the fifth lowest tax burden, just after the Netherlands and before Germany and France. IAS/IFRS-based tax accounting should not change the current tax competitive ranking of countries. Since the use of IAS/IFRS broadens the tax base, a reduction of the Belgian corporate income tax rate could be done to help companies to switch to IAS/IFRS and improve the attractiveness of Belgium.

Swenson and Lee (2009) indicated cash taxes, Lifo VS FIFO, fair value measurement, uncertain tax position, and a host of other issues should the US adopt IFRS over GAAP.

Some sectors like construction and automotive vehicles see much larger increases in effective tax burdens than others but the impact remains in general relatively important.

There is need to carry out studies on IFRS and Tax as it is an under researched area to facilitate better conclusions especially in Africa and other emerging markets.

Foreign Direct Investments (FDI) and Economic Growth

Investors abroad are faced with information asymmetries that are to the disadvantage of the foreign investor or where there are additional costs involved in obtaining information about foreign investments as per ICAEW (2014). If the purpose of IFRS is to ensure disclosures, transparency and comparability, it should then follow that foreign investors problem is solved by IFRS adoption. This assumes that IFRS reduces information asymmetries leading investors to allocate capital with consequences of capital flow between countries when deciding on FDI or portfolio investment.

Foreign Direct investments (FDI) is one of the strong reasons for the advocacy of IFRS and South Africa is one of those countries that has been argued adopted IFRS to attract foreign investments following the many years of sanctions against apartheid. The arguments for FDI stem from the fact that financial statements upon which decisions are made are quality i.e. faithful, relevant, reliable, comparable, understood and timely and hence value relevant. International agencies such as the World Bank and the International Organization of Securities Commissions (IOSCO) promote the adoption of International Financial Reporting Standards (IFRS) to create a solid international financial infrastructure, which in turn should stimulate economic development of the adopting countries (Collins, 1989; Wyatt et al., 1993). Both papers argue that the IFRS fosters world trade and development of global financial markets which are prerequisites for economic growth.

Efobi et al. (2014) looked at 42 African countries with data between 2001 and 2012 on the impact of IFRS on FDI flows against the institutional plague of corruption in Africa. Their initial findings show that African countries will benefit more from IFRS by improving their institutional framework, than by having a static institutional framework and then adopting IFRS. This finding corroborates other results in other parts of the world that IFRS per se is not sufficient to provide the benefits if the institutions (supervision and enforcement), investor protection and the letter and spirit of good governance is missing.

In a 135 country study, Gresilova (2013) applied a 2 stage least squares regression model to examine the direction of the relationship between foreign direct investments and international financial reporting within the framework of countries economic level of development. Her study answer three questions, whether the causality of IFRS and FDI goes in both directions, whether there is a distinct effect for developing and developed countries and whether the non-linearity of the FDI effect increases the likelihood of IFRS implementation. Her findings show that causality goes in both directions, but only for developing countries. In other words, developing countries benefit both from IFRS adoption in terms of increasing FDI inflows, and at the same time, higher level of FDI inflows raises the likelihood of adopting IFRS by developing countries. The latter effect, however, holds only till FDI inflow reaches 0.5 to 1.6 billion USD per year. FDI inflows beyond that level do not affect the probability of IFRS implementation in developing countries

Lous et al. (2013) in a 20 country worldwide survey on whether the 2005 mandatory adoption of IFRS is associated with an increase in cross-border acquisitions into the adopting countries and whether any documented effect is driven by concurrent enforcement changes using the exogeneity of a firm's listing status. They document a significant increase in cross-border acquisitions of listed targets from the adopting countries and no evidence that the IFRS effect is driven by those countries that apparently bundled the IFRS adoption with enforcement changes. Chen et al. (2014) in a 30 country survey measuring in and outflow between pairs and countries whose economies converged to IFRS for 2000-2005 find a positive association between FDI and IFRS especially in countries with stronger convergence and stronger institutions. Flourou et al. (2011) reported increases in ownership and consequently show that IFRS affect allocation decisions of institutional investors. They state that IFRS related ownership changes are higher for value and growth investors who are more likely to make use of financial statements in their investment decisions.

Amiram (2012) in a 104 country survey on the effects of mandatory IFRS adoption on foreign portfolio investments in equities finds that foreign equity portfolio investments (FPI) increase in countries that adopt IFRS. He also finds that the relation is driven by foreign investors from countries that also use IFRS. Moreover, the effect of accounting familiarity is more pronounced when investor and investee countries share language, legal origin, culture, and region. He also finds that countries with lower corruption and better investor protection experience larger increases in FPI after they adopt IFRS relative to other IFRS users, a finding that supports Efobi et al. (2014)

Huerta et al. (2013) for a 172 country study, estimate a two stage least square regression to test if the adoption of IFRS increases the economic growth of the adopting countries. They find partial support for the hypothesis that adoption of IFRS increases the economic growth of the adopting countries but this is mainly due to major data limitations.

From this evidence there are suggestions that IFRS adoption is associated with both increased FDI and increased international portfolio investment. It appears the FDI cases provide strong evidence of IFRS impact.

IFRS Adoption and the Environment

The initial idea of IFRS was to assist the preparation of financial statements that would provide reliable information and foster confidence in capital markets and protect investor interest. This section traces possibilities of IFRS adoption impact on the environment or environmental issues such as pollution, depletion of the ozone layer and other associated events. Negash (2012) indicated that a comprehensive review of academic and professional literature indicates that the IFRS regime provides useful conceptual and practical frameworks for monitoring firms that are operating in environmentally sensitive industries.

The Chair of the IASB board on a visit to China in 2012 remarked that the public interest role of accounting standards is deeper than is defined and that sound economies rely on the provision of faithful, reliable financial information to maintain public trust and ensure the flow of capital to fuel growth, Hoogervorst (2011:2). Efobi (2014) has taken this a notch higher by looking at the relationship between IFRS adoption and environmental pollution in Africa which by extension attributes market confidence to concern and attention for the environment. They apply data from 47 countries between 2001-2013 using System Generalized Method of Moments (SMMN) technique and find a positive and significant linkage exist between IFRS adoption and environmental pollution. The interactive variable also shows that the effect of IFRS on the environment will reduce when institutions quality (in the form of bureaucratic corruption) is addressed. The main channel through which IFRS adoption affects the environment is through the attractiveness of FDI.

IFRS Fair Value Accounting and the Global Financial Crisis: Is IFRS Responsible?

Fair value is a rational and unbiased estimate of the potential market price of a good, service, or asset and many practitioners have described it as the practice of measuring assets and liabilities at estimates of their current value and recognizing changes in fair value as gains and losses in the income statement. Fair value accounting has been one of the most controversial issues in accounting because of the way it is determined in practice and one of consequences of IFRS has been over or under valuation of assets leading to unfair distribution of firm residues and ultimate melt down of corporations with devastating impacts in the economy. Stock market crashes and financial crises have had many occurrences in the world with the 2008 crisis appearing to have originated in the US following a credit crunch and the securitization of debts. Attempts have been made to associate this crisis with accounting standards, in particular IAS 39 (Fair value accounting), which has been accused of being responsible for volatility in profits especially when markets are depressed and illiquid. Another closely related standard is IFRS 7 that deals with risk disclosure in financial instruments. Both the Asian financial crisis of 1997and the global financial crisis of 2008 has led to questions on whether the adoption and implementation of IFRS would have prevented the crisis. In Kenya, the 2008/2009 financial crisis resulted in a major drop in the stock exchange index with many people agonizing as their wealth kept evaporating day by day. These global financial crises have been partly explained by the view that weaker regulation and weak enforcement of IFRS and rules as opposed to the lack of them are the main causes of financial crisis.

How is IFRS associated with financial crisis? ICAEW (2014) suggested two reasons. First, they argue that the use of IFRS fair values for some financial instruments overstated profits before the crisis, adding to the atmosphere of excessive optimism and risk-taking in banking, and leading to excessive remuneration and distributions, which left banks with inadequate capital to face the crisis. At the same time, it led to overstated losses during the crisis, reducing banks' capital ratios and undermining confidence in the banks. The second reason has been stated as the incurred loss method of calculating loan loss provisions also led to overstated profits before the crisis, again adding to the atmosphere of excessive optimism and risk-taking, and leading to excessive remuneration and distributions, but resulting in capital inadequacy when in due course more realistic provisions had to be recognized after the crisis had struck.

Leventis et al. (2011), in a study of 18 European countries on the effect of mandatory adoption of IFRS on banks' loan loss provisions for the period 1999-2008 found that earnings management significantly reduced after IFRS adoption. They also find that earnings management is more pronounced for riskier banks which may actually lead to a crisis.

Amir et al. (2013) looking at the impact of fair value accounting on the failure of Northern Bank in the UK conclude that its failure could not be attributed to fair value accounting because it had cash flow issues leading to insolvency.

Applying descriptive and empirical evidence that sheds light on the role of fair value accounting for U.S. banks, Laux et al. (2010) found little evidence that the financial crisis occurred as a direct result of IFRS fair-value accounting or that the problems would have been less severe under historical-cost accounting. Banks were highly levered during the boom and relied heavily on collateralized repurchase agreements. Barth et al. (2010) scrutinize the role that financial reporting relating to fair values, asset securitizations, and derivatives played in contributing to the financial crisis. They conclude that because the objectives of bank regulation and financial reporting differ, changes in financial reporting needed to improve transparency of information provided to the capital markets likely will not be identical to changes in bank regulations needed to strengthen the stability of the banking sector. Although accounting standard setters and bank regulators should find a common ground, it is the responsibility of bank regulators, not accounting standard setters, to ensure the stability of the financial system. Barth (2010) and Lauz (2010) conclude that contrary to what many critics of fair value contend, fair value accounting played little or no role in the financial crisis.

The role of fair value accounting has received more research in the US than any other part of the world with few cases noted in the EU and unknown cases in Africa and other parts of the world. While US is not an IFRS zone, it should be clear that the convergence project of IASB and FASB at some point merged on the reporting criteria for financial instruments so that the requirements for IFRS are as a good as SFAS[4] of the US. At the moment it can therefore be concluded that there is insufficient evidence that IFRS reporting especially fair value are related to the financial crisis.

FUTURE RESEARCH DIRECTIONS

As can be seen in this chapter, there are still a numbers of issues to be addressed through research. These are issues that arise from each research and they remain without clarity.

One of the areas is the inconsistencies where several researches show different results for the same test and no explanation is offered. For example accounting approaches such as variability in income might show that income is significantly variable after IFRS adoption but same test for variability in income in relation to cash flow shows insignificant variability. Currently, no research exists to resolve such findings and it is possible a big picture of IFRS consequences might be realized by addressing such gaps.

Part of the reason given for lack of confidence in isolating IFRS as the sole reason for the consequences is the competing institutions and directives. For example in Kenya, when IFRS resolution was passed by local professional accounting institute (ICPAK), the Capital Market Authority (CMA) and the Central Bank also issued other reform directives and current research has not delved into identifying the exact roles of each of these different directives on the adoption of IFRS.

Since each of the countries are different from the institutions, incentives, economics and politics, it might be worthwhile to continue with research at Individual country level so that the total of all these individual country researches, their differences and similarities can shed more light on IFRS consequences.

So far there is less work on direct consequences of IFRS on economic development at country and regional levels. Additional evidence from research may be helpful in providing insights on how far IFRS has contributed towards economic development of each country or region.

Other areas that still need more research include unintended consequences such as IFRS and the environment, pay compensation, financial crisis and recurring costs.

CONCLUSION

This chapter looks at the consequences of IFRS adoption by reviewing circumstances under which the benefits and costs accrue to firms, countries and the world. It discusses the research approaches applied to arrive at the consequences. From all the matters raised, it can be concluded that the consequences of IFRS are transparency, comparability, FDI, cost of capital, taxes, and other intended and unintended effects. Furthermore, these consequences differ from firm to firm, from country to country and from study to study. Research findings also indicate that these consequences at best, arise when there is strong legal enforcement and investor protection while others find that they arise in spite of any conditions. Inconsistencies in findings are explained as possibly arising from differences in samples, quality of data, periods covered, methodologies applied and there is every chance that these differences are being resolved. Other reasons advanced for the failure to realize full consequences of IFRS include accounting alternatives resulting in less true and faithful representation of the firms underlying economics. Also the principle-base nature of IFRS leads to professional judgment which creates opportunities for earnings management. Finally, weak enforcement mechanisms of adopting nations can also reduce anticipated consequences, even when high quality IFRS are implemented. It is these cocktail of positives and caveats that leads to the notion that IFRS is a myth and a reality as some researchers find excellent consequences on one continuum while another group does challenges the outcomes.

The reasons for the mixed findings are also delicate. Research is sometimes based on larger listed companies with abilities to follow and benefit from IFRS adoption unlike their counterparts especially in emerging and frontier economies where the quality of data and expertise may not be as efficient as in the developed world. Variations in findings are bound to occur because of this scale of differences.

The chapter concludes that whilst IFRS was a key decision in the EU for preparation of consolidated financial statements, other countries without capacity to develop their standards tagged along. The end result has been a world wide spread of IFRS. Notwithstanding, all issues raised about the consequences, IFRS adoption has had positive consequences and no wonder nearly 120 countries around the world and significant markets have adopted it.

This chapter contributes to our increased understanding of consequences IFRS adoption across the globe based on existing research. The findings are useful to a wide constituency including regulators, academics, boards and management of companies who are keen to know that their investments in IFRS are justified and that matters arising are continuously resolved. Governments and development partners such as the World Bank will also find this chapter useful given the detailed explanations provided on what works and what doesn't where IFRS adoption is concerned.

REFERENCES

Agami, A. (2007). *Compliance of Companies Listed on Stock Exchanges in Emerging Markets With financial Reporting Standards: The case of Egypt*. Paper presented at the World Confederation of Accountants (WCA), Istanbul, Turkey.

Albrecht, D. (2010). *Economic Consequences and the Political Nature of Accounting Standard Setting*. Retrieved from: https://profalbrecht.wordpress.com/2010/01/06/economic-consequences-and-the-political-nature-of-accounting-standard-setting/

Ames, D. (2013). IFRS adoption and accounting quality: The case of South Africa. *Journal of Applied Economics and Business Research*, *3*(3), 154–165.

Amir, A., & Meeks, G. (2013). Bank failure, mark-to-market and the financial crisis. *Abacus*, *49*(3), 308–339. doi:10.1111/abac.12011

Amiram, D. (2012). Financial information globalization and foreign investment decisions. *Journal of International Accounting Research*, *11*(2), 57–81. doi:10.2308/jiar-50282

Armstrong, C., Barth, M., Jagonlinzer, A., & Riedl, E. (2010). Market Reaction to the Adoption of IFRS in Europe. *The Accounting Review American Accounting Association*, *85*(1), 31–61. doi:10.2308/accr.2010.85.1.31

Barth, M., Landsman, R., Young, D., & Zhuang, Z. (2011). *Relevance of Differences Between Net Income Based on IFRS and Domestic Standards for European firms*. International Accounting e-Journal.

Barth, M., & Landsman, W. (2010). How did financial reporting contribute to the financial crisis? *European Accounting Review*, *19*(3), 399–423. doi:10.1080/09638180.2010.498619

Barth, M., & Schipper, K. (2008). Financial Reporting Transparency. *Journal of Accounting, Auditing & Finance*, *23*, 173–190.

Brochet, F., Jagolinzer, A., & Riedl, E. (2011). *Mandatory IFRS Adoption and Financial Statement Comparability.* Harvard Business Review Working Paper 11-109.

Brown, P. (2011). International Financial Reporting: What are the benefits? *Accounting and Business Review*, *41*(3), 269–285. doi:10.1080/00014788.2011.569054

Brown, P. (2013). Some Observations on Research on the Benefits to Nations of Adopting IFRS. *Japanese Accounting Review*. Doi:10.11640/tjar.3.2013.01

Brüggemann, U., Hitz, J., & Sellhorn, T. (2013). Intended and Unintended Consequences of Mandatory IFRS Adoption: A Review of Extant Evidence and Suggestions for Future Research. *European Accounting Review*, *22*(1), 1–37. doi:10.1080/09638180.2012.718487

Callao, S., Jarne, J., & Lainez, A. (2007). Adoption of IFRS in Spain: Effect on the comparability and relevance of financial reporting. *Journal of International Accounting, Auditing & Taxation*, *16*(2), 148–178. doi:10.1016/j.intaccaudtax.2007.06.002

Camfferman, K., & Zeff, S. (2007). *Financial Reporting and Global Capital Markets-A History of the International Accounting standards committee*. London: Oxford University Press. doi:10.1093/acprof:oso/9780199296293.001.0001

Cascino, S., & Gassen, J. (2012). *Comparability Effects of Mandatory IFRS Adoption*. SFB 649 Discussion Paper 2012-009. Retrieved 14 November 2014 from: http://sfb649.wiwi.hu-berlin.de/papers/pdf/SFB649DP2012-009.pdf

Chen, P., Yuan, D., & Bin, X. (2014). Convergence of accounting standards and foreign direct investment. *The International Journal of Accounting*, *49*(1), 53–86. doi:10.1016/j.intacc.2014.01.007

Collins, S. (1989). The Move to Globalization: Is a Common International Accounting Language Feasible? *Journal of Accountancy*, *167*, 82–85.

Daske, H., Hall, L., Leuz, C., & Verdi, R. (2008). Mandatory IFRS Reporting around the World: Early Evidence on the Economic Consequences. *Journal of Accounting Research*, *46*, 1085–1142.

Daske, H., Luzi, H., Leuz, C., & Verdi, R. (2013). Adopting a label: Heterogeneity in the economic consequences around IAS/IFRS adoptions. *Journal of Accounting Research*, *51*(3), 495–547. doi:10.1111/1475-679X.12005

Efobi, U. (2014). *IFRS Adoption and the Environment: Is Africa closing her Eyes to Something?* Working paper available at SSRN.

Efobi, U., Iyoha, F., & Mukoro, D. (2014). *IFRS Adoption and Foreign Investment in Africa: Institutions also Matter.* Working paper available at SSRN.

Elbannan, M. (2011). Accounting and Stock Market Effects of International Accounting Standards Adoption in an Emerging Economy. *Review of Quantitative Finance and Accounting*, *1*(36), 207–245. doi:10.1007/s11156-010-0176-1

Florou, A., & Pope, P. (2012). Mandatory IFRS adoption and institutional investment decisions. *Accounting Review*, *87*(6), 1993–2025. doi:10.2308/accr-50225

Fox, A, Helliar, C, Veneziani, M and Hannah, G. (2013). The Costs and Benefits of IFRS Implementation in the UK and Italy. *Journal of Applied Accounting Research*, *14*(1).

Francis, J., Lafond, R., Olsson, P., & Schipper, K. (2004). Costs of Equity and Earning Attributes. *Accounting Review*, *79*(4), 967–1010. doi:10.2308/accr.2004.79.4.967

Gresilova, I. (2013). *Chicken Or Egg? The Relationship Between IFRS Adoption And FDI.* A Thesis submitted in partial fulfillment of the requirements for the degree of MA in Financial Economics. Kyiv School of Economics. Retrieved from www.kse.org.ua/download.php?downloadid=299

Haverals, J. (2005). IAS/IFRS. In *Belgium: Quantitative Analysis Of The Impact On The Tax Burden Of Companies. '1 Université Libre de Bruxelles – Centre Emile Bernheim*. SBS.

Herbert, W. & Tsegba, N. (2013). Economic Consequences of International Financial Reporting Standards (IFRS) Adoption: Evidence from a Developing Country. *European Journal of Business and Management*, *5*(28).

Huerta, E., & Zaidi, S. (2014). IFRS Adoption and Enforcement as Antecedents of Economic Growth. *International Journal of Accounting and Financial Reporting*, *4*(1). DOI: 10.5296/ijafr.v4i1.5410

ICAEW. (2007). *EU Implementation of IFRS and the fair value directive*. A report for the European Commission. Available from http://ec.europa.eu/internal_market/accounting/docs/studies/2007-eu_implementation_of_ifrs.pdf

ICAEW. (2014). The Effects of Mandatory IFRS Adoption in the EU: A Review of Empirical Research. ICAEW. Available from http://www.icaew.com/~/media/Files/Technical/Financial-reporting/Information for better markets/IFBM/effects-of-mandatory-ifrs-adoption-oct2014-

IMF. (2009). *London Summit – Leaders' Statement*. Retrieved from https://www.imf.org/external/np/sec/pr/2009/pdf/g20_040209.pdf

Johnson, S., & Leone, M. (2009). *CFO's on IFRS: Forget about It*. Retrieved from http://www.cfo.com/article.cfm/13517383?f=home_featured

Jones, S., & Higgins, D. (2006). Australia's Switch to International Financial Reporting Standards: A perspective from Account Preparers. *Journal of Accounting, Auditing & Finance*, *20*, 95–119.

Laux, C., & Leuz, C. (2010). Did fair-value accounting contribute to the financial Crisis?. *The Journal of Economic Perspectives*, *24*(1), 93–118. doi:10.1257/jep.24.1.93

Lee, E., Walker, M., & Zeng, C. (2013). *Does IFRS Convergence Affect Financial Reporting Quality in China?. Research report 131. The Association of Certified* Public Accountants.

Leventis, S., Dimitropoulos, P., & Anandarajan, A. (2011). Loan loss provisions, earnings management and capital management under IFRS: The case of EU Commercial banks. *Journal of Financial Services Research, 40*(1-2), 103–122. doi:10.1007/s10693-010-0096-1

Louis, H., & Urcan, O. (2012). *The Effect of IFRS on Foreign Direct Investment: Evidence from Cross-Border Acquisitions*. Paper presented at Singapore Management University.

Negash, M. (2012). IFRS and environmental accounting. *Management Research Review, 35*(Iss: 7), 577–601. doi:10.1108/01409171211238811

Oduware, U. (2012). *Comparability of IFRS Financial Statements*. Retrieved from https://www.deloitte.com/assets/Dcom-

Outa, E. (2011). *The Impact of International Financial Reporting Standards (IFRS) Adoption on the Accounting Quality of Listed Companies in Kenya*. Available at http://ssrn.com/abstract=1976146

Phan, D., Mascitelli, B., & Barut, M. (2014, March). Perceptions Towards International Financial Reporting Standards (IFRS): The Case of Vietnam. *Global Review of Accounting and Finance., 5*(1), 132–152.

Pope, P., & McLeay, S. (2011). The European IFRS Experiment: Objectives, Research, Challenges and some early Evidence. *Accounting and Business Review, 41*(3), 233–266. doi:10.1080/00014788.2011.575002

Ramanna, K., & Sletten, E. (2009). Why do countries adopt International Financial Reporting Standards? Harvard Business School 09-102.

Swenson, C., & Lee, N. (2009). How Will IFRS Affect Accounting for Income Taxes? *Corporate Taxation Insider.* Available from: http://www.cpa2biz.com/Content/media/PRODUCER_CONTENT/Newsletters/

Tarca, A. (2012). *The Case for Global Accounting Standards: Arguments and Evidence*. Available at SSRN: http://ssrn.com/abstract=2204889

Tweedie, D. (2009). Sir David Tweedie Takes On IFRS. *AICPA Corporate Finance Insider*. Retrieved from http://www.ifrs.com/overview/general_listing.html

Tweedie, D., & Seidensttein, T. (2005). Setting a global standard: The case for Accounting Convergence. *Northwestern Journal of International Law and Business, 25*(3), 589.

UNCTAD. (2006). *Review of Practical Implementation Issues Of International Financial Reporting Standards - Case Study In Kenya*. Washington, DC: UNCTAD. Retrieved from www.unctad.org/en/docs/c2isard37_en.pdf

Veron, N. (2007). *The Global Accounting Experiment*. Brussels: Bruegel Blue Print Series.

Wyatt, A., & Yospe, J. (1993). Wake-up Call to American Business: International Accounting Standards are on the Way. *Journal of Accountancy*, 80–85.

Zeff, S. (2007). Some obstacles to global financial reporting comparability and Convergence at a high Level of quality. *The British Accounting Review, 39*(4), 290–302. doi:10.1016/j.bar.2007.08.001

KEY TERMS AND DEFINITIONS

Asset Securitizations: The process of promoting liquidity by combining other financial assets and then marketing different tiers of the repackaged instruments to investors.

Collateralized Repurchase Agreements: The sale of securities together with an agreement for the seller to buy back the securities at a later date. The difference between the repurchase price and the sale price is interest.

Convergence: The goal of establishing a single set of high-quality accounting standards to be used internationally, and the efforts of standard-setters towards achieving that goal.

Cost of Capital: Refers to the cost of funds used for financing a business and in this case the cost of equity. Theoretically it is the rate of return demanded by equity investors and it is made up of Risk-free rate + (Company's Beta x Risk Premium).

Derivative: A contract between two or more parties and includes futures contracts, forward contracts, options and swaps and are used as an instrument to hedge risk, but can also be used for speculative purposes.

FDI: Short for foreign direct investments. An investment that carries less than 10% of the voting power in the investee is conventionally regarded as a portfolio investment, while one that gives 10% or more is regarded as FDI.

Financial Instruments: A document representing some monetary value and can be classified as equity based representing ownership of the asset, or debt based, representing a loan made by an investor to the owner of the asset. It is also a contractual right to receive or deliver cash.

Loan Loss Provisions: An allowance set aside in case customer defaults and in International accounting standards it was described as backward due to the provision being calculated on the basis of the current loan balance. In the revised IFRS, it is futuristic as it is based on the future ability of the loan to be fully repaid.

ENDNOTES

1 The term IFRS refer to both IFRS issued by the International Accounting Standards Board (IASB) and International Accounting Standards (IAS) issued by IASC (the predecessor of IASB).

2 ICAEW stands for Institute of Chartered Accountants in England and Wales and this citation refers to a report by its faculty.

3 Most of the history of IFRS are based on the works of Camferman and Zeff (2007), *Financial Reporting and Global Capital Markets-A History of the International Accounting standards committee*. London: Oxford University Press and Zeff (2007) on the Evolution of the IASC into the IASB, and the Challenges.

4 SFAS-Stands for statement of financial accounting standards- the accounting standards issued in the US by FASB.

Chapter 4
Determinants of and Obstacles to the Adoption of International Financial Reporting Standards in Africa

Lesley Stainbank
Durban University of Technology, South Africa

Venancio Tauringana
Bournemouth University, UK

ABSTRACT

This chapter investigates the determinants of and obstacles to the adoption of International Financial Reporting Standards (IFRSs) in Africa. Specifically we investigate whether English as an official language, educational levels, existence of a capital market, economic openness and economic growth are associated with the probability of a country adopting IFRSs with a sample of 46 African countries. Binary logistics regression was used to analyze the data. The results suggest that only English as one of the official languages was associated with the likelihood of a country adopting IFRSs. Through an examination of the Reports on the Observance of Standards and Codes of the World Bank, we document that the major obstacles to adopting IFRSs are the lack of enabling legislation for its adoption and a lack of capacity in all aspects of the accounting supply chain. The chapter concludes that more research is needed at a continent level given that most of the determinants we investigated are not associated with the likelihood of a country adopting IFRSs.

INTRODUCTION

The benefits of adoption of International Financial Reporting Standards (IFRSs) have been well documented. For example, Barth, Landsman and Lang (2008) investigated whether the adoption of IFRSs is associated with higher earnings quality. They found that firms applying international accounting standards in 21 countries generally evidenced less earnings management, more timely loss recognition,

DOI: 10.4018/978-1-4666-9876-5.ch004

and more value relevance accounting amounts than do matched firms applying non-United States (US) domestic standards. Armstrong, Barth, Jagolinzer and Riedl (2010) investigated the market reaction to the adoption of IFRSs in Europe. They suggest that markets in Europe would react positively to movement toward IFRSs adoption if, for example, investors expected application of IFRSs to result in higher quality financial reporting information. The study found that the markets reacted positively to firms with lower quality pre-adoption information and with higher pre-adoption information asymmetry, consistent with investors expecting net information quality benefits from IFRSs adoption. Another study by Daske, Hail, Leuz and Verdi (2008) examined the economic consequences of mandatory IFRSs reporting around the world by analyzing the effects on market liquidity, cost of capital and Tobin's *q* in 26 countries. Their findings suggest that on average, market liquidity increases around the time of introduction of IFRSs and that the cost of the firms' capital decreases and the equity valuations increases.

However, while the benefits of adoption of IFRSs in developed countries are undisputed, IFRSs adoption and use in developing countries has been subject of much debate. For example, some academics have suggested that the international accounting standards may not be applicable to developing countries (e.g., Briston, 1978; Hove, 1986; Perera, 1989). Such questioning of the relevance of international accounting standards has come both from a general perspective, analysis of a group of developing countries and examination of specific developing countries (Cairns, 1990; Hove, 1986; Samuels and Oliga, 1982; Perera, 1985). However, Chamisa (2000) cogently argues the case for applicability of international standards to developing nations using Zimbabwe as an example. Chamisa (2000, p. 274) suggests that '.. developing countries (such as Zimbabwe and many others) in which the private sector dominates the economy (resembling the sector ownership patterns found in the UK and US), the IASC standards (which are oriented towards information needs of the private sector) are judged to be relevant'. Tyrrall, Woodward and Rakhimbekova (2007) who examined the relevance and implementation of IFRSs between 1991 and 2006 in Kazakhstan, however, concluded that although a strong case for IFRSs cannot be made, even by 2006, Kazakhstan had little choice but to proceed with IFRSs.

Despite the controversy discussed above as to whether IFRSs are relevant to developing countries, some developing countries have adopted IFRSs while others have not. The pertinent question therefore is why some developing countries have opted to adopt and what are the obstacles for those that may want to adopt but have not done so. There are a few studies that have investigated the determinants of IFRSs adoption (e.g. Ding, Jeanjean & Stolowy, 2005; Zeghal & Mhedhbi, 2006; Hope, Jin & Kang, 2006; Ramanna & Sletten, 2009; Judge, Li & Pinsker, 2010). However, all these studies except Stainbank (2014) are not continent specific. For example, Zeghal and Mhedhbi (2006) included 21 African countries in their sample of 64 countries. Ramanna and Sletten (2009) included 24 African countries in their final sample of 102 non-European Union countries. Judge *et al.* (2010) included 22 African countries in their end sample of 109 countries. These studies did not attempt to isolate factors that may be more significant in one particular continent. Other empirical research usually includes only the larger more developed African countries, such as South Africa and Kenya, in their data sets. The purpose of this research is to focus only on African countries and identify factors influencing the adoption of IFRSs in African countries.

The contribution of this study is that it extends the work by Stainbank (2014) who investigated the determinants of adoption of IFRSs by 32 countries (or 59% of all African countries) due to limited data set. We extend that study by investigating the determinants of adoption by a larger data set of 46 (or 85%) of all African countries. We also contribute by including two new variables that were not part of the study by Stainbank (2014). In addition to investigating the determinants, we also investigate the possible barriers to IFRSs adoption. Investigating the possible barriers is important as it will open up avenues for further empirical investigation.

Extending the Stainbank (2014) study is important as (1) it adds to the IFRSs adoption literature and its relevant consequences in understanding specific factors that motivates countries' adoption of IFRSs and the possible barriers affecting its adoption from the African continent perspective; (2) adding more variables provides a deeper insight into issues that are peculiar to African countries; and (3) it helps in increasing the degree of freedom for the regression analysis and therefore a more reliable inference can be drawn from the analysis. This current study provides policy makers, development agencies and the International Accounting Standards Board (IASB) with further insight into understanding possible constraints to adoption of IFRSs by African countries and assist in strategies to circumvent such challenges.

The remainder of this paper is organized as follows. Firstly, prior studies on accounting development are reviewed together with studies that attempt to explain why a country might adopt IFRSs. This is then followed by the development of the hypotheses. Thereafter, the research methodology and results are discussed followed by the conclusion and limitations.

LITERATURE REVIEW AND HYPOTHESES DEVELOPMENT

Literature Review

Only a small number of previous studies have specifically investigated the determinants of adoption of IFRSs. One such study was by Hope *et al.* (2006) who argued that investigating the determinants of IFRSs adoption was pertinent to standard-setters because a better understanding of the motivation for adoption would enable them to promote IFRSs more effectively to countries that do not currently employ IFRSs. The sample for their study consisted of 38 countries of which 12 countries had adopted IFRSs by 2004. Their results revealed a significant negative association between adoption of IFRSs and poor disclosure rules and anti-director rights – a variable which was used as proxy for investor protection. The study interpreted these findings as an indication that countries with weaker shareholder protection bond themselves to superior accounting standards in order to access international investors and/or markets. Further, Hope *et al.* (2006) also found that countries providing better access to their stock market for international investors were more likely to adopt IFRSs.

Zeghal and Mhedhbi (2006) also investigated the factors that could explain the adoption of international accounting standards in developing countries. Specifically, the study investigated the factors of economic growth, education level, the degree of external economic openness, cultural membership in a group of countries, and the existence of a capital market. The results indicated that developing countries with the highest literacy rates, have capital markets and have Anglo-American culture are most likely to adopt international standards. Ramanna and Sletten (2009) used a sample of 102 non-European countries also to investigate what influences countries to adopt international accounting standards. The study used the economic theory of networks to develop the hypotheses. Economic network theory predicts that in addition to network benefits (synchronization value), a product with network effects can be adopted due to its direct benefits (autarky value) (Katz & Shapiro, 1985; Liebowitz & Margolis, 1994). The study focused on the analysis of network effects at regional and trade levels. The results indicate that the likelihood of IFRSs adoption for a given country increases with the number of IFRSs adopters in its geographical region and with IFRSs adoption among its trading partners.

Clements, Neill and Stovall (2010) investigated the IFRSs adoption decision by 61 countries. They, in particular, examined the influence of cultural diversity and country size. Their results suggest that the IFRSs adoption decision was significantly associated with country size but not with cultural influences. They concluded that their findings were consistent with the notion that larger countries have a well-established set of financial accounting and reporting standards already in place, and therefore would be reluctant to incur the cost of changing to an international set of standards.

Judge *et al.* (2010) suggest that while there has been considerable research on the effects of IFRSs adoption, there has been relative little systematic research on the antecedents of IFRSs adoption. The study therefore sought to find out why some countries quickly embraced IFRSs while other partially adopted and others continued to resist. The study used the Deloitte 2008 database to identify the 132 countries included in the final sample. Using logistics regression and controlling for market capitalization and GDP growth, their findings suggest that foreign aid, import penetration and level of education achieved within a national economy were all predictive of the degree to which IFRSs were adopted across the 132 transitional, developing and developed countries.

The only study to date that is continent specific is that by Stainbank (2014). The population for the study was all 48 African countries in the Deloitte (2011) dataset. However, due to problems in obtaining the necessary data for all of these countries meant that only 32 countries comprised the final data set. The study examined whether economic growth, adult literacy, foreign direct investment, culture and capital market capitalization significantly determined whether the country adopted IFRSs. Using logistics regression, the findings suggest that only culture was a significant determinant of the decision to adopt IFRSs.

Hypotheses Development

Official Language

Language has been widely cited as a possible barrier to accounting hamonization throughout the world (Nobes & Parker, 2010). Abd-Elsalam and Weetman (2003) suggest that familiarity with new legislation is more problematic when the authoritative source material is not in the local language. This means that countries where English is not one of the official languages may find it difficult to adopt IFRSs since IFRSs are issued in English language. Moreover, according to Alver, Alver, Mackevičius, Paupa and Bailey (1998) language barrier in the context of accounting harmonization and a market economy, means that it may well remain a puzzlement in the absence of an adequate informative literature in the official Estonian, Latvian and Lithuanian languages and with some Western accounting materials being accessible only in Russian or Polish languages. Using archival data of the Translation Review Committee (TRC) and translation guidelines and other materials provided by the IASB, as well as interviews, Kettunen (2011) shows that the quality of translation is far from a straightforward issue because translation cannot be accomplished without interpretation of the original standards and thus target language text is a compromise between those who participate in the translation process. While most African countries have a number of indigenous languages, many have adopted English as an official language. Elad (2015) argues that in the African Franc Zone countries, the approach to financial accounting is still modelled on French traditions. Given the difficulty in translation it can be argued that countries where English is among the official languages are more likely to adopt IFRSs compared to other countries. It is therefore hypothesized that:

H_1: *The probability of an African country adopting IFRSs increases if English is one of the official languages.*

Education Level

Zeghal and Mhedhbi (2006) suggest that the adoption of International Accounting Standards (IASs) is a strategic and critical decision and that it requires high level of education, competence, and expertise to enable to understand, interpret and then make use of these standards. Hegarty, Gielen and Barros (2004) also point out that the application of IFRSs requires certain minimum levels of capacity (i.e., appropriately qualified individuals), which depends on the availability of opportunities for relevant and adequate education, training and experience. This is consistent with Gernon, Meek and Mueller (1987) who found that there is a positive relationship between education level and the competence of professional accountants. Since highly qualified accountants and well trained users must exercise professional judgement (Street, 2002), it is expected that in countries where the educational level is low and expertise weak, there is a real barrier to the adoption of IAS (Zeghal & Mhedhbi, 2006). It is therefore hypothesized that:

H_2: *The probability of an African country adopting IFRSs increases with education levels.*

Existence of a Capital Market

The existence of a capital market is likely to increase the probability of a country adopting IFRSs for a number of reasons. First, according to Gray, McSwenney and Shaw (1984), investors require quality financial information in order to make optimal investment decisions when they analyze investment opportunities. Given that at least some of those investors who participate of the capital market are foreign investors, it is likely that they will put pressure for firms to adopt high quality IFRSs. Second, Adhikari and Tondkar (1992) suggested that in countries with a capital market, standard–setting bodies tend to establish sophisticated accounting systems in order to guarantee the production and disclosure of quality financial information that will be potentially useful for investors in making their decisions. This may well entail adoption of high quality IFRSs. Third, in the context of Africa, in general and Zimbabwe specifically, Chamisa (2000) suggests that IASs are relevant to capital markets of developing countries even if they are underdeveloped. This suggests that those countries in Africa with a capital market are likely to see the need for adopting IASs to improve the functioning of such capital markets. It is therefore hypothesized that:

H_3: *The probability of an African country adopting IFRSs increases with the presence of a capital market.*

External Economic Openness

The reasoning for expecting external economic openness to influence the likelihood of adoption of IFRSs is based on 'mimetic' isomorphism. This is the tendency of social actors to imitate those other actors (i.e., individuals, organizations and nations) which are viewed as successful and legitimate. These successful multinationals that come from foreign locations are likely to conform to IFRSs and domestic competitors may imitate these successful multinational firms (El-Gazzar, Finn & Jacob, 1999). Consistent with this argument, Wei, Liu, Song and Romilly (2001) demonstrated that a region's openness to foreign competition and trade exposes firms to a wider array of 'best practices'. Judge *et al.* (2010) cites anecdotal evidence to support the hypothesized relationship of mimetic pressure arising from foreign direct investments and adoption of international accounting standards. Specifically they cited the case of Iran and Bangladesh which had relatively little inward Foreign Direct Investment (FDI) as examples of countries that continued to shun IFRSs practices and norms. On the other hand, Judge *et al.* (2010) cited the case of the United Kingdom (UK) and Ireland which have open economies and considerable inward FDI as examples of countries that had fully embraced IFRSs practices.

Zeghal and Mhedhbi (2006) also argue that external pressures, such as the degree of economic openness, will expose the country to diverse international pressures such as that by 'foreign investors, multinational corporations, international accounting firms and world financial institutions'. Their study found external economic openness to be statistically insignificant. It is therefore hypothesized that:

H_4: *The probability of an African country adopting IFRSs increases with a high degree of external economic openness.*

Economic Growth

The relationship between economic growth and adoption of IFRSs is expected on the basis that higher accounting quality may help lower the cost of capital, and thus leads to economic growth (Mueller, Gernon & Meek, 1994). Zeghal and Mhedhbi (2006) also suggest that economic conditions are a major determinant in the development of a country's accounting system. Consistent with this notion Adhikari and Tondkar (1992) established that a country's level of economic growth has a positive effect on the development of accounting systems and practices. Moreover, where information plays a critical role, the accounting system will undergo significant changes in response to demands of the changing economic conditions of a more dynamic business environment. Previous empirical research on the relationship between economic growth and adoption of IFRSs is, however, contradictory. For example, Zeghal and Mhedhbi (2006) and Stainbank (2014) did not find a significant relationship. It is therefore hypothesized that:

H_5: *The probability of an African country adopting IFRSs increases with economic growth of that country.*

RESEARCH METHODOLOGY

Population and Sample

As at 31st December, 2014 there were 54 independent nations on the African continent. While all 54 African countries were chosen, difficulties in obtaining the necessary data for all of them meant that 46 countries comprised the final data set. Despite not having 100% of the African countries, our sample represents a considerable increase in data set compared to the 32 countries included in a similar study by Stainbank (2014). The countries included are shown in Table 1.

The fourteen countries that are included in the current study but not included in the study by Stainbank (2014) are: Central African Republic, Republic of Congo, Equatorial Guinea, Eritrea, Ethiopia, Republic of Guinea, Guinea Bissau, Lesotho, Liberia, Libya, Madagascar, Mauritania, Mauritius and Zimbabwe.

Table 1. Countries in Africa and whether or not IFRSs adopted

Country[1]	IFRSs Adopted	Year of Adoption
Algeria	0	
Angola	1	2009: Accounting standard regulators in Angola started to adopt IFRSs.
Benin	0	
Botswana	1	2009: IFRSs required for some, permitted for others.
Burkina Faso	0	
Burundi	0	
Cameroon	0	
Central Africa Rep.	0	
Chad	0	
Congo (Rep. of)	0	
Democratic Republic of Congo (DRC)	0	
Egypt	0	
Equatorial Guinea	0	
Eritrea	0	
Ethiopia	0	
Gabon	0	
Gambia	1	2007: Central Bank of Gambia started adopting IFRS in 2007. Mandatory from 2009.
Ghana	1	2007: Required for some entities from 2007, and for all others from 2009.
Guinea (Rep. of)	0	
Guinea-Bissau	1	2014: The Conseil Comptable Ouest Africain (CCOA), the regional standard-setting body, is converging its regional accounting standards (known as SYSCOA) towards IFRSs starting in 2014.
Ivory Coast (Côte D'Ivoire)	0	
Kenya	1	1998[2]: IFRSs was set to be the accounting standard in Kenya in 1998 by the council of the Institute of Certified Public Accountants of Kenya.
Lesotho	1	2001: The Council of the Lesotho Institute of Accountants voted for the adoption of IFRSs in 2001.
Liberia	1	2012: IFRSs required for all banks from 2012.
Libya	1	2005: IFRSs required for all listed companies.
Malawi	1	2001: Following a Society of Accountants in Malawi decision in 2001, corporate entities of all types and size that are listed in the market, are producing financial statements in accordance with the IFRSs.
Mali	0	
Madagascar	0	
Mauritania	0	
Mauritius	1	2001: The Companies Act 2001 requires all companies with annual revenue over 50 million rupees (approximately US$ 1.5 million) to use IFRSs (some exceptions apply).

Table 1. Continued

Country[1]	IFRSs Adopted	Year of Adoption
Morocco	1	2004: In 2004, the Moroccan Stock Exchange Law was established and this required that all companies (except banks and financial institutions) listed on the Casablanca Stock Exchange prepare their financial statements using either IFRSs or Moroccan GAAP.
Mozambique	1	2007: IFRSs permitted, required for banks 2007.
Namibia	1	2005: In January 1, 2005, IFRSs became required for listed companies under the Namibia Stock Exchange.
Niger	0	
Nigeria	1	2010: Required from 2010 and implemented from 2012 onwards.
Rwanda	1	2008: From 2008 accounting standards were consistent with IFRSs.
Senegal	0	
Sierra Leone	1	2006: In July 2006, Sierra Leone adopted IFRSs as its national standard.
South Africa	1	1993[3]: Followed IAS, but renumbered and adapted.
Swaziland	1	2008: IFRSs permitted.
Togo	0	
Tanzania	1	2002: Local standards based on IFRSs. IFRSs and IAS formally adopted as national standards in 2004.
Tunisia	0	
Uganda	1	1999: IFRSs permitted. Formally legislated in 2004 for financial institutions.
Zambia	1	2005: The Zambia Institute of Chartered Accountants permits all corporate entities, including commercial banks and non-bank financial institutions registered and operating in Zambia, to adopt IFRSs for reporting periods beginning on or after 1 January 2005.
Zimbabwe	1	1993: IFRSs were formally adopted for use in Zimbabwe in 1993.

Measurement of Dependent Variable

The dichotomous approach was used to measure the dependent variable, IFRSs adoption (ADOP). Countries that have adopted IFRSs were coded '1'; '0' otherwise. According to Stainbank (2014) an examination of the IASplus website and the adoptifrs website and the descriptions of a country's adoption show that there are many levels of adoption. She classified whether or not a country had adopted IFRSs using *Use of IFRSs by Jurisdiction* webpage (Deloitte, 2011) on the IASplus website, together with data from the website www.adoptifrs.org (this website is the outcome of a research project conducted at Simon Fraser University in Canada) and prior literature. Similarly, this is the approach that was followed by the current study in coding adopting and non-adopting countries. The adoption dates we used are the dates from which the country permitted IFRS or legislated the use of IFRS, whichever was the earlier. The adoption dates, together with a brief explanation are shown in Table 1.

Measurement of Independent Variables and Sources of Data

All the data extracted for the variables were available on the World Bank website (http://data.worldbank.org/data-catalog/africa-development-indicators), with the exception of official language where a different website was used. The way all independent variables were measured is explained in Table 2.

Model Specification

To determine whether the selected independent variables determine whether the country adopts IFRSs we used logistics regression analysis. Logistics regression analysis is suitable for the study because our dependent variable (IFRSs adoption) is a categorical dichotomy and therefore the alternative such as ordinary least squares (OLS) regression was considered inappropriate (Myers, 1990). According to Tabachnick and Fidell (1996), when the dependent variable is dichotomous, logistic regression yields estimators that are asymptotically efficient and normally distributed. This makes it feasible to construct an appropriate large sample confidence bounds and tests of hypotheses for parameters. To test the hypotheses, the study specified the following logistic regression model:

$$\text{Adopt} = \beta 0 + \beta_1 \text{LANG} + \beta_2\ \text{EDLE} + \beta_3\ \text{EXCM} + \beta 4\ \text{ECOP} + \beta_5 \text{ECGR} + \varepsilon$$

RESULTS AND DISCUSSION

Descriptive Statistics

The descriptive statistics of the continuous variables in respect of those countries that have adopted IFRSs and those that have not are presented in Table 3. The results show that the education level (EDLE) measured by literacy rates is higher for those countries that have adopted IFRSs with a mean of 68.22% compared to 56.54% for those countries that have not adopted. Similarly, the median is higher for adopters at 69% compared to 55% for non-adopters. The t-test results show that there is a significant difference in

Table 2. Definitions of variables included in the logistic regression model

Adop	IFRSs adoption coded '1' if the country has adopted IFRSs; '0' otherwise
$\beta 0$	Intercept
β_1LANG	Official language is coded as '1' if English is one of the official languages of the country; '0' otherwise
β_2 EDLE	Education levels measured by the adult literacy rate in the country.
β_3 EXCM	Existence of a capital market in a country coded '1' if the country has a capital market; '0' otherwise
$\beta 4$ ECOP	Economic openness measured as foreign direct investment as a proportion of GDP
β_5ECGR	Economic growth was measured as the average annual increase in the per capita GDP of each country in the last five years leading to adoption of the IFRS. If a country had not adopted IFRS, the last five years of GDP growth (2009 – 2013) were used
ε	Error term

Table 3. Descriptive statistics of adopters and non-adopting African countries: continuous variables

Variables	Adopters			Non-Adopters			
	Mean	Std Dev	Median	Mean	Std Dev	Median	t-test
EDLE	.6822	0.1598	.6900	0.5654	0.1986	0.55	2.196*
ECOP	0.0483	0.0858	0.0188	0.0535	0.0550	0.0266	-0.249
ECGR	0.0310	0.0310	0.0283	0.0098	0.0215	0.0129	2.573*

*Significant at 5%

mean values at the 5% level between the two groups. The results in Table 3, however, reveal that there is no significant difference in respect of economic openness (ECOP) measured as foreign direct investment as a proportion of the country's GDP.

Although the difference is not significant, the results indicate that the non-adopters have a slightly higher ECOP of 5.4% compared to 4.8% for those countries that have adopted. In respect of economic growth (ECGR) the results show that those countries adopting IFRSs experienced a higher economic growth, on average, five years prior to adoption compared to non-adopters. Specifically, the results show that the average economic growth rate five years prior to adoption was 3.1% for adopters compared to 1.0% for non-adopters.

Table 4 shows the descriptive statistics in respect of English as one of the official language (LANG) and existence of capital market (EXCM) which are categorical variables. The results show that 78.3% of the countries in which English is among the official languages adopted IFRSs compared to 8.7% countries which adopted IFRSs where English is not one of the official languages. The results also show that 21.7% of the countries where English is not one of the official languages did not adopt IFRSs compared to 91.3% of countries for non-adopters.

The chi-square result shows that there is a significant difference between adopters and non-adopters in the likelihood of a country adopting IFRSs depending on whether English is one of the official language at the 1% level. The descriptive statistics in respect of EXCM show that there are very little differences between adopters and non-adopters. For example, the results show that 69.6% of the countries which have a capital market adopted IFRSs compared to 65.2% for non-adopters. Similarly, 30.4% of countries which have a capital market did not adopt compared to 34.8% which have no capital market. Not surprisingly, the chi-square test result shows that the percentage difference in the two groups of countries is not significant.

Table 5 presents the Spearman's rho correlations between the dependent and independent variables. The results show that LANG is significantly correlated with ADOP at 1% level. Further, the results also show that ADOP is also significantly correlated with EDLE and ECGR at 5% level.

Table 4. Descriptive statistics of adopting and non-adopting countries: categorical variables

Variables		Adopters	Non-Adopters	Chi-Square
LANG	Coded 1 Coded 0	78.3% 21.7%	8.7% 91.3%	25.310**
EXCM	Coded 1 Coded 0	69.6% 30.4%	65.2% 34.8%	0.099

*Significant at the 10% level (two-tailed); ***Significant at the 1% level (two-tailed).

Table 5. Correlation matrix among the independent and dependent variables

	ADOP	LANG	EDLE	EXCM	ECOP	ECGR
ADOP	1.0000					
LANG	0.702**	1.0000				
EDLE	0.314*	0.334*	1.0000			
EXCM	0.046	0.049	0.253	1.0000		
ECOP	-0.037	0.030	-0.123	-0.308*	1.0000	
ECGR	0.362*	0.140	0.033	-0.246	0.084	1.0000

In terms of correlations among the independent variables, the results in Table 5 show that there are significant correlations between EDLE and LANG of 0.334 and between ECOP and EXCM of -0.308. Although these correlations are significant at 5%, they are not high to cause multicolinearity problems in our model. As a rule of thumb, multicollinearity in regression analysis is considered harmful only when they exceed 0.8 or 0.9 (Belsey, Kuhn and Welsch, 1980). In addition, the variance inflation factor (VIF) for each independent variable was computed and in all cases the VIFs was below the critical value of 10 (Myers, 1990).

Logistics Regression Results

The logistic regression results are shown in Table 6. The results show that the overall fit for the model is 87% and that the model explains relatively very little of the variation in IFRSs adoption as indicated with the pseudo R^2 of 17.86%. The results in Table 6 also show that the probability of a country adopting IFRSs increases where English is one of the official languages (LANG). This means that hypotheses 1 (H_1) is confirmed. The results also show that the relationship between IFRSs adoption and economic growth (ECGR) is only significant at the 10% level which means H_5 is not confirmed. Table 6 also show

Table 6. Logistic regression results

	Coefficient.	Std. Error	Wald $_x{}^2$	Sig.	95% Confidence Interval	
					Lower	Upper
LANG	3.785	1.078	12.319	0.000	5.320	364.572
EDLE	1.530	2.854	0.287	0.592	0.017	1240.424
EXCH	0.688	1.124	0.374	0.541	0.220	18.024
ECOP	-3.146	7.848	0.161	0.689	0.000	206267.486
ECGR	46.414	25.741	3.251	0.071	0.018	1.169
Constant	-3.700	1.959	3.567	0.059		
Constant (-2LL) 31.336						
Model $_x{}^2$ 5.597						
Pseudo R^2 0.1786						
Overall fit 87%						

that the other independent variables incorporated in our model are not significantly associated with IFRSs adoption. Therefore, H_2, H_3 and H_4 are not confirmed.

The significant result in respect of English as an official language (LANG) is consistent with the argument that language is a barrier in accounting harmonization as the result suggests that those countries where English is not an official language are unlikely to adopt IFRSs. In a sense, the fact that those countries where English is not one of the official languages are unlikely to adopt IFRSs is an indication of translation difficulties. For example, Kettunen (2011) suggests that the quality of translation is far from a straight forward issue because translation cannot be accomplished without interpretation of the original standards and thus target language text is a compromise among the participants.

The results in respect of education level (EDLE) which show that the variable is not a significant influence are inconsistent with Zeghal and Mhedhbi (2006) who found a significant positive relationship. However, they are contradictory to our arguments that higher education levels will lead to a country adopting IFRSs. This is also contrary to the suggestion by Zeghal and Mhedhbi (2006) that since highly qualified accountants and well trained users must exercise judgement, it is expected that countries where the education level is low and expertise weak, there is a real barrier to adoption of IAS. However, our results may have been influenced by the way we measured the variable. Literacy rates may not be a good proxy for the strength of the accounting profession which may be expected to influence the adoption of IFRSs. However, the figures for the strength of accounting profession are not available for all the countries in our study.

The insignificant existence of capital market (EXCM) result is contradictory to our suggestion that since capital markets require quality information and that market participants especially foreigners would pressurize firms and regulators to adopt high quality IFRSs. The result is also contradictory to the suggestion by Chamisa (2000) that IFRSs are relevant for capital markets even in developing countries. Further, the results also contradict the suggestion by Adhikari and Tondkar (1992) that in countries with capital markets, the standard-setters tend to establish sophisticated accounting systems which means that adoption of international accounting standards was likely. The results are also inconsistent with Zeghal and Mhedhbi (2006) who found that the existence of a stock market increases the probability of a country adopting IFRSs.

Our result which suggests that the degree of the country's economic openness does not significantly influence a country to adopt IFRSs is contrary to Judge *et al.* (2010) who cite anecdotal evidence indicating that mimetic pressure emanating from foreign direct investments may be related to the adoption of international accounting standards. Our finding is, however, consistent with the results reported by Zeghal and Mhedhbi (2006) and Stainbank (2014). Finally, the result reported by this study suggest that economic growth is only significantly related to the choice by countries to adopt international accounting standards at the 10% level are contradictory to those reported by Stainbank (2014). They are also contrary to Mueller *et al.* (1994) who suggested that economic growth and adoption of international accounting standards may be expected on the reasoning that higher accounting quality may help lower the cost of capital and thus leads to economic growth.

Obstacles to IFRS Adoption

To probe qualitative reasons why African countries may be experiencing difficulties in adopting IFRSs, the Reports on the Observance of Standards and Codes (ROSC) – Accounting and Auditing for African countries were accessed on the World Bank website. The objectives of the ROSC program are firstly to compare critically the national accounting and auditing standards with international standards, determine the degree of compliance, and assess any strengths and weaknesses of the institutional framework in the support of high-quality financial reporting; and secondly to assist the country in developing and implementing a country action plan to improve institutional capacity so as to strengthen the country's corporate financial reporting regime (World Bank, 2015).

Where more than one ROSC report had been issued, only the most ROSC report was used. Thirty-three (33) ROSC reports were identified on the website of which seven were in French. Thus a total of twenty-six (26) reports were examined. The reports were spread over the years 2002 – 2014, with 12 reports issued in the first six years and 14 reports issued in the last six years. No reports were issued in 2009. Five countries had more than one report.

The most common obstacle to the successful adoption and implementation of IFRSs are the outdated laws in certain countries. A number of the ROSCs mentioned that the Companies Act or similar was outdated, or that it made no mention of the enabling provisions for the adoption of IFRSs. In effect, in many countries there is no legal mandate for the adoption of IFRSs and which body in the country has the authority for the adoption and implementation of accounting and auditing standards. The ROSCs also noted that some countries have no standard-setting arrangements.

Even if the country has adopted IFRSs, the ROSCs noted that an impediment to its successful implementation is the lack of technical capacity in the country. This affects adoption in a number of ways as successful adoption and implementation needs a critical mass of technically up-to-date accountants and auditors in the country. To get to this critical mass, countries could offer their own professional qualifications or enter into professional mutual recognition agreements with other countries. Looking firstly at whether a country could offer its own professional accounting education programme, a number of the ROSCs noted that some countries do not offer any country qualifications and that universities lack the human, physical and financial resources to implement existing education programmes or enhance the programmes already being offered. Some ROSCs noted that some countries had arrangements for the mutual recognition of each other's professional qualification.

Furthermore, in the ROSCs it was noted that many professional accountancy organizations (PAOs) lack technical capacity (and often human and financial capacity) to support the successful adoption of IFRSs. Some PAOs did not meet the International Federation of Accountants' (IFAC) requirements for membership and in a number of PAOs, it was noted that there was room for improvement. A strong PAO could assist in growing the number of accountants and auditors in the country and provide implementation guidance on IFRSs for its members. The lack of implementation guidance was also noted in some of the ROSC reports as a weakness.

The ROSC reports also noted that in some countries, regulators lack capacity to monitor and enforce the standards even when adopted, leading to compliance gaps in the financial statements when compared to IFRSs. Twelve of the ROSCs noted that there was a shortage of qualified professionals in the country, and also made mention of the inadequate technical capacity of auditors, regulators and accountants. Monitoring and enforcement of international standards is also critical to the successful implementation of IFRSs. A number of countries do not have enforcement mechanisms, and where they existed they were considered weak or inadequate by the ROSC teams of the World Bank. Linked to this were other findings such as the lack of any monitoring, the lack of or inadequate oversight and the lack of sanctions for entities that fail to comply with IFRSs.

SUMMARY AND CONCLUSION

This study investigated the possible determinants of the decision to adopt IFRSs using a sample of 46 African countries. Specifically, the study examined if English as one of official language, education level, existence of a capital market, economic openness and economic growth are associated with IFRSs adoption. The findings suggest that only English as one of the official languages was associated with the adoption of IFRSs. Although no study has investigated the use of English as a possible determinant of IFRSs adoption, the findings are consistent with existing literature that suggest that language may be a barrier to accounting harmonization. Also it is consistent with Stainbank (2014) who found that those countries that were former colonies of the UK (and presumably use English as one of the official languages) were more likely to have adopted IFRSs.

According to the ROSCs we examined, a lack of enabling legislation means that in many countries there is no legal mandate for the adoption and implementation of IFRSs. Furthermore there is a lack of capacity in all aspects of the accounting supply chain.

The results reported by this study should be interpreted in the light of a three main limitations we identified. First, we based our classification of whether or not a country had adopted IFRSs on the basis of information on websites such as the IASplus (www.iasplus.com) and AdoptIFRS (www.AdoptIFRS.org) which may not always be accurate. For example, Ramanna and Sletten (2009) report that information on the IASplus website was not correct when independently verified. Our study is therefore limited in the sense that we did not attempt to independently verify the adoption status of the countries other than by using different websites to cross check the information. Second, similar to previous studies, we used a dichotomous approach in measuring adoption of IFRSs. However, in some instances there are different levels of IFRSs adoption such as IFRSs adoption without implementation, or implementation without enforcement or IFRSs adoption for listed firms only. Third, the way we measured some of our independent variables may have affected the results. For example, for education levels we took literacy rates. However, literacy rates may not be a good measure of the likelihood of adoption of IFRSs. The strength of the accounting profession may be a better measure when it comes to influencing the decision to adopt IFRSs. However, as already pointed out, the information on the strength of accounting profession was not available for all the countries investigated. Finally, more research is needed at a continent level given that most of the determinants we investigated are not associated with the likelihood of a country adopting IFRSs.

REFERENCES

Abd-Elsalam, O. H., & Weetman, P. (2003). Introducing international accounting standards to an emerging capital market: Relative familiarity and language effect in Egypt. *Journal of International Accounting, Auditing & Taxation*, *12*(1), 63–84. doi:10.1016/S1061-9518(03)00002-8

Adhikari, A., & Tondkar, R. H. (1992). Environmental factors influencing accounting disclosure requirements of global stock exchanges. *Journal of International Financial Management and Accounting*, *4*(2), 75–105. doi:10.1111/j.1467-646X.1992.tb00024.x

Alver, A., Alver, L., Mackevičius, J., Paupa, V., & Bailey, D. (1998). Baltic states. In D. Alexander & S. Archer (Eds.), *European accounting guide* (3rd ed.; pp. 1464–1475). Miller.

Armstrong, C. S., Barth, M. E., Jagolinzer, A. D., & Riedl, E. J. (2010). Market reaction to the adoption of IFRS in Europe. *Accounting Review*, *85*(1), 31–61. doi:10.2308/accr.2010.85.1.31

Barth, M. E., Landsman, W. R., & Lang, M. H. (2008). International accounting standards and accounting quality. *Journal of Accounting Research*, *46*(3), 467–498. doi:10.1111/j.1475-679X.2008.00287.x

Belsey, D. A., Kuhn, E., & Welsch, R. E. (1980). *Regression diagnostics, identifying influential data and sources of collinearity*. New York: John Wiley & Sons. doi:10.1002/0471725153

Briston, R.J. (1978). The evolution of accounting in developing countries, *International Journal of Accounting: Education and Research*, (Fall), 105-120.

Cairns, D. (1990). Aid for the developing world. *Accountancy*, (March), 82-85.

Chamisa, E. E. (2000). The relevance and observance of the IASC Standards in developing countries and the particular case of Zimbabwe. *The International Journal of Accounting*, *35*(2), 267–286. doi:10.1016/S0020-7063(00)00049-2

Clements, C. E., Neill, J. D., & Stovall, O. S. (2010). Cultural diversity, country size, and the IFRS adoption decision. *Journal of Applied Business Research*, *26*(2), 115–126.

Daske, H., Hail, L., Leuz, C., & Verdi, R. (2008). Mandatory IFRS reporting around the world: Early evidence on the economic consequences. *Journal of Accounting Research*, *46*(5), 1085–1142.

Deloitte. (2011). *Use of IFRSs by jurisdiction*. Available from: http://www.iasplus.com/country/useias.htm

Ding, Y., Jeanjean, T., & Stolowy, H. (2005). Why do national GAAP differ from IAS? *The International Journal of Accounting*, *40*(4), 325–350. doi:10.1016/j.intacc.2005.09.004

El-Gazzar, S. M., Finn, P. M., & Jacob, R. (1999). An empirical investigation of multinational firms' compliance with International Accounting Standards. *The International Journal of Accounting*, *34*(2), 239–248. doi:10.1016/S0020-7063(99)00005-9

Elad, C. (2015). The development of accounting in Franc Zone countries in Africa. *The International Journal of Accounting*, *50*(1), 75–100. doi:10.1016/j.intacc.2014.12.006

Gernon, H., Meek, G., & Mueller, G. (1987). Accounting: an international perspective. Homewood, IL: Irwin.

Gray, S. G., McSwenney, L. B., & Shaw, J. C. (1984). *Information disclosure and the multinational corporation*. London: John Wiley and Sons.

Hegarty, J., Gielen, F., & Barros, A. C. H. (2004). *Implementation of International Accounting and Auditing Standards: lessons learned from the World Bank's Accounting and Auditing ROSC Program*. Washington, DC: World Bank. Retrieved 1 December 2012 from: http://www.worldbank.org/ifa/LessonsLearned_ROSC_AA.pdf

Hope, O., Jin, J., & Kang, T. (2006). Empirical evidence on jurisdictions that adopt IFRS. *Journal of International Accounting Research*, *5*(2), 1–20. doi:10.2308/jiar.2006.5.2.1

Hove, M. R. (1986). Accounting practices in developing countries: Colonialism's legacy of inappropriate technologies. In Readings in International Accounting (pp. 81-100). London: International Thomson Business Press.

Judge, W., Li, S., & Pinsker, R. (2010). National adoption of International Accounting Standards: An institutional perspective. *Corporate Governance International Review (Steubenville, Ohio)*, *18*(3), 161–174.

Katz, M. L., & Shapiro, C. (1985). Network externalities, competition, and compatibility. *The American Economic Review*, *75*, 424–440.

Kettunen, J. (2011). *Translation of IFRS standards into local languages: understanding problematics of translation*. Retrieved 1 April 2015 from: http://www.lse.ac.uk/accounting/pdf/Kettunen.pdf

Liebowitz, S. J., & Margolis, S. E. (1994). Network externality: An uncommon tragedy. *The Journal of Economic Perspectives*, *8*(2), 133–150. doi:10.1257/jep.8.2.133

Mueller, G., Gernon, H., & Meek, G. (1994). *Accounting: an international perspective*. Burr Ridge, IL: Irwin.

Myers, R. (1990). *Classical and modern regression with applications*. Boston, MA: Duxbury.

Nobes, C., & Parker, R. (2010). *Comparative international accounting* (11th ed.). London: Prentice-Hall.

Perera, M. H. B. (1985). *The relevance of International Accounting Standards to developing countries*. Working Paper. University of Glasgow.

Perera, M. H. B. (1989). Accounting in developing countries: A case for localized uniformity. *The British Accounting Review*, *21*(2), 141–158. doi:10.1016/0890-8389(89)90193-5

Ramanna, K., & Sletten, E. (2009). *Why do countries adopt International Financial Reporting Standards?* Harvard Business School Working Paper, 9-102.

Samuels, J.M., & Oliga, J.C. (1982). Accounting standards in developing countries. *International Journal of Accounting Education and Research*, (Fall), 69-88.

Stainbank, L. J. (2014). Factors influencing the adoption of International Financial Reporting Standards by African countries. *SA Journal of Accounting Research*, *28*(1), 79–95.

Street, D. L. (2002). GAAP 2001: Benchmarking national accounting standards against IAS: Summary of results. *Journal of International Accounting, Auditing & Taxation*, *11*(1), 77–90. doi:10.1016/S1061-9518(02)00055-1

Tabachnick, B. G., & Fidell, L. S. (1996). *Using multivariate statistics*. New York: HarperCollins.

Tyrrall, D., Woodward, D., & Rakhimbekova, A. (2007). The relevance of International Financial Reporting Standards to a developing country: Evidence from Kazakhstan. *The International Journal of Accounting*, *42*(1), 82–110. doi:10.1016/j.intacc.2006.12.004

Wei, Y., Liu, X., Song, H., & Romilly, P. (2001). Endogenous innovation growth theory and regional income convergence in China. *Journal of International Development*, *13*(2), 153–170. doi:10.1002/jid.721

World Bank. (2015). *Reports on the Observance of Standards & Codes. Topics: Accounting and auditing*. Retrieved 1 April 2015 from: http://www.worldbank.org/ifa/rosc_aa.html

Zeghal, D., & Mhedhbi, K. (2006). An analysis of the factors affecting the adoption of international accounting standards by developing countries. *The International Journal of Accounting*, *41*(4), 373–386. doi:10.1016/j.intacc.2006.09.009

ENDNOTES

1 All the countries are classified as developing. Source: World Bank, January 2011. Geographic classifications and data reported for geographic regions are for low-income and middle-income economies, as defined by the World Bank - http://web.worldbank.org/.

2 Zeghal and Mhedhbi (2006).

3 Zeghal and Mhedhbi (2006).

Chapter 5
IFRS, Foreign Investment, and Prevailing Institutional Structure in Africa

Efobi Uchenna
Covenant University, Nigeria

Francis Iyoha
Covenant University, Nigeria

ABSTRACT

We revisit the effectiveness of IFRS adoption for FDI attractiveness by considering the adopting country's institutional structure. Attention was on the extent of corruption control (as a measure of institutional structure). Data was tested on 42 African countries for the period 2001-2012. Using the Panel Corrected Standard Error (PSCE) estimation technique, our result suggest that the effect of IFRS adoption on foreign investment differs based on the level of corruption control instituted in the sample countries. When the variable – IFRS adoption, was tested for the sample with corruption control below the median value, the coefficient was either negative or insignificant. However, the opposite was seen for the category of countries with corruption control above the median value. This result was robust to the inclusion of alternative measures of corruption, foreign investment, and control of global financial crisis and legal origin of the country.

1. INTRODUCTION[1]

Since the promulgation of the International Financial Reporting Standard (IFRS) following the creation of the International Accounting Standard Board from the International Accounting Standard Committee in 2001, there has been an improvement in the global capital flow as one of the bi-product from the usage of IFRS for global financial reporting practice. IFRS was adjudged as a better form of financial reporting practice that applies more realistic measure of accounting numbers and promotes better disclosure of accounting transactions; thus reducing information asymmetry between preparers and users of financial information (Portes & Rey, 2005; Ramos, 2010; Wysocki, 2011; Gordon, Loeb & Zhu, 2012). Recent

DOI: 10.4018/978-1-4666-9876-5.ch005

studies (e.g. Gordon, Loeb & Zhu, 2012; Chen, Ding & Xu, 2014) have emphasized the role of IFRS adoption as a catalyst to spur foreign investment. The main argument is that – since IFRS promotes better disclosure – then it reduces the cost of monitoring of subsidiaries and information barriers to cross border investments. Foreign investors – therefore – will be able to have access to high-quality information that enables them to make decisions as regards the prospects of their investments at a lower cost.

Institutions, on the other hand, includes those structures and frameworks by which authorities are exercised to provide incentives for productive economic activities. It includes those rules, decrees, policies, guidelines and frameworks, which shapes relationships among economic agents, ensures security of property rights and reduces any form of losses as a result of opportunistic behaviours of economic agents (see North, 1991; Williamson, 2000; Osabuohien & Efobi, 2013; Osabuohien, 2014; Efobi, 2015a). There are recounting empirical evidences suggesting a strong correlation between institutions and foreign investment (Asiedu, 2006; Busse & Hefeker, 2007; Asiedu & Lien, 2011; Anyanwu, 2012; Bandyopadhyay, Sandler & Younas, 2014). Investors seek to protect their investment and maximise their returns, and therefore will prefer to flow into countries that have a strong institutional structure to set up their investment.

Pointing directly at the main concern raised by Wysocki (2011)[2], this chapter looks at the extent to which the resulting FDI benefit from the adoption of IFRS is affected by the prevailing institutional structure in Africa. The main issue addressed is whether the prevailing institutional structures interferes with the extent to which IFRS adoption can inform foreign capital flow to Africa. This issue is of utmost importance in the African setting because of the increasing wave of the number of IFRS adopting countries in this region and the underlining reason being to improve financial reporting infrastructure in order to be able to attract more foreign investors. More frantic, some experts in the International Accounting Standards Board (IASB)[3] encourages African countries to see the adoption of IFRS as an opportunity for deepen their capital market participation, enhance inward investment to foster the growth of the private sector and provide a suitable investment climate for multinationals who would like to set-up their operations in Africa. This therefore makes the improvement of the volume of investment in Africa the central reason for the drive towards IFRS adoption. However, the quality of institutions in this region questions the realisation of the FDI benefit from IFRS adoption.

Focusing on corruption: this represents one of the main institutional palaver in most African countries and has been charged for the slow developmental process of these countries (Fosu, 2011; Asongu, 2012; Ackah, Turkson & Opoku, 2013; Asongu, 2013, 2014; Efobi, 2015a). There are incidences in some African countries where political leaders divert developmental resources for private interest (Easterly, 2008). The spill-over effect of the reoccurrence of such incidences is that the complimentary structures like infrastructure, human capital development, among others, will be unattended to thereby creating an unfavourable environment for investment and creating a disincentive for foreign investment inflow. More so, corruption erodes the capacity of the state to deliver efficient services to economic agents that would have hitherto desired to invest in such country. For instance, corruption increases the transaction cost of setting up an investment since those who control regulatory authorities can possibly circumvent instituted guidelines in order to derive specific rents. In contrast, countries with lower corruption will experience reduced transaction cost for investors as the requisite guidelines to be followed in setting up investment is rid of unnecessary delays and procedures to attract rent from the investors. Being this the case, we suspect that African countries may not be able to realise the FDI benefit from the adoption of IFRS as a result of the prevailing institutional structure and bearing in mind its effect on investment decisions.

There are three plausible ways through which the prevailing institutional structure in African countries affects the FDI outcome from IFRS adoption. First, IFRS is more of principle based regulations that allows professionals to apply their value judgement in interpreting/applying the standard (Collins, Pasewark & Riley, 2012). The danger in this is that in countries with poor institutional frameworks, professionals can still perpetrate in opportunistic behaviours and thus, progress the occurrence of information asymmetry which defeats the objective of IFRS adoption. Second, for African countries to attract FDI from their adoption of IFRS, they will require the development of their institutional structure in order to reduce resultant associative transaction cost. The increased transaction cost from poor institutions signals the incidence of poor investment climate to other investors who would have wanted to invest in the affected country: thus investment is diverted to other locations with lower transaction cost and improved institutions (Bandyopadhyay, Sandler & Younas, 2014). Considering the adoption of IFRS in isolation cannot reduce such transaction cost as it is embedded in the requisite framework that is charged with investment set-up processes like licensing, documentation, legal procedures, among others. Third, in a country with poor institutions - like the prevalence of corruption – there is a higher incentive to divert public fund from development projects (such as infrastructural provisions and human capital development) to personal benefit of public officers. Consequently, such developmental projects, which would have induced foreign investment flow, will be lacking and the adoption of IFRS will matter insignificantly in informing FDI flow.

This chapter therefore presents an empirical investigation into this tripartite issues by including the three variables in an empirical model and from the analysis, learn more about the relative importance of institutional structure in the IFRS adopting country. There are a number of conceptual and empirical challenges that such an investigation has to overcome. The first is in the measurement of the concepts - IFRS adoption. There are potential overlap to the identification of the exact indicator for this concept. Nevertheless, the literature provides adequate guidance to some of the indicators that suffices in measuring IFRS. For IFRS adoption, Gordon, Loeb and Zhu (2012) proposes the use of a dummy variable where 1 connotes the period for adoption of IFRS and 0 otherwise. This is unlike Chen, Ding and Xu (2014) that applied Ding *et al* (2005) national accounting standards conformity with IFRS index, which reports the number of points on which the national accounting conforms with IFRS. While the later presents a more recent and robust measure to identify IFRS adoption, it only captures the extent of convergence of national accounting standard with IFRS and does not show the extent of adoption like most African countries are currently doing. So we recourse to the former, but faces another challenge of identifying the year to use as a base for IFRS adoption. Two options are available: the first is to capture IFRS adoption year as the year the country's Security and Exchange Commission (SEC) publicly declares its legal adoption of IFRS, while the second is to use the year the country's SEC mandates all publicly quoted entities to report their financial statements using IFRS. In this chapter, we categorise the two periods as the year of IFRS adoption and the year of implementation. We prefer to use the former for two reasons: first, it represents the year the country legally and statutorily adopts IFRS. Second, the dataset that presents the IFRS legal adoption status of countries did not explicitly state the year the country is expected to implement IFRS, which most times are within two year of the legal declaration of adoption of IFRS. Therefore, when a country declares its legal adoption of IFRS, it signals some extent of favourability of some institutional infrastructure that attracts foreign investment and improves the localisation advantage for the FDI presence (Chen, Ding & Xu, 2014; Efobi, 2015b).

The second challenge is to examine the effect of corruption either as a conditioning factor or at varying thresholds. The first considers the relationship between IFRS adoption and FDI conditioned on corruption. This includes the indirect or intervening effect of corruption on the IFRS-FDI nexus. The second is to consider different thresholds of corruption and examine the behaviour of IFRS adoption and FDI. In this case, only the direct effect of IFRS adoption on FDI is considered but at varying thresholds of corruption. Of course, with this kind of analysis, we are able to see how the effect of IFRS adoption on FDI diminishes (or improves) across the different corruption thresholds. This fits more to the emphasis of this chapter.

Using a sample of 49 African countries for which data was available, and controlling for other FDI determinants identified by literature, we obtain result generally consistent with our expectations. Specifically, our cross-section analysis generally shows that IFRS adoption is visibly important in attracting FDI flow to countries with stronger institutional structures. Furthermore, this relationship is found to be consistent irrespective of the combination of the covariates. Also, the result does not change even when we controlled for the global economic crisis shocks.

This chapter contributes to policy and literature in some important ways. First, the effect of the institutional structure in the IFRS adopting country and how it affects the FDI outcome have not received empirical attention. Most influential studies concludes by advocating for better institutions to enhance the effect of IFRS on FDI[4]. This is without empirical estimations of the behaviour of the nexus when considering different thresholds of institutional development. We take this further by being the first (to the best of our knowledge) to provide such empirical clarifications. Second, since the focus of this chapter is on African countries; considering the institutional structure and its attendant consequence will receive influential policy attention. This is because the region have since seen ineffective institutions as a major challenge impeding development processes. Third, the chapter also advanced the theoretical explanations on the factors that determine the location of FDI by considering IFRS and institutional infrastructure as an important framework.

The contributions of this chapter is important because foreign investment presents one of the foremost developmental finance relevant for African economy. The United Nations Millennium Declaration clearly points out that an increase in the volume of foreign capital flow to Africa will aid in the speedy achievement of the Millennium Development Goals (MDG), which includes poverty reduction by at-least half in 2015[5]. Asiedu (2006) also points out that the resource gap needed to attain broad economic goals of African countries will be substantially improved if foreign capital inflow is stimulated. No wonder some of the African countries are seeing the improvement of their financial reporting infrastructure as a veritable tool for attracting foreign capital flow. This is even reverberated by the recounting push by international organisations like the World Bank, World Trade Organisation and United Nations Conference on Trade and Development (UNCTAD) for the need to improve the business environment – by adopting IFRS – in order to be capable of attracting FDI. The remainder of the chapter is organised as follows: the next section presents the development of the hypothesis. The research method, which includes the econometric model and variables, the data and the estimation technique are in the third section. The main empirical results is presented and discussed in the fourth section. The fifth section concludes with policy recommendations.

2. REVIEW OF RELATED LITERATURE AND HYPOTHESIS DEVELOPMENT

There is an increased range of literature that has related institutions to the growth of foreign capital inflow to countries especially African countries. Prominent among them include Morisset (2000), Li and Resnick (2003), Asiedu (2004), Busse and Hofeker (2005), Daude and Stein (2007), Asiedu and Lien (2011), Bandyopadhyay, Sandler and Younas (2014). These authors observe that the improvement of the institutional framework of a country tend to provide a conducive environment that reduces the transaction cost on investment and improves the overall returns from investment. Based on this, it is usual to expect that a country with better institutions will attract FDI. This is so since governance structures that are reform oriented and pro-active with policies, will gain the trust of foreign investors. More so, such countries will create location-specific benefits and internationalization advantages to encourage the inflow of investment.

IFRS, on the other hand, is a global financial reporting standard that is intended to ensure better transparency and information disclosure, aimed at improving the flow of foreign investment and ensuring improved global capital mobility. The prominent contributors to this nascent body of knowledge include Barth et al (2008), Beneish *et al* (2010), Ramos (2010), Prochazka and Ilinitchi (2011), Gordon, Loeb and Zhu (2012), Chen, Ding and Xu (2014), Efobi (2015b), who all concluded that the convergence of national accounting standards with IFRS/or the adoption of IFRS promotes foreign investment by reducing information processing costs that would hitherto have been heightened if local standards were maintained. As it is well known, multinationals require transparent and comparable accounting standards in order to minimize the cost of translating financial information.

Despite the budding empirical evidence supporting the claim that improved FDI flow stems from IFRS adoption, it is essential to note that other structural factors affect the extent to which this relationship can be substantiated. An important structural factor (being considered in this chapter) is the prevalence of corruption. We argue that apart from the accounting reporting standards that is expected to affect the extent of transparency and disclosure of accounting information, foreign investment will still dwindle (or not be improved) in the face of heightened corruption.

Some studies have attempted to carry on this enquiry but without substantial empirical justification. For instance, the influential study by Chen, Ding and Xu (2014), concluded that accounting standards have no major impact on accounting quality per se, but there is the need to control for the institutional factors as a possible reporting incentives that can have an impact on foreign investors. Wysocki (2011) earlier concluded that observed outcomes from the adoption of IFRS will be more effective when benchmarked against institutions. Some other studies like Louis and Urcan (2013), Gordon, Loeb and Zhu (2012), and Hail, Leuz and Wysocki (2010) have reached similar conclusions. A common peculiarity across these studies is that there are no empirical justification to validate this relationship.

The closest attempt was Chen, Ding and Xu (2014) and Gordon, Loeb and Zhu (2012), who used rule of law variable and other measures of institutions. Since this chapter is interested in corruption control for obvious reasons, we are not able to rely on their conclusions for the African sample. More so, these authors included the measure of institution in a linear model framework, where their measures of institutions were included as part of the explanatory variable. The concern with this approach is that we are not able to empirically isolate the effect of IFRS adoption on FDI when considering the conditioning effect of institutions (or corruption control). Therefore, it will be difficult to see how the effect of IFRS adoption on FDI changes when considering different regimes of institution. Based on this, we present the main hypothesis of this chapter as:

Hypothesis One: African countries will attract more FDI if they adopt IFRS and improve on the institutional structures that controls for corruption.

3. RESEARCH METHOD

To begin with, an econometric model was formulated to conceptualise the main aim of this chapter. The main objective is to examine the linkage between IFRS adoption and foreign investment, taking into consideration the quality of institutions in the selected sampled countries. The econometric model is a standard foreign capital explained model that is augmented by including the institutional structure. Asiedu (2006) presents a background for the formulation of an FDI explained model for African countries. This is because the model includes the prominent factors that inform the attractiveness of foreign investor into African countries. Asiedu's model is such that foreign investment into African countries is explained by structural, policy and institutional variables. Thus:

$$FDI_{it} = \alpha_1 + \beta \text{EconomicStructure}_{it} + \gamma \text{EconomicPolicy}_{it} + \delta \text{InstitutionalVariable}_{it} + \varepsilon_i \quad (1)$$

This model was extended by including the IFRS adoption variable in Equation (1). Therefore Equation (1) is transformed as:

$$FDI_{it} = \alpha_1 + \partial IFRS\text{Adoption}_{it} + \beta \text{EconomicStructure}_{it} + \gamma \text{EconomicPolicy}_{it} + \delta \text{GovernanceVariable}_{it} + \varepsilon_i \quad (2)$$

This model, at this point, cannot effectively explain the effect of IFRS adoption on FDI when considering corruption. To effectively accentuate this, we first of all estimate the baseline model in Equation 2 at varying thresholds of corruption, to understand how IFRS adoption variable reacts at different levels of corruption. In essence, we expect that at higher thresholds of corruption, the effect of IFRS adoption on FDI becomes insignificant due to the deteriorating effect corruption has on FDI attractiveness. On the other hand, we expect a significant and positive effect of the IFRS adoption variable on FDI when considering lower corruption thresholds.

The variables are defined as follows: *FDI* is used as an indicator of foreign investment. The reason for this is because the OECD definition of foreign investment considers FDI as a major indicator due to its long lasting relationship with the host country's enterprise and the magnitude of influence that usually comes with such relationship[6]. In measuring FDI flow, we follow the approach of Asiedu (2006) and Bandyopadhyay, Sandler and Younas (2014), where FDI is measured as the net inflow of FDI as percentage of GDP. This approach captures the volume of FDI inflow that remains in the country as a percentage of the total income of the country. A second measure was also used for sensitivity checks: net FDI inflow, computed as the net FDI flow without it being considered as a percentage of GDP.

IFRS Adoption variable was measured as earlier defined. A dummy variable structure is applied to capture this variable, where the value 1 was assigned to the year the country's Security and Exchange Commission (SEC) legally adopts the standard and 0 to other years when the standard was not adopted. This approach has received credence in Gordon, Loeb and Zhu (2012).

The variables economic structure and economic policy were included as control variables. The variable economic structure include those variables that reflects the structure of the economy in terms of the extent of *natural resource dependence* and *market size. Natural resource* was measured as the percentage of fuel and minerals in total export, while the *market size* was computed as the value of per capita GDP in constant 2005 USD. The economic policy variables include variables that are influenced by government policies and which can affect the extent of FDI flow to the country. Popular measure of this variable is the *FDI policy* (i.e. total trade to GDP). These control variables are popular covariates included in FDI models in previous studies that have focused on the determinants of FDI flow to African countries (e.g. Asiedu, 2006; Asiedu and Lien, 2011; Anyanwu, 2012).

The variable 'governance structure' is the second main explanatory variable. The variable 'rule of law' was used to capture the governance structure of the country. The reason being that it effectively captures the extent to which economic agents have confidence in and abide by the rules of society, and in particular the quality of contract enforcement, property rights, the police, and the courts, as well as the likelihood of crime and violence. This effectively explains the quality of governance in the respective countries.

Two approaches are applied in understanding corruption control in the respective countries. They are the control of corruption indicator from the World Bank World Governance Indicator (WGI) – by Kaufmann, Kraay and Mastruzzi (2010) and the corruption perception index as reported by the Transparency International. This approach has its advantage over other sources like the Transparency International and International Country Risk Guide (ICRG), especially because of the substantive nature of the methodology that was applied in generating the scores (Rohwer, 2009). More so, Glaeser et al (2004) lend support to the use of WGI measure of corruption other than the ICRG. The measure of corruption, as reported by WGI, is captured as -2.5 (increased corruption) to + 2.5 (reduced corruption). While that of the Transparency International is as defined: where higher values signify reduced corruption and vice versa.

To test the models in this chapter, data was gathered for 49 African countries for which data was available. Small countries – with population that is less than 500, 000 – were excluded from the sample, since idiosyncratic factors are likely to be a major influencer of their economic policies and decisions. For instance, countries like Cape Verde, Mayotte, Sao Tome and Principe, and Seychelles, fall into this category. The full list of the sampled countries are presented in Table 1. The period selected is between 2001 and 2012. The choice of this period was because IFRS came to existence after the formation of IASB in 2001, and 2012 was the latest year for which data was available for the variables of interest. Furthermore, to allow for longer span of variation, the selected period fits this objective.

Table 1. Mean statistics of sampled countries' variables

	FDI	Years of IFRS Adoption	Natural Resource	Market Size	FDI Policy	Corruption
All Sampled Countries *(Mean)*	4.69	1.58	17.52	1597.60	78.26	3.12
(Standard Deviation-SD)	7.94	2.64	17.52	2354.27	36.34	0.54
(Median)	42.93	6.00	49.83	7509.99	115.42	2.71
Algeria	1.42	1.75	97.34	2923.93	63.30	3.08
Angola	6.05	0.83	0.00	1933.91	127.31	3.80
Benin	1.05	1.25	0.40	538.81	48.03	3.14
Botswana	4.12	1.75	0.17	5566.18	86.31	1.54
Burkina Faso	0.57	0.00	0.32	406.09	36.78	2.73
Burundi	0.16	3.75	1.34	148.86	37.82	3.52
Cameroon	1.75	0.83	39.41	912.50	55.07	3.50

continued on following page

Table 1. Continued

	FDI	Years of IFRS Adoption	Natural Resource	Market Size	FDI Policy	Corruption
Central African Republic	2.92	0.00	0.19	357.50	35.60	3.54
Chad	14.13	4.58	0.00	437.69	87.49	3.78
Comoros	0.70	0.00	0.01	629.38	54.65	3.27
Congo	14.27	0.00	77.37	1723.16	133.63	3.54
DRC	7.07	0.00	0.00	135.31	89.31	3.86
Cote D'Ivoire	1.90	0.50	24.12	951.43	85.10	3.59
Djibouti	7.68	0.00	6.47	951.93	94.25	3.01
Egypt	3.39	2.33	41.43	1323.17	53.53	3.04
Equatorial Guinea	13.77	0.00	0.00	11554.97	153.63	4.03
Eritrea	1.11	0.00	0.01	218.65	NA	2.76
Ethiopia	2.58	0.00	0.01	176.88	43.41	3.19
Gabon	1.93	0.83	76.92	6307.96	92.95	3.26
Gambia	7.19	1.75	0.28	439.64	68.43	3.11
Ghana	4.51	1.75	8.53	527.12	87.53	2.61
Guinea Bissau	1.13	0.00	0.81	416.89	85.32	3.56
Kenya	0.60	5.50	9.07	534.41	62.16	3.43
Lesotho	5.07	6.50	0.08	746.71	175.81	2.57
Liberia	27.38	1.25	NA	200.79	110.07	3.30
Libya	2.15	0.00	97.24	7627.84	84.67	3.48
Madagascar	5.92	3.00	4.07	277.66	68.65	2.58
Malawi	2.57	6.50	0.11	228.57	68.74	3.11
Mali	2.20	0.00	2.41	460.20	66.41	2.98
Mauritania	9.00	0.00	13.12	735.34	106.68	2.88
Mauritius	1.98	3.00	0.04	5508.44	120.26	2.00
Morocco	2.34	3.75	2.22	2092.04	72.90	2.76
Mozambique	7.09	2.33	14.22	332.84	74.67	3.01
Namibia	4.90	3.00	0.74	3719.11	94.01	2.29
Niger	5.13	0.00	1.85	256.70	52.98	3.31
Nigeria	3.41	0.50	93.54	851.76	72.00	3.60
Rwanda	1.01	0.83	0.04	300.61	38.02	2.70
Senegal	2.01	0.00	17.94	766.07	68.92	2.80
Sierra Leone	5.45	2.33	NA	338.58	45.34	3.41
South Africa	1.82	3.00	10.57	5420.00	59.35	2.19
Sudan	8.18	0.25	87.13	720.12	36.76	3.78
Swaziland	2.24	0.83	0.80	2351.23	161.20	2.83
Tanzania	4.63	3.75	0.95	397.65	56.98	3.04
Togo	3.39	0.00	1.27	390.42	93.08	3.43

continued on following page

Table 1. Continued

	FDI	Years of IFRS Adoption	Natural Resource	Market Size	FDI Policy	Corruption
Tunisia	3.46	0.00	12.73	3377.84	96.56	2.45
Uganda	4.85	3.75	3.11	343.50	47.09	3.32
Zambia	6.90	3.00	0.86	667.05	75.35	3.17
Zimbabwe	1.50	0.83	4.49	462.78	93.24	3.84

Note: FDI was measured as the percentage of net FDI flow to GDP; IFRS Adoption was measured as the number of years post the year the country legally adopts IFRS; Natural resource was measured as the percentage of fuel and minerals in total export; Market size (per capita GDP in constant 2005 USD); infrastructure was measured as number of telephone usage per 100 population; macroeconomic stability was measured as inflation rate and FDI policy was measured as percentage of total trade to GDP. Other variables are as earlier defined.

The data was collected from several sources. The data for the explained variable, economic structure and policy variables, was gathered from the World Bank 'World Development Indicators,' 2012 version. The data for IFRS adoption was gathered from various sources including the IFRS website (www.ifrs.org), Deloitte IASPlus (www.iasplus.com) and World Bank Group Report on Standards and Codes (www.worldbank.org/ifa/rosc). Finally, the data for governance structure and institutions was gathered from the World Bank 'World Governance Indicators'.

A brief descriptive statistics of some of the key variables are also presented in Table 1. The mean net FDI inflow as a percentage of GDP for the entire sample is 4.69 percent. The net FDI flow of the individual countries, scaled by their GDP, is presented in the same Table. On the average, the entire sampled countries have since adopted IFRS for about 2 years. Some countries like Malawi and Lesotho have longer IFRS adoption period. Moving on to the measure of corruption as reported by WGI, the level of corruption in the sampled countries is still high.

The form of the model for this chapter is such that considers IFRS adoption as a global accounting standard that is expected to bring about linkages in the accounting framework across countries. As a result of this, it is expected that the error term in the estimable model (Equation 2) may be contemporaneously correlated across countries as a result of the increasing inter-country similarity in their financial reporting framework. We therefore estimate this relationship using the Panel Corrected Standard Errors (PCSE) procedure, which allows for disturbances across the sample, and that are heteroscedastic and contemporaneously correlated. The PCSE corrects for first-order autocorrelation (AR1) that are specific to each country.

Since we intend observing the behaviour of IFRS adoption on FDI at varying thresholds of corruption, it will be important to consider how the thresholds are determined. In this chapter, we consider the thresholds above and below the median values of the corruption indicators. The reason for this is the size of our sample, which is relatively small and somewhat homogenous – in terms of corruption incidences (see Table 1). This will not allow for the considerations of thresholds at the 25%, 75% and 90%, because the sample countries that fall into these thresholds are minimal and may be affected by the degree of freedom for accurate predictions. As a result of this, we considered only thresholds lower and above the median values of the measures of corruption. In essence, countries lower than the median value for the WGI and CPI measure of corruption are termed high corrupt countries and those higher than the median are termed low corrupt countries.

4. EMPIRICAL RESULTS

The empirical results are discussed beginning with the correlation analysis, then followed by the main regression analysis. The robustness checks are then reported afterwards.

4.1 Correlation Analysis

The correlation matrix is presented in Table 7 in the appendix. The first panel of the Table for the entire sample and the thresholds of corruption are presented in Panels A-C. The essence being to have a foresight as to the bivariate behaviour of the main variables and to check for the existence of multicollinearity among the explanatory variables. From the Table, the bivariate association between the variables IFRS adoption and FDI as a percentage of GDP was positive in all the Panels except for Panel B, which presents the estimates for countries that are below the median value for corruption. Countries within this category can best be defined as those experiencing high rate of corruption (or poor rate of corruption control). In essence, the result suggest that – in these countries, IFRS adoption was not able to exert a positive influence on FDI inflow. This is unlike countries in Panel C, where the IFRS adoption variable was positively associated with FDI inflow.

Considering the issue of multicollinearity, the behaviour of the variables in all the Panels of Table 7, shows that the explanatory variables were all individually identified. Their behaviours in the model did not show possibilities of being *multicollineared*. This implies that the variables can all be included in a single model and their behaviours will be independent of themselves. Since it is only the bivariate relationships that are presented in Table 7, we may not be able to draw accurate inference as to the behaviour of IFRS adoption and FDI when considering the varying corruption thresholds. Therefore, we go further to present the PCSE estimations in Table 2.

4.2 Main Regression Result

The PCSE estimates are presented in Table 2. For robustness and sensitivity checks, two (2) indicators are included as a measure of FDI inflow, representing the two *Panels* in the Table. *Panel A* of Table 2 represents the FDI as a percentage of GDP, while the *B Panel* represents the aggregate net FDI inflow, which is logged because of the nature of this data[7]. The *Wald* statistics and its significant values are presented in the lower segment of the two panels. The significant values shows the overall fitness of the estimated model; implying the reliability of the estimates. The coefficient and significant values of the covariates are considered to ensure their consistency with theoretical expectations.

In most of the columns, the variables *Natural Resources*, *GDP Growth*, *FDI Policy* and *Governance* follow theoretical predictions (i.e. Morrisset, 2000; Asiedu, 2004; Asiedu, 2006; Asiedu & Lien, 2011; Bandyopadhyay, Sandler & Younas 2014), since they displayed a significant association with the variable 'FDI inflow' to African countries and their signs were consistent as well. This suggest that in the African context, natural resource, the GDP growth rate (measure of economic buoyancy), FDI policy and governance are important determinant of the inflow of foreign investment. The infrastructural development 'infrastructure' displayed an inconsistent behaviour in most part of the columns in both *Panels* of Table 2. Perhaps, we infer that the extent of the development of complementary factor input like infrastructure dissuades the extent of FDI inflow into African countries. This is contrary to the findings by Asiedu (2006) and Asiedu and Lien (2011), who found a positive association between the

Table 2. Panel corrected standard errors estimations

	Panel A: FDI as a % of GDP					**Panel B: Net FDI Inflow**				
		<=3.18	*<=27*	*>3.18*	*>27*		*<=3.18*	*<=27*	*>3.18*	*>27*
	All	*WGI*	*CPI*	*WGI*	*CPI*	*All*	*WGI*	*CPI*	*WGI*	*CPI*
IFRS Adoption	1.020* (0.006)	-0.645 (0.444)	0.255 (0.791)	2.204* (0.004)	1.761** (0.022)	0.549*** (0.084)	-0.992*** (0.064)	-0.489 (0.138)	1.372* (0.000)	1.232* (0.002)
Natural Resource	0.043* (0.000)	0.056* (0.000)	0.073* (0.000)	-0.005 (0.775)	0.001 (0.934)	0.039 (0.000)	0.033* (0.000)	0.039* (0.000)	0.026*** (0.057)	0.028** (0.017)
GDP growth	0.170* (0.002)	0.252* (0.004)	0.151*** (0.098)	0.016 (0.847)	0.022 (0.743)	0.058 (0.073)	0.132* (0.009)	0.096** (0.018)	0.011 (0.776)	0.020 (0.646)
FDI Policy	0.046* (0.000)	0.062* (0.000)	0.067* (0.000)	0.026** (0.018)	0.033* (0.001)	0.005 (0.463)	0.010 (0.340)	0.020* (0.002)	-0.006 (0.459)	-0.009 (0.299)
Infrastructure	-0.194* (0.006)	-0.174 (0.210)	-0.660* (0.000)	-0.131 (0.133)	-0.111*** (0.100)	-0.004 (0.931)	0.123 (0.220)	-0.029 (0.758)	0.015 (0.812)	0.015 (0.806)
Governance	0.979 (0.177)	1.939*** (0.076)	2.239*** (0.073)	0.327 (0.813)	0.382 (0.707)	0.941** (0.039)	0.893 (0.172)	1.126* (0.002)	0.387 (0.690)	0.678 (0.426)
Constant	-0.429 (0.650)	-0.448 (0.740)	-0.040 (0.979)	1.263 (0.252)	0.709 (0.494)	18.309* (0.000)	17.906* (0.000)	17.672* (0.000)	19.130* (0.000)	19.399* (0.000)
R^2	0.198	0.366	0.339	0.204	0.184	0.328	0.503	0.453	0.311	0.313
Wald	53.770	62.760	43.740	19.040	25.090	44.850	48.610	166.490	18.100	17.900
Prob. Value	0.000	0.000	0.000	0.004	0.000	0.000	0.000	0.000	0.006	0.000

Note: the columns 'All' imply the estimation of the baseline model without considerations of the different thresholds; '*<=3.18* and *<=27*' include the estimations below the median value for corruption when considering the definitions by World Governance Indicator – WGI, and by Transparency International Corruption Perception Index – CPI. On the other hand, '*>3.18* and *>27*' imply the estimates above the median value for both WGI and CPI. In essence, the median for WGI and CPI are 3.18 and 27 respectively.
The superscripts *, **, and *** imply the significant values at 1, 5 and 10 percent respectively. The values in parenthesis are the probability values.

two variables. However, to ensure that our result is not affected by the inclusion of this variable, we go further to present the estimations (in Table 2) when this variable is excluded from the model.

Moving on to the variable of interest – *IFRS Adoption* – Table 2 reports that when considering the effect of IFRS adoption on FDI (see the columns identified as 'all' in *Panel A* and *B*) irrespective of the prevalence of corruption, the result reveal that there is a positive effect on FDI inflow. This result supports the findings of Gordon, Loeb and Zhu (2012) and Efobi (2015b), who observed that IFRS adoption has a positive influence on the volume of FDI inflow. In essence, the adoption of IFRS improves the information environment in the adopting country and makes it easier for parent firms to monitor their subsidiaries, which raises their incentives to increase their investment capitals. The findings we will like to highlight, however, are the behaviours of IFRS adoption on FDI when considering the extent of corruption in the sampled African countries.

As earlier argued, we expect that the extent to which IFRS adopting country is able to attract FDI is highly dependent on the extent of institutional framework within the country. In this case, we are particular about the prevalence of corruption and substantial argument have earlier been presented on the reasons why this form of institutional framework is most important in Africa. Our result in both *Panels* of Table 2 reveals that in countries with higher prevalence of corruption (i.e. countries that are below the median value of corruption for WGI and CPI), IFRS adoption has either an insignificant effect on

FDI flow or at best the relative effect is negative. However, when considering the countries with lower prevalence of corruption (i.e. countries that are above the median score of corruption for WGI and CPI), the IFRS adoption variable were consistently having a positive effect on FDI inflow. This suggest that in these countries, the adoption of IFRS will most likely attract more FDI than in countries with higher prevalence of corruption. It is important to highlight that in this sample, the effect of some of the covariates were absorbed and their levels of significance were no longer visible.

Table 3 presents the regression analysis to check the behaviour of the IFRS adoption variable by re-estimating the model when the *infrastructure* variable was excluded from the model. As earlier pointed out, the infrastructure variable did not follow theoretical expectation and it is likely that its presence in the model may disturb the behaviour of the other explanatory variables, including the IFRS adoption variable. From the Table, it is evident that IFRS adoption had a significant and positive impact on FDI flow in the columns that represents better corruption control, compared to those with lower corruption control. In essence, the IFRS adoption variable was not positive and significant in the columns that includes countries with lower than median values for the *WGI* and *CPI* measures of corruption. Contrary result that are consistent with the outlook in Table 2 was observed for countries with corruption values that are higher than the mean value for the *WGI* and *CPI* measures of corruption. Therefore, irrespective of the inclusion (or exclusion) of infrastructure variable, IFRS adoption will have a better impact on FDI in countries with better control of corruption (or lower incidence of corruption).

Table 3. Panel corrected standard errors estimations excluding infrastructure variable

	Panel A: FDI as a % of GDP					**Panel B: Net FDI Inflow**				
		<=3.18	*<=27*	*>3.18*	*>27*		*<=3.18*	*<=27*	*>3.18*	*>27*
	All	*WGI*	*CPI*	*WGI*	*CPI*	*All*	*WGI*	*CPI*	*WGI*	*CPI*
IFRS Adoption	0.927 (0.113)	-0.793 (0.340)	0.211 (0.818)	2.122* (0.007)	1.668* (0.005)	0.547*** (0.084)	-0.887*** (0.085)	-0.491 (0.129)	1.383* (0.000)	1.242* (0.001)
Natural Resource	0.031* (0.007)	0.050* (0.000)	0.056* (0.000)	0.019 (0.298)	0.010 (0.503)	0.039* (0.000)	0.037* (0.000)	0.039* (0.000)	0.028** (0.023)	0.029* (0.007)
GDP growth	0.226* (0.000)	0.277* (0.001)	0.218* (0.006)	0.027 (0.744)	0.037 (0.588)	0.059*** (0.073)	0.114** (0.027)	0.099** (0.011)	0.013 (0.751)	0.022 (0.612)
FDI Policy	0.038* (0.000)	0.057* (0.000)	0.050** (0.011)	0.021*** (0.095)	0.030* (0.005)	0.004 (0.473)	0.014 (0.185)	0.019** (0.022)	-0.006 (0.492)	0.008 (0.313)
Governance	0.414 (0.450)	1.564 (0.129)	1.568 (0.195)	1.295 (0.165)	0.991 (0.190)	0.913* (0.010)	1.159*** (0.057)	1.096* (0.002)	0.584 (0.365)	0.861 (0.140)
Constant	-1.279 (0.195)	-0.708 (0.590)	-0.357 (0.799)	0.834 (0.482)	0.179 (0.867)	18.292* (0.000)	18.091* (0.000)	17.657* (0.000)	19.184* (0.000)	19.467* (0.000)
R^2	0.158	0.358	0.272	0.178	0.159	0.328	0.487	0.452	0.309	0.312
Wald	41.310	63.440	40.140	13.400	16.910	44.620	49.220	160.800	18.150	17.610
Prob. Value	0.000	0.000	0.000	0.020	0.005	0.000	0.000	0.000	0.003	0.004

Note: the columns 'All' imply the estimation of the baseline model without considerations of the different thresholds; '*<=3.18* and *<=27*' include the estimations below the median value for corruption when considering the definitions by World Governance Indicator – WGI, and the Transparency International Corruption Perception Index – CPI. On the other hand, '*>3.18* and *>27*' imply the estimates above the median value for both WGI and CPI. In essence, the median for WGI and CPI are 3.18 and 27 respectively.
The superscripts *, **, and *** imply the significant values at 1, 5 and 10 percent respectively. The values in parenthesis are the probability values.

An important feature of countries with higher incidence of corruption is that the transaction cost of doing businesses is higher compared to countries with lower prevalence of corruption. Some of these transaction cost can be seen in the risks associative with expropriation, cost of investment, such as licensing, securing property and land, cost of accessing public services and utilities (christened cost of doing business), among others. In such a situation, a foreign investment that hitherto was attracted to invest in an IFRS adopting country, will incur a higher opportunity cost when the institutional framework in such a country is low. These investors would rather prefer to invest in countries with better institution (reduction of corruption) and that have adopted IFRS.

Further Robustness Checks

This sub-section further checks the robustness of our results. Three main items are likely to play central roles in the determination of our results. The first is the effect of the disturbances that are likely to occur in the FDI trend as a result of the inclusion of the period of financial crisis in the sampled time period. Second is the consideration of other measures of governance, since the measure of governance included is an important variable that determines the behaviour of FDI flow in empirical analysis. Third is the control of the legal origin of the sampled countries, which may likely inform the outlook of our result. We devote some space to each of these variables by discussing how they may likely affect our result and then consequently, observe consistency of the results when considering each of these variables.

Financial Crisis Dummy

The global financial crisis was triggered by the United States housing bubble in 2007 and soon after, in September 2008, the financial turmoil erupts and contagion over the European Union's member countries escalated into the named global financial crisis. The effect of the crisis include the collapse of asset markets, decline of industrial productivity and employment and increase in government debt as a result of decline in fiscal inflows (see Reinhart & Rogoff, 2009). Consequently, to mitigate this crises, some of the prosperous countries who participated in development assistance to developing countries and whose nationals/ investors were engaged in foreign investments, took fiscal austerity measures and some extent of investment repatriations. Atleast, it was reported that FDI flows decreased by 10 percent in 2008 and the foreign financial flow that sustained developing countries development capital were drastically affected as a result of the economic recession in 2008 and 2009 (UNCTAD, 2009; Das & Dutta, 2012; Osabuohien & Efobi, 2014).

The effect of this crisis on our result is that there may be disturbances that are contained in the dataset as a result of the inclusion of the period of the financial crisis (2007-2009) in our dataset. Therefore, to check whether our results are sensitive to the inclusion of this period, we created a dummy called the *financial crisis* dummy. A similar approach has been used by Osabuohien and Efobi (2014). This dummy was then included in the estimations that are reported in Table 2. The main function of this variable in the model is to control for the effect of the financial crisis that are typical with the years 2007-2009, which may not be captured by the other control variables.

Table 4 reports the robustness check result that examines foreign investment as a percentage of GDP (see *Panel A* in Table 4) and the logarithm value of FDI (see *Panel B* in Table 4): we find that the behaviour of IFRS adoption (our main explanatory variable) are essentially the same as those presented in Tables 2 and 3. In particular, IFRS adoption is found to exert a positive and significant effect on FDI inflow in

Table 4. Robustness check (PCSE estimations controlling for financial crisis period)

	Panel A: FDI as a % of GDP					**Panel B: Net FDI Inflow**				
		<=3.18	*<=27*	*>3.18*	*>27*		*<=3.18*	*<=27*	*>3.18*	*>27*
	All	*WGI*	*CPI*	*WGI*	*CPI*	*All*	*WGI*	*CPI*	*WGI*	*CPI*
IFRS Adoption	0.791 (0.153)	-0.670 (0.431)	-0.512 (0.633)	1.975* (0.007)	1.366** (0.015)	0.418 (0.193)	-0.978*** (0.070)	-0.624*** (0.095)	1.213* (0.002)	1.053* (0.009)
Natural Resource	0.041* (0.000)	0.055* (0.000)	0.073* (0.000)	0.004 (0.804)	0.001 (0.967)	0.038* (0.000)	0.034* (0.000)	0.040* (0.000)	0.026** (0.050)	0.028** (0.015)
GDP growth	0.177* (0.001)	0.253* (0.003)	0.164*** (0.093)	0.023 (0.773)	0.034 (0.604)	0.061*** (0.054)	0.132* (0.009)	0.093** (0.022)	0.007 (0.859)	0.014 (0.743)
FDI Policy	0.044* (0.000)	0.061* (0.000)	0.082* (0.000)	0.026** (0.018)	0.030* (0.001)	0.003 (0.607)	0.011 (0.337)	0.019* (0.007)	0.007 (0.419)	0.010 (0.239)
Infrastructure	-0.190* (0.007)	-0.179 (0.207)	-0.635* (0.001)	-0.131 (0.128)	-0.116*** (0.080)	-0.002 (0.962)	0.126 (0.227)	-0.007 (0.944)	0.015 (0.810)	0.012 (0.836)
Governance	1.003 (0.165)	1.935*** (0.075)	3.090** (0.012)	0.432 (0.751)	0.716 (0.473)	0.958** (0.033)	0.896 (0.174)	1.218* (0.001)	0.460 (0.630)	0.830 (0.324)
Financial Crisis	0.892** (0.025)	0.178 (0.762)	0.650 (0.413)	0.704 (0.206)	1.366* (0.001)	0.484* (0.010)	-0.097 (0.828)	0.169 (0.741)	0.468** (0.029)	0.592* (0.002)
Constant	-0.503 (0.593)	-0.442 (0.744)	-0.029 (0.984)	1.096 (0.313)	0.621 (0.532)	18.288* (0.000)	17.904* (0.000)	17.702* (0.000)	19.047* (0.000)	19.341* (0.000)
R^2	0.210	0.366	0.404	0.213	0.229	0.341	0.503	0.464	0.328	0.341
Wald	59.670	67.240	63.200	20.000	36.700	59.130	47.960	129.820	32.410	56.060
Prob. Value	0.000	0.000	0.000	0.006	0.000	0.000	0.000	0.000	0.000	0.000

Note: the columns 'All' imply the estimation of the baseline model without considerations of the different thresholds; '*<=3.18* and *<=27'* include the estimations below the median value for corruption when considering the definitions by World Governance Indicator – WGI, and the Transparency International Corruption Perception Index – CPI. On the other hand, '*>3.18* and *>27*' imply the estimates above the median value for both WGI and CPI. In essence, the median for WGI and CPI are 3.18 and 27 respectively.
The Pairwise correlation was first carried out to ensure that the financial crisis dummy was not multicollineared with any of the other explanatory variables. This was not reported for space.
The superscripts *, **, and *** imply the significant values at 1, 5 and 10 percent respectively. The values in parenthesis are the probability values.

countries with lower corruption (or higher control of corruption), and the result becomes insignificant and to some extent, negative, when considering the impact of IFRS adoption on FDI in countries with higher corruption. In essence, we surmise that the result is not affected by the disturbances caused in the trend of FDI as a result of the financial crisis.

Other Measures of Governance

In as much as we controlled for governance in model (2), by including the indicator - rule of law, it is important that we draw attention to some of the shortcomings of using one indicator to represent this complex concept that has faced many criticism. The concept "governance" is a framework that shows the extent of institutional development in a country, which aims at protecting the rights of economic agents and reducing economic losses from human interactions. Noting the importance of this concept in studying economic phenomenon (as earlier discussed in previous section), studies have warned that the concept cannot be adequately measured by relying on some secondary databases for which the methodology in explaining its computation cannot be readily verified. For instance, the construct validity of some of these measures, regarding their ability to measure what they purport to measure, have received heavy criticism by authors such as Knack (2006), Rohwer (2009), Thomas (2010), among others. As a result of this, empirical models that include these measures may likely be confronted with the possibility of bias estimates. However, the prevailing conclusions in some of these studies is that each measure of governance by different sources have their relative strengths and weaknesses, and it will be important to take account of this fact when applying the measures for policy research.

One possible way of reducing the likelihood of presenting a biased estimate is to use alternative measures of governance, and check if the results still remains consistent. This approach have been favoured by Asiedu (2006), Asiedu and Lien (2011) and Efobi (2015a). In this chapter, an alternative measure of governance is applied: it is the use of the measure of democracy, which is the average of the Freedom House's political rights and civil liberties[8]. Table 5 reports the result when this measure of governance is included in the empirical model (i.e. Equation 2).

From Table 5, the result shows that when including another measure of governance, the effect of IFRS adoption on FDI still remained consistent across the different thresholds of the prevalence of corruption. For countries with lower prevalence of corruption (i.e. higher control of corruption and CPI score), the

Table 5. Robustness check (PCSE estimations including other measures of governance)

	Panel A: FDI as a % of GDP					Panel B: Net FDI Inflow				
		<=3.18	*<=27*	*>3.18*	*>27*		*<=3.18*	*<=27*	*>3.18*	*>27*
	All	*WGI*	*CPI*	*WGI*	*CPI*	*All*	*WGI*	*CPI*	*WGI*	*CPI*
IFRS Adoption	1.116** (0.048)	-0.088 (0.924)	0.512 (0.622)	2.239* (0.003)	1.811* (0.001)	0.576*** (0.078)	-0.902 (0.122)	-0.648*** (0.062)	1.380* (0.000)	1.233* (0.000)
Natural Resource	0.032* (0.005)	0.040* (0.005)	0.055* (0.001)	-0.011 (0.498)	0.010 (0.480)	0.032* (0.000)	0.029* (0.001)	0.034* (0.000)	0.021*** (0.086)	0.020*** (0.058)
GDP growth	0.213* (0.000)	0.366* (0.000)	0.256** (0.018)	0.015 (0.853)	0.016 (0.800)	0.088** (0.011)	0.170* (0.001)	0.127* (0.002)	0.013 (0.729)	0.023 (0.561)
FDI Policy	0.047* (0.000)	0.057* (0.000)	0.059* (0.000)	0.026** (0.017)	0.035* (0.000)	0.005 (0.448)	0.008 (0.467)	0.016* (0.007)	0.006 (0.466)	0.007 (0.343)
Infrastructure	-0.122 (0.163)	-0.155 (0.303)	-0.659* (0.002)	-0.109** (0.033)	-0.086** (0.046)	0.056 (0.136)	0.156 (0.137)	0.036 (0.717)	0.036 (0.359)	0.049 (0.182)
Democracy	0.473 (0.165)	0.687* (0.009)	0.529 (0.286)	0.142 (0.577)	0.291 (0.170)	0.006 (0.967)	0.064 (0.798)	-0.036 (0.786)	0.087 (0.637)	0.114 (0.513)
Constant	-1.934 (0.128)	-5.615* (0.006)	-4.327*** (0.078)	0.665 (0.625)	-0.538 (0.672)	17.579* (0.000)	16.742* (0.000)	16.874* (0.000)	18.668* (0.000)	18.689* (0.000)
R^2	0.192	0.369	0.328	0.206	0.199	0.295	0.487	0.434	0.312	0.310
Wald	52.860	66.270	38.720	19.510	27.280	39.770	43.420	27.640	21.210	20.830
Prob. Value	0.000	0.000	0.000	0.000	0.000	0.000	0.000	0.000	0.002	0.002

Note: the columns 'All' imply the estimation of the baseline model without considerations of the different thresholds; '<=*3.18* and <=*27*' include the estimations below the median value for corruption when considering the definitions by World Governance Indicator – WGI, and the Transparency International Corruption Perception Index – CPI. On the other hand, '>*3.18* and >*27*' imply the estimates above the median value for both WGI and CPI. In essence, the median for WGI and CPI are 3.18 and 27 respectively.
The Pairwise correlation was first carried out to ensure that the financial crisis dummy was not multicollineared with any of the other explanatory variables. This was not reported for space.
The superscripts *, **, and *** imply the significant values at 1, 5 and 10 percent respectively. The values in parenthesis are the probability values.

effect of IFRS adoption on FDI remained consistently positive – just as it is for Tables 2-4. Likewise, for countries with higher prevalence of corruption (i.e. lower corruption control and CPI score), the effect of IFRS adoption on FDI remained insignificant. Therefore the result is robust and not driven by the type of governance measure included in our empirical model.

Controlling for the Legal Origin of Sampled Countries

The legal origin of the IFRS adopting country connotes the existent jurisdictional differences that explains some fundamental structures that affects investment within the country. These differences are seen in the structure of the legal system, which explains how economic and social life should be organised (Asongu, 2011). The legal origin also explains the legal protection of outside investors and limits the risk of expropriation. Empirical documentations (e.g. La Porta et al, 1997, 1998; La Porta et al, 2008) suggest that some legal origin that are tied to the English Common Law are more protective of outside investors than the civil law- particularly the French civil laws. More so, some legal jurisdiction – like the civil law, have more government involvement in the market, thereby resulting to higher incidences of corruption and larger unofficial economy (La Porta et al, 2008). From yet another stand point, countries with common law legal structure, have lower formalism of judicial procedures and higher judicial independence, than the countries with civil law legal structure (Djankov et al, 2003; La Porta et al, 2004; Osabuohien, 2011).

Noting these issues, a regression analysis that does not control for the legal origin of countries will likely be omitting an important variable that is supposed to account for the behaviour of foreign investment as a result of their sensitivity to the extent of contract enforcement and security of property rights. Foreign investors consider these issues as an important determinant of the direction of FDI flow (Busse and Hefeker, 2007; Asiedu and Lien, 2011). Following Asongu (2014) approach, we classified the legal origin of our sample into English Common Law "*English_Law*" as 1, while 0 otherwise.

From Table 6, the legal origin variable was positive in most of the column, suggesting that legal origin that are tied to the English common law had a positive influence on the volume of FDI. However, the significant values are not verified except for some of the columns (see columns 2 and 3 in Panel B). We focus on the main variable of interest (i.e. IFRS adoption), From the Table, the signs and significant values of the IFRS adoption variable remained consistent like it has been in the previous Tables. This suggest that the effect of IFRS adoption on FDI does not change even when the legal origin of the sampled country are controlled for. Hence, we conclude that the results conform to our hypothesis irrespective of the checks conducted and the approach of measuring foreign investment.

CONCLUSION

This chapter investigates the impact of IFRS adoption on FDI when considering the prevailing institutional structure (or corruption control) of African countries. We apply IFRS adoption data for forty two (42) African countries for the period 2001-2012. More so, alternative measures of FDI was included and further robustness checks to ensure the consistency of our estimates. This chapter distinguishes the effect of IFRS adoption on FDI across sampled countries depending on the level of corruption control in the country. Put differently, this effect was tested on countries with low corruption control (i.e. high

Table 6. Robustness check (PCSE estimations including legal origin dummy)

	Panel A: FDI as a % of GDP					Panel B: Net FDI Inflow				
		<=3.18	*<=27*	*>3.18*	*>27*		*<=3.18*	*<=27*	*>3.18*	*>27*
	All	*WGI*	*CPI*	*WGI*	*CPI*	*All*	*WGI*	*CPI*	*WGI*	*CPI*
IFRS Adoption	0.951*** (0.100)	-0.859 (0.352)	0.298 (0.772)	2.344* (0.003)	1.826* (0.003)	0.451 (0.193)	-1.712* (0.001)	-1.014* (0.010)	1.388* (0.000)	1.294* (0.001)
Natural Resource	0.036* (0.000)	0.044* (0.001)	0.061* (0.000)	-0.011 (0.507)	0.003 (0.820)	0.032* (0.000)	0.023* (0.000)	0.029* (0.000)	0.022*** (0.083)	0.021*** (0.051)
GDP growth	0.200* (0.000)	0.331* (0.000)	0.227** (0.035)	0.023 (0.722)	0.027 (0.699)	0.086** (0.018)	0.184* (0.000)	0.142* (0.000)	0.011 (0.787)	0.017 (0.691)
Trade Openness	0.045* (0.000)	0.058* (0.000)	0.061* (0.000)	0.028** (0.017)	0.034* (0.001)	0.004 (0.586)	0.011 (0.289)	0.017** (0.026)	0.005 (0.543)	0.006 (0.433)
Infrastructure	0.018 (0.319)	-0.054 (0.689)	-0.590* (0.001)	-0.109** (0.035)	-0.091** (0.047)	0.055 (0.153)	0.238* (0.003)	0.037 (0.596)	0.035 (0.405)	0.048 (0.215)
Legal Origin	0.627 (0.627)	0.787 (0.433)	0.174 (0.883)	0.520 (0.577)	-0.267 (0.724)	0.419 (0.351)	1.740* (0.000)	1.406* (0.000)	0.129 (0.845)	0.269 (0.653)
Constant	-1.216 (0.152)	-2.617** (0.046)	-1.859 (0.206)	1.084 (0.293)	0.517 (0.579)	17.510* (0.000)	16.282* (0.000)	16.258* (0.000)	18.989* (0.000)	19.098* (0.000)
R^2	0.190	0.351	0.314	0.207	0.184	0.305	0.596	0.505	0.308	0.306
Wald	50.330	58.680	37.330	19.550	24.150	35.900	79.630	22.960	19.600	19.810
Prob. Value	0.000	0.000	0.000	0.000	0.001	0.000	0.000	0.000	0.000	0.000

Note: as usual, the columns 'All' imply the estimation of the baseline model without considerations of the different thresholds; '*<=3.18* and *<=27*' include the estimations below the median value for corruption when considering the definitions by World Governance Indicator – WGI, and the Transparency International Corruption Perception Index – CPI. On the other hand, '*>3.18* and *>27*' imply the estimates above the median value for both WGI and CPI. In essence, the median for WGI and CPI are 3.18 and 27 respectively.
The Pairwise correlation was first carried out to ensure that the financial crisis dummy was not multicollineared with any of the other explanatory variables. This was not reported for space.
The superscripts *, **, and *** imply the significant values at 1, 5 and 10 percent respectively. The values in parenthesis are the probability values.

prevalence of corruption) and countries with high corruption control (i.e. low prevalence of corruption). The result suggest that in countries with high corruption control, the incidence of IFRS adoption will have a higher and positive effect on FDI flow. This was contrary when considering countries with lower corruption control. This result validates the conceptual submission of Wysocki (2011) that there is a complimentary impact of institutional development on IFRS effect on FDI.

This result has diverse implications for African countries. The desire to adopt IFRS in order to improve the financial statement reporting framework, and with the utmost intention of attracting foreign investors will not be effective by disregarding the underlining role of improved institutions (in the form of corruption control). There is the need for policies to address the issue of corruption control in African countries. This, of course, will require the government commitment to setting up structures that discourages rent-seeking behaviour of any form. In essence, just as most African government are desiring to address the state of financial reporting in their countries by adopting IFRS, it should not be assumed that the state of corruption in these countries does not matter.

This chapter has suggestions for future enquiries. The main area of critical focus is to examine a case study type of inquiry, with objectives that are streamlined on country specific cases. The aim of such enquiry should be to ensure, and validate, the findings from this study. In essence, the main enquiry will be to observe whether the result remains the same when focusing on case studies of African countries that have adopted IFRS.

REFERENCES

Ackah, C., Turkson, F., & Opoku, K. (2013). Trade Costs and Intra-Regional Trade Flows in ECOWAS. *Journal of West African Integration*, *1*(1), 1–43.

Anyanwu, J. C. (2012). Why does Foreign Direct Investment Go Where It Goes? New Evidence from African Countries. *Annals of Economics and Finance*, *13*(2), 425–462.

Asiedu, E. (2004). Policy Reform and Foreign Direct Investment in Africa: Absolute Progress but Relative Decline. *Development Policy Review*, *22*(1), 41–48. doi:10.1111/j.1467-8659.2004.00237.x

Asiedu, E. (2006). Foreign Direct Investment in Africa: The Role of Natural Resources, Market Size, Government Policy, Institutions and Political Instability. *World Economy*, *29*(1), 63–77. doi:10.1111/j.1467-9701.2006.00758.x

Asiedu, E., & Lien, D. (2011). Democracy, Foreign Direct Investment and Natural Resources. *Journal of International Economics*, *84*(1), 99–111. doi:10.1016/j.jinteco.2010.12.001

Asongu, S. (2011). *Law, Finance and Investment: Does Legal Origin Matter?* Retrieved from http://mpra.ub.uni-muenchen.de/34698/

Asongu, S. (2012). On the effect of foreign aid on corruption. *Economic Bulletin*, *32*(3), 2174–2180.

Asongu, S. (2013). Fighting corruption when existing corruption-control levels matter. What do wealth-effects tell us in Africa? *Institutions, Etc.*, *5*(3), 53–74.

Asongu, S. (2014). Fighting African corruption when existing corruption-control levels matter in a dynamic cultural setting. *International Journal of Social Economics*, *41*(10), 906–922. doi:10.1108/IJSE-05-2013-0117

Bandyopadhyay, S., Sandler, T., & Younas, J. (2014). Foreign Direct Investment, aid and terrorism. *Oxford Economic Papers*, *66*(1), 25–50. doi:10.1093/oep/gpt026

Barth, M. E., Landsman, W. R., & Lang, M. H. (2008). International accounting standards and accounting quality. *Journal of Accounting Research*, *46*(3), 467–498. doi:10.1111/j.1475-679X.2008.00287.x

Beneish, M. D., Miller, B. P., & Yohn, T. L. (2010). *IFRS Adoption and Cross-Border Investment in Equity and Debt Markets*. Available at SSRN: http://ssrn.com/abstract=1403451

Busse, M., & Hefeker, C. (2007). Political risk, institutions and foreign direct investment. *European Journal of Political Economy*, *23*(2), 397–415. doi:10.1016/j.ejpoleco.2006.02.003

Chen, C. J., Ding, Y., & Xu, B. (2014). Convergence of Accounting Standards and Foreign Direct Investment. *The International Journal of Accounting*, *49*(1), 53–86. doi:10.1016/j.intacc.2014.01.007

Collins, D. L., Pasewark, W. R., & Riley, M. E. (2012). Financial Reporting Outcomes under Rules-Based and Principles-Based Accounting Standards. *Accounting Horizons*, *26*(4), 681–705. doi:10.2308/acch-50266

Das, K. D., & Dutta, C. B. (2012). *Global Financial Crisis and Foreign Development Assistance Shocks in Least Developed Countries*. Retrieved from http://mpra.ub.uni-muenchen.de/id/eprint/40281

Daude, C., & Stein, E. (2007). The Quality of Institutions and Foreign Direct Investment. *Economics and Politics*, *19*(3), 317–344. doi:10.1111/j.1468-0343.2007.00318.x

Ding, Y., Jeanjean, T., & Stolowy, H. (2005). Why do national GAAP differ from IAS? The role of culture. *The International Journal of Accounting*, *40*(4), 325–350. doi:10.1016/j.intacc.2005.09.004

Djankov, S., La Porta, R., Florencio, L., & Andrei, S. (2003). Courts. *The Quarterly Journal of Economics*, *118*(2), 453–517. doi:10.1162/003355303321675437

Easterly, W. (2008). Introduction. In W. Easterl (Ed.), *Reinventing Foreign Aid*. Cambridge, MA: The MIT Press.

Efobi, U. R. (2015a). Politicians' Attributes and Institutional Quality in Africa: A Focus on Corruption. *Journal of Economic Issues*, *49*(3), 787–813. doi:10.1080/00213624.2015.1072393

Efobi, U. R. (2015b). IFRS Adoption and the Environment: Is Africa Closing Her Eyes to Something? In Beyond the UN Global Compact: Institutions and Regulations (pp. 169-195). doi:10.1108/S2051-503020150000017016

Fosu, A. K. (2011). *Terms of trade and growth of resource economies: A tale of two countries*. UNU-WIDER Working Paper No.2011/28

Glaeser, E., La Porta, R., Lopez-De-Silanes, F., & Shleifer, A. (2004). Do institutions cause growth? *Journal of Economic Growth*, *9*(3), 271–303. doi:10.1023/B:JOEG.0000038933.16398.ed

Gordon, L. A., Loeb, M. P., & Zhu, W. (2012). The Impact of IFRS Adoption on Foreign Direct Investment. *Journal of Accounting and Public Policy*, *31*(4), 374–398. doi:10.1016/j.jaccpubpol.2012.06.001

Hail, L., Leuz, C., & Wysocki, P. (2010). Global Accounting Convergence and the Potential Adoption of IFRS by the US: Conceptual Underpinning and Economic Analysis. *Accounting Horizons*, *24*(3), 428–454. doi:10.2308/acch.2010.24.3.355

Kaufmann, D., Kraay, A., & Mastruzzi, M. (2010). *The World Governance Indicators: Methodology and Analytical Issues*. World Bank Policy Research Working Paper, No. 5430. Retrieved from: SSRN: http://ssrn.com/abstract=1682130

Knack, S. (2006). *Measuring Corruption in Eastern Europe and Central Asia: A Critique of the Cross Country Indicators*. Washington, DC: World Bank. doi:10.1596/1813-9450-3968

La Porta, R., Florencio, L., & Andrei, S. (2008). The Economic Consequences of Legal Origins. *Journal of Economic Literature*, *46*(2), 285–332. doi:10.1257/jel.46.2.285

La Porta, R., Florencio, L., Andrei, S., & Robert, W. V. (1997). Legal Determinants of External Finance. *The Journal of Finance*, *52*(3), 1131–1150. doi:10.1111/j.1540-6261.1997.tb02727.x

La Porta, R., Florencio, L., Andrei, S., & Robert, W. V. (1998). Law and Finance. *Journal of Political Economy, 106*(6), 1113–1155. doi:10.1086/250042

La Porta, R., Florencio, L., Cristian, P., & Andrei, S. (2004). Judicial Checks and Balances. *Journal of Political Economy, 112*(2), 445–470. doi:10.1086/381480

Li, Q., & Resnick, A. (2003). Reversal of Fortunes: Democratic Institutions and Foreign Direct Investment Inflows to Developing Countries. *International Organization, 57*(1), 175–211. doi:10.1017/S0020818303571077

Louis, H., & Urcan, O. (2013). *The Effect of IFRS on Foreign Direct Investments: Evidence from Cross-Border Acquisitions*. Available at SSRN: http://ssrn.com/abstract=2164995 or10.2139/ssrn.2164995

Morrisset, J. (2000). Foreign Direct Investment in Africa: Policies also Matter. *Transnational Corporation, 9*(2), 107–125.

North, D. C. (1991). Institutions. *The Journal of Economic Perspectives, 5*(1), 97–112. doi:10.1257/jep.5.1.97

Osabuohien, E. (2011). *Analysis of International Trade Performance in SSA: Impact of Institutional Framework*. (Unpublished Thesis). Covenant University.

Osabuohien, E., & Efobi, U. (2013). Africa's Money in Africa. *The South African Journal of Economics, 81*(2), 291–306. doi:10.1111/saje.12012

Osabuohien, E., & Efobi, U. (2014). Assessment of Trade Performance of OIC African Members in the Face of Global Economic Crisis. *Journal of Economic Cooperation and Development, 35*(1), 1–22.

Osabuohien, E. S. (2014). Large-Scale Agricultural Land Investments and Local Institutions in Africa: The Nigerian Case. *Land Use Policy, 39*, 155–165. doi:10.1016/j.landusepol.2014.02.019

Portes, R., & Rey, H. (2005). The determinants of cross-border equity flows. *Journal of International Economics, 65*(2), 269–296. doi:10.1016/j.jinteco.2004.05.002

Prochazka, D., & Ilinitchi, C. P. (2011). The Theoretical Relationships among Foreign Direct Investments, Migration and IFRS Adoption. *European Financial and Accounting Journal, 4*, 85–100.

Ramos, L. M. (2008). *The Effect of IFRS Adoption on Trade and Foreign Direct Investments*. International Trade and Finance Association Working Paper No. 19.

Ramos, L. M. (2010). *European Accounting Harmonization: Consequences of IFRS Adoption on Trade in Goods and Foreign Direct Investments*. Retrieved from: www.alde.es/encuentros/anteriores/xiiieea/trabajos/pdf/046.pdf

Reinhart, C., & Rogoff, K. (2009). *The Aftermath of Financial Crises*. National Bureau of Economic Research Working Paper 14656.

Rohwer, A. (2009). *Measuring Corruption: A Comparison between the Transparency International's Corruption Perception Index and the World Bank's Worldwide Governance Indicators*. CESifo DICE Research Report 3/2009. Retrieved September 6 2014 from: https://www.cesifo-group.de/portal/pls/portal/docs/1/1192926.PDF

Thomas, M. A. (2010). What do the World Governance Indicators Measure? *European Journal of Development Research*, *22*(1), 31–54. doi:10.1057/ejdr.2009.32

UNCTAD. (2009). World Investment Report 2009. Geneva, Switzerland: UNCTAD.

Williamson, O. E. (2000). The new institutional economics: Taking stock, looking ahead. *Journal of Economic Literature*, *38*(3), 595–613. doi:10.1257/jel.38.3.595

Wysocki, P. (2011). New Institutional Accounting and IFRS. *Accounting and Business Review*, *41*(3), 309–328. doi:10.1080/00014788.2011.575298

ENDNOTES

1 Foreign investment, and foreign capital are used interchangeably throughout the chapter.

2 Wysocki (2011) noted that more empirical emphasizes should be placed on some unanswered questions about the structure, types, causation, interdependency and efficiency of observed accounting framework like IFRS on economic outcomes (e.g. FDI) and how institutional structures in the IFRS adopting country interplays.

3 see http://www.ifrs.org/news/features/Pages/africa-embraces-ifrss.aspx

4 See Wysocki (2011); Gordon, Loeb and Zhu (2012).

5 Asiedu (2006) for more discussion of the role of FDI in improving development resources in Africa.

6 OECD (2014) Define foreign investments as cross-border investment by a resident entity in one economy with the objective of obtaining a lasting interest in an enterprise resident in another economy. The lasting interest implies the existence of a long-term relationship between the direct investor and the enterprise and a significant degree of influence by the direct investor on the management of the enterprise. Ownership of at least 10% of the voting power, representing the influence by the investor, is the basic criterion used.

7 The aggregate FDI inflow was presented in Billion USD.

8 Political right measures the extent to which a particular country allows for the freedom of the electoral process, political pluralism and participation, as well as the presence of a functioning government. On the other hand, the civil liberty variable captures the freedom of expression and belief, freedom to join an association and organization, the prevalence of the rule of law and other forms of personal autonomy and individual rights.

APPENDIX

Table 7. Correlation for the entire sample, sub-sample below and above median corruption thresholds

	FDI_GDP	IFRS Adoption	Natural Resource	GDP Growth	Trade Openness	Infrastructure	Governance
Panel A: Entire Sample							
FDI_GDP	1.000	---	---	---	---	---	---
IFRS Adoption	0.054	1.000	---	---	---	---	---
Natural Resource	0.245	0.075	1.000	---	---	---	---
GDP growth	-0.116	0.075	-0.088	1.000	---	---	---
Trade Openness	0.197	-0.221	-0.021	0.054	1.000	---	---
Infrastructure	0.335	0.003	0.020	0.205	-0.038	1.000	
Governance	-0.099	0.236	0.002	0.588	-0.361	0.005	1.000
Panel B: Below Median WGI (i.e. <=3.18)							
FDI_GDP	1.000	---	---	---	---	---	---
IFRS Adoption	-0.115	1.000	---	---	---	---	---
Natural Resource	0.257	0.075	1.000	---	---	---	---
GDP growth	-0.051	-0.081	-0.045	1.000	---	---	---
Trade Openness	0.417	-0.307	0.090	0.334	1.000	---	---
Infrastructure	0.334	-0.232	0.038	0.108	0.185	1.000	---
Governance	-0.040	0.289	0.048	0.216	-0.237	-0.338	1.000
Panel C: Above Median WGI (>3.18)							
FDI_GDP	1.000	---	---	---	---	---	---
IFRS Adoption	0.265	1.000	---	---	---	---	---
Natural Resource	0.228	0.095	1.000	---	---	---	---
GDP growth	-0.158	0.083	-0.157	1.000	---	---	---
Trade Openness	-0.141	-0.077	-0.128	0.110	1.000	---	---
Infrastructure	0.358	0.196	-0.004	0.256	-0.139	1.000	---
Governance	-0.150	0.094	-0.028	0.716	-0.288	0.198	1.000

Chapter 6
Economic and Political Implications of IFRS Adoption in the Czech Republic

Irena Jindrichovska
Anglo-American University, Czech Republic

Dana Kubickova
University of Finance and Administration, Czech Republic

ABSTRACT

This chapter analyses the political and economic impact of IFRS adoption in the Czech Republic. It contributes to the current understanding of IFRS adoption from the perspective of a small European transitional market, where local accounting standards were previously well developed and still play a major role in financial reporting mainly, however for local taxation purposes. Although there has been an observable increase in the country's exports, FDI and international trade since the beginning of the 1990s, the direct impact of IFRS is difficult to discern, because of many political and institutional changes that have taken place concurrently. However, it is clear that adoption of IFRS has contributed to greater cultivation of the economic environment and facilitated international operations. IFRS adoption is not highly prevalent but is gradually increasing. This is apparent mainly in Czech companies with foreign parents that are in any event required to report in IFRS.

INTRODUCTION

The main goal of this chapter is to characterize the political and economic impact of IFRS adoption in the Czech Republic - a small European country in transition. The Czech Republic is considered to be a transitional country as a member of the group of CEE countries (countries of Central and Eastern Europe). The CR is a member of the OECD since December 21, 1995. The socio-economic and political background is characterized by changing from a centrally-planned to a market based economy where market mechanisms, principles and institutions do not work properly as yet[1]. It should be highlighted at the outset that the impact of these new regulations (international accounting standards) will have

DOI: 10.4018/978-1-4666-9876-5.ch006

disparate impacts depending on the environment where the changes are implemented (Nobes, 2012). As we are dealing with the Czech Republic where the economy was transformed from a state-regulated centralized regime to a market-based economy, one can expect influences of previous arrangements to survive for a substantial period of time. Further, institutional settings do not change instantly, but also take time to modify - due to inertia and resistance of existing institutions and habits - in order to adapt to new conditions. Furthermore, the economics of the "outside world" is becoming more complicated with globalization and the impact of new technologies, and even traditional laws of economics are changing even in developed countries, e.g. Stiglitz 2003 and 2010; Gatti *et al.*, 2012; Komlos, 2015 and others.

IFRS adoption has been influenced to a great extent by change of ownership structure, with 58 per cent of companies in foreign hands (Ernest, 2014). This has been generated by previous mass privatization and the influence of FDIs. This has influenced the scope of implementation or adoption of IFRS in the Czech Republic.

The expected macroeconomic impact of IFRS can be seen in terms of increased foreign direct investment, greater volumes of international trade and higher levels of international mobility of people see e.g. Hail *et al.*, 2010; Beneish, *et al.*, 2010; Liu, *et al.*, 2011; Brüggemann *et al.*, 2013. In the Czech Republic there were recent conceptual publications by, Ištvánfyová *et al.*, 2010; and more analytical publications by Prochazka & Prochazkova Ilinitchi, 2012; Prochazka, 2014, Jindrichovska *et al.*, 2014, and Prochazka & Pelak, 2015.

The methodology of this conceptual paper is based on critical analysis of historical development of the local economy, reviewing macro-economic development inside the country, and making a connection with development of accounting practices. The chapter concentrates on the impact of IFRS introduction into the Czech Republic during the transitional period in terms of changing rules and regulations. It also investigates practical interpretation and application of these items. Analysis of real data and particular regulations and contemporary materials is based on holistic methods. It also includes a backward analysis of development process involving accounting harmonization at European and global levels from the perspective of the current level of knowledge and experience. The chapter is complemented by a summary of the present stage of IFRS adoption in Czech companies. The perceived pros and cons from the perspective of Czech companies were analysed by using a questionnaire survey.

The Czech Republic is characterized as an open economy, dependent to a large extent on international trade. The majority of exports are in the machinery and automotive industries. An important feature of the Czech economy is also the ownership structure of Czech companies that were privatized at the beginning of 1990s. The majority of Czech companies are now in foreign hands, which makes the country´s economic planning and strategic development difficult. Foreign interests also dominate the banking sector, where 97 per cent of Czech banking assets is in foreign hands. The overall structure of the economy is now becoming more traditional, with greater emphasis on industrial sectors providing greater value- addition.

An important step in the process of transition toward a market economy was the reconstitution of the Czech capital market. The Prague Stock Exchange was re-established in 1993 after a fifty-year break. After the first couple of years of rather successful trading, the value of trades decreased mainly due to the concentration of ownership and delisting of companies listed during the mass coupon privatisation. An important negative aspect was non-transparent trading and lack of regulations. Introduction of IFRS did not stimulate an increase in trading volumes on the Prague Stock Exchange. Now, there are very few companies listed at the Prague stock exchange, and these companies are not there for financial reasons – to list more shares and obtain new capital (there have been only ten IPOs since the restart of PSE operations). This is further explained in the relevant paragraph on the development of Czech capital market.

Toward the end of the 20th century, the economies of Central and Eastern Europe failed to deliver economic growth. Political changes started with the dismantling of the Berlin Wall. Central European countries and some Eastern European countries under Soviet domination initiated political change, which subsequently created opportunities to change the economic system.

After initial reform of accounting regulations, which commenced at the beginning of the 1990s, Czech regulations were first transformed from centrally planned rules to market-based principles. Subsequently, IFRS was introduced to Czech accounting as a voluntary means of reporting in 2003 and 2005 obligatory for listed companies. At the same time there was and still is an obligation to report according to Czech national GAAP for tax purposes. Therefore, as the Czech companies do not clearly see the benefits of IFRS introduction, they are rather hesitant to invest in this new reporting activity.

In general, the number of companies reporting according to IFRS is not much, even though their percentage is increasing. There are three principal reasons why using IFRS is less frequent:

1. The capital market where IFRS reporting would be compulsory is not very active,
2. Industrial relations with foreign entities do not necessarily require more frequent use of IFRS, and
3. Perceptions of extra costs associated with implementation of IFRS were verified by recent research survey on a representative sample of 258 Czech companies. The reason for extra perceived costs is valid particularly for SMEs but not for subsidiaries of foreign parent companies, where these costs were already covered by the needs of consolidation. In these cases the lack of interest in IFRS reporting was caused by lack of perceived benefits.

As a follow-on from the proceeding debate, this chapter intends to achieve the following objectives:

1. To present an assessment of the impact of IFRS reporting in the Czech Republic through macroeconomic indicators.
2. To assess the importance of IFRS adoption, which is perceived as a measure generally resulting in reduction of information asymmetries between firms and external parties and which in turn contributes to positive changes in the country's institutional environment (Gordon *et al.*, 2012; Brüggemann *et al.*, 2014; and Márquez-Ramos, 2011).
3. To assess the impact of IAS/IFRS on the Czech capital market following incorporation of international standards into Czech accounting in 2005, when issuers of securities became obligated to prepare consolidated financial statements in accordance with international principles.
4. To offer an overview of development of Czech accounting, concentrating on implementation of IFRS in the accounting system. This includes legal adjustments to regulations and the current state of opinions and perceptions of IFRS within a sample of Czech companies, together with a cost-benefit analysis of IFRS adoption by small and medium-sized companies and general influence of IFRS adoption.

IFRS ADOPTION and FDI: An Overview

The need to harmonize accounting worldwide has emerged as increased international trade generated a need to finance industrial companies and corporations across borders. The need for harmonization started in the second half of 20th century (Miller, 1990; Emenyonu & Gray, 1992; Hopwood, 1994; Taylor Zarzeski, 1996) and it was formally enabled in Europe by EC directives. Officially, harmonization of financial accounting was regulated in the EU by two EU directives of the Council of Ministers: the Fourth Directive on the annual accounts of companies (July 1978) and the Seventh Directive on consolidated accounts (June 1983).

The rationale was based on differences in national accounting standards which create potential difficulties for users of financial information requiring comparisons of data from different countries, and for companies wishing to engage in cross-border activities, such as raising capital in more than one country (Thorell & Whittington, 1994; Hopwood, 1994; Miller, 1990).

In general, expected changes can occur on three levels through introduction of IFRS - increase in international trade; positive impact on export and FDI; and easing institutional settings for enterprises. However, with a transitory economy such as the Czech Republic, as one might expect, political and economic policies dominated change pursuant to disintegration of the centralized regime. This further led to major changes in structures of ownership after privatization and thus enabling a major influx of international companies. Therefore, this change can be considered a result of political changes rather than changes in accounting regulations (enabling of IFRS).

From the current perspective, macroeconomic impact of IFRS introduction cannot be clearly isolated in the Czech Republic, because concurrently there were changes in pro–export policy and ambitious efforts to attract FDI. Accounting standards represent just one part of changes in the overall macroeconomic environment that started in 2000. Compulsory compliance with IFRS was introduced for companies listed on stock exchanges in 2005. But very few companies in the Czech Republic to date are in that category.

Many international studies have recently focused on the relationship between IFRS and FDI and/or other macroeconomic factors worldwide. Overall it was found that there was a positive correlation of these elements.

A broadly based study by Márquez-Ramos (2011) found that International Financial Reporting Standards (IFRS) adoption reduces information costs among countries and is, therefore, an important way to encourage international trade in goods and investments. The results indicate that benefits exist in terms of trade in goods and FDI when IFRS is adopted. The paper shows that accounting harmonisation in Europe is a way to reduce information costs and unfamiliarity between countries and, thus it becomes an important way of encouraging international trade and foreign direct investments. Here the results show that transitioning economies have benefited most from IFRS adoption in terms of trade in goods and FDI inflows from 2002 onwards.

Gordon, *et al.*, 2012, analysed the impact of IFRS adoption on foreign direct investment using a panel data set of over 1300 observations covering 124 countries, from 1996 through 2009, to assess the impact of adopting IFRS on overall country FDI inflows, and to determine if this impact varies based on whether a country is classified as having a developing or developed economy. Based on an empirical study, the argument that the overall FDI inflows are positively associated with a country's decision to adopt IFRS appears valid. However, as anticipated, this support is statistically significant for those countries classified as developing economies, but not for countries classified as developed economies.

The study by Beneish *et al.*, 2012, contrasted the impact of IFRS adoption on Equity and debt markets The authors find that mandatory adoption of IFRS is associated with an increase in total foreign portfolio investment into a country's capital markets, however IFRS adoption has a significantly greater effect on foreign investment into a country's debt market than into its equity market. The authors also found that the increase in foreign debt investment around IFRS adoption is not associated with quality of governance, economic development, or creditor rights prior to IFRS adoption. In contrast, they have found that post-adoption increase in foreign equity investment is positively associated with a country's governance quality, economic development, and creditor rights prior to IFRS adoption. This evidence suggests that the increase in foreign investment is more likely a result of improved financial reporting quality rather than increased comparability.

An empirical paper by Brüggemann *et al.*, 2014, analysed the evidence of economic consequences of mandatory adoption of IFRS in the European Union. The paper stated that empirical research on intended consequences generally fails to document an increase in comparability or transparency of financial statements. However, the authors find rich and almost unanimous evidence of positive effects on capital markets and in macroeconomic data.

Chen *et al.*, 2014, considered accounting standards as a component of the institutional infrastructure of a location and hypothesize that the convergence of domestic and International Financial Reporting Standards (IFRS) promotes FDI as it reduces information processing costs for foreign investors. The authors determined if the effect of reduced information costs was stronger for partner countries in which accounting systems showed greater pre-convergence differences. The authors used bilateral FDI data from 30 OECD countries between 2000 and 2005, and find evidence generally consistent with these hypotheses. As these results were obtained after allowing for other determinants of FDI - in particular the rule of law - it was arguable that accounting standards represent a specific component of institutional infrastructure that is important for FDI.

PREVIOUS CZECH RESEARCH STUDIES ON THE IMPACT OF IFRS ADOPTION

Previous Czech studies on the impact of changes to accounting and the impact of IFRS (or rather the association of IFRS with political and economic changes) were written by Schroll, 1995; Daniel *at al.*, 2001, Sucher and Jindrichovska, 2004, Zarova 2008, Zarova & Mejzlik, 2009 and 2011; Zarova *et al.*, 2010 and others, and more recently by Istvanfyova 2010. Contemporary analytical studies were written by Prochazka & Ilinitchi, 2011 and 2012; Zarova *et al.*, 2014; Prochazka 2014; Jindrichovska, *et al.*, 2014, and Prochazka and Pelak, 2015.

The first group of mentioned studies was more involved with reforms in Czech accounting standards characteristic of transition from a centrally planned economy to a market-based one. The more recent studies examine implementation or adoption of IFRS and its implications.

In their 2011 study, Prochazka & Ilinitchi argue that globalization of the world economy is accompanied by changes in volume and structure of international trade, capital flows and human migration. The paper focuses on theoretical aspects of recent changes to international harmonization of accounting through adoption of International Financial Reporting Standards (IFRS), migration and foreign direct investment with emphasis on mutual interdependencies. The paper concludes that adoption of IFRS is only the first step in a more complex process. Due to cultural differences, some discrepancies are inherent in the quality of IFRS implementation in financial statements of companies under consideration. The authors claim, that use of IFRS may be helpful in attracting FDI. However, easing legal approval of IFRS as the financial reporting system in a particular country is not the sole factor influencing the decision, which involves allocation of scarce domestic resources.

In a subsequent study from 2012, the same team of authors sought the connection between the IFRS adoption, FDI and migration. Here they concluded that the global economy brings new challenges in presentation of financial statements, because users need more high-quality financial information. Adoption of IFRS has important microeconomic and macro-economic effects and it influences the mutual relationship of financial and management accounting systems. The paper outlines possible links with a triangle consisting of "IFRS adoption – FDI flows – migration" and it concludes that because of cultural differences, the discrepancies in the actual quality of IFRS implementation in financial statements exist amongst various countries.

Zarova *et al.*, 2014, focused on the political and socio-economic aspects of development of the new economic system and argue that changes in accounting and introduction of IFRS brought new quality to Czech financial reporting and accelerated its transformation to a market economy. Not only value relevant inputs were brought to financial reporting, but implementation of IFRS brought positive elements to internal management accounting and allowed more accurate performance valuation.

Prochazka, 2014, asserts that IFRS adoption has improved the quality of accounting information significantly. However, huge costs were incurred by all subjects involved. The process has also considerable consequences for national tax systems because corporate income tax systems in code law countries are closely related to accounting regulation. Governments are now forced to decide whether and how companies using financial statements under IFRS should reflect IFRS- based figures on their income tax returns. The author suggests that the Czech Republic - a small open economy with a decisive share of foreign capital in company ownership, may benefit from this step by increasing understanding and transparency of the taxation system in relation to corporate accounting.

Jindrichovska *et al.*, 2014, focused on development of rules and practices of accounting and on the application of IFRS in the Czech Republic. Analysis of development of accounting regulations and the broader historical context indicate that the majority of Czech companies nowadays have little motivation to switch to international reporting standards, especially if there are no compelling reasons to do so, such as legal requirement, presence in capital markets or strong business partners - e.g. foreign parents requiring the Czech entity to report using IFRS.

Prochazka & Pelak, 2015, in their recent conference paper investigated the impact of IFRS adoption on capital markets of the new EU countries. The authors begin with the premise that globalisation of capital markets strongly favours harmonised accounting to reduce information risk of foreign investors. The authors researched whether IFRS adoption in new EU countries had any impact on the size of regulated capital markets. The authors conclude that IFRS adoption has a rather negative impact on these markets, indicating "absolute losers": Czech Republic, Slovakia, Latvia, and Lithuania, "a relative loser": Slovenia, "relative winners": Hungary, Estonia and "an absolute winner": Poland. In addition the authors conclude that there was observable shrinkage of capital markets because of implementation of new rules and compliance costs. The results of this study raise cardinal questions for empirical research on the effects of IFRS adoption, as almost 10 per cent of German companies left capital markets during the transition period (2002-2005). These are most likely companies foregoing expected positive benefits from the changeover to IFRS.

Other studies investigating IFRS adoption looked at different aspects. The majority of them were conceptual and concentrated on: 1) interpretation of IFRS principles in the respective national language and alignment with national Financial Reporting Principles; 2. dealing with a particular reporting feature; 3. exploring issues of application of IFRS to SMEs; 4. exploring the effects of IFRS application in the Czech Republic and the EU; 5. assessing cultural differences and their impact on IFRS usage, and 6. dealing with the impact of f IFRS on assessment of financial situations of companies. For more details see Jindrichovska, *et al.*, 2014.

MACRO-ECONOMIC BACKGROUND OF THE CZECH REPUBLIC

Economic development of the Czech Republic should be assessed in the context of developments in other countries due to the economic crisis that began in 2008 and affected most countries, especially developed countries. It is considered the deepest crisis in the post-war period. As for the Czech Republic, after a deep recession in 2009 there came only a moderate recovery in 2010, and in 2011 growth momentum was already lost - as in most EU countries.

According to the recent reports by European Commission, the Czech economy returned to growth in 2014, after two years of contraction. Previously the macroeconomic situation was negatively influenced by the financial crisis of 2007-2010, which in the Czech case was extended to 2012-2013 (European Commission, 2015, 1). The new recession was caused by a combination of unfavourable internal and external influences. While the crisis in 2009 was caused predominantly by external conditions, industrial production dropped in 2012 as a result of a new recession caused by internal measures that strongly reduced domestic demand and, were it not for positive influence of international trade, the decline in Czech GDP would have be more pronounced (Spevacek, 2013).

However, after this slowdown, government policy changed following fresh elections. As a result, investment activity started to grow in 2014. The domestic environment improved, foreign industrial orders picked up and the government increased its efforts to make use of expiring EU funds. In general the domestic environment improved. The trade surplus also continued to grow steadily; however, this was also due to favourable impact on prices caused by devaluation of Czech Crown in the second half of 2013 (table 1).

The Czech Republic is considered an open economy dependent to a large extent on international trade. It is a small open economy with important exports mainly in machinery. Parallel movements of GDP and size of export can be observed in macroeconomic data. National GDP is sustained by exports - predominantly machinery and automotive exports, which represented about 62 – 67 per cent of total exports in 2005 through 2014 (figure 1).

Major export destinations are neighbouring countries: Germany, Slovakia, Austria and Poland. These countries receive almost half total Czech exports. Main exports are cars and accompanying parts for production, electrical energy, cement and fertilizers. Figure 2 below shows the dominant position of manufacturing exports.

Regarding the macroeconomic environment, there are obvious reasons to suggest that IFRS may well be an additional contributing driver of FDI flows (figure 3). However in the Czech Republic, IFRS was not one of the main drivers. The development of inward FDI shows that Czech Republic was an important target country for FDIs in the region and the greatest importance in the picture was played by business opportunities supported by a pro-export government policy also supporting FDIs. Inflow from FDIs slowed down marginally in 2011 - 2013, when the country was experiencing problems due to restrictive budget policy. In general, profitability of FDIs was also above average as described by KPMG (KPMG, 2014).

FDIs react to economic and political changes and to developments in the "outside world". There was the apparent influence of the global financial crisis and also the local political cycle and changes in support of pro-export policy and the negative impact of the EU embargo against Russia (despite Russia not being a major export country).

Table 1. Development of GDP and GDP per capita

		1993	1994	1995	1996	1997	1998	1999	2000	2001	2002	2003
GDP	Bil CZK, real.	1 195,8	1 364,8	1 580,1	1 812,6	1 953,3	2 142,6	2 237,3	2 372,6	2 562,7	2 674,6	2 801,2
GDP per cap	CZK, real.	115 754	132 043	152 952	175 721	189 575	208 120	217 577	230 969	250 649	262 199	274 579
GDP	Increase %, real.	1,0	2,4	6,2	4,3	-0,7	-0,3	1,4	4,3	3,1	1,6	3,6
		2004	2005	2006	2007	2008	2009	2010	2011	2012	2013	2014
GDP	Bil CZK, real.	3 057,7	3 258,0	3 507,1	3 831,8	4 015,3	3 921,8	3 953,7	4 022,4	4 047,7	4 086,3	4 266,1
GDP per cap.	CZK, real.	299 567	318 345	341 604	371 204	384 992	373 810	375 921	383 208	385 152	388 771	405 342
GDP	Increase %, real.	4,9	6,4	6,9	5,5	2,7	-4,8	2,3	2,0	-0,8	-0,7	2,0

Source: Czech National Bank

Figure 1. Development of GDP and export after 1995
Source: Czech statistical office

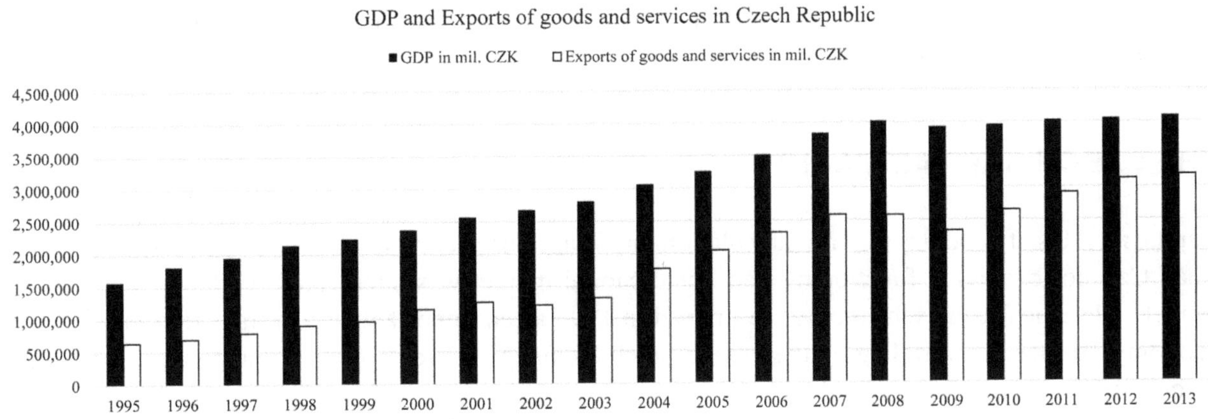

Figure 2. Manufacturing and non-manufacturing export
Source MPO - Ministry of industry and trade

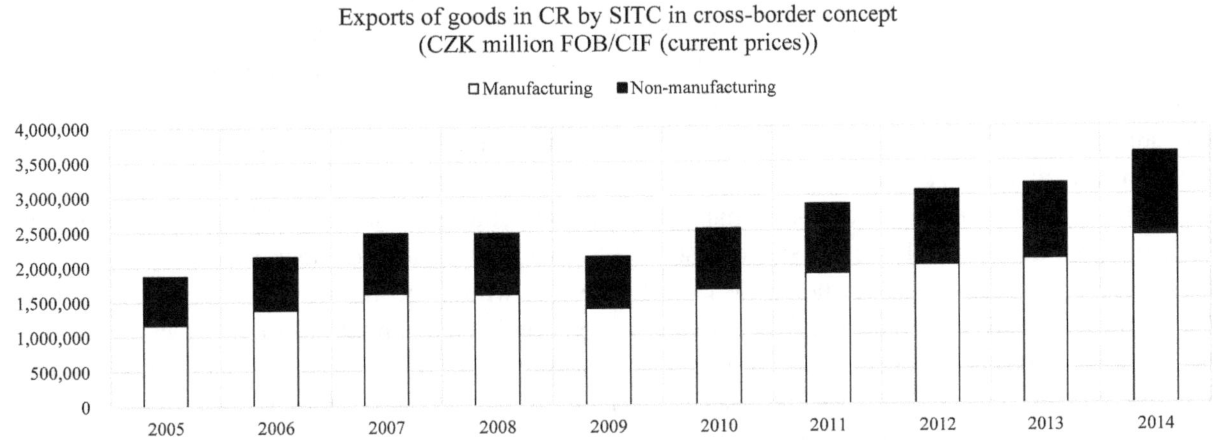

Figure 3. Characteristic of FDI (1995 - 2014)
Source: Czech National Bank

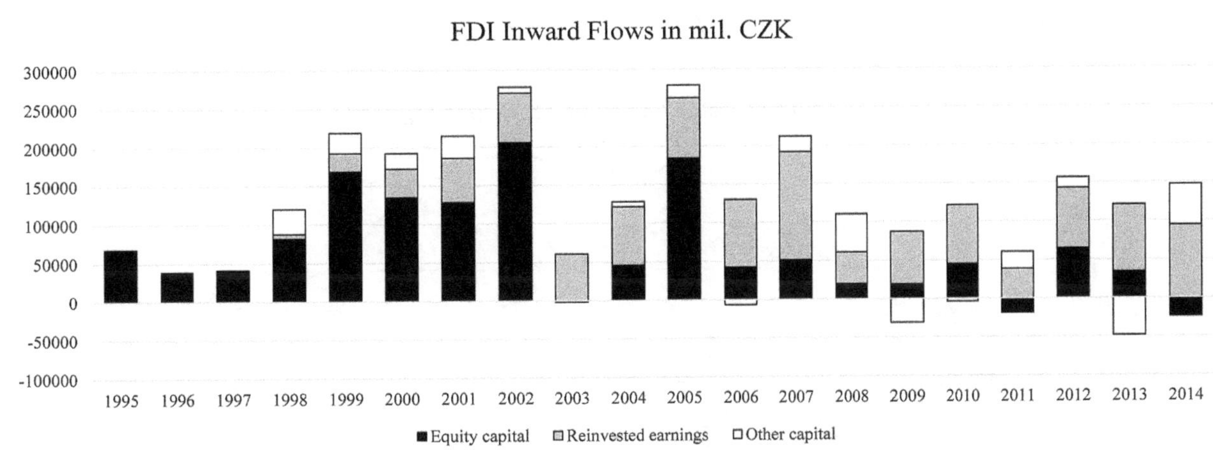

The option of allowing Czech companies to adopt IFRS did not prevent the economic crisis. According to the graph, the mode of FDI is changing. This is mostly in response to changes in the political climate - a reflection of the domestic political cycle and other strong influences - the (external) financial crisis and devaluation of Czech currency.

THE CZECH CAPITAL MARKET

Capital markets of a country traditionally play an important role in attracting FDIs. In the Czech Republic (then Czechoslovakia), a functioning traditional capital market was interrupted by the Second World War. The Prague Stock exchange was re-opened in 1993 as an important step in transition to a market economy. At inception, trading on the Prague Stock Exchange started with 955 companies listed from so-called "Great Privatization".

Although trading reached relatively high volumes in 1997 – 2009, the Prague Stock Exchange did not alter its system of operation, and a lack of standard capital market regulations impacted on trading results with low liquidity. At the same time, because of complicated internal regulatory conditions, there were precious few incentives for companies seeking new capital to issue new stocks. Few IPOs have been floated (only ten since inception). The reason was not only due to a historical tradition of the financial system being essentially bank-based, but it also was a result of the privatization process. Concentration of ownership fell into the hands of a relatively small number of investment groups which were allowed to acquire shares at very low prices. This effectively led to bankruptcy and liquidation of many Czech companies in all sectors (figure 4).

The fact book for the Prague Stock Exchange lists 20 companies representing 99.87 per cent of market capitalization, out of which the top six represent 91.82 per cent as at December 31. 2014. At present, the Prague Stock Exchange is owned by Wiener Börse AG, which became its majority shareholder on December 2008 and now holds a 92.739 per cent Stake in registered capital of Prague Stock Exchange. Presently the market does not effectively provide capital to industrial companies. As previously mentioned, only ten IPOs have occurred since the restart of operations. The Prague Stock Exchange is now part of CEESEG AG, where the exchanges of Budapest, Ljubljana, and Vienna are also equal subsidiaries.

Figure 4. Trading volume at the Prague Stock Exchange (1993 - 2013) (In billions of CZK)
Source: Prague Stock Exchange and own research

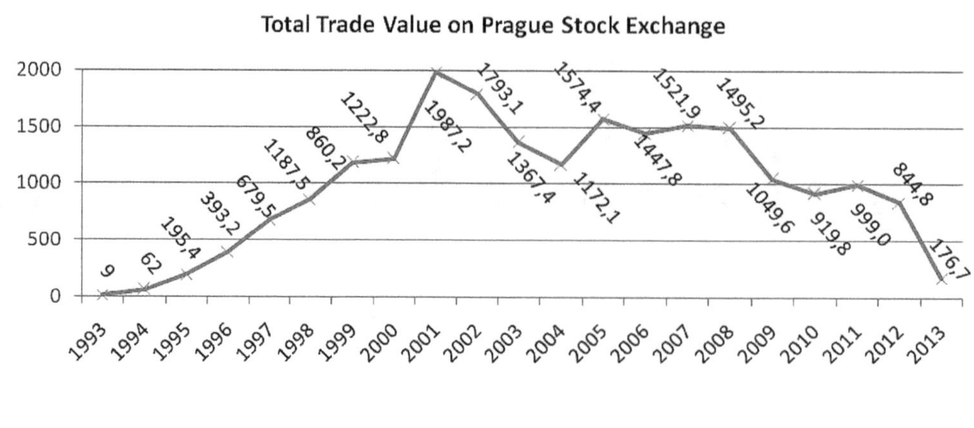

CONDITIONS OF IFRS IMPLEMENTATION IN THE CZECH ACCOUNTING SYSTEM

Financial reporting differs in various countries due to historical and socio-economic context. Although the general purpose of accounting and preparation of financial statements is similar in most countries, many differences occur for the following reasons:

- Character of the legal system (code law *vs.* common law),
- Character and historical development of the economy (industrial economy with several dominant branches),
- Different systemic reallocation of available sources (i.e. how organized is the movement of temporarily free capital to areas where required),
- Close connection to tax reporting,
- Cultural dynamics.

For more details see e.g. Wohe & Kislingerová (2007); Nobes, 2012; Nobes & Parker, (2012); Zarova (2014).

The decisive factor underlying construction of the accounting system in the Czech Republic and its regulation in all historical periods was the fact that it belongs to countries with dominant Roman law (code law).[2]

The economy of the Czech Republic (first as part of the Austrian and then the Austro-Hungarian monarchy) developed rapidly based on manual and industrial production since the 17th century. The growth of enterprises and increasing complexity of their management was accompanied by changes in the system of business management and separation of ownership and managerial functions (Wöhe & Kislingerová, 2007; Vochozka, 2011). This was accompanied by the development of the legal system, especially by Commercial Law, which set forth basic conditions for economic activities, amongst which was bookkeeping.

The need for additional capital has increased with growth of enterprises and capital intensity of production. Free capital sources were in the hands of financial houses and banks. After being released from limitations of religious covenants, banks became the main provider of capital, mainly in form of loans. This is why the modern Czech accounting system was built predominantly from the creditors' perspective. Annual reports were not initially prepared to provide information for the needs of equity investors and the capital market, as opposed to the Anglo-Saxon model. Financial data was primarily needed to assess a borrower's ability to satisfy creditors' claims through both property and performance.

In the 19th and 20th centuries, accounting and its development in the Bohemian region was deeply rooted in strong domestic industry. Czechs excelled especially in machinery, automotive and avionics. Companies like CKD, Skoda, OKD, Poldi, T. Bata, Electro Praga, Letov, Aero, Walter Jinonice and Tatra took the lead in innovative production. The accounting system was constructed to support operation of these industrial companies. The entire accounting system was initially based on French, German and Italian accounting practices.

The most important aspect of the Czech accounting system from its early days is its close connection with tax reporting. This usually leads to the fact that many accounting decisions become tax influenced or even tax biased. This link between accounting and tax regulations is found in many European countries, most often in those that do not have explicit investor approach (e.g. Strouhal *et al.*, 2009; Pasekova *et al.* 2010; Strouhal, 2011).

The main features of Czech accounting development that was transferred to the next stage can be summarized as follows:

- Emphasis on creditor protection and tax collection,
- Absence of a sophisticated capital market,
- Preference for national charts of accounts.

Czech Accounting after the Political Changes in 1989

During forty years of a centrally planned economy, accounting and financial reporting played rather passive role in companies´ economic decision-making. State enterprises were obliged to produce financial statements for tax and statistical authorities, which treated as private information. Provision of a true and fair representation of financial stability and performance of enterprises for the general public simply did not exist.

In the early years of economic transformation, accounting underwent efforts to transform the existing system into a form suitable for a market economy. The transformations occurred in various fields at different times concurrently with other significant changes in the external economic environment (e.g. increasing globalization, development of information technology, influence of financial markets etc.). Accounting and applicable regulation were reformed in the context of these changes.

The development of accounting after 1989 can be split into two phases. The aim of the first stage from 1989 to 2000 was an attempt to adapt the existing accounting system to a market-driven system. The second phase (2000 to date) is focused on adaptation and implementation of IFRS.

The first significant step was passage of The Act on Accounting, which sought to adjust basic financial reporting principles to the new economic environment. It came into force on January 1, 1993. It was based on the principle of providing appropriate information to financial managers to enable them to make financial decisions for their companies (Schroll, 1995). The concept of a 'true and fair view' was declared as the core principle (but it became part of the wording of the Act only several years later). Even during this period, the Act contained permission to use the other Czech accounting standards: "In addition to financial statements prepared in compliance with the Act on Accounting, accounting units may also provide accounting information those are prepared in compliance with IFRS or other internationally recognised accounting."

At the same time other new acts were prepared - the Act on Income Tax, a starting point for calculation of income tax of legal entities, established accounting profit. As a result of this financial reporting fell under the influence of tax rules.

Restoration of the Prague Stock Exchange was underway at that time. Thus, the adjustments to the Act on Accounting partially reflected the needs of capital markets. But it is necessary to state that the management of companies, the Czech capital market, investors, and business partners were not adequately prepared to use the accounting information effectively.

In subsequent years the Act on Accounting enacted and fully endorsed in 1993, has been modified several times and supplemented by other regulations.

After 2000, the changes in the accounting regulation were prepared under the influence of development in IAS/IFRS. In particular, there was the strategy of "Way Forward" adopted by the EU in the year 2000 and Regulation EC 1606/2002 on the use of International Accounting Standards approved by the EU in 2000. The main incentive was the prospect of EU membership and the obligation of OECD membership. These influences resulted in extensive changes in wording of the Act on Accounting since 2002 and 2004.

In this period the system of accounting regulation was rebuilt as a three level system (Zarova, 2014, p. 34). This type of regulation included Act on Accounting, Decrees and Czech accounting standards.

The Act covered all accounting entities, including business enterprises, banks, insurance companies, public entities (budgetary), non-profit organisations, municipalities, national property funds, and even small entities using cash-based accounting (cash-based accounting was excluded in 2004).

Specific decrees were issued by the Ministry of Finance to cover different sectors of economy (business entities, banks, insurance companies, health insurance companies, public entities, and non-profit organization), and to specify the accounting procedures given by the Act on Accounting (chart of accounts, layout of financial statements, etc.)

Separate national accounting standards were issued by the Ministry of Finance for four types of entities: (general business entities, banks and financial institutions, insurance companies, and public entities). They determined acceptable accounting methods and/or procedures.

The whole new system of accounting regulation was partially based on the Fourth and Seventh European Directives and on International Accounting Standards. However, some pre-1989 measures, which were included into new laws, could be identified (Seal *et al.*, 1995). This practice is similar to other continental European countries - there still remains a close link between accounting and tax and relatively small importance associated with the data in financial statements.

The Implementation of IFRS into Czech Accounting System

Forms of IFRS Implementation

The three level system of regulation coming in force in 2004 the implementation of IFRS was realised in two forms:

1. Firstly in the form of definitive adoption, according to which companies were obliged to prepare their financial statements in accordance with IFRS (as a part of Act on Accounting),
2. Secondly in form of adjustments of accounting practices (as part of Decrees and Czech accounting standards), where the regulation became a direct part of Czech accounting system.
3. And lastly full incorporation of IFRS into the Czech accounting standards (which is the case of financial institutions).

Concurrently, however, Act 586/1992 Coll., Income Tax Law as amended and valid as of January 1, 2011, stipulated that the tax base should be established from the results according to procedures laid down by Decree, i.e. based on Czech accounting standards:

To determine the tax base is based on: a) the result (profit or loss), and always without the influence of international accounting standards, for taxpayers who keep accounting records. A taxpayer who prepares the financial statements in accordance with International Accounting Standards, for the purposes of this

Act shall apply to determine profit by special legislation. (I.e. Decree No. 500, 501, and 502). b) The difference between revenues and expenditures for taxpayers, who do not keep accounts.

A. Degree of IFRS Implementation

The actual status of IFRS implementation in the Czech accounting system can be assessed either based on the provisions of the Act on Accounting as the highest regulatory instrument and the other level of regulation, or on the real use of IFRS in business practice. In this section, we focus on the current provisions of the Accounting Act. In the following section we will describe the real state of practical use of IFRS in Czech companies. In this assessment it is also important to distinguish implementation in the form of compilation of statements on one hand and in the form of record-keeping during the reporting period and the subsequent report on the other. Both forms are acceptable and represent different stages of implementation: compilation of reports can be based on accounting data recorded by other reporting systems (CAS), followed by their transformation into accounting statements according to IFRS principles (i.e. with the use of a transformation bridge).

Implementation of IAS/IFRS in the Czech national accounting system is influenced by ownership structure, which has been changing since the time of mass privatization and gradual transition to market principles. The change of ownership structure continued with subsequent activities of Czech government, which sold Czech state enterprises and Czech banks to foreign investors. The current ownership structure is indicates 58 per cent share of foreign ownership (Ernest, 2014). Foreign owners naturally prefer their own reporting style, which is sometimes in accordance with IFRS but not necessarily. Furthermore, Czech regulatory authorities (Ministry of Finance) do not push for the compulsory use of IFRS, mainly for the reasons of tax reporting.

According to the provisions of Act on Accounting the use of IAS/IFRS, with regards to the ownership structure of Czech companies can be distinguished in three types of companies (adapted by Zarova, 2014):

Category I

This category usually represents big companies that are issuers of securities listed on regulated securities exchanges in the EU. These companies are obliged to keep accounts and to compile the financial statement in accordance with IAS/IFRS. According to a provision of the Act on Accounting (as amended), this group is comprised of two types of entities:

1. Companies and financial groups, that are issuers of securities listed on regulated capital exchanges in the EU (i.e. publicly traded companies according to the Regulation 1606/2002), that have to prepare consolidated financial statements in accordance with IAS/IFRS.
2. Independent (individual) trading companies, that are issuers of securities listed on regulated capital exchanges in the EU. [3]

Both these groups have to show pre-tax income on the income tax report in accordance with Czech accounting standards (decrees) for the tax purposes.

Category II

This category includes very different companies. Their common feature is that they are not direct issuers of publicly traded securities, but they are the subsidiaries of parent companies that are issuers and as such they are required to prepare consolidated financial statements in accordance with IAS/IFRS. Therefore, the companies in this category shall prepare individual financial statements in accordance with the CAS (for statutory purposes and tax calculation). And in addition, they shall provide their parent companies with financial statements and other information needed for consolidation in compliance with IFRS. The Act on Accounting does not permit voluntary application of the IFRS instead of Czech accounting standards for these entities. Consolidated entities that are not issuers of publicly traded securities may be also included to this category - companies that can use the IAS/IFRS for consolidated financial statements voluntarily.

To this category can be included both individual and financial group companies, which are not issuers of publicly traded securities on regulated capital markets temporarily in the EU member states, i. e. securities trading that terminates on organized exchanges during the accounting period or applications to be admitted to public trading in EU capital markets or interruption of trading on an EU capital exchange. These companies can use IAS/IFRS voluntarily if they are applying to be admitted to public trading within the next 3 (4) years. If they are not applying to be admitted to the public trading or after the fourth year when the trading was ended, they are obliged to use/return to CAS.

Also these entities are obliged to account their pre-tax income for the income tax purposes based on the Czech accounting standards (decrees).

Category III

This category includes small and family owned companies and other companies that are neither direct, nor indirect issuer of publicly traded securities. They shall keep accounts and prepare their financial statements in accordance with the CAS and there is no possibility to apply the IFRS voluntarily.

Special Category: Financial Institutions and Banks

Banks and other financial institutions form a special category, which includes various types of financial institutions and banks. Accounting in the financial sector has changed substantially. The financial reporting of these companies is regulated by a special decree and accounting standards (standards for financial institutions) that respect the special character of the business process in these companies. According to current accounting practice, banks and some financial institutions (i. e. regulated financial institutions except insurance companies) have to report their financial position in accordance with IFRS rules since January 1st 2002. Mandatory reporting in accordance with the IFRS for the vast majority of Czech banks started on January 1, 2005. Czech accounting standards for this sector prepared in that time are fully harmonized and are in compliance with the principles of IFRS - in contrast to the other sectors for which the Czech accounting standards were harmonized with IFRS only in selected areas (Jílek & Svobodová, 2013).

In the amendment of Act of Accounting in the 2002 a preparation the Decrees and Czech accounting standards for these types of entities IFRS principles were directly involved in the provision of these regulation tools (decrees and standards). This means that regulatory tools are indeed tools of national

Table 2. IFRS in the financial reporting system in the Czech Republic

Category	Companies of the Category	Extent of Use IFRS	IFRS	
			Mandatory	Voluntary
I.	Big companies, issuers of publicly traded securities, both individual entities and financial groups	Individual and consolidated financial statements, keeping accounts	x	x
II.	Medium companies, not issuers of publicly traded securities (definitely, temporarily), subsidiary of the parent companies-issuers of publicly trading securities	Individual and consolidated financial statements, keeping accounts, special items/reports	x (according to parent companies)	x (in case of temporarily interruption of trading)
III.	Small and family owned companies which are not issuers of publicly traded securities,	Individual financial statements	-	-
Special treatment	Financial institutions (banks, insurance companies)	Individual and consolidated financial statements, keeping accounts	x (IFRS=CAS)	-

Source: own elaboration Notes: CAS – Czech Accounting Standards;

regulation, but contain principles and rules of IFRS. The implementation of IFRS was in that case included right into the national rules (Jílek & Svobodová, 2013).

Classification of types of companies with regard to compulsory/voluntary application of the IFRS and CAS is summarised in table 2.

Nevertheless, the actual extent of the IFRS use outside the mandatory group of companies listed on the EU capital market is very low. The interest in voluntary adoption of IFRS for preparation of financial statements is also very low – the reasons are investigated in the next chapter. The causes of this reality can be identified in many aspects and characteristics of the Czech economy and treatment of Czech accounting regulations. Some of these causes were discussed in the first part of the chapter: underdeveloped capital markets; the ownership structure of Czech companies, the industrial structure of the economy and foreign trade; and last, but not least, lack of trust in the accounting system and lack of perceived benefits, which in turn, is further weakened by subordination to tax reporting purposes. Serious impediments are also the significant differences between Czech accounting procedures and the procedures that required by the IFRS system.

B. Degree of IFRS Implementation in the Czech Accounting Standards

Besides the provision on what entities are obliged or can voluntary use the IFRS for preparing financial statement, implementation of IFRS into the Czech accounting system is carried out in another form. This form consists of implemention elements of IFRS principles directly into the Czech accounting standards, which are used by significant majority of accounting units. As example of these standards can be listed the principles of

- Depreciation of fixed assets (economic useful life, residual value),
- Component depreciation, valuation of financial instruments,
- Fair value (for financial instruments),

- Goodwill.

And also such principles as

- True and fair view,
- Data reliability,
- Business year,
- And many others.

It is very hard to distinguish between changes resulting from evolution of Czech accounting thought and those from implementation of elements of IFRS principles into the Czech accounting regulation. These changes cover a broad scope of corrections that were made to the Act on Accounting, from defining the concept of business entity to the changes in the principles of valuation of assets, financial instruments and to the introduction of the primarily concept of accounting (true and fair view) etc. All of these corrections resulted in the gradual improvement of the Czech accounting regulations and Czech system of financial reporting (Prochazka, 2010, Zárova *et al.*, 2014).

CURRENT STATE OF IFRS ADOPTION IN THE CZECH ENVIRONMENT

The method of research survey was used to investigate the current state of adoption of IFRS by Czech enterprises. The survey was conducted in March and April of 2015 using an online questionnaire. The questionnaire was originally developed from previous research concentrating primarily on Czech SMEs and international studies on IFRS adoption (Mullerova, *et al.*, 2010; Pasekova, 2012 and Albu, N. *et al.*, 2011). Further, the research was broadened to other enterprises and subsidiaries of international companies, which were originally Czech SMEs and then became part of international groups mostly for business reasons. Some became suppliers or clients of foreign companies.

Thus, a database containing 1,613 medium and large firms was used with e-mail contacts to chief financial officers and chief accountants. In total we processed 258 completed questionnaires. This means a response rate of 15.99 per cent. The sample included 77 companies which exceed the thresholds for SME definition, i.e. belong to big firms. The predominant share of the sample represented medium business, small firms represented less than 15%, and there were only a small number of micro firms. The structure of the respondents according to industrial sector is in table 3.

The questionnaire consisted of five parts: the first part was aimed at identifying the respondents. The second part investigated the potential reasons for IFRS adoption, i.e. cooperation with the foreign partners (suppliers, customers), being a subsidiaries of parent company or an intention to issue securities. The third part investigated the degree of involvement of IFRS in companies accounting practice - how are the accounts kept. The fourth part concentrated on the most demanding issue in accounting, and the question in the fifth part investigated in more details the experience with and the view on IFRS usage.

The structure of a set of respondents describes the data gathered in the first part, which is presented in table 3. The results of the other parts of the questionnaire are in subsequent tables. The results of the second part showed that more than half of the companies (63%) have business contacts abroad (suppliers, customers, parent). The foreign contacts were established mainly with important suppliers, followed by links to the parent company, and major customers. The results show that the nature of international

Table 3. Sample characteristics

Company	Number of Respondents	Industrial Sector				
		Manufacturing	Trade	Services	Construction	Agriculture/ Other
Micro	6	0	1	4	1	0
Small	37	8	15	11	3	0
Medium	138	73	20	23	13	9
Big	77	49	6	18	4	0
Total	258	130	42	56	21	9

Source: own research

contacts almost always represent the commercial interests of the company rather than improvement of access to sources on capital markets. This corresponds to the nature of the Czech economy with a large export segment. Foreign contacts are of various kinds - one company can have multiple links: a contact to its parent company as well as to foreign suppliers and customers.

The third part investigated the state of IFRS adoption. The question was whether companies report additionally under other than Czech accounting standards. There were 81 firms i.e. 34 per cent of companies prepare financial statements in accordance with CAS plus another system of accounting standards. These companies prepare statements mostly according to IFRS (28 per cent), and only a small percentage of firms use US GAAP or other standards (6 per cent). For preparation of financial statements in accordance with IFRS, firms most often use the so-called "transformation bridge" (48 per cent), i.e. they do not use IFRS to track transactions, but rather financial statements are recalculated from original Czech accounting. Other firms prepare two sets of accounting books (28 per cent), and 14 per cent of firms report only selected items in accordance with IFRS. (For more details see table 4)/

Awareness of IFRS through completion of IFRS training by firm employees has been found in 90 companies, i.e. 35 per cent. However, 168 respondents (65 per cent) confirm only basic or no information (47 and 18 per cent respectively). Interest in attending such training was identified in 35 companies (13 per cent). Therefore it seems clear that awareness amongst company managements and accounting departments is relatively high, even if the firms do not report under IFRS. But on the other hand there are other firms that have little or no information and have no interest in IFRS (61 per cent, and 12 per cent from the whole sample). It is surprising that 95 of the respondents from IFRS non-adopters (i.e. 66 per cent and 38 per cent of the sample) do not see any benefits to reporting according to IFRS despite the fact that they have contact with foreign customers or suppliers or intend to establish such contact. This was confirmed by 108 and 129 respondents in the sample respectively (i.e. 41 and 50 per cent). Thus it can be concluded that firms still do not associate cooperation with a foreign partner with mandatory IFRS reporting. This also implies that foreign entities still do not require transparent and comparable information from Czech partners.

The last part of the questionnaire investigated the reasons for IFRS adoption and perceived benefits. In total, 147 respondents, i.e. 57 per cent, answered that they did not use IFRS. This interesting revelation on the use of IFRS in practice raises the question: what advantages or benefits are perceived by respondents in connection with the use of IFRS (companies that still do not use the IFRS answered). Only five per cent of IFRS non-adopters consider the adoption of IFRS in the future. Only 17 per cent of

Table 4. Usage of IFRS according to company characteristics

Sample characteristics					
Sample characteristics					
Accounting standards used besides CAS		*IAS/ IFRS%(abs.)*	*US GAAP %(abs.)*	*Other %(abs.)*	*No %(abs.)*
		27 (70)	*4 (10)*	*3 (9)*	*66 (169)*
Company location					
	Small city in CR	27,1	3,9	3,5	65,5
	Regional city in CR	22,5	2,8	3,5	71,1
	Prague	24,6	1,6	3,3	70,5
	Foreign country	50	50	-	-
Business sector					
	Manufacturing	27,7	5,4	5,4	61,5
	Trade	28,6	4,8	2,4	64,3
	Services	33,9	-	1,8	64,3
	Construction	9,5	4,8	-	85,7
	Agriculture	14,3	-	-	85,7
Potential reasons of IFRS adoption					
	Foreign customers				
	Yes	28,1	4,	4,3	62,7
	No	24,7	1,4	1,4	72,6
	Foreign suppliers				
	Yes	27,4	4,7	4,2	63,7
	No	26,1	-	-	73,9
Practice of accounting					
Accounting kept by:	Own employees	Accounting firm	Individual accountant		
	92% (238)	6% (16)*	2% (4)		
Creation of financial statements:					
	Transformation bridge from CAS	48	40	67	-
	Keeping two independent accounting books	28	20	11	-
	Translation of selected items only	14	20	11	-
	Different way	10	20	11	-
Knowledge of IFRS					
		Yes	Basic knowledge	No	
Having enough information about IAS		35%	47%	18%	
			Yes %	No %	
Participation in a training	Questioned persons		45	55	
	Other employees		33	67	
Want to participate in a training in future			39	61	

Source: own research *Note: Just five operating accounting firms offer preparation in IAS/IFRS; value in brackets represents number of answers

respondents perceive some benefits of using IFRS, while 83 per cent see no positive effects in the use of IFRS. From eight listed benefits for the use of IFRS the respondents most frequently chose the reason: “Better comparison of accounting data” (69 per cent) and:”Easier reporting“(66 per cent).

Knowledge of the potential benefits reflects an awareness of IFRS at least at a general level (83 per cent). The second most frequently quoted benefit is “Higher credibility for business partners“(47 per cent). Interesting findings follow from the response that 28 and 22 per cent of respondents connect IFRS reporting with better use of internal data for in-house managerial accounting and internal reporting respectively. This aspect has been already discussed by Prochazka, 2010 and Zarova 2014. A very low number of respondents perceived the importance of use of IFRS for easier access to bank loans (3 per cent). This can be understood as a reflection of the basic designation of the IFRS, but it is also a reflection of the fact that from the standpoint of banks IFRS is not required as reliable statements of financial position. (For more details – see table 5).

The adopters of IFRS were asked about difficulties in connection with IFRS adoption. Regarding costs associated with transition to IFRS, they most frequently report costs in the range of 5 per cent of firm turnover (in case of 31 per cent of respondents). The most frequently reported kinds of costs are cost of training (67 per cent), consulting services (51 per cent) and IT adjustments (43 per cent). Meanwhile, the main positive effects of IFRS adoption perceived by IFRS adopters are: “Getting loans easier”, “Easier increase of equity capital”, “Easier issuance of bonds”, “Better access to EU funding” (3.4 and 3.6 per cent) – see table 6.

To sum up the empirical findings: The findings are more or less in line with expectations. Use of IFRS is still relatively low, even though it has increased in comparison to previous studies from 2010 and 2013 (from 16 per cent to 28 per cent). The most important reason for not reporting in accordance with IAS / IFRS is the perceived absence of any benefits for companies. Offers to prepare statements according to it IFRS by professional accounting firms are minimal; therefore 93 per cent of all companies prepare their financial statements internally - predominantly using the transformation bridge. There are

Table 5. Characteristics of IFRS non-adopters

Non-adopters (147 companies)					
Will you consider IFRS adoption?			Are there any benefits from IFRS adoption for your company?		
Yes	No		Yes	No	
5%	95%		17%	83%	
Main reasons for not adopting IFRS		%	**What are the benefits of IFRS adoption?**		%
No benefits for company		38	Better comparison of accounting data		69
Don’t know about benefits from IFRS usage		29	Easier reporting		66
Company is not issuer of securities		14	Higher credibility for business partners		47
Other		11	Better public perception		28
Don’t have a foreign business partner		9	Better usage of data for business management		28
			Better quality of inter-company information		22
			Better access to EU funding		13
			Getting loans easier		3

Source: own research

Table 6. Characteristics of IFRS adopters

IFRS Adopters (71 companies)					
Costs of implementation [% of business turnover]	< 0,05	0,05 – 0,5	0,5 – 1	> 1	Couldn't estimate
	31%	12%	1%	1%	54%
Types of costs %	Consultancy	IT	Training	Salary	Other
Preparation of IFRS statements	51	43	67	20	6
Implementation of other standards	33	29	20	13	6
Problems	%	**Evaluation**			*
CAS is subordinate to tax reporting	36	Easier reporting			1.6
Complicated terms under IAS/IFRS	25	Better comparison of accounting data			2.1
Different problem	16	Better quality of inter-company information			2.7
Big difference between CAS and IFRS	10	Better usage of data for business management			2.7
Insufficient instruction for first adoption	6	Higher credibility for business partners			2.9
Difficult translation	4	Better public perception			2.9
Nonexistence of some transactions used in IFRS	3	Getting loans easier			3.4
Insufficiently developed capital market	0	Easier increase of equity capital			3.4
Investors and users are satisfied with CAS	0	Easier issuance of bonds			3.6
		Better access to EU funding			3.4

Source: own research
*Note: average mark from 68 companies on a scale from 1 (means yes) to 5 (means no).

some differences between the IFRS adopters and non-adopters with regards to perceived benefits of the use of IFRS, but the most significant reasons are similar for both groups. Macroeconomic changes and increased proportion of foreign companies through the increase FDIs plays a decisive role in the format of company reporting. And foreign companies do not always chose to use full IFRS, especially if they need only some complementary information for their own consolidation.

CONCLUSION AND RECOMMENDATIONS

Regarding the impact of IFRS on a macro-economic level, evidence of any positive impact is obfuscated because there were many political and economic measures implemented concurrently. For international investors, the decisive factor is the quality of potential investment opportunity and not the use or lack of use of IFRS. This is perceived as a minor obstacle. According to accounting professionals, a more structured implementation of IFRS in the Czech environment is recommended.

IFRS has brought a new quality to financial reporting in the Czech Republic and accelerated the process of transformation to a market economy. The implementation of IFRS brought positive features also in the operation of internal management accounting and performance valuation (Zarova, *et al.*, 2014; Prochazka, 2010). IFRS adoption brings a new variable to managerial decision-making, especially of small and medium companies and to the organization of their information systems. In many companies such an improved quality in financial reporting standards is used for internal purposes. External users are satisfied with the financial statements based on local standards. From this point of view, the latest Amendment of the Act on Accounting, effective from 2011 and 2014, has to be considered as giving more leeway to companies when deciding how to organize internal information systems in order to meet information needs of all users.

FUTURE RESEARCH DIRECTIONS

As for further development of Czech accounting research, there is the question of how to implement international standards – the question of convergence *versus* adoption. Learning from reactions of Czech companies thus far, there seems to be a practical prevalence for slow convergence to IFRS, starting with the firms with international ownership, where international practices have already been adopted.

The next stage of investigation with regards to future research opportunities IFRS adoption should be analysed according to its impact on the business environment. It would be desirable to concentrate on the positive effects of the use of IFRS for Czech companies and for the whole economy. And within the domain of the topic further analysis should concentrate on additional changes in the environment contrasting especially Czech SMEs to big companies.

There is also an unknown area concerning the cultural influences and real implementation of principles on which reporting according to IFRS is based. It might be interesting to investigate the influence of national culture and different types of economic thought in the usage of IFRS including the absence of the detailed rules to which accounting environment is accustomed.

The reasons for infrequent usage of IFRS in the Czech Republic have been previously identified by Zarova, *et al.*, 2014; Mullerová *et al.*, 2010; Kubickova 2012 and others. The most frequently cited reasons from the corporations stand point are:

- Higher demands on enterprise information systems;
- Requirement of further increase of qualifications of accounting staff;
- Incomparability of accounting data in time series;
- Incomparability of reported data within groups;
- Impact on strategic management of companies;
- Discontinuity of accounting policies (distribution of profit, motivations systems etc.);
- Organizational problems in bookkeeping systems of companies (financial statements translation in groups, accounting for tax purposes etc.);
- Lack of understanding of IFRS principles in accounting profession.

Furthermore it is not explained how to implement IFRS in particular national conditions. Therefore, it is necessary to take in consideration specific cultural features of particular country because as it has been observed cultural features have bigger impact than expected at the beginning of accounting harmonization effort (Brüggemann *et al.*, 2013).

Czech national accounting standards and as well as practical bookkeeping are regulated by the Act on Accounting of 1993. Similar normative regulation does not exist for the use of IFRS. More regulations are needed, at least on the level of best practices recommendation for practical use of Czech companies.

In the Czech Republic IFRS is not used very frequently and one may identify more detailed reasons for this state of affairs. One is the perceived costs related to IFRS adoption. Furthermore there is the ownership structure of companies where big ones are predominantly foreign owned, which solves capital needs in the capital markets in the other countries, there is also slow development of capital markets that would require IFRS usage. And last but not least, Czech accounting firms are not really prepared to provide IFRS accounting for their clients. Graduates of both secondary schools and the universities are also poorly prepared.

Looking at companies, IFRS implementation in the Czech economy is limited by some important factors:

- Limited and slow development of the capital market (limited domestic ownership of firms, impact of big international firms, insufficient legislative regulation, inadequate protection of investors, and lack of experience).
- Inadequate economic incentives and lack of interest for effective use of financial information in business.
- Significant differences between accounting practices used locally and by the IFRS (current development suggests that international principles of financial reporting will not be fully accepted even by the next generation of accountants).
- Weak position of the accounting profession and lack of ambition to improve practices, regulation and surveillance of accounting practice (slow process of implementation of IFRS knowledge into the curricula of secondary schools and universities, lack of recommendation at least on the level of best practices of bookkeeping in accordance with IFRS).

On the macro-economic level, international investors do not expect too much from implementation of IFRS in terms of better access to financial or capital markets. The main role in decision making, whether to invest in Czech Republic or not, is certainly not in whether the company does or does not report using IFRS but the potential opening of an investment opportunity. As can be seen from the practical research especially in small and medium Czech firms, if accounting does not play an important role, international standards do not have too much impact in general. However even if the IFRS adoption is not very high it is gradually rising which is apparent mainly in Czech companies with foreign parents that have to report in IFRS themselves.

ACKNOWLEDGMENT

The authors acknowledge the support of Research project IGA VŠFS Prague No 7762 funded by the institutional support for long-term strategic development research organization University of Finance and Administration, Prague. This research has been also supported by the Anglo-American University in Prague. We would also like to thank the Editor of the book for guidance and one anonymous referee for insightful comments. Further acknowledgement needs to be extended for technical assistance of our two collaborators Barbora Ulehlova and Martin Kohout.

REFERENCES

Albu, N., Albu, C. N., Bunea, S., St. Calu, D. A., & Girbina, M. M. (2011). A story about IAS/IFRS implementation in Romania. *Journal of Accounting in Emerging Economies*, *1*(1), 76–100. doi:10.1108/20421161111107868

Beneish, M. D., Miller, B. P., & Yohn, T. L. (2012). The impact of financial reporting on equity versus debt markets: Macroeconomic evidence from mandatory IFRS adoption. *Journal of Accounting and Public Policy, 34*(2015), 1–27.

Bohusová, H. (2008). The empirical study of the SMEs position in the process of IFRS for SME application in the Czech Republic. *Economics and Management*, *1*, 157–162.

Brüggemann, U., Hitz, J. M., & Sellhorn, T. (2013). Intended and unintended consequences of mandatory IFRS adoption: A review of extant evidence and suggestions for future research. *European Accounting Review*, *22*(1), 1–37. doi:10.1080/09638180.2012.718487

Chen, C. J., Ding, Y., & Xu, B. (2014). Convergence of accounting standards and foreign direct investment. *The International Journal of Accounting*, *49*(1), 53–86. doi:10.1016/j.intacc.2014.01.007

Daniel, P., Suranova, Z., & De Beelde, I. (2001). The development of accounting in Slovakia. *European Accounting Review*, *10*(2), 343–359. doi:10.1080/09638180126639

Emenyonu, E. N., & Gray, S. J. (1992). EC accounting harmonisation: An empirical study of measurement practices in France, Germany and the UK. *Accounting and Business Review*, *23*(89), 49–58. doi:10.1080/00014788.1992.9729860

Ernest, J. (2014). Český průmysl je náš jen z poloviny [Czech industry is our only half]. *Statistika & My, 4*(10), 8-19. Retrieved June 7 2015 from: http://www.statistikaamy.cz/wp-content/uploads/2014/12/18041410.pdf

European Commission. (2015). *Country Report Czech Republic 2015*. Retrieved from: http://ec.europa.eu/europe2020/pdf/csr2015/cr2015_czech_en.pdf

Gatti, D. D., Gallegati, M., Greenwald, B. C., Russo, A., & Stiglitz, J. E. (2012). Mobility constraints, productivity trends, and extended crises. *Journal of Economic Behavior & Organization*, *83*(3), 375–393. doi:10.1016/j.jebo.2012.03.011

Gordon, L. A., Loeb, M. P., & Zhu, W. (2012). The impact of IFRS adoption on foreign direct investment. *Journal of Accounting and Public Policy*, *31*(4), 374–398. doi:10.1016/j.jaccpubpol.2012.06.001

Hail, L., Leuz, C., & Wysocki, P. (2010). Global accounting convergence and the potential adoption of IFRS by the US (Part I): Conceptual underpinnings and economic analysis. *Accounting Horizons*, *24*(3), 355–394. doi:10.2308/acch.2010.24.3.355

Hibbard, R. L., II. (2012). *Global Implementation of IFRS*. University of Tennessee Honors Thesis Projects. Retrieved June 26, 2015 from: http://trace.tennessee.edu/utk_chanhonoproj/1485

Hopwood, A. G. (1994). Some reflections on 'The harmonization of accounting within the EU'. *European Accounting Review*, *3*(2), 241–254.

Istvánfyová, J., Mejzlik, L., & Pelak, J. (2010). Progression of Financial Reporting in Czech Republic and its Regulation. *European Financial and Accounting Journal*, *5*(1), 64–77.

Jindrichovska, I., Kubickova, D., & Kocmanova, S. (2014). The development of accounting and application of IFRS in the Czech Republic. *Accounting and Management Information Systems*, *13*(2), 198–235.

Komlos, J. (2015). How Natural Is the Natural Rate of Unemployment? *Challenge*, *8*(2), 160–167. doi:10.1080/05775132.2015.998151

Liu, C., Yao, L. J., Hu, N., & Liu, L. (2011). The impact of IFRS on accounting quality in a regulated market: An empirical study of China. *Journal of Accounting, Auditing & Finance*.

Márquez-Ramos, L. (2011). European accounting harmonization: consequences of IFRS adoption on trade in goods and foreign direct investments. *Emerging Markets Finance and Trade, 47*(sup4), 42-57.

Mullerova, L., Pasekova, M., & Kubickova, D. (2010). Analysis of Differences in Reporting According to IFRS in SMEs in the Czech Republic and its influence on Performance. *ACTA VŠFS*, (2), 106-125.

Nobes, C., & Parker, R. (2012). *Comparative International Accounting* (12th ed.). Pearson Education Limited. Retrieved from: https://www.kpmg.com/CZ/cs/IssuesAndInsights/ArticlesPublications/Factsheets/Documents/KPMG-Investment-in-the-Czech-Republic-2014.pdf

Pasekova, M. (2012). *Implementace IFRS do malých a středních podniků* [Implementation of IFRS in small and medium enterprices]. Prague: Wolters Kluwer.

Pasekova, M., Bialic-Davendra, M., Müllerová, L., Hvastová, J., Manova, E., Sowa, B., & Cizevska, L. (2010). IFRS for SMES: Current issues in reporting of SMES in the Czech Republic, Slovak Republic, Poland and Ukraine. In *Proceedings of the 5th International Conference, Accounting and Management Information Systems (AMIS 2010)*. Editura Ase.

Prochazka, D. (2014). The IFRS as Tax Base: Potential Impact on a Small Open Economy. *European Financial and Accounting Journal*, *9*(4), 59–75.

Prochazka, D. & Ilinitchi, C. P. (2011). The Theoretical Relationships among Foreign Direct Investments, Migration and IFRS Adoption. *European Financial and Accounting Journal, 2011*(4), 85-100.

Prochazka, D., & Ilinitchi, C. P. (2012). Is any connection between the IFRS adoption and foreign direct investments/migration? *AMIS*, *2012*, 903–917.

Prochazka, D., & Pelak, J. (2015). Impact of IFRS Adoption on Capital Markets of the New EU Countries. In *Finance and Performance of Firms in Science, Education and Practice*. Zlín: T. Bata University, FAME. Retrieved from: http://ufu.utb.cz/konference/sbornik2015.pdf)

Schroll, R. (1995). The new accounting system in the Czech Republic. *European Accounting Review*, *4*(4), 827–832. doi:10.1080/09638189500000052

Stiglitz, J. E. (2002). *Globalization and its Discontents*. New York.

Stiglitz, J. E. (2010). *Freefall: America, free markets, and the sinking of the world economy*. WW Norton & Company.

Strouhal, J. (2011). *Harmonization of SME's Financial Reporting in Emerging CEE Countries* (1st ed.). Wisconsin: WSEAS.

Sucher, P., & Jindrichovska, I. (2004). Implementing IFRS: a case study of the Czech Republic. *Accounting in Europe*, *1*, 109–141.

Taylor Zarzeski, M. (1996). Spontaneous harmonization effects of culture and market forces on accounting disclosures practices. *Accounting Horizons*, *10*(1).

Thorell, P., & Whittington, G. (1994). The harmonization of accounting within the EU: Problems, perspectives and strategies. *European Accounting Review*, *3*(2), 215–240. doi:10.1080/09638189400000019

Zarova, M. (2008). Accounting Reform in the Czech Republic. In R. W. McGee (Ed.), *Accounting Reform in Transition and Developing Economies* (pp. 89–100). Miami, FL: Springer.

Zarova, M., & Mejzlik, L. (2009). Have IFRS Positive Impact on the Regulatory Accounting Systems in Continental European Countries? *European Financial and Accounting Journal*, *2009*(1), 5-24.

Zarova, M., Prochazka, D., & Roe, J. (2010). *Financial reporting and management in Central and Eastern Europe*. Praha: Nakladatelství Oeconomica.

ADDITIONAL READING

Bailey, D. (1995). Accounting in transition in the transitional economy. *European Accounting Review*, *4*(4), 595–623. doi:10.1080/09638189500000042

Bohusova, H. (2008). *Harmonizace účetnictví a aplikace IAS/IFRS: vybrané IAS/IFRS v podmínkách českých podniků* [Accounting harmonization and applications of IAS/IFRS]. Prague: ASPI.

Bohusova, H., Nerudova, D., & Svoboda, P. (2013). *Konvergence systémů IFRS a US GAAP pro vznik jediného systému finančního výkaznictví* [Convergence of IFRS and US GAAP systems for creation of united system of financial reporting]. Brno: Policy Research Center.

Bonaci, C. G., Matis, D., & J. Strouhal (2008). Financial reporting paradigms for financial instruments: Empirical study on the Czech and Romanian regulations. *Journal of international trade law and policy*, *7*(2), 101-122.

Borker, D. R. (2012). Accounting, Culture and Emerging Economies: IFRS in Central and Eastern Europe. *International Business and Economics Research Journal*, *11*(9), 1003–1018.

Efobi, U., Iyoha, F., & Mukoro, D. (2011). *IFRS Adoption and Foreign Investment in Africa: Institutions also Matter.* Retrieved April 26, 2015 from: http://ssrn.com/abstract=2492235

Horvatova, E., & Pilch, C. (2013). Behavior investors on financial markets, In Finacial Management of firms and finacial institutions, Proceedings, Part II, Ostrava, ČR: VŠB Ostrava, Economic faculty, 675-680.

Jindrichovska I. (2011). *Transformation of Czech Financial and Capital Markets at the Break of the New Millenium, Study of the Czech Financial Environment*, Saarbrucken, Německo: LAP Lambert-academic-publishing.

Larson, R. K., & Street, D. L. (2004). Convergence with IFRS in an expanding Europe: Progress and obstacles identified by large accounting firms' survey. *Journal of International Accounting, Auditing & Taxation, 13*(2), 89–119. doi:10.1016/j.intaccaudtax.2004.09.002

Mackevicius, J., Strouhal, J., & Zverovich, S. (2008). Comparative analysis of the national accounting standards of the Czech Republic and Lithuania. *European Financial and Accounting Journal, 3*(4), 22–44.

Mejzlik, L., & Zarova, M. (2009). *Impact of IFRS Implementation on the Architecture of the Regulatory Accounting System in the Czech Republic*, In: Proceedings of EAA - 32nd Annual Congress. Tampere: EAA.

Nerudova, D. (2009). *Harmonizace účetních standardů pro malé a střední podniky* [Harmonization of accounting standards for small and medium sized enterprises]. Prague: Wolters Kluwer.

Prochazka, D. (2010). The Development of Financial and Management Accounting After the IFRS Adoption: A Case from the Czech Republic. Retrieved from: SSRN: http://ssrn.com/ abstract=1660122 or10.2139/ssrn.1660122

Prochazka, D. (2012). Výkaz o úplném výsledku hospodaření dle IFRS. [Statement on complete economic result in accordance with IFRS] In: Randakova, M. (ed.). Sborník pedagogické konference Nové požadavky na účetní výkazy v ČR. In: *Proceedings of educational conference New requirements on accounting statements in the Czech Republic*, Prague: Oeconomica Publishers, 79-83.

Prochazka, D. (2013). Proč se novelizují účetní pravidla pro vykazování výnosů [Why are the rules for reporting returns getting novelized]. *Auditor, 20*(2), 17–20.

Seal, W., Sucher, P., & Zelenka, I. (1995). The changing organization of Czech accounting. *European Accounting Review, 4*(4), 659–684. doi:10.1080/09638189500000044

Strouhal, J. (2009). Reporting Frameworks for Financial Instruments in Czech: Czech Accounting Practices versus International Financial Reporting Standards. *WSEAS Transactions on Business and Economics, 6*(7), 352–361.

Strouhal, J. (2011). *Harmonization of SME's Financial Reporting in Emerging CEE Countries. 1. vyd.* Wisconsin: WSEAS.

Struharova, K., Steker, K., & Otrusinova, M. (2010). Challenges and opportunities represented by shift to IFRS in the Czech Republic. In: *Proceedings of the 5th International Conference on Economy and Management Transformation, WSEAS.*

Sucher, P., & Jindrichovska I. (2004). Implementing IFRS: a case study of the Czech Republic. *Accounting in Europe*, No. 1, 109–141.

Zarova M. (2009). Dopad směrnice ES na vykazování účetních informací pro malé a střední podniky, [Impact of the EU regulation on reporting of accounting information for small and medium sized enterprises] *Český finanční a účetní časopis, [Czech financial and accounting journal]* 4(3), 73-77.

Zarova, M. (2013a). Can the Academic Research Contribute to the Legislative Change in Accounting Topics? In: E. Jircikova, A. Knapkova, & E. Pastuszkova (Ed.), *Proceedings of the 6th International Scientific Conference: Finance and the performance of Firms in Science, Education and Practice*, Zlín: Tomáš Baťa University, FAME, 827-836.

Zarova, M. (2013b). Could New Accounting Directive Improve European Financial Reporting? *European Financial and Accounting Journal*, *8*(2), 4–6.

KEY TERMS AND DEFINITIONS

Accounting System: System of rules and principles, which together determine the form of financial statements and the method of their preparation and presentation.

Czech Accounting Standards: A set of rules for maintaining accounting records and preparing financial statements that is based on the historical roots (enshrined in the Law on Accounting and decrees) and adapted to the needs of current stage of development of economic and financial system.

Economic Transformation: A long-term process of changes in national economy of the countries in central and eastern Europe with the aim to rebuilt its institutional and legal basis from the one based on public ownership and central planning, in which the state is dominating, to the one in which the economic activities react and are influenced by market situation.

Effect of IFRS Adoption: Phenomena in various areas of economic, political and social system, which can be reasonably assigned to the fact that some of the companies or all businesses adopted principles of international financial reporting (IFRS).

FDI (Foreign Direct Investment): Capital movement between two or more countries, that are designed to achieve economic return in a non-domestic environment.

Harmonization of Accounting: Process of development and implementation of the system of financial reporting standards that are acceptable for entities reporting in different countries (a process of increasing compatibility of accounting practices by setting bounds to their degree of variation). Harmonization is more than standardization. It includes harmonization of rules and principles, and also the way of their application in practice.

IFRS Adoption: A case when accounting entity prepares financial statements based on principles given by International Financial Reporting Standards (IFRS) and for this purposes keep adequate chart of accounts and performs of measurements of accounting variables.

ENDNOTES

1. Note: Since the Centre for Co-operation with European Economies in Transition was established in 1990 in the OECD.
2. The code law system originated in Roman law and has developed in the majority of continental countries in Europe. It is characterized by a wide set of rules which attempt to give guidance in all situations in the treated area (as opposed to the common law, based on the rules and principles, which develops case by case and which does not prescribe general rules, which could be applied to all cases, used in the Anglo-Saxon countries).

3 In this provision the regulator, the Ministry of Finance, expanded the wording of the Regulation 1606/2002 twofold. This Regulation contains a duty to prepare consolidated financial statements by publicly traded companies. Czech regulator in this case uses the possibility to broaden the scope of entities, which are obliged/allowed to apply the IFRS to prepare the individual (not consolidated) financial statements. The second extension is that the entities are obliged not only to prepare the financial statements, but also to keep accounts in accordance with IAS/IFRS: "entities, which are business companies and which are the issuers of publicly traded securities listed on a regulated market in the member states of the European Union, shall apply the International Accounting Standard as adopted by the EU for keeping their accounts and for preparation of financial statements" (Act on Accounting as amended, § 19, article 9). In this provision the regulator - Ministry of Finance, expanded wording of the Regulation 1606/2002 – also on keeping of accounts according to IAS/IFRS.

Chapter 7
IFRS Adoption in the EU and the Challenge of Nomenclature Evidence from the UK, France, and Germany

Matthias Nnadi
Rivers State University of Science and Technology, Nigeria

Sailesh Tanna
Coventry University, Nigeria

ABSTRACT

Since the adoption of International Financial Reporting Standards (IFRS) and the subsequent directive by the European Union (EU), all companies operating in the EU are required to report their consolidated financial statements in line with the IFRS. This study examines the consolidated financial statements of the top 170 listed companies in three major EU stock exchanges (UK, France and Germany) and uncovered a disparity in the use of common nomenclatures. The findings reveal that the inconsistencies in the application of terminologies such as statement of financial position instead of balance sheet and sequence of arrangement of assets in order of liquidity constitute the main differences for entities operating in the three countries. Such differences pose an imminent challenge in the comparability and interpretation of financial results.

1. INTRODUCTION

Starting from the 2005 financial year[1], all companies listed in the European Union stock markets are required to present their consolidated financial statements in compliance with the IFRS. The endorsement of the IFRS by the European Commission (EC) follows a long process of debate, negotiation and extensive consultation with the European Financial Reporting Advisory Group, a body charged with the enormous responsibility of advising the EC on accounting standards. Thus under this agreement, compliance with the IFRS becomes mandatory rather than optional for all publicly listed firms.

DOI: 10.4018/978-1-4666-9876-5.ch007

The main purpose of enforcement of the IFRS by the EU on companies within its domain is to protect investors and promote market confidence (CESR, 2003). In addition, the adoption of IFRS should improve the international comparability of financial reporting and enhance harmonisation. However, if the implementation of the Standard is perceived to be non-value creating to European shareholders, then the purpose of adopting IFRS will be self-defeating. Hence, the road to convergence of nation members' accounting systems into a harmonised form through the adoption of IFRS can be quite challenging (Alp & Ustundag, 2007). The major challenge is the implementation of the Standards such that all member nations freely accept the legal and professional obligations to comply wholly, rather than their domestic national standards (Wong, 2004). Such compliance will be reflected in strict adherence to the provisions and guidelines of the IFRS, with punitive measures put in place to ensure compliance and discourage dissidence by firms.

Prior research in the harmonisation of EU accounting practices, particularly in the UK, France and Germany, has focused on differences in methods of stock valuation; depreciation; treatments of goodwill; research and development; valuation of fixed assets; and treatment of extraordinary or exceptional items of listed companies in the three countries (Emenyonu & Gray, 1992; Kvaal & Nobes, 2010). In essence, these studies examined the pattern of usage of assets and profit measurement practices by large companies in France, Germany and the UK. Their findings indicate significant differences in the measurement and treatment of a number of key items among the three countries. The differences confirm the assertion that the measurement provisions of the EC Fourth Directive (Nobes, 2010) are inherently flexible.

In fact, the adoption of the IFRS since 2005 does not in itself give a blanket assurance that all companies in the EU countries will implement the Standards as required. As noted by Christensen & Nikolaev (2008) and Chen et al (2014), countries may still be influenced by their traditional GAAP practices rather than follow the dictates of the IFRS and listed companies in the EU may be influenced by general accounting conservatism in their country of operation or incorporation. Thorell and Whittington (1994) observe that although French and German accounting reporting traditions reflect the EU format, they have different rules for the balance sheet and the profit and loss account. They require detailed statutory prescription of formats, disclosures and options to meet the needs of divergent national regulation and practice. The differences in the accounting system of the three countries are even more apparent in the extent of their requirements in disclosing important items. For instance, whilst France and UK have similar strict regulations on environmental disclosure, Germany offers a distinctively different and less stringent requirement (Barbu et al, 2014). Such national influence on accounting reporting requirement is apparent in the application of the IFRS among the respective countries (Nobes, 2006), despite signing up to a global and regional compliance.

According to Nobes (2006), differences in financial reporting between the UK and Germany are palpable and significant; and such differences reflect the purpose of their preparation and use. For instance, published accounts of German companies are used for fiscal purposes and require strict emphasis on historical costs, as increases in asset values lead to a higher tax charge. In addition, a significant proportion of the shares of large German listed companies is held through the intermediation of banks and other large companies, some of which have representatives on their boards of directors.

Furthermore, while assets impairment is tax deductible in Germany, this is not allowable in the UK. In contrast, the UK GAAP places greater importance on investors by its emphasis on reporting to the shareholders who have no other direct source of information about the company except for those disclosed in financial statements. Since investors' protection measures are considered to be high in English Common Law according to La Porta et al (2000), companies operating in UK are under a greater obligation for more disclosure to investors than in France and Germany.

Although IFRS does not prescribe a particular format for reporting financial statements, the choice in style for reporting these statements and valuing inventories vary greatly among the EU countries. For instance the UK uses FIFO in stock valuation, while Germany favours weighted average method. The two methods have tax implications in the both countries (Kesti, 2005). In addition, German firms are more likely to write off goodwill than French firms. Both practices will have a significant impact on the financial results.

Irrespective of the aforementioned differences, the adoption of the IFRS by the EU implies that all companies in the economic region are required to adhere closely to the guidelines on reporting their consolidated statements, which will include the use of uniform terminologies, similarities in the arrangements of items in financial reports, as well as all required disclosures. In this paper, we examine the challenges of uniformity in accounting nomenclatures of 270 listed companies based in the UK, France and Germany is used to evaluate the extent of congruence and uniformity in the use of terminologies and arrangement of items in the financial statements.

2. REVIEW OF LITERATURE

2.1 Discrepancies in Adoption: A Historical and Ongoing Perspective

The difference in the accounting regulations among the three countries is observable in their application of the EU Economic Commission Directives on consolidated accounting guidelines. Emenyonu and Gray (1992) noted that the 1983 measurement provisions, which were incorporated in the 7th EC Directive, were implemented in different years by the three countries. The UK was the last to implement the directive in 1989; France implemented it in 1986 and Germany in 1985. The staggered implementations could explain the slow pace of application of the relevant IFRS by firms operating within EU borders as directed by the EC. In addition, there are also significant variations in the extent of disclosure requirements among the countries.

Parker (1996) compared the notes to the accounts of UK and French companies and observed that while UK companies are required to provide one set of notes to accompany both the financial statements of the parent company and those of the group, French companies with subsidiaries are obliged to provide two notes: one for the parent company accounts and another for the consolidated accounts. Similar observations have been made of the UK and German accounting systems. Christensen, Lee and Walker (2007) observed that if the perceived net benefit of IFRS adoption is at least partly determined by extent of accounting measurement and disclosures which are unlikely to be identical for Germany and the UK, due to their institutional differences. Some accounting principles may be less applicable to the UK than Germany, as both countries differ in their approach to accounting regulations. The UK Common Laws are more akin to the IFRS in comparison with Germany.

The non-harmonisation in accounting reporting before the adoption of IFRS among EU countries has been well documented in accounting studies. Hoogendoorn (1996) studied accounting and taxation treatments among thirteen European countries and observed that only Netherlands and Norway bear some similarities in the treatments. Despite the general adoption of IFRS by all EU countries, differences in the inherent accounting traditions of member countries cannot be totally ignored; and such differences can have a substantial influence on their reporting and financial results. Brown and Tarca (2007) observe that differences within and between countries may affect the level of gap in their financial reporting. The observation supports the assertion of Fields, Lys & Vincent (2001) that firms choose accounting policies in response to a series of administrative, business and country-level inducements which predicate their needs. Such needs are institutional infrastructures upon which the accounting standards are laid and thus reflects the need of the country (Chen et al, 2014).

Some aspects of the IFRS were adopted by some EU companies only three years after the IASB and EU directives. Across the companies sampled, the following sections of the Standards were reluctantly adopted:

1. **IFRS 8:** Operating Segments, which replaces IAS 14 (Segment Reporting). The Standard specifies how an entity should report information about its operating segments, based on information relating to the components of the entity that management uses to make important business decisions.
2. **IFRS 10:** Interim Financial Reporting and Impairment, which replaces IAS 36 and 39[2] (Impairment of Assets and Financial Instruments: Recognition and Measurement). The Standard sets out the treatment of any impairment losses recognised in an interim annual report in respect of goodwill (IAS 36) and other financial assets (IAS 39).
3. **IFRS 11:** Group and Treasury Share Transaction, which replaces (Share-based Payment). The Standard provides for a share-based payment arrangement in which an entity receives goods and services as a form of payment for its own equity instruments. It also addresses issues relating to share-based payments regarding transactions with the parents company, whether such a settlement should be treated as cash or equity settlements.
4. **IFRS 12:** Service Concession Arrangement. The Standard provides guidance on service concession arrangements where a public enterprise offers contracts for the supply of public services to a private enterprise.

The above illustrate the reluctance by some of the EU companies to comply immediately with the Directive. Although the implementation of the Standards was due to take effect at the end of 2006, some listed companies did not adopt these Standards until 2009. The reluctance of some companies in the three countries to fully implement the IFRS also raises questions about the ability of the EU compliance machinery to monitor and enforce compliance. A loose compliance signals weakness in the regulatory machinery and threatens the quest for harmonisation of financial Standards in the region. In the next section, we draw attention to some of the key differences between the IFRS and US GAAP to offer an explanation for the 'loose compliance' among some EU countries.

The gains of adoption are quite numerous in the long-run but there are some areas of uncertainty, so firms must be appropriately cautious in applying the Standards. Francis et al. (2004) examined the relationship between earnings attributes and the implied cost of equity, and found that a lower quality of information is associated with a higher cost of capital. This implies that the extent of disclosure as required under the IFRS will have an impact on the financial results of firms. Dargenidou, Mcleay, and Raonic (2006) also used a sample of European companies to test how the change from local GAAP to international accounting affected the estimated cost of capital. They concluded that such a change has a significant impact on the financial results of firms adhering strictly to the Standards.

2.2 Issue of Nomenclature

The IFRS created a new system of classification which differentiates it from the US GAAP and other national standards. The adoption of the IFRS, therefore, implies that all companies in the EU have to follow the IFRS system of nomenclature in their financial statements. The Standards outline assets to be arranged in their order of liquidity instead of solidity in the consolidated financial statements.[3]

Under the IFRS, the profit and loss account statement becomes the income statement and the statement of financial position replaces the balance sheet. The title 'income statement' better conveys the idea of the content of the financial report, as it does not solely focus on whether profit or loss has been made but chronicles all incomes earned and expenses incurred during the period by a firm. In the same vein, the 'statement of financial position' conjures more the state of affairs of a company's assets, liabilities and equity. Though the wisdom of inventing new nomenclature has remained unquestioned in accounting literature, it does however, pose a challenge for companies to comply. Most companies in the EU have either inconsistently applied the new nomenclature or are still at the bottom end of the learning curve of using the terminologies since its adoption in the EU.

The IFRS guideline for arranging current assets is the direct opposite of the US GAAP style. The IFRS suggests that current assets need to be arranged in descending order of liquidity with bank, cash and cash equivalents positioned at the bottom of the current assets. In contrast, the US GAAP requires the current assets to be arranged in ascending order of liquidity. With bank, cash and cash equivalents are placed on top of the current assets list, and more solid assets at the bottom. The term non-current assets is preferred to fixed assets, creditors to payables, debtors to receivables and stock to inventory in the IFRS. Other terminologies include non-controlling interest instead of minority interest, earnings before interest and tax instead of profit before interest and tax.

3. DATA AND METHOD

Data for the study is collected from three leading stock markets of the UK, Germany and France. Our sample comprise of top capitalised companies listed in the UK FTSE, France CAC and Germany DAX. The companies are from different industries and their financial statements are available online with periods covering from 2005 to 2014. The sample from each stock market comprises of 100 from the FTSE, 40 from CAC and 30 from DAX.

Another set of 130 companies was taken as control sample from the US stock markets, comprising of 100 from S&P and 30 from the Dow Jones respectively. The top capitalised companies were selected in the survey as they are known to influence accounting and financial policy and disclosure (Meek, Roberts & Gray, 2005). Large companies are more likely to be affected by differences between the IFRS and their respective national GAAP (Stenka, Ormrod & Chan, 2008). Thus, the sample selection is appropriate for examining the level of application.

We use summative content analysis technique to examine each financial statement of the 170 companies in our sample. Our focus is to determine the level of harmonisation and compliance by companies in the three countries in the use of terminologies suggested by the IASB. The technique involves comparisons of keywords, contents and interpretation of the underlying context (Hsieh & Shannon, 2005; Samra, Bottle & Ayim, 2015).

The content analysis examines the arrangement of items in the financial statements of EU members, and the application of common terminologies. We compare our results with the arrangement of similar items in the US companies listed in Dow Jones and S&P. Our findings reveal significant difference among EU countries in the arrangement and use of accounting nomenclature. However, the US listed firms are consistent in the application of both terminologies and arrangement of items in financial statements.

We also examine the discrepancies in the adoption of the IFRS as directed by EC and the challenges of harmonisation based on differences in nomenclature among the three EU countries (UK, France and Germany). In particular, differences in use of terminologies and arrangement of items in the financial statements by companies are identified and examined. The content analysis carefully examines companies' level of adherence to the IFRS. Specifically, we examine the consistency in the presentation of current assets in their order of liquidity and the use of such terminologies as income statement (as against profit and loss account), statement of financial position (as against balance sheet) and other nomenclature as suggested by the IFRS.

4. DISCUSSION OF FINDING

However, the extent of arranging these items has remained quite inconsistent among EU companies. Of the 270 companies' financial statements surveyed, 68% comply with the descending order of liquidity in their statement of financial position or balance sheet; while the remaining 32% still adhere to the old format or the US GAAP. The nomenclatural and categorisation challenge still remains obvious as 73% of EU companies in the sample are yet to change from title of 'balance sheet' to 'statement of financial position'. Only 27% companies have changed from the term 'balance sheet' to 'statement of financial position' and most are yet to replace 'fixed assets' with 'non-current assets'. The level of application varies among the three EU countries surveyed. Table 1 summarises the percentage of application by firms listed in FTSE (UK), CAC (France) and DAX (Germany).

The application of the some of the changes in nomenclature remains the least complied across the countries. Most companies follow the IFRS format in the order of liquidity in their current assets, with France being the most compliant in both the order of liquidity and nomenclature. German companies are the least complaint with the IFRS format of descending order of liquidity, but better than the UK companies in following the correct nomenclature - such as the change from balance sheet to statement of financial position. The majority of UK companies still favour the term 'balance sheet' rather than 'statement of financial position'.

Table 1. Level of IFRS Application by listed companies in UK, France and Germany

Country	Order of Liquidity		Application with Nomenclature	
	Percentage of Application %	Non-Application %	Percentage of Application %	Non-Application %
UK (FTSE)	75	25	12	88
France (CAC)	86	14	43	57
Germany (DAX)	67	33	17	83
S&P	98	2	100	-
Dow Jones	100	-	100	-

The reluctance of some EU companies to adopt the new terminology of statement of financial position puts a question mark on the essence of change by IASB. If IFRS compliant countries still struggle to imbibe such changes, it becomes very instructive to retain the old term - balance sheet - in alliance with the US GAAP. Interestingly, 100% of listed companies on the US Dow Jones and S&P consistently use the term 'balance sheet' and 98% of listed firms in the S&P maintain the ascending order of liquidity in their financial statements. Such consistency is lacking among EU firms, a situation which may portray the EU enforcement as weak and threaten the essence of a global and harmonised accounting system as canvassed by IASB.

An average of 76% of the top capitalised companies across the three countries still retains and prefers the use of 'balance sheet'. The preference for the balance sheet instead of the 'statement of financial position' is overwhelming and encourages the reinstatement of the terminology. Although French listed companies apply the new terminologies more than in the UK and Germany, 57% of companies in the CAC still use the old terminology. In general, French companies comply more closely with both the order of current assets arrangement and the use of the appropriate terminology as recommended by IFRS.

As noted by Nobes (2006), IASB tells entities to choose accounting policies when no other part of the Standard applies. This allows entities freehand to manoeuvre or choose which they prefer. This could lead in creating differences in the application of the Standards. More than few terminologies have created opportunities for such manoeuvring. For instance, IAS 7 which deals with Cash Flow Statements requires reconciling 'cash and cash equivalent' of an entity. Cash equivalent is defined in the Standards as an investment with 'a short maturity of, say, three months'. The word 'say' instead of 'normally' creates some level of ambiguity as it leaves room for manoeuvring. The Portuguese translation of this Standard for instance, omits 'say' which then gives the definition of cash equivalent a slightly different meaning.

In the same vein IAS 41 which deals with government grants describes biological assets which are recognised as income when the grants are 'receivable'. The terms 'receivable' and 'received' are different words which could be applied differently. Some European countries, for example Norway, have preference for 'received' instead of the prescribed term of 'receivable' (Nobes, 2006).

This contrasts with the level of application and compliance observed in the 130 listed companies in the US stock markets in the control sample. This indicates that the US GAAP monitoring machinery is stronger than that in the EU. The majority of US companies are found to adhere to the FASB guidelines on consolidated financial statements terminologies and the order of current assets arrangement.

5. CONCLUSION AND IMPLICATION OF FINDINGS

This paper has sought to examine the consolidated financial statements of top 170 listed companies in three major EU stock exchanges (UK, France and Germany) and revealed the disparity in the use of common nomenclatures as well as the inconsistencies in the application of terminologies required for adoption of the IFRS as endorsed by the EU. The EU plays a key role in the economic activities of European countries and its influence is felt extensively outside Europe. It is, therefore, the most significant harmonizing force of the IFRS among major economies. However, the success of the IFRS harmonization can only be achieved through the implementation of directives and regulations which have been imposed by the EU (Alves &Antunes, 2011).

Although the harmonisation of the IFRS will help in achieving a standardised global financial reporting system, some of its provision may be more stringent for businesses compared with those operating under the US GAAP system. However, while most companies across the three countries in the sample examined adhere strictly to the order of liquidity of current assets, the percentage of non-application in the use of IFRS terminology is overwhelmingly high. For example, the majority of firms prefer 'balance sheet' to the 'statement of financial position'. This indicates that the implementations of the IFRS by EU companies have remained inconsistent and threatens the harmonisation. Jemakkowicz and Gornik (2004) used social survey to examine implementation of (IFRS) among (EU) companies and confirmed that majority of respondent firms have adopted the IFRS for more than just consolidation purposes. In addition, a majority of respondents would not adopt IFRS if not required by the EU Regulation. The complexity of the IFRS, as well as the lack of implementation guidance and uniform interpretation, remains key challenges in accounting harmonisation.

There is however, merit in advocating the retention of balance sheet terminology. The nomenclature is quite traditional and widely popular across the globe. The items contained in the balance sheet are the same as those in the statement of financial position and, therefore, retain the same values. The UK, France and Germany are key influential members of the EU; as such, the preference for balance sheet terminology by firms listed in their stock exchanges will imply a similar preference for listed firms in other EU countries.

In order to overcome these challenges, the EU could ensure adherence to the implementation of the IFRS guidelines by companies through a system of strict and close monitoring of listed firms' consolidated financial statements. If a strong adherence to the IFRS is achieved, the attainment of harmonisation becomes more feasible.

REFERENCES

Alp, A., & Ustundag, S. (2007). Financial reporting, transformation: Experience of Turkey. *Critical Perspectives on Accounting*, 2–17.

Alves, M., & Antunes, E. (2011). International Accounting Standards in Europe: A Comparative Study. *International Research Journal of Finance and Economics*, *61*, 64–73.

Barbu, E. M., Dumontier, P., Feleaga, N., & Feleaga, L. (2014). Mandantory environment disclosures by companies complying with IASs/IFRSs: The cases of France, Germany and the UK. *The International Journal of Accounting*, *49*(2), 231–247. doi:10.1016/j.intacc.2014.04.003

Brown & Tarca. (2007). A Commentary on Issues Relating to the Enforcement of International Financial Reporting Standards in the EU. *European Accounting Review*, *14*(1), 181–212.

CESR-The Committee of European Securities Regulations (2003). *Standard nº1 on Financial Information – Enforcement of Standards on Financial Information in Europe*. Author.

Chen, C. J. P., Ding, Y., & Xu, B. (2014). Convergence of accounting standards and foreign direct investment. *The International Journal of Accounting*, *49*(1), 53–86. doi:10.1016/j.intacc.2014.01.007

Christensen, H., & Nikolaev, V. (2008). *Who uses fair value accounting for non-financial assets after IFRS adoption?* University of Chicago, Booth School of Business, working paper, No 09-12.

Christensen, H. B., Lee, E., & Walker, M. (2007). Cross-sectional variation in the economic consequences of international accounting harmonization: The case of mandatory IFRS adoption in the UK. *The International Journal of Accounting*, *42*(4), 341–379. doi:10.1016/j.intacc.2007.09.007

Dargenidou, C., Mcleay, S. & Raonic, I. (2006). *Expected Earnings Growth and the Cost of Capital: An Analysis of Accounting Regime Change in the European Financial Market*. Academic Press.

Emenyonu, E. N., & Gray, S. J. (1992). EC Accounting Harmonisation: An Empirical Study of Measurement Practices in France, Germany and the UK. *Accounting and Business Review*, *23*(89), 49–58. doi: 10.1080/00014788.1992.9729860

Field, T., Lys, T., & Vincent, L. (2001). Empirical research on accounting choice. *Journal of Accounting and Economics*, *31*(1-3), 255–307. doi:10.1016/S0165-4101(01)00028-3

Francis, J., LaFond, R., Olsson, P., & Schipper, K. (2004). Costs of equity and earnings attributes. *Accounting Review*, *7*(4), 967–1010. doi:10.2308/accr.2004.79.4.967

Hoogendoorn, M. N. (1996). Accounting and taxation in Europe-A comparative overview. *European Accounting Review*, *5*(sup1), 783–794. doi:10.1080/09638189600000050

Hsieh, H., & Shannon, S. E. (2005). Three approaches to qualitative content analysis. *Qualitative Health Research*, (Nov): 15, 1277–1288. PMID:16204405

Jemakowicz, E. K., & Gornik, T. S. (2004). Implementing IFRS from the perspective of EU publicly traded companies. *Journal of International Accounting, Auditing & Taxation*, *15*(2), 170–192. doi:10.1016/j.intaccaudtax.2006.08.003

Kesti, J. (2005) Germany in European Tax Handbook. Amsterdam: International Bureau of Fiscal Documentation. Part A.1.3.4.

Kvaal, E., & Nobes, C. (2010). International differences in IFRS policy choice: A research note. *Accounting and Business Review*, *40*(2), 173–187. doi:10.1080/00014788.2010.9663390

La Porta, R., Florenico, L., Shleifer, A., & Vishny, R. W. (2000). Agency problems and dividend policies around the world. *The Journal of Finance*, *55*(1), 1–33. doi:10.1111/0022-1082.00199

Meek, G. K., Roberts, C. B., & Gray, S. J. (2005). Factors Influencing Voluntary Annual Report Disclosures by U.S., U.K. and Continental European Multinational Corporations. *Journal of International Business Studies*, *26*(3), 555–572. doi:10.1057/palgrave.jibs.8490186

Nobes, C. (2006). The survival of international differences under IFRS: Towards a research agenda. *Accounting and Business Review*, *36*(3), 233–245. doi:10.1080/00014788.2006.9730023

Parker, R. H. (1996). Harmonising the notes in the UK and France: A case study in de jure harmonisation. *European Accounting Review*, *5*(2), 317–337. doi:10.1080/09638189600000019

Samra, R., Bottle, A., & Aylin, P. (2015). Monitoring patient safety in primary care: An exploratory study using in-depth semistructured interviews. *BMJ Open*, *5*(9), e008128. doi:10.1136/bmjopen-2015-008128 PMID:26362663

Stenka, R., Ormrod, P., & Chan, A. (2008) *Accounting for business combinations – the consequences of IFRS adoption for UK listed entities*. Working paper, SSRN.

Thorell, P., & Whittington, G. (1994). The harmonization of accounting within the EU Problems, perspectives and strategies. *European Accounting Review*, *3*(2), 215–239. doi:10.1080/09638189400000019

Wong, P. (2004). *Challenges and Successes in Implementing International: Standards Achieving Convergence to IFRSs and IASs*. IFAC -International Federation of Accountants.

Zeff, S. A. (2002). Political Lobbying on Proposed Standards: A Challenge to the IASB. *Accounting Horizons*, *16*(1), 43–54. doi:10.2308/acch.2002.16.1.43

ENDNOTES

1 Certain international conglomerates, listed in US markets and trading on debt securities were given an extended compliance period, no later than the 2007 financial year.

2 There were controversies surrounding the initial adoption of IAS 32 and IAS 39. However the Standards were endorsed at end of 2004 financial year, and compliance and implementation were to be immediate. The delay by listed companies in the UK, France and Germany may be explained by the reluctance with which the EU adopted these sections of the IFRS. The controversies surrounding the adoption of IAS 32 and 39 are not within the scope of this study.

3 The IFRS as a principle based standards does not mandate entities to follows the individual standards with precision. Our paper however examines whether firms operating within the EU consistently apply the principles in the same way, and the extent to which the differences can affect the comparability in their financial results.

Chapter 8
IFRS Adoption in Poland in the Light of Empirical Research

Konrad Grabiński
Cracow University of Economics, Poland

Marcin Kędzior
Cracow University of Economics, Poland

Joanna Krasodomska
Cracow University of Economics, Poland

ABSTRACT

The aim of this chapter is to present Polish experience of the IFRS adoption process. The first part characterizes a cultural background of the Polish society. Using Hofstede and Inglehart cultural dimensions Poland is compared to other European countries. The impact of time on national culture is taken into consideration as well as its influence on financial reporting. The authors believe that the culture has a profound impact on the accounting practice and, therefore it can impede or ease the process of the IFRS adoption. In the second part the history of Polish accounting is presented as well as the evolution of an accounting regulatory framework. A special emphasis is put on the scope of the IFRS application in Poland and the issue of IFRS vs. Polish GAAP comparability. The last and the most extensive part is devoted to the positive and negative consequences of the IFRS application in Poland from the perspective of empirical research.

1. INTRODUCTION

Poland is one of the biggest post-communist countries in Central Europe. Although after the World War II it was formally an independent state, it remained in the zone of Soviet influences, as other countries of that region. Year 1989 was an important year in the history of Europe. For lots of countries of that region it meant they became independent of the Soviet influences and beginning of political and economic transformations, in majority of cases achieved by peaceful means. Those changes facilitated unification of Germany and began a process of enlargement of the European Union (EU).

DOI: 10.4018/978-1-4666-9876-5.ch008

In the political scope, the countries of that region commenced to build democratic structures, whereas in the economic scope - to create the free market system. For majority of the countries of that region those changes also meant that their economies opened to foreign contacts, trade increase and a greater competition from the part of foreign enterprises. Opening was not easy for domestic enterprises based on the centrally planned economy system. In majority of CEE countries (CEE countries - Central-Eastern Europe countries) the state was an owner of lots of medium and big enterprises before year 1989, only small businesses were left in the private hands. For a great number of the state enterprises, opening of the economy meant lots of problems with selling their products and a necessity of their restructuring, due to lack of competitiveness.

In Poland, the beginning of 90-ies was time of economic problems, bankruptcy of lots of unprofitable state enterprises and privatization of profitable ones. Those changes resulted in unemployment which was a phenomenon unknown previously in the centrally planned communist economy. Economic problem effects also included an inflation phenomenon, piling up social tensions, or structural budget imbalance which limited possibilities of the government. The first years of the transformation were exceptionally difficult what was reflected by the real decrease in the GDP per capita in the first years of the transformations. The Polish state undertook activities simultaneously to form structures and free market institutions. A characteristic feature for Poland which distinguishes it from other countries of that region is a strong development of the capital market - the Warsaw Stock Exchange. The 1990s were a period of building the free market economy. The process was not devoid of mistakes and entailed high social costs.

. Poland like other countries of the region started from a very low economic development level comparing to the developed economies of Western Europe. For an example according to the data of the World Bank in year 1990 GDP per capita of the United States was 14 times higher than Polish one, and GDP per capita of Great Britain almost 11 times higher. Generally GDP per capita of Poland was 2.5 times lower than the world average.

Wide opening of the economy outside and the quick transition to the principles of the free market in the economy were characterized as a shock therapy. In Poland this policy has not been assessed unequivocally so far, first of all, because of high social costs. However, it is a fact that after the transition to the free market principles the Polish economy entered a pathway of high growth after a few years. It can be seen in doubling of the GDP indicators and GDP per capita in Poland in the period between year 1989 and year 2014. For year 2013 GDP per capita of the United States is only 4 times higher than Polish, and GDP per capita of Great Britain only 3 times higher than Polish one. Generally, per capita of Poland is significantly higher than the world average.

In the last 25 years a significant aspect of the Polish economy was a large inflow of direct foreign investments. For example, in 1990, the level of foreign investment inflow to Poland was about 100 million USD. According to the report produced by the United Nations Conference on Trade and Development (UNCTAD), a total of 230 604 million USD flowed into Poland in 2012.

In the last 25 years the most important events were accession of Poland to North Atlantic Treaty Organization (NATO) and the EU. In particular, the last event was the culmination of the long period of the economic transformation. It also enabled to procure the EU structural funds which boost the economic development even more and linked the Polish economy with economies of other EU countries, particularly with the German economy. As it is indicated by the German minister for economy, Sigmar Gabriel, the Germany-Poland trade exchange is greater than the Germany-Russia exchange, or Germany-Japan (Osiński, 2015).

The dynamic change of the economic conditions also constituted a challenge for accounting in Poland, which had to adopt to challenges and needs of the economic life. The accession of Poland to the EU had a great significance in the field of financial reporting. History of Poland in this scope is similar to other countries of this region, as Czech, Slovakia, Hungary, Romania and Bulgaria and others. Those countries have common experiences in the scope of the centrally planned economy and move in the same direction – the free market economy. However, among this group of the countries, Poland is often quoted as an example of the economic success and use of opportunities provided. As far as the IFRS-based financial reporting is concerned Poland definitely belongs to the leaders of the region, owing to the strong capital market. At present at the Warsaw Stock Exchange there are more than 450 companies listed, and lots of them use international regulations in the their financial reporting, In this respect it is a fundamental advantage which differentiates Poland from other countries of the region.

The aim of the chapter is to present and assess the IFRS adoption in Poland. The differences in the implementation of IFRS among countries may result from a number of external circumstances. The chapter discusses the institutional environment and cultural conditions as well as the specific features of the accounting system in Poland. Authors also carry out an extensive review of the results of empirical research related to the IFRS adoption. For economic entities operating in Poland, this was a process of crucial importance, leading primarily to an increase in the comparability of financial statements on an international level. It also turned out to be a long and labour-intensive procedure, especially for smaller companies. The chapter presents the empirical research concerning issues related to the IFRS adoption in Poland, the results of which are of great importance to legislators, financial statement preparers and users. Referring to them in the chapter allows for the practical aspects of this process to be presented to a wider, international audience.

The chapter is organized as follows. The second section discusses cultural determiners in Polish society. In the third section some basic information on financial accounting regulations in Poland is provided. Finally, the fourth, and the most extensive section, presents the results of empirical studies on the IFRS implementation in Poland.

2. CULTURAL CONDITIONINGS OF POLAND ON THE BACKGROUND OF OTHER COUNTRIES

The empirical studies in the scope of a quality of the reported financial result indicate that the standardization process of the financial accounting regulations is only one of the conditions of achieving complete comparability (Leuz, 2003). However, it is not the sufficient condition, other key elements influencing the accounting practice can include the institutional environment and cultural conditionings. The institutional environment is connected with power and independence of the institutions safeguarding the broadly defined public interest. This applies in particular to the public supervision bodies, a quality of the mandatory law and effectiveness of its enforcement what affects directly a legal protection level of individual investors, and also a quality of the ownership supervision system. In this respect a great role is also played by the professional organizations of accountants and certified public auditors which have an influence on the social position of these professions. The second element – cultural conditionings are recognized presently as important determinants of the accounting practice, which influence significantly a quality of the reporting process in the specific country. Both factors – the institutional environment and cultural conditionings – are interconnected and in the empirical research it is very difficult to separate an influence of both elements on the accounting practice.

Schwarz (2006, p. 138) defines culture as a rich and complex set of meanings, beliefs and practices, symbols, standards and values prevailing in the given society. This set should be internally coherent, and particular elements of the culture should support one another. Lack of cohesion of particular elements may lead to the social tensions, and in turn, they should result in eliminating reasons for the tensions. In consequence a culture evolution should cause a development of coherent values and ideals of a specific culture. A manifestation of the most important values for the specific society frequently constitutes the most distinct and characteristic feature of the culture. For example, emphasizing such values as the good work organization in the German society is reflected in lots of aspects of social behavior and the proverbially high quality of German products. In turn, attachment to the free market ideals is changed into high competitiveness in the American society, which in other cultures can be even perceived as an expression of excessive ambition, aggressiveness, or a desire of dominance.

The cultural values determine the evaluation criteria of social behavior, what is good and what bad. They also determine social ideals - what is appropriate for a broadly defined social, cultural or state development. They constitute a justification for activities undertaken and determine a hierarchy of the goals accepted. For example, with reference to the targets set for business entities, there are other expectations of the British, Japanese or German society. Generally, it is assumed that in the case of the British companies the most important target is profitability and maximization of a shareholder value. In the case of the Japanese companies a market position of a company is more important than profitability. In the case of the German companies a significant target of enterprise existence is to provide workplaces. Interestingly, in each society those targets are recognized as convergent with the public interest. Polish economy undergoes a process of dynamic changes, what is also reflected by social attitudes and targets of the business entities. The initial period of the transformation was characterized by profit orientation at any price, maximization of a shareholder value and market survival. Providing workplaces or other social targets were seldom taken into account by management of the business entities.

As a result of opening of the economy outside the foreign capital took over majority of the business entities, including the banking sector. Relatively low labor costs comparing to the economies of Western Europe are the main asset of the Polish economy. It was accompanied by a possibility of procuring well-educated employees. Owing to it the foreign corporations can achieve significant savings. It is manifested clearly by a dynamic development of outsourcing services, and Poland becomes slowly one of the world leaders in this field.

The cultural conditionings, as Schwarz (2006, p. 139) indicates, are a resultant of a social structure, a history of the nation, demographic conditions and a configuration and conditions of the natural environment. For example, traditional societies based on agriculture, such as e.g. the Chinese society has been used to laborious and regular work on the land for a few thousand years. Success, prosperity, and sometimes survival often depended on the weather prevailing in the given year. The environmental conditions have a direct influence on characteristics of the Chinese society, which is recognized as hard working, methodical and peaceable. In turn the nations of northern Europe, such as e.g. the Scandinavian countries, were oriented towards hunting and surviving a hard and long winter. In consequence people living in the north spent seemingly idle a great part of a year, waiting for a spring. However, idleness bore new ideas, inventions, curiosity, undertaking new challenges in a form of crusades, or trade expeditions, which the famous Vikings made. Nowadays the Scandinavian societies are recognized as one of the most innovative in the world, and the corporations from this region as very competitive. Other elements influencing the culture of the country include a geo-political location of the nation and the religion prevailing in the country.

The political location of Poland between two very powerful countries: Germany and Russia, resulted historically in many problems. Experiences of the Polish society are abundant with fighting for independence, and during the occupation, or the partitions are characterized by the underground activity and coping with adversities. In the Polish society those experiences resulted in forming a great distrust for state machinery and the authority, keeping distance towards the law and tendency to act less formally and opportunism to the top-down imposed solutions. On the other hand difficult past formed an ability to cope in the difficult situation, flexibility and high competitiveness.

In the subject literature a disputable issue is durability of the cultural values and their change. It is accepted generally that the cultural value changes in the society is slow, gradual, and in the majority of cases the cultural values and other aspects of the culture are characterized by stability in time. Moreover, each culture affects to a lower to higher degree and is a subject of an influence of other cultural circles. A situation of an isolated culture for a long period of time seldom happens, although such cases occur, as it is in North Korea. As Tang (2008: 1060) indicate, the cultural value change is influenced by economic growth and a level of wealth measured by the GDP per capita. Durability of the cultural values can be reinforced by a strong and stable institutional environment. In the case of Poland these both factors influence the change of the cultural conditioning. As it has been indicated previously, for the last 25-years Poland has been undergoing a phase of a quick transformation and dynamic economic growth what also is transformed into quick enrichment of the society. For over 10 years Poland has been an active member of the EU, what leads to a change of the institutional environment and intensification of trade and social contacts with other cultural circles in the EU. A significant social phenomenon in Poland is also a big wave of emigration of the young generation to other richer EU countries, especially to the United Kingdom and Germany. The young people assimilate values of other cultural circles, and some of them return to their motherland with wealth of experience and other cultural values. Undoubtedly, those factors have an influence on a change of attitudes and cultural values in the Polish society.

The theory of Hofstede, the theory of Schwarz and the theory of Inglehart should be included into the most important theories of the cultural conditionings.

The theory of Inglehart (2001, p.17) postulates two classification groups of the cultural conditionings:

- Traditional vs. secular-rational and
- Survival vs. self-expression

The traditional societies are characterized by a high level of authoritarian, dominance of men in the public life, an attachment to a religion and lack of tolerance for divorces and abortions. The secular-rational societies have totally different characteristics. The Polish society is characterized by the traditional approach. According to the Inglehart-Welzel cultural map of the world, the Polish society is positioned as one of the most traditional European societies (see Figure 1). The cultural values determined here as traditional are resistant to time elapse, at least within the period of the last 20 years. We would expect that according to the theory of Inglehart, Poland would be included into a group of Catholic Europe countries. However, because of its very traditional values it is positioned among the countries of Latin America, close to Argentina and Brazil. It may be connected with the strongly rooted catholic religion in Poland and a figure of pope John Paul II which is important for the history of Poland. It is difficult here to find any rendering on the quality of the financial statements and trace the factors of the implementation of

Figure 1. Traditional vs. secular rational values
Source: The Hofstede Center (2015)

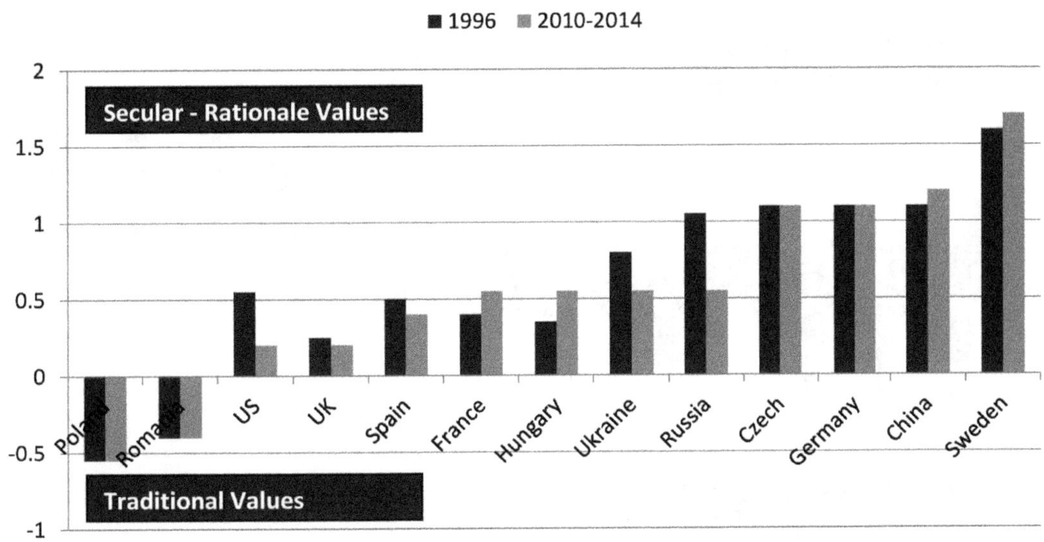

the international regulations. It coincides with the investigation results of Callen and al. (2011, p. 118), who stated that a level of religiousness and the professed religion did not have a direct influence on the accounting practice and earnings quality, particularly on the phenomenon of the earnings management.

Another cultural aspect concerns polarization between the values oriented at materialism and post-materialism, which are included into so called societies oriented at surviving and societies oriented at self-expression, and realization of their needs, respectively. The last group concerns more modern and more economically developed societies, so called post industrial ones, where a survival ability in the economic sense does not constitute a problem. A greater interest in matter of the environment protection, emancipation of women, a greater activity of civil movements and activity in the public life can be observed in that group. Such societies are more oriented at consumption of services and a quality of life than at a purchase of material goods. In a wider scope work of people is connected with communication with other persons and information processing and it is characterized by a greater trust in contacts with other persons. The Scandinavian countries are given as the typical examples of the postindustrial countries.

The societies determined as oriented at surviving - refer to poorer countries where economic survival is not guaranteed, it requires hard work and a daily struggle. In the social contacts, including trading, use of the limited trust principles can be observed. In the case of this dimension a big change can be observed in Poland. In the mid-1990s Poland was classified among the countries where the characteristics appropriate for the survival value dimension were dominant. At present, in the classification being prepared for the period of 2010-2014 Poland inclines slightly more towards the self-expression value dimension (see Figure 2).The main reason for the change may be that fact that the society gets richer and there is an influence of the European integration and contacts of the young generation with their peers from other countries.

The Hofstede cultural dimensions are the most frequently used in the studies of an influence of the cultural factors on accounting practice. It results from the fact that those dimensions refer to the zone of

Figure 2. Survival vs. self-expression values
Source: World Value Survey (2015)

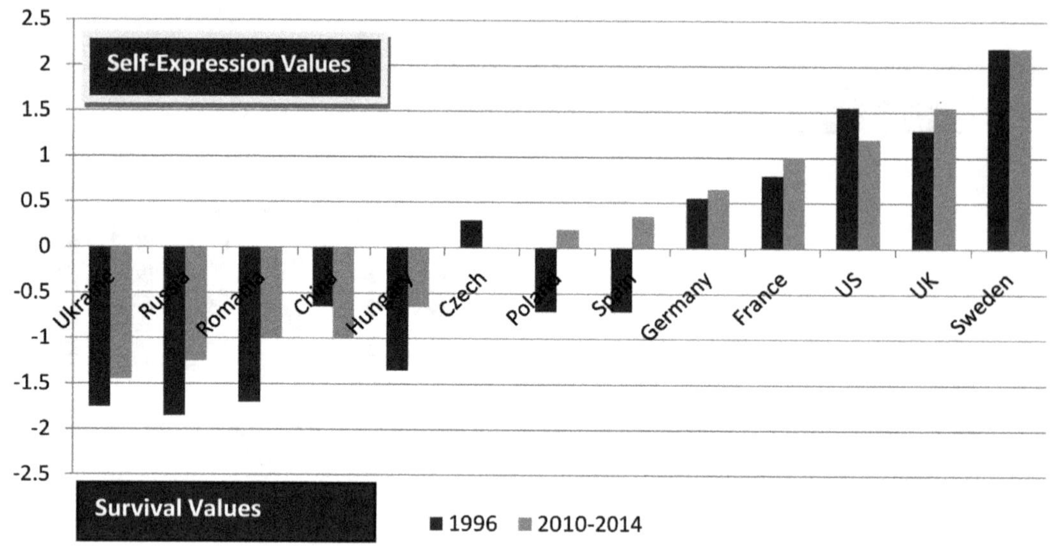

management of economic entities. At present the following six cultural dimensions are distinguished: power distance, individualism, masculinity, uncertainty avoidance, long-term orientation and indulgence.

The power distance determines social acceptance for an unequal division of power. The societies characterized by a high level of the power distance accept existing social hierarchy and do not expect its justification. In the societies of a low level of the power distance individuals try to equate the division of power in the society, and any inequalities in this scope require justification. According to the Hofstede classification (http://geert-hofstede.com/poland.html) the Polish society accepts an unequal division of power, subordinates expect clear instructions from their supervisors, centralization of power is popular, and a friendly autocrat is deemed to be an ideal supervisor. As far as the power distance is concerned Poland does not distinguish itself on the background of other countries, it is at a similar level as France, Czech and Spain (see Figure 3). From the point of view of an implementation of IFRSs, which are based on general principles and professional judgments, a relatively high power distance may cause some problems in implementing international regulations.

Another cultural dimension: *individualism vs. collectivism* determines how an individual defines himself with reference to a society, more individually as 'I', or as 'we'. In the societies characterized by a high level of individualism, individuals take care mainly about themselves and their closest family. In the collective societies an individual takes care about his local society in a wider scope. The Polish society is classified as individualistic (see Figure 4), what means that activities of the individuals are directed at personal benefit, and social welfare is less important. In that regard Poland does not stand out from other countries like Germany, Czech or Spain. The investigation results of Callen and al. (2011, p.118) illustrate that a high level of individualism is correlated negatively with a phenomenon of earnings management. From the point of view of an implementation of IFRSs, which are based on the professional judgment to a higher degree comparing to the Polish regulations, the high level of individualism can have a positive influence on earnings quality.

Figure 3. Power distance in Polish society on the background of other European countries
Source: The Hofstede Center (2015)

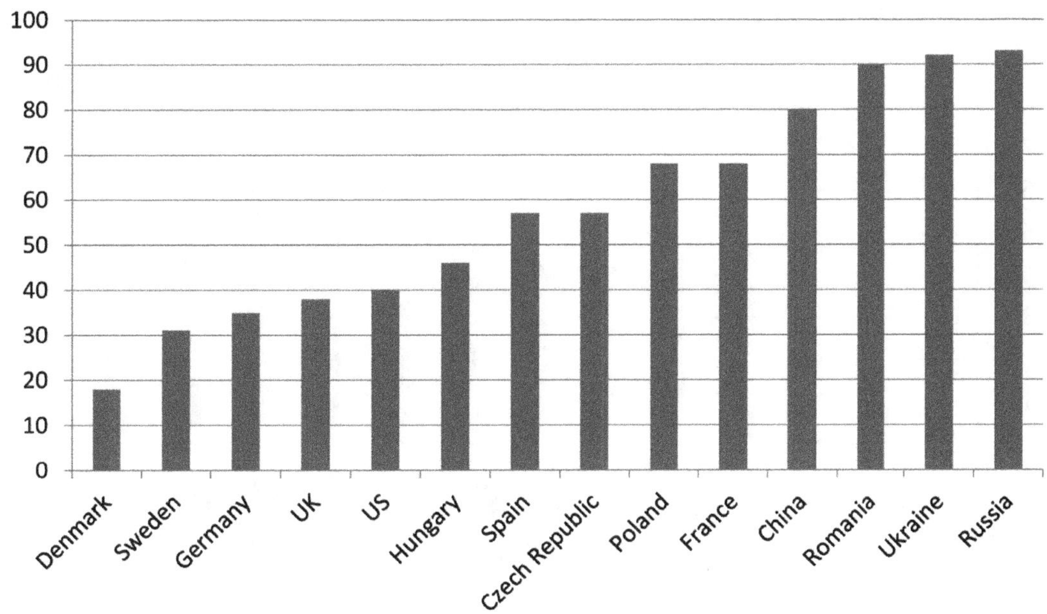

Figure 4. Individualism in Polish society on the background of other European countries
Source: The Hofstede Center (2015)

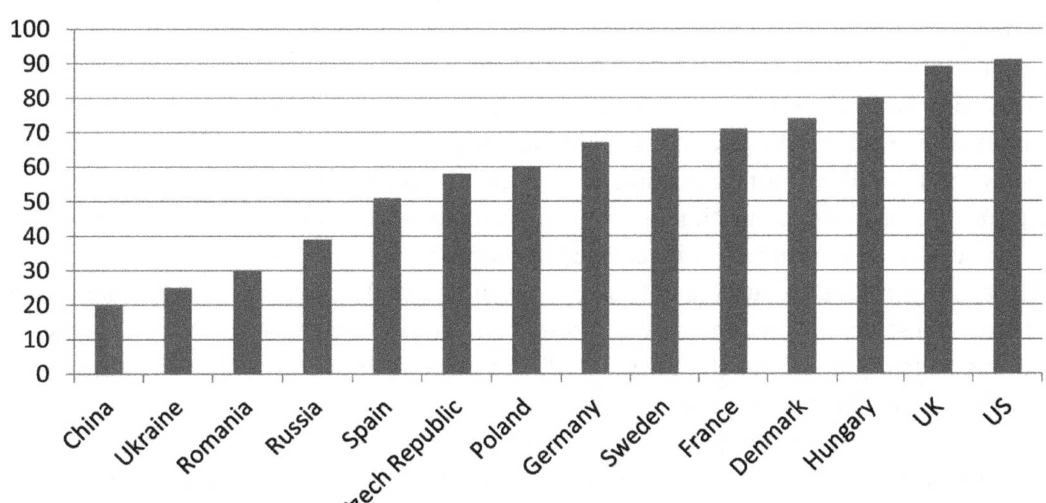

The masculinity dimension determines how social activities can be driven by competitiveness and a need to achieve success, a need to be the best. In turn, low values of this feature means a society in which a quality of life and what you do are a sign of success. The Polish society is a typical masculine society, where you live to work, decisiveness and assertiveness are expected from managers. In this aspect Poland does not differ much from Germany or Czech (see Figure 5).

Figure 5. Masculinity in Polish society on the background of other countries
Source: The Hofstede Center (2015)

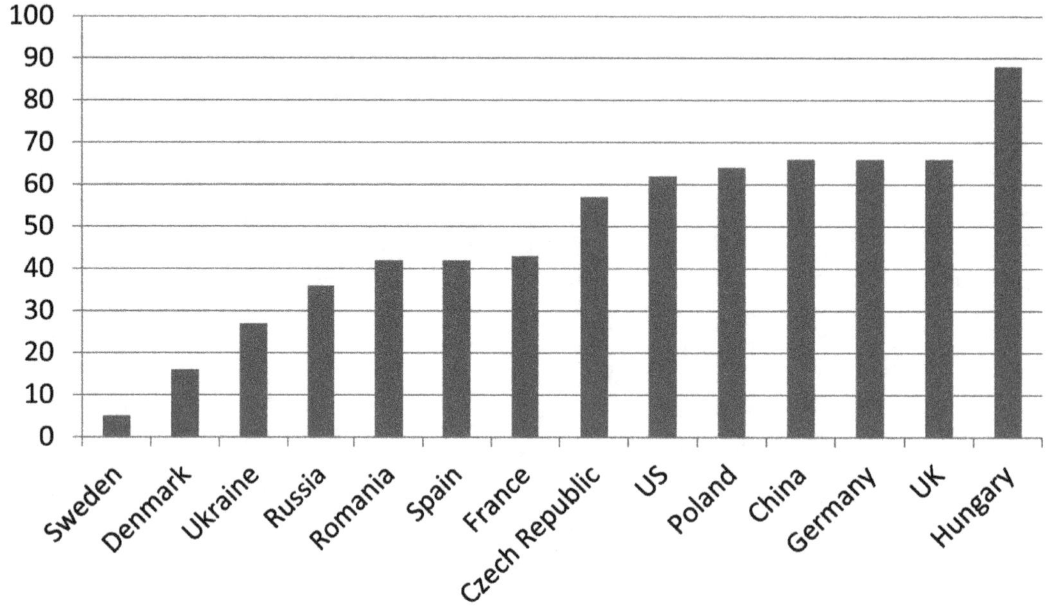

Uncertainty avoidance dimension indicates how members of a society deal with uncertainty, the future which cannot be predicted. The Polish society like the societies of Ukraine and Russia are characterized by a very high level of uncertainty avoidance (see Figure 6). It means that these societies need very detailed regulations to solve uncertain situations. Moreover, they are characterized by lack of tolerance of untypical behavior and try to avoid ambiguous situations at work. They attach a great importance to punctuality, precision, hard work and sense of security. The high level of this feature can limit innovativeness and flexibility. From this point of view the IFRS implementation can be problematic. Its example is arbitrariness of presentation of financial statements according to IFRS, where there is only a general scope of information which is required in the financial statement what is criticized much in Poland. Expectations of the accounts in Poland are to include templates of the financial statement presentation, what would solve the dilemma: how to present a balance-sheet, or a profit and loss account. The investigation results of Callen and al. (2011, p.118) show that the high level of this feature is correlated positively with the earnings management.

The long-term orientation dimension determines how a society maintains bonds with the past while solving current and future problems. The societies characterized by a low level of this feature attach importance to tradition and approach novelty with suspicion. The societies characterized by a high level of this feature use a more pragmatic approach, they rely on the modern education to a higher degree, which can meet challenges of the future. The Polish society shows a great attachment to tradition and is oriented at achieving quick effects (see Figure 7). In this respect the Polish society is closer to the Anglo-Saxon culture. From the point of view of the IFRS implementation it can mean problems which can be perceived suspiciously as a kind of novelty in the financial reporting. Moreover, the IFRS implementation is perceived as a costly process, and positive results are deferred in time.

Figure 6. Uncertainty avoidance in Polish society on the background of other countries
Source: The Hofstede Center (2015)

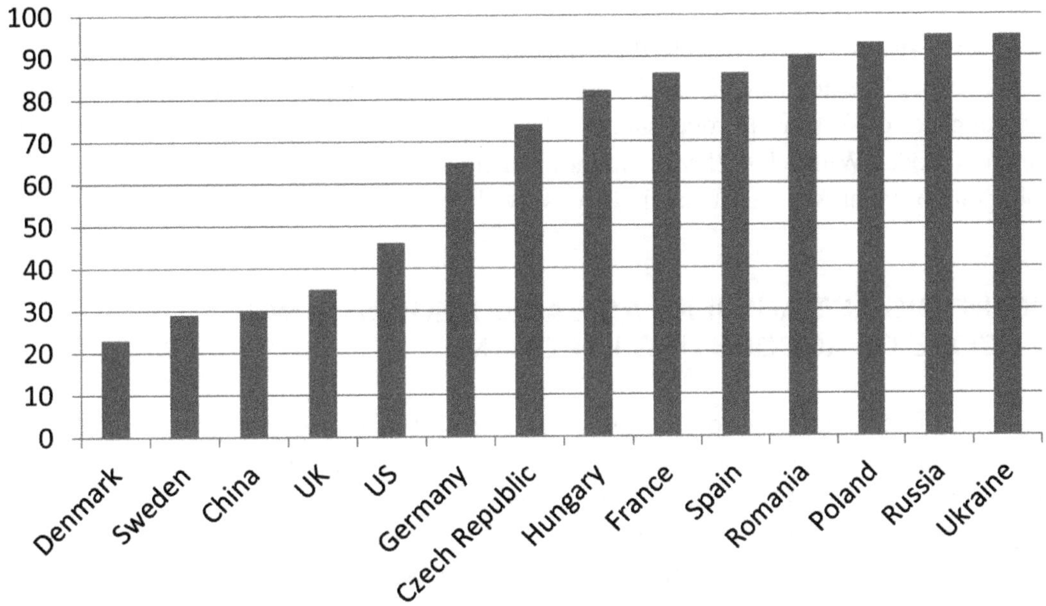

Figure 7. Long-term orientation in Polish society on the background of other countries
Source: The Hofstede Center (2015)

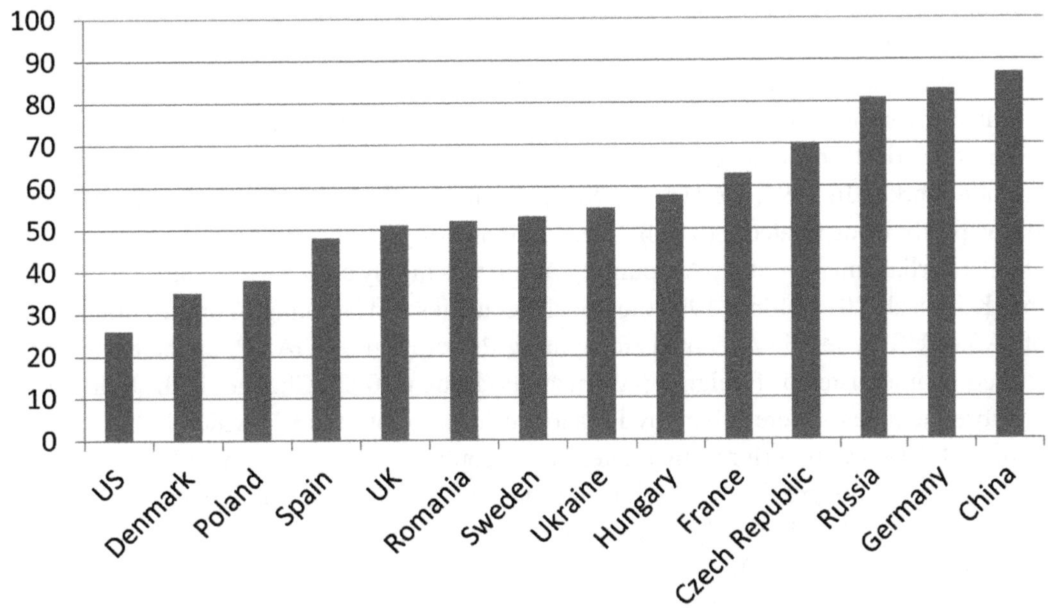

The indulgence dimension describes to what extent members of a society control their desires and drives on basis how they were brought up and formed. A low level of control means a high level of indulgence, and a low level of 'restraint. The Polish society is classified as 'restraint', what means tendency to pessimism and cynicism. In this scope it is difficult to find rendering into the accounting practice, it may result in a higher level of conservatism in accounting. However, this problem has not been dealt in the empirical investigations so far.

On basis of the analysis above it results that Poland is included admittedly in the group of the emerging economies in the CEE region (see Figure 8), however regarding cultural conditionings it is closer to the developed countries of Western Europe, such as Germany, Spain, or France, that is countries classified to a continental model. Within last 25 years cultural changes which are an effect of the economic growth and membership of Poland in the EU could be observed.

3. ACCOUNTING ACT AND IFRS AS BASIC REGULATIONS IN THE SCOPE OF ACCOUNTING IN POLAND

The beginnings of accounting in Poland date back to the XV century, and its evolution is connected closely with the historical events, such as partitions, wars and influences of other countries. The communist system and isolation from Western influence had a great impact on the status and the role of accounting in Poland. In a centrally planned economy, companies were relegated to the role of operating units where the fulfillment of political function was more important than the economic goals (Obloj & Kostera, 1993). The accounting system was perceived as a method of authorities control and a source of statistical information for planning purposes. In the most cases the prices were set artificially and therefore there was little need for information that would aid decision-making. Rather, the accountant was responsible for safeguarding the assets of the enterprise and the reporting of input costs (Vellam 2004). Accountancy chiefly served tax needs, which resulted in the fact that financial statements were audited to suit fiscal requirements (Jaruga et al, 1996).

The year 1989 marked the end of the centrally planned economy and the beginning of a political and economic transformation in Poland. The process of adapting Polish legislation to the requirements of the EU started in the early 1990s and brought the Polish economy closer to the standards, norms and rules of the common market. In 1991, the Warsaw Stock Exchange was established and the 4th Accounting Directive was partly incorporated into Polish legislation (Jaruga et al., 2004).

In 1994, the Parliament passed the Accounting Act. It was highly conservative, and leaned towards tax accounting (Klimczak, 2011). Since 1998 the Polish Securities and Exchange Commission has permitted the use of IAS or US Generally Accepted Accounting Principles (US GAAP) as the basis for financial reporting of companies listed on foreign capital markets (Jaruga, 2002). Changes in the Polish accounting system in subsequent years were driven by Poland's efforts to join the EU which led to the successful accession in 2004. Two years prior to that date, the Accounting Act was amended, with changes made to almost all articles of the previous act. It has introduced a great number of new terms and solutions in compliance with the IAS and identifying explicit differences between tax and accounting regulations (Grabiński et al. 2014, p.283-284).

It should be stressed that the Act is subject to continuous changes which adjust it to the EU regulations and IFRS. The last amendment was made in July 2014 and brought major simplifications of reporting of the micro-entities. These simplifications do not only include a possibility of a significantly shortened financial statement, but a ban to use valuation of assets and liabilities according to a fair value and amortized cost as well.

Figure 8. Indulgence dimension in Polish society on the background of other countries
Source: The Hofstede Center (2015)

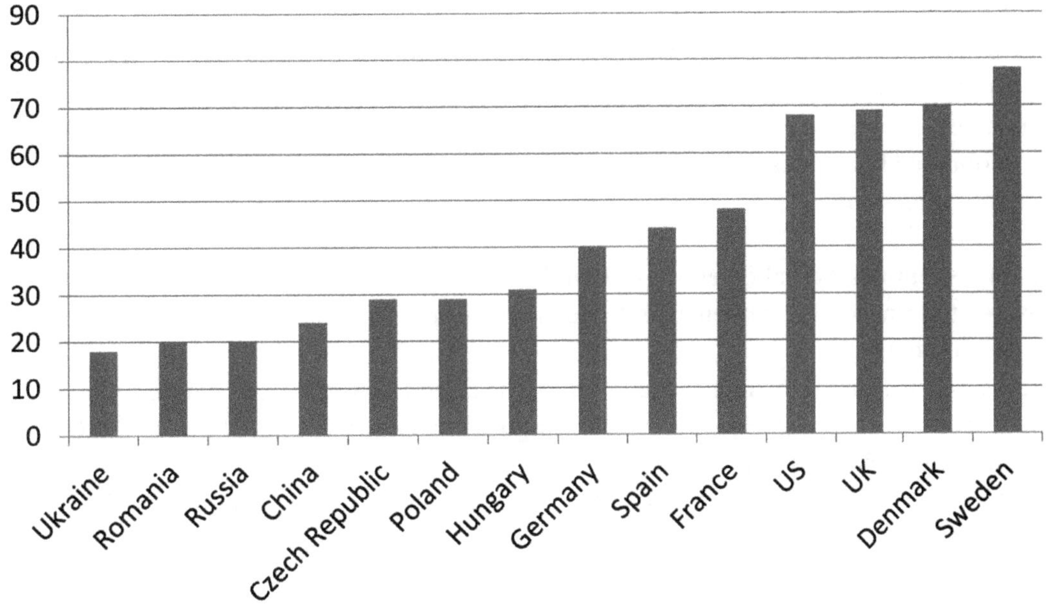

The Accounting Act specifies accounting principles, procedures of auditing by certified auditors and principles of conducting an activity in a scope of providing book-keeping services. It contains general provisions, including definitions of basic terms (chapter 1), book-keeping (chapter 2) stocktaking (chapter 3), valuation of assets and liabilities and determining the financial result (chapter 4), and also issues concerning merger of companies (chapter 4a), financial statements of undertakings (chapter 5), consolidated financial statements of a capital group (chapter 6), auditing, submitting of financial statements to an appropriate court register and their publishing (chapter 7), book-keeping services (chapter 8a), criminal liability (chapter 9). The act contains 4 annexes, presenting a scope of the information shown in the financial statements:

1. Undertakings other than banks, insurance companies and reinsurance companies and micro-entities,
2. Banks,
3. Insurance companies and reinsurance companies,
4. Micro-entities.

Following other European countries, in 2001, the Polish Accounting Standards Committee (ASC) which regulates the National Accounting Standards (NAS) was established. The Accounting Standards Committee has carried out its activities within the Ministry of Finance since 2002. Up to now, 9 standards have been issued, and the subsequent ones are being developed. The Committee's members are the experts in accounting who represent accounting regulatory bodies (the Ministry of Finance, the Ministry of State Treasury, the National Bank of Poland, and the Banking Supervision Commission), the major professional organizations (Accountants Association in Poland and the National Chamber of Mandatory Auditors) as well as academics and the representative of auditing companies (Grabiński et al. 2014, p.288). NAS are based on IFRS adopted by the European Commission, and provide additional commentary and guidelines to assist implementation. They are published in the Official Journal of the Ministry of Finance (Jaruga et al., 2005).

By summing up it should be stated that to 2006, the Accounting Act was the only law that regulated accounting policies. Pursuant to Regulation 1606/2002 of the European Parliament and the Council listed companies, issuers of securities admitted to public trading and banks were obliged to apply IFRS in their consolidated financial statements. From the perspective of IFRS application, Polish entities can be divided into three groups:

- The largest entities, so called entities of public interest, which are obliged to apply IFRS in their consolidated financial statements, and which may apply international standards in non-consolidated statements;
- Entities which aspire to belong to the group of the largest companies, or entities constituting their capital structure, and the subsidiaries of foreign companies which apply IFRS in their financial statements may choose to apply IFRS;
- The remaining entities which apply the Act on accounting and in matters not regulated by the Act apply National Accounting Standards, and if this is not sufficient, refer to IFRS (table 1).

As a result of the mandatory application of IFRS in specific cases, the Polish accounting regulations were developed in two directions. Accounting systems in most small and medium size business entities are regulated by the Accounting Act. Additionally, there are several regulations of the Council of Ministers and the Minister of Finance related to specific accounting issues. The majority of big companies which are listed prepare their financial statements according to IFRS (figure 9).

Benefits derived from IFRS implementation vary depending on an entity size and its financial structures as well as the sources of a foreign investment. Overall, large companies are likely to benefit most. The benefits derived from IFRS implementation can be mainly attributed to the application of higher quality accounting standards, which leads to a higher comparability of the financial statements. As a result, the IFRS adoption increases the attractiveness of Polish listed companies as investment targets for foreign investors, increase the liquidity of their shares and, consequently, reduce the cost of capital and risk levels. In the case of the groups of companies, the voluntary implementation of non-consolidated statements leads to substantial savings in consolidating financial statements (Grabiński et al. 2014, p.292-295).

Table 1. The scope of IFRS application in Polish financial reporting

Obligatory	**Voluntary**	
Consolidated Financial Statements	**Non-Consolidated Financial Statements**	**Consolidated Financial Statements**
• Issuers of securities admitted to public trading • Banks	• Issuers of securities admitted to public trading • Foreign company's subsidiaries if this company applies IFRS • Entities applying to be admitted to public trading • Entities, members of a group of companies in which the dominant entity applies IFRS in its consolidated financial statements	• Entities applying to be admitted to public trading • Members of a group of companies in which a parent company applies IFRS in financial statements

Source: Helin, (2006, p.24).

Figure 9. Duplication of accounting principles of the entities operating in Poland
Source: the authors' own elaboration

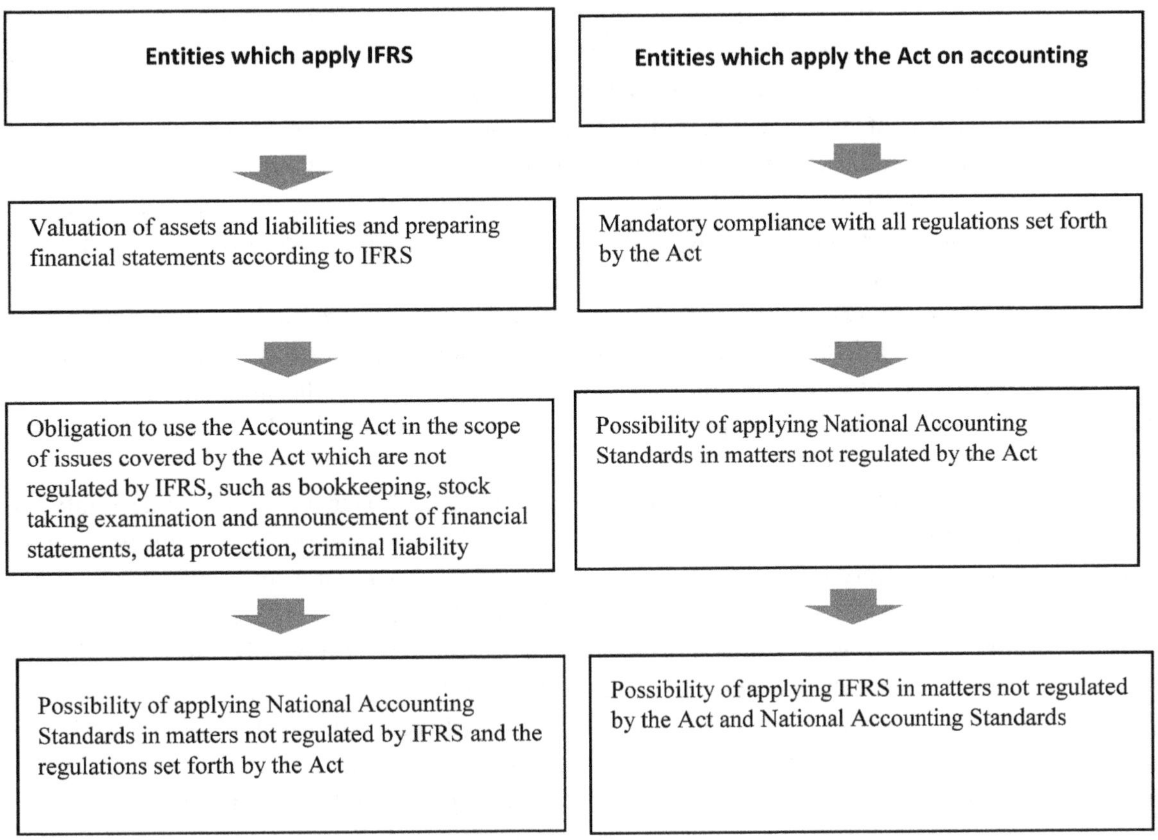

4. IFRS IMPLEMENTATION IN POLAND IN THE LIGHT OF EMPIRICAL STUDIES

There are often essential differences between the Polish Accounting Act and IFRS regarding specificity and complexity of regulations and requirements in a scope of mandatory disclosures. It should be emphasized that the differences are minimized largely, if IFRSs are compared jointly with the Accounting Act and the National Accounting Standards (Kamieniecka, 2009, p. 35-45). The above statements were proved by the empirical studies conducted by Judkowiak (2014, p. 91-105). The author confirmed that the financial statements of the Polish economic entities did not provide a lot of information on the financial instruments. The economic entities which prepare their IFRS based financial statements include much more detailed information on this subject. In the world literature the Polish accounting standards were not compared with IFRS. Comparisons dealt mostly with IFRS and US GAAP. The latter ones are deemed as more detailed and more rigorous comparing to IFRS (Anderson, 1993, p. 52). Despite that there are differences between US GAAP and IFRS they are getting smaller and smaller with time (Street, Gray, 1999, p. 133).

In the Polish literature IFRSs are recognized as the most developed form of harmonization of the world accounting standards (Messner, 2002, p. 41). The world harmonization of accounting concentrates on minimizing potential contradictory rules, conventions and principles, without total unification of the accounting standards. There is consent to alternative solutions which are not mutually exclusive and can be used parallel by diverse economic entities (Ignatowski, 2012, p. 33-53). Total elimination of the differences between particular countries should not be an end in itself, but their significant limitation. In practice this approach is represented by the IFRS originators. Similar views are represented by Kędzior, Grabiński (2011, p. 55-88). Harmonization of standards of accounting seems to be a desirable phenomenon for lots of participants of market gambling such as investors, auditing companies etc. However, it is worthwhile asking a question if the accounting standards should be identical in most of the world countries, without considering such factors as diverse economic legal, tax, political cultural or other systems. The standards should not be uniform for big and small economic entities, even when they are both listed on a stock exchange.

Even greater controversies can be caused by creating the same conceptual frameworks of the accounting for listed and non-listed companies. There are also adversaries of this approach, who assume creating uniform, unified, global accounting standards (World GAAP). In the situation of numerous accountant scandals in the American companies IFRSs as more flexible standards are closer to a practical application in the world (Ignatowski, 2012, p. 33-53).

Similar views can be found in the world literature on this subject. Harmonization of accounting is a complex and long-term phenomenon. You cannot expect total unification of the accounting standards, due to numerous local difference of an economic character and others, present in particular countries of the world (McCombie, Deo, 2005, p. 154). According to Ball (2006, p. 5-27) the IFRS prevalence in over 100 countries of the world can be regarded as a great success. It should be emphasized that the IFRS-based harmonization means creating a global, complex set of the standards of a high quality. Winney, Marshall, Bender, Swiger (2010, 167-178) underline that there are substantial differences between aims and guidelines of persons responsible for creating standards and practice of their use (as: Carmona, Trombetta, 2008, p. 455-461). Hence, the differences between the particular countries (presented above) cause the diverse IFRS implementation in particular states (compare: Fox, Hannah, Helliar, Veneziani, 2013, p. 86-101). IFRSs can constitute a significant challenge, in particular, for the economic entities coming from the emerging (Al-Hashim, 1994, p. 28 – 35).

A controversial phenomenon identified with the IFRS application in Poland is valuation based on a fair value. In the opinion of the Polish authors the fair value is difficult to be verified, and it should be emphasized that its definition is inaccurate and is most useful mainly for investors, not necessarily for other users of economic information (Gmytrasiewicz, 2009, p. 63-70). There is a rather big group of economic entities which have considerable practical problems with objective valuation on basis of the fair value (Kucharczyk, 2009, p. 89-103). It is also significant that in order to valuate lots of assets there is no active market. Those situations cause understandable difficulties for the employees of the financial-accounting departments of the Polish enterprises (Kiziukiewicz, 2009, p. 99-108). Investigations on the real application of the fair value characteristic for IFRS were performed by Kucharczyk (2009, p. 89-103). A range of use of this valuation in the banking sector was about 18%-19% of the balance sheet total in years 2007-2008, for the liabilities it is about 3-7%. Banks resign willingly from the fair value-based valuation, if a standard provides it. In the Polish conditions the fair value is not used for negatively understood creative accounting. Pielichaty (2008, 173-183) also criticized broad use of the fair value. It may result in worsening of an image quality of assets and equity standing. Reliability and objectivity of valuation based on the fair value of diverse balance sheet items are also evaluated negatively.

Use of the fair value in the valuation process is also evaluated as controversial in the world literature. Jain (2011, p. 125 – 136) draws attention to frequent use of this valuation method in the financial statements prepared according to IFRS. The fair value results in a greater variability and subjectivity of the financial reporting. Lots of the entities from the emerging economies using mostly valuation based on historical cost face serious problems connected with use of the fair value. Ball (2006, p. 5-27) holds similar views. Valuation and auditing of the fair value constitutes a great challenge for auditors too. A range of subjective decisions in accounting and a possibility of manipulating the estimated values increase. Values of the specific assets at a high fluctuation of markets can be correlated inappropriately many times with the market realities. (Akgün, Pehlivanlı, Gürünlü, 2011, p. 163). However, its greater potential useful value for investors in estimating future cash flows is in favor for use of the fair value. (Bonaci, Tudor, 2011, p. 197 – 206).

Gmytrasiewicz (2009, p. 63-70) points out to significant changes in a scope of conception of calculating a financial result and changes in basic accounting principles in reporting according to IFRS. A departure from conception of prudent valuation is particularly noteworthy (like Sobańska, Michalak, 2009, p. 219-237). In the author's opinion such an approach can be both advantageous and disadvantageous. Studies in a scope of conservatism of the Polish Accounting Act and IFRS were made by Krzywda and Schroeder (2007, p. 79–107). The authors verified empirically that the equity values were about 6%-9% lower on basis of the Polish Accounting Act, whereas the value of the reported net profits was about 35% higher. Then, Jaruga, Fijalkowska, Jaruga-Baranowska, Frendzel (2007, p. 67–78) confirmed that for majority of the companies analyzed after adopting IFRS a higher value of the equity and values of the generated profit were noticed. Similar results were obtained by Fijałkowska, Jaruga-Baranowska (2007, p. 97-114). Therefore, what is surprising a level of conservatism decreased after implementing IFRS in the Polish listed companies. Similar results were obtained by Grabiński, Kędzior (2007a, 2007b, p. 7-21; 2007). While analyzing profitability ratios calculated on basis of the Polish Accounting Act and IFRS Grabiński and Kędzior (2007c) did not find any significant differences, in spite of the fact that these differences should be considered as statistically significant. The greatest diversity concerned the ROE ratio. Kabalski (2007, p. 131-141) emphasizes the IFRS-based financial reporting shows repeatedly tendency to earnings smoothing. An example of such practices is interest capitalization, instead of including it directly into the financial result. In such a way risk can be reduced, although a question should be asked if its minimization by activities in the operational zone would not be a better solution. In spite of the diverse results of the empirical works a higher level of conservatism for the Polish Accounting Act in relation to IFRS should be confirmed. However, those difference should not be considered as very significant.

In the world literature a level of conservatism of the local accounting standards and IFRS was also a subject of investigations. Since IFRS should be recognized as standards close to the Anglo-Saxon accounting tradition, the IFRS conservatism level should be lower in relation to lots of local accounting standards. For the Spanish companies using IFRS creation of more conservative financial reporting was confirmed surprisingly. (Callao, Jarne, Laínez, 2007, p. 148-178). Behind it there area cultural traditions and factors of a legal character, determining a selection of a treatment and valuation of financial items in the accounting. Studies of similar issues were performed for the Greek enterprises. Iatridis, Dalla (2011, p. 284-303). The authors investigated an influence of the IFRS use on the liquidity and debt ratios. The results of the empirical investigations confirmed that the liquidity ratios decreased, whereas the debt ratios increased. Therefore, the IFRS implementation causes more conservative influence on the liquidity and debt ratios, which is a manifestation of greater conservatism of the accounting according to IFRS in relation to the Greek accounting standards. Thus, the results obtained in the Polish conditions are not quite identical with ones obtained in other countries.

A range of the real IFRS implementation in the Polish practice can be determined at a level of particular economic entities, as unknown until the end or even uncertain. (Kucharczyk, 2009, p. 89-103). IFRSs provide a possibility of forming an individualized image of an economic situation of an economic entity, which in practice does not always mean comparability of financial data. IFRS should be considered as more flexible standards, not as rigid and rigorous ones as for example US GAAP (Masztalerz, 2012, p. 123-131). Therefore, it cannot be surprising that in practice their comparability can be limited. The principles provide only general guidelines, whereas rules indicate definite ways of proceeding, are more precise, costly, but the financial information included in them is comparable to much higher degree. (as: Ignatowski, 2012, p. 33; more on this subject Masztalerz, 2012, p. 123-131). Similar views are presented by Markiewicz-Rudnicka, Piotrowska (2009, p. 119-128). Changes in the financial reporting should provide an increase in transparency and unification of the accounting practice, it is not in practice though. In the author's opinion this is comparability of information in the financial statement according to IFRS which deserves criticism.

Ryba (2011, p. 251-264) points out that a diverse way of calculation of depreciation of fixed assets, allowed in IFRS limits largely or even precludes direct comparability of financial statements of enterprises for the same reporting period. In turn, Kalinowski (2011, p. 145-168) draws attention to specificity of keeping accounts in the branch of developers. The author emphasizes significant differences between reporting based on the Polish Accounting Act and based on IFRS. This situation decreases comparability of financial statements and as a consequence worsens a flow and allocation of capital. A quality of the financial information in this branch seems to be key one, because this is a sector, which is a specific barometer of the economic situation and the branch which is exceptionally susceptible to economic risk. However, according to the author some differences in the international financial reporting as a result of the IFRS implementation were reduced. An issue of comparability of IFRS with the Polish Accounting Act deserves a separate analysis. Grabiński, Kędzior (2007a, p. 7-21) examined differences in values of balance sheet items for 30 biggest listed companies prepared on basis of IFRS and the Polish Accounting Act. Majority of the items showed the differences at a level of 2.5%. High comparability of the balance sheets made according to the Polish solutions and world solutions results from the fact the Polish Accounting Act refers directly to IFRS in the issues not governed by it.

It should be noticed that use of the same accounting standards does not mean an automatic improvement of comparability of financial reporting (Dobija, 2010, p. 5-14). Some people supporting use of IFRS point out to their higher comparability or transparency. However, numerous empirical studies do not confirm it. The economic entities on which an obligation is imposed to use identical accounting standards differ among themselves in a scope of the accounting practice. Substantial differences in bookkeeping are also present at a level of particular countries. Those differences are influenced not only by economic, political and social factors but cultural ones as well.

The IFRS implementation does not have to mean an achievement of total comparability of the financial statements (Ignatowski, 2008, p. 91-100). The success of the whole undertaking depends on uniform and consistent use of IFRS. A support of various institutions at a global, regional and country level or particular branches and sectors of the economy are essential in the whole process. Achieving total convergence of comparability of the accounting standards under the IFRS leadership can be problematic at present. There are lots of factors disrupting the process of the financial statement comparability. They include, among others, a diverse level of the economic growth in the particular countries of the world or diverse characteristics of a local economic-institutional environment.

An analysis of the international literature dealing with comparability of the local accounting standards and IFRS is also ambiguous, although majority of the authors agree with its increase after implementing IFRS. According to Jain (2011, p.125 – 136) reporting of the economic entities which use IFRS is convergent to a greater extent. A comparison of a financial situation of two entities using IFRS becomes easier. DeFond, Hu, Hung, Li (2011, p. 240-258) confirmed an increased comparability of the financial statements as a result of mandatory IFRS implementation on the EU territory. The authors have noticed an increased capital commitment of foreign investment funds, if the IFRS implementation resulted in an improvement of the international comparability of the financial statements. Similar investigation results were presented by Horton, Serafeim, Serafeim (2013, p. 388-423). The authors indicate the increased comparability and accounting information quality on the capital markets as a result of the mandatory IFRS implementation on the EU territory. Yip, Young (2012, p. 1767-1789) also confirmed empirically the increased comparability of the IFRS-based financial statements. The higher quality and accounting convergence are factors determining the reporting comparability. The convergent areas of accounting became much more comparable, whereas the discrepancies were not intensified.

Then, Callao, Jarne, Laínez (2007, p. 148-178) draw attention to worsening of comparability of the national financial statements. An implementation of reforms bringing closer the local accounting legislation to the international standards seems to be necessary. This situation also takes place in Poland. The listed companies use mostly IFRS, while the non-listed companies use the local accounting regulations. Brüggemann, Hitz, Sellhorn (2013, p. 1-37) emphasize that the analysis of the empirical investigations dealing with comparability of the financial statements according to IFRS does not provide generally evidence that the mandatory IFRS implementation increases comparability of the financial statements. Greater comparability will probably, be possible among the companies coming from various countries.

Relevance of the financial information on the capital markets generated by accounting was also a matter of research in the Polish literature on the subject. Sobańska, Michalak (2009, p. 219-237) emphasize an increasing scope of prospective information disclosed in the IFRS-based financial statements. However, it should be pointed out that this information can be more prone to manipulations and can cause understandable difficulties in the scope of its verification. This conception causes that credibility of the financial statements can be limited. Among the advantages of providing information oriented at the future its greater usability for needs of investors should be, undoubtedly, mentioned. In the opinion of Ignatowski (2008, p. 5-24) one of the fundamental premises of the IFRS implementation on lots of capital markets was to increase relevance of the information provided for the stock exchange investors. Therefore, an attempt to answer the question if the IFRS implementation is linked with a positive reaction of the capital markets, expressed by fluctuations in share prices seems to be purposeful. The author points out that in the literature there are definitively studies predominant which connect the IFRS implementation with a positive reaction of stock exchanges. The reactions of the capital markets are usually stronger in the situations when there is a significant qualitative difference between the accounting standards used so far by a company and IFRS. Advantages from the IFRS use are the greater the earlier in time the information about their implementation is provided. An additional support of the national institutions and regulators is also important in the whole process. The positive reaction of the capital markets to the IFRS implementation cannot be surprising. They contribute usually to a decrease in the capital cost, especially in the situation of lack of the convergence of the local accounting standards and IFRS. Additionally, use of IFRS increase liquidity of the stock exchanges and the companies themselves.

The IFRS relevance depends mostly on a quality of their implementation (Zimnicki, Sojak, 2008, p. 135-163). Their inappropriate or superficial implementation does not generate an added value for the investors. On basis of the investigations dealing with the segment reporting implementation in the practice of the Polish entities the authors emphasize that a degree of a real information disclosure in relation to the standard requirements is low. A total disclosure of the required financial information was not observed in any company. The disclosures dealt mostly with the segment revenues, although even this item was not shown by all the enterprises being an object of the studies. The authors conclude that the incomplete disclosures in relation to the standard requirements decrease significantly relevance of the information generated by the economic entities. Klimczak (2011, p. 228–248) performed investigations on reactions of the capital markets to the IFRS implementation into the Polish listed companies. The investigation results confirm rather a slight reaction of the capital markets themselves. Effectiveness of the capital market in Poland, an easy access to the financial information and its effective processing influence undoubtedly the investigation results. Effectiveness of the capital markets and value relevance of earnings was also investigate in the Polish conditions. The empirical studies confirm effectiveness of the capital markets and value relevance of earnings, phenomena were not caused by the IFRS implementation though. (Dobija, Klimczak, 2010, p. 356–374). A subject of interest of the Polish researchers was an influence of the IFRS use on the profit quality. Waniak-Michalak, Czajor, Michalak (2012, p. 63-82) noticed a slight statistically significant relationship between the mandatory IFRS use since 2005 and the profit quality.

In the Polish literature on the subject you can find disputable articles if a real objective of accounting and reporting should be to provide information about a growth potential of a goodwill in the future. (Sobańska, Michalak, 2009, p. 219-237). It is worth considering if accounting should be an information system about value or an information system about economic facts, and a user of the financial statement should make valuation and a capital evaluation himself. (Gmytrasiewicz, 2009, p. 63-70). Lots of arguments for and against the suggestions above can be presented with no doubt.

The world literature on this subject also describes mainly a positive influence of the IFRS use on relevance of the financial information and a positive reaction of the capital markets to the information on their future implementation. Aharony, Barniv, Falk (2010, p. 535-578) confirmed an increase in the value relevance for the accounting information on an example of expenditures on the research and development, goodwill and asset revaluation for the entities which began to use IFRS mandatorily. Brüggemann, Hitz, Sellhorn, 2013, p. 1-37) also verified the increased value relevance following the mandatory IFRS adoption on the capital markets. It should be pointed out that some of the effects described are characteristic for the states with powerful legal enforcement. In turn Callao, Jarne, Laínez (2007, p. 148-178) did not confirm an increase in the relevance of financial reporting on the local capital markets. Despite that the increased relevance of financial reporting has not been not observed in a short period of time, it can be higher in the long-term period..

Christensen, Lee, Walker (2007, p. 341-379) noticed a positive reaction of the capital market to the information on the future IFRS implementation. Similar investigations were conducted by Armstrong, Barth, Jagolinzer, Riedl (2010, p. 31-61). A reaction of the investors to the events which increased a probability of the IFRS use were positive or negative, if they decreased a probability of their implementation. A reaction of the capital market participants was stronger for the entities with a lower quality of accounting before the IFRS implementation, higher information asymmetry and for the entities from the common law countries. Daske, Hail, Leuz, Verdi (2008, p. 1085-1142) also underline the fact that advantages from the IFRS use on the capital markets are not noticeable in all countries. They take place in the countries where there is special motivation of the enterprises to implement transparent accounting at. strong legal enforcement. The capital markets react to the IFRS use stronger when it is a voluntary implementation.

Other IFRS aspects being a subject of evaluation in the Polish literature on this subject also deserve attention. An important standard in Poland due to importance of the food, agriculture sector is IFRS 41 Agriculture. Bieniasz, Gołaś, Czerwińska-Kayzer (2011, p. 9-24) draw attention to inaccuracy of wordings and a controversial character of this standard. The classification of the specific components of the property connected with the agricultural activity should be more precise, because this classification determines the accepted valuation methods. Lack of precise information on a way of presenting these items in the standard results in their diverse presentation by particular companies. In such a situation the information included in the statement becomes unclear and difficult to be compared with other companies in this branch. Lack of use professional vocabulary within the discussed matters, available in other legal regulations in the accounting scope, deserves a negative assessment as well. Kiziukiewicz (2009, p. 99-108) emphasized particularly difficulties of valuation of *biological assets* on basis of the fair value. According to the author disclosures of the biological assets should not be limited to a balance sheet and additional information. Specially developed reports on the biological assets which increase the information value of the data disclosed in this scope seem to be purposeful.

Gmytrasiewicz (2009, p. 63-70) points out to the fact that a number and a scope of particular accounting standards grow steadily, whereas a number of the accounting principles which should constitute basis for creating particular standards does not change. Lack or inappropriate defining of many key items in the accounting such as equity or liabilities also deserves critical evaluation (like Kędzior, Grabiński, 2011, p. 55-88). Pielichaty (2008, 173-183) also criticized some IFRS areas. The author drew attention to objective difficulties of many enterprises in a scope of preparing a lot of new financial information, which should be disclosed in a different and uniform way. Toborek-Mazur (2014, p. 89-114) makes critical remarks on the selected aspects of the IFRS-based financial statement consolidation.

5. CONCLUSION

IFRSs were implemented into the accounting reporting in Poland more than 10 years ago, mainly in relation to big economic entities, listed companies and banks. At the moment of implementation the Polish accounting in its assumptions had already been based on the international regulations for a long time. For this reason the IFRS implementation did not constitute a big qualitative change. The results of the empirical investigations presented did not find any significant differences in the reaction of the capital market to the information presented in the financial statements made acc. the national and international accounting regulations. No significant differences were found in the financial result quality. Only in the case of the entities which decided to implement IFRS voluntarily a slightly higher earnings quality could be seen. A level of the disclosure is the area which differentiates significantly the Polish and international regulations. It can be stated that the financial statement made acc. IFRS is characterized by a higher level of disclosures.

A wide scope of the IFRS use in Poland comparing to other countries of the region should be pointed out. It results from the fact that there is a strong capital market in Poland, which is not always a rule in the developing countries of the CEE region. The listed companies are obliged to make consolidated statements according to IFRS, whereas in the case of individual statements they have such a possibility and they use it increasingly. Like in other European countries a quick IFRS implementation for the SMEs should not be expected.

Institutional and social changes in Poland which bring cultural conditionings and legal solutions more and more closer to ones functioning in the western part of Europe should be pointed out too. As a consequence you can expect a greater comparability of the financial statements of the Polish listed companies in relation to the statements of the companies from other EU countries. From the economic point of view the IFRS implementation can be viewed as an asset in a form of an increase in attractiveness of the Polish economy for foreign investments.

REFERENCES

Akgün M., Pehlivanlı D., Gürünlü M. (2011). A Process Design for Auditing Fair Value. *International Journal of Economics and Finance, 3*(3).

AlHashim, D. D. (1994). International Dimensions in Accounting and Implications for Developing Nations. *Management International Review, 34*, 28–35.

Anderson, N. (1993). *The Globalization GAAP* (Vol. 75). Management Accounting.

Armstrong, C. S., Barth, M. E., Jagolinzer, A. D., & Riedl, E. J. (2010). Market reaction to the adoption of IFRS in Europe. *Accounting Review, 85*(1), 31–61. doi:10.2308/accr.2010.85.1.31

Ball, R. (2006). International Financial Reporting Standards (IFRS): pros and cons for investors. *Accounting and Business Research, 36*(sup1), 5-27.

Bieniasz, A., Gołaś, Z., & Czerwińska-Kayzer, D. (2011). Klasyfikacja i prezentacja aktywów rolniczych w sprawozdaniu finansowym według polskich i międzynarodowych regulacji rachunkowości. *Zeszyty Teoretyczne Rachunkowości*, (64), 9-24.

Bonaci, C. G., & Tudor, A. T. (2011). Fair Value Empirical Studies: An Overview on Accounting Research Literature. *Annales Universitatis Apulensis Series Oeconomica, 2*(13), 197 – 206.

Brüggemann, U., Hitz, J. M., & Sellhorn, T. (2013). Intended and unintended consequences of mandatory IFRS adoption: A review of extant evidence and suggestions for future research. *European Accounting Review, 22*(1), 1–37. doi:10.1080/09638180.2012.718487

Callao, S., Jarne, J. I., & Laínez, J. A. (2007). Adoption of IFRS in Spain: Effect on the comparability and relevance of financial reporting. *Journal of International Accounting, Auditing & Taxation, 16*(2), 148–178. doi:10.1016/j.intaccaudtax.2007.06.002

Callen, J. L., Morel, M., & Richardson, G. (2011). Do culture and religion mitigate earings management? Evidence from a cross-country analysis. *International Journal of Disclosure and Governance, 8*(2), 103–121. doi:10.1057/jdg.2010.31

Carmona, S., & Trombetta, M. (2008). On the global acceptance of IAS/IFRS accounting standards: The logic and implications of the principles-based system. *Journal of Accounting and Public Policy, 27*(6), 455–461. doi:10.1016/j.jaccpubpol.2008.09.003

Christensen, H. B., Lee, E., & Walker, M. (2007). Cross-sectional variation in the economic consequences of international accounting harmonization: The case of mandatory IFRS adoption in the UK. *The International Journal of Accounting*, *42*(4), 341–379. doi:10.1016/j.intacc.2007.09.007

Daske, H., Hail, L., Leuz, C., & Verdi, R. (2008). Mandatory IFRS reporting around the world: Early evidence on the economic consequences. *Journal of Accounting Research*, *46*(5), 1085–1142.

DeFond, M., Hu, X., Hung, M., & Li, S. (2011). The impact of mandatory IFRS adoption on foreign mutual fund ownership: The role of comparability. *Journal of Accounting and Economics*, *51*(3), 240–258. doi:10.1016/j.jacceco.2011.02.001

Dobija, D. (2010). Dylematy standaryzacji sprawozdawczości finansowej, wyceny i pomiaru ryzyka. *Zeszyty Teoretyczne Rachunkowości*, (57), 5-14.

Dobija, D., & Klimczak, K. K. (2010). Development of accounting in Poland: Market efficiency and the value relevance of reported earnings. *The International Journal of Accounting*, *45*(3), 356–374. doi:10.1016/j.intacc.2010.06.010

Fijałkowska J., Jaruga-Baranowska M. (2007). The Impact of IAS/IFRS Adoption on the Presentation of the Financial Position and Performance of Polish Listed Companies. *Theoretical Journal of Accounting*, (41), 97-114.

Fox, A., Hannah, G., Helliar, C., & Veneziani, M. (2013). The costs and benefits of IFRS implementation in the UK and Italy. *Journal of Applied Accounting Research*, *14*(1), 86–101. doi:10.1108/09675421311282568

Gmytrasiewicz, M. (2009). Dyskusyjne metody ustalania i prezentacji wartości według Międzynarodowych Standardów Sprawozdawczości Finansowej. *Zeszyty Teoretyczne Rachunkowości*, (53), 63-70.

Grabiński, K., & Kędzior, M. (2007a). An empirical evidence on convergence of Polish Accounting Rules and International Financial Reporting Standards on the basis of Polish PLC listed on the Warsaw Stock Exchange. *30th Annual Congress*, European Accounting Association, Lisbon.

Grabiński, K., & Kędzior, M. (2007b). Bilanse według ustawy o rachunkowości i Międzynarodowych Standardów Rachunkowości. *Rachunkowość, 11*, 7-21.

Grabiński, K., & Kędzior, M. (2007c). *Wpływ zastosowania Międzynarodowych Standardów Rachunkowości na wartość analityczną sprawozdań finansowych spółek notowanych na Giełdzie Papierów Wartościowych w Warszawie. In Rachunkowość w teorii i praktyce*. Poznań: Wydawnictwo Akademii Ekonomicznej w Poznaniu.

Grabiński, K., Kędzior, M., & Krasodomska, J. (2014). The Polish accounting system and IFRS implementation process in the view of empirical research. *Accounting and Management Information Systems*, *13*(2), 281–310.

Helin, A. (2006). Sprawozdanie finansowe według MSSF. Zasady sporządzania i prezentacji. C.H.Beck.

Hofstede Center. (2015). *Poland.* Retrieved from: http://geert-hofstede.com/poland.html

Horton, J., Serafeim, G., & Serafeim, I. (2013). Does Mandatory IFRS Adoption Improve the Information Environment? *Contemporary Accounting Research, 30*(1), 388–423. doi:10.1111/j.1911-3846.2012.01159.x

Iatridis, G., & Dalla, K. (2011). The impact of IFRS implementation on Greek listed companies: An industrial sector and stock market index analysis. *International Journal of Managerial Finance, 7*(3), 284-303.

Ignatowski, R. (2008). Instytucjonalne działania na rzecz spójności w stosowaniu MSR. *Zeszyty Teoretyczne Rachunkowości*, (44), 91-100.

Ignatowski, R. (2008). Reakcja rynków kapitałowych na stosowanie MSR. Przegląd badań empirycznych. *Zeszyty Teoretyczne Rachunkowości*, (43), 5-24.

Ignatowski, R. (2012). Światowa harmonizacja rachunkowości w perspektywie teoretycznej. *Zeszyty Teoretyczne Rachunkowości, 67*, 33–53.

Inglehart, E., & Baker, W. E. (2001). Modernization's Challenge to Traditional Values: Who's Afraid of Ronald McDonald? *The Futurist, 2001*, 16–21.

Jain, P. (2011, March). IFRS implementation in India: Opportunities and challenges. *World Journal of Social Sciences, 1*(1), 125–136.

Jaruga, A. (Ed.). (2002). *Międzynarodowe regulacje rachunkowości. Wpływ na rozwiązania krajowe*. Warszawa: C. H. Beck.

Jaruga, A. (2004). *Polish capital market and earnings management: evidence from Warsaw Stock Exchange*. Paper presented at the 27th European Accounting Association Congress, Prague, Czech Republic.

Jaruga, A. (2005). Adoption of IAS/IFRS in Poland: Challenges and problems. In M. Dobija (Ed.), *General Theory of Accounting*. Krakow: Academy of Economics.

Jaruga, A., Fijalkowska, J., Jaruga-Baranowska, M., & Frendzel, M. (2007). The Impact of IAS/IFRS on Polish Accounting Regulations and their Practical Implementation in Poland. *Accounting in Europe, 4*(1), 67–78. doi:10.1080/17449480701308675

Jaruga, A., Walinska, E., & Bankiewich, A. (1996). The relationship between accounting and taxation in Poland. *European Accounting Review, 5*(sup1), 883–897. doi:10.1080/09638189600000057

Judkowiak, A. (2014). Informacja o instrumentach finansowych w sprawozdaniach finansowych sporządzanych zgodnie z MSSF i polskimi zasadami rachunkowości. *Zeszyty Teoretyczne Rachunkowości, 77*, 91–105.

Kabalski, P. (2007). Dylematy ujmowania kosztów finansowania zewnętrznego w kontekście nowelizacji MSR 23. *Zeszyty Teoretyczne Rachunkowości*, (41), 131-141.

Kalinowski, J. (2011). Porównywalność sprawozdań finansowych firm deweloperskich na tle krajowych i międzynarodowych regulacji rachunkowości. *Zeszyty Teoretyczne Rachunkowości, 60*, 145–168.

Kamieniecka, M. (2009). Odroczony podatek dochodowy w międzynarodowych i krajowych uregulowaniach rachunkowości – podobieństwa i różnice. *Zeszyty Teoretyczne Rachunkowości, 51*, 35–45.

Kędzior, M., & Grabiński, K. (2011). Ocena opracowywanego przez IASB i FASB projektu założeń koncepcyjnych sprawozdawczości finansowej. *Zeszyty Teoretyczne Rachunkowości*, *61*, 55–88.

Kiziukiewicz, T. (2009). Zasady ujawniania aktywów biologicznych w sprawozdaniach finansowych jednostek rolniczych według Międzynarodowych Standardów Sprawozdawczości Finansowej. *Zeszyty Teoretyczne Rachunkowości*, *49*, 99–108.

Klimczak, K. M. (2011). Market Reaction to Mandatory IFRS Adoption: Evidence from Poland. *Accounting and Management Information Systems*, *10*(2), 228–248.

Kucharczyk, B. (2009). Wartość godziwa w wycenie aktywów finansowych – praktyka banków polskich. *Zeszyty Teoretyczne Rachunkowości*, *52*, 89–103.

Markiewicz-Rudnicka, D., & Piotrowska, K. (2009). Sprawozdanie finansowe a zmiany w Międzynarodowych Standardach Sprawozdawczości Finansowej. *Zeszyty Teoretyczne Rachunkowości*, *51*, 119–128.

Masztalerz, M. (2012). O standardach rachunkowości - zasady czy reguły. *Zeszyty Teoretyczne Rachunkowości*, *66*, 123–131.

McCombie. K., & Deo, H. (2005). The International Harmonization of Accounting Standards: Making progress in Accounting Practice or an Endless Struggle?. *Journal of American Academy of Business*, *7*.

Messner, Z. (2002). Komitet Standardów Rachunkowości. *Rachunkowość*, (10).

Obloj, K., & Kostera, M. (1993). Polish privatisation, action, symbolism and cultural barriers. *Industrial and Environmental Crisis Quarterly*, *7*(3), 7–21.

Osiński, Ł. (2015). *Minister gospodarki Niemiec: Nasz handel z Polską jest większy od wymiany handlowej z Rosją*. Gazeta Wyborcza. Retrieved from: http://wyborcza.biz/biznes/1,100896,17883053,Minister_gospodarki_Niemiec__Nasz_handel_z_Polska.html

Pielichaty, E. (2008). Skutki przekwalifikowania instrumentów finansowych w wyniku zmiany intencji inwestora w świetle Międzynarodowych Standardów Rachunkowości. *Zeszyty Teoretyczne Rachunkowości*, *44*, 173–183.

Ryba, A. (2011). Zmiana metody wyceny środków trwałych zgodnie z Międzynarodowymi Standardami Sprawozdawczości Finansowej a porównywalność sprawozdań finansowych. *Zeszyty Teoretyczne Rachunkowości*, *60*, 251–264.

Sobańska, I., & Michalak, M. (2009). Wykorzystanie informacji prospektywnych w sprawozdawczości finansowej zorientowanej na wartość na przykładzie MSR 36 Utrata wartości aktywów. *Zeszyty Teoretyczne Rachunkowości*, (53), 219-237.

Street, D. L., & Gray, S. J. (1999). How Wide Is the Gap Between IASC and U.S. GAAP? Impact of IASC Comparability Project and Recent International Developments. *Journal of International Accounting, Auditing & Taxation, 8*(1).

Tang, L., & Koveos, P. E. (2008). A Framework to Update Hofstede's Cultural Value Indices: Economic Dynamics and Institutional Stability. *Journal of International Business Studies*, *39*(6), 1045–1063. doi:10.1057/palgrave.jibs.8400399

Toborek-Mazur, J. (2014). Wpływ koncepcji konsolidacji sprawozdań finansowych na zmiany w międzynarodowych standardach rachunkowości. *Zeszyty Teoretyczne Rachunkowości*, *76*(76(132)), 89–114. doi:10.5604/16414381.1108293

Vellam, I. (2004). Implementation of International Accounting Standards in Poland: Can True Convergence be achieved in Practice? *Accounting in Europe*, *1*(1), 143–167. doi:10.1080/0963818042000262784

Waniak-Michalak, H., Czajor, P., & Michalak, J. (2012). *Impact of mandatory IFRS implementation on earnings quality. Evidence from the Warsaw Stock Exchange*. World Value Survey. Retrieved from http://www.worldvaluessurvey.org/

Winney, K., Marshall, D., Bender, B., & Swiger, J. (2010). Accounting globalization: Roadblocks to IFRS adoption in the United States. *Global Review of Accounting and Finance*, *1*(1), 167–178.

Yip, R. W., & Young, D. (2012). Does mandatory IFRS adoption improve information comparability? *Accounting Review*, *87*(5), 1767–1789. doi:10.2308/accr-50192

Zimnicki, T., & Sojak, S. (2008). Wartość dodana sprawozdań finansowych wynikająca z ujawnienia segmentów działalności według MSR 14. *Zeszyty Teoretyczne Rachunkowości*, *46*, 135–163.

Chapter 9
IFRS Convergence and Revisions:
Evidence of Accounting Information Quality from East Africa

Erick R. Outa
Strathmore University, Kenya

Nelson M. Waweru
York University, Canada

ABSTRACT

This chapter is aimed at examining the impact of IFRS convergence and revisions on the financial statements of companies listed in East Africa. This was achieved by determining whether firms report losses (LNEG) when they occur (timely loss recognition) or report small positive income (SPOS) or whether incomes reported exhibit variability in net income (NI) over time. Simultaneously, the chapter tests whether there is any influence of corporate governance on these three measures which are considered indicators of financial reporting quality. Four models applying GLS random effects are applied on 520 firm year observations for firms listed in Nairobi Securities Exchange (NSE) between 2005 and 2014. The result shows that a positive coefficient on frequency of large losses reported in the finding interpreted as firms with converged and revised IFRS recognize large losses (LNEG) as they occur. The findings also show a negative coefficient on small positive income (SPOS) interpreted as firms applying non-converged and revised standards manage earnings towards small positive amounts more than firms applying converged standards. The post convergence\revisions are significant for Chi, R^2 and the residual which suggest that variability in net income (NI) improved in the post convergence period while corporate governance show insignificant mixed coefficient with the three indicators.

DOI: 10.4018/978-1-4666-9876-5.ch009

INTRODUCTION

The objective of this chapter is to examine the impact of IFRS convergence and revisions on the financial statements of listed companies in East Africa. Specifically, the study attempts to determine whether firms in East Africa report losses when they occur (timely loss recognition) or report small positive income, and whether incomes reported exhibit variability in net income (NI) over time. The study also checks whether there is any influence of corporate governance on these three measures that are considered indicators of financial reporting quality in line with Chen and Rezaee (2012). The authors state that effective internal corporate governance helps companies to be more aligned with IFRS and thus provides high quality financial information. The study is motivated by the lack of direct measures on the impact of convergence and revisions. Kaboyo (2014) reported that 69 of listed companies in East African practice earnings management, Ernst &Young (2013) in a global survey involving 100 Kenyan firms, reported that 53 per cent of managers believed their companies over-report their financial performance, driven by increased pressures to hit targets in an increasingly challenging business environment. Paanen et al. (2008) attributes the untimely loss recognition and increased earnings management in post IFRS Germany to changes in IFRS, a finding that needs to be closely monitored. The study is also timely as IASB continues with reforming its conceptual framework where accounting conservatism is featuring and raising questions.

The current study looks at two time periods, 2005-2009 and 2010-2014, and the compares how the three indicators have changed over the two time periods as the revisions and convergence to IFRS occur and are implemented. During this period, there was accelerated issuance of IFRS to close off the convergence period and also address some of the controversies arising from the financial crisis of 2008. Francis et al. (2004) and Lee (2013) have shown that financial reporting quality measures can either be market based or conservative with conservative measures being timely loss recognition, earnings management and discretionary accruals. The two authors have criticized conservative measures for not providing direct evidence of the usefulness of accounting information to its end users. On the other hand, they have indicated market based approaches as value relevance and liquidity studies and the measures have the advantages of directly addressing end users but are criticized for the fair value weaknesses. Fair values can provide managers with more discretion in accounting, which might diminish the quality of accounting information because of increased earnings management (Ormrod and Taylor. 2004). This chapter takes the conservative approach on the basis of difficulties of applying fair value approaches in less developed markets such as those of East Africa.

Very few studies have been undertaken in this area in East Africa. A related study by Outa (2011) focused on the impact of IFRS/IAS adoption on the accounting quality before and after IFRS adoption from the perceived low quality standards issued by International Accounting Standards Committee (IASC). The period '1995-2004' is based on an outdated data given the changes that have taken place in the standards, the firms and the economy in general. The data for the current study is up to 2014, with improved methodology that is designed to demonstrate how the revisions and convergence to the standards are applied in developing markets, and how it impacts on the financial reporting quality. Capital Markets of East Africa exist in the four countries except Burundi and Sudan but Nairobi Securities exchange (NSE) remains the biggest. Furthermore, East Africa is becoming a key economy that deserves attention. Oil and gas discoveries together with major infrastructure developments is putting spotlight in the region hence the need to assess how financial reporting which is critical to investors, is in tandem with these dynamics and global aspirations.

The current study differs from previous studies because of the exclusive focus on a single region applying revisions to standards arising from convergence efforts, all of which are presumed to be quality standards under IASB as opposed to IASC whose standards were not well regarded as quality. The study applies balanced panel sample to mitigate the effects of lack of comparable data given that East Africa applies IFRS only and so there are no non IFRS firms to act as control. The findings from the study indicates that the observed changes in financial reporting relating to timely loss recognition, small positive income and variability in earnings in East Africa are primarily due to IFRS revisions rather than managerial incentives, legal or institutional mechanisms. Also by applying quality metrics on recent data after the convergence MOU in 2006 between IASB and FASB, the results are robust with and without financial services with a design that reasonably controlled for many of the confounding factors.

The rest of the paper is organized as follows. In the next section, we present a narrative review of literature relevant to this topic and the resulting hypothesis to be tested. Methodology applied in the study including design, population, sampling and descriptive statistics are reported in section 3.This section also discusses reasons for the choices made. The fourth section presents and discusses the results. The last section concludes and discusses the contribution, implications as well as recommendations for future work.

THEORY AND LITERATURE REVIEW

Theory

According to Riro *et al.,* (*forthcoming*) there are four main theories that explain why companies disclose information. These include agency theory, signaling theory, political cost theory and proprietary cost theory. Agency theory proposes that disclosure of corporate information is a way of controlling managers' actions and aligning incentives for managers and owners (Jensen and Meckling, 1976) and specifies mechanisms, which reduce agency losses. The theory argues that, in the presence of information asymmetries, managers will choose the set of decisions required to maximize their usefulness. It conceives disclosure as a mechanism, which decreases the costs resulting from conflicts between managers and shareholders (compensation contracts) and from conflicts between the firm and its creditors (debt contracts). Therefore, disclosure works as a mechanism to control manager's performance. The theory is designed on rational people, seeking to maximise their utility with the least possible expenditure and to attain rewards and avoid punishments (Jensen and Meckling, 1976).

Signaling theory argues that the disclosure of information by companies is a signal to capital markets, sent to decrease the asymmetry of information, which often exists between managers and other stakeholders, to optimise financing costs and to increase corporate value (A´lvarez *et al.,* 2008). The theory is based on the assumption that information is not equally available to all parties at the same time, and that information asymmetry is the rule (Riro et al., *forthcoming*). Information asymmetries can result in very low valuations or a sub-optimum investment policy. These signals are the cornerstone of financial communications policy. Managers can be motivated to disclose private information voluntarily as they expect this to provide a good signal about their company's performance to the market.

The political cost theory stipulates that companies will disclose information to avoid the shifting of business wealth towards the public and/or political sector. Companies will disclose when this leads to an improvement in the relationships with governments and the public sector by decreasing political costs (for example taxes) and obtaining certain advantages; for example subsidies and governmental actions that are in the favour of the corporation (A´lvarez, *et al.,* 2008). The theory predicts that large firms, rather than small firms, are more likely to use accounting choices that reduce reported profits.

Proprietary costs theory argues that the disclosure of information may be a disadvantage because of the likely detrimental use of this information by some external users such as shareholders, employees, and competitors (A´lvarez *et al.,* 2008, Riro *et al., forthcoming*). The theory concludes that firms have an incentive not to disclose information that will reduce their competitive position, even if it makes it more costly to raise additional equity. Darrough (1993) noted that a firm's decision to disclose information to investors could damage its competitive position. As a result, in the presence of proprietary costs, a firm has to trade off the positive effects of disclosure against the negative effects (Riro *et al., forthcoming*).

Institutional Setup and Accounting in East Africa

East Africa is made of 5 countries namely Kenya, Uganda, Tanzania, Rwanda and Burundi, although Sudan is in the waiting with Kenya having the biggest economy. The market operations can be described as common law, a term that denotes strong orientation towards shareholders investors like in the US and the UK. Under common law, there are higher incentives such as minimizing taxes or reserve accounting which are used to reduce volatility in earnings and create more wealth for the shareholders unlike in the code law countries where reporting is driven by tax regulations, conservative behavior and broader stakeholder orientation Under code law, the government, shareholders, debt holders, employees and managers are viewed as stakeholders relying less on public information because they have access to that information internally. Following the arguments of Prather et al. (2008), IFRS are investor\ shareholder oriented, it would then appear that IFRS convergence and revisions may have less impact in common law countries because their framework will already be in sync with IFRS and hence suggest that East Africa may not benefit much from IFRS revisions.

The Institutional framework explains how accounting is organized in East Africa, countries that have been closely linked ever since the East Africa Community in 1960s, leading to many similarities and commonness in institutions and businesses. The institutional framework of accounting in East Africa is made up of four elements including the statutes governing the accounting profession, the financial reporting framework, industry regulation and the constitution. The statutory framework is the law that creates the professional accounting institutes and grants them mandate to oversee the profession and make accounting standards as well over see exams leading to qualification as an accountant. They consist of institute of certified public accountants in Kenya, Uganda and Rwanda, and the national board of accountants and auditors in Tanzania. In all these countries accounting is a self-regulating profession and set the standards, registration and disciplinary process while working with the global accounting standard setting body. The financial reporting framework is driven by company law and defines corporate and financial reporting requirements but has been criticized for falling short of International best practice. Industry specific laws refer to regulators of various sectors such as capital markets, insurance, banking, central banks and cooperatives all of which relate to accounting and require financial reports as defined by relevant statutes. The constitution is the supreme law and defines what all entities need to do and provides for the position of auditor general for state corporations and in Kenya has laid down the requirements for leadership and ethical behavior.

Convergence and Revisions to Accounting Standards

There is need to distinguish between convergence and revisions from IFRS adoption. Annual and continuous revisions of IFRS by IASB are understood in the context that they are set of rules which are based on a system of continuous improvement by attempting to adjust rules to the real world economic issues or economic problems. Convergence on the other hand has been explained by (FASB, 2012) as the goal of establishing a single set of high-quality accounting standards to be used internationally, and the efforts of standard-setters towards achieving that goal. Some countries have therefore decided to upgrade their local standards to the level of IFRS instead of outright declaration of adoption of IFRS as produced by IASB, but some differences still exist. East Africa is one such region where there is full adoption as opposed to convergence like China where Chinese Accounting Standards (CAS) has been regarded by Qu and Zhang (2010) to have a convergence with a coefficient of 0.7497 regarded as high degree of convergence.

According to AICPA (2008), convergence projects aim to either improve respective accounting standards or aim to reduce the difference between them. The overall objective of convergence remains the production of comparable financial statements of different firms. Convergence has been criticized for its costs, pace, complexity and the idea that the resultant comparability may not be that strong according to Goldstein (2009) and AICPA (2008). The outcome of comparability studies remain the subject of research with differing outcomes. Many questions have been raised about convergence projects with SEC believing it will result in increased comparability between financial statements of different firms. Many critics have been harsh on these projects with some saying it is European focused with IASB conceding too much in vain attempt to win over the US but the US still believes the chosen routes will not improve US GAAP.

The current study focuses on the initiated convergence and revisions between 2005 and 2014 and the adoption of the resulting standards even though convergence history goes back to the 1950s. In 2006, IASB and the Financial Accounting Standards Board (FASB) signed an MOU on convergence projects and there was accelerated review to the standards since then. In a report published in 2012, the projects outlined in 2006 memorandum had been completed paving way for long term projects. The critical projects completed covered segment reporting (IFRS 8 issued in 2006) and fair value option amended in 2007 all of which led to the revised IAS 39 and IFRS 7. According to IASB, their work program are divided into three areas covering financial crisis related projects (financial instruments, consolidation and fair value), MOU projects (mainly convergence related to financial statement presentation, leases, revenue recognition, joint ventures and employee benefits) and the last referred to as others cover mainly annual improvements. As at the mid-2015, there were 15 IFRS and most of the revised converged standards had effective dates after 2009.Research on whether the revision of a particular IFRS improves financial reporting quality is sparse and reporting financial results not consistent with the economic reality of the firm is not new. Ball, et al. (2015) investigate the effect of mandatory IFRS adoption on debt contracting in a sample of new debt issues from 2001 to 2010 in 22 IFRS-adopting countries and 21 non-IFRS-adopting countries. They report a significant reduction in the use of accounting-based debt covenants and increase in non-accounting-based covenants following mandatory IFRS adoption. They do not observe such effects in non-adopting countries. Arguably, then, financial reporting quality in lending markets was reduced by IFRS revisions. On the other hand Chalmers et al. (2011) show that impairment charges from revised IFRS indicate better accounting information. Robert (2011) show that fraudulent reporting was first exposed after the US great economic crash in 1929 and has been noticed in the Savings & Loans financial scandals in the 1980s and the dot-com bubble of the early 1990s and the financial crisis of 2000s.

Timely Loss Recognition, Variability, and Small Positive Income and Corporate Governance

Leuz et al. (2003) and Lang et al. (2003) posit that firms reporting high quality earnings exhibit timely loss recognition because losses are recognized as they occur rather than being deferred to future periods. The arguments follow that if earnings are smoothed, then large losses should be rare. This leads to the prediction that East African firms that apply converged and revised standards are unlikely to report large losses with higher frequency. The authors indicate that firms with less earnings smoothing exhibit more earnings variability. In view of the objectives of IASB for developing IFRS, it is expected that the revised and converged IFRS will limit management discretion to report earnings that does not reflect the firm's economic performance. It is therefore expected that East African listed companies are likely to exhibit high variability in earnings.

Leuz et al. (2003) and Barth et al. (2008) identified positive income as a practice where firms produce financial results with small positive incomes in particular to avoid reporting a loss. High frequency of small positive net income is regarded as evidence of managing earnings according to Leuz et al. (2003) and therefore our prediction is that East African firms that apply converged and revised standards should exhibit low frequency of small positive income.

Fewer studies have been carried out to determine relationships between corporate governance and financial reporting. Leung et al. (2013) posit that information asymmetry between the agent and principal is the major reason why agent can take advantages from adverse selection and moral hazard, which is the obvious problem in recent accounting scandals. They found mixed results in a study whether firms adopting IFRS with corporate governance regimes can reduce information asymmetry by making themselves more transparent. The reasons included complex and inter-related nature of corporate governance systems including single-country or cross-country studies, self-constructed or comprehensive corporate governance metrics and whether self-selection and endogeneity can be controlled in modeling.

Habib and Jiang. (2015) posit that one of the desirable properties of good corporate governance is to improve financial reporting quality for facilitating efficient resource allocation decisions by corporate managers. They observe a lack of any comprehensive review of the governance-reporting quality literature in China. Lin et al. (2012) in a German study found that IFRS adoption appears to result in a greater increase in comparability than convergence, a finding which may suggest that countries should adopt IFRS rather than converge their standards. Houqe and Easton (2013) find that the mandatory adoption of IFRS in low investor protection countries will lead to an improvement in information quality and international comparability. Chalmers et al. (2013) on a similar note found that the association between firms' goodwill charges against income and the firms' investment opportunities is stronger during the IFRS regime than the AGAAP regime implying the revised IFRS produce financial statements that better reflect the economic position of the firm.

Chen et al. (2010) in a 15 country study in the EU found that there is less earnings management towards a target (SPOS) after IFRS between 2000-2007.They also found that firms recognize losses in a less timely manner (LNEG) in post IFRS periods. In a meta-analysis of 88 papers on IFRS adoption effects, Ahmed et al. (2013) findings suggest that discretionary accruals which impact the three indicators under our investigations did not reduce. Pannanen (2008) on accounting quality in Sweden found a significant decrease in variability in earnings which contradicts the hypothesis. She also found higher occurrence of small positive earnings and an insignificant prevalence of large negative income both of which suggest a low accounting information in post IFRS. They found similar results in Germany. Elbanannan (2010) in Egyptian study found insignificant empirical evidence that earnings management decreases post adoption, while Ames (2013) finds mixed results in South Africa.

In East Africa, little academic work has been undertaken in relation to IFRS convergence, revisions, accounting information and corporate governance. Outa (2011) found high variability in earnings, a positive coefficient on LNEG implying quality decline and an insignificant SPOS with the overall conclusion that IFRS did not improve financial reporting quality significantly. Ndirangu (2014) in testing for accounting quality did find that there was timely loss recognition even though she focused on cross listed firms only. The latest World Bank report on Kenya known as Report on Observance of Standards and Codes (ROSC) (2010) indicated reluctance of top management to comply with the full disclosure and transparency requirements of IFRS and that the differences existed between disclosed accounting policies and actual practices. Challenges in compliance with the impairment of assets, segment information, financial instruments and taxation were also noted by the report. Disclosure as to whether actuarial or other forms of valuation had been used in quantifying outstanding liabilities for post-employment benefits as required by IAS 19 has not been clear and disclosure of contingent liabilities has been reported as inadequate. A similar report on Uganda, ROSC (2014) stated that a number of financial statements of banks had elaborate disclosures in the notes that are not relevant to a bank, inadequate disclosure of credit risk, liquidity risk and market risk relating to financial instruments, three financial statements did not disclose the basis of revenue recognition in the accounting policies. The report noted quality of disclosure of significant judgment's and estimates made by management needed improvement in most financial statements reviewed while related party disclosures and segment information disclosed were generally below that required by the relevant IFRSs.

Recent ROSC as well studies on IFRS compliance for Tanzania and Rwanda have raised almost similar issues. In general the UNCTAD (2014) report on human capacity development in accounting and corporate reporting indicated there are a number of human capacity related challenges that countries face when implementing corporate reporting standards and codes developed at a global level and it is possible that as East Africa continues the uptake of revisions and convergence, inadequate human skills may impact the outcome. In view of the fact that East Africa abandoned their local standard setting process and adopts IFRS as issued by IASB, it might be prudent to argue that adoption is the same as convergence and revisions in this region.

As the standard setting board revises the standards and works on convergence to minimize alternatives and choices, and to focus on a single set of high quality standards, this study hypothesizes that the quality of accounting information has improved as a result of the revisions and changes made to the standards and specifically states:

H_1: Firms with higher accounting quality information exhibit more variability in change in NI (ΔNI) in common law East African countries.

H_2: Firms with higher accounting quality information exhibit large frequency of large losses (LNEG) in common law East African countries.

H_3: Firms with higher accounting quality information exhibit low frequency of small positive income (SPOS) in common law East African countries.

H_4: Corporate Governance influences quality of financial reporting as measured by variability of change in NI, frequency of large losses and frequency of small positive income in common law East African countries

RESEARCH METHODOLOGY

Research Design

In the current study, the quality of accounting information represented by more variability of change in NI, large frequency of large losses and low frequency of small positive income is investigated against revised\converged IFRS. These information quality constructs have previously been applied by Lang et al. (2003), and Barth et al. (2008), among others. The current design also incorporates corporate governance disclosure indices to test for influence of corporate governance.

Variability in Change in NI

It is not possible to observe variability in earnings and so our study applies constructs in extant literature as in Lang et al. (2003) and Barth et al. (2008) with the modified regression being:

$$\Delta NI_{it} = \alpha_{0+} \alpha_1 \text{ SIZE} + \alpha_2 \text{ Growth} + \alpha_3 \text{ EIssue} + \alpha_4 \text{ LEV} + \alpha_5 \text{ DIssue} + \alpha_6 \text{ Turn} + \alpha_7 \text{ CF} + \alpha_8 \text{ AUD} + \alpha_9 \text{ NUMEX} + \alpha_{10} \text{ Corporate Governance} + \varepsilon)_{it} \quad (1)$$

where:

ΔNI_{it}: Change in annual earnings (based on end of year total assets) for firm i year t.
SIZE: is the natural logarithm of assets in millions of shillings as of year end.
GROWTH: Annual percentage (%) of change in sales.
EISSUE: annual percentage (%) change in Shares.
LEV: end year total liabilities divided by end year book value of equity.
DISSUE: annual percentage (%) change in total liabilities.
TURN: Sales divided by end of year total assets.
CF: Annual net cash flow from operating activities scaled by end of year total assets.
AUD: an indicator that equals 1 if the auditor is one of the large international accounting firms.
NUMEX: Number of exchange listings.
Corporate Governance: represents the corporate governance compliance indices from corporate governance guidelines.

The intuition behind this model is that if firms smooth their earnings, then the resulting reporting earnings should be less volatile. Previous studies also indicates that variability in earnings is driven by many factors and hence the need to control for them as shown in the regression equation 1. The resulting variance which is picked from the residuals is then compared in the pre and post convergence with higher residual being an indicator of high variability hence higher accounting quality information. The Corporate governance variable is added to determine the extent to which corporate governance can impact variability.

Frequency of Reporting Small Positive Earnings

This measure is driven by the arguments that management prefers to report small positive income as opposed to a loss and again it is not a direct measure. Based on prior studies, the following equation is derived where a dummy variable indicating small positive earnings is assigned 1 when NI based on assets is between 0 and 0.01 and zero otherwise as applied by Barth et al. (2008). A negative coefficient on SPOS indicates that pre convergence\revised IFRS firms manage earnings towards small positive amounts more frequently than do post convergence firms.

$$\text{IAS }(0,1)_{it} = \alpha_{0+} \alpha_1 SPOS_{+} \alpha_2 SIZE + \alpha_3 Growth + \alpha_4 EIssue + \alpha_5 LEV + \alpha_6 DIssue + \alpha_7 Turn + \alpha_8 CF + \alpha_9 AUD + \alpha_{10} NUMEX + \alpha_{11} Corporate\ Governance + \varepsilon)_{it} \quad (2)$$

where the additional variable 'IAS (0,1)' is an indicator variable that equals 1 for 2005-2009 period firms and Zero for 2010-2014 period and SPOS $_{it}$ is an indicator variable that equals 1 if net income scaled by total assets is between 0 and 0.01. The numbers between 0 and 0.01 are regarded as small positive income.

$$\text{POST }(0,1)_{it} = \alpha_{0+} \alpha_1 SPOS_{+} \alpha_2 SIZE + \alpha_3 Growth + \alpha_4 EIssue + \alpha_5 LEV + \alpha_6 DIssue + \alpha_7 Turn + \alpha_8 CF + \alpha_9 AUD + \alpha_{10} NUMEX + \alpha_{11} Corporate\ Governance + \varepsilon)_{it} \quad (3)$$

where POST (0, 1) is an indicator variable that equals one for observations in the post revision period and zero and otherwise and SPOS is an indicator that equals one for observations in the post revision period. SPOS is indicator variables that equals one for observations where net income scaled by total assets is between 0 and.01.A negative coefficient on SPOS indicates that post revision firms manage earnings towards small positive amounts more frequently than do post revision firms.

Timely Loss Recognition

Firms with higher accounting quality show a large frequency of large losses

$$\text{IAS }(0,1)_{it} = \alpha_{0+} \alpha_1 LNEG_{+} \alpha_2 SIZE + \alpha_3 Growth + \alpha_4 EIssue + \alpha_5 LEV + \alpha_6 DIssue + \alpha_7 Turn + \alpha_8 CF + \alpha_9 AUD + \alpha_{10} Corporate\ Governance + \varepsilon)_{it} \quad (4)$$

A positive coefficient on LNEG indicates that post revision\convergence firms recognize large losses more frequently than pre convergence firms.

LNEG is an indicator variable that equals 1 for observations for which annual net income scaled by total assets is less than -.20 and zero otherwise. A positive coefficient on LNEG indicates that post converged\revised firms recognize large losses more frequently than pre firms.

$$\text{POST }(0,1)_{it} = f(\alpha_{0+} \alpha_1 LNEG_{+} \alpha_2 SIZE + \alpha_3 Growth + \alpha_4 EIssue + \alpha_5 LEV + \alpha_6 DIssue + \alpha_7 Turn + \alpha_8 CF + \alpha_9 AUD + \alpha_{10} Corporate\ Governance + \varepsilon)_{it} \quad (5)$$

where LNEG is an indicator variable that equals 1 for observations in which annual net income scaled by total assets is less than -0.20 and zero otherwise. A positive coefficient on LNEG suggests that conversed\IFRS firms recognize large losses more frequently in the post revision period than they do in the pre period. A positive coefficient on LNEG indicates that post convergence\revision firms recognize large losses more frequently in the post revision period than they do in the pre revision period.

Influence of Corporate Governance Disclosure Guidelines

A fourth variable corporate governance was introduced to the 3 regressions to determine corporate governance influence on variability of reported NI, large negative income and small positive net income. This is measured by the level of disclosure of the firm's adherence to the corporate governance code.

Population, Sampling and Descriptive Statistics

The sample consists of all companies listed in Nairobi Securities Exchange (NSE) between 2005 and 2014 who comply with IFRS/IAS. Four of the companies are listed in Uganda, Tanzania and Rwanda. Fifty two out of fifty eight companies were included, while 8 were left out due to missing data (balanced data requirements). Data could not be found for both the pre and post convergence\revision period. The 52 out of the 58 firms are 89% of the market and this provided 520 firm year observations included in the study and this is considered adequate for normality tests. GLS random effects were run to generate descriptive statistics and other regressions. In order to decide between random and fixed effects model, since both were used to estimate the coefficients for the model, Hausman test was performed. The Hausman test did not reject the null hypothesis that the unobserved heterogeneity is uncorrelated with the regressors meaning that the random and the fixed effects were not significantly different. According to Princeton (2007) the rationale behind random effects model is that, unlike the fixed effects model, the variation across entities is assumed to be random and uncorrelated with the predictor or independent variables included in the model. In this case the random effects model was more consistent and efficient to use.

Sector analysis is shown in tables 1 and 2.

Descriptive statistics from GLS random effects output are shown in table 3 are divided into pre revision (2005/2009) and post revision (2010/2014) and further divided into test and control variables. There were a total of 520 firm year observations from 52 firms listed between 2005 and 2014 in East Africa. The sample size reflects a balanced panel data used to construct our indicators to mitigate effects of autocorrelation and homoscedasticity. Table 3 shows variability in income (ΔNI) improved from a mean of -0.747 to 0.0039 in the post revision period suggesting higher variability in the post revision and convergence. LNEG increased from.0077 to.0352 reflecting courage to report negative income when that is the case. SPOS improved from 0.0115 to 0.0155. These indicators seem to suggest that financial reporting quality may have improved following revisions and convergence of IFRS.

Table 1. Sample selection process

	Pre Revision (2005-2009)		Post Revision (2010-2014)		Total Observations	
	Firms	Firm Years	Firms	Firm Years	Firms	Firm Years
Total Firms	60	300	60	300	60	600
missing data\mismatch	(8)	(40)	(8)	(40)	(8)	(80)
Total Sample	52	260	52	260	52	520

Source: Author

Table 2. Sector analysis

Sector	Number of Firm Years	% in Sample
Automobile and accessories	39	7.5%
Agriculture	71	13.7%
Banking	99	19.0%
Commercial & Allied	70	13.5%
Construction & Allied	50	9.6%
Energy and Petroleum	41	7.9%
Insurance	40	7.7%
Investment	20	3.8%
Manufacturing & Allied	70	13.5%
Telecom & Technology	20	3.8%
Total	520	100.0%

Source: Author

Another indicator of interest is corporate governance which slightly improved over the two periods. Size and leverage also improved suggesting this was a growth period especially growth in assets which could have been financed from debt or which could benefited from fair value effects of the revised standards.

RESULTS AND DISCUSSION

The results from the analysis are presented in two parts. The first is to test the association between the variables of interest and to determine the presence (or absence) of multicollinearity. The second involves the regression analysis, which will be used in testing the hypothesis.

Pearson Correlations

Table 4 shows Pearson Correlations for the variables used in the study. Almost all correlations are low and negative suggesting that there are no problems of multicollinearity. However there is only one high correlation between corporate governance and size which may suggest that good corporate governance is related to the size of the firms: this may explain higher asset reporting being related to good corporate governance.

Regression Outputs

Table 5 shows the random effects *GLS* regression output for equation on variability of income. The chi square for the pre convergence of 0.3963 is above 0.05 suggesting the results are not significant. R^2 is 10.7 percent (%) while the residual is 0.5507. The post convergence\revisions are significant both for Chi, R^2 and the residual which seem to suggest that variability in NI improved in the post convergence period. This finding concurs with the aggregate results which show that the chi is significant and that corporate governance has a positive coefficient in relation to reporting variability in NI.

Table 3. Descriptive statistics

		Pre Revision(2005-2009)				Post Revision (2010-2014)			
	N	Min	Maxm	Mean	Std. Deviation	Min	Maxm	Mean	Std. Deviation
Test Variables									
ΔNI	260	-5.757	.6346	-.0747	.5485	-.6119	.4887	.0039	.0997
SPOS	260	.000	1.000	.0115	.1070	.000	1.000	.0155	.1240
LNEG	260	.000	1.000	.0077	.0877	.000	1.000	.0352	.1848
Control Variables									
CG	260	.000	.804	.5917	.1871	.000	.804	.5933	.1866
SIZE	260	10.78	19.08	15.72	1.764	10.964	19.616	16.106	1.819
LEV	260	-8.945	11.777	2.255	2.871	-6.943	64.965	3.069	7.160
GROWTH	260	-.994	29.79	.353	2.266	-.694	2.378	.1555	.393
AUD	260	.000	1.000	.961	.1930	.000	1.000	.946	.225
NUMEX	260	1.000	4.000	1.212	.632	1.000	4.000	1.298	.755
EISSUES	260	-1.278	40.611	.704	4.075	-6.928	3.865	.070	.828
DISSUES	260	-.996	28.766	.702	3.152	-.849	15.266	.421	1.605
TURN	260	.051	4.854	.959	.988	.039	5.564	.843	.871

Source: Author- GLS Data output

Tabulated statistics are for the listed firms matched in the pre revision 2005-2009 and post revision 2010-2014.

Test Variables

1. ΔNI -Change in annual earnings (based on end of year total assets).
2. SPOS- An indicator that equals 1 for observations with annual earnings scaled by total assets between 0.00 and 0.01.
3. LNEG- An indicator that equals 1 for observations with annual earnings scaled by total assets less than 0.20.

Control Variables

4. Corporate Governance
5. SIZE-is the natural logarithm of market value of equity in millions of shillings as of year end
6. LEV-end year total liabilities divided by end year book value of equity.
7. GROWTH-Annual % of change in sales.
8. AUD- an indicator that equals 1 if the auditor is one of the large international accounting firms.
9. NUMEX- Number of exchange listings.
10. EISSUE-annual % change in Shareholders' equity
11. DISSUE-annual % change in total liabilities
12. TURN-Sales divided by end of year total assets

Table 6 shows the results for tests for reporting large negative income. In line with prediction, a positive coefficient on *LNEG* implies that firms with converged and revised IFRS recognize large losses more frequently suggesting better financing reporting quality.

Table 7 for testing firms reporting small positive income is also in line with prediction. A negative coefficient on *SPOS* is interpreted that firms applying non-converged and revised standards manage earnings towards small positive amounts than firms applying converged standards. This finding suggests that there is less management of earnings towards small positive amounts in the post convergence firms.

Table 4. Random-effects GLS regression results: Pearson correlations

	NI	Numex	Aud	Turn	Dissue	Eissue	CG	Converg	Growth	DE	Size	LNEG	SPOS
NI	1												
Numex	0.0365	1											
Aud	0.0143	0.0671	1										
Turn	-0.0267	-0.0914	-0.146	1									
Dissue	0.0445	0.0616	0.0238	-0.0191	1								
Eissue	-0.0121	-0.0187	0.0114	-0.0287	0.0022	1							
CG	0.094	0.1553	0.3064	-0.1231	0.0104	-0.0396	1						
Convergence	0.127	-0.0068	-0.0027	-0.0739	-0.0773	-0.0657	0.0065	1					
Growth	0.0878	-0.0118	0.0528	0.0328	0.0902	0.0035	0.0233	-0.0805	1				
De 9	0.0095	0.1691	0.0059	-0.3358	0.0646	-0.004	0.307	-0.0039	-0.0265	1			
Size	0.1152	0.322	0.2669	-0.2764	0.0297	-0.0645	0.7143	0.2071	0.0197	0.5039	1		
LNEG	-0.0395	-0.0495	-0.2483	-0.0488	-0.0159	-0.0085	-0.1637	0.095	-0.036	0.0137	-0.1102	1	
SPOS	0.0055	-0.0126	-0.0632	-0.0486	-0.0049	-0.006	-0.0741	-0.0054	-0.1081	-0.484	-0.0335	-0.1174	1

Table 5. Random-effects GLS regression results: Variability in NI

	Variable	Prediction	Post Convergence 2010-2014(N= 260)	Pre Convergence 2005-2009(N= 260)	Aggregate Sample 2005-2014(N= 520)
1	CG		-.05632	.3233	.15162
2	Residual	Post>Pre	.10303	.5507	.39524
3	R^2		38.67	10.7	0.1280
4	Prob > chi2		0.0001	0.3963	0.0350

Table 6. Random-effects GLS regression: Timely loss recognition-Large negative income

	Pre	Post	Aggregate
Prediction	+	+	+
LNEG Coefficient	.3074	.00497	.32907
CG Coefficient		.02549	-.7889
R^2	55.30	0.5049	0.1418
Prob > chi2	0.2487	0.0000	0.0000

*Table 7. Random-effects GLS regression: Frequency of Small Positive Income (SPOS)**

	Pre	Post	Aggregate
Prediction	-	-	-
SPOS Coefficient	-.2769112	.0031549	-.1002778 (0.05)**
CG Coefficient	-.3447208	.0254132	-.8156306 (0.000)**
R^2	5.039	0.5048	0.1338
Prob > chi2	0.2349	0.0000	

*All tests carried out at.05 levels

** Significant as $p<0.05$

Tabulated statistics are for the sample of listed firms matched in the pre revision 2005-2009 and post revision 2010-2014.

1. Variability of ΔNI – Variance of the residuals from the regression of ΔNI on the control variables.

2. SPOS-Small positive Net Income- Regression based on indicator variable that equal 1 for pre revision firms and 0 for post revision firms. The reading is based on the coefficient of SPOS on the regression output.

3. LNEG- an indicator variable that equals 1 if net income scaled by total assets is between 0 and 0.01 and the reading is based on the coefficient of 1 on the regression output.

Discussion of the Results

Our first objective is to find out whether there is variability in NIs reported in financial statements following the revision and convergence of IFRS adopted by listed firms in East Africa. The results show significant improvements in the post convergence period, a finding which is an improvement over previous studies when mixed results were obtained. The model is fit and explains up to 38.67 percent (%) of the variability while the rest is explained by other factors. This finding is consistent with Outa (2011) who reported higher variability in the post adoption period with the explanation that improved IFRS have the ability to minimize managerial discretion and accounting choices. This finding concurs with Chen et al.

(2010) for the EU, but contradicts Paananen (2008) for Germany and Sweden, and contradicts Elbannan (2010) for Egypt and Ames (2013) for South Africa.

The second objective is to determine whether financial statements report large negative income in the post convergence\revision period as compared to the pre. The results show that large negative incomes are reported in the post revision period a finding consistent with outa (2011). This finding concurs with Chen et al., (2010) for the EU, but contradicts Paananen and Lin (2008) for Germany and, Ahmed (2013) who used meta-analysis, Elbannan (2010) for Egypt, and Ames (2013) for South Africa.

The third objective is to determine whether financial statements report small positive incomes (SPOS) following convergence and revisions to the standards. The results show negative coefficients which are interpreted as quality reporting. This finding contradicts Outa (2011) who found positive coefficients for the data between 1995 and 2004. This result concurs with Chen (2010), but contradicts Pannanen for Germany and Sweden and contradicts Elbannan (2010) for Egypt, and Ames (2013) for South Africa. These results show that IFRS convergence and revisions based on the latest data and institutional changes together with their implementation has actually improved financial reporting in East Africa.

The fourth objective is to determine the influence of corporate governance disclosure guidelines on variability of reported NI, large negative income and small positive net income. The results show that *CG* has a mixed coefficient (negative and positive) and insignificant with *NI* variability, *LNEG* and *SPOS*. The Pearson correlation for *LNEG* and *SPOS* are negative while *NI* is low and positive which suggest low impact of corporate governance. While corporate governance has medium score of 57% (Outa, forthcoming), it is possible that the medium scores imply that corporate governance has not driven up financial reporting as expected and so East Africa needs to push up corporate governance practices to bolster financial reporting. This finding contradicts Cormier (2013) who found that the advent of IFRS reduces the impact of corporate governance on information asymmetry and that earnings value is relevant only for firms with good corporate governance. The findings concur with Outa (forthcoming) that corporate governance is yet to impact fully on IFRS indicators. However the findings show better results from Outa (2011) when mixed findings were obtained.

These findings are an improvement over the previous study and suggest that based on the three indicators examined, quality of accounting information has improved. Possible explanation could be that the study by Outa (2011) applied data between 1995 and 2004 when standards and institutions were being set up. It is possible that recent data with IASB, IFRS standards may have improved. Some of the reasons for the insignificant improvement in earlier studies were inadequate compliance with IFRS, conflict between regulators and IFRS (IAS 39) and enforcement. The findings of Pananen (2008) and the qualitative findings by Kaboyo and Wamwea (2013) and Ernst and Young (2013) have been challenged by this study. While Pannanen findings are contradicted by Chen (2010) too, it is possible their findings fall within the explanations of methodologies and cross country differences while Kaboyo and Wamwea (2014) and Ernst & Young (2013) findings could be due to personal perceptions of managers not supported by any tangible significant scientific evidence. The recent arguments by Christensen et al. (2013) that enforcement play a much more critical role in consequences of adoption appears to be defied in Kenya. Kenya does not have a robust enforcement mechanism as those prescribed by the EU, and probably the US so other factors discussed seem to weigh out over enforcement.

Daske et al. (2008) argued that firms have considerable discretion on how they adopt IFRS leading to serious and label adopters a view held by Prather et al. (2008). It can therefore, be argued that some Kenyan listed companies may have been label adopters in the earlier years but changed over time as the IFRS tune gathered momentum thus becoming serious adopters leading to improved quality in later years. Convergence and revisions has increased quality of standards and improved methodology leading to better quality indicators. Over this period, the Institutes of Certified Public Accountants in East Africa may have also improved their surveillance role, investors became more informed, people learned from their mistakes and IFRS education improved and more accountants were trained.

From an emerging market perspective, Elbannan (2011) attributes the lack of improvement to the lack of enforcement of these standards by regulators and inadequate training of practitioners while Ames (2013) mixed results in South Africa are explained by data quality and methodology. Zhou et al. (2009) who examined the impact of adopting IFRS on earnings management in a sample of Chinese firms found they were rule-based compared to the principle-based IFRS. They found that post-adoption, earnings are less smooth, consistent with a decrease in earnings management. However, they did not observe an improvement in the timeliness of loss recognition. They conclude that the improvements of IFRS adoption are at least somewhat neutralized by more opportunities for earnings management under IFRS. From Corporate governance angle, the findings seem to agree with agency theory, signaling theory, political cost theory and proprietary cost theory which may suggest that East African firm managers are responding to the difficulties and scandals of the past by ensuring that information asymmetries are kept at minimum.

Robustness

Apart from the validity and control conditions applied in the test, we run a number of robustness tests that addresses some concerns noted in previous literature. Sample size was reduced for example to exclude banks and manufacturing sectors. We also run three sectors together with highly reduced sample size. We run the regression excluding the banks which are thought to have higher enforcement and other regulatory measures over and above other listed companies. In all cases results though slightly different in values, still confirm the statistics as showing better quality in the post revision\convergence.

5. CONCLUSION

The study set out to determine whether convergence projects and annual revision to IASB accounting standards improved the financial statement as measured by variability in income, LNEG and SPOS for firms listed in the East Africa's Security Exchanges. The findings show increased variability of change in NI, the firms report large negative incomes and there is less small positive net income in the post convergence and revisions period leading to the conclusion that convergence and revision have improved financial reporting quality in East Africa. The findings on impact of corporate governance are mixed leading to the conclusion that the role of corporate governance in financial reporting quality is yet to be realized. Regulators in East Africa including Accounting Institutes, Capital Markets Authority, banking and insurance regulators should continue enforcing IFRS to enhance quality of reporting and confidence in the capital markets. The report can also be useful to standard setters where issues on accounting conservatism are being explored and how they can be included in the conceptual framework. The findings have to be read with the caveat that the data is obtained from the public domain and it is possible other information with the firms may alter these findings. Areas for further research may need to look at why reported quality show improvements while exploratory studies claims that firms are managing earnings. Further research could also be carried out to determine why the relationship between corporate governance and financial reporting quality is insignificant in East Africa when corporate governance should be a key influencer in financial reporting.

REFERENCES

Ahmed, K., Chalmers, K., & Khlif, H. (2013). A meta-analysis of IFRS adoption Effects. *The International Journal of Accounting*, *48*(2), 173–217. doi:10.1016/j.intacc.2013.04.002

AICPA. (2008). *Convergence with International Accounting Standards*. Retrieved from http://www.ifrs.com/updates/aicpa/Convergence_Accounting_Std.html

A´lvarez, G., Sa´nchez, M., & Rodrı´guez, D. (2008). Voluntary and compulsory Information disclosed online. The effect of industry concentration and other explanatory factors. *Online Information Review, 32*(5), 601-616.

Ames, D. (2013). IFRS adoption and accounting quality: The case of South Africa. *Journal of Applied Economics and Business Research*, *3*(3), 154–165.

Ball, R., Li, X., & Shivakumar, L. (2015). *Contractibility of Financial Statement Information Prepared Under IFRS: Evidence from Debt Contracts*. Retrieved from http://ssrn.com/abstract=2278946

Barth, M., Landsman, W., & Lang, M. (2008). International Accounting Standards and Accounting Quality. *Journal of Accounting Research*, *46*(3), 467–728. doi:10.1111/j.1475-679X.2008.00287.x

Chalmers, K. G., Godfrey, J. M., & Webster, J. C. (2011). Does a goodwill impairment regime better reflect the underlying economic attributes of goodwill? *Accounting and Finance*, *51*(3), 634–660. doi:10.1111/j.1467-629X.2010.00364.x

Chen, H., Tang, Q., Jiang, Y., & Lin, Z. (2010). The Role of International Financial Reporting Standards in Accounting Quality: Evidence from the European Union. *Journal of International Financial Management and Accounting*, *21*(3), 220–278. doi:10.1111/j.1467-646X.2010.01041.x

Chen, Y., & Rezaee, Z. (2012). The role of corporate governance in convergence with IFRS: Evidence from China. *International Journal of Accounting and Information Management, Vol*, *20*(2), 171–188. doi:10.1108/18347641211218470

Christensen, H., Lee, E., & Walker, M. (2008). *Incentives or standards: What determines Accounting quality changes around IFRS adoption*? Presented at the annual meeting of the American Accounting Association, Anaheim, CA.

Cormier, D. (2014). *The Incidence of Corporate Governance and IFRS on Information Asymmetry and the Value Relevance of Earnings: Some Canadian Evidence.* Retrieved from www.cifo.uqam.ca/publications/pdf/2014-01.pdf

Darrough, M. (1993). Disclosure policy and competition: Cournot vs. Bertrand. *Accounting Review*, *68*, 534–561.

Daske, H., Hall, L., Leuz, C., & Verdi, R. (2008). Mandatory IFRS Reporting around the World: Early evidence on the Economic Consequences. *Journal of Accounting Research*, *46*, 1085–1142.

Elbannan, M. (2011). Accounting and Stock Market Effects of International Accounting Standards Adoption in an Emerging Economy. *Review of Quantitative Finance and Accounting*, *1*(36), 207–245. doi:10.1007/s11156-010-0176-1

Ernst & Young. (2013). Kenya firms post false company results. Ernst & Young's 2013 Europe, Middle East, India and Africa Fraud Survey. *Navigating Today's Complex Business Risks*. Retrieved from http://www.theeastafrican.co.ke/news/Kenya-firms-post-false-company-results-/-/2558/1862740/-/ji0al/-/index.html

FASB. (2012). *International Convergence of Accounting Standards*. Retrieved from http://www.fasb.org/jsp/FASB/Page/SectionPage&cid=1176156245663

Francis, J., Lafond, R., Olsson, P., & Schipper, K. (2004). Costs of Equity and Earning Attributes. *Accounting Review*, *79*(4), 967–1010. doi:10.2308/accr.2004.79.4.967

Goldstein, M. (2009). *Drive for Accounting Convergence Slows, G20 key*. Retrieved from http://www.reuters.com/article/reuters

Habib, A., & Jiang, H. (2015). Corporate governance and financial reporting quality in China: A survey of recent evidence. *Journal of International Accounting, Auditing & Taxation*, *24*, 29–45. doi:10.1016/j.intaccaudtax.2014.12.002

Houqe, M., & Easton, S. (2013). *Does Mandatory IFRS Adoption improve Information Quality in Low Investor Protection Countries? Evidence from France, Sweden and Switzerland*. Available at: http://ssrn.com/abstract=2224278

Jensen, M., & Meckling, W. H. (1976). Theory of the firm: Managerial behavior, agency costs, and ownership structure. *Journal of Financial Economics*, *11*(4), 305–360. doi:10.1016/0304-405X(76)90026-X

Kaboyo, O., & Wamwea, G. (2014). *Motivation Factors For Earning Management Practice In Public Listed Companies in Kenya*. A Research Paper Presented at the 5th African International Business and Management (AIBUMA) Conference. Retrieved from business.uonbi.ac.ke/.../MotivationFactorsForEarning

Lang, M., Raedy, J., & Yetman, M. (2003). How Representative are Firms that are Cross Listed In the United States? An analysis of Accounting Quality. *Accountability in Research*, *41*, 363–386.

Lee, E., Walker, M., & Zeng, C. (2013). *Does IFRS Convergence Affect Financial Reporting Quality in China? Research report 131. The Association of Certified* Public Accountants.

Leung, R., & Ilsever, J. (2013). Review of Evidence between Corporate Governance and Mandatory IFRS Adoption from the Perspective of Agency Theory and Information Asymmetry. *Universal Journal of Accounting and Finance*, *1*(3), 85–94.

Leuz, C., Nanda, D., & Wysocki, P. (2003). Earnings Management and Investor Protection: An International Comparison. *Financial Economics*, *69*(3), 505–527. doi:10.1016/S0304-405X(03)00121-1

Lin, S., Riccardi, W., & Wang, C. (2012). Does accounting quality change following a switch from US GAAP to IFRS? Evidence from Germany. *Journal of Accounting and Public Policy*, *31*(6), 641–657. doi:10.1016/j.jaccpubpol.2012.10.006

Ndirangu, E. (2014). *The Effect of Cross Listing on the Accounting Quality Of Firms Cross Listed in East African Markets*. Master's thesis at the University of Nairobi. Retrieved from erepository.uonbi.ac.ke/handle/11295/77882

Ormrod, P., & Taylor, P. (2004). The Impact of the Change to International Accounting Standards on Loan Covenants in the UK. *Accounting in Europe*, *1*, 71–94. doi:10.1080/0963818042000262775

Outa, E. (2011). The Impact of IFRS adoption on the accounting quality of Companies listed in Kenya. *The International Journal of Accounting and Financial Reporting*, *1*(1). Retrieved from http://www.macrothink.org/journal/index.php/ijafr/article/view/1096/905

Outa, E. (in press). Earnings Management & Corporate governance Disclosures: Empirical evidence from East Africa. *Journal of Accounting in Emerging Economies*.

Paananen, M., & Lin, C. (2008). *The Development of Accounting Quality of IAS and IFRS Over time: The case of Germany*. Presented at the annual meeting of the American Accounting Association, Anaheim, CA.

Prather-Kinsey, J., Jermakowicz, E., & Vongphanith, T. (2008). *Capital Market Consequences of European Firms Mandatory Adoption of IFRS*. Presented at the annual Meeting of the American Accounting Association, Anaheim, CA.

Princeton. (2007). *Panel Data Analysis Fixed and Random Effects using Stata* (v. 4.2). Retrieved from http://www.princeton.edu/~otorres/Panel101.pdf

Qu, X., & Zhang, G. (2010). Measuring the Convergence of National Accounting Standards with International Financial Reporting Standards: The Application of Fuzzy Clustering Analysis. *The International Journal of Accounting*, *45*(3), 334–355. doi:10.1016/j.intacc.2010.06.008

Riro, G., Waweru, N., & Uliana, E. O. (in press). Quality of financial reporting: Case Studies from an emerging market. *Afro Asian Journal of Finance and Accounting*.

Robert, C. (2011). *The Financial Crisis Report- US government.* Retrieved from www.gpo.gov/fdsys/pkg/GPO-FCIC/pdf/GPO-FCIC.pd

ROSC. (2010). *Report on the Observance of Standards and Codes (ROSC) on Kenya Accounting and Auditing Standards*. Washington, DC: World Bank.

ROSC. (2014). *Report on the Observance of Standards and Codes (ROSC) on Uganda Accounting and Auditing Standards*. Washington, DC: World Bank.

UNCTAD. (2014). *Report on human capacity development in accounting and corporate reporting*. Retrieved from http://www.iasplus.com/en/news/2014/05/unctad

Zhou, H., Xiong, Y., & Ganguli, G. (2009). Does The Adoption Of International Financial Reporting Standards Restrain Earnings Management? Evidence from an Emerging Market. *Academy of Accounting and Financial Studies Journal*, *13*, 43–56.

KEY TERMS AND DEFINITIONS

Convergence: The goal of establishing a single set of high-quality accounting standards to be used internationally, and the efforts of standard-setters towards achieving that goal. It is achieved through elimination of significant differences between IASB's standards and local standards.

Corporate Governance: Generally defined as the systems by which companies are directed and controlled and this system is mainly acknowledged as the role of the board of directors. In the recent times corporate governance guidelines have been issued to guide the process.

East Africa: The formalized relationship of the Republics of Burundi, Kenya, Rwanda, the United Republic of Tanzania, and the Republic of Uganda, with its headquarters in Arusha, Tanzania.

GLS: Acronym for Generalized Least Squares. It is a technique for estimating the unknown parameters in a linear regression model and is generally applied when there is a certain degree of correlation between the observations and the ordinary least squares and weighted least squares are not statistically efficient.

International Financial Reporting Standards (IFRS): A set of standards stating how particular types of transactions and other events should be reflected in financial statements, issued by the International Accounting standards Board (IASB) and previously issued by International Accounting Standards Committee (IASC) as IAS.

Large Negative Income (LNEG): An expression in earnings management to denote a situation where a firm reports negative results as they occur. It means the firms are sincere in their reporting.

Small Positive Income (SPOS): An expression in earnings management to denote a situation where a firm reports small positive income. It means the firms are smoothing their reporting and so the resulting financial statements are not high quality.

APPENDIX

Table 8. Summary of IFRS Revisions 2005- 2009

	IFRS/IAS	W.e.f	Focus	Revision
1	IAS1- Presentation of Financial Statements.	1/1/2005	Presentations and disclosures	1.IFRS5,IAS 19, IFRS 7 and IAS 23 2. Disclosure of critical management judgments and uncertainties. 3. Transfer policies related estimates and errors to IAS 8.
2	IAS2-Inventories	1/1/2005	Inventory valuation	Prohibition of LIFO
3	IAS8-Accounting Policies, Changes in Accounting Estimates	1/1/2005	Changes in Accounting Policies, estimates and correction for prior years.	Fundamental errors and changes in Accounting policy.
4	IAS10-Events after the Reporting Period.	1/1/2005	Adjustments and disclosures for after reporting period	Presentation of proposed dividends.
5	IAS16-Property, Plant and Equipment.	1/1/2005	Treatment, recognition& disclosure for PPE	1.Disclosure of comparative figures for movements in PPE 2. Capitalization of dismantlement, removal or restoration. 3.Fair value if it can be measured 4. Depreciation at the point when asset is in use.
6	IAS19-Employee benefits.	1/1/2006	Actuarial gain	Recognize actuarial gains and losses in Equity.
7	IAS24-Related Party Disclosures.	1/1/2006	Identify relationships and transactions.	Disclosure of compensation for Key personnel
8	IAS39- Financial Instruments: Recognition& Measurement.	1/1/2006	Fair value hedge accounting, reclassification of financial assets, fair value options, cash flow hedge	Restricted use of fair value to eliminate accounting or economic mismatches.
9	IFR 5-Noncurrent assets held for sale.	1/1/2006		IFRS7,IFRS 8,IAS 8, IAS 1
10	IFR 6-Exploration and evaluation of mineral resources.	1/1/2006		Regulation
11	IFR 7-Financails Instruments Disclosure	1/1/2007	Risk Disclosure-Credit, market and liquidity risks	Nature and extent of risks arising from financial instruments

Table 9. Summary of IFRS Revisions 2010-2014

	IFRS/IAS	W.e.f	Focus	Revision
1	IAS 1-Presentation of financial statements.	1/1/2009	Comprehensive income	1. Analysis into equity between owners and non-owner's transactions. 2. Disclosure of puttable instruments and obligations arising on liquidation.
2	IAS 23-Borrowing Costs	1/1/2009	Borrowing costs	Prohibits immediate expensing of borrowing costs relating to qualifying assets.
3	IAS 24-Related Party Disclosures.	1/1/2011		1.change definition of related party 2. Partial exemption from disclosure of government t related entities.

continued on following pge

Table 9. Continued

	IFRS/IAS	W.e.f	Focus	Revision
4	IAS27-Consolidated & Separate Financial statements.	1/1/2009	Amendments to IFRS 3	
5	IAS 28-Investment in Associates	1/7/2009	Amendments to IFRS 3	
6	IAS 31-Interests in Joint ventures	1/7/2009	Amendments to IFRS 3	
7	IAS 32-Financial Instruments: Presentation	1/7/2009	Classification of rights issues	Disclosure of puttable instruments and obligations arising on liquidation
8	IAS 39-Financial Instruments: Recognition& Measurement	1/7/2009	Fair value thru Profit or loss	1.Reclassification of financial Assets 2.Eligible hedged items 3.Embeded derivatives when reclassifying financial instruments
9	IFRS 1-First Time adoption of IFRS	1/7/2010		Apply IFRS in Measuring all recognized assets and liabilities
10	IFRS 2 Share based payment	1/7/2010	Group Cash settled share based payment transactions	Share based payments for acquiree's employees
11	IFRS 3-Business Combinations	1/7/2009	Choices for non-controlling interests & IAS 36.	1.Applying the acquisition method 2. Discontinuation of Amortization of goodwill & impairment tests for goodwill.
12	IFRS 7-Financial Instruments: Disclosures	1/1/2009	Enhancing disclosures about fair values and liquidity risk	
11	IFRS 8-Operating segments.	1/1/2009	Management approach	Presented on same basis for internal reporting.
12	IFRS 9 Financial Instruments	1/1/2013		
13	IFRS 10 Consolidated Financial statement	1/1/2013		
14	IFRS 11Joint Arrangements	1/1/2013		
15	IFRS 12 Disclosure of Interest in other Entities	1/1/2013		
16	IFRS 13 Fair Value Measurement	1/1/2013		

Source: Compiled by Author from various published audited accounts and IFRS materials

Chapter 10
Impact of Adopting IFRS in Ghana:
Empirical Evidence

Ben K. Agyei-Mensah
Solbridge International School of Business, South Korea

ABSTRACT

This chapter reports on the impact of the adoption of IFRS in Ghana. It first traced the history of accounting standards in Ghana and the reason for the adoption of IFRS in 2007. One of the key issues that IFRS talk about is the disclosure of financial and non financial information in corporate financial reports. Hence this chapter provides evidence on the extent of disclosures, the quality of the disclosures and the determinants of the disclosures. The disclosure of financial ratios, forward-looking information and internal control information in corporate annual reports were extensively studied and findings reported in this chapter. The results of the quality of financial information disclosure mean of 76.80% (pre adoption) and 87.09% (post adoption) for the two years indicate that the quality of financial reports has improved significantly after adopting IFRSs. The findings thus confirms that the implementation of IFRSs generally reinforce accounting disclosure quality. However, the low levels of other disclosures (accounting ratio disclosure quality 6.64%, level of disclosure 60%; forward looking information 35%; internal control information 42%) by listed firms in Ghana do not support signaling theory which suggests that firms with good performance will wish to signal their quality to investors, hence are more likely to disclose their performance by disclosing more voluntary information. It is therefore important for the SEC and The Ghana Stock Exchange to do more by enforcing adherence to the corporate code of corporate governance.

INTRODUCTION

The adoption of the International Financial Reporting Standards (IFRS) has revolutionalised the content of corporate financial reports in Ghana. Financial information disclosure is defined as the release of information concerning the economic performance, position or prospects particularly as measured in monetary terms (Gibbins et al., 1990). This chapter traces the development of IFRS adoption, economic

DOI: 10.4018/978-1-4666-9876-5.ch010

benefits, demerits, extent and quality of disclosures in corporate financial reports. The chapter excludes the consideration of detailed and specific accounting principles and application of the International Financial Reporting Standards.

Among the factors noted to be influencing the adoption of IAS in developing countries, Zeghal, D. and Mhedhbi, K. (2006), singled out availability of capital market, as very cogent.

According to Chamisa (2000) the key determinants of the relevance of IAS in developing countries are:

- The accounting needs of the country,
- The size of the private or public sector,
- The existence of capital market, and
- The similar environment argument.

Prior to the adoption of IFRS in Ghana, the Generally Accepted Accounting Principles used was the Ghana National Accounting Standards. The Ghana National Accounting Standards was partly based on UK accounting standards; Statements of Standard Accounting Practices (SSAPs) and pre-IFRS, International Accounting Standards.

In 2004, the World Bank conducted a review of accounting and auditing practices in Ghana which was presented in its Report on Observance of Standards and Codes. This was to "evaluate the weaknesses and strengths of the accounting and auditing requirements, and to review the reporting requirements against actual practices" (ROSC, 2004). One of the major weaknesses identified in the report was that, the Ghana National Accounting Standards was outdated and differ significantly with International Accounting Standards. The World Bank therefore recommended that Ghana should adopt the IFRS. Hence The Institute of Chartered Accountants' proclamation that all financial reports from 2007 onwards should comply with the IFRS.

In justifying the adoption of IFRS in developing countries, Ball (2006) stated that many developing countries where the quality of local governance institutions is low, the decision to adopt IFRS will be beneficial.

According to Chamisa (2000), "When developing countries adopt the IASC standards as national standards, the primary objective is not to achieve international accounting harmonization, but to meet their need for appropriate accounting and reporting standards".

The International Accounting Standards Board's (IASB) Framework states that;

The objective of financial statements is to provide information about the financial position, performance and changes in financial position of an entity that is useful to a wide range of users in making economic decisions.

Publicly traded companies (that is, companies listed on the stock market) are required to make more financial statement disclosure (compared to privately held companies) for the benefit of outside investors. Since the accounting scandals of Enron and WorldCom, the regulatory bodies have focused on companies disclosing information about the relationship with their public audit firm to determine proper independence.

The International Accounting Standards Committee (IASC) was established in mid-1973 with the mandate of developing new international standards, which would be accepted and implemented globally. The IASC lasted 27 years until March 2001, where IASC foundation, a not for Profit Corporation incorporated in the USA and the parent entity of International Accounting Standards Board (IASB) was restructured to become IASB. A series of accounting standards, known as the International Accounting Standards, were released by the IASC between 1973 and 2000, and were sequentially numbered. The series started with IAS 1, and concluded with the IAS 41, in December 2000. Thus prior to 2003 standards were issued as International Accounting Standards (AISs). In 2003 IFRS 1 was issued and all new standards are now designated as IFRSs.

The objectives of the IASB are:

- To develop, in the public interest, a single set of high quality, understandable and enforceable global accounting standards that require high quality, transparent and comparable information in financial statements and other financial reporting to help participants in the world's capital markets and other users make economic decisions.
- To promote the use and rigorous application of those standards.
- To bring about convergence of national accounting standards and international financial reporting standards to high quality solutions.

The International Accounting Standards (IAS) defines the minimum level of disclosure in corporate annual reports expected by regulatory forces and they are stated in distinct sections of each standard and prescribe what information should be presented in the financial statements.

IAS 1 requires that an entity whose financial statements comply with IFRSs make an explicit and unreserved statement of such compliance in notes. Financial statements shall not be described as complying with IFRSs unless they comply with all the requirements of IFRSs. To be able to meet the needs of the users, the financial statements must not only comply with the International Financial Reporting Standards (IFRS), but also be of high quality.

The quality of financial reports is measured using four key qualitative characteristics of financial information embedded within the Framework for the Preparation and Presentation of Financial Statements issued by International Accounting Standards Board (IASB 2010). These qualitative characteristics are relevance, faithful representation, comparability and understandability. According to the (IASB 2010) relevance and faithful representation are the fundamental qualities, whilst comparability and understandability are enhancing qualities. The Framework states that the qualitative characteristics are the attributes that make the information provided in financial statements useful to users.

Accounting information has the quality of relevance when it makes a difference in a business decision; it provides information that has predictive value and has confirmatory value (IASB 2010).

Accounting information has the quality of faithful representation when it accurately depicts what really happened; nothing important has been omitted (i.e. complete); and is not biased toward one position or another (i.e. neutral) (IASB 2010).

An enhancing quality of the information provided in financial statements is that it should be presented in such a way that it is readily understandable by users, i.e. it should be presented in a clear and concise fashion (IASB 2010).

Another enhancing quality of accounting information is that of comparability. Users must be able to compare the financial statements of an enterprise over time to identify trends in its financial position and performance. Users must also be able to compare the financial statements of different enterprises to evaluate their relative financial position, performance and financial adaptability. Consistency is therefore required, (IASB 2010).

Several studies have been conducted using the IASB's qualitative characteristics to determine the quality of corporate reports. These findings will be reviewed in this chapter.

The data used in this chapter are; World Bank Reports, Newspaper reports during the launch of Ghana's adoption of IFRS and research papers on the adoption of IFRS in Ghana both published and unpublished.

HISTORY OF IASB AND GHANA'S ADOPTION OF THE IFRS

Companies in Ghana are required to prepare accounts in accordance with both local and international regulations. For example, The Companies Act 179, 1963 Section 123 requires every company to maintain proper books of accounts of its assets and liabilities, income and expense. Section 124: requires companies to publish Statement of profit and other comprehensive income, Statement of financial position, statement of changes in equity, Cash flow statement and notes to the accounts to members not later 18 months after incorporation and annually subsequently. Sections 125, 126. and 127 deals with the presentation and components of Income statement, statement of financial position and group accounts respectively. the Banking act 2004, Act 673 as amended in 2007 Act 738, insurance act 724, 2006 and other similar legislation have sections dealing with financial reporting in line with the company's act of Ghana and the required accounting framework.

The International Accounting Standards Board (IASB) was established in 2001 to develop International Financial Reporting Standards (IFRS). The first IFRS was issued in 2003, by which time at least 19 countries required compliance with the international standards. Since then, nearly 70 countries (including Ghana) have mandated IFRS for all listed companies. As of 2007, at least 40 countries continue to require domestically developed accounting standards over IFRS, and this list includes some large economies like Brazil, Canada, China, Japan, India, and the US.

In 2004, the World Bank conducted a review of accounting and auditing practices in Ghana which was presented in its Report on Observance of Standards and Codes. This was to "evaluate the weaknesses and strengths of the accounting and auditing requirements, and to review the reporting requirements against actual practices" (ROSC, 2004). The World Bank used the International Financial Reporting Standards (IFRSs) and International Standards on Auditing as the benchmarks for assessing national standards. The Report on the Observance of Standards and Codes published by the World Bank in June, 2004 was the results of the assessment of the Ghanaian accounting and auditing standards and contained policy recommendations to improve the financial reporting framework in Ghana.

Report on Observance of Standards and Codes (ROSC)

The review demanded an evaluation exercise that;

- Assessed the strengths and weaknesses of existing institutional frameworks that underpin financial accounting and auditing practices;
- Determined the comparability of national accounting and auditing standards with internationally recognized standards (International Accounting Standards (IAS) and International Standards on Auditing (ISA);
- Examined the degree of compliance with national accounting and auditing standards; and

- Evaluated the effectiveness of enforcement mechanisms for ensuring compliance with existing national standards, rules, and regulations.
- It also aimed at measuring the extent to which the Ghana National Accounting Standards match up to internationally accepted accounting standards.

The World Bank, after its evaluation of the Ghana National Accounting and Auditing Standards made several recommendations which was meant to bring the Ghana accounting system in line with international standards. These recommendations served as the main guidelines to Ghana's adoption and compliance with International Financial Reporting Standards. The recommendations are summarized in the following.

Recommendation 1

Raise awareness of investors, directors, managers and auditors to improve the degree of compliance with financial reporting requirements by publicly traded companies. Regulators of the financial system create the awareness among investors, directors, managers, and auditors on the merits of financial statements and the compliance with accounting requirements.

Recommendation 2

Improve the statutory framework of accounting and auditing in the country and this requires that the following actions be taken:

- Fully adopt International Accounting Standards/International Financial Reporting Standards (IFRS) without modifications and ensure mandatory observance of these standards. It was prescribed that Ghana should put in place measures to fully adopt IAS/IFRS and its related interpretations issued by the IASB as legally enforceable standards applicable to the preparation of the legal entity and consolidated financial statements of companies including government owned enterprises.
- Agree to a simplified financial reporting framework for small and medium enterprises. Another recommendation was that Ghana should develop a simplified financial reporting framework for Small and Medium Entities. The Ghana national accounting standard-setters should design specific standards for small-and medium-size enterprises. However, this provision was to be temporal since at that time, the international standard for small and Medium Scale Entities were not ready. However, it was mentioned that when these standards come into force, Ghana must make sure that these standards for small entities comply with them.

Recommendation 3

Establish an independent oversight body to monitor and enforce accounting and auditing standards and codes. Ghana was recommended to set up a Financial Reporting Act which would have a new independent oversight body, called the Financial Reporting Council. The Financial Reporting Council should be made up of mostly practicing auditors. However, other members of the council can be chosen from

Securities and Exchange Commission, Ghana, Ghana Stock Exchange, Bank of Ghana, Institute of Chartered Accountants Ghana, the legal profession, and the academia.

The main task of the council would be to set accounting and auditing standards. The Council will also be responsible for the adoption of IAS/IFRS without modification as well as IFAC's Code of Ethics Professional Accountants and ensure the compliance with the set standards. The council would also develop the implementation guidelines for IAS/IFRS in Ghana so as to facilitate easy and thorough compliance to these standards.

Recommendation 4

Enhance professional education and training. Changes in the global accounting trends must be reflected in the education and training arrangements by ICAG on a timely basis. "Tertiary institutions should be supported to improve accountancy education and appropriate accreditation of external education and training providers should be introduced. The ICAG needs more rigorous arrangements to regularly monitor the quality of practical training provided by authorized training providers" (ROSC, 2004).

Other Recommendations

Other recommendations given by the World Bank include the following:

- Continued professional education in Ghana should be regularly monitored so as to ensure that they correspond to IFAC's curriculum.
- Ghana should make arrangements for improving ICAG's capacity to assist practice development and quality enhancement of its members.
- Strengthen capacity of the regulatory bodies.
- Strengthen ICAG's capacity by establishing affiliations with the developed professional accountancy bodies.

It was based on these recommendations that led to adoption of IFRS in Ghana in 2007.

CASE STUDIES ON EXTENT OF MANDATORY AND VOLUNTARY DISCLOSURE OF FINANCIAL AND NON FINANCIAL INFORMATION IN CORPORATE FINANCIAL REPORTS AFTER ADOPTION OF IFRS IN GHANA

This section of the chapter reports on research by the author on mandatory and voluntary disclosures in Ghana.

Methods Used in Disclosure Studies

Researchers have investigated the disclosure of financial and non financial information in corporate financial reports in two main directions according to Citro, F. (2013, p199):

- Disclosure level evaluation, i.e. analyzing the approach firms have adopted towards accounting (mandatory and voluntary) disclosure.
- Disclosure determinant analysis, i.e. investigating the reasons why some firms disclose more or less information than others.

Generally speaking there are two main approaches to developing a scoring scheme to capture levels of disclosure; content analysis and disclosure indices.

Content analysis is a research technique that make inferences on data obtained from published financial reports. A discussion of this research technique is provided by [Holsti, O.R. (1969); Krippendorff, K. (1980); Weber, R.P. (1986) and Boyatzis, R.E. (1998)].

According to Martson, C.L. (1991) disclosure indices are extensive lists of selected items, which may be disclosed in a company's financial report. The disclosures can cover mandatory or voluntary or both.

$$\text{Disclosure Index} = \frac{\text{Actual Disclosure}}{\text{Total Possible Disclosure}} = \frac{\sum_{1}^{m} di}{\sum_{1}^{n} \text{di}}$$

where:

d_i = 1 if the item *di* is disclosed (0 if not disclosed)
m = number of items disclosed;
n = maximum number of disclosure items possible

It is important to note that the research findings reported in this section used the methodology described above.

Case Study 1: Extent and Quality of Financial Reports after Adopting IFRS in Ghana

This section reports on research to establish the extent and quality of financial reports published by listed firms on the Ghana Stock exchange before and after adopting IFRS. The hypotheses tested were:

H1: *Liquidity is positively associated with the quality of financial and non-financial statement disclosure.*
H2: *Company size is positively associated with the quality of financial and non-financial statement disclosure.*
H3: *Profitability is positively associated with the quality of financial statement disclosure.*
H4: *Auditor type is positively associated with the quality of financial statement disclosure*
H5: *Leverage is positively associated with the quality of financial statement disclosure.*

Quality of Disclosure

Table 1 displays the industry classification of firms listed on the Ghana Stock Exchange (GSE). 31.4% are from the Finance / Insurance category; 17.2% from Manufacturing / Trading category; 14.3% from Paper conversion/Information Technology and Pharmacy / Beverages categories. 11.4% from Agric. / Agro processing and Metals and Oils categories.

From Table 2, 83% of the firms listed on the Ghana Stock Exchange are being audited by Audit firms with international affiliations.

From Table 3, the mean score for the quality disclosure index for the pre-official IFRS adoption period, 2006 is 60.61% and the maximum is 61%, with a standard deviation of 0.0006592. For the post IFRS adoption period, 2008 the mean is 87.09% and maximum of 95.24% and a standard deviation of 5.62%.The results of the quality of disclosure level, mean of 87.09%, for 2008 indicate a significant improvement in the quality of financial reports after adopting IFRS in 2007. It also indicates that most of the firms listed on the Ghana Stock Exchange are not only overwhelmingly complying with the IAS 1 disclosure requirements but also satisfying the IASB's IFRS qualitative characteristics of relevance, faithful representation, understandability, and comparability.

Table 1. Industry classification of Ghana listed companies

Industry Type	Frequency	Percentage (%)
Finance / Insurance	11	31.4
Paper Conversion / IT	5	14.3
Manufacturing / Trading	6	17.2
Agric / Agro processing	4	11.4
Metals / oils	4	11.4
Pharmacy / Beverages	5	14.3
TOTAL	35	100

Table 2. Auditor affiliation by industrial sector

Industry	Auditor Affiliated with International Auditing Firm Frequency %	Auditor Not Affiliated with International Auditing Firm Frequency %	Total
Finance and insurance	11	-	11
Paper conversion/ IT	2	3	5
Manufacturing/trading	6	-	6
Agric/agro processing	1	3	4
Metals/oils	4	-	4
Pharmacy/Beverages	5	-	5
TOTAL	**29 (83)**	**6 (7)**	**35 (100%)**

Table 3. Disclosure Index (2006 and 2008)

YEAR	N	MIN	MAX	MEAN	SD
2006	35	0.7061	0.8100	0.76805	0.000659
2008	35	0.7619	0.9524	0.870949	0.562126

A regression analysis was performed on the dependent and independent variables to check on the existence of the multi-colinearity problem. In a multiple regression model, multicollinearity exists when two independent variables are perfectly correlated with each other. The result is shown in the Table 4.

The variable inflation factor (VIF) in excess of 10 should be considered an indication of harmful multi-colinearity according to Neter et al. (1989). All the VIF are less than 10 and the average VIF is 1.1796 therefore, it can be said that there is no multi-colinearity problem for the model. The results of the regression analysis can therefore be interpreted with a greater degree of confidence. The Durbin-Watson value of 1.723 (Table 5) indicates that the data has no serial correlation or autocorrelation problem. The multiple regression model is highly significant ($p \leq 0.000$). The coefficient of determination (R^2) indicates that 14.1% of the variation in dependent variable is explained by variation in the independent variables.

In order to test the specified hypotheses the stepwise method was used. The great advantage that this method has is that, it optimizes the econometric model so that all statistically non significant variables are eliminated from the model.

Table 4. Multiple regression analysis results (multi-colinearity check)

Model	Coefficients[a]	Unstandardized Coefficients		Standardized Coefficients			Collinearity Statistics	
		B	**Std. Error**	**Beta**	**t**	**Sig.**	**Tolerance**	**VIF**
1	(Constant)	0.641	0.048		13.232	0.000		
	RETURN ON CAPITAL EMPLOYED	-0.001	0.001	-0.306	-1.667	0.106	0.808	1.237
	DEBT EQUITY RATIO	0.010	0.010	0.170	0.933	0.358	0.822	1.216
	AUDITOR	-0.006	0.047	-0.024	-0.137	0.892	0.887	1.128
	NET ASSETS	-2E-07	0.000	-0.222	-1.271	0.214	0.893	1.120
	LIQUIDITY	0.057	0.056	0.184	1.019	0.316	0.835	1.197

a. **Dependent Variable:** Quality of Disclosure

Table5. Model Summary[c]

Model	R	R Square	Adjusted R Square	Std. Error of the Estimate	Durbin-Watson
1	.538(a)	.290	.268	.0480892	
2	.612(b)	.375	.336	.0458038	1.425

a. **Predictors:** (Constant), Auditor
b. **Predictors:** (Constant), Auditor, Net Assets
c. **Dependent Variable:** Quality of Disclosure

The results of the multiple regression analysis shown in Tables 5, 6 and 7 below, show that type of auditor and firm size (represented by Net Assets) are associated on a statistically significant level as far as the quality of disclosure is concerned.

Therefore hypotheses;

H2: *Company size is positively associated with the quality of financial and non-financial statement disclosure*

and

H4: *Auditor type is positively associated with the quality of financial statement disclosure,*

are accepted and the others cannot be accepted. The findings is consistent with earlier research by (Singhvi and Desai 1971; Ahmed and Nicolls 1994, Wallace and Naser 1995, Meek 1995, Inchausti 1997; Dumontier and Raffournier 1998, Naser et al. 2002, Camfferman and Cooke 2002)who found similar results for compliance from companies in many countries.

The findings go on to support the idea that the size of a company's audit firm and its international link do influence the quality of information disclosed in the annual reports. Thus big companies audited

Table 6. ANOVA[c]

Model		Sum of Squares	df	Mean Square	F	Sig.
1	Regression	.031	1	.031	13.457	.001(a)
	Residual	.076	33	.002		
	Total	**.107**	**34**			
2	Regression	.040	2	.020	9.604	.001(b)
	Residual	.067	32	.002		
	Total	**.107**	**34**			

a. **Predictors:** (Constant), Auditor
b. **Predictors:** (Constant), Auditor, Net Assets
c. **Dependent Variable:** Quality of Disclosure

Table 7.

Model	Coefficients[a]	Unstandardized Coefficients		Standardized Coefficients		
		B	Std. Error	Beta	T	Sig.
1	(Constant)	0.9365	0.0196		47.7021	5.05E-32
	AUDITOR	-0.0791	0.0216	-0.5382	-3.6684	0.0009
2	(Constant)	0.9325	0.0188		49.6149	7.62E-32
	AUDITOR	-0.0843	0.0207	-0.5738	-4.0759	0.0003
	NET ASSETS	1.809E-07	8.65E-08	0.2945	2.0917	0.0445

a. **Dependent Variable:** Quality of Disclosure

Table 8. Excluded variables

Model	Excluded Variables[c]	Beta In	T	Sig.	Partial Correlation	Collinearity Statistics Tolerance
1	NET ASSETS	0.2945	2.0917	0.0445	0.3468	0.9854
	RETURN ON EQUITY	0.1246	0.8176	0.4196	0.1430	0.9358
	DEBT EQUITY RATIO	-0.1226	-0.8274	0.4142	-0.1447	0.9901
	LIQUIDITY	-0.0085	-0.0565	0.9553	-0.0100	0.9875
2	RETURN ON EQUITY	0.1895	1.3015	0.2027	0.2276	0.9014
	DEBT EQUITY RATIO	-0.0791	-0.5501	0.5862	-0.0983	0.9664
	LIQUIDITY	0.0136	0.0948	0.9251	0.0170	0.9820

a. **Predictors in the Model:** (Constant), Auditor
b. **Predictors in the Model:** (Constant), Auditor, Net Assets
c. **Dependent Variable:** Quality of Disclosure

by the big audit firms with international links do produce quality financial reports in accordance with IAS 1 and the IASB's qualitative characteristics of relevance, faithful representation, understandability and comparability. According to (Tasios and Bekiaris 2012,14)

Auditors perceive qualitative characteristics as important quality factors of financial reports, considering faithful representation as the most important of them.

Case Study 2: Financial Ratio Disclosure after Adopting IFRS in Ghana

This section reports the empirical findings of a research directed to the investigation of factors that explain the extent and quality of financial ratios disclosed in corporate financial reports in Ghana.

Since the users of the financial statements don't have access to the accounting records, they rely solely on the information disclosed in the financial statements to make informed decisions. Disclosure in the view of, Ho & Wong, (2001) is the best vehicle for communicating with investors. Therefore, adequate disclosure of financial and non-financial information is essential if users are to judge properly the opportunities and risks of investing in the company.

One of the means used to disclose financial information in the annual financial reports of companies is the use of financial ratios. The disclosure of financial ratios in the annual reports helps users in several ways.

- Financial ratio disclosures can enhance the understanding of stakeholders by providing them with a quick and simple tool highlighting firms' performance. Assessment of firm performance can be further enhanced if the ratio data is presented using graphs or tables that depict changes over time. Courtis,(1996).
- Communicating financial ratio information can provide users of financial statements with new information that is not comprehensively presented in any single media, Watson et al. (2002). This information is likely to be even more meaningful for non-sophisticated users in evaluating and making informed investment decisions.

- Ratios allow comparison with peers through inter-firm comparison schemes and comparison with industry averages so that possible strengths and weaknesses can be identified. Elliot, B. and Elliot, J (2013).
- According to Elliot, B. and Elliot, J (2013, p.704) "accounting ratios enable the comparison of entities of different sizes. For example, it is very difficult to compare the absolute profits of two entities without an appreciation of how 'large' one entity is relative to another".

Regulation is the most effective way to ensure that firms disclose sufficient information but currently there is only one regulation,(IAS 33) that compels firms to provide Earnings per Share (EPS) ratios as part of their reporting requirements. Though there is no regulation (financial reporting standard) that compels firms to disclose financial ratios in their annual reports, firms voluntarily do so. Even though users of these annual reports tend to benefit from adequate financial ratio disclosures, the extensiveness and quality of the ratios disclosed tend to be questionable. The question that can be asked therefore is; what is the motivation behind such voluntary disclosures? The study therefore seeks to answer the following questions:

1. What is the extent of disclosures of financial ratio information in the annual reports of firms listed on the GSE?
2. What is the quality of disclosures of financial ratio information in the annual reports of firms listed on the GSE?
3. What are the significant predictors influencing the extent of financial ratio disclosures in the annual reports of firms listed on the GSE?
4. What are the significant predictors influencing the quality of financial ratio disclosures in the annual reports of firms listed on the GSE?

The hypotheses tested were:

H1a: *The extent of financial ratio disclosures is positively associated with firm size.*
H1b: *The quality of financial ratio disclosures is positively associated with firm size.*
H2a: *The extent of financial ratio disclosure is positively associated with return on capital employed.*
H2b: *The quality of financial ratio disclosure is positively associated with return on capital employed.*
H3a: *The extent of financial ratio disclosure is positively associated with return on investment*
H3b: *The quality of financial ratio disclosure is positively associated with return on investment.*
H4a: *The extent of financial ratio disclosure is positively associated with return on assets.*
H4b: *The quality of financial ratio disclosure is positively associated with return on assets.*
H5a: *The extent of financial ratio disclosure is positively associated with liquidity of the firm.*
H5b: *The quality of financial ratio disclosure is positively associated with the liquidity of the firm.*
H6a: *The extent of financial ratio disclosure is positively associated with the leverage of the firm.*
H6b: *The quality of financial ratio disclosure is positively associated with the leverage of the firm.*
H7a: *The extent of financial ratio disclosures is positively associated with a higher ownership concentration.*
H7b: *The quality of financial ratio disclosures is positively associated with a higher ownership concentration.*

H8a: *The extent of financial ratio disclosures is positively associated with the proportion of independent directors on the board. (Board composition)*

H8b: *The quality of financial ratio disclosures is positively associated with the proportion of independent directors on the board.*

Findings

Descriptive Statistics

The descriptive statistics for the variables are presented in Table 9. The first dependent variable, EFRD has a mean of 62.78% with a standard deviation of 8.13%. This level of disclosure is higher than the 9.2% reported by Aripin, Tower and Taylor (2009). A minimum score for the EFRD is 50% and the maximum extent of financial ratios disclosed of 75%. QFRD measures the quality of financial ratio disclosures. The minimum quality for financial ratio disclosure is 2%, the mean score for this variable is 6.6% with standard deviation of 6.1%, with the maximum being 32% The quality of disclosure is lower than 32.2% reported by Aripin, Tower and Taylor (2009). The board composition (BODCOMP) mean score is 66.75 with a standard deviation of 11.37. Average OCS (Top20 shareholding) is 84.2% with standard deviation of 10.5%.

Univariate Analysis

Before running the regression analysis there was the need to verify the correlation between the variables. Table 10 reports on the Spearman's rho correlation indices for all the test variables. The Spearman's rho is very commonly used by researchers. This has been used because of the small sample size and the Spearman's rho will help in getting a clear result. It has been suggested by Bryman and Cramer (2007) that Spearman's rho is a powerful non-parametric method dealing with data, which means they can be used in a wide variety of contexts since they make fewer assumptions about variables.

The analysis shows that Return on capital employed (ROCE) has a significant relationship with Net Assets at 5% level (p=0.020). Return on capital employed (ROCE) also has a significant relationship

Table 9. Descriptive statistics

	N	Minimum	Maximum	Mean	Std. Deviation
NET ASSETS	28	4,449.00	9,381,800.00	1,157,623.54	2,035,039.35
ROCE	28	-8.0	33.0	7.393	8.4518
CUR	28	.3	16.9	2.787	3.9521
TD/TA	28	.1	2.8	.807	.5242
ROA	28	-8.0	33.0	7.243	9.0626
EFRD	28	50.0	75.0	62.786	8.1393
QRFD	28	2.0	32.0	6.643	6.1114
DIV/SHAR	28	0.0	1.3	.169	.2754
OCS	28	56.6	97.1	84.222	10.5312
BODCOM	28	50.0	86.0	66.750	11.3713
Valid N (listwise)	28				

Table 10. Spearman's rho correlations

		NET ASSETS	ROCE	CUR	TD/TA	ROA	EFRD	QFRD	DIV/SHAR	OC	BODCOM
NET ASSETS	Correlation Coefficient	1.000	-.437*	-.010	.333	-.219	-.063	.053	.344	.009	-.111
	Sig. (2-tailed)	-	.020	.961	.084	.263	.750	.787	.073	.962	.574
	N	28	28	28	28	28	28	28	28	28	28
ROCE	Correlation Coefficient	-.437*	1.000	.165	-.416*	.739**	.122	.138	.426*	.006	-.172
	Sig. (2-tailed)	.020	-	.401	.028	.000	.537	.484	.024	.977	.382
	N	28	28	28	28	28	28	28	28	28	28
CUR	Correlation Coefficient	-.010	.165	1.000	-.137	.467*	-.076	.008	.112	.008	-.073
	Sig. (2-tailed)	.961	.401	-	.487	.012	.702	.969	.570	.969	.714
	N	28	28	28	28	28	28	28	28	28	28
TD/TA	Correlation Coefficient	.333	-.416*	-.137	1.000	-.183	.369	-.114	.023	-.196	-.002
	Sig. (2-tailed)	.084	.028	.487	-	.350	.054	.563	.909	.318	.992
	N	28	28	28	28	28	28	28	28	28	28
ROA	Correlation Coefficient	-.219	.739**	.467*	-.183	1.000	.010	.072	.301	-.038	-.223
	Sig. (2-tailed)	.263	.000	.012	.350	-	.959	.717	.120	.848	.253
	N	28	28	28	28	28	28	28	28	28	28
EFRD	Correlation Coefficient	-.063	.122	-.076	.369	.010	1.000	.150	.300	.058	-.033
	Sig. (2-tailed)	.750	.537	.702	.054	.959	-	.445	.121	.771	.868
	N	28	28	28	28	28	28	28	28	28	28
QFRD	Correlation Coefficient	.053	.138	.008	-.114	.072	.150	1.000	.132	-.038	.037
	Sig. (2-tailed)	.787	.484	.969	.563	.717	.445	-	.503	.202	.102
	N	28	28	28	28	28	28	28	28	28	28
DIV/SHAR	Correlation Coefficient	.344	.426*	.112	.023	.301	.300	.132	1.000	-.042	-.061
	Sig. (2-tailed)	.073	.024	.570	.909	.120	.121	.503	-	.833	.757
	N	28	28	28	28	28	28	28	28	28	28
OC	Correlation Coefficient	.009	.006	.008	-.196	-.038	.058	-.038	-.042	1.000	-.251
	Sig. (2-tailed)	.962	.977	.969	.318	.848	.771	.202	.833	-	.198
	N	28	28	28	28	28	28	28	28	28	28

continued on following page

Table 10. Continued

		NET ASSETS	ROCE	CUR	TD/TA	ROA	EFRD	QFRD	DIV/SHAR	OC	BODCOM
BODCOM	Correlation Coefficient	-.111	-.172	-.073	-.002	-.223	-.033	.037	-.061	-.251	1.000
	Sig. (2-tailed)	.574	.382	.714	.992	.253	.868	.102	.757	.198	-
	N	28	28	28	28	28	28	28	28	28	28

*. Correlation is significant at the 0.05 level (2-tailed).
**. Correlation is significant at the 0.01 level (2-tailed).

Table 11.

Model	Coefficients[a]	Unstandardized Coefficients		Standardized Coefficients			Collinearity Statistics	
		B	Std. Error	Beta	T	Sig.	Tolerance	VIF
1	(Constant)	34.202	19.817		1.726	.101		
	FIRM SIZE	-4.673E-07	.000	-.117	-.556	.584	.791	1.264
	RETURN ON CAPITAL EMPLOYED	.279	.402	.289	.693	.497	.200	3.002
	CURRENT RATIO	.130	.473	.063	.274	.787	.661	1.513
	DEBT RATIO	6.394	3.198	.412	1.999	.060	.822	1.216
	RETURN ON ASSETS	-.221	.376	-.246	-.589	.563	.199	2.022
	RETURN ON INVESTMENT	11.575	6.027	.392	1.920	.070	.839	1.192
	OWNERSHIP CONCENTRATION	.139	.156	.180	.891	.384	.852	1.173
	NON EXECUTIVE DIRECTORS	.142	.146	.198	.970	.344	.840	1.191

a. Dependent Variable: Extent of Financial Ratio Disclosure

with Leverage (Total debts/ Total Assets) at 5% level (p=0.000). ROCE also has a significant relationship with return on assets (ROA) at 1% level (p=0.000). ROCE also has a significant relationship with Dividend per share (DIV/SHAR) at 5% level (p= 0.000). Finally, ROA also has a significant relationship with current ratio (CUR) at 5% level (p=0.012).The other variables do not seem to have significant relationship among each other. These results indicate the need to pay attention to possible multi-co linearity problem in the regression analysis.

A regression analysis was performed on the dependent and independent variables to check on the existence of the multi-co linearity and serial or autocorrelation problems. In a multiple regression model, multicollinearity exists when two independent variables are perfectly correlated with each other. Drury (2007, p.1046) sums up the multicollinearity in multiple regression analysis as follows:

Multiple regression analysis is based on the assumption that the independent variables are not correlated with each other. When the independent variables are highly correlated with each other, it is very difficult, and sometimes impossible, to separate the effects of each of these variables on the dependent variable. This occurs when there is a simultaneous movement of two or more independent variables in the same direction and at approximately the same rate.

Methods for correcting multicollinearity include computing variable inflation factor (VIF), dropping one or more of the independent variables from the model or enlarging the sample size. Since it is not possible to increase the sample size at this stage of the research, the first two methods were adopted. As a rule of thumb a variable inflation factor (VIF) in excess of 5 is considered an indication of harmful multi-co linearity, Zikmund et al. (2010). All the VIF (Table 10) are less than 5 and the average VIF is 1.5716 therefore it can be said that there is no multi-co linearity problem for the model. The results of the regression analysis can therefore be interpreted with a greater degree of confidence.

The Durbin -Watson statistic was also used to test for autocorrelation. The Durbin-Watson value of 1.283 (Table 11) indicates that the data has no serial correlation or autocorrelation problem.

Extent of Financial Ratio Disclosure

Overall, the sampled firms show a moderate level of financial ratio disclosure in their annual reports. The level of financial ratio disclosure ranges between 50% and 75% with an average of 60% (SD = 8.13). This level of disclosure is higher than the 9.2% reported by Aripin, Tower and Taylor (2009).

Table 11 shows a negative relationship between firm size and level of financial ratio disclosure, (β= -.117) but statistically insignificant at.05 level (p=.584). Therefore Hypothesis 1a is not supported. This is at variance with what researchers like ; (Inchausti, 1997; Owusu-Ansah, 1998; Ashbaugh, 2001; Al-saeed, 2006; Barako et al. (2006) found that firm size is positively associated with voluntary disclosure in financial reports.

Table 11 shows a positive relationship between profitability, represented by ROCE and extent of financial ratio disclosure, (β=.289). However, statistically, it is insignificant (p=.497). Thus hypothesis H2a is not supported.

Return on investment represented by dividend per share also have a significant positive relationship with the extent of financial ratio disclosure ((β=1.920, p=.070). Hence hypothesis H3a is accepted. This finding is consistent with Singhvi & Desai's (1971) study which found a significant positive relationship between profitability and return on investment and quality of disclosure.

Table 11 also shows a negative relationship between return on assets (β=-.246) and the extent of financial ratio disclosure but statistically insignificant (p=-563). Thus hypothesis H4a is not supported, hence rejected.

Table 11 also shows a positive relationship between liquidity, represented by current ratio and the extent of financial ratio disclosure (β=.063), but statistically insignificant (p=.787). Thus hypothesis H5a is not supported, hence rejected. This finding is consistent with Belkaoui & Kahl (1978) who found an insignificant positive relationship between liquidity and disclosure.

The findings also show that there is a significant positive relationship between leverage (debt ratio) and the extent of financial ratio disclosure (β=.412, p=.060). Thus hypothesis H6a is accepted. This is inconsistent with Belkaoui & Kahl's (1978) findings which showed a negative relationship between financial leverage and disclosure.

The two board composition ratios, ownership concentration (β=.891, p=.384), and proportion of non-executive directors (β=.970, p=.344), though have positive relationships with the extent of financial ratio disclosure they are not significant. Hence hypotheses H7a and H8a are not supported and therefore rejected.

Quality of Financial Ratio Disclosure

QFRD measured the quality of financial ratio disclosures. The minimum quality for financial ratio disclosure is 2%, the mean score for this variable is 6.6% with standard deviation of 6.1%, with the maximum being 32% The quality of disclosure is lower than 32.2% reported by Aripin, Tower and Taylor (2009).

Table 12 shows a positive relationship between firm size and quality of financial ratio disclosure, (β=.165) but statistically insignificant at.05 level (p=.463). Therefore Hypothesis 1b is not supported, hence rejected.

Table 12 shows a positive relationship between profitability, represented by ROCE and the quality of financial ratio disclosure, (β=.404). However, statistically, it is insignificant (p=.368). Thus hypothesis 2b is not supported, hence rejected. Return on investment represented by dividend per share also have a positive relationship with the quality of financial ratio disclosure ((β=.163) but statistically insignificant (p=.455). Hence hypothesis H3b is not supported hence rejected. These findings support Inchausti (1997) who found no relationship between disclosure and profitability. These findings are however inconsistent with Gray & Robert (1989) and Singhvi & Desai (1971) who found a positive relationship between profitability and return on investment

Return on Assets (ROA) has a negative relationship (β=-.350) with the quality of financial ratio disclosure, but statistically insignificant (p=.436). Thus hypothesis H4b is not supported, hence rejected.

Table 12. Model Summary[b]

Model	R	R Square	Adjusted R Square	Std. Error of the Estimate	Durbin-Watson
1	.581[a]	.337	.058	7.8991	1.689

a. **Predictors:** (Constant), Non Executive Directors, Liquidity, Firm Size, Leverage, Return on Investment, Ownership Concentration, Debt Ratio, Profitability

b. **Dependent Variable:** Extent of Financial Ratio Disclosure

Table 12 also shows a positive relationship between liquidity, represented by current ratio and the quality of financial ratio disclosure (β=.116), but statistically insignificant (p=.636). Thus hypothesis H5b is not supported, hence rejected.

The findings also show that there is a positive relationship between leverage (debt ratio) (β=.044) and the quality of financial ratio disclosure, but statistically insignificant (p=.842). Thus hypothesis 6b is not supported, hence rejected.

The findings (Table 13) show that there is a significant negative relationship between ownership concentration and the quality of financial ratio disclosure (β=-.254, p=.017). Thus hypothesis 7b is not supported and rejected. This means that under a higher level of ownership concentration less quality financial ratios are disclosed. This finding is in line with what other empirical studies (e.g., Sartawi, et. al. 2014; Jahmani, 2013; Chakroun, 2013; Lakhal, 2007; Aripin, N., et. al., 2009). This thus supports (Bangho & Plenborg, 2008) argument that the presence of large shareholders encourages "information retention", since they can rely on internal sources to obtain information.

The findings also show that there is a significant positive relationship between board composition (proportion of non-executive directors) and the quality of financial ratio disclosure (β=.246, p=.024). Thus hypothesis H8b is accepted. This finding is consistent with what Aripin, N., et. al., (2009) found in their research. According to Aripin, N., et. al., (2009) the higher proportion of independent directors on the board may mitigate the agency problem through voluntary financial reporting, in this case financial ratio disclosures. The adoption of good corporate governance practices appears to enhance the provision of quality accounting information. These results support the notion that governance plays a key role in enhancing quality financial reporting.

Table 13. Regression results for QFRD

Model	Coefficients[a]	Unstandardized Coefficients B	Unstandardized Coefficients Std. Error	Standardized Coefficients Beta	t	Sig.	Collinearity Statistics Tolerance	Collinearity Statistics VIF
1	(Constant)	7.663	15.636		.490	.630		
	FIRM SIZE	4.968E-07	.000	.165	.750	.463	.791	1.264
	RETURN ON CAPITAL EMPLOYED	.292	.317	.404	.921	.368	.200	2.002
	CURRENT RATIO	.179	.373	.116	.480	.636	.661	1.513
	DEBT RATIO	.509	2.523	.044	.202	.842	.822	1.216
	RETURN ON ASSETS	-.236	.297	-.350	-.795	.436	.199	1.022
	RETURN ON INVESTMENT	3.628	4.755	.163	.763	.455	.839	1.192
	OWNERSHIP CONCENTRATION	.147	.123	-.254	-1.194	.017	.852	1.173
	NON EXECUTIVE DIRECTORS	.132	.115	.246	1.150	.024	.840	1.191

a. **Dependent Variable:** Quality of Financial Ratio Disclosure

Case Study 3: Forward Looking Information Disclosures after Adopting IFRS in Ghana

This section reports on the research conducted to examine the disclosure of forward looking information by listed firms after adopting IFRS in Ghana.

Besides the historical information which is largely provided by financial statements and narrative sections of annual reports, stakeholders want to know what projections firm managers make for the future operations. Especially, investors need such information in making buying or selling decisions about shares of a given firm. They are willing to invest in companies which promise high future performance. The implication is that financial statements that disclose forward-looking information would be most useful to existing and potential investors in particular and other users in general.

The Private Securities Litigation Reform Act of 1995 defines forward-looking information, which can be oral or written as:

- A statement containing a projection of revenues, income (including income loss), earnings (including earnings loss) per share, capital expenditures, dividends, capital structure, or other financial items;
- A statement of the plans and objectives of management for future operations, including plans or objectives relating to the products or services of the issuer;
- A statement of the future economic performance, including any such statement contained in a discussion and analysis of financial condition by the management.

Financial information disclosure is defined as the release of information concerning the economic performance, position or prospects particularly as measured in monetary terms (Gibbins et al., 1990). Forward-looking information disclosure refers to providing information which enables stakeholders to evaluate future performance of a company. Such forward-looking disclosure might involve both financial forecasts such as -financial information such as risks and uncertainties that are likely to affect performance of the firm (Aljifri and Hussainey, 2007).

Since the users of the financial statements don't have access to the accounting records, they rely solely on the information disclosed in the financial statements to make informed decisions. Disclosure of financial and non financial information by companies, in the view of (Ho & Wong, 2001) is the best vehicle for communicating with investors. Therefore, adequate disclosure of financial and non financial information is essential if users are to judge properly the opportunities and risks of investing in the company.

The focus of this report is, therefore, to investigate whether firms listed on the Ghana Stock Exchange are voluntarily adopting the principles of disclosure of forward-looking information reporting. By investigating this phenomenon the researcher intends to provoke debate and discussion on the need for directors to identify, quantify and report publicly on their strategy, the resources and the relationships – financial and non-financial information that they rely upon to implement their strategy, and the risks they face - all with an emphasis on the past and the future.

The hypotheses tested were:

H1: *There is a significant positive association between board size and disclosure of forward-looking information.*

H2: *There is a significant positive association between proportion of non-executive directors and disclosure of forward-looking information.*
H3: *There is a significant positive association between proportion of institutional ownership and disclosure of forward-looking information.*
H4: *There is a significant positive association between higher ownership concentration and disclosure of forward-looking information.*
H5: *There is a significant positive association between Firm size and the disclosure of forward-looking information.*
H6: *There is a significant positive association between the size of the audit firm and the disclosure of forward-looking information.*
H7: *There is a significant positive association between Leverage and the disclosure of forward-looking information.*
H8: *There is a significant positive association between Profitability and the disclosure of forward-looking information.*
H9: *There is a significant positive association between Liquidity and the disclosure of forward looking information.*

Study Results and Analysis

Descriptive Statistics

The descriptive statistics for the variables are presented in Table 14. The dependent variable, DFLI has a mean of 35%, the minimum is 14%, the maximum being 71% with a standard deviation of 21%. This level of disclosure is higher than the 21% reported by Uyar and Kilic (2012). The board composition (BODCOMP) mean score is 66.75 with a standard deviation of 11.37. Average BOC (Top20 shareholding) is 84.2% with standard deviation of 10.5%.

Table 14. Descriptive statistics

	Minimum	Maximum	Mean	Std Deviation	Skewness	Kurtosis
NET ASSETS	4,449.000	9,381,800	1,277,923.37	2,039,053.99	2.535	7.825
ROCE	(8.000)	33.0	6.74	8.529	1.351	2.939
CUR	0.201	16.9	2.66	3.847	2.783	7.566
TD/TA	0.060	2.8	0.88	0.575	1.711	3.529
ROA	(8.000)	33.0	6.70	8.983	1.457	2.431
AUDITOR	-	1.0	0.80	0.407	-1.580	.527
DFLI	0.143	.71	0.35	0.211	.549	-1.130
QOD	2.000	32.0	6.33	6.013	2.846	11.044
DIV/SHAR	-	1.3	0.16	0.269	2.705	8.841
BOC	54.950	97.1	84.26	11.150	-1.467	1.860
BODCOM	14.000	86.0	65.27	14.711	-1.154	3.740
BODS	4.000	18.0	8.60	2.811	1.059	2.938
INSTO	1.000	96.55	75.21	22.604	-1.807	3.190

The low level (35%) of forward looking information disclosure makes it very difficult for the firms' stakeholders to determine future performance of the company. It is interesting to note that majority of the disclosures (90%) is qualitative and all the firms gave good news, none disclosed bad news. These findings are consistent with the findings of earlier studies.

Univariate Analysis

Before running the regression analysis there was the need to verify the correlation between the variables. The Spearman's rho was also used to test whether there is an econometric problem in the model used to determine the firm characteristics affecting the disclosure of forward looking information. Table 15 reports on the Spearman's rho correlation indices for all the test variables. The Spearman's rho is very commonly used by researchers. This has been used because of the small sample size and the Spearman's rho will help in getting a clear result. It has been suggested by Bryman and Cramer (2007) that Spearman's rho is a powerful non-parametric method dealing with data, which means they can be used in a wide variety of contexts since they make fewer assumptions about variables.

The analysis shows that Disclosure of Forward Looking Information (DFLI) has a significant relationship with Board Ownership Concentration (BOC) at 1% level (p=0.000). Net Assets has a significant relationship with ROCE at 1% level (p=0.009); with TD/TA at 5% level (p=0.033) and BODS at 1% level (p=0.004). ROCE has a significant relationship with TD/TA at 1% level (p=0.007); ROA at 1% level (p=0.000) and DIV/SHAR at 1% level (p=0.003).

These results indicate the need to pay attention to possible multi-co linearity problem in the regression analysis. A regression analysis was performed on the dependent and independent variables to check on the existence of the multi-co linearity and serial or autocorrelation problems.

Methods for correcting multicollinearity include computing variable inflation factor (VIF), dropping one or more of the independent variables from the model or enlarging the sample size. Since it is not possible to increase the sample size at this stage of the research, the first two methods were adopted. As a rule of thumb a variable inflation factor (VIF) in excess of 5 is considered an indication of harmful multi-co linearity, Zikmund et al. (2010, p588). All the VIF are less than 5 and the highest VIF is 1.248 therefore it can be said that there is no multi-co linearity problem for the model. The results of the regression analysis can therefore be interpreted with a greater degree of confidence.

The Durbin -Watson statistic was also used to test for autocorrelation. The Durbin-Watson value of 1.704 (Table 16) indicates that the data has no serial correlation or autocorrelation problem.

According to the regression analysis Adjusted R-Squared is 36.7%. That means that 36.7% of the variations in the DFLI could be explained by this model. With regards to the direction of relationship between the dependent variable (DFLI) and the independent variables, the regression results are as are shown in Table 19.

Table 19 (excluded variables), shows a positive relationship between disclosure of forward looking information and board size, (β=0.055) but statistically insignificant at.05 level (p=0.729). Therefore, hypothesis 1 is not supported, hence rejected.

Table 19 (excluded variables), shows a negative relationship between disclosure of forward looking information and board composition (proportion of non-executive directors), (β= -0.082) but statistically insignificant at.05 level (p=0.600). Therefore, hypothesis 2 is not supported, hence rejected. This findings question the monitoring role of independent directors and contribute to the debate on the benefits obtained from having a financial expert serving on the audit committee, as defined by the Sarbanes-Oxley Act.

Table 15. Correlations (Spearman's rho)

		NET ASSETS	ROCE	CUR	TD/TA	ROA	AUDITOR	DFLI	DIV/SHAR	BOC	BODCOM	BODS	INSTO
NET ASSETS	Correlation Coefficient	1.	-.468**	-.011	.390*	-.267	.058	-.070	.199	.001	-.122	.506**	-.012
	Sig. (2-tailed)		.009	.955	.033	.154	.762	.714	.292	.995	.520	.004	.951
	N	30	30	30	30	30	30	30	30	30	30	30	30
ROCE	Correlation Coefficient	-.468**	1.	.182	-.481**	.788**	.150	.136	.518**	-.008	-.127	-.029	.211
	Sig. (2-tailed)	.009		.335	.007	.000	.429	.475	.003	.966	.504	.879	.264
	N	30	30	30	30	30	30	30	30	30	30	30	30
CUR	Correlation Coefficient	-.011	.182	1.	-.167	.439*	.202	.034	.144	-.040	.051	-.260	-.058
	Sig. (2-tailed)	.955	.335		.378	.015	.284	.859	.447	.833	.790	.165	.761
	N	30	30	30	30	30	30	30	30	30	30	30	30
TD/TA	Correlation Coefficient	.390*	-.481**	-.167	1.	-.279	-.043	-.108	-.134	-.147	-.072	-.026	-.159
	Sig. (2-tailed)	.033	.007	.378		.135	.820	.569	.481	.438	.705	.891	.401
	N	30	30	30	30	30	30	30	30	30	30	30	30
ROA	Correlation Coefficient	-.267	.788**	.439*	-.279	1.	.101	.067	.415*	-.053	-.171	-.152	.052
	Sig. (2-tailed)	.154	.000	.015	.135		.594	.726	.022	.783	.367	.424	.785
	N	30	30	30	30	30	30	30	30	30	30	30	30
AUDITOR	Correlation Coefficient	.058	.150	.202	-.043	.101	1.	.235	.305	-.337	.048	.322	-.058
	Sig. (2-tailed)	.762	.429	.284	.820	.594		.211	.101	.068	.799	.083	.762
	N	30	30	30	30	30	30	30	30	30	30	30	30
DFLI	Correlation Coefficient	-.070	.136	.034	-.108	.067	.235	1.	.238	.616**	.002	.242	-.267
	Sig. (2-tailed)	.714	.475	.859	.569	.726	.211		.205	.000	.990	.198	.153
	N	30	30	30	30	30	30	30	30	30	30	30	30
DIV/SHAR	Correlation Coefficient	.199	.518**	.144	-.134	.415*	.305	.238	1.	-.080	-.005	.545**	.294
	Sig. (2-tailed)	.292	.003	.447	.481	.022	.101	.205		.676	.978	.002	.115
	N	30	30	30	30	30	30	30	30	30	30	30	30

continued on following page

Table 15. Continued

		NET ASSETS	ROCE	CUR	TD/TA	ROA	AUDITOR	DFLI	DIV/SHAR	BOC	BODCOM	BODS	INSTO
BOC	Correlation Coefficient	.001	-.008	-.040	-.147	-.053	-.337	.616**	-.080	1.	-.289	-.020	.781**
	Sig. (2-tailed)	.995	.966	.833	.438	.783	.068	.000	.676		.121	.916	.000
	N	30	30	30	30	30	30	30	30	30	30	30	30
BODCOM	Correlation Coefficient	-.122	-.127	.051	-.072	-.171	.048	.002	-.005	-.289	1.	-.190	-.196
	Sig. (2-tailed)	.520	.504	.790	.705	.367	.799	.990	.978	.121		.315	.298
	N	30	30	30	30	30	30	30	30	30	30	30	30
BODS	Correlation Coefficient	.506**	-.029	-.260	-.026	-.152	.322	.242	.545**	-.020	-.190	1.	.294
	Sig. (2-tailed)	.004	.879	.165	.891	.424	.083	.198	.002	.916	.315		.115
	N	30	30	30	30	30	30	30	30	30	30	30	30
INSTO	Correlation Coefficient	-.012	.211	-.058	-.159	.052	-.058	-.267	.294	.781**	-.196	.294	1.000
	Sig. (2-tailed)	.951	.264	.761	.401	.785	.762	.153	.115	.000	.298	.115	
	N	30	30	30	30	30	30	30	30	30	30	30	30

**. Correlation is significant at the 0.01 level (2-tailed).

*. Correlation is significant at the 0.05 level (2-tailed).

Table 16. Model Summary[b]

Model	R	R Square	Adjusted R Square	Std. Error of the Estimate	Durbin-Watson
1	.624[a]	.389	.367	.16780	1.704

a. **Predictors:** (Constant), BOC
b. **Dependent Variable:** DFLI

Table 17. ANOVA[a]

Model		Sum of Squares	df	Mean Square	F	Sig.
1	Regression	.502	1	.502	17.815	.000[b]
	Residual	.788	28	.028		
	Total	1.290	29			

a. **Dependent Variable:** DFLI
b. **Predictors:** (Constant), BOC

Table 18. Coefficients[a]

Model		Unstandardized Coefficients		Standardized Coefficients			Collinearity Statistics	
		B	Std. Error	Beta	T	Sig.	Tolerance	VIF
1	(Constant)	1.341	.237		5.649	.000		
	BOC	.012	.003	.624	4.221	.000	1.000	1.000

a. **Dependent Variable:** DFLI

Table 19. Excluded Variables[a]

Model		Beta In	T	Sig.	Partial Correlation	Collinearity Statistics		
						Tolerance	VIF	Minimum Tolerance
1	NET ASSETS	.015[b]	.098	.923	.019	.994	1.006	.994
	ROCE	.041[b]	.274	.786	.053	.988	1.012	.988
	CUR	.010[b]	.067	.947	.013	.971	1.030	.971
	TD/TA	-.001[b]	-.007	.995	-.001	1.000	1.000	1.000
	ROA	-.012[b]	-.078	.938	-.015	1.000	1.000	1.000
	AUDITOR	.091[b]	.581	.566	.111	.916	1.092	.916
	DIV/SHAR	.053[b]	.347	.731	.067	.974	1.027	.974
	BODCOM	-.082[b]	-.531	.600	-.102	.937	1.067	.937
	BODS	.055[b]	.350	.729	.067	.921	1.086	.921
	INSTO	.009[b]	.053	.958	.010	.801	1.248	.801

a. **Dependent Variable:** DFLI
b. **Predictors in the Model:** (Constant), BOC

Table 19 (excluded variables), shows a positive relationship between disclosure of forward looking information and institutional ownership, (β=0.009) but statistically insignificant at.05 level (p=0.958). Therefore, hypothesis 3 is not supported, hence rejected.

Table 18, shows a positive relationship between disclosure of forward looking information and board ownership concentration, (β=.624) but statistically significant at.05 level (p=0.000). This means that under a higher level of ownership concentration more forward looking information is disclosed. Thus Hypothesis 4 is supported hence accepted. This finding is in consonant with Haniffa and Cooke (2002) and who found a significant positive association between the extent of disclosure and the proportion of shares held by top 10 shareholders (ratio of total shares owned by top 10 shareholders to a total number of shares issued). It is also consistent with Chau, G., & Gray, S.J. (2010) who found a positive association between board ownership concentration and disclosure of voluntary information. This finding is also inconsistent with what has been reported by other empirical studies (e.g., Abdur Rouf & Al Harun, 2011; Yanesari, Gerayli, Ma'atoofi, & Abadi, 2012; Chakroun, 2013; Jahmani, 2013).

Table 19 (excluded variables), shows a positive relationship between disclosure of forward looking information and firm size, (β=0.015) but statistically insignificant at.05 level (p=0.923). Therefore, hypothesis 5 is not supported, hence rejected.

Table 19 (excluded variables), shows a positive relationship between disclosure of forward looking information and size of audit firm, (β=0.091) but statistically insignificant at.05 level (p=0.566). Therefore, hypothesis 6 is not supported, hence rejected.

Table 19 (excluded variables), shows a positive relationship between disclosure of forward looking information and leverage, (β=0.053) but statistically insignificant at.05 level (p=0.995). Therefore, hypothesis 7 is not supported, hence rejected.

Table 19 (excluded variables), shows a positive relationship between disclosure of forward looking information and (ROCE), (β=0.041); but statistically insignificant at.05 level (p=0.786). Therefore, hypothesis 8 is not supported, hence rejected.

Table 19 (excluded variables), shows a positive relationship between disclosure of forward looking information and liquidity (CUR), (β=.010); but statistically insignificant at.05 level (p=0.947). Therefore, hypothesis 9 is not supported, hence rejected.

Case Study 4: Internal Control Information Disclosures after Adopting IFRS in Ghana

This section reports on the research conducted to examine the disclosure of internal control information by listed firms after adopting IFRS in Ghana.

A key issue of corporate governance relate to how a company complies with rules and principles. According to (Kaen, 2003) the actual value of a corporate business is what capital providers or investors will make available to the corporate business on the basis of its anticipated returns to its owners. In all countries listed firms are required to operate systems of corporate governance laid down either by statute or professional organisations such as Securities and Exchange Commission (SEC) and the Stock Exchange. It is important to note that corporate governance has links to risks and internal controls. Whilst good corporate governance cannot stop company failure or prevent companies failing to achieve their objectives, it is a major help, and well-run companies tend to achieve their objectives in a less risky way. As a result it is part of risk reduction strategy for major companies.

When a company collapsed unexpectedly, there is always a suspicion that the internal control system was ineffective. There usually appears to have been inadequate risk management generally.

The primary objective of financial reporting is to provide information that will be useful to financial statement users in making economic decisions. Existing and potential shareholders use company annual reports to evaluate the investment potential of a company's shares, creditors and lenders to assess the creditworthiness and liquidity, government to administer the company law. One of the essential aspects of providing complete and reliable information which are taken seriously by the financial community is to have a set of rigorous internal controls (Elliot and Elliot 2013). The collapse of Enron Corporation fully exposed the malpractices of the company's internal control system by authorities and the formalism of information disclosure of internal control. According to (Deumes, 2004) reporting on internal control improves the quality of financial reporting and reduces governance problems.

Although different countries have corporate governance requirements relating to internal controls and risk management, the UK guidelines provide a useful benchmark. The UK Corporate Governance Code (September 2014) states that:

- *The board is responsible for determining the nature and extent of the principal risks it is willing to take in achieving its strategic objectives. The board should maintain sound risk management and internal control systems.*
- *The board should monitor the company's risk management and internal control systems and, at least annually, carry out a review of their effectiveness, and report on that review in the annual report. The monitoring and review should cover all material controls, including financial, operational and compliance controls.*

Ashbaugh-Skaife et al (2008) found that markets respond negatively to internal control weaknesses.

The Committee of Sponsoring Organisations of the Treadway Commission, (COSO) defines internal control as,

a process, effected by an entity's board of directors, management and other personnel, designed to provide reasonable assurance regarding the achievement of objectives in the following categories:
- *Effectiveness and efficiency of operations*
- *Reliability of financial reporting*
- *Compliance with applicable laws and regulations*

Effective internal control can help an organisation to achieve its performance and profitability targets, and thus prevent loss of resources (COSO 1992).

Internal control according COSO consists of five interrelated components:

- Control environment
- Risk assessment
- Control activities
- Information and communication
- Monitoring.

Bryan and Lilien (2005) examined public filing of firms with internal control weaknesses and found that they were generally smaller, riskier and not high performers in their industry. Thus confirming the importance of internal control in organisations.

The disclosure of internal control information in corporate annual reports and its determinants have attracted the attention of many researchers because of the mixed results produced and this study is thus set to add to the existing knowledge. According to (Kiyanga, B.P.L 2014 73) 'with globalisation, comparative disclosure cannot be ignored as it provides a means of benchmarking disclosure regimes against others with a view to improving the quality of disclosure'.

The objective of this study is to examine whether firms listed on the Ghana Stock Exchange are meeting the corporate governance requirements of internal control disclosures. Thus this study empirically examined the influence of corporate governance structure, on internal control information disclosures of these listed firms. This will help provide some reference information for stakeholders and regulators of these financial reports. Lord Kelvin (19th century English physicist) once said, if you cannot measure it, you cannot improve it. There is therefore, the need to assess (measure) the disclosure of internal control information by firms listed on the GSE so that they can be improved.

Research Questions

The research study intends to find answers to the following questions:

1. Are firms listed on the GSE reporting sufficient internal control information in their annual reports? (i.e. extent of disclosure)
2. Can the information be used by stakeholders to determine level of corporate governance practices in the listed companies? (i.e. effectiveness)
3. What are the drivers of internal control information disclosures? (i.e. determinants).

Corporate Governance in Ghana

The regulatory framework for an effective corporate governance practice in Ghana is contained in the Companies code 1963 (Act 179), Securities Industry Law 1993 (PNDCL 333) as revised by the Securities Industry (Amendment) Act, 2000 (Act 590) and the listing regulations, 1990 (L.I. 1509) of the Ghana Stock Exchange. Section IV of the Code of Best Practices on Corporate Governance states that, 'the primary responsibility for ensuring that good corporate governance prevails lies with the board of directors of the corporate body (SEC 2005 p. 12). The code recommends that there should be a separation between the role of the chairman and the Chief Executive Officer. Section V states that, 'the annual report should contain a statement from the board as to the adequacy of the internal control mechanism and procedures of the corporate body'. The World Bank's 2005 assessment of corporate governance in Ghana made the following disparaging statement;

The annual report does not contain company objectives, stakeholder issues, or governance policies, but must reflect risk factors, RPTs, director and executive pay, and direct (not ultimate) ownership. A Management Discussion and Analysis(MD&A) is normally covered by the Chairman report. SEC enforcement is predicated on capacity and expertise. Compliance with non-financial disclosures is weak.

The provisions in the corporate governance frameworks in the two countries were used as the compliance test in this study. As suggested by (KPMG P.55), 'Companies that are confident of the strength of their governance should maximise the value by informing investors through clear and meaningful disclosure'.

The hypotheses tested were:

H1: *There is a significant positive association between board size and disclosure of internal control information.*
H2: *There is a significant positive association between proportion of non-executive directors and disclosure of internal control information.*
H3: *There is a significant positive association between proportion of institutional ownership and disclosure of internal control information.*
H4: *There is a significant positive association between higher ownership concentration and disclosure of internal control information.*
H5: *There is a significant positive association between Firm size and the disclosure of internal control information.*
H6: *There is a significant positive association between the size of the audit firm and the disclosure of internal control information.*
H7: *There is a significant positive association between Leverage and the disclosure of internal control information.*
H8: *There is a significant positive association between Profitability and the disclosure of internal control information.*
H9: *There is a significant positive association between Liquidity and the disclosure of internal control information.*

Method

Sample

The population of the study includes all the 33 and 35 firms listed on the BSE and GSE respectively, at the end of 2013. Firms with unavailable data were excluded. Applying this criteria resulted in a sample of 28 and 30 firms on the BSE and GSE respectively. The annual reports and data used in this study were obtained from African financials database (www.africanfinacials.com). Annual reports for the financial year 2013 were downloaded from the web site of African financials.com. Only one year was selected because disclosure practices and directors of a firm are relatively stable over time. Each annual report was individually examined and coded in order to obtain the disclosure of internal control information. For the purpose of this article, dummy variables are assigned to represent whether or not an item is used, if an item is used 1 is assigned to that item and zero if an item is not used. The values assigned are then summed up to represent the total score for each company. This is mathematically presented as follows:

The disclosure index = Total internal control items disclosed / Maximum (8) items disclosed for each company. This can mathematically be stated as follows:

$$\text{Disclosure Index} = \frac{\text{Actual Disclosure}}{\text{Total Possible Disclosure}} = \frac{\sum_{1}^{m} di}{\sum_{1}^{n} \mathrm{di}}$$

where:

d_i = 1 if the item *di* is disclosed (0 if not disclosed)
m = number of items disclosed;
n = maximum number of disclosure items possible

Table 20 shows the internal control disclosure evaluation criteria used in the study.

Model Development

The following model was used to examine the relationship between board composition and firm characteristics on the disclosure of internal control information.

$$DICI=\beta_0 + \beta_1\,BODS + \beta_2\,PNED + \beta_3\,INSTO + \beta_4\,BOC + \beta_5\,FSIZE + \beta_6\,AUDT + \beta_7\,LEV + \beta_8\,PROF + \beta_9\,LIQDT + \varepsilon$$

Table 20. Internal control evaluation sheet

Item	Content	Scores
Internal Environment	Corporate governance structure, human resources policies, corporate culture	Disclosing =1, Otherwise =0
Risk Evaluation	Identification of internal and external risk, risk analysis, risk responses	Disclosing =1, Otherwise =0
Control Activities	Internal control activities based on risk evaluation	Disclosing =1, Otherwise =0
Information and Communication	The establishment of information and communication system	Disclosing =1, Otherwise =0
Internal Supervision	Internal supervision from internal audit department	Disclosing =1, Otherwise =0
Internal control defects	The defects or abnormal items in internal control and the improvement methods	Disclosing =1, Otherwise =0
Internal assessment	Assessment from board of directors	Disclosing =1, Otherwise =0
External assessment	External auditor's assessment	Disclosing =1, Otherwise =0

Adapted from: Jainfei Leng and Yiran Ding (2011)

Table 21. The definitions and proxies of independent variables

Variable	Definition/Proxy
Board size	Total number of directors on the board
Board Independence	The proportion of non-executive directors to total number of board members
Institutional Ownership	Percentage of institutional ownership.
Board Ownership Concentration	Total shareholding of top 20 shareholders divided by the total number of shares outstanding
Firm size	The firm's total assets
Auditor size	Dummy variable: 1=Big 4 audit firms, 0= other audit firms
Leverage	Ratio of non-current liabilities to shareholder's equity
Profitability	Return on assets / Return on Capital Employed
Liquidity	The ratio of current assets to current liabilities

where:

DICI = Disclosure of internal control information
BODS = Board size
PNED = Proportion of non-executive directors
INSTO = Institutional ownership
BOC = Board ownership concentration
FSIZE = Firm size
AUDT = Auditing firm
LEV = Firm financial leverage
PROF = Firm profitability
LIQDT = Firm liquidity
β_0 = Regression coefficients
ε = Error term.

Descriptive Statistics

Table 22 shows the descriptive statistics of dependent variable (DICI) and nine independent variables of the 30 sampled listed companies. The DICI mean of 41.80% (SD=.208) implies that voluntary disclosure of internal control information in financial reports of firms listed on the GSE is not very high. The maximum profitability (ROA) is 23.86%, the minimum is negative -53%, with the mean of 5.39% indicates that operating results of listed firms vary significantly. The average profitability is not good enough. On the average 72% of the board members are independent directors, which is good for effective corporate governance. The Securities and Exchange Commission (SEC) and the GSE listing standards require a majority of independent directors on listed companies boards. The INSTO mean of 67.62% indicates that more than two-thirds of the shares are owned by institutional shareholders. The financial leverage (LEV) has a mean of 13.15%, with the minimum of 1.2% and the maximum being 51.57%.

Correlation analysis of DICI and independent variables is shown in Table 23.

Table 22. Descriptive Statistics

	N	Minimum	Maximum	Mean	Std. Deviation	Skewness	Kurtosis
TD/TA	30	0.06	2.77	0.88	0.58	1.71	3.53
ROA	30	(8.00)	33.00	6.70	8.98	1.46	2.43
AUDITOR	30	-	1.00	0.80	0.41	(1.58)	0.53
DICI	30	0.14	0.71	0.42	0.15	(0.03)	(1.35)
DIV/SHAR	30	-	1.25	0.16	0.27	2.70	8.84
OC	30	54.95	97.05	84.26	11.15	(1.47)	1.86
BODS	30	4.00	18.00	8.60	2.81	1.06	2.94
INSTO	30	1.00	96.55	75.21	22.60	(1.81)	3.19
Valid N (listwise)	30						

Table 23. Spearman's rho correlation

		TOTAL ASSETS	CUR	TD/ TA	ROA	AUDITOR	DICI	PNED	BOC	BODS	INSTO
TOTAL ASSETS	Correlation Coefficient	1.000	-.011	.390*	-.267	.058	-.050	.199	.001	.506**	-.012
	Sig. (2-tailed)		.955	.033	.154	.762	.791	.292	.995	.004	.951
	N	30	30	30	30	30	30	30	30	30	30
CUR	Correlation Coefficient	-.011	1.000	-.167	.439*	.202	.041	.144	-.040	-.260	-.058
	Sig. (2-tailed)	.955		.378	.015	.284	.829	.447	.833	.165	.761
	N	30	30	30	30	30	30	30	30	30	30
TD/TA	Correlation Coefficient	.390*	-.167	1.000	-.279	-.043	-.160	-.134	-.147	-.026	-.159
	Sig. (2-tailed)	.033	.378		.135	.820	.397	.481	.438	.891	.401
	N	30	30	30	30	30	30	30	30	30	30
ROA	Correlation Coefficient	-.267	.439*	-.279	1.000	.101	.177	.415*	-.053	-.152	.052
	Sig. (2-tailed)	.154	.015	.135		.594	.348	.022	.783	.424	.785
	N	30	30	30	30	30	30	30	30	30	30
AUDITOR	Correlation Coefficient	.058	.202	-.043	.101	1.000	.310	.305	-.337	.322	-.058
	Sig. (2-tailed)	.762	.284	.820	.594		.095	.101	.068	.083	.762
	N	30	30	30	30	30	30	30	30	30	30
DICI	Correlation Coefficient	-.050	.041	-.160	.177	.310	1.000	.112	.094	.257	.217
	Sig. (2-tailed)	.791	.829	.397	.348	.095		.557	.621	.171	.249
	N	30	30	30	30	30	30	30	30	30	30
PNED	Correlation Coefficient	.199	.144	-.134	.415*	.305	.112	1.000	-.080	.545**	.294
	Sig. (2-tailed)	.292	.447	.481	.022	.101	.557		.676	.002	.115
	N	30	30	30	30	30	30	30	30	30	30
BOC	Correlation Coefficient	.001	-.040	-.147	-.053	-.337	.094	-.080	1.000	-.020	.781**
	Sig. (2-tailed)	.995	.833	.438	.783	.068	.621	.676		.916	.000
	N	30	30	30	30	30	30	30	30	30	30
BODS	Correlation Coefficient	.506**	-.260	-.026	-.152	.322	.257	.545**	-.020	1.000	.294
	Sig. (2-tailed)	.004	.165	.891	.424	.083	.171	.002	.916		.115
	N	30	30	30	30	30	30	30	30	30	30
INSTO	Correlation Coefficient	-.012	-.058	-.159	.052	-.058	.217	.294	.781**	.294	1.000
	Sig. (2-tailed)	.951	.761	.401	.785	.762	.249	.115	.000	.115	
	N	30	30	30	30	30	30	30	30	30	30

**. Correlation is significant at the 0.01 level (2-tailed).

*. Correlation is significant at the 0.05 level (2-tailed).

The correlation analysis (Table 23) shows that FSIZE (TOTAL ASSETS) has a significant relationship with TD/TA at 5% level (p=0.033). BODS has a significant relationship with FSIZE (TOTAL ASSETS) at 1% level (p=0.004). CUR has a significant relationship with ROA at 5% level (p=0.015). PNED also has a significant relationship with ROA at 5% level (p=0.022) and BOC has a significant relationship with INSTO at 1% level (p=0.000).

These results indicate the need to pay attention to possible multi-co linearity problem in the regression analysis. A regression analysis was performed on the dependent and independent variables to check on the existence of the multi-co linearity and serial or autocorrelation problems. However, the VIF value of 1.000 and Durbin Watson value of 1.985 show that there is no econometric problem with the model.

Regression Analysis Results

Tables 24-26 contain information about the regression results for DICI. According to the regression analysis Adjusted R-Squared is 0.158. That means that 15.80% of the variations in the DFLI could be explained by this model. With regards to the direction of relationship between the dependent variable (DFLI) and the independent variables, the regression results are shown in Tales 24, 25, and 26.

Table 24, shows a positive relationship between disclosure of internal control information and leverage (TD/TA), (β=0.443) and statistically significant at.05 level (p=0.034). Hypothesis 7 is supported, therefore accepted. This implies that firms with high leverage are willing to disclose internal control information. This is inconsistent with (Xiaowen, 2013) who posits that companies with high leverage are not willing to disclose internal control information.

Table 25, shows a negative relationship between disclosure of internal control information and (BODS) board size, (β=-0.167) but it is statistically insignificant at.05 level (p=0.408). Therefore, hypothesis 1 is not supported, hence rejected.

Table 26, shows a positive relationship between disclosure of internal control information and (PNED) board independence (proportion of non-executive directors), (β= 0.220) but it is statistically insignificant at.05 level (p=0.301). Therefore, the hypothesis 2 is not supported hence rejected.

Table 24. Model Summary[b]

Model	R	R Square	Adjusted R Square	Std. Error of the Estimate	Durbin-Watson
1	.443[a]	.196	.158	.11378	1.985

a. **Predictors:** (Constant), TD/TA
b. **Dependent Variable:** DICI

Table 25. Coefficients[a]

Model		Unstandardized Coefficients		Standardized Coefficients			
		B	Std. Error	Beta	T	Sig.	VIF
1	(Constant)	.788	.047		16.703	.000	
	TD/TA	.109	.048	.443	2.265	.034	1.000

a. **Dependent Variable:** DICI

Table 26. Excluded Variables[a]

Model		Beta In	T	Sig.	Partial Correlation	Collinearity Statistics	
						Tolerance	Minimum Tolerance
1	NET ASSETS	-.165[b]	-.778	.446	-.171	.863	.863
	PNED	.220[b]	1.061	.301	.231	.881	.881
	CUR	-.060[b]	-.293	.772	-.065	.948	.948
	ROA	.085[b]	.408	.688	.091	.926	.926
	AUDITOR	.270[b]	1.384	.182	.296	.962	.962
	BOC	-.169[b]	-.858	.401	-.188	.997	.997
	BODS	.167[b]	.845	.408	.186	.993	.993
	INSTO	.019[b]	.093	.927	.021	.925	.925

a. **Dependent Variable:** DICI
b. **Predictors in the Model:** (Constant), TD/TA

Table 26, shows a negative relationship between disclosure of internal control information and (INSTO) institutional ownership, (β=-0.054) but it is statistically insignificant at.05 level (p=0.838). Therefore, hypothesis 3 is not supported, hence rejected.

Table 26, shows a positive relationship between disclosure of internal control information and (BOC) board ownership concentration, (β=.169) but statistically insignificant at.05 level (p=0.401). Therefore, hypothesis 4 is not supported, hence rejected.

Table 26, shows a negative relationship between disclosure of internal control information and (NET ASSETS) firm size, (β=-.165) but it is statistically insignificant at.05 level (p=0.446). Therefore, hypothesis 5 is not supported, therefore rejected. This finding is inconsistent with that of (Kent and Ung, 2003; Celik, et al 2006; O'Sullivan et al. 2008).

Table 26, shows a positive relationship between disclosure of internal control information and (AUDT) size of audit firm, (β=0.270) but it is statistically insignificant at.05 level (p=0.182). Therefore, hypothesis 6 is not supported, hence rejected.

Table 26, shows a positive relationship between disclosure of internal control information (PROF), profitability (β=0.085); but it is statistically insignificant at.05 level (p=0.688). Therefore, hypothesis 8 is not supported, hence rejected.

Table 26, shows a negative relationship between disclosure of internal control information and liquidity (CUR), (β=-0.060); but it is statistically insignificant at.05 level (p=0.772). Therefore, hypothesis 9 is not supported, hence rejected.

FUTURE RESEARCH DIRECTIONS

One of the shortcomings of the case studies cited in this chapter is fact that it was limited to firms listed on the Ghana Stock Exchange. This makes it very difficult to generalize the findings. The author therefore, recommends that other researchers consider working with a bigger sample comprising some of the unlisted firms in Ghana. Further longitudinal studies might be conducted to investigate disclosure patterns of companies across years. The results may differ across different years if multiple years are considered.

CONCLUSION

The results of the quality of financial information disclosure mean of 87.09% for year 2009 as against 76.8% for 2006 indicates significant improvement in the quality of financial reports after adopting IFRS in Ghana. It also indicates overwhelming compliance with the IASB's IFRS Framework. The study confirms that the implementation of IFRSs generally reinforce accounting quality. With the improvement in the quality of the financial reports after adopting IFRSs users are assured of useful information for financial decision-making.

The results of the multiple regression analysis shows that company size, represented by net assets and Auditor type were found to be statistically associated with the quality of financial information disclosed. This means that big firms audited by big audit firms tend to produce high quality accounting reports. Thus fulfilling the requirements of not only the qualitative characteristics of financial statements but also the tenets of agency theory.

As a result of asymmetric information and self-interests, the principals (shareholders) should have reasons not to trust the agents (the managers). In this sense, certain mechanisms (auditors) are put in place to align the interests of agents with those of the principals, thus reducing the possibility of information asymmetry, as well as opportunistic behaviors (ICAEW, 2005).

This second case study provided evidence on the extent and quality of financial ratio disclosures in the annual reports of firms listed on the Ghana Stock Exchange. Agency and Signaling theories were used to test the relationship between firm size, profitability, liquidity, leverage, board composition and ownership concentration with the dependent variables, EFRD and QFRD.

The multiple regression results indicate that leverage and profitability are significant in predicting the extent of financial ratio disclosures. This is consistent with agency theory where highly leveraged firms may deal with higher agency costs due to higher auditing fees; therefore, they will have to disclose more information, including financial ratios. Firms with high profits also tend to disclose more information, including financial ratios thus signaling their performance in order to attract investments and gain shareholder confidence.

For the quality of financial ratios disclosures, the corporate governance mechanism do have predictive properties. The findings show that there is a significant positive relationship between board composition (proportion of non-executive directors) and the quality of financial ratio Whereas, ownership concentration is significantly affect the quality of financial ratio disclosures but in opposite direction with the expectation. The findings from this research are potentially important for regulatory bodies, professional accounting bodies, listed companies, business communities including shareholders. In addition, the existence of the Conceptual Framework by the IASB should be more fully utilized. These valuable framework documents should be regarded as vitally important guidelines for the preparers of financial statements to ensure that users are provided with quality information. Thus, the elements of relevance, reliability, comparability and understandability should be more inculcated into accounting research as well as listed firms' financial reporting communication practices. More extensive and higher quality dissemination of financial ratios disclosures would provide greater transparency for all stakeholders.

The third case study investigated the influence of firm-specific characteristics which include, Board size proportion of Non-Executive Directors, Institutional ownership, ownership concentration, firm size, profitability, debt equity ratio, liquidity and leverage on the disclosure of forward looking information by firms listed on the Ghana Stock Exchange for the year ending December 2013. The study provides empirical evidence in relation to the impact of these variables on the information disclosure level.

This study extends the literature on corporate governance and disclosure by showing the association between forward-looking information disclosure and directors' characteristics. The results of the disclosure of forward looking information, mean of 35%, indicate that most of the firms listed on the Ghana Stock Exchange did not disclose sufficient forward looking information in their annual reports. The low level (35%) of forward looking information disclosure makes it very difficult for the firms' stakeholders to determine future performance of the company. This low forward looking disclosure level might be attributed to pessimism in future expectations, unwillingness to disclose too much information which might weaken competitive position in the marketplace, litigation costs due to wrong projections, or some other reasons. The finding does not support IASB's strategy of encouraging more voluntary disclosures of nonfinancial and forward looking information to satisfy the information needs of users of financial statements. The finding also does not support signaling theory which suggests that firms with good performance will wish to signal their quality to investors, hence are more likely to disclose their performance by disclosing more forward looking information.

The study provides empirical evidence in relation to the impact of these variables on the information disclosure level. The results of the regression analysis indicate that board ownership concentration is the significant variable that explain the level of forward looking information disclosure; the eight other variables are statistically insignificant.

The study found that board independence is not associated with the disclosure of forward-looking information. This finding question the monitoring role of independent directors and contribute to the debate on the benefits obtained from having a financial expert serving on the audit committee, as defined by the Sarbanes-Oxley Act. The study is based on data for the year 2013. Further longitudinal studies might be conducted to investigate disclosure patterns of companies across years. This study used only the annual reports of firms as the information disclosure source; other sources such as web sites, press releases, and prospectuses were not utilized. Future research can be conducted using these other sources to improve the findings. This research study adds to the prior literature by exploring the effect of firm characteristics on the disclosure of forward-looking information. It is believed that this study will improve the insight of the variables that could impact on forward-looking information in listed companies in countries south of the Sahara.

The fourth case study investigated the influence of corporate governance and firm-specific characteristics which include, Board size proportion of Non-Executive Directors, Institutional ownership, ownership concentration, firm size, profitability, debt equity ratio, liquidity and leverage on the disclosure of internal control information by firms listed on the Ghana Stock Exchange for the year ending December 2013. The study provides empirical evidence in relation to the impact of these variables on the internal control disclosure level.

This study extends the literature on corporate governance and disclosure by showing the association between internal control disclosure and directors' characteristics. The results of the disclosure of internal control information, mean of 42% is not encouraging. The implication is that corporate governance in Ghana is not taken serious by the listed firms. This findings confirms the World Banks study which found the disclosure of non-financial information in financial reports of listed firms as weak.

The finding does not support IASB's strategy of encouraging more voluntary disclosures of nonfinancial and internal control information to satisfy the information needs of users of financial statements. The low level of disclosure by listed firms in Ghana does not support *signaling theory which suggests that firms with good performance will wish to signal their quality to investors, hence are more likely to disclose their performance by disclosing more internal control information.* It is therefore important for the SEC and Stock Exchange to do more by enforcing adherence to the corporate code of corporate governance. The SEC and the other supervisory authorities should be resourced to help them meet their regulatory tasks in order to help the listed firms improve on their corporate governance practices. Special attention should also be paid on the quality of information disclosed by listed firms. The results show that in the case of Ghana, board composition is not related to the disclosure of internal control information. Further longitudinal studies might be conducted to investigate disclosure patterns of companies across years. The results may differ across different years if multiple years are considered. This study used only the annual reports of firms as the information disclosure source; other sources such as web sites, press releases, and prospectuses were not utilized. Future research can be conducted using these other sources to improve the findings. This research study adds to the prior literature by exploring the effect of firm characteristics on the disclosure of internal control information in emerging markets. It is believed that this study will improve the insight of the variables that could impact on internal control information disclosure in listed companies in countries south of the Sahara. The researcher on the basis of the findings suggest that listed firms in Ghana should improve their corporate governance and internal control systems for health and sustainable development of the firms.

REFERENCES

Abdur Rouf, M., & Al Harun, A. (2011). Ownership structure and voluntary disclosure in annual reports of Bangladesh. *Pakistan Journal of Commerce and Social Sciences*, *5*(1), 129–139.

Agyei-Mensah, B. K. (2013). Adoption of International Financial Reporting Standard (IFRS) in Ghana and the Quality of Financial Statement Disclosures. *The International Journal of Accounting and Financial Reporting*, *3*(2), 269–286. doi:10.5296/ijafr.v3i2.4489

Agyei-Mensah, B. K. (2015). The determinants of Financial Ratio Disclosures and Quality: Evidence from an Emerging Market. *International Journal of Accounting and Financial Reporting*, *5*(1), 188–211. doi:10.5296/ijafr.v5i1.7267

Agyeman, O. S., Aboagye, E., & Ahali, A. Y. O. (2013). Prospect and Challenges of Corporate Governance in Ghana. *International Journal of Scientific and Research Publications*, *3*(5), 1–9.

Ahmed, K., & Courtis, J. K. (1999). Association Between Corporate Characteristics and Disclosure Levels in Annual Reports: A Meta-Analysis. *The British Accounting Review*, *132*(1), 35–61. doi:10.1006/bare.1998.0082

Ajinkya, Bhojraj, & Sengupta. (2005). The association between outside directors, institutional investors and the properties of management earnings forecast. *Journal of Accounting Research, 43*(3), 343-375.

Akhtaruddin, M., & Haron, H. (2010). Board composition, audit committees' effectiveness and corporate voluntary disclosure. *Asian Review of Accounting*, *18*(1), 68–82. doi:10.1108/13217341011046015

Al-Ajmi, J. (2008). The usefulness of corporate governance and financial ratios to credit and financial analysts: Evidence from Bahrain. European *Journal of Economics Finance and Administrative Sciences*, *11*(September), 107–125.

Aljifri, K., & Hussainey, K. (2007). The determinants of forward-looking information in annual reports of UAE companies. *Managerial Auditing Journal*, *22*(9), 881–894. doi:10.1108/02686900710829390

Alsaeed, K. (2006). The association between firm-specific characteristics and disclosure. *Managerial Auditing Journal*, *21*(5), 476–496. doi:10.1108/02686900610667256

Aripin, N., Tower, G., & Taylor, G. (2009). *Reporting financial ratios in annual reports: Voluntary disclosure perspective*. In Asian Academic Accounting Association (AAAA) Annual Conference, Istanbul, Turkey.

Ashbaugh-Skaife, H., Collins, D., Kinney, W., & Lanfond, R. (2008). The Effect of SOX internal control deficiencies on firm risk and cost of equity. *Journal of Accounting Research*, *47*(1), 1–43. doi:10.1111/j.1475-679X.2008.00315.x

Assenso-Okofo O., Ali J. M., & Ahmed K. (2009). The Development of Accounting and Reporting in Ghana. *The International Journal of Accounting, 46*(2011), 459-480.

Ball, R. (2006). International Financial Reporting Standards (IFRS): Pros and cons for investors. *Accounting and Business Review*, *36*(sup1), 5–27. doi:10.1080/00014788.2006.9730040

Bangho, J., & Plenborg, T. (2008). Value relevance of voluntary disclosure in the annual report. *Accounting and Finance*, *48*(2), 159–180. doi:10.1111/j.1467-629X.2007.00240.x

Barako, D. G. (2007). Determinants of voluntary disclosures in Kenyan companies annual reports. *African Journal of Business Management*, *1*(5), 113–128.

Belkaoui, A., & Kahl, A. (1978). *Corporate financial disclosure in Canada*. CCGAA Research Monograph.

Boyatzis, R. E. (1998). *Transforming qualitative information: Thematic analysis and code development*. Thousand Oaks, CA: Sage Publications.

Bryman, A., & Cramer, D. (2007). *Quantitative data analysis with SPSS for windows*. London: Routledge.

Chakroun, R. (2013). Family control, board of directors‘ independence and extent of voluntary disclosure in the annual reports: Case of Tunisian companies. *Journal of Business Studies Quarterly*, *5*(1), 22–42.

Chamisa. (2000). *The Relevance of and Observance of the IASC Standards in Developing Countries and the Particular Case of Zimbabwe*. University of Illinois.

Chau, G., & Gray, S. J. (2010). Ownership structure and corporate voluntary disclosure in Hong Kong and Singapore. *The International Journal of Accounting*, *37*(2), 247–265. doi:10.1016/S0020-7063(02)00153-X

Cheng, E., & Courtenay, S. (2006). Board composition, regulatory regime and voluntary disclosure. *The International Journal of Accounting*, *41*(3), 262–289. doi:10.1016/j.intacc.2006.07.001

Chow, C. W., & Wong-Boren, A. (1987). Voluntary financial disclosure by Mexican corporations. *Accounting Review*, *62*(3), 533–541.

Cinca, C. S., Molinero, C. M., & Larraz, J. L. G. (2005). Country and size effects in financial ratios: A European perspective. *Global Finance Journal*, *16*(1), 26–47. doi:10.1016/j.gfj.2005.05.003

Cooke, T. (1991). An assessment of voluntary disclosure in annual reports of Japanese corporations. *The International Journal of Accounting*, *26*(3), 174–189.

Cooke, T. E. (1989). Voluntary corporate disclosure by Swedish companies. *Journal of International Financial Management and Accounting*, *1*(2), 171–195. doi:10.1111/j.1467-646X.1989.tb00009.x

Drury, C. (2007). *Management and Cost Accounting* (6th ed.). London: Thomson Learning.

Dumontier, P., & Raffournier, B. (1998). Why firms comply voluntarily with IAS: An empirical analysis with Swiss data. *Journal of International Financial Management & Accounting*, *9*(3), 216–245. doi:10.1111/1467-646X.00038

Eng, L. L., & Mak, Y. T. (2003). Corporate governance and voluntary disclosure. *Journal of Accounting and Public Policy*, *22*(4), 325–345. doi:10.1016/S0278-4254(03)00037-1

Gibbins, M., Richardson, A., & Waterhouse, J. (1990). The Management of Corporate Financial Disclosures: Opportunism, Ritualism, Policies and Processes. *Journal of Accounting Research*, *28*(1), 121–143. doi:10.2307/2491219

Gul, F. A., & Leung, S. (2004). Board leadership, outside directors' expertise and voluntary disclosures. *Journal of Accounting and Public Policy*, *23*(5), 351–379. doi:10.1016/j.jaccpubpol.2004.07.001

Habib, A., & Azim, I. (2008). Corporate governance and the value relevance of accounting information: Evidence from Australia. *Accounting Research Journal*, *21*(2), 167–194. doi:10.1108/10309610810905944

Haniffa, R. M., & Cooke, T. E. (2002). Culture, corporate governance and disclosure in Malaysian Corporations. *Abacus*, *38*(3), 317–349. doi:10.1111/1467-6281.00112

Ho, S. M. S., & Wong, K. R. (2001). A study of the relationship between corporate governance structures and the extent of voluntary disclosure. *Journal of International Accounting, Auditing & Taxation*, *10*(2), 139–156. doi:10.1016/S1061-9518(01)00041-6

Holsti, O.R. (1969). *Content analysis for the social sciences and humanities*. Reading, MA: Addison-Wesley.

Hossain, M., Perera, M. H. B., & Rahmam, A. R. (1995). Voluntary disclosure in the annual reports of New Zealand companies. *Journal of International Financial Management and Accounting*, *6*(1), 69–85. doi:10.1111/j.1467-646X.1995.tb00050.x

IASB. (2010). *The Conceptual Framework for Financial Reporting*. London: IASB.

Inchausti, B. (1997). The influence of company characteristics and accounting regulations on information disclosure by Spanish firms. *European Accounting Review*, *6*(1), 45–68. doi:10.1080/096381897336863

Jahmani, O. (2013). Ownership structure and corporate voluntary disclosure: Evidence from Bahrain. *International Journal of Accounting and Financial Reporting*, *3*(2), 133–148. doi:10.5296/ijafr.v3i2.4088

Jensen, M. C., & Meckling, W. H. (1976). Theory of the firm: Managerial behaviour, agency costs and ownership structure. *Journal of Financial Economics, 3*(4), 305–360. doi:10.1016/0304-405X(76)90026-X

Krippendorff, K. (1980). *Content analysis: an introduction to its methodology*. Beverly Hills, CA: Sage Publications.

Lakhal, F. (2007). Ownership structure and voluntary disclosures: the case of French-listed firms. *Corporate Ownership and Control, 5*(1), 131-138.

Lundholm, R., & Winkle, M. V. (2006). Motives for disclosure and non-disclosure: A framework and review of the evidence. *Accounting and Business Review*, *36*(Special issue), 43–48. doi:10.1080/00014788.2006.9730044

Malone, D., Fries, C., & Jones, T. (1993). An Empirical investigation of the extent of corporate financial disclosure in the oil and gas industry. *Journal of Accounting, Auditing & Finance*, *8*(3), 249–273.

McKinnon, J. L., & Dalimunthe, L. (1993). Voluntary disclosure of segment information by Australian diversified companies. *Accounting and Finance*, *33*(1), 33–50. doi:10.1111/j.1467-629X.1993.tb00192.x

Meek, G. K., Gray, S. J., & Roberts, C. B. (1995). Factors influencing voluntary annual report disclosures by US, UK and continental European multinational corporations. *Journal of International Business Studies*, *26*(3), 555–572. doi:10.1057/palgrave.jibs.8490186

Mitchell, J. (2006). Selective reporting of financial ratios in Australian annual reports: Evidence from a voluntary reporting environment. *Accounting Research Journal*, *19*(1), 5–30.

Myers, S., & Majluf, N. (1984). Corporate financing and investment decisions when firms have information that investors do not have. *Journal of Financial Economics*, *13*(2), 187–221. doi:10.1016/0304-405X(84)90023-0

Okpala, K.E. (2012). Adoption of IFRS and Financial Statement effects: The Perceived Implications on FDI and Nigeria Economy. *Australian Journal of Business and Management Research, 2*(5), 76-83.

Owusu-Ansah, S. (1998). The impact of corporate attributes on the extent of mandatory disclosure and reporting by listed companies in Zimbabwe. *The International Journal of Accounting*, *33*(5), 605–631. doi:10.1016/S0020-7063(98)90015-2

Private Securities Litigation Reform Act of 1995. (n.d.). Retrieved from www.cga.ct.gov/2002.rpt.2002-R-0695.htm

Ross, S. A. (1977). The determination of financial structure: The incentive signaling approach. *The Bell Journal of Economics*, *8*(Spring), 23–40. doi:10.2307/3003485

Sartawi, I. S. M., Hindawi, R. M., Bsoul, R., & Jamil Ali, A. (2014). Board Composition, Firm characteristics, and voluntary disclosure: The case of Jordanian firms listed on the Amman stock exchange. *International Business Research*, *7*(6), 67–82. doi:10.5539/ibr.v7n6p67

Singhvi, S. S., & Desai, H. B. (1971). An empirical analysis of the quality of corporate financial disclosure. *Accounting Review*, *46*(1), 129–138.

Song, J., & Windram, B. (2004). Benchmarking audit committee effectiveness in financial reporting. *International Journal of Auditing*, *8*(3), 195–205. doi:10.1111/j.1099-1123.2004.00090.x

Tasios, S., & Bekiaris, M. (2012). Auditor's perceptions of financial reporting quality: The case of Greece. *International Journal of Accounting and Financial Reporting*, *2*(1), 57–74. doi:10.5296/ijafr.v2i1.1286

Taylor, G., Tower, G., Van Der Zahn, M., & Neilson, J. (2008). Corporate governance determinants on Australian resource companies' financial instrument disclosure practices. *Asian Review of Accounting*, *16*(1), 56–73. doi:10.1108/13217340810872472

Wallace, R. S. O., Naser, K., & Mora, A. (1995). The relationship between the comprehensiveness of corporate annual reports and firm characteristics in Spain. *Accounting and Business Review*, *25*(97), 41–53. doi:10.1080/00014788.1994.9729927

Watson, A., Shrives, P., & Marston, C. (2002). Voluntary disclosure of accounting ratios in the UK. *The British Accounting Review*, *34*(4), 289–313. doi:10.1006/bare.2002.0213

Weber, R. P. (1986). *Basic content analysis, quantitative applications in the social sciences* (Vol. 49). Sage Publications.

World Bank. (2005). Report on Observance of Standards and Codes. Ghana: World Bank.

Yanesari, A., Gerayli, M., Ma'atoofi, A., & Abadi, A. (2012). Board characteristics and corporate voluntary disclosure: An Iranian perspective. *Archives des Sciences*, *64*(5), 478–484.

Zeghal, D., & Mhedhbi, K. (2006). *An analysis of the factors affecting the adoption of international accounting standards by developing countries*. University of Illinois.

Zikmund, W. G. (2010). *Business Research Methods* (6th ed.). Fort Worth, TX: Harcourt College Publisher.

Chapter 11
International Accounting Standards:
Adoption, Implementation and Challenges

Essa R El-Firjani
Tripoli University, Libya

Shamsaddeen M. Faraj
Al-Gabal Al-Garbi University, Libya

ABSTRACT

This chapter aims, to highlight a review of IAS history, followed by approaches of accounting regulations. The development of accounting regulation within developing countries is also highlighted and discussed in the context of cultural diversity. It also aims to shed light into the motives that drive the adoption and implementation of IASs/IFRS. The political nature of lobbying and accounting standards setting process is also discussed in this chapter. In addition, the chapter discusses those factors that may be perceived as challenges which may delay or even block the convergence into the IASs/IFRS. Finally the authors provide key remarks about the IASs and venues for future research.

INTRODUCTION

Accounting standards as a form of regulation, determines how and what corporate information is presented as well as provide a higher quality and quantity of corporate information (Tower, 1993). However, the accounting information produced by national accounting standards may be insufficient for users to make decisions due to the growth of international trade and globalization of businesses, (Zeghal and Mhedhbi, 2006). In the context of the agency theory of (Jensen and Meckling 1976) accounting regulation exists to mitigate the agency costs that occur due to conflict of interest between contracting parties e.g. owners and agents.

An effective regulation is affected by internal environment variables such as the stage of economic development; the goals of society; culture and the underlying legal rules or common law and external environmental variables include colonial ties that can transfer accounting systems; international move-

DOI: 10.4018/978-1-4666-9876-5.ch011

ments of accounting professionals and firms; internationalization of world trade and stock markets and membership and participation bodies that set international accounting standards, Cooke and Wallace (1990). Moreover, the development of a new financial accounting regulation process in different countries is influenced by different factors which include social and cultural values, legal systems, the economic and political environment changes and conditions, capital markets, structure of ownership, standards setting process, and international efforts towards accounting regulation (Sawani 2009; Ashraf and Ghani, 2005; Chamisa, 2000).

The review of the accounting literature reveals that the accounting regulation approaches have varied across countries. In this respect, it can be argued that these approaches of accounting regulation is expected to provide high quality of financial reporting. Financial reporting has been considered as the main source of information for users groups when making decisions (Alrazeen and Karbhari, 2004). Therefore, IASs adopted by some developing countries because they believe that the adoption of IASs is economical and less time-consuming than preparing their own standards, and it has great advantages in facilitating both national and foreign firms and international connections, (Tan et al, 2009; Mashayekhi and Mashayekhi, 2008; Nobes and Parker, 2002).

In this respect, IASs reduce international differences in accounting standards which assist in removing barriers to cross-border acquisitions Ball (2006). Furthermore, IASs provide more information than the national accounting standards and are good value for investors (Rawashdeh 2003). The remaining of this chapter will be structured as follows: the next section will cover history of IASs, then in section three the accounting regulation and its approaches will be addressed. Section four will be devoted to accounting development and culture. Section 5 will shed light into accounting regulation in developing countries. Section six is devoted to IASs. The following section will discuss accounting standards setting process. Section eight will explain the challenges that face IASs implementation the last section concludes the chapter.

HISTORY OF IASs/IFRS

International accounting standards are issued by the International Accounting Standards Committee (IASC). The IASC was established in 1973 as a private organisation by agreement of accountancy bodies of the following nine countries: Australia, Canada, France, Germany, the UK and Ireland, the US, Japan, Mexico and the Netherlands, (IASB 2008; IASC 1995). IASC aims to formulate and publish in the public interest accounting standards to be observed in the presentation of financial statements and to promote their worldwide acceptance and observance. To work generally for the improvement and harmonization of regulations, accounting standards and procedures relating to the presentation of financial statements.

The members of the IASC has increased over the period from its establishment to 2001 and the members were accountancy bodies from various countries worldwide. It had 16 members from nine countries in 1973. From 1995 it had 110 members within 82 countries. By 1999 they were 143 members from 104 countries, and by 2001, its members were 150 members from 110 countries, (Nobes and Parker, 2002; Chamisa, 2000; IASC 1995; Mueller et al, 1987). During the period from 1973 to 2000, the IASC issued forty-one IASs to guide accountants, globally on financial statements preparation and presentation, (Aljifri and Khasharmeh, 2006; Mir and Rahaman, 2005).

The International Accounting Standards Board (IASB), was replaced the IASC in 2001 as the standard-setting body of the IASC foundation, an independent private sector body and observed by the

Trustees of IASC, (IASB, 2008). It was formed as a restructured, accounting standard setter that has achieved much since the IASC formation in 1973 to issue IFRS (Street and Gray, 2002). In this respect, Mackenzie et al (2013) state that both IFRS foundation and the IASB aim to develop a framework of high-quality, understandable, enforceable and globally accepted financial reporting standards based upon clearly articulated principles. IASB issued 13 IFRS, since its established.

THE ACCOUNTING REGULATION

Regulation is defined as "intentional restriction of a subject's choice of activity, by an entity not directly party to or involved in the activity", (Rahman, et al, 2002). Development of accounting regulation has been influenced by the growth of business enterprises and the general philosophy prevailing in society. It has also come about in response to shocks experienced in the financial reporting environment. These shocks have largely come in the form of scandals or important business failures, (Taylor and Turley, 1986).

Accounting regulations are important because accounting information users need to be able to have confidence that the information is a fair representation and has not been manipulated by management (Elliott and Elliott, 2007). The development of a new financial accounting regulation process in different countries is influenced by the economic and political environment changes, the demand for and use of financial information, (Ashraf and Ghani, 2005; Chamisa, 2000). The approaches of accounting regulation have varied from country to country. In some countries, for example, the UK and the US, accounting regulations were developed by the accounting profession (self-regulation) (Day, 2000). In other countries, like France, accounting regulation was developed by legislation (legal regulation) (Mcleay et al, 1999).

Self-Regulation Approach

Self-regulation is "the form of regulation in which both the regulator and regulated are from the private sector", (Velayutham, 1996: 354). Velayutham, (1996) argues that self-regulation is usually initiated by the organisation's members (individuals or business units) involved in a particular activity when the activity is threatened by public regulation, or the members feel there is some benefit to be obtained from this regulation. With this approach accounting regulation is carried out by the accounting profession, independent of legal direction or government intervention. Accounting standards are established entirely by expert professional accountants. Accounting standards, as a form of regulation, restrict choice in how and, in what manner, corporate information is presented. In a free market economy with a strong capital market (e,g. the UK and the US) accounting standards were purposely prepared to provide information for specific groups of users and the operation of accounting systems is based on the belief that economic resource allocation can be achieved by the operation of the free market, (Tower, 1993). Watts (1993: 200) states that: "Accounting standards are concerned with the development of uniform rules for external financial reporting, presumably with the objective of making accounts more meaningful to users".

Accounting regulation is intended to narrow the differences in practice and to protect the interests of the public. By its nature, self-regulation involves the activities of various individuals and private/government agencies including the capital market, the accountancy profession, financial accounting users, management/preparers, independent professional accountants and regulators in the implementation of regulatory activity, (Kwok and Sharp, 2005; Cooper and Robson, 2006).

In the USA, The Securities and Exchange Commission (SEC) was established by the US Congress in 1934. The SEC could prescribe the format and content of financial statements and the earnings statement (Higson, 2003). The SEC was very important for the New York Stock Exchange (NYSE) to restore public confidence in investing in corporations (Gaffikin, 2006).

In 1938, the AICPA's Committee and Accounting Procedures (CAP) commenced issuing Accounting Research Bulletins. This body was the first private-sector body involved in US accounting standards. The CAP was replaced by the establishment of the Accounting Principles Board (APB) and the Accounting Research Division in 1959 with the mission to advance the written expression of what constitutes generally accepted accounting principles (GAAP) (Higson, 2003; Nobes and Parker, 2006).

As the APB was dominated by the accounting profession, there were insufficient provisions to ensure that the opinion of other interested parties were taken into account. The Wheat Committee's report in 1972 'Establishing Financial Accounting Standards' led to the formation of three new bodies: the FASB responsible for setting standards; the Financial Accounting Foundation (FAF) responsible for appointing members of the FASB and the Financial Accounting Standards Advisory Council (FASAC) as advisory body (Nobes and Parker, 2006). Therefore, the Accounting Principles Board was superseded by the Financial Accounting Standards Board (FASB) in 1973.

In 2001, due to the spectacular collapses of some large companies like Enron the difference between US standards and IASB standards was highlighted. In 2002, the FASB announced a joint project with the IASB to remove as many differences as possible between their standards by 2005, and then to work on further convergence in the medium term (Nobes and Parker, 2006).

In the UK, the Institute of Chartered Accountants in England and Wales (ICAEW) was provided (under title the English Institute) in 1880. Therefore, the UK has been one of the earliest countries to establish professional accounting associations. Due to the absence of an effective law to sort out all accounting problems, the development of the accounting profession in the UK has been the responsibility of the professional accounting bodies, and, particularly, the ICAEW (Taylor and Turley, 1986). The UK profession's power is a great factor in the use of self-regulation as opposed to government regulation of accounting details. He also indicates that the regulatory framework has changed significantly since the 1854 Companies Act marked the first formal control over accounting, (Day 2000).

The accounting development in the UK started with the standards setting process. The ICAEW was the first body involved in this process, in 1942. In 1942, the ICAEW produced many recommendations on Accounting Principles, and they gave general guidance to Institute's members. 29 recommendations were issued by 1969, but they were not mandatory (Higson, 2003; Mcleay et al, 1999). As the result of a number of financial scandals in 1960s and the flexibility of accounting practice, the need for standardization of accounting was increased to deal with those problems: the flexibility and the deficiencies in accounting practice.

In 1970, the Accounting Standards Steering Committee (ASSC) was formed as a committee of the ICAEW. The ASSC rapidly incorporated members from other accountancy bodies were: the Institute of Chartered Accountants of Scotland; the Institute of Chartered Accountants in Ireland; the Association of Chartered Certified Accountants; and the Chartered Institute of Management Accountants (Higson, 2003). By 1974 the Chartered Institute of Public Finance and Accountancy had joined with the five accounting bodies. These six governing bodies of the ASSC worked together and formed the Consultative Committee of Accountancy Bodies (CCAB) (Mcleay, 1999; and Nobes and Parker, 2006), later (in 1976) the ASSC was renamed the Accounting Standards Committee (ASC) to prepare a draft standard for the six professional accounting bodies (Elliott and Elliott, 2007). This body was reconstituted as a joint committee of the CCAB, equivalent in function, (Nobes and Parker, 2006). The ASC established as a response to government and audit requirements, (Mcleay, et al 1999).

The main objective of the ASC was the development of the Statements of Standard Accounting Practice and ensuring these standards are accepted within and outside the accounting profession and influence in the regulation of practice, (Taylor and Turley, 1986). This is supported by Nobes and Parker (2006: 284) who state that "The role of the ASC was confined to developing Statements of Standard Accounting Practice (SSAPs) with adoption and enforcement remaining the responsibility of the six professional bodies". In 1990, the ASC was replaced by the Accounting Standards Board (ASB). The ASB is supervised by the Financial Reporting Council (FRC), independent of the profession, and it has its own authority and power to issue accounting standards, (Nobes and Parker, 2006).

Legal Regulation Approach

Under this approach, government plays a crucial role in the control of economic activities, and accounting standards become part of the legal framework. Therefore, the accounting profession may become relatively weak or has a limited role, (Mueller et al, 1987). In this situation, a government is a single authority (usually the nation's national planning board) which exercises control over accounting information. This approach is usually adopted in a centralised economic system. Accountants under this economic system develop accounting policies through an authoritative, comprehensive chart of accounting processes. In France and Germany for example, external accounting is dominated by a comprehensive chart of accounts, (Nobes and Parker, 2002; Taylor and Turley, 1986).

In contrast to the self-regulation approach, uniformity is the main feature of accounting systems under the legal regulation approach. In this respect, Wallace (1993) argues that France believed in planning and controlling the allocation of the resources of its environment by following a uniform accounting plan for micro and/or macro control in purposes. The uniform accounting system is likely to have a different set of characteristics. Its extent is wider than financial reporting and external auditing, financial statements are prepared for a wide range of users (e.g. national planners; shareholders; management and society at large), normally include information related to budget and accounting being shaped by legal requirements It may be inflexible and difficult to apply (Mueller et al, 1987; Taylor and Turley, 1986).

In the seventeenth century, several attempts were made in France to regulate accounting through legislation. This started in 1673 when the government issued the first decree ' Ordonnance de Colbert' made obligatory for all business to keep books of accounts and register them with a national plan authority, Mcleay et al, (1999). This decree formed the basis for the Napoleonic Commercial Code (code de commerce) of 1807, (Nobes and Parker, 2006). Prior to the 1940's, an annual financial report was presented by directors to company's annual meeting as response to the Companies Law of 1867, and it applied until 1919 (Mcleay et al, 1999).

A set of generally accepted accounting principles did not exist in France, mostly because of there was no accounting standards body like in the UK and the USA (e.g. FASB and ASB) to regulate accounting standards in the country. Thus accounting in France has been influenced by laws rather than the profession. Therefore, the National Accounting Plan was the most important source for accounting regulation, (Nobes and Parker, 2006). In 1946, a new national accounting code was formulated by the Commission de Normalisation des Comptabilités which was established by the French government. The implementation and development of this code was vested in the 'Conseil de Sécurité de la Comptabilité ' (CSC) (Mcleay et al, 1999).

The 1947 Plan Comptable Général (PCG) was the first comprehensive effort for accounting regulation in France. The plan was administered by the National Council of Accountancy (Conseil National de la Comptabilité [CNC]) to commence the standardization of accounting practice in France. The membership of the PCG includes accountants; industrialists; and civil servants. It is organized and controlled by the Ministry of Finance in France, (Alhashim and Arpan, 1992; Nobes and Parker, 2006). With issuance of the Companies Law of 1966 (amended in 1967) all business in France had to prepare an activities report, a profit and loss account and a balance sheet at the end of the fiscal year. It also clarified when financial statements of large and medium firms should be checked by their external auditors and regulated the appointment and responsibilities of those auditors, (Alhashim and Arpan, 1992).

The French government established the Stock Exchange Commission (Commission des Operations de Bourse, COB) in 1967, modeled on the SEC in the USA. This resulted in the marked development of the securities markets and the appearance of detailed financial information. Within 1999 the COB greatly increased its powers to take on control of financial markets and related information. It provides regulations, carries out investigations, and imposes fines. It also updated the previous plans' explanation of accounting terms, valuation rules, codes of accounts, and the contents and formats of required financial statements (Nobes and Parker, 2006).

In June 2000 the EU Commission announced its intention to adopt IFRS as part of its policy of encouraging free movement of capital (Welbenberger et al, 2004; Whittington, 2005; Fearnley et al, 2006). In 2002 the EU's Council of Ministers approved the regulation No. 1606/2002, which makes the mandatory application of IFRS by all companies listed on EU stock markets from 2005 onwards to prepare their consolidated financial statements under these standards, (Callao et al, 2007; Haller, 2002; Schipper, 2005; Whittington, 2005; Weibenberger et al, 2004; Larson and Street, 2004; Fearnley, et al, 2006). France as a member of the EU its regulatory framework has been influenced by the new EU regulation No. 1606/2002. Therefore, all listed companies in France are required to prepare their consolidated financial reports in accordance with IFRS from beginning or after January 2005.

In the UK, legal regulation of the accounting profession contains regular changes and improvements in the content of accounts required by both law and the objectives of the statutes. Therefore, company's activities in the UK are primarily controlled by the Companies Acts (Taylor and Turley, 1986). Day (2000) found in his study on the UK accounting regulation that the UK has a commercial legal system relying on a limited amount of statute law. The Companies' Act of 1948 was more comprehensive and provided that the 'true and fair view'. With the Companies' Act of 1981, accounting standards and procedures became incorporated in legislation in the UK. Any variation in accounting practice from these standards and procedures must be explicitly justified in the essence of the 'true and fair view' override law if necessary clause which emphasizes the quality of information, (Alhashim and Apran, 1992).

These Acts also required the appointment of an external auditor for a company. This auditor must clarify whether company's financial statements are prepared within the Acts requirements, and whether they give a 'true and fair view' of the company's financial position and the outcomes of its operations, (Alhashim and Arpan, 1992). The Fourth Directive of the EU required from its members such as the UK, its legislation must incorporate EU Directives. Furthermore, the UK made many modifications to its companies' laws in order to standardize the content and presentation of corporate financial statements and to bring its legislation closer to European Community Directives such as the Companies Act of 1989, (Glautier and Underdown, 2001).

The UK regulatory system has witnessed significant change including the adoption of IAS in 2000 through the EU authorities. (Fearnley et al, 2006; Jermarkowicz and Tomaszewski, 2006; Welbenberger et al, 2004; Whittington, 2005). This regulation requires all EU-listed companies to prepare their consolidated financial reports in accordance with IFRS by beginning on or after January 2005 (Jermarkowicz and Tomaszewski, 2006; Fearnley et al, 2006; Callao et al, 2007; Haller, 2002; Schipper, 2005; Whittington, 2005; Weibenberger et al, 2004; Larson and Street, 2004). Fearnley et al, (2006) state that as the UK has the largest stock market in the EU therefore this new regulation is extremely significant in the UK. Hence, one could state that IASs adoption cross countries, represents cultural challenge.

ACCOUNTING DEVELOPMENT AND CULTURE

The influence of culture on the accounting profession is introduced by several researchers (Gray, 1988; Salter and Niswander, 1995). Therefore, one can argue that the development of accounting is influenced by culture. Culture is defined as 'the collective programming of the mind which distinguishes the members of one group or category of people from another' (Hofstede 1997, p:5). The programming is apparent in the values and beliefs of a society. Values are the propensity of an individual to prefer certain states of affairs over others (Cohen et al., 1993). Accounting systems within a society is linked to the cultural values as classified by Hofstede (1980, 1984). These values are (1) Individualism; (2) Uncertainty Avoidance (UA); (3) Power Distance and (4) Masculinity and (5) long and short term orientation. The study of Askary (2006) examined the effect of national culture on accounting professionalism in twelve developing countries by using Gray's 1988 model of accounting values, concluded that 'culture in different societies can strongly impact national accounting systems' (p: 102). In addition, Askary et al. (2008) suggest that cultural and country-specific values affect the accounting system development.

Furthermore, Tsakumis (2007) investigated the influence of national culture on accountants' application of accounting rules across two countries which are Greece and the USA. The results indicate that Greek accountants would be less likely to disclose the existence of both contingent assets and liability than US accountants. This is because 'national culture does play a role in accountants' disclosure judgment [and that] uniform accounting standards may not result in similar disclosure decisions being made across countries' (p: 44). Moreover, Gray's (1988) model proposes four accounting values which are professionalism, uniformity, conservatism and secrecy, which are linked to Hofstede's (1980) cultural values. These accounting values have two opposite ends as defined by Gray (1988: 8):

- **Professional versus Statutory Control:** A preference for the exercise of individual professional judgment and the maintenance of professional self-regulation as opposed to compliance with prescriptive legal requirements and statutory control.
- **Uniformity versus Flexibility:** A preference for the enforcement of uniform accounting practices between companies and the consistent use of such practices over time as opposed to flexibility in accordance with the perceived circumstances of individual companies.
- **Conservatism versus Optimism:** A preference for a cautious approach to measurement so as to cope with the uncertainty of future events as opposed to a more optimistic, laissez-faire, risk-taking approach.
- **Secrecy versus Transparency:** A preference for confidentiality and the restriction of disclosure of information about the business only to those who are closely involved with its management and financing as opposed to a more transparent, open and publicly accountable approach.

Linking these accounting values to Hofstede's (1980) social values, allowed Gray (1988) to suggest a number of hypotheses relating to the relationship between the social values (Uncertainty Avoidance (UA), Power Distance (PD), individualism and masculinity) and accounting values which are:

1. A country with a higher rank on individualism and a lower rank in UA and PD, is expected to express a high rank in terms of professionalism (lower uniformity);
2. A country with a higher rank in UA and PD and the lower rank in terms of individualism, is expected to demonstrate a high rank in terms of uniformity (lower professionalism);
3. A country with a higher rank in UA and a lower rank in terms of individualism and masculinity, is expected to demonstrate a high rank in terms of conservatism; and
4. A country with a lower rank in UA and the lower rank in terms of individualism and masculinity, is expected to demonstrate a high rank in terms of secrecy.

In measuring professionalism, Salter and Niswander (1995) examined Gray's (1988) model by using the control of entry into the profession (exam) and auditor's opinion (Auditor Judgment) on corporations' financial reports (true and fair view), in twenty nine countries from developed and developing countries. They found that professionalism is influenced by the Uncertainty Avoidance (UA) level. UA was strongly and negatively related to both setting exams and auditors' practice of the accounting profession. In other words, countries that exhibit high UA appear to have accounting systems that are ordered by legal requirements [for accounting practice] and statutory control [for the auditing profession]. Moreover, Cohen et al., (1993) argue that individuals from cultures having weak UA fail to accept consistent procedures. Individuals from strong UA cultures 'focus on rules to the exclusion of asking whether the procedure leads to an ethical outcome' (p: 11).

ACCOUNTING REGULATION IN DEVELOPING COUNTRIES

Accounting regulation development research, in emerging economies, needs more research to examine the accounting standards harmonization, (El-Firjani & Faraj, 2014; Faraj & El-Firjani, 2014). However, there is some handful empirical research on some developing countries. For instance, Mashayekhi and Mashayekhi (2008) show that the audit organisation in Iran has played its role in developing national accounting standards. Another example in Libya, Faraj and El-Firjani (2014) state that Libyan listed companies are following the GAAP though they are required to comply with IASs. Libyan listed companies in stead, comply with certain laws (like commercial law and tax law) and financial regulations when preparing accounts, and they are applied prior to the GAAP.

In Similar context, Al-Qahtani (2005) addressed the development of the accounting regulation in Gulf Cooperation Council (GCC) countries including Bahrain; Kuwait; Qatar; United Arab Emirates (UAE); Saudi Arabia; and Oman. In this region, the regulation of the accounting profession is still influenced by the codes of commercial laws in all the GCC countries except Saudi Arabia which regulates its accounting profession by the power of Government by giving authority to the Saudi Organisation for Certified Public Accountants (SOCPA) (including reviewing, preparing and endorsing of accounting standards). In the same region, Al-Shammari et al (2007) show that the governments of the GCC countries are involved in regulation of the financial reports and they control the accounting and auditing professions.

Therefore, one may articulate that political influence, on accounting regulation, can be highlighted through the power of these governments.

In similar context, the impact of the environmental factors on accounting development in Egypt has been discussed by HassabElnaby, et al (2003). They show that the level of the economy and the political environment are positively correlated with accounting development. While in Jordon Al-Akra, et al (2009) demonstrate that the accounting profession which is regulated by the Jordanian Association of Certified Public Accountants (JACPA) has played an important role in facilitating the adoption of IASs/IFRS. They also indicate that the political and economic factors which led to privatization have an impact on accounting practices and regulation in Jordon.

In a different context, Dobija and Klimczak (2010) pointed out that Poland changed its accounting regulations which permit to use IAS/IFRS before it adopted IFRS in 2005 which had taken steps to reduce the gap between National Accounting Regulation and IAS (e.g. a significant increase in transparency and public disclosure of accounting policies and put greater emphasis on fair value instead of historical cost accounting).

Moreover, in Slovakia, Daniel and Suranova (2001) show that Slovak Ministry of Finance played a key role in the development of accounting practices and regulation. All its regulations are generally obligatory for all companies. It co-operated with the Slovak accounting profession to prepare the legal acts concerning accounting. They also show that the Slovak accounting system is influenced by the commercial code and accounting law which is generally based on IASs. Similarly, in Brazil, Radebaugh and Gray (2002) point out that accounting development has been influenced by the commercial code and the Companies' Law which includes the basic requirements governing the preparation of financial statements and disclosures for public companies. While listed companies are required to comply with the national accounting standards that are approved by the Securities Exchange Commission.

THE ADOPTION OF IASs/IFRS

Many countries do not have adequate standards of accounting and auditing (Riahi-Belkaoui, 2000). Therefore, IASs have been adopted by some developing countries without any modifications such as Bahrain, Jordan, Malaysia, Thailand, Pakistan, Bangladesh, Nigeria, the Arab Gulf Countries Co-operation Council member states (GCC) and Singapore, (Joshi and Ramadhan, 2002; Ashraf and Ghani, 2005), or with a view modifications to ensure that it is consistent with local laws and regulations such as in Zimbabwe and Iran (Chamisa, 2000; Mashayekhi and Mashayekhi, 2008). The adoption of IASs/IFRS in developing countries is enforced by country authorities or a group of companies, (Zeghal and Mhedhbi, 2006).

The adoption of IASs/IFRS is driven by some factors such as foreign investments, the financial reports quality, accounting education, economic growth, external auditors, international legislation, and harmonization, (El-Firjani and Faraj 2014). For instance, the involvement and increasing number of foreign banks in Qatar and Saudi Arabia that voluntarily used IASs led their governments to require all banks to adopt IASs. This is attributed to the pressure from multinational corporations in the GCC countries, which led to the adoption of IASs by their governments Al-Shammari et al (2007). In Iran, Mashayekhi and Mashayekhi (2008) argue that to attract foreign direct investment, financial reporting should follow accepted accounting standards like IASs. With respect to the accounting harmonization, Poland issued new regulations that allow using IAS/IFRS, which has facilitated foreign investment (Dobija and Klimczak 2010).

The financial reports quality, also to some extent, drives the adoption of IASs/IFRS. Commonly, the quality of financial reporting is accompanied by the quality of the accepted accounting standards such as IASs/IFRS. For example, Joshi and Ramadhan (2002) show that the factors which influence the decision to adopt IASs are: the expectation of improving the efficiency and effectiveness of financial reporting and achieving the company's objectives. IASs/IFRS have been adopted by developed and developing countries for improving their companies financial reporting. Another example, the IFRS are expected to have the greatest impact on existing financial reporting practices in areas where there are no equivalent Australian accounting standards Jones and Higgins (2006).

The accounting quality improvements are confined to German firms with incentives to adopt IAS, Christensen, et al, (2008). In Belgium Jermakowicz (2004) state that the adoption of IFRS increases comparability of consolidated accounts as well as levels of transparency for many Belgian companies. In different, context, the positive impact of IASs adoption is also addressed by (Rawashdeh 2003) on the Amman Stock Exchange in Jordan, as the IASs provide more information than the local Jordanian accounting standards. However, Pakistan, has adopted IASs as national standards, but the quality of financial reporting did not improve, Ashraf and Ghani (2005).

The accounting standards adoption is also driven by accounting education. In this regard, Archambault and Archambault (2009) show that literacy rates positively influence the decision to adopt IFRS in 120 countries. Similarly, Al-Akra et al (2009) argue that accounting education may prevent the successful implementation of IASs/IFRS due to the quality of teaching in accounting and auditing, particularly at university level suffers from a lack of modern curricula and too few teachers and focus on elementary topics and not include IASs/IFRS.

Economic growth is another factor that may perceived to drive the adoption of IASs/IFRS. For instance, Cooke and Wallace (1990) argue that accounting not only affects economic growth but it is also affected by economic growth and the interaction of other environmental factors of each country such as the levels of political, educational, and technological development. Furthermore, Gray and Roberts (1991) point out that an appropriate accounting system is important, because inadequate accounting systems may obstruct economic growth. For instance, in Slovakia, the development of economic growth led to the development of accounting Daniel and Suranova (2001). However, economic growth and external economic openness may not have a significant impact on the adoption of IASs in emerging economies (Zeghal and Mhedhbi 2006). In addition, Larson and Kenny (1995) argue that the adoption of IASs alone did not guarantee increased economic growth.

External auditors like Big-4 auditors may have an impact on the adoption of IASs/IFRS. For example, Al-Basteki (1995) states that external auditors influence their clients' decisions to adopt IASs in Bahrain, and the IASC/IASB could encourage various countries to accept its standards through close cooperation with auditors practicing in these countries. Another example in Bahrain Joshi and Ramadhan (2000) show that external auditors have a positive influence, on their clients, towards the adoption of IASs. While Srijunpetch (2004) argues that national external auditors in Thailand may have some influence on the extent of IAS compliance. However, international audit firms are the most influential factor in the adopting of IASs in the country, and are perceived as more credible than local audit firms.

For instance, in the Middle East countries where a number of governments have embarked on privatization programs, most of the national auditors are partnered with big international audit firms and this has a positive impact on corporate reporting particularly in improving the level of disclosure Nasser and Nuseibeh (2003). External auditors influence, on the IASs/ IFRS adoption, is attributed to the role played by these auditors in the establishment of the IASC in 1973 and they are still the main supporters of the IASB Rahman et al (2002).

The international legislations are also regarded as one of the motives that lead to the adoption of IASs/IFRS. For example, within developing country context, Mir and Rahman (2005) states that Bangladesh government and professional accounting bodies enact institutional legislations which facilitate the adoption of IASs/IFRS. These legislations are perceived as a major factor that drives the decision of adoption because of the pressure of the key international lending institutions on the Bangladesh government. Similarly in Bahrain, (Joshi and Ramadhan 2002) argue that international financial institution e.g. Banks require local borrows and investors to adopt IASs in Bahrain. Another example is of Thailand where international lenders exert their pressure on local borrows towards the adoption of IASs (Srijunpetch 2004).

International financial institutions such as the World Bank (WB) and the International Monetary Fund (IMF) demanded certain conditions in most Asian countries during the Asian economic crisis in 1997 Rahman (2000). The WB and IMF convinced the ministers of finance, ministers of trade and industry and securities commissions in developing countries that accounting reform is a major part of financial reform. Thus WB and IMF are insisting on the use of IASs by recipients of their finance (Chamisa 2000).

In addition, harmonization of accounting standards may facilitate internationalization of capital markets and foreign business because it can give comparable financial information for several international users (Choi and Levich, 1991; and Nobes, 1995). Harmonization is also intended to facilitate economic growth and world trade by presenting financial information of corporations located in different countries (Larson 1993 and Purvis et al, 1991). Similarly, Rahman et al (2002) addressed accounting harmonization between Australian and New Zealand companies as they share similar environmental factors which led to accounting practice harmony. Another example, in Belgium implementing IFRS changes dramatically the way companies design both their internal and external reporting activities as well as created harmonization of these reports, Jermakowicz (2004).

ACCOUNTING STANDARDS SETTING PROCESS

The accounting standard setting is directly affected by a perception that it is the role of accountants to develop accounting standards or the role of one's association to represent one's interests. (Durocher et al, 2007). In this respect, Fogarty et al (1994) state that many professional leaders believe that the accounting standard setting process should be insulated from politics, as such, standard setters may be required to trade off relevance against the need to satisfy several constituencies with conflicting interests of several groups including e.g. investors, creditors, auditors). However, one may argue that the standard setting process represents a political nature that has made it difficult to isolate the process from political systems. In this respect, (Johnson, 2011) argues that lobbying activity, with conflicting-interests of diverse influential veto amongst parties, may result in delay or blocking of policies or/and standards.

For instance, in New Zealand Rahman et al (1994) argue that low participation by users may result from a perceived absence of economic consequences for user of participation in the standard setting process by users and academic groups. in addition, Weetman et al (1996) indicate that the reasons for users' low participation levels were a tradition of non-response to exposure drafts, a lack of time and the fact that participation happens through informal meetings with standard setters.

Accounting standards setting participations by academics is highlighted by Tandy and Wilburn (1992). They conclude that the academics had a low level of participation. The low level is attributed to the following reasons: the lack of understanding or interest in the perceived political nature of the FASB's process and the low expectations of affecting the FASB's decisions, inadequate academic rewards for this activity at their universities, the absence of a relationship between the issues and research or teaching, the feeling of being unable to contribute, and lack of time or resources. Similarly, Mcleay et al (2000) emphasized that the academic group exerted relatively little influence on the standard setting decisions of the German legislature. However, in the USA academic accountants have played an important role in accounting standard-setting (Nobes and Parker, 2006).

The role played by auditors in the accounting standards setting process is varied across countries. For instance, Daniel and Suranova (2001) state that the Slovak Chamber of Auditors (SKAU) has a role in accounting standard setting. SKAU created special committees that discuss specific legal topics with the Ministry of Finance and then prepare accounting standards in their specific field of interest. In addition, auditors in Iran are considered as the main participants in accounting standard setting process. Accounting standard drafts in Iran should be prepared based on the results of studies of committees of the audit organisation about accounting problems (Mashayekhi and Mashayekhi 2008). Moreover, Van (1997) highlighted that lobbying activities of various interest groups on the dissemination of Dutch financial reporting regulations for companies engaging in banking and insurance activities, and show that most report users was not intensive, but authors and preparers of accounts seem to have greater possibilities to participate.

A key role is apparent through preparers' participation in accounting standards setting process. For instance in Germany, Mcleay et al (2000) highlighted that the preparers group had a strong influence on the standard setting decisions of the German legislature. This is because company lobbying on accounting standards may involve a number of interconnected issues. This lobbying would be carried out by submitting comment letters or meeting with the standard setters (Georgiou, 2004). Similarly, Nobes and Parker (2006) show that USA company managers were more likely to influence standard setters. While in the UK the level of lobbying activity carried out by investment management firms, relatively to that of other interest groups such as financial statement preparers, is low, (Georgiou 2010).

Government intervention affects the accounting standards setting process. For example, Ball et al (2003) indicate that the governments in Malaysia and Singapore have taken more intervention roles in accounting standard setting. In addition, Kosonboon (2004) state that the Institute of Certified Accountants and Auditors of Thailand (ICAAT) is responsible for establishing standards. Though, the government is directly strongly involved in accounting standard setting through the Ministry of Commerce and the stock market regulator, and the final accounting standard draft is required to be approved under the Ministry of Commerce.

CHALLENGES OF IASs/IFRS IMPLEMENTATION

Many developed and developing economies are required to follow IFRS (Clements et al 2010). In this regards, the debate about IASs/IFRS is increasingly taking place amongst academics and professional as these standards are being used as the reporting framework in most developed nations, such as UK, France, Germany and Australia (Mulyadi, et al 2012). However, in developing countries such as Pakistan, Libya and Kuwait, companies compliance to the IASs/IFRSs face some obstacles and problems

(Albu and Albu 2012). For example, in Libya as a developing country, the existing laws in the country influence the IASs/IFRS applications by Libyan listed companies, (Faraj and El-Firjani 2014). Thus, it can be said that the convergence process to IASs represents great challenge and difficulty.

Several researchers have examined the implementation of IASs/IFRS, in developing countries such as Libya, Nigeria, Algeria, Pakistan, and Kuwait (Faraj and EL-Firjani 2014; Kapoor, and Ruhela, 2013; Saidi, 2013; Akdogan, 2007; Gonen, and Ugurluel, 2007). They found that there are some obstacles and problems caused difficulties to comply with these standards. These obstacles represent: lack of training programmes, outmoded accounting education curriculum, which consequently resulted in a lack of awareness and understanding of the importance of these standards. Moreover, difficulties in using English language by preparers, managers and auditors, also represent another challenge in the process of IASs/IFRS adoption and application within non Anglo Saxon countries, while the contrary is right in the Anglo Saxon countries (Boolaky, 2012; Zeghal, D. and Mhedhbi, 2006).

In the context of cultural diversity, one may argue that culture is another challenge facing the IASs/ IFRS adoption and implementation. For instance, (Kangarlouei et al 2013) argue that to ensure successful IASs/IFRS adoption, it is better to consider environmental issues such as political system, social and economic factors and culture. However, Clements et al (2010) failed to document any relationship between culture effect and adoption decision amongst 151 countries worldwide. Thus, it can be argued that successful international and local standards implementation can be achieved through efficient enforcement (Ball et al, 2003).

In this regard, Rahman (2000) highlights the efficiency of the enforcement mechanism through the interaction between three parties which include: company management, external auditors and regulatory authorities; and that if one party is missing, enforcement would be weakened. Therefore, one could argue that countries that fail to converge to IASs, have weak enforcement mechanism such as Pakistan and Libya (Faraj and EL-Firjani 2014; and Ashraf and Ghani 2005). While other developing countries such as Thailand that possess strong enforcement system have achieved IASs implementation (Srijunpetch, 2004).

CONCLUSION

This chapter aimed to shed light on the topic of IAS/IFRS adoption and implementation. It also highlighted the factors that are perceived as motives which drive the adoption of IASs/IFRS. This chapter also illustrates the accounting profession development from the perspective of cultural diversity cross societies. In addition, it also discusses the political nature of the lobbying and accounting standards setting process. The challenges or obstacles that may prevent or limit the convergence to IASs/IFRS are also portrayed. From the above discussion, it can be concluded that when countries plan to converge to IASs, environmental factors, within countries, have to be borne in mind. For instance national laws and legislations may need amendment when they prevent or limit the process of implementation of IAS. It is recommended that future empirical research may reveal uncovered contextual factors, which may influence IAS implementation, worldwide. It is also worth studying the mechanism of adoption and standards setting process in developing countries. Professional bodies and standards setting agencies may benefit from these insights and discussions.

REFERENCES

Akdogan, N. (2007). Accounting in Turkey/Financial Reporting Standards Application Process: Problems, Solutions. *Journal of Financial Solutions*, *80*, 101–117.

Al-Akra, M., Ali, M. J., & Marashdeh, O. (2009). Development of Accounting Regulation in Jordan. *The International Journal of Accounting*, *44*(2), 163–186. doi:10.1016/j.intacc.2009.03.003

Al-Basteki, H. (1995). The Voluntary Adoption of International Accounting Standards by Bahrain Corporations. *Advances in International Accounting*, *8*, 47–64.

Al-Qahtani, A. K. (2005). The Development of Accounting Regulation in the GCC. *Managerial Auditing Journal*, *20*(3), 217–226. doi:10.1108/02686900510585564

Al-Shammari, B., Brown, P. R., & Tarca, A. (2007). *Development of Enforcement Mechanisms Following Adoption of International Accounting Standards in the Gulf Co-Operation Council Member States.* Working Paper. Gulf Co-Operation Council Member States.

Albu, N., & Albu, C. N. (2012). International Financial Reporting Standards in an Emarging Economy: Lessons from Romania. *Australian Accounting Review*, *22*(63), 341–352. doi:10.1111/j.1835-2561.2012.00196.x

Alhashim, D. D., & Arpan, J. S. (1992). International Dimension of Accounting (3rd ed). PWS-Kent Publishing Co.

Aljifri, K., & Khasharmeh, H. (2006). An Investigation into the Suitability of the International Accounting Standards to the United Arab Emirates Environment. *International Business Review*, *15*(5), 505–526. doi:10.1016/j.ibusrev.2006.05.009

Alrazeen, A., & Karbhari, Y. (2004). Users' perceptions of Corporate Information in Saudi Arabia: An Empirical Analysis. *International Journal of Commerce and Management*, *14*(3), 41–57. doi:10.1108/10569210480000183

Archambault, J. J., & Archambault, M. E. (2009). An Analysis of Social Factors Influencing the Adoption of International Financial Reporting Standards. Journal for Global Business Advancement, 2(1-2).

Ashraf, J., & Ghani, W. I. (2005). Accounting Development in Pakistan. *The International Journal of Accounting, 40*, 175-201.

Askary, S. (2006). Accounting professionalism – a cultural perspective of developing countries. *Managerial Auditing Journal*, *21*(1), 102–111. doi:10.1108/02686900610634784

Askary, S., Pounder, J. S., & Yazdifar, H. (2008). Influence of Culture on Accounting Uniformity among Arabic Nations. *Education, Business and Society: Contemporary Middle Eastern Issues*, *1*(2), 145–154. doi:10.1108/17537980810890329

Ball, R. (2006). *International Financial Reporting Standards (IFRS): Pros and Cons for Investors.* Accounting and Business Research.

Ball, R., Robin, A., & Wu, J. S. (2003). Incentives Versus Standards: Properties of Accounting Income in four East Asian Countries. *Journal of Accounting and Economics*, *36*(1-3), 235–270. doi:10.1016/j.jacceco.2003.10.003

Boolaky, P. K. (2012). Accounting Development and International Financial Reporting Standards in Small Island Economies: The Case of Mauritius between 1960-2008. *Journal of Accounting in Emerging Economies*, *2*(1), 4–29. doi:10.1108/20421161211196102

Callao, S., Jarne, J. I., & Lainez, J. A. (2007). Adoption of IFRS in Spain: Effect on the Comparability and Relevance of Financial Reporting. *Journal of International Accounting, Auditing & Taxation*, *16*(2), 148–178. doi:10.1016/j.intaccaudtax.2007.06.002

Chamisa, E. E. (2000). The Relevance and Observance of the IASC Standards in Developing Countries and the Particular Case of Zimbabwe. *The International Journal of Accounting*, *35*(2), 267 – 286.

Choi, F. D., & Levich, R. M. (1991). Behavioral Effects of International Accounting Diversity. *Accounting Horizons*, *5*(2), 1–13.

Christensen, H. B., Lee, E., & Walker, M. (2008). *Incentives or Standards: What Determines Accounting Quality Changes Around IFRS Adoption?*. Available at: http://ssrn.com/abstract=1013054

Clements, C. E., Neill, J. D., & Stovall, O. (2010). Cultural Diversity, Country Size, And The IFRS Adoption Decision. *Journal of Applied Business Research*, *26*(2), 115–126. doi:10.19030/jabr.v26i2.288

Cohen, J. R., Pant, L. W., & Sharp, D. J. (1993). Culture-Based Ethical Conflicts Confronting Multinational Accounting Firms. *Accounting Horizons*, *7*(3), 1–13.

Cooke, T. E., & Wallace, R. S. O. (1990). Financial Disclosure Regulation and Its Environment: A Review and Further Analysis. *Journal of Accounting and Public Policy*, *9*(2), 79–110. doi:10.1016/0278-4254(90)90013-P

Cooper, D. J., & Robson, K. (2006). Accounting, Profession and Regulation: Locating the Sites of Professionalization. *Accounting, Organizations and Society*, *31*(4-5), 415–444. doi:10.1016/j.aos.2006.03.003

Daniel, P., Suranova, Z., & De Beelde, I. (2001). The Development of Accounting in Slovakia. *European Accounting Review*, *10*(2), 343–359. doi:10.1080/09638180126639

Day, R. G. (2000). *UK Accounting Regulation: An Historical Perspective. Working Paper Series*. Bournemouth University, School of Finance & Law.

Dobija, D., & Klimczak, K. M. (2010). Development of Accounting in Poland: Market efficiency and the Value Relevance of Reported Earnings. *The International Journal of Accounting*, *45*(3), 356–374. doi:10.1016/j.intacc.2010.06.010

Durocher, S., Fortin, A., & Cote, L. (2007). Users' participation in the Accounting Standard-setting Process: A Theory-building Study. *Accounting, Organizations and Society*, *32*(1-2), 29–59. doi:10.1016/j.aos.2006.03.004

El-Firjani, E., & Faraj, S. (2014). *An Empirical Investigation into the Motives for the Adoption of International Accounting Standards (IASs) Within Developing Countries: The Case of Libya*. Paper presented at the British Accounting & Finance Association 50th Annual Conference, London, UK.

Elliott, B., & Elliott, J. (2007). Financial Accounting and Reporting (11th ed). Prentice Hall.

Faraj, S., & El-Firjani, E. (2014). Challenges Facing IASs/IFRS Implementation by Libyan Listed Companies. *Universal Journal of Accounting and Finance*, *2*, 57–63.

Fearnley, S., Gillies, A., Hines, T., & Willett, C. (2006). *Bewildered but Better Informed: A Qualitative, Interview-based Study into the Attitudes of some UK Accountants and Regulators to the EU IFRS Conversion Project Prior to its Implementation in the UK.* Working Paper. University of Portsmouth, Business School.

Fogarty, T. J., Hussein, M. E. A., & Ketz, J. E. (1994). Political Aspects of Financial Accounting Standard Setting in the USA. *Accounting, Auditing & Accountability Journal*, *7*(4), 24–46. doi:10.1108/09513579410069830

Gaffikin, M. (2006). *Regulation: Standardising Accounting Practice. Working Papers Series*. School of Accounting & Finance, University of Wollongong.

Georgiou, G. (2004). Corporate Lobbying on Accounting Standards: Methods, Timing and Perceived Effectiveness. *Abacus*, *40*(2), 219–237. doi:10.1111/j.1467-6281.2004.00152.x

Georgiou, G. (2010). The IASB Standard-setting Process: Participation and Perceptions of Financial Statement Users. *The British Accounting Review*, *42*(2), 103–118. doi:10.1016/j.bar.2010.02.003

Glautier, M. W. E., & Underdown, B. (2001). *Accounting Theory and Practice (7th ed.)* London: Prentice Hall.

Gonen, S., & Ugurluel, G. (2007). Turkey, International Financial Reporting Standards (IFRS) Transition Challenges Facing Applications and Solutions. *Journal of World Tax*, *316*, 229–236.

Gray, S. J. (1988). Towards a Theory of Cultural Influence Internationally on the Development of Accounting Systems Internationally. *Abacus*, *24*(I), 1–15. doi:10.1111/j.1467-6281.1988.tb00200.x

Gray, S. J., & Roberts, C. B. (1991). East-West Accounting Issues: A New Agenda. *Accounting Horizons*, *5*(March), 42–50.

Haller, A. (2002). Financial Accounting Developments in the European Union: Past Events and Future Prospects. *The European Accounting Review*, *11*, 1-153.

HassabElnaby, H. R., Epps, R. W., & Said, A. A. (2003). The Impact of Environmental Factors on Accounting Development: An Egyptian Longitudinal Study. *Critical Perspectives on Accounting*, *14*(3), 273–292. doi:10.1006/cpac.2002.0530

Higson, A. (2003). *Corporate Financial Reporting: Theory and Practice*. London: SAGE Publications.

Hill, N. T., Shelton, S. W., & Stevens, K. T. (2002). Corporate Lobbying Behaviour on Accounting for Stock-Based Compensation: Venue and Format Choices. *Abacus*, *38*(1), 78–90. doi:10.1111/1467-6281.00098

Hofstede, G. (1980). *Culture's Consequences: International Differences in Work Related Values*. Beverly Hills, CA: Sage Publications.

Hofstede, G. (1984). *Culture's Consequences: International Differences in Work-Related Values*. Beverly Hills, CA: Sage Oublications.

Hofstede, G. (1997). *Cultures and Organisations: Software of Mind*. New York: McGraw-Hill.

IASB. (2008). *IASB and FASB to Hold First Round Table on Global Financial Crisis in London on 14 November*. Press Release. Retrieved from www.iasb.org

IASC. (1995). The full text of all International Standards extant at 1 January 1995 and current Exposure Drafts. London, UK: IASC.

Jensen, M. C., & Meckling, W. H. (1976). Theory of the Firm: Managerial Behaviour, Agency Costs, and Ownership Structure. *Journal of Financial Economics*, *3*(4), 305–360. doi:10.1016/0304-405X(76)90026-X

Jermakowicz, E. K. (2004). Effects of Adoption of International Financial Reporting Standards in Belgium: The Evidence from BEL-20 Companies. *Accounting in Europe*, *1*(1), 53–70. doi:10.1080/0963818042000270811

Jermakowicz, E. K., & Tomaszewski, S. G. (2006). Implementing IFRS from the Perspective of EU Publicly Traded Companies. *Journal of International Accounting and Taxation*, *15*(2), 170–196. doi:10.1016/j.intaccaudtax.2006.08.003

Johnson, D. C. (2011). *Political Systems, Lobbying, and the Adoption of International Financial Reporting Standards*. doi:10.2139/ssrn.1753225

Jones, S., & Higgins, A. D. (2006). Australia's Switch to International Financial Trporting Standards: A Perspective from Account Preparers. *Accounting and Finance*, *46*(4), 629–652. doi:10.1111/j.1467-629X.2006.00186.x

Joshi, P. L., & Ramadhan, S. (2002). The Adoption of International Accounting Standards by Small and Closely Held Companies: Evidence from Bahrain. *The International Journal of Accounting*, *37*, 429–440.

Kangarlouei, S. J., Agababa, M., & Motavassel, M. (2013). Assessment of Social, Economic and Political Impact of Adopting International Accounting Standards in Iran. *World Applied Sciences Journal*, *21*(2), 214–220.

Kapoor, B., & Ruhela, J. (2013). IFRS Implementation – Issues and Challenges for India. *International Journal of Business and Management Research*, *3*(2), 103–106.

Kosonboon, L. D. (2004). *The Relevance of International Accounting Standards for Developing Countries: The Case of IAS 41 in Thailand*. (Ph.D Thesis). University of Strathclyde, Glasgow, UK.

Kwok, W. C. C., & Sharp, D. (2005). Power and International Accounting Standard Setting Evidence from Segment Reporting and Intangible Assets Projects. *Accounting Aedlting & Accotftability Journal*, *18*(1), 74–99. doi:10.1108/09513570510584665

Larson, R., & Street, D. (2004). Convergence with IFRS in an Expanding Europe: Progress and Obstacles Identified by Large Accounting Firms' survey. *Journal of International Accounting, Auditing & Taxation, 13*(2), 89–119. doi:10.1016/j.intaccaudtax.2004.09.002

Larson, R. K. (1993). International Accounting Standards and Economic Growth: An Empirical Investigation of their Relationship in Africa. In R. S. O. Wallace (Ed.), *Research in Third World Accounting* (Vol. 2, pp. 27–43). JAI Press Ltd.

Larson, R. K., & Kenny, S. Y. (1995). An Empirical Analysis of International Accounting Standards, Equity Markets, and Economic Growth in Developing Countries. *Journal of International Financial Management and Accounting*, *6*(2), 130–157. doi:10.1111/j.1467-646X.1995.tb00054.x

Mackenzie, B., Coetsee, D., Njikizana, T., Selbst, E., Chamboko, R., Colyvas, B., & Hanekom, B. (2013). Interpretation and Application of International Financial Reporting Standards. John Wiley & Sons, Inc.

Mashayekhi, B., & Mashayekhi, S. (2008). Development of Accounting in Iran. *The International Journal of Accounting*, *43*(1), 66–86. doi:10.1016/j.intacc.2008.01.004

Mcleay, S., Neal, D., & Ajd Tollington, T. (1999). International Standardisation and Harmonisation: A New Measurement Technique. *Journal of International Financial Management and Accounting*, *10*(1), 42–70. doi:10.1111/1467-646X.00042

Mcleay, S., Ordelheide, D., & Young, S. (2000). Constituent Lobbying and its Impact oj the Development of Financial Reporting Regulations: Evidence from Eermani. *Journal of Accounting, Organizations and Society*, *25*(1), 79–98. doi:10.1016/S0361-3682(99)00028-8

Mir, M. Z., & Rahaman, A. S. (2005). The Adoption of International Accounting Standards in Bangladesh. *Accounting, Auditing & Accountability Journal*, *18*(6), 816–841. doi:10.1108/09513570510627720

Mueller, G. G., Gernon, H., & Meek, G. (1987). *Accounting: An International Perspective*. IRWIN.

Mulyadi, M. S., Soepriyanto, G., & Anwar, Y. (2012). IFRS adoption and taxation issue. *International Journal of Arts and Commerce*, *1*(7), 159–165.

Naser, K., & Nuseibeh, R. (2003). Quality of Financial Reporting: Evidence from the Listed Saudi nonfinancial Companies. *The International Journal of Accounting, 38*, 41-69.

Nobes, C., & Parker, R. (1995). *Comparative International Accounting* (5th ed.). London: Prentice Hall.

Nobes, C., & Parker, R. (2002). *Comparative International Accounting* (7th ed.). London: Prentice Hall.

Nobes, C., & Parker, R. (2006). *Comparative International Accounting* (9th ed.). London: Prentice Hall.

Purvis, S. E. C., Gernon, H., & Diamond, M. A. (1991). The IASC and its Comparability Project Prerequisites for Success. *Accounting Horizons*, *5*(2), 25–44.

Radebaugh, L. H., & Gray, S. J. (2002). International Accounting & Multinational Enterprises (5th ed.). Hermitage Publishing Services.

Rahman, A., Perera, H., & Ganesh, S. (2002). Accounting Practice Harmony, Accounting Regulation and Firm Characteristics. *Abacus*, *38*(1), 46–77. doi:10.1111/1467-6281.00097

Rahman, A. R., Ng, L. W., & Tower, G. D. (1994). Public Choice and Accounting Standard Setting in New Zealand: An Exploratory Study. *Abacus*, *30*(1), 98–117. doi:10.1111/j.1467-6281.1994.tb00345.x

Rahman, M. Z. (2000). *Accounting Standards in the East Asia Region*. Paper presented to the Second Asian Roundtable on Corporate Governance "The Role of Disclosure in Strengthening Corporate Governance and Accountability", Hong Kong.

Rawashdeh, M. (2003). Effects of Introducing International Accounting Standards on Amman Stock Exchange. *Journal of American Academy of Business, 3*(1-2), 361−366.

Riahi-Belkaoui, A. (2000). Accounting Theory (4th ed.). London: Business Press.

Saidi, F. (2013). Accounting Developments in Algeria: The Road to IFRS. *International Research Journal of Applied Finance*, *4*, 124–142.

Salter, B. S., & Niswander, F. (1995). Cultural Influence on the Development of Accounting Systems Internationally: A Test of Gray's (1998) Theory. *Journal of International Business Studies, 26*(2), 379 – 397.

Sawani, A. (2009). The Changing Accounting Environment: International Accounting Standards and US implementation. *Journal of Finance and Accountancy*, *1*(August), 1–9.

Schipper, K. (2005). The Introduction of International Accounting Standards in Europe: Implications for International Convergence. *European Accounting Review*, *14*(1), 101–126. doi:10.1080/0963818042000338013

Srijunpetch, S. (2004). *The Implementation of International Accounting Standards in Thailand*. (Unpublished PhD Thesis). The University of Manchester, Manchester, UK.

Street, D. L., & Gray, S. J. (2002). Factors Influencing the Extent of Corporate Compliance with International Accounting Standards: Summary of a Research Monograph. *Journal of International Accounting, Auditing & Taxation*, *11*(1), 51–76. doi:10.1016/S1061-9518(02)00054-X

Tan, H., Wang, S., & Welker, M. (2009). *Foreign Analyst Following and Forecast Accuracy around Mandated IFRS Adoptions*. Working Paper. Available at: http://www.bus.wisc.edu/accounting/faculty/documents/PaperMikeWelker17-09.pdf

Tandy, P. R., & Wilburn, N. L. (1992). Constituent Participation in Standard setting: The FASB's first 100 Statements. *Accounting Horizons*, (June): 47–58.

Taylor, P., & Turley, S. (1986). *The Regulation of Accounting*. New York: Blackwell Inc.

Tower, G. (1993). A Public Accountability Model of Accounting Regulation. *The British Accounting Review*, *25*(1), 61–85. doi:10.1006/bare.1993.1006

Tsakumis, G. T. (2007). The Influence of Culture on Accountants' Application of Financial Reporting Rules. *Abacus*, *43*(1), 27–48. doi:10.1111/j.1467-6281.2007.00216.x

Van Lent, L. (1997). Pressure and Politics in Financial Accounting Regulation: The Case of the Financial Conglomerates in the Netherlands. *Abacus*, *33*(1), 88–114. doi:10.1111/1467-6281.00005

Velayutham, S. (1996). Corporatization and the Regulation of Accounting Services. *The British Accounting Review*, *28*(4), 351–368. doi:10.1006/bare.1996.0023

Wallace, R. S. (1993). Development of Accounting Standards for Developing and Newly Industrialized Countries. *Research in Third World Accounting, 2*, 121-165.

Watts, J. (1993). *Accounting in the Business Environment*. London: Pitman Publishing.

Weetman, P., Davie, E. S., & Collins, W. (1996). Lobbying on Accounting Issues Preparer/user Imbalance in the Case of the Operating and Financial Review. *Accounting, Auditing & Accountability Journal*, *9*(1), 59–76. doi:10.1108/09513579610109978

Welbenberger, B. E., Stahl, A. B., & Vorstius, S. (2004). Changing from German GAAP to IFRS or US GAAP: A Survey of German Companies. *Accounting in Europe*, *1*(1), 169–189. doi:10.1080/0963818042000262748

Whittington, G. (2005). The Adoption of International Accounting Standards in the European Union. *European Accounting Review*, *14*(1), 127–153. doi:10.1080/0963818042000338022

Zeghal, D., & Mhedhbi, K. (2006). An Analysis of the Factors Affecting the Adoption of International Accounting Standards by Developing Countries. *The International Journal of Accounting*, *41*(4), 373–386. doi:10.1016/j.intacc.2006.09.009

Chapter 12
Are IFRS Adoption Benefits in Developing Countries a Time-Lag?
A Critical Review of the Case of Nigeria

Koholga Ormin
Adamawa State University, Nigeria

ABSTRACT

The IFRS is a useful international financial reporting framework that ensures comparable and quality financial information disclosure. IFRS perceived benefits compare to local and regional accounting standards has led to its adoption and implementation by several countries around the globe. However, IFRS is argued to benefit the developed countries the most due to their strong market and institutional settings (He, Wong & Young, 2009). This paper critically explores the question of whether IFRS adoption benefits in a developing country such as Nigeria is time-lag. The paper is a library research thus inferences were drawn deductively base on previous works conducted in Nigeria and elsewhere on IFRS adoption. This approach was further complimented by the conduct of interview with three professional accountants in practice and two economics analysts. It was revealed and concluded that due to their weak market, institutional settings and other factors, a time-lag is necessary for Nigeria and indeed all other developing countries to fully maximise the benefits of IFRS adoption and implementation. Notwithstanding, the paper recommends that to fast track IFRS benefits, developing countries and Nigeria in particular, should overhaul capital market infrastructure and ensure a strong ethical and good corporate governance environment as well as strict compliance with IFRS requirements through increase monitoring and use of sanctions by regulators.

INTRODUCTION

Financial reporting has been governed by the accounting and other regulatory statutes of each country, or at most, regional frameworks for a long time. Though, specific-country accounting standards and statutory regulations reflects the unique economic, social, political, cultural and legal environment thereby

DOI: 10.4018/978-1-4666-9876-5.ch012

the relevance and usefulness of financial reporting to users, globalization have challenged the worth of such standards particularly for foreign investors decision making. The IFRS is evolved to harmonized accounting standards globally in order to among others allow investors explore cross-broader investment opportunities (Bhattacharjee & Islam, 2009).

Prior to IFRS introduction, restatement of financial statements was core to investors of other nationalities to make meaning out of the accounting information disclosed by companies in nations they desire to have business dealings. In other words, as Ocansey & Enahorol (2014) puts it, financial statements comparism was not only difficulty but meaningless without adjustments. Bhattacharjee and Islam (2009) posits that, for usefulness, the information disclosed need not only be intelligible but comparable such that investment and credit decisions are facilitated globally. The need for a single set of financial information which is reliable, understandable, and comparable globally underpinned the introduction of the IFRS.

Daske, Hail, Leuz & Verdi (2008) notes IFRS introduction as one of the most significant regulatory changes ever witness in the history of accounting. IFRS has been described as an international financial reporting standard of the International Accounting Standards Board (IASB) that regulates financial reporting by public entities globally. The IASB is an independent organization registered in the United States of America but based in London, United Kingdom (Oduware, 2012). According to Okpala (2012), IFRS is a principles-based and globally accepted standard issued by the IASB aimed to enhance preparation and presentation of high quality, transparent and comparable financial statements. The adoption of IFRS for financial reporting is stated to have several other benefits.

There is evidence that since introduction, over 120 countries require the use of IFRS by listed companies within their jurisdiction while over 70 countries use the IFRS for Small and Medium Enterprises (Bewaji, 2012). Terzi, Oktem & Sen (2013) documented that about 27 member countries of the European Union prepare financial reports using IFRS with many countries in Africa, Asia, Australia, and America sacrificing local GAAP for IFRS. Nigeria adopted IFRS in 2012 with the expectation to reap the acclaimed benefits of the global standard. However, there are indications that IFRS may benefit the developed countries the most than developing countries due to market and institutional settings (He, Wong & Young, 2009). Impliedly, until developing countries like Nigeria are able to adjust their market and other institutional settings, they may not fully reap the benefits of IFRS adoption. In fact, Cuijipers and Buijinks (2005) cited in Atanassova (2008) pointed out that IFRS adoption benefits will take some time to fully materialized. Several studies have been conducted on the economic consequences of IFRS adoption in different countries including its effect on financial reporting quality (Chan, 2001; Morais & Curto, 2008; Brochet, Jagolinzer & Riedl, 2011; Morunga & Bradbury, 2012; Ames, 2013; Barth, Landsman, Lang & Williams, 2013; Umoren & Enang, 2015), capital market (Li, 2009; Cai & Wong, 2010; Okpala, 2012; Dhaliwal, Wen, Li & Pereira, 2013), tax (Gee, Haller & Nobes, 2010; Roe, 2014) and corporate governance (Cormier, 2013). However, little comprehensive evidence exists as to whether a time-lag is required for IFRS adoption to produce benefits in developing countries since they have weak market and institutional settings compared to their developed counterparts (He, Wong & Young, 2009). Empirically, Li (2009) provides evidence of IFRS adoption reducing firms cost of equity but in countries with strong legal enforcement. Also, Beneish, Miller & Yohn (2015) found that IFRS adoption significantly increase foreign equity investment but this effect is limited to countries with higher governance quality, economic development and creditor rights.

This paper therefore reviews the case of Nigeria with a view to understanding whether developing countries that adopted IFRS will require some time-lag before fully reaping the associated benefits.

This paper is significant because it shades light on the issue of whether a time-lag is necessary for less developed countries who adopted IFRS to derive its full benefits. This insight is considered important because many countries especially within Africa are striving to position themselves on the path of development. If IFRS adoption is seen as one of the instruments for achieving this objective, where these benefits do not seems apparent in the early years of adoption, it could be frustrating and at the same time discouraging to other countries contemplating doing so. This is likely to be so because IFRS adoption has cost implications (McGregor, 2012; Morunga & Bradbury, 2012). Moreover, the paper provides a road map of what needs to be done by developing countries to fast track IFRS adoption benefits.

The rest of the paper is structured into literature review, methodology, discussion, conclusion and recommendations, and frontier for further research.

LITERATURE REVIEW

Rationale for IFRS Adoption in Nigeria

There is evidence that only a 10% of countries globally will not participate in the IFRS (Fosbre, Kraft & Fosbre, 2009 in Ocansey & Enahorol, 2014). This means that about 90% of countries globally will or are participating either by way of adoption or convergence to the IFRS. It is also implicit that IFRS offers considerable benefits otherwise a majority of countries will not embrace it to the sacrifice of their national or regional accounting standards that have been in operation for long.

Financial reporting in Nigeria has been regulated by Statement of Accounting Standards (SASs) issued by the Nigerian Accounting Standards Board (NASB) established under the NASB Act of 2003. In its existence, the NASB had issued several standards covering various subject matters on accounting. Nigeria transition to IFRS began in 2010. The Nigeria's Federal Executive Council (FEC) endorsed the adoption of IFRS following the blue print of the IFRS adoption roadmap committee. The adoption was to proceed in three phases. The first phase targeted listed entities and significant public interest entities. This group of entities were required to adopt IFRS by 1st January, 2012. Phase two targeted all other public interest entities excluded in the first phase. This category of entities was to implement IFRS by the 1st January, 2013. While the third phase targeted Small and Medium Scale Enterprises (SMEs). The SMEs were to implement IFRS by 1st January, 2014. Preparatory to mandatory IFRS implementation, listed entities were required to prepare their closing balances as at 31st December, 2010 based on IFRS which was to become IFRS opening balances as at 1st January, 2011. As a follow up, the Nigeria Stock Exchange (NSE) urged all quoted companies to comply with IFRS by 2011 while the Central Bank of Nigeria (CBN) was more proactive by requiring banks to do so by December, 2010.

Bala (2013) stated that Nigeria's Generally Accepted Accounting Principles (GAAP) requirements were grossly inadequate to effectively bridge information asymmetry between reporting entities and users of financial reports. IFRS addresses this problem by requiring more disclosure on the activities of companies. In fact, prior to the Nigeria government resolve to adopt IFRS, the Nigerian financial reporting system (ie SAS) had no equivalents of IAS 18, Revenue; IAS 20, Accounting for Government Grants and Disclosure Assistance; IAS 23, Borrowing Costs; IAS 24, Related Party Disclosure; IFRS 7, Financial Instruments: Recognition and Measurement; and IAS 36, Impairment of Assets. These subject matters that SASs did not incorporate but will be reported by IFRS are a clear indication that greater value will be derived by users of financial information in the country.

Okafor & Ogiedu (2011) indicate that IFRS will benefit in the areas of international capital mobility, greater comparability of financial statements, and better integration with global operations than the use of Nigeria GAAP in financial reporting. Oduware (2012) opined the IFRS benefits to Nigeria in the areas of boost in the country's Foreign Direct Investments (FDIs), useful and meaningful investment portfolio decisions, easier access to external capital, reduce cost of doing business internationally as a result of elimination of supplementary information in the country and enhance knowledge of global financial reporting standards by tertiary institutions. Arguing with particular respect to FDI, Oduware (2012) stressed that FDI is hindered where financial reports are prepared under different national accounting rules because the information disclose contains little or no meaning, is difficult to interpret and costly to obtain. With IFRS, the application of same rules enhances transparency and comparability globally thereby confidence hence increase the flow of FDIs.

According to Bala (2013), IFRS was meant to improve the quality of financial reporting of Nigerian companies, the comparability and transparency of financial reports and reduced information asymmetry. Another benefit of IFRS adoption relates to the cost savings associated with developing local standards by the NASB now Financial Reporting Council of Nigeria (FRCN). A considerable amount of resources is involved in the process of developing and issuing accounting standards. Since, IFRSs are developed by the IASB and are either adopted wholly or with amendments to reflect peculiarities; cost will be saved by the local accounting standards setting bodies.

Empirical evidence on the rationalization of IFRS adoption by Nigeria is limited. This may not be far from the fact that IFRS was implemented in the country only in 2012 and sometime passage is necessary to warrant genuine assessment. Okafor & Ogiedu (2011) examine the potential effects of the adoption and implementation of IFRS in Nigeria. The study surveyed 54 respondents comprising of accounting lecturers, auditors and accountants and found that IFRS has potential to yield greater benefits than the use of Nigeria GAAP. In addition, it was reported that IFRS can improve business performance management, and besides financial reporting, impact other business functions such as business process and operations, the finance function, information technology and human resources. Furthermore, it was revealed that IFRS adoption will create financial reporting complexities but increase compliance with accounting standards. In another study, Okpala (2012) found that IFRS implementation has significant effect on FDI inflows and economic growth in Nigeria. The study administered questionnaire to 123 preparers (companies quoted on the NSE) and users (investment analysts) and utilized Pearson correlation statistics to analyse the data. Uromen and Enang (2015) also found earnings reported being more informative to equity investors in determining banks value in the post-IFRS period.

It is worth pointing out that though several reasons could be advanced for Nigeria's adoption of IFRS, the prime rationale is the country's quest to be one of the top twenty economies in the world by the year 2020 as articulated in the country version 202020. The adoption of IFRS provides a veritable platform for achieving this version.

Conditions for Beneficial IFRS Adoption

The review of available literature suggests that countries likely to benefit the most and timely from IFRS adoption will have an enabling environment. Because the prevailing economic, social, political, ethical and legal conditions differ from country to country, IFRS adoption may not benefit countries equally and within the same time. Advanced or developed economies with strong, reliable and stable capital markets, institutional settings and whose local GAAP is compatible with IFRS are likely to find IFRS implementation more successful and beneficial (He, Wong & Young, 2009; Gee, Haller & Nobes, 2010; Beneish, Miller & Yohn, 2015). This also implies that emerging or developing countries in which these conditions do not perfectly exist may derive benefits from IFRS adoption but perhaps after a longer time than their developed counterparts. Notwithstanding, so far as IFRS benefits exceeds the use of local GAAP, its adoption is ideal even for developing countries.

Some of the identified conditions necessary for IFRS success and timely benefits include; openness of economy, sophistication of investors, level of development of capital market and depth of accounting development and regulation (He, Wong & Young, 2009; Ikpefan & Akande, 2012; Siqili, 2010 in Pawan, 2011).

The countries whose economies are receptive to foreign investment and operate beyond the shore of the national bounders will reap benefits from IFRS than those in which these conditions are lacking. Some important benefits that IFRS offer adopters are increase FDI, enhance access and reduce cost of capital by companies (Okafor & Ogiedu, 2011; Okpala, 2012; Atanassova, 2008; Pawan, 2011; Beneish, Miller & Yohn, 2015). Okpala (2012) document that IFRS adoption increases FDI in Nigeria while Siqili (2010) cited in Pawan (2011) provide evidence from 1084 European Union firms during the period 1995 to 2006 suggesting that firms adopting IFRS on average significantly experience reduction in cost of raising equity.

Also, a shallow and less vibrant capital market will not create substantial benefits from IFRS adoption. He, Wong & Young (2009) document that many previous studies established that IFRS adoption has positive effects particularly in developed markets. This is because investors trust and confidence is dependent on the resilience of the capital market.

The sophistication of investors and other users of financial statements in terms of financial literacy is yet another condition for beneficial IFRS adoption. Financial reporting under IFRS produces complex financial information that may not be easily understood by investors and other users. Australia adopted IFRS in 2005 and due to its complex disclosure; investors made little use of the statements when making investment decisions. This cumulated to some leading accountants and business people in that country questioning the usefulness of financial statements prepared on the basis of IFRS for investors (McGregor, 2012). McGregor (2012) documents that the IASB recognize the associated complexity of IFRS reporting when the body clearly states that IFRS financial statements are directed at investors who have reasonable level of financial sophistication or literacy. Invariably, in countries where investors possess less than the expected level of financial literacy, IFRS adoption will add cost to information processing and acquisition hence the benefit. To bridge the literacy gap, Ikpefan & Akande (2012) submitted that considerable time will be required to educate investors, lenders, employees, auditors, audit committees, and other stakeholders during the transition and early post IFRS adoption.

The depth of accounting development and regulation also dictates IFRS adoption benefits. The countries with independent and equipped accounting standards setting machinery and whose standards are compatible with IFRS will find it easy and less costly to converge to IFRS (He, Wong & Young, 2009; Gee, Haller & Nobes, 2010). Moreover, the effectiveness with which accounting regulators discharge their responsibilities will go a long way to determine compliance and eliminate unethical practices that may affect the success of IFRS adoption. Li (2009) showed that the IFRS benefit of reduce cost of equity is present only in countries with strong legal enforcement.

An evaluation of Nigeria along these conditions would reveal that a perfect environment for IFRS success was lacking when the country adopted the international reporting framework. This explains why the relevant stakeholders had to pull resources and other logistics preparatory to implementation and will continue to do so in order to obtain the benefits of IFRS adoption.

Challenges of IFRS Adoption in Nigeria

IFRS adoption has associated difficulties and challenges (Ocansey & Enahorol, 2014). The evidence in the literature suggests that the practical challenges of IFRS adoption are quite similar across the countries. However, the challenges prevalent in the developed countries are much more similar and less pronounced compare to the developing countries (He, Wong & Young, 2009).

A fundamental practical challenge of IFRS adoption is dealing with the problem of complexity in financial information disclosure. Okafor & Ogiedu (2011) described complexity in financial reporting as the difficulty for stakeholders to grasp the economic substance of a transaction or event of a company under the IFRS regime. According to Okafor & Ogiedu (2011), the complexity of IFRS is derived on its fair value accounting relating to revenue recognition, financial liabilities and equity, and consolidations. Whereas IFRS disclosure presents complexity, previous studies indicate that generally the level of readability and understandability of financial information by users is poor (Schroeder & Gilbson, 1990 in Morunga & Bradbury, 2012). This complexity is not limited to users but also affects preparers' of financial reports due to the valuation requirements. Tackling this challenge will require extensive user's enlightenment by regulators.

In fact, the fair value accounting approach of the IFRS can further create serious earnings management problems (Ball, 2006 in He, Wong & Young, 2009). This situation will result to lower quality of financial reporting. Research evidence on effect of IFRS on financial reporting quality is rather mixed. For example, Barth et al. (2008) and Zhou et al. (2009) both cited in Pawan (2011), Umoren & Enang (2015) document positive impact while Lin (2009) also in Pawan (2011) and Ames (2013) found decease in financial reporting quality in Germany and South Africa respectively post IFRS adoption.

Generally, Ocansey & Enahorol (2014) identified the challenges to include; demands of a new set of skills and expertise, transitional challenges in the area of change management bottlenecks, inconsistencies in applicable laws, emerging technical areas and terminologies, frequent reviews of standards cost verse benefit analysis, and higher demand on auditors. Other challenges are the problem of aligning to IFRS since international accounting has language problem, resistance to change, problems of technical accounting tax implications, internal processes and statutory reporting, technology infrastructure, and organizational issues (Okpala, 2012). Ikpefan & Akande (2012) enumerated the challenges to IFRS adoption and implementation to include awareness about international practices, training, taxation, fair value, management compensation plan and reporting system.

Specifically within the Nigeria context, Oduware (2012) stated the challenges to include unsophisticated accounting systems and poor record keeping, lack of sufficient technical expertise, lack of documented risk management framework, inertia for change, lack of cooperation from non-finance units, lack of robust accounting system, tax implication, complexity of post-employment benefits, delays in release of regulatory guidance and general apathy towards technical research.

It is worth remarking that while Nigeria has fully transited to IFRS, some of these challenges will continue to impact the attendant benefits of IFRS adoption until they are comprehensively addressed.

Financial Reporting under the Nigeria GAAP And IFRS

There are significant differences in financial reporting requirements and content under IFRS compared to the Nigeria GAAP (ie SASs). Ikpefan & Akande (2012) stated that the major differences in IFRS and SASs are the extensive use of fair value reporting under IFRS which results to differences in income recognition and carrying values of assets and liabilities and further difference in current and deferred tax liability or assets. Simply put, IFRS emphasis fair value accounting reporting as against Nigeria GAAP historical value accounting. Fair value accounting is an approach whereby assets or securities valuation is updated on a regular basis, usually with reference to current prices of similar assets or securities established in the context of a liquid market while historical value accounting method records the value of an asset using the price at which it was originally acquired (Greenberg, Helland, Clancy & Dertouzous, 2013). The fair value and historical value accounting differences is likely to cause changes in key accounting ratios that are useful for evaluating firm's performance by investors and other users of financial information.

In terms of content, there is no value added statement and five-year financial summary under IFRS which are part of the Nigeria GAAP and several other differences exists in measurement (Ikpefan & Akande, 2012). Furthermore, financial reporting under IFRS regime cover accounting subject matters such as Revenue (IAS 18), Accounting for Government Grants and Disclosure of Government Assistance (IAS 20), Borrowing Costs (IAS 23), Related Party Disclosure (IAS 24), Financial Instruments: Disclosure and Presentation (IFRS 7), Financial Instruments: Recognition and Measurement (IAS 39), and Impairment of Assets (IAS 36). These were not covered by the Nigerian GAAP. Similarly, financial reporting under the Nigeria GAAP covers topics such as Accounting in the Petroleum Industry-Upstream (SAS 14), Accounting in the Petroleum Industry-Downstream Activities (SAS 17), Accounting for Insurance Business (SAS 16) and Abridge Financial Statements (SAS 20) which IFRS does not cover. The implication is that the inclusion of more subject matters to be reported upon under IFRS and the differences in measurement may have far reaching effect on the quality of financial reports, volume of information disclosure and user's information search and analytical skills.

Implications of IFRS Adoption

The change from local or regional accounting standards to IFRS has economic consequences on reporting entities, government and investor's decision making. Accounting standards change may have effect on the value of firms and wealth of those who make decisions using accounting information (Leftwitch, 1983). The introduction and adoption of IFRS has stimulated research that had examined the financial reporting, capital market, macroeconomic, tax reporting and corporate governance effects. The results of these studies are mixed suggesting impart that certain conditions are necessary to hold for IFRS benefits to be maximised.

The quality of financial reporting is fundamental to the decision accuracy of investors and other users of accounting information. A key objective of IFRS is to enhance financial reporting quality (IASB, 2008). The effect of IFRS on the quality of financial reporting has been estimated through earnings management, value relevance, comparability, and information overload. Morais & Curto (2008) examined the effect of IFRS adoption on accounting quality proxy by earnings smoothness of 30 Portuguese listed firms. The results indicated a decrease in earnings smoothness implying IFRS improves accounting quality. Similarly, Chiha, Trabelsi & Hamza (2013) investigation of 113 listed companies on the Paris

Stock Exchange during a nine year period spanning 2002 to 2010 indicated IFRS to improve accounting information quality. Brochet, Jagolinzer & Riedl (2011) examined mandatory IFRS adoption and financial statement comparability in the UK. The results revealed that IFRS adoption lead to enhanced comparability in the study area. Barth, Landsman, Lang & Williams (2013) study of whether the adoption of IFRS increased comparability of accounting amounts by non-US firms found that the accounting amounts of firms that voluntarily adopted IFRS afterwards become more comparable to earlier adopters and less comparable to non-adopting firms applying domestic standards in preparing financial reports.

In Nigeria, Umoren & Enang (2015) investigated whether mandatory IFRS adoption has improved the value relevance of financial information disclosed in the financial statements of listed banks. Using a sample of 12 banks with 2010 and 2011 as the pre-adoption period and 2012 and 2013 as the post-adoption period and utilizing descriptive and OLS regression, IFRS was found to have enhanced the accounting quality of Nigerian banks. Specifically, equity value and earnings of banks was shown to be relatively value relevant to share prices in the IFRS regime than under the Nigerian SAS era. Also, earnings per share was found to be incrementally value relevant post-IFRS whereas book value of equity per share incrementally less relevant post-IFRS. A situation interpreted to mean earnings reported being more informative to equity investors in determining bank value in the post-IFRS period.

Contrarily to studies that established IFRS enhancing financial reporting quality, Morunga & Bradbury (2010) who examined the implication of IFRS on information overload in New Zealand found that the annual reports for over 92% of the sample firms increased. This means that IFRS contributed to information overload hence adversely affected financial reporting quality. In the area of earnings management, Wang & Campbell (2012) study of 1329 listed companies from 1998 to 2009 in China did not find evidence that IFRS implementation reduced the incidence of earnings management. Also, Ames (2013) sampled 3950 COMPUSTAT global firms in South Africa during the period 2000 to 2011 found no significant improvement in earnings quality post IFRS adoption.

Studies that examined the effect of IFRS on capital markets include among others Daske, Hail, Leuz & Verdi (2008), Li (2009), Cai & Wong (2010), Barth, Landsman, Lang & Williams (2013), Dhaliwal, Wen, Li, Pereira (2013) and Beneish, Miller & Yohn (2015). Daske, Hail, Leuz & Verdi (2008) examined the capital market effect of mandatory IFRS adoption and found IFRS to be associated with increase market liquidity, decrease cost of firms capital and increase in equity valuation. Li (2009) study of 1084 EU firms during the period 1995 to 2006 found that on average IFRS adoption significantly reduces the cost of equity for mandatory adopters by 47 basis points. Dhaliwal, Wen, Li, Pereira (2013) examined the role of mandatory adoption of IFRS on financial market integration. Market integration was proxy by the extent to which the global factor explains local stock returns and the speed with which local stock returns incorporate global factors. It was found that a positive association exists between IFRS adoption and market integration. The association was further shown to be particularly significant where major differences in terms of quality exists between IFRS and local accounting standards and a stronger legal enforcement prevailed. To corroborate Dhaliwal, Wen, Li, Pereira (2013), Cai & Wong (2010) also established more financial integration between listed companies in countries that adopted IFRS than those using local accounting standards.

Barth, Landsman, Lang & Williams (2013) comparatively examined whether IFRS adoption has attendant capital market benefits such as increase liquidity, share turnover and firm specific information by non-US firms by adopting, earlier adopters and non-IFRS adopting firms. The study reported that relative to earlier and non-adopting firms, firms adopting IFRS exhibits increased capital market benefits of liquidity, share turnover and firm specific information. Conversely to the aforementioned studies, Hung & Subramanyan (2007), Clarkson, Hanna, Richardson & Thompson (2011) did not suggest IFRS adoption to have caused a significant improvement on the value relevance of book value of equity.

With respect to macroeconomic effect, Beneish, Miller & Yohn (2015) investigated the association between mandatory IFRS adoption and foreign portfolio investment into the adopting country's debt and equity markets. It was found that IFRS adoption has a significantly greater effect on foreign debt than on foreign equity investment flows. They also found that increase in foreign equity investment around IFRS adoption is limited to countries that had higher governance quality, economic development and creditor rights prior to adoption. Okpala (2012) also found that IFRS adoption has significant effect on FDI in Nigeria.

Taxation has a strong relationship with financial reporting. Changes in accounting rules are bound to have tax effect just as changes in tax rules may affect financial reporting practice both in terms of the presentation and information content of financial statements. Roe (2014) theoretically concluded that transiting from US GAAP to IFRS will have significant effect on tax because of the relationship of tax rules and regulations with US GAAP and the heavy reliance on financial reporting in tax compliance and regulation in the US. Empirically, Gee, Haller & Nobes (2010) examined the tax differences of IFRS consolidated financial statements of German and UK firms. The result showed German IFRS statements to exhibit tax influence while that of UK devoid of such influence. The study explained this to be so because unlike the case of UK, German tax practices are based on commercial code (Handelsgesetzbuch) which is significantly different from IFRS.

Corporate governance plays a crucial role in financial reporting quality. Cormier (2013) study of corporate governance and information asymmetry in Canada found that the introduction of IFRS reduced the impact of corporate governance on information asymmetry. This means that IFRS does not enhance corporate governance.

METHODOLOGY

This paper is a critical review on the question of whether due to their weak architecture, a time-lag is necessary for IFRS adoption and implementation in developing countries to yield the expected benefits. The paper sought evidence from Nigeria's adoption and implementation of IFRS in 2012. The work is essentially a library research. Thus, draws extensively on the evidence documented in the literature both in Nigeria and other countries that have adopted IFRS. The knowledge of the researcher on the Nigerian financial reporting system and general economic, political, social, ethical, cultural and legal environment was brought to bear in making inferences from the available literature. But to ensure non-misleading conclusions, this approach was further complimented by an interaction with three professional accountants in practice and two economics analysts. In particular, the interviewee opinion was sought on how soon IFRS adoption by Nigeria will yield the benefits of improved financial reporting quality and decision making by investors and other users (issues of comparability and understandability), increase FDI, greater compliance, and easy access to capital by companies. The selection of the interviewee was based on convenience and willingness to provide information. The interviewees were drawn from Yola, Adamawa State and Makurdi, Benue State, Nigeria. Deductive reasoning was adopted by the paper in reaching conclusion. By this approach, the paper explores on the position of existing literature to draw conclusion.

DISCUSSION

Nigeria like other developing countries is believed to lack an enabling environment that would maximize the benefits of IFRS adoption and implementation, particularly during the initial years. This is evident from He, Wong & Young (2009) contention that due to market and institutional settings, the effect of IFRS adoption in emerging markets may differ from those of mature markets. This section provides a critical review on the question of whether or not IFRS adoption benefits in developing countries such as Nigeria is time-lag due to their weak market, institutional settings and other factors.

The IFRS emphasis fair value accounting. Oduware (2012) state this approach to constitute a serious challenge to Nigerian companies due to lack of qualified and sufficient technical expertise and robust accounting system required for its implementation. Impliedly, companies will have to create the enabling environment by investing heavily on accounting personnel training, acquiring information technology and restructuring accounting and internal control system. In a study, Price Waterhouse Coopers (PWC, 2004) pointed out that at the stage of the change process to IFRS, firms will experience low internal controls and until they implement full controls and procedures in line with IFRS requirements, no benefits will be derived (Okafor & Ogiedu, 2011). There is report of Australian businesses incurring significant cost in transiting to IFRS (McGregor, 2012). The situation in Nigeria may not be any different as companies have invested in manpower training, altering of existing financial reporting structures and other logistics. This initial cost will certainly outweigh any probable benefits derivable from IFRS adoption in the short-run.

Ocansey & Enahorol (2014) argue that large and medium scale firms especially those with subsidiaries in other countries or that sought international finance stand to reap the desired benefits from IFRS adoption. Therefore, while it may be appreciated that the depth of capital market is important to IFRS increasing access to capital by companies; of even more fundamental importance is the operation of companies on the international scene. Unfortunately, many Nigerian companies do not operate beyond the shore of the country boundaries but rather companies of other nationalities are dominant in key sectors like the oil and gas. It is only of recent that more Nigerian banks and the Dangote Group are beginning to explore the international scene. Thus, until these companies become well established and recognize at the international scene, the expected benefit of access to capital may not be optimised.

In relation to users, the convergence to IFRS requires at the initial stage greater reporting with respect to changes in presenting items in the accounts, their valuation cum effect, accompanied by fair value valuation of assets, liabilities and equities as well as more subject matters compare to the repealed SASs. Ikpefan & Akande (2012) point out most of the significant differences of the new IFRS reporting and old Nigeria GAAP. The implication is that the nature of IFRS reporting may likely lead to information overload in the annual reports and accounts. Morunga & Bradbury (2012) document that IFRS creates information overload. Furthermore, IFRS has terminology problem. Since Nigerian users (investors in particular) cannot be considered highly sophisticated in terms of financial literacy, at least within the first few years, they will experience difficulty in reading and understanding the information disclosed. This might necessitate their resorting to information experts such as financial analysts for effective decision making. This option will however end in increase cost of information acquisition. Put differently, Nigerian investors and other users may require time to be conversant and develop better information search strategies to fully ascertain benefits from IFRS adoption.

The benefit of IFRS adoption causing an increase in financial reporting quality is also a doubt in its early years of implementation in a developing country like Nigeria. IFRS offer more discretion in financial reporting (Okafor & Ogiedu, 2011) and due to the weak ethics and corporate governance prevalence; managers may have opportunity to engage in earnings management practices (Ames, 2013). In fact, studies on IFRS adoption and financial reporting quality are inconclusive. Whereas, the studies of Barth et al (2009) and Zhou et al (2009) both documented in Pawan (2011), Brochet, Jagolinzer & Riedl (2011) show IFRS adoption to significantly improve financial reporting quality (proxy by earnings management), that of Wang & Campbell (2012) and Ames (2013) does not find such evidence. Though, few known evidence exists in Nigeria of IFRS enhancing financial reporting quality (Umoren & Enang, 2015), the weak ethics and corporate governance couple with further weakness in regulatory supervision and enforcement in the country means financial reporting quality may likely be negatively affected until regulators adjust to prevent these practices. It is in the same vein, that Pawan (2011) concluded that the achievement of high quality financial reporting environment under IFRS, is dependent on the effectiveness of controls and enforcement mechanisms.

Furthermore, timeliness of release of financial statement is an important quality of financial reporting (Beest, Braam & Boelens, 2009; Iyoha, 2012). The tedious valuation process and other detailed disclosure (accounting policies) due to switch to IFRS may mean that more time will be spent on information accumulation by companies for the purposes of disclosure. Notwithstanding that no empirical evidence exist that examine the timeliness of financial reporting pre-and post IFRS adoption in the country, the mentioned issues may likely affect the timeliness of corporate disclosure. However, with time, when experience and expertise is gained and detailed disclosure on effect regarding changes in accounting policies is no longer required, no much time may be taken in financial statements preparation.

Regulatory wise, the creation of awareness, adoption and modification of IFRS to suit local context have significant financial and other resource implications. Moreover, several statutes such as CAMA, SEC, NSE, NDIC, NAICOM, PENCON, BOFIA, CBN Act among others need to be amended in order to harmonise with IFRS and indeed make IFRS superior to the local GAAPs. Unfortunately, up to date, the required amendments to these statutes are yet to be effected. This is already a lapse and an indication that IFRS adoption requires time for the benefits to be derived.

With respect to FDI, though Okpala (2012) provides evidence of IFRS adoption in Nigeria increasing FDI in the early years, this finding is questionable. This is because the current political dispensation of President Goodluck E. Jonathan and the previous had made concerted efforts in terms of infrastructure and other incentives to attract foreign investors in the country. Since Okpala (2012) study did not control for all noise variables, some which may impact FDI than IFRS adoption, the results could be taken to provide only a partial explanation of the substance. Moreover, the increased insecurity; particularly in the north-east part of the country at the time of IFRS adoption would most likely affect whatever benefits in attracting FDI in the immediate time.

The issue of IFRS adoption impacting government tax revenue in the country is also pertinent. IFRS adoption is noted to affect financial reporting structure which also affects the tax laws hence procedure for determining corporate tax liability (Fowokan, 2011; Ikpefan & Akande, 2012). Whereas, IFRS is implemented in the country, the tax laws are yet to be amended. More so, since IFRS is associated with greater flexibility, there is a question of whether corporate management will not take advantage by manipulating and disclosing in ways that results to lesser tax liability thus government tax revenue. This scenario has implications on the country's economic growth and development. Impliedly, more time is required by the tax authorities to adjust tax laws in line with IFRS information disclosure.

The interview conducted confirms most of the inferences drawn. Specifically, it was a shared view of the interviewees that due to the fact that IFRS increase the subject matters to be reported on which previously were not covered by SASs, and the expected greater searchlight by regulators, financial reporting quality will increase. Comparability was identified as the main quality of financial reporting that will be enhanced. But that the increase in financial reporting quality will be dependent on the accuracy of fair value accounting valuation and level of compliance with IFRS requirements. The issue of accuracy of fair value accounting valuation is instructive that a time-lag is necessary to maximize the benefit.

On FDI, the respondents do not believe that any increase in the country at the moment is attributable to IFRS adoption, but rather to other economic policies of the federal government aimed at attracting foreign investors into the oil and gas, agricultural and other sectors of the economy. It was also revealed that easy and more access to capital will be enhanced if Nigeria companies expand the boundaries of their operations by setting up subsidiaries in other countries of the world especially the developing economies were investment opportunities abound and there are lesser investment constraints.

The finding with respect to users and tax revenue also indicated the necessity of a time-lag. In particular, it was gathered that not only investors but professional financial analysts who are not knowledgeable on IFRS will all find difficulty in understanding the financial reports. However, some of the interviewees believe that the awareness so far created which is still on-going will address this timely. It was also indicated that IFRS has taxation effect but majority of the interviewees expect the tax authorities to respond appropriately to prevent decline in government tax revenue.

By and large, the interviewees believe in the potential of IFRS adoption to accrued substantial benefits in a developing country like Nigeria in the long-run than may be the case in the short-run. It was also their submission that the identification of impeding challenges through continue review and sustained commitment by the regulatory bodies and government will surely yield the anticipated benefits. Invariably, the views disclosed in this paper corroborates Cuijipers & Buijink (2005) who suggest that IFRS adoption benefits will take some time to fully materialise (Atanassova, 2008).

The findings of this study basically have regulatory and academic research implications. It is indicative that effective regulation is at the heart of not only IFRS adoption success but the maximisation of the benefits of its implementation. From the academic research dimension, it reiterates the widely held notion that when a policy is developed and implemented, reasonable time is require to lapse for genuine empirical research evidence. Put differently, research on the impact of IFRS adoption in developing counties may not produce valid findings until a reasonable time period lapses from the date of implementation. Therefore, within the first five years, explorative studies are more useful.

CONCLUSION AND RECOMMENDATIONS

The adoption and convergence to IFRS by the different countries of the world may have the fundamental objective of achieving comparability and improving the quality of financial reporting (Bala, 2013), but there are many more benefits associated with the use of IFRS in financial reporting. However, to implement IFRS and reap the benefits in the short-run, an enabling environment must be in place. This environment is found in the developed countries but lacking in the developing countries. Therefore, the benefits derivable from IFRS adoption and implementation in developing countries such as Nigeria will necessarily require a time-lag to be maximised.

Notwithstanding, developing countries, Nigeria in particular, can work to timely maximise IFRS adoption benefits by overhauling capital market infrastructure and ensuring a strong ethical and good corporate governance environment. This will not only spur investors' confidence in the system but also ensure better oversight on financial reporting in the country hence accrue more timely the benefits of adopting IFRS. Furthermore, regulatory authorities should ensure strict compliance with IFRS requirements by companies through increase monitoring and use of sanctions on defaulters.

FRONTIER FOR FURTHER RESEARCH

The adoption of IFRS by Nigerian listed companies offers several research opportunities. This paper theoretically examined whether as a developing nation, a time-lag is necessarily for listed companies and the Nigerian economy as a whole to experience significant benefits of applying the IFRS in financial reporting. Further empirical studies are required into the extent of IFRS adoption, the firm's characteristics that influence IFRS adoption and effects of IFRS adoption on financial reporting quality, capital market, corporate governance and tax in the country.

REFERENCES

Ames, D. (2013). IFRS adoption and accounting quality: The case of South Africa. *Journal of Applied Economies and Business Research*, *3*(3), 154–165.

Atanassova, A. (2008). *IFRS adoption in Bulgarian banks: Non-numerical disclosure evidence*. Working Paper. University of Economics Varna.

Bala, M. (2013). Effects of IFRS adoption on the financial reports of Nigerian listed entities: The case of oil and gas companies. *The Macrotheme Review*, *2*(7), 9–26.

Barth, M. E., Landsman, W. R., Lang, M. H., & Williams, C. D. (2013). *Effects on comparability and capital market benefits of voluntary adoption of IFRS by US firms: Insight from voluntary adoption of IFRS by non-US firms*. Working Paper No. 3074.

Beest, F., Braam, G., & Boelens, S. (2009). *Quality of financial reporting: Measuring qualitative characteristics*. Nice Working Paper 09-108.

Beneish, M. D., Miller, B. P., & Yohn, T. L. (2015). Macroeconomic evidence on the impact of mandatory IFRS adoption on equity and debt markets. *Journal of Accounting and Public Policy*, *34*(1), 1–27. doi:10.1016/j.jaccpubpol.2014.10.002

Bewaji, O. (2012). *The international financial reporting standards: Implication for the Nigerian accountants*. Paper presented at the 49th induction ceremony of the Institute of Chartered Accountants of Nigeria (ICAN).

Bhattacharjee, S., & Islam, M. Z. (2009). Problems of adoption and application of international financial reporting standards (IFRS) in Bangladesh. *International Journal of Business and Management*, *4*(12), 165–175. doi:10.5539/ijbm.v4n12p165

Brochet, F., Jagolinzer, A., & Riedl, E. J. (2011). *Mandatory IFRS adoption and financial statement comparability*. Working Paper, 11-109.

Cai, F., & Wong, H. (2010). The effect of IFRS adoption on global market integration. *International Business and Economics Research Journal, 9*(10), 25–34.

Chan, S. Y. (2001). The use of graphs as decision aids in relation to information overload and managerial decision quality. *Journal of Information Science, 27*(6), 417–425. doi:10.1177/016555150102700607

Charkson, P., Hanna, J. D., Richardson, G. D., & Thompson, R. (2011). The impact of IFRS adoption on the value relavence of book value and earnings. *Journal of Contemporary Accounting and Economics, 7*(1), 1–17. doi:10.1016/j.jcae.2011.03.001

Chiha, H., Trabelsi, N. S., & Hamza, S. E. (2013). The effect of IFRS on earnings quality in a European stock market: Evidence from France. *Interdisciplinary Journal of Research in Business, 2*(12), 35–47.

Cormier, D. (2013). *The incidence of corporate governance and IFRS on information asymmetry and the value relevance of earnings: Some Canadian evidence.* Cahier de Recherche 2014-01.

Daske, H., Hail, L., Leuz, C., & Verdi, R. (2008). Mandatory IFRS reporting around the world: Early evidence on the economic consequences. *Journal of Accounting Research, 46*(5), 1085–1142.

Dhaliwal, D., Wen, H., Li, Y., & Pereira, R. (2013). *Does mandatory IFRS adoption facilitate financial market integration?* Paper presented at the American Accounting Association (AAA) Annual meeting and Conference, Consequences of IFRS Adoption, California.

Fowokan, T. (2011). *IFRS adoption in Nigeria-tax implications.* Paper presented at CITN Seminar on IFRS adoption in Nigeria. Retrieved July 30, 2012 from http://www.docstoc.com/docs/89676635/IFRS-Adoption-in-Nigeria-Tax-Implications-Paper-presented-by-Mrs-Titilayo-Fowokan-ACA-ACTI-CITN-Seminar-on-IFRS-Adoption-in-Nigeria-Overview-%EF%82%97-Introdu

Gee, M., Haller, A., & Nobes, C. (2010). The influence of tax on IFRS consolidated statements: The convergence of Germany and the UK. *Accounting in Europe, 7*(1), 97–122. doi:10.1080/17449480.2010.485382

Greenberg, M. D., Helland, E., Clancy, N., & Dertouzes, J. N. (2013). *Fair value accounting, historical cost accounting, and systemic risk: Policy issues and options for strengthening valuation and reducing risk.* RAND Centre for Corporate Ethics and Governance. Retrieved December 28, 2014 from: www.rand.org

He, X., Wong, T., & Young, D. (2009). *Challenges for implementation of fair value accounting in emerging markets: Evidence from IFRS adoption in China.* Retrieved December 28, 2014 from https://tippie.uiowa.edu/accounting/mcgladrey/pdf/wong_tj.pdf

Hung, M., & Subramanyam, K. R. (2007). Financial statement effect of adopting internation accounting standards: The case of Germany. *Review of Accounting Studies, 12*(4), 623–657. doi:10.1007/s11142-007-9049-9

IASB. (2008). Exposure draft on an improved conceptual framework for financial reporting: The objective of financial reporting and qualitative characteristics of decision-useful financial reporting information. London: IASB.

Ikpefan, O. A., & Akande, A. O. (2012). International financial reporting standard (IFRS): Benefits, obstacles and intrigues for implementation. *Research Journal of Finance and Accounting*, *3*(10), 143–151.

Iyoha, F. O. (2012). Company attributes and the timeliness of financial reporting in Nigeria. *Business Intelligence Journal*, *5*(1), 41–49.

Leftwitch, R. W. (1983). Accounting information in private markets: Evidence from private lending agreements. *Accounting Review*, *58*(1), 23–42.

Li, S. (2009, September). Does mandatory adoption of international financial reporting standards in the European union reduce the cost of equity capital? *The Accounting Review*.

McGregor, W. (2012). *In defence of IFRS financial statements*. CPA Australia Ltd.

Morais, A. I., & Curto, J. D. (2008). Accounting quality and the adoption of IASB standards: *Portuguese evidence. Revista Contabilidade and Financas*, *19*(48), 103–111. doi:10.1590/S1519-70772008000300009

Morunga, M., & Bradbury, M. E. (2010). *Has IFRS resulted in information overload?* Discussion Paper Series 221.

Morunga, M., & Bradbury, M. E. (2012). The impact of IFRS on annual report length. *Australasian Accounting. Business and Finance Journal*, *6*(5), 47–62.

Ocansey, E. O. N. D., & Enahorol, J. A. (2014). Comparative study of the international financial reporting standard implementation in Ghana and Nigeria. *European Scientific Journal*, *10*(13), 529–546.

Oduware, U. (2012). *IFRS adoption in Nigeria & optimising the gains of global investment climate*. Retrieved December 28 2014 from https://www.wecadeloitte.com/extranet/data/ifrsacademy/content/_1355906750_30C8SXR170.pdf Accessed.

Okafor, C., & Ogiedu, K. O. (2011). Potential effects of the adoption and implementation of international financial accounting standards (IFRS) in Nigeria. *JORIND*, *9*(2), 345–358.

Okpala, K. E. (2012). Adoption of IFRS and financial statements effects: The perceived implications on FDI and Nigerian economy. *Australian Journal of Business and Management Research*, *2*(5), 76–83.

Pawan, J. (2011). IFRS implementation in India: Opportunities and Challenges. *World Journal of Social Sciences*, *1*(1), 125–136.

Roe, J. (2014). Transition from US GAAP to IFRS: Analysis of impact on income tax administration in USA. *European Financial and Accounting Journal*, *9*(4), 86–109.

Terzi, S., Oktem, R., & Sen, I. K. (2013). Impact of adopting international financial reporting standards: Empirical evidence from Turkey. *International Business Research*, *6*(4), 55–66. doi:10.5539/ibr.v6n4p55

Umoren, A. O., & Enang, E. R. (2015). IFRS adoption and value relevance of financial statements of Nigerian listed banks. *International Journal of Finance and Accounting*, *4*(1), 1–7.

Wang, Y., & Campbell, M. (2012). Corporate governance, earnings management, and IFRS: Empirical evidence from Chinese domestically listed companies. *Advances in Accounting, Incorporating. Advances in International Accounting*, *28*(1), 189–192. doi:10.1016/j.adiac.2012.03.007

Chapter 13
International Financial Reporting Standards (IFRS) Adoption in Vietnam:
From Isolation to Isomorphism

Duc Hong Thi Phan
RMIT University, Vietnam

Mahesh Joshi
RMIT University, Australia

Bruno Mascitelli
Swinburne University, Australia

ABSTRACT

The chapter is aimed at analyzing the collective perception of the accounting community of Vietnam towards the adoption of International Financial Reporting Standards (IFRS). This perception is premised on the twin issues of legitimacy and isomorphism. A broad sample survey of 728 persons out of 3000 accountants, auditors and academics was undertaken with a detailed questionnaire sent to each. With a net response rate of 24 per cent from this community, there emerged a definite influence of coercive, mimetic and normative isomorphisms as well as legitimacy motives. The study provides practical implications for the policymakers of Vietnam for the transformation of the accounting profession in the country and the strategic planning towards full mandatory IFRS adoption by 2020.

INTRODUCTION

The adoption of International Financial Reporting Standards (IFRS) in developing countries is a well-known area of research. Despite its across-the-globe presence, the trajectory of adoption is not similar with developing countries. One of the major impacting factors is the pressure imposed by the lending institutions like the World Bank and the International Monetary Fund (IMF). A series of studies related

DOI: 10.4018/978-1-4666-9876-5.ch013

to Egypt (Hassan 2008), Bangladesh (Mir & Rahaman 2005); Czech Republic, Hungary, Turkey, and Romania (Albu et al. 2013); Zimbabwe (Chamisa 2000); and Ghana (Assenso-Okofo, Ali & Ahmed 2011), have confirmed the presence of this factor behind the adoption of IFRS in these countries. For instance, the World Bank and IMF were using the access to developmental assistance and finance as a major threat for countries to adopt IFRS. As a result of such financial pressures, since 2005, more developing countries chose to adopt IFRS. Yet, limited study has been undertaken in the case of Vietnam and whether the policymakers, auditing and academic communities are influenced in a similar ways or not is still to be ascertained (Phan, Mascitelli & Barut 2014a).

IFRS are not required or allowed in Vietnam as the financial reporting rules. All Vietnamese businesses are required to report under VAS. There are significant differences between the current VAS and IFRS. This is because VAS is generally based on the international accounting standards (IAS) issued prior to 2003 with adjustments for Vietnamese economic, finance and accounting conditions. According to Pham (2012), the overall de jure convergence (convergence by accounting regulation) of VAS and IFRS is about 66 per cent in which the measurement convergence is at a higher rate (75.8 per cent) and the disclosure convergence is at lower rate (61.9 per cent). The findings of Phan, Mascitelli and Barut (2013) revealed that disclosure convergence between VAS and IFRS is significantly lower because most of the IASB standards require additional disclosure relative to its equivalent VAS. This disparity leads to the concern that financial statements prepared under VAS may not fully need the external users' needs for accounting information. Thus, it is not uncommon practice in Vietnam that companies prepare two separate financial statements, one under mandatory VAS and the other voluntarily compliant with IFRS for overseas financing purposes.

The timing of this research in Vietnam is appropriate because the Vietnamese accounting system is in a phase of transition towards IFRS (Phan & Mascitelli 2014). The Ministry of Finance, recently, made a decision to mandate full IFRS adoption for public enterprises (banking, insurance and publicly listed companies) by 2020 and allow these public enterprises to early adopt IFRS in 2017 (Vo 2014). Recent economic history of Vietnam has been full of economic stop and starts, particularly, its jump from a centrally planned economy to a more market-friendly one. This kind of externalization has created a significant number of changes in the accounting practices of the country (Bui 2011). This metamorphosis is still in progress as to how this eventual alignment with IFRS would occur. There is no clear-cut feedback about how the key stakeholders are thinking about these changes and what are the key impacting factors working behind their choices (Phan 2014). So, there is a much needed perception-based study to understand the attitudes of all the members associated with the accounting profession in Vietnam. The current study goes precisely in this direction so as to ascertain the responses of all the stakeholders.

A survey approach was undertaken to explore the perceptions through a detailed questionnaire. It revealed that the most coercive influence came from the World Bank and the World Trade Organization according to the key members of the accounting community of Vietnam. It was followed by the Asian Development Bank, International Monetary Fund and the International Financial Corporation. Continuing with isomorphic behavior, the mimetic isomorphism too was reported to be equally influential. The case of those countries that underwent successful IFRS, the adoption process was also considered to be a major impacting factor in the perception of many responses. Vietnam was expected not to be a laggard; if other countries could achieve some benefits from IFRS adoption, there was no reason for Vietnam not doing so. But out of three forms of institutional isomorphism, the lowest impact came from the normative isomorphism. The predominance of Vietnamese accounting bodies towards the adoption of IFRS was not particularly noteworthy. There was a consensus among all surveyed groups that Vietnam would finally adopt IFRS in its march towards globalization as it seeks to attract foreign investment, increase the credibility of its stock market and raise its national importance in the global environment.

This chapter is divided into six sections. Section one begins with the introduction followed by a brief literature review of the institutional isomorphism and legitimacy theories. This is followed by the empirical evidence that allows for the development of the required hypotheses. This is followed by a section that outlines the research methodology along with a discussion on the findings of the analyses. In the final section comes the conclusion wherein a summary of the entire research outcomes along with the limitations of the study and the scope for future research.

LITERATURE REVIEW AND HYPOTHESIS DEVELOPMENT

The broader domain of this chapter lies within the disciplinary confines of "New Institutional Accounting" (NIA) as used by Leuz and Wysocki (2008) and Wysocki (2011). NIA's domain lies around the interaction of market forces, regulatory frameworks, standards, enforcements and other institutions, that affect corporate financial reporting and disclosure outcomes. The core of NIA draws its strength from recent advances in institutional economics literature. Here, there is some differentiation as this study is focused on the role of accounting in social legitimacy and interactional accounting standards and specifically prefers to align with the institutional theory of Di Maggio and Powell (1983) and the Legitimacy theory of Schuman (1995). The basic proposition of this study is that any decision for or against the adoption of an accounting change is deeply responsive to institutional pressures and legitimacy as well as economic logic. The theoretical work undertaken by Di Maggio and Powell (1983) states that there are three mechanisms through which institutions are reproduced elsewhere; these are coercive, mimetic and normative isomorphisms, each with its own antecedents. The first, coercive isomorphism comes from the formal and informal pressures exerted on one unit by other units upon which they are dependent. Mimetic isomorphism results from a standard response to uncertainty. It is like saying "do what others do when faced with a similar challenge". Normative isomorphism is the result of internal evolution of a professional community as to what kind of expertise they regard sufficient for legitimacy as Schuman (1995) defined it as "a generalised perception or assumption that the actions of an entity are desirable, proper, or appropriate within some socially constructed system of norms, values, beliefs, and definitions" (p.574).

There have been a number of studies which reveal that a developing country is quite vulnerable to coercive, mimetic and normative institutional pressures from multinational lending agencies, international capital markets, the Big Four accounting firms and the IASB (Irvine 2008; Judge, Li & Pinsker 2010). All of these can be regarded as factors/agents that affect the adoption trajectory of financial reporting under IFRS in developing countries. The following section will discuss each element of institutional isomorphism, its relevance and effects upon the possibility of IFRS adoption.

Coercive Isomorphism

For developing countries, two organizations namely the International Monetary Fund (IMF) and the World Bank are the most powerful coercive forces. Their role as international lending agencies has in some circumstances created a debtor trap of "do as directed". The choice was to either accept IFRS completely or adapt the national accounting standard in line with IFRS (Hegarty, Gielen & Barros 2004;

Perera & Baydoun 2007; Hassan 2008; Al-Omari 2010). To exemplify it further, Perera and Baydoun (2007) mention the case of Indonesia. In 1997 during the Asian Financial Crisis, the country was forced to depend upon the IMF for a quick financial salvaging operation. However the deal came with conditions, one being of a need to change financial reporting practices to incorporate the international best practice and therefore consider the adoption of international accounting standards. The evidence also extends to the World Bank that pushed developing countries to adopt IFRS or develop national standards based on IFRS, for example in Jordan (Al-Omari 2010), in Egypt (Hassan 2008), and in Bangladesh (Mir & Rahaman 2005). In some countries, the World Bank made the adoption of IFRS as a requirement of its loans (Hegarty, Gielen & Barros 2004). In short multinational financial institutions have come to believe that developing nations with weaker forms of financial reporting processes must be encouraged to adopt IFRS or move towards harmonization of a global standard. Therefore, it is suggested that Vietnam is also under similar pressure from these financial aid providers to accept IFRS or to develop Vietnamese accounting standards in line with IFRS. Thus, it was hypothesised that

H1: There is the existence of coercive isomorphism upon the consideration of IFRS adoption in Vietnam.

Mimetic Isomorphism

The pressure from trade partners and the multinational companies (Al-Omari 2010) creates much pressure to adapt to a similarity of business practices. There has been a near-consensus on the issue that as trade becomes entrenched by globally multinational corporations, the desire to expand and express financial statements through IFRS also increases (Gelb, Holtzman & Mest 2008; Irvine 2008). Current corporate governance not only pushes the reporting and disclosure mechanisms by following IFRS but also creates a culture of 'do as the best do' among those national companies who want to reach global standards. This becomes both desirable and the essential models of success. Additional evidence for the same has been provided by authors (Irvine 2008; Ramanna & Sletten 2009) that a country is more likely to adopt IFRS if its trade partners or countries within its geographical region are IFRS adopters. Companies tend to model themselves on fellow organizations they consider being more legitimate, large or successful in the same sector. For example, IFRS are only mandatory for publicly listed companies in countries within the European Union (EU). Non-listed companies in the EU are permitted, but are not required, to use IFRS since 2005. However, many authors (Kumar, Wilder & Stocks 2008; Wang, Sewon & Claiborne 2008; Karamanou & Nishiotis 2009) observed that the unlisted companies within the EU and listed companies from developing countries (where IFRS is not required) also voluntarily adopt IFRS in their consolidated financial statements to enhance their image and perceived legitimacy. Mimicking in response to uncertainty and seeking legitimacy is expected to become more prominent in the coming years (Rodrigues & Craig 2007). Therefore, it was suggested that Vietnam may also be under pressure from different mimetic forces to accept IFRS or to develop Vietnamese accounting standards based on IFRS. Thus, it was hypothesised that

H2: There is the existence of mimetic isomorphism upon the consideration of IFRS adoption in Vietnam.

Normative Isomorphism

Every developing economy has its own professional ecosystem accounting community that comprises of professional bodies, university educators, professional training programs and more. There is a collective but singular strain behind such a large and diverse entity. It has been found in many countries that this creates normative pressures to converge the national accounting standards with IFRS. For example, normative isomorphism is found;

- In the preferences of large international accounting firms towards IFRS by advising their customers to adopt IFRS where choice is permitted;
- In the presence of IFRS, either full or limited coverage, in accounting curricula in universities; and
- In the lobby of professional accounting bodies urging the standard setters to adopt or converge towards IFRS (Rodrigues & Craig 2007).

Much academic research is reaching consensus on the fact that the Big Four accounting firms (i.e. PricewaterhouseCoopers, Deloitte Touche Tohmatsu, KPMG and Ernst & Young) play an important role in the homogenization of accounting standards and represent the normative pressures within the accounting community (Street & Gray 2002; Chand, Patel & Patel 2005; Gillis 2011). In particular, according to Al-Omari (2010), the debt conditions, set by the World Bank, were demanding from companies to be audited and certified by internationally renowned accounting firms. This requirement aided and supported the international operations and auditing procedures of the Big Four accounting firms. Moreover, it is evidenced in Gillis (2011) how the Big Four accounting firms came to be accepted as a normative function within the Chinese accounting professional society and gained access to the coercive power of the Chinese government. In other words, the Big Four accounting firms are considered to be one of the many international forces behind the process and advancement of convergence of accounting standards (Chand, Patel & Patel 2005).

The case of Vietnam is a bit more nuanced towards normative isomorphism. Here, the role of two internationally accredited accounting professional institutions ACCA and CPA Australia are quite prominent. They tend to influence the accounting community in Vietnam. As these two professional elites follow international best practices and transfer their know-how to the Vietnamese counterparts, it creates much synergy. Vietnam is also a member of the International Federation of Accountants (IFAC) and it is committed to complying with the international accounting practices. Therefore, it is suggested that Vietnam may be under pressure from professional accounting bodies as well as accounting/consulting firms to accept IFRS or to develop Vietnamese accounting standards based on IFRS. Thus, it was hypothesised that

H3: There is the existence of normative isomorphism upon the decision of IFRS adoption in Vietnam.

Legitimacy

It is clear in the literature that legitimacy is an inter-related part of institutional isomorphism. For example, coercive isomorphism was explained as a form of legitimacy that a developing country seeks by following mandatory regulations and policies (Phan 2014). Mimetic isomorphism was explained as a form of legitimacy that a country ensures via models diffused through successful companies working on a global scale. Normative isomorphism was explained as the legitimacy of the national professional bodies by seeking alignment with international standards-setting agencies and code of conduct.

There is now a sufficient body of evidence and literature to show that most of the developing countries tend to choose international accounting practices not out of their free will rather they tend to follow a certain pattern that emerges because of institutional isomorphism. The entire source of legitimacy is drawn from this tendency. A complete chain of institutions like the World Trade Organization (WTO), the Organization for Economic Co-operation and Development (OECD), the International Monetary Fund (IMF), the World Bank (WB), the International Accounting Standards Board (IASB), the European Union (EU), the International Organization of Securities Commissions (IOSCO), and the United Nations (UN) back this trend.

The vulnerability of developing countries makes them prone to accepting IFRS. Because of their limited ability to produce their own high quality national accounting standards, they consider IFRS as a legitimate, modern and high quality set of accounting standards (Irvine 2008; Lasmin 2011). As a result, more developing countries choose to adopt IFRS to enhance their national reputation and legitimacy. This discussion is not at all different from the results of recent studies (Hassan 2008; Danjou & Walton 2012; Sanada 2012). These scholars argued that the decision of countries to adopt IFRS is motivated more by social pressures of legitimacy, and less by any direct economic logic. Furthermore, the literature provided demonstrates that macro-economic fundamental like Gross Domestic Product (GDP) growth and Foreign Direct Investment (FDI) are not significantly related to developing countries' decisions to adopt IFRS (Zeghal & Mhedhbi 2006). However, over a hundred countries permitted or adopted IFRS as they do not only seek to achieve high quality standards but they ultimately seek legitimacy and social acceptance as credible global trade partners (Chua & Taylor 2008; Hassan 2008).

From the above discussion, it is suggested that Vietnam may be seeking legitimacy through accepting IFRS or developing Vietnamese accounting standards based on IFRS. Thus, it was hypothesised that

H4: There is the existence of legitimacy upon the consideration of IFRS adoption in Vietnam.

METHODOLOGY

This kind of study was in need of testing amongst the survey cohorts. Accountants, auditors and academics were the three main groups who were the best targets for any perception based study. To encapsulate the results of above-mentioned theoretical underpinnings behind IFRS adoption, a survey instrument with 30 potential influential factors was used (Phan 2014). The questions are designed using five point Likert scales so that the individuals' perceptions could easily be determined. The questionnaire was self-administered as this design was considered preferable for a large number of responses, allowing conclusions to be drawn with greater confidence. Also, the data analysed could be used for comparison across groups. Creswell and Clark (2007) concluded that the self-administered questionnaire was an appropriate method for analysing a large volume of data or number of people.

A pre-test in both English and Vietnamese was conducted with 30 members of the accounting community (10 from each accountant group). This study has adopted both back-translation and additional rewrite processes. The process involved a group of professional translators, accounting practitioners and academics. The target audiences of the survey are categorised in three different sub-groups: (i) 1,000 accountants in public-practice, members of Vietnam Association of Certified Public Auditors (VACPA); (ii)

1,000 accountants in industry, members of the Association of Chartered Certified Accountants (ACCA) and CPA Australia; and (iii) 1,000 accounting lecturers from universities across Vietnam.

A total of 728 usable responses received from 3,000 sent questionnaires producing an effective response rate of 24 per cent. The data analysis was performed using descriptive statistics on the Statistical Package for the Social Sciences (SPSS) software. Some survey responses were received after the cut-off date. These late responses were compared with other responses at five per cent of statistical significance. The differences between these responses were insignificant and it is reasonable to conclude that the error due to non-response bias was negligible or insignificant.

FINDINGS

Perceived Coercive Isomorphism

To test the impact of coercive isomorphism, a list of nine potential agencies were chosen for the respondents. Beginning with the World Bank, the World Trade Organization and the International Monetary Fund, it went on to include the Asian Development Bank and the International Financial Corporation as well. An analysis of the results showed that seven of the nine coercive isomorphism items (Mean > 3.00) listed in Table 1 were perceived as having a significant effect with regards to the adoption of IFRS in Vietnam.

Respondents perceived the World Trade Organization (Mean 3.60, SD 1.001) as having a slightly stronger coercive pressure than the World Bank (Mean 3.50, SD 1.247) and other financial institutions and creditors (Mean 3.52, SD 1.017). The Asian Development Bank (Mean 3.41, SD 1.240), the International Monetary Fund (Mean 3.40, SD 1.203), and the International Finance Corporation (Mean 3.29, SD 1.175) were also perceived to play significant coercive roles on the widespread adoption of IFRS in Vietnam. In comparison to other multinational agencies, the effects of official development assistance (ODA) providers such as Japanese ODA (Mean 2.91, SD 1.123) and Korean ODA (Mean 2.82, SD 1.088) were perceived as being of lower significance in terms of institutional pressure.

Table 1. Perceived coercive isomorphism

Ranked Order	Description	Min	Max	Mean	S.D	Variance	Skewness	Kurtosis
1	Coercive - World Trade Organisation	1	5	3.60	1.001	1.002	-0.982	0.821
2	Coercive - Financial institutions and creditors	1	5	3.52	1.017	1.034	-0.685	-0.044
3	Coercive - World Bank	1	5	3.51	1.247	1.554	-0.844	-0.312
4	Coercive - Asian Development Bank	1	5	3.41	1.240	1.537	-0.735	-0.47
5	Coercive - International Monetary Fund	1	5	3.40	1.203	1.446	-0.725	-0.401
6	Coercive - International Finance Corporation	1	5	3.29	1.175	1.38	-0.57	-0.497
7	Coercive - State Regulatory Authorities	1	5	3.12	1.045	1.093	-0.217	-0.438
8	Coercive - Japanese ODA fund	1	5	2.91	1.123	1.261	-0.142	-0.559
9	Coercive - Korean ODA fund	1	5	2.82	1.088	1.184	-0.147	-0.578

Source: Authors

The survey findings support the hypothesis *H1: There is the existence of coercive isomorphism upon the consideration of IFRS adoption in Vietnam.* These findings provide empirical evidence to support the arguments of Di Maggio & Powell (1983, p.154) "The greater an organization depends on another organization, the more similar it will become to that organization in structure, climate, and behavior focus". The fact that World Bank, International Monetary Fund and Asian Development Bank require financial statements complied with IFRS as one of the requirements to access their developmental assistance and financial aids, provide further supporting evidence for the hypothesis H1 (Phan 2014).

Perceived Mimetic Isomorphism

To test the hypothesis regarding the influences of mimetic isomorphism on the adoption of IFRS by Vietnam, seven mimetic isomorphism items were tested (Table 2). Results showed that the influence levels of all mimetic isomorphic sources were perceived as significant in the adoption of IFRS in Vietnam (Mean >3.00).

The two highest influential mimetic isomorphisms include "mimicking IFRS successful adopters over the world" (Mean 3.55, SD 0.938), and "mimicking successful adopters in Asia" (Mean 3.41, S.D 1.009). Perceptions of the importance of the other five mimetic factors were ranked at lower levels. These results may be explained by the dominance of the Vietnamese government upon the standard setting process, thereby rendering the perceived influence levels from industry leaders, leading listed companies, leading foreign invested enterprises as weaker.

The survey results support the hypothesis *H2: There is the existence of mimetic isomorphism upon the consideration of IFRS adoption in Vietnam.* The argument of Di Maggio and Powell (1983) that the country or the organization mimics the other country or organization in the uncertainty circumstances was supported in this study. Di Maggio and Powell (1983) proposed "The more ambiguous the goals of an organization, the greater the extent to which the organization will model itself after organizations that it perceives to be successful" (p.155). The fact that Vietnamese standard setters announced its strategic intention to allow IFRS voluntary adoption by 2017 and require IFRS mandatory adoption by 2020 for public-interest entities (Vo 2014) provide collaborating supporting evidence for the hypothesis H2 (Phan 2014).

Table 2. Perceived mimetic isomorphism

Ranked Order	Description	Min	Max	Mean	S.D	Variance	Skewness	Kurtosis
1	Mimetic - Mimicking IFRS successful adopters over the world	1	5	3.55	0.938	0.88	-0.452	-0.447
2	Mimetic – Mimicking successful adopters in Asia	1	5	3.41	1.009	1.017	-0.377	-0.485
3	Mimetic – Multinational Corporations	1	5	3.32	1.057	1.116	-0.374	-0.631
4	Mimetic - Trading Alliances	1	5	3.30	1.022	1.044	-0.532	-0.182
5	Mimetic - Lobby from leading foreign companies	1	5	3.16	0.961	0.923	-0.357	-0.119
6	Mimetic - Lobby from leading listed entities	1	5	3.13	0.947	0.896	-0.261	-0.033
7	Mimetic - Industry Leading Enterprises	1	5	3.08	1.031	1.063	-0.128	-0.687

Source: Authors

Perceived Normative Isomorphism

To test the hypothesis regarding the influences of normative isomorphism on the adoption of IFRS by Vietnam, ten items were tested (Table 3). Results showed that the three professional bodies, the International Federation of Accountants - IFAC (Mean 3.69, SD 0.949), the Vietnam Accounting Association – VAA (Mean 3.47, SD 0.992) and the International Accounting Standards Board – IASB (Mean 3.44, SD 1.078) were perceived to have the strongest influences of the ten listed bodies on the possibility of IFRS adoption in Vietnam. Respondents also perceived other professional bodies including the Association of Chartered Certified Accountants - - ACCA (Mean 3.29, SD 0.947), CPA Australia (Mean 3.08, SD 1.035), the Asian Federation of Accounting - AFA (Mean 3.29, SD 0.888) as having a significant influence upon IFRS adoption decision. The only organization that was perceived with insignificant influence is the Asian-Oceanian Standard-Setters Group AOSSG (Mean 2.97, SD 0.947). It could be explained by the less active involvement in discussing issues and sharing experiences on its convergence progress towards IFRS adoption in Vietnam. Although Vietnam is a member of AOSSG, none of Vietnamese accountancy professional bodies is an active organization member of this standard-setters group (AOSSG 2015).

The survey results support hypothesis *H3: There is the existence of normative isomorphism upon the consideration of IFRS adoption in Vietnam.* The results lend support to the argument of Di Maggio and Powell (1983) that the greater the participation of organizational managers in trade and professional associations, the more likely the organization will be, or will become, like other organizations in its field. Di Maggio and Powell (1983) stated "The greater the extent of professionalization in a field, the greater the amount of institutional isomorphic change" (p.155). The result reflects the divided views of Vietnamese accountants on the roles of Vietnamese professional accountancy bodies in the standard setting process (Phan 2014).

Table 3. Perceived normative isomorphism

Ranked Order	Description	Min	Max	Mean	S.D	Variance	Skewness	Kurtosis
1	Normative - IFAC	1	5	3.69	0.949	0.901	-0.429	-0.21
2	Normative - VAA	1	5	3.47	0.992	0.984	-0.536	-0.112
3	Normative - IASB	1	5	3.44	1.078	1.163	-0.325	-0.416
4	Normative - VACPA	1	5	3.32	1.039	1.08	-0.174	-0.608
5	Normative - ACCA	1	5	3.29	0.947	0.897	-0.197	-0.21
6	Normative - AFA	1	5	3.29	0.888	0.789	-0.291	0.165
7	Normative - Big Four	1	5	3.28	1.11	1.231	-0.173	-0.756
8	Normative - Academics	1	5	3.11	0.947	0.897	-0.233	-0.418
9	Normative - CPA Australia	1	5	3.08	1.035	1.072	-0.233	-0.247
10	Normative - AOSSG	1	5	2.97	0.947	0.897	-0.029	-0.12

Source: Authors

Perceived Legitimacy

Four items were chosen for testing the hypothesis regarding perceptions of legitimacy on the adoption of IFRS by Vietnam (Table 4). There was strong support for all four factors showing that the majority of the respondents perceived that Vietnam would eventually adopt IFRS to raise finance overseas (Mean 3.84, SD 1.043), to enhance national reputation (Mean 3.82, SD 1.009), to attract foreign investment (Mean 3.76, SD 1.046), and to enhance the Vietnamese stock market (Mean 3.75, SD 0.906).

The survey results support the hypothesis *H4: There is the existence of legitimacy upon the consideration of IFRS adoption in Vietnam.* These findings support the suggestion in Judge, Li and Pinsker (2010) that IFRS adoption process is driven by both institutional isomorphisms and social legitimisation. The results indicate a strong desire from the Vietnamese accounting community and urge the Vietnamese policymakers to consider a decision of IFRS adoption in the near term (Phan 2014).

DISCUSSIONS

The survey clearly pointed out that the context of isomorphism does exist and can shape the eventual outcomes. There was a definite coercive pressure upon the Vietnamese accounting legislation and service community from the multinational agencies. For example, Vietnam had committed itself to the World Trade Organization (WTO) that it would open its services sector to allow foreign investment in insurance, accounting, auditing and taxation services. To meet this commitment, Vietnam allowed foreign auditors and foreign accounting firms offering accounting, auditing consulting services to operate with Vietnamese businesses. With small adaptations, they have aligned themselves with this emerging reality. "Vietnam has just issued the new independent auditing law. Those who want to conduct auditing in Vietnam would have to sit the test in Vietnamese. According to the old law, those who hold a Western qualification could convert them into Vietnamese CPA by sitting the test (100 multiple choice questions in English)… However the law has changed. The test is now in Vietnamese" (Interviewee 39 cited in Nguyen, Hooper & Sinclair 2013, p. 479).

The Vietnamese government has been trying hard to deal with the dominance of Western organizations such as the World Bank, the International Monetary Fund, the World Trade Organization, Big Four and second tier accounting firms, international accounting professional bodies such as ACCA and CPA

Table 4. Perceived legitimacy

Ranked Order	Description	Min	Max	Mean	S.D	Variance	Skewness	Kurtosis
1	Legitimate - Desire to raise finance overseas	1	5	3.84	1.043	1.089	-1.039	0.727
2	Legitimate - Desire to enhance national reputation	1	5	3.82	1.009	1.018	-1.121	1.066
3	Legitimate - Desire to attract FDI	1	5	3.76	1.046	1.095	-0.975	0.522
4	Legitimate - Desire to enhance stock market	1	5	3.75	0.906	0.821	-0.741	0.65

Source: Authors

Australia. To this end the government has revised and amended existing legislation as well as issuing new legal regulations as a defensive response. As noted earlier, the Independent Auditing Law with a change of language from English to Vietnamese in the Vietnamese CPA exam for an overseas CPA license holder is an example of a defensive response from the Vietnamese regulators. This kind of calibrating from the current system is what the keystone of the isomorphic context becomes. Additionally, there may be a need to consider internal factors, as the results of the study showed that the role of the state is perceived to be less critical (at 37 per cent) than the pressures of other internal coercive isomorphisms, the roles of financial institutions and major creditors (at 61 per cent). This result would explain why Vietnamese businesses voluntarily prepare IFRS statements. This result could also have implications for policy and practice and be useful for state regulatory authorities to perform macro governance and control. For instance, in the banking regulatory regime, the State Bank of Vietnam may require commercial banks to implement IAS 29 Financial Reporting in Hyperinflationary Economies because Vietnam has high levels of inflation with the consumer price index up to 18 per cent and the current Vietnamese accounting legislation does not have any guidance to address this issue (Pham 2010).

Two professional bodies, the International Federation of Accountants (IFAC) and the Vietnam Accounting Association (VAA), were perceived to have strong influences on the possibility of IFRS adoption in Vietnam. In particular, the IFAC was perceived by 60 per cent of respondents as playing the influential role in shaping accounting and auditing standards in Vietnam. The influential roles of the VAA, as one of the largest professional bodies of Vietnam were also perceived by 55 per cent of the respondents. Overall, the view of the respondents upon normative isomorphism is divided with no clear strong outcome for any of the ten bodies. One reason for this result could be the strong intervention from the government and the weak influential role from the professional bodies in the standard setting process in Vietnam. This result again confirms the viewpoint that IFRS implementation is challenging if the government does not support the changes to protect their power, as discussed earlier (Phan 2014).

There are several pieces of evidence that further lend support for the existence of institutional isomorphism in accounting regulation activities in Vietnam.

1. Vietnam has improved its income distribution from low-income to lower middle-income as classified by the World Bank since 2010. The country has received lower official development assistance (ODA) funds and higher levels of technical assistance from World Bank and other multinational donors to improve its capabilities (World Bank 2012).
2. Since 2007, Vietnam has become the 150th member of the World Trade Organization. Vietnam and has made some commitments with the World Trade Organization to open its market for accounting, auditing, and insurance services. Between the years 2001 to 2006, prior to joining the World Trade Organization, Vietnam speedily issued 26 VAS and achieved a convergence of 84 per cent with international accounting rules (mostly pre-2003 IAS).
3. During 2007-2012, Vietnam slowed down its convergence process and none of the amendments of International Accounting Standards and new IFRS announced by the IASB were reflected in the current VAS. In July 2013, the Ministry of Finance joined with the SSC to introduce the drafting of six forthcoming standards and interpretations for the capital market. The technical and financial assistance of the Asian Development Bank, the World Bank were again acknowledged in the new phase of Vietnamese standards setting (MoF 2013).

The proposed new Vietnamese standards include the following:

- VAS 32 "Financial Instruments: Presentation";
- VAS 39 "Financial Instruments: Recognition and Measurement";
- VFRS 7 "Financial Instruments: Disclosures";
- VFRS 9 "Financial Instruments";
- VFRS 13 "Fair Value Measurements; and
- VFRIC 19 "Extinguishing Financial Liabilities with Equity Instruments".

The names of these forthcoming standards are not different from the corresponding IFRS, thus it could be envisaged that in the content as well, there will be a high degree of convergence between these Vietnamese standards and IFRS (CafeF 2013). Additionally, the international commercial banks, the international accounting firms, and their branches in Vietnam also played a critical role in providing technical assistance and expertise during the process (ECOVIS 2013).

We anticipate that upon the strong influence of institutional isomorphism and strong legitimacy motivate, a convergence of Vietnamese accounting standards in accordance with IFRS is only a matter of time. This anticipation turned out in real life when the Ministry of Finance recently issued Circular 210/2009/TT-BTC. The legislation allows companies to decide whether they want voluntarily compliance with IFRS for financial instrument transactions in the absence of equivalent guidance in Vietnamese accounting legislation. Since the Vietnamese policymakers decided to move forward with IFRS adoption, greater clarification and better enforcement of accounting regulations will be required.

CONCLUSION

The trajectory of IFRS adoption in Vietnam is strongly influenced by institutional isomorphism. The survey confirms that the accounting and auditing community of Vietnam will be affected by the coercive, mimetic and normative isomorphisms and legitimacy motives. The role of the World Bank and the World Trade Organization (WTO) was found to be the strongest of the coercive forces behind IFRS adoption in Vietnam. The broader belief among the respondents showing mimetic isomorphism was being guided by other successful IFRS adopting nations and the multinational corporations who were preparing their consolidated financial statements using the best global standards. The normative influence was strongly present in the two Vietnamese accounting professional bodies namely the International Federation of Accountants (IFAC) and the Vietnam Accounting Associations (VAA).

Despite its best efforts this study acknowledges the existence of certain limitations in the study possible in a single survey method conducted through questionnaires. It has to be expected that a single questionnaire, and its representative sample may not fully reflect the views of the full range of the intended population. This absence can be tackled by undertaking further research wherein a larger sample could be undertaken and within that, other relevant groups like investors, financial brokers, institutional lenders, regulators and others could be involved. This quantitative survey can be further supplanted with the qualitative methods so as to have a better understanding as to how the IFRS adoption in Vietnam would relate with the wider sections of the economy.

REFERENCES

Al-Omari, A. M. (2010). The Institutional Framework of Financial Reporting in Jordan. *European Journal of Economics Finance And Administrative Sciences*, *1*(22), 32–50.

Albu, C. N., Alb, N., Pali-Pista, S. F., Gîrbină, M. M., Selimoglu, S. K., & Kovács, D. M. et al. (2013). Implementation of IFRS for SMEs in Emerging Economies: Stakeholder Perceptions in the Czech Republic, Hungary, Romania and Turkey. *Journal of International Financial Management & Accounting*, *24*(2), 140–175. doi:10.1111/jifm.12008

AOSSG. (2015). *Member Organisations*. Retrieved 18 Mar 2015 from: http://www.aossg.org/about-us/member-organisations

Assenso-Okofo, O., Ali, M. J., & Ahmed, K. (2011). The Development of Accounting and Reporting in Ghana. *The International Journal of Accounting*, *46*(4), 459–480. doi:10.1016/j.intacc.2011.09.010

Bui, T. M. V. (2011). *A study of the development of accounting in Vietnam*. (PhD thesis). RMIT University, Melbourne, Australia.

Cafe, F. (2013). *Propose Vietnamese Accounting Standards for capital market*. Retrieved from http://cafef.vn/pageprintnews.aspx?news_id=201307160018200179

Chamisa, E. E. (2000). The Relevance and Observance of the IASC Standards in Developing Countries and the Particular Case of Zimbabwe. *The International Journal of Accounting*, *35*(2), 267–286. doi:10.1016/S0020-7063(00)00049-2

Chand, P., Patel, C., & Patel, A. (2005). *Judgements of Professional Accountants in Fiji: Implications for Convergence of Accounting Standards*. Academic Press.

Chua, W. F., & Taylor, S. L. (2008). The rise and rise of IFRS: An examination of IFRS diffusion. *Journal of Accounting and Public Policy*, *27*(6), 462–473. doi:10.1016/j.jaccpubpol.2008.09.004

Danjou, P., & Walton, P. (2012, June 1). The Legitimacy of the IASB. *Accounting in Europe*, *9*(1), 1–15. doi:10.1080/17449480.2012.664396

Di Maggio, P. J., & Powell, W. W. (1983, April). The Iron Cage Revisited: Institutional Isomorphism and Collective Rationality in Organizational Fields. *American Sociological Review*, *48*(2), 147–160. doi:10.2307/2095101

ECOVIS SV. (2013, January). *The Ministry of Finance shall amend the 37 Vietnamese Standards on Auditing (VSA) and 26 Vietnamese Accounting Standards (VAS) in 2013*. Newsletter.

Gelb, D., Holtzman, M. P., & Mest, D. (2008, December). International operations and voluntary disclosures by U.S.-based multinational corporations. *Advances in Accounting*, *24*(2), 243–249. doi:10.1016/j.adiac.2008.09.002

Gillis, P. L. (2011). *The Big Four in China: Hegemony and Counter- hegemony in the Development of the Accounting Profession in China*. (PhD thesis). Macquarie Graduate School of Management, Macquarie University, Sydney, Australia.

Hassan, M. K. (2008). The development of accounting regulations in Egypt: Legitimating the International Accounting Standards. *Managerial Auditing Journal*, *23*(5), 467–484. doi:10.1108/02686900810875299

Hegarty, J., Gielen, F., & Barros, A.C.H. (2004). *Implementation of International Accounting and Auditing Standards: Lessons learned from the World Bank's Accounting and Auditing ROSC Program.* Academic Press.

Irvine, H. (2008). The global institutionalization of financial reporting: The case of the United Arab Emirates. *Accounting Forum*, *32*(2), 125–142. doi:10.1016/j.accfor.2007.12.003

Judge, W., Li, S., & Pinsker, R. (2010). National Adoption of International Accounting Standards: An Institutional Perspective. *Corporate Governance International Review (Steubenville, Ohio)*, *18*(3), 161–174.

Karamanou, I., & Nishiotis, G. P. (2009). Disclosure and the Cost of Capital: Evidence from the Market's Reaction to Firm Voluntary Adoption of IAS. *Journal of Business Finance & Accounting*, *36*(7-8), 793–821. doi:10.1111/j.1468-5957.2009.02154.x

Kumar, G., Wilder, M., & Stocks, M. (2008). Voluntary Accounting Disclosures by U.S.-Listed Asian Companies. *Journal of International Accounting Research*, *7*(1), 25–50. doi:10.2308/jiar.2008.7.1.25

Lasmin. (2011). An institutional perspective on International Financial Reporting Standards adoption in developing countries. *Academy of Accounting & Financial Studies Journal*, 61-71.

Leuz, C., & Wysocki, P. D. (2008). *Economic Consequences of Financial Reporting and Disclosure Regulation: A Review and Suggestions for Future Research.* SSRN eLibrary.

Mir, M. Z., & Rahaman, A. S. (2005). The adoption of international accounting standards in Bangladesh: An exploration of rationale and process. *Accounting, Auditing & Accountability Journal*, *18*(6), 816–841.

MoF. (2013). *Proposed Draft for the Circular of amendment 8 VAS in Stage 1.* Retrieved from http://www.mof.gov.vn/portal/page/portal/mof_vn/Suggestion_Legal?p_detail=1&p_topic_id=7378

Nguyen, L., Hooper, K., & Sinclair, R. (2013). Conservatism versus Change in the Vietnamese Accounting Field. *Corporate Ownership & Control*, *11*(1), 471–482.

Perera, H., & Baydoun, N. (2007). Convergence with International Financial Reporting Standards: The Case of Indonesia. *Advances in International Accounting*, *20*(1), 201–224. doi:10.1016/S0897-3660(07)20007-8

Pham, T. (2010). *International Financial Reporting Standards effects on banks in Vietnam.* (Bachelor thesis). International Business, JAMK University of Applied Sciences, Finland.

Phan, D. (2010). *The Relevance of International Financial Reporting Standards in Vietnam.* Paper presented at the 2nd Engaging with Vietnam Conference by Monash University and Vietnam National University, Hanoi, Vietnam.

Phan, D. (2014). What Factors are Perceived to Influence Consideration of IFRS Adoption by Vietnamese Policymakers?. *Journal of Contemporary Issues in Business and Government*, *20*(1), 27-40.

Phan, D., & Mascitelli, B. (2014a). Optimal approach and timeline for IFRS adoption in Vietnam: Perceptions of accounting professionals. *Research in Accounting Regulation Journal*, *26*(2), 222-229.

Phan, D., & Mascitelli, B. (2014b). IFRS adoption in Vietnam: If, When and How?. *Corporate Ownership & Control, 11*(4), 428-436.

Phan, D., Mascitelli, B., & Barut, M. (2013). *Perceptions of Accounting Professionals towards International Financial Reporting Standards (IFRS) in Developing Country: Evidence from Vietnam.* Paper presented at the 3rd Global Accounting, Finance and Economics Conference, Rydges Melbourne, Australia.

Phan, D., Mascitelli, B., & Barut, M. (2014). Perceptions Toward International Financial Reporting Standards (IFRS): The Case of Vietnam. *The Global Review of Accounting and Finance, 5*(1), 132-152.

Ramanna, K., & Sletten, E. (2009). *Why do countries adopt International Financial Reporting Standards?* Harvard Business School Working Paper 09(10).

Rodrigues, L. L., & Craig, R. (2007). Assessing international accounting harmonization using Hegelian dialectic, isomorphism and Foucault. *Critical Perspectives on Accounting, 18*(6), 739–757.

Sanada, M. (2012). *Legitimacy of Global Accounting Standards: A New Analytical Framework.* Academic Press.

Street, D. L., & Gray, S. J. (2002). Factors influencing the extent of corporate compliance with International Accounting Standards: Summary of a research monograph. *Journal of International Accounting, Auditing & Taxation, 11*(1), 51–76. doi:10.1016/S1061-9518(02)00054-X

Suchman, M. C. (1995). Managing Legitimacy: Strategic and Insititutional Approaches. *Academy of Management Review, 20*(3), 571–610.

VCCI. (2011). *ACCA - A Strategic Partner of Vietnam in Developing Local Accounting and Audit Profession to Global Standards.* Vietnam Business Forum.

Vo, V. T. H. (2014). *Follow-up on the Accounting Development Tool (ADT) - Enhancing Vietnam's capacity for producing high-quality corporate reports.* Geneva: ISAR.

Wang, K., Sewon, O., & Claiborne, C. (2008). Determinants and consequences of voluntary disclosure in an emerging market: Evidence from China. *Journal of International Accounting, Auditing & Taxation, 17*(1), 14–30. doi:10.1016/j.intaccaudtax.2008.01.001

World Bank. (2012). *Market economy for a middle-income Vietnam.* Joint Donor Report to the Vietnam Consultative Group Meeting.

Wysocki, P. D. (2011, July 4). New Institutional Accounting and IFRS. *Accounting and Business Review, 41*(3), 309–328. doi:10.1080/00014788.2011.575298

Zeghal, D., & Mhedhbi, K. (2006). An analysis of the factors affecting the adoption of international accounting standards by developing countries. *The International Journal of Accounting, 41*(4), 373–386. doi:10.1016/j.intacc.2006.09.009

APPENDIX

Table 5. List of influential factors on IFRS adoption in Vietnam

Ranked Order	Description	Min	Max	Mean	S.D	Variance	Skewness	Kurtosis
01	Legitimate - Desire to raise finance overseas	1	5	3.84	1.043	1.089	-1.039	0.727
02	Legitimate - Desire to enhance national reputation	1	5	3.82	1.009	1.018	-1.121	1.066
03	Legitimate - Desire to attract FDI	1	5	3.76	1.046	1.095	-0.975	0.522
04	Legitimate - Desire to enhance stock market	1	5	3.75	0.906	0.821	-0.741	0.65
05	Normative - IFAC	1	5	3.69	0.949	0.901	-0.429	-0.21
06	Coercive - World Trade Organisation	1	5	3.60	1.001	1.002	-0.982	0.821
07	Mimetic - Follow trend of 120 countries permit/require IFRS	1	5	3.55	0.938	0.88	-0.452	-0.447
08	Coercive - Financial institutions and creditors	1	5	3.52	1.017	1.034	-0.685	-0.044
09	Coercive - World Bank	1	5	3.51	1.247	1.554	-0.844	-0.312
10	Normative - VAA	1	5	3.47	0.992	0.984	-0.536	-0.112
11	Normative - IASB	1	5	3.44	1.078	1.163	-0.325	-0.416
12	Mimetic - Follow Asian successful adopters	1	5	3.41	1.009	1.017	-0.377	-0.485
13	Coercive - Asian Development Bank	1	5	3.41	1.24	1.537	-0.735	-0.47
14	Coercive - International Monetary Fund	1	5	3.40	1.203	1.446	-0.725	-0.401
15	Normative - VACPA	1	5	3.32	1.039	1.08	-0.174	-0.608
16	Mimetic - MNC	1	5	3.32	1.057	1.116	-0.374	-0.631
17	Mimetic - Trading Alliances	1	5	3.30	1.022	1.044	-0.532	-0.182
18	Coercive - International Finance Corporation	1	5	3.29	1.175	1.38	-0.57	-0.497
19	Normative - ACCA	1	5	3.29	0.947	0.897	-0.197	-0.21
20	Normative - AFA	1	5	3.29	0.888	0.789	-0.291	0.165
21	Normative - Big Four	1	5	3.28	1.11	1.231	-0.173	-0.756
22	Mimetic - Lobby from leading foreign companies	1	5	3.16	0.961	0.923	-0.357	-0.119
23	Mimetic - Lobby from leading listed entities	1	5	3.13	0.947	0.896	-0.261	-0.033
24	Coercive - State Regulatory Authorities	1	5	3.12	1.045	1.093	-0.217	-0.438
25	Normative - Academics	1	5	3.11	0.947	0.897	-0.233	-0.418
26	Normative - CPA Australia	1	5	3.08	1.035	1.072	-0.233	-0.247
27	Mimetic - Industry Leading Enterprises	1	5	3.08	1.031	1.063	-0.128	-0.687
28	Normative - AOSSG	1	5	2.97	0.947	0.897	-0.029	-0.12
29	Coercive - Japanese ODA fund	1	5	2.91	1.123	1.261	-0.142	-0.559
30	Coercive - Korean ODA fund	1	5	2.82	1.088	1.184	-0.147	-0.578

Chapter 14
Rational Asymmetric Development:
Transfer Mispricing and Sub-Saharan Africa's Extreme Poverty Tragedy

Simplice A. Asongu
African Governance and Development Institute, Cameroon

ABSTRACT

A recent publication by the World Bank on Millennium Development Goals (MDGs) has established that extreme poverty has been decreasing in all regions of the world with the exception of sub-Saharan Africa (SSA), in spite of over two decades of growth resurgence. This chapter explores the role of transfer mispricing in SSA's extreme poverty tragedy. The analytical structure entails: (1) emphasis of rational asymmetric development as the dark side of transfer pricing; (2) linkages between financial reporting, international financial reporting standards (IFRS), transfer pricing and poverty; (3) evidence that the recent growth resurgence in African countries has been driven substantially by resource-rich countries which are experiencing high levels of exclusive growth and extreme poverty; (4) the practice of transfer mispricing by multinationals operating in resource-rich countries of SSA and (5) a Zambian case study of extreme poverty and transfer mispricing schemes by Glencore in the copper industry. While transfer mispricing is contributing to diminishing African growth, available evidence shows that the component of growth that is not captured by transfer mispricing does not trickle down to the poor because the African elite is also animated by practices of rational asymmetric development. Policy implications for the fight against extreme poverty are discussed.

1. INTRODUCTION

A recent publication by the World Bank on Millennium Development Goals (MDGs) has established that extreme poverty has been decreasing in all regions of the world with the exception of sub-Saharan Africa (SSA) (Caulderwood, 2015; World Bank, 2015). Consistent with Asongu and Kodila-Tedika (2015),

DOI: 10.4018/978-1-4666-9876-5.ch014

about 45% of nations in the sub-region are substantially off-track from attaining the MDGs extreme poverty target. From the evidence provided by Figure 1, it can be noticed that, but for SSA, extreme poverty has been decreasing in all other regions of the world. This is an unfortunate tendency, despite about two decades of growth resurgence that began in the mid 1990s (Alan & Carlyn, 2015, p. 598). In the light of these observations optimistic narratives about African rising should be treated with extreme caution, notably: (i) Pinkivskiy & Sala-i-Martin (2014) on all African countries attaining the MDGs extreme poverty target by 2014, with the exception of the Democratic Republic of Congo; (ii) Leautier (2012) on Africa's growing leadership role in the World and (iii) the continent witnessing considerable poverty decline compared to other world regions (Fosu, 2015a). It should be noted that the cautious position of Fosu is much more articulated in Chapter 1 (Fosu, 2015b) of his recent book on 'growth and institutions in Africa'(Fosu, 2015c). Nonetheless, such overly optimistic positions may have been motivated by a stream of the literature on 'the African growth miracle' (Young, 2012): a motivational current in the literature which is likely to be more concerned about promoting the interest of neoliberal ideology and capital accumulation. Therefore, neglecting fundamental ethical concerns like: ecological crisis, inequality and sustainability in job creation (Obeng-Odoom, 2013, 2014).

Over the past decades, a lot of scholarly attention has focused on the causes of African poverty (Englebert, 2002; Jerven, 2011; Kodila-Tedika & Agbor, 2014; Asongu & Kodila-Tedika, 2015). The plethora of studies has either been based on the existence of an African dummy or the assumption that the continent is fundamentally different from other regions of the world. Some of the documented reasons for persisting poverty include: social barriers to economic growth and technological change (Amavilah, 2015); deinstitutionalization of Africa (Nunn, 2008, 2009; Nunn & Puga, 2012) and/or loss of traditional African institutions (Amavilah, 2014a, 2006; Lewis, 1955); inability to make a clear distinction between 'private property rights' and 'private use rights' (Amavilah, 2015); overvaluation of foreign knowledge and undervaluation of local knowledge (Brush & Stabinsky, 1996; Raseroka, 2008; Lwoga

Figure 1. Comparative regional poverty levels
Source: World Bank PovcalNet

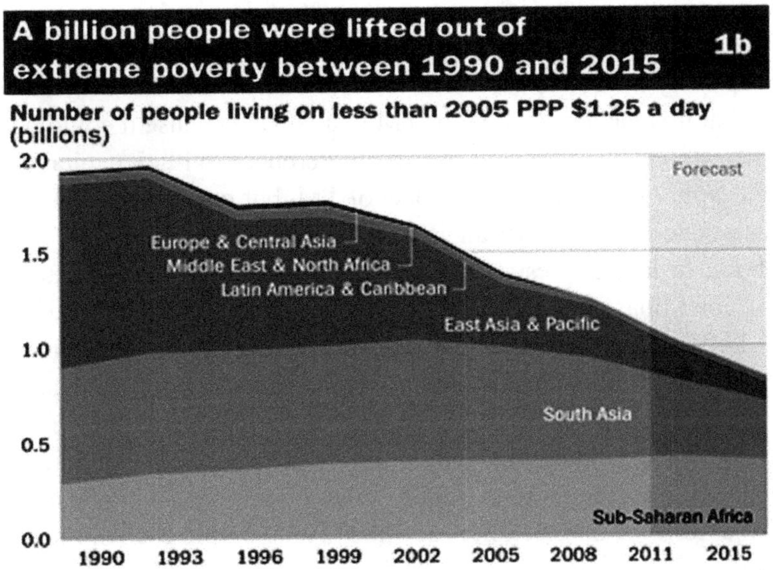

et al., 2010; Asongu, 2014a; Tchamyou, 2014; Amavilah et al., 2014; Asongu et al., 2014); over-idleness of natural resources (Doftman, 1939; Lewis, 1955; Amavilah, 2014a); 'Ignoring art as an expression of technological knowledge' (Amavilah, 2014a); excessive consumption of luxury (Adewole & Osabuohien, 2007; Efobi et al., 2013); lack of capacity to acknowledge scarcity (Lewis, 1955; Dorfman, 1939; Lucas, 1993; America, 2013; Drine, 2013; Looney, 2013; Asongu, 2014ab); negative influences from colonialism and noecolonialsm (Ndlovu-Gatsheni, 2013); false economics of preconditions (Monga, 2014); lost decades of policy prescriptions from the Washington Consensus (Lin, 2015; Asongu and Ssozi, 2015); less self-reliance (Fofack, 2014) and over-dependence on development assistance (Moyo, 2009; Obeng-Odoom, 2013; Asongu, 2014c); absence of qualitative measurements in African paradigms of development (Obeng-Odoom, 2013); inability to effectively negotiate for foreign aid, absence of favourable local conditions and presence of fragile institutions (Kayizzi-Mugerwa, 2001); low levels of regional integration (Kayizzi-Mugerwa, et al., 2014); corruption in international trade (Musila & Sigué, 2010) and asymmetric globalisation-fuelled policies that are more favourable to developed countries (Asongu, 2015a), inter alia.

To the best of our knowledge, the role of 'transfer mispricing' (hence TM) has not been substantially explored as a fundamental cause of African poverty. It is important to position a TM-related line of inquiry on Africa because with the continent's growth resurgence, Multinational corporations (MNCs) are expected to increases their presence in the region (Curtis and Todorova, 2011, p. 2).

According to Sikka and Willmott (2010, p. 342), in the conventional literature on accounting, transfer pricing (TP) is a technique that is employed by multinationals to optimally allocate revenues and costs across joint ventures, subsidiaries and among divisions within a group of entities that are related. Consistent with the authors, these representations of TP illustrate how multinational companies are substantially involved in processes of wealth retentiveness which enable corporations to avoid taxes and ease capital flight. In essence, while a conception of purely technical nature of computing TP could abstract from the politico-economic contexts of their development and usage, the context much reflects contemporary business activities or an époque of globalised trade combined with interactions among tax authorities of the state, shareholders and other stakeholders of the business practicing TP. It is acknowledged that the practices determine economic opportunities in ways that are critical in augmenting private gains, hence, contributing to social impoverishment of developing countries through tax avoidance (Nkurunziza, 2012). It is also worthwhile to note that TP is a legitimate business practice as it is a necessary accounting entry needed to ascertain profit arising from different jurisdictions. Therefore, TP in itself is not bad but it is the abuse of TP or TM that is bad because it could be a cause of poverty in SSA. While the interested reader may find recurrent references to illicit capital flight, it is important to also note that illicit capital flight is only an aspect of TM, but has been documented to represent the most substantial consequence of TM (Nkurunziza, 2012).

In light of the above, to logically establish that TM may be a source of extreme poverty in SSA countries, at least five conditions are necessary: (i) evidence of rational asymmetric development as the dark-side of TP; (ii) linkages between financial reporting, international financial reporting standards (IFRS), TP and poverty, (iii) establishing that the recent growth resurgence in African countries has been driven substantially by resource-rich countries which are experiencing high levels of exclusive growth and extreme poverty, (iv) substantiating that TM is practiced by foreign multinational in resource-rich countries in SSA and (v) a case study of a resource-rich country for which we clearly articulate the first-four points. In what follows, one section is devoted to elucidating each of the five points, while the last section concludes.

2. FINANCIAL REPORTING, IFRS, TRANSFER PRICING, AND POVERTY IN AFRICA

We discuss this section in five strands, notably: (i) the reason TP is important in Africa, (ii) TP schemes/regimes, (iii) challenges to TP, (iv) future of TP and (v) linkages between TM, tax evasion and poverty in the continent.

In the first strand, TP is important for African countries essentially because at the advent of globalisation, MNCs are increasingly playing an important role in the economic growth of most countries (Curtis and Todorova, 2011). According to the narrative, as of 2011, more than two-third of transactions in the world, were related to MNCs. The authors sustain that attaining the MDGs requires, inter alia: increasing domestic revenues and consolidating domestic tax bases. This entails, tailoring TP policies such that domestic tax revenue is protected without disincentivising foreign direct investment (FDI) and international trade.

The second strand engages TP regimes in Africa. Curtis and Todorova (2011) have outlined various stages in the adoption of TP reform, namely: Stage 1, Stage 2 and Stage 3 respectively 'Developing countries that do not have TP legislation in place', 'Developing countries that are on the verge of implementing TP legislation' and 'Countries with existing TP legislation'. Accordingly, stages of development are the basis for categorising a given TP regime corresponding to the specific country. In Africa, the picture is mixed at best. The perspective is the following for some countries, inter alia: well established referenced TP regimes (Kenya and South Africa); recently passed TP legislation (Uganda); expectations of enacting TP legislation (Nigeria and Zimbabwe); tax code provisions that mention TP (Mozambique and Algeria) and no TP regulation/legislation (Libya and Sudan). This heterogeneity among countries represents substantial challenges to harmonizing TP policies across the continent.

Challenges for African TP regimes in the third strand have inevitable consequences like tax evasion which has substantial poverty externalities (Nkurunziza, 2012). Documented challenges by Curtis and Todorova, (2011) include: lack of comparable transactions, lack of knowledge and resources, the intangible economy or intellectual property (IP) regimes which skew most taxable income to developed countries, concerns with location of savings and lack of comprehensive tax treaties.

The fourth strand relates to the future of TP in Africa. According to Curtis and Todorova, (2011), since more African countries engaging-in and/or speeding-up the adoption process of TP regimes, it is imperative for the underlying TP policies to be harmonized at some point in time. The integration process of the continent into the global economy would require, inter alia, the adoption of comprehensive and harmonized TP policies. To this end, strategic safeguard harbours with which to ease capacity and compliance concerns have been documented by Curtis and Todorova (p.11).

Harmonizing TP policies is very crucial because according to Donnelly (2015), the 2015 African Economic Outlook report has revealed that TM is substantially retarding the continent's development because of the absence of a monitoring capacity which focuses on tax avoidance. The report is jointly published by the Organisation for Economic Co-operation and Development (OECD), the African Development Bank (AfDB) and the United Nations Development Programme (UNDP). The authors sustain that 'illicit flows of tax revenue collection' is continuously falling short of the needs of countries. According to the narrative, there has been an extensive abuse of TP and only three African countries are currently in possession of TP units in their internal revenue services': "Lack of official monitoring capacity leaves African countries highly vulnerable to these tax avoidance practices".

This leads us to the fifth strand on linkages between TM, tax evasion and poverty. Donnelly (2015) have recently reported on the abusive TP and tax evasion that are contributing to substantial losses of income that would have been invested on the poor in African countries, notably: more than 60 billion USD annually. We articulate the report by Donnelly (2015) with numbers to enhance clarity. The issues of illicit financial flows from the continent are in the neighbourhood of 4% of Gross Domestic Product (GDP): outstripping FDI and official development assistance (ODA). The unlawful money flows entail practices that build around tax evasion, via, inter alia: abusive transfer pricing, trade misinvoicing, bribery and money laundering by international companies. According to the report, in 2012, illicit flows from SSA stood at about 68.6 billion USD, compared to 35.4 billion USD and 41.1 billion in FDI and ODA respectively. Moreover, given that these unlawful transactions are surreptitious, there is a high likelihood that the actual scales of the illicit financial outflows are being substantially under-reported.

On the nexus with poverty, the corresponding research estimates that the stock of African capital would have increased by more than 60% had the underlying illicit funds been retained in the continent, whereas GDP would have been about 15% higher. Given that economic growth is needed for poverty reduction, the link between illicit capital flows and poverty cannot be denied. Donnelly (2015) further reports that commercial corporations account for a substantial portion (approximately 65% of illicit capital flows), followed by organised crime (about 30%) and corruption-related practices (5%). Moreover, trade misinvoicing or the deliberate under- and over-invoicing of trade transactions has been the most widely documented method of the illegal transfer of money across borders, representing about 67.4% of corresponding illegal outflows during the period 2003 to 2012.

The deplorable linkages between TP, tax losses in domestic economies and negative externalities on economic development have been articulated in a recent report by renowned economists who have qualified the international tax system as 'repulsive and inequitable' (Walsh, 2015). According to Nobel Prize laureate Joseph Stiglitz, the manner in which MNCs are taxed is 'repulsive, inequitable and inefficient'. Stiglitz emphasises that, whereas tax systems are national, MNCs and their capital are global; hence, they have "free rein to move their money around to the low-cost jurisdictions" (Walsh, 2015).

This tendency deprives developing countries (especially in Africa) of the capital needed for investments in education, health and development programs. According to Stiglitz, "it undermines the social and economic fiber of a country". Moreover, he articulates that endowing MNCs with tax breaks and implicitly allowing them to engage in schemes of TM makes domestic companies less willing to comply with their own tax obligations: "If multinational companies are escaping taxation, domestic firms are put in an unfair competitive position and it distorts the economy". For brevity and lack of space, we invite the interested reader to get more insights into country-specific consequences of TM in Ndikumana & Boyce (2012a). Diak (2014) posits that, had the tax revenues lost to TM been spent on healthcare since the year 2000, with incremental tax revenue from avoidance of capital flight, approximately 350 000 children could have been saved on a yearly basis.

Fofack and Ndikumana (2010) have estimated that if a quarter of capital flight was repatriated to Africa, the continent's domestic investment as a percentage of GDP would increase from about 19% to 35%. Channels via which capital flight increases poverty have been documented by Nkurunziza (2012) who has empirically examined linkages between capital flight and poverty in Africa. According to the author, TM (e.g illicit financial flows) increases uncertainty and risk in the domestic economy, thereby discouraging investment and its potential appealing impact on the mitigation of poverty. Moreover, countries with high corruption levels in which the governing elite have more opportunities of unlawfully appropriating resources and transferring them to save havens abroad, there are limited or decreased incentives to put in place socio-economic measures for poverty reduction. This is essentially because the corresponding elites may easily recourse abroad for services that are lacking domestically.

3. RATIONAL ASYMMETRIC DEVELOPMENT AND THE DARK SIDE OF TRANSFER PRICING

In this section, we: (i) clarify the concept of rational asymmetric development; (ii) elucidate the correlation between rational asymmetric development and TM and (iii) engage the dark side of TP.

Consistent with Asongu (2015a), rational asymmetric development "refers to unfair practices of globalisation adopted by advanced nations to the detriment and impoverishment of less developed countries" (p. 14). The author refers the interested reader to find more insights into the phenomenon in studies focused on capitalism-oriented rational asymmetry. Some examples include: 'Making Globalisation Work' by Stiglitz (2007) which documents that "The average European cow gets a subsidy of $2 a day; more than half of the people in the developing world live on less than that. It appears that it is better to be a cow in Europe than to be a poor person in a developing country" (p. 85). Additionally, "Without subsidies, it would not pay for the Unites States to produce cotton; with them, the United States is, as we have noted, the world's largest cotton exporter" (p.85). Moreover, the Chang (2008) 'Bad Samaritans: The Myth of Free Trade and the Secret History of Capitalism' also provides insights into the underlying concept. Mshomba (2011) has also provided an African specific-perspective with a systematic review of how the World Trade Organisation (WTO) policies are affecting Africa while Asongu (2015a) has extended the celebrated Piketty (2014) literature to elucidate the spirit of African poverty.

Drawing from the above, in the second strand there are grounds on which to sustain that capitalism-fuelled TM is fundamentally motivated by rational corporate policies from multinational companies which are primarily concerned about increasing shareholder value, with little regard over how such practices (like tax evasion) affect the livelihoods of the poor in the less developed world from which they operate. According to Osabuohien et al. (2013, 2014, 2015), multinational corporations in African countries have been increasingly employing very questionable accounting practises that enable them to declare minimum profits and therefore liable to low taxes to African governments. The dichotomy between less developed and more advanced countries comes-in when such rational corporate practices are destined to increase tax revenues in more advanced countries, to the detriment of their less developed counterparts. In this light, owing to accounting malpractices, a substantial chunk of wealth from African countries ends-up in offshore financial centres that are for the most part under the jurisdictions of the OECD nations (Boyce & Ndikumana, 2003, 2010; Fofack & Ndikumana, 2010). Given that, these offshore financial centres are economically and politically managed by OECD countries, it follows that advanced nations are the primary beneficiaries of these rational corporate practices. Hence, the term: 'rational asymmetric development'.

The European Network on Debt and Development (EURODAD, 2008) has provided an interesting literature on how the 'black hole' of asymmetric development can be tackled through capital flight regulation. It is important to note that more than 50% of illicit capital flight from developing countries involves questionable accounting practices by corporations (EURODAD, 2008, p. 7). Some characteristics of capitalism-driven illicit capital flight practices documented in the study include: (i) speculation and volatility, (ii) tax havens, tax concessions, investment and abusive TP, (iii) emergence of hedge funds and private equity, (iv) capital account liberalisation and its implications, (v) failure by the International Monetary Fund (IMF) to enhance financial surveillance and regulation and (vi) European nations easing conditions for regulatory inefficiencies in hedge funds and private equity, as well as facilitating capital flight from less developed countries. From the above narrative, asymmetric development between rich (high-income) and poor (low-income) countries is fundamentally driven by capitalism-oriented policies, with TM fundamentally motivating the flow of illicit capital flight from less developed to developed countries.

Borrowing from Sikka and Willmott (2010), we engage the dark side of TP in the third strand. According to the authors, TP is of growing relevance to companies in the globalised world where their operations are not limited to a single country, but extended to nations with differing regulation capacities and regimes of taxation. The narrative sustains that, in the pursuit of cash flows, marketing goals, joint ventures, profits, inter alia, corporations are obliged to recourse to rational measures of taxable profits and cost performance. Under such environmental conditions, multinational corporations develop processes of overhead- and cost-allocation as well as design strategies with which to transfer commodities. Given the subjective nature of overhead and cost allocation channels, companies enjoy some discretion in tailoring them towards specific geographical jurisdictions and commodities. Such discretion allows them to keep taxes at minimum, hence, increasing profits. The strategy consists of allocating most profits to low-risk and low-tax jurisdictions. While there is some consensus that TP can help companies mitigate the negative effects of double taxation, the practice is substantially abused as it is: (i) used to shift profits by virtually every multinational company in the world (Baker, 2005) and (ii) increasingly being employed to artificially shift profits to low- from high-tax jurisdictions, thereby maximizing income in the former and expenses in the latter. Ultimately, TP remains the most important issue of international taxation that Multinational Enterprises (MNEs) are increasingly being confronted with (Ernst & Young, 2006). This is essentially because it is very instrumental in tax avoidance (Ernst & Young, 2005), which has consequences in the distribution of public commodities and wealth in low-income countries.

Globalization has brought about new dimensions in the politics of TP (Sikka and Willmott, 2010). Extricated from the constraints of territorial jurisdictions, MNEs find it easier to establish joint ventures, trust, special purpose entities, affiliates and subsidiaries that enable them to take advantage of favorable subsidies and taxes in certain geographic locations. Hence, global production has brought new and extensive avenues for TP schemes that enable MNEs to avoid taxes in less desirable locations and shift profits to more desirable areas. The sheer complexity, power and scale of globalization represents a significant challenge to mainstream thinking on TP, essentially because owing to complex production and exchange networks: (i) domestic corporations now have transnational and multinational tendencies and (ii) foreign corporations either work with local companies through joint ventures or establish fresh businesses in new jurisdictions.

The overwhelming increases in corporate power and global trade has provided many avenues for crafting 'tax avoidance' TP strategies, especially with the tendency of MNEs exploiting natural resources in less developed countries. Hence, developing nations are substantially vulnerable to TP practices of illicit capital flight and/or tax avoidance (Borkowski, 1997). The evidence of manipulation by MNEs in developing countries has been documented in a broad stream of literature. First, the IMF's position that the globalization of trade has emerged in tandem with numerous issues for national tax authorities, accruing from the abuse and potential use of TP by MNEs, entailing, the allocation of fixed costs, loans, patents and trademark valuations (Sikka & Willmott, 2010). Second, a plethora of tax administrators are involved in TP practices (Tanzi, 2000).

The strength of MNEs is consolidated with the ideologies of capitalism, as nation-states are obliged to compete in order to attract the investment needed to boost domestic economies. This competition engenders avenues by which MNEs devise TP strategies, rationally needed to take advantage of differences in taxes across nation-states (Sikka & Willmott, 2010). In addition, the opportunities provided by TP are beginning to facilitate the birth of microstates, which are known as 'tax havens' or offshore financial centers. These microstates are instrumented by advanced nations with legislative powers to provide less tight regulation, preserve secrecy and impose no/low taxes which are attractive to MNEs seeking blur administrative structures. The secrecy represents a fertile ground for creative TP schemes that are being exploited for tax avoidance. No wonder approximately half of global trade transactions transit via offshore financial centers, despite these jurisdictions accounting only for about 3% of World GDP. While microstates represent only 1.2% of the global population, they account for 26% (31%) of assets (net profits from American MNEs) (Sikka & Willmott, 2010).

We end this section by providing some stylized facts on the increasing power of microstates and growing influence of MNEs vis-à-vis nation states. First, consistent with Sikka and Willmott (2010), every year about 200 000 new corporations are created in microstates, with a cumulative number of about 3000 000 after the turn of the millennium according to Baker (2005). Consistent with the narrative, some cases in point include: (i) a building in Caymans registering about 18, 857 corporations, including major global MNEs (US Government Accountability Office, 2008); (ii) the British Virgin Islands (Caymans) having 3389 (182) corporations by per 100 people and (iii) the 575 residents of Sark Island (part of the Channel Islands) having some 15,000 companies which are non-resident corporations for the most part (UK Home Office, 1998). A common denominator among these tax havens is that they do not impose taxes on the profits of corporations and hence, local tax authorities are not concerned about TM practices. Second, at the start of the third millennium, of the 100 largest economies, 51% were not nation states but MNEs with a considerable exercise of power (Anderson et al., 2005). We engage the narrative in five points. First, the 100 biggest companies controlled about $3400 billion worth of assets, of which about 40% are not located within domestic economies. Second, the top 200 companies represented about 28% of the world economy. Third, the top 500 controlled 70% of global trade, 80% of FDI, 30% of world GDP, about 33.3% of manufactured exports, 75% of trade in goods and services and approximately 80% of trade in technical and management services. Fourth, less developed countries which are dependent on agriculture are left to the whims and caprices of MNEs because, only 20 controlled the trade of coffee, 6 influenced 70% of trade in wheat, 1 controlled about 98% of packed tea production and 2 companies influenced about 80% of world grain which was distributed by two MNEs. Fifth, intellectual property rights (IPRs) were essentially monopolized at about 97% by OECD nations, of which 90% were held by powerful MNEs (Anderson et al., 2005).

4. AFRICA RISING, RESOURCE-RICH SSA COUNTRIES, EXCLUSIVE GROWTH, AND POVERTY

In this section, drawing from the evidence that most of Africa's growth has been driven by resource-wealthy countries with oil, mining and gas industries (Deaton, 1999; Veselinovic, 2015), we present evidence that underlying countries are characterised with exclusive growth and poverty. We have shown above that the growth resurgence in the sub-region has been fundamentally driven by resource-rich nations owing to increasing commodity prices (Boyce & Ndikumana, 2012ab; Asongu, 2014d). Unfortunately, these wealthy nations are also plagued by substantial extreme poverty, with comparatively lower social and health amenities. Putting the account into greater perspective (Ndikumana & Boyce, 2012b): the Republic of Congo, Gabon and Equatorial Guinea are among these countries with per capita incomes (wealth rank) of respectively \$1,253 (15th), \$4,176 (5th) and \$8,649 (2nd) and oil reserve ranks of 8th (Congo), 7th (Gabon) and 10th (Equatorial Guinea). Consistent with the account, a great portion of the population in these nations still live in very abject poverty. Accordingly, the lack of basic social services, drinkable water, elementary schools and decent sanitation are eloquent testimonies. For example, Gabon and Equatorial Guinea both rank second- and third-to-the last with 55% and 51% respectively of immunization rates against measles. Moreover, the probability of a child reaching his/her fifth birthday in Equatorial Guinea is lower than the average of the SSA sub-region.

Evidence of exclusive growth is provided by a recent global ranking on 'quality of growth' provided by the IMF (Mlachila et al., 2014, p. 27)[1]. Drawing from time-dynamic assessments of the performance from 93 developing nations in terms of 'quality of growth', rankings of the highlighted oil-wealthy nations have been deteriorating substantially. In essence, evidence from 1990-1994, 1995-1999, 2000-2004 and 2005-2011 shows increasing exclusive growth: Congo Republic (59th, 70th, 74th & 84th), Gabon (58th, 61st, 67th & 69th) and Equatorial Guinea (76th, 73rd, 76th & 88th).

In light of the above, the position of SSA countries in Figure 1 is not surprising, given that the two decades of growth resurgence has been marred by inequality[2]. The stance can be elucidated on two counts: (i) the relationships among, growth, inequality and poverty and (ii) evidence that growth in the sub-region has been marred by inequality which justifies the growing extreme poverty.

First, inequality substantially affects the relationship of growth on poverty because the inequality elasticity of poverty is higher than the growth elasticity of poverty (Asongu & Kodila-Tedika, 2014). In more specific terms: "The study finds that the responsiveness of poverty to income is a decreasing function of inequality" (Fosu, 2010a, p. 818); "The responsiveness of poverty to income is a decreasing function of inequality, and the inequality elasticity of poverty is actually larger than the income elasticity of poverty" (Fosu, 2010b, p. 1432); and "In general, high initial levels of inequality limit the effectiveness of growth in reducing poverty while growing inequality increases poverty directly for a given level of growth" (Fosu, 2011, p. 11). This evidence is consistent with studies focusing on Africa (Fosu, 2010ac) and a broad sample of developing nations (Fosu, 2010b; Asongu et al., 2014).

Second, Africa's growth resurgence has been marred by inequality (Blas, 2014; Veselinovic, 2015). According to Veselinovic (2015), Africa's growth has been characterised by the rich getting richer and the poor getting poorer. According to the narrative, the continent is characterised with inter alia, (i) seven of the 10 fastest-growing economies in the world, (ii) the highest expected-increase in the number of multimillionaires over the next 10 years (59%) and (iii) 6 of the 10 countries with the highest inequalities, notably: South Africa (65), Namibia (61.3), Botswana (60.5), Zambia (57.5), Central African Republic (56.3) and Lesotho (54.2).

The facts on inequality substantially contrast with a recent strand of literature on Africa rising (Young, 2012; Leautier, 2012; Alan & Carlyn, 2015; Fosu, 2015a). The continent is becoming the destination for luxury commodities (e.g Nigeria being a top Champagne market) and about 45% of Africans are still living in extreme poverty (Asongu & Kodila-Tedika, 2015). It follows that, the fruits of economic prosperity gathered in recent decades have not rolled-down to the poor. Moreover, the resource-industries driving African growth (Bond et al., 2010), intuitively do not employ a substantial bulk of the population because they are capital-intensive for the most part. Hence, the growth is not broad-based as only a few elite are benefiting from the economic prosperity.

5. RESOURCE-RICH COUNTRIES, TRANSFER MISPRICING (TM), AND CAPITAL FLIGHT

Consistent with the caution in the introduction, illicit capital flight is only an aspect of TM. We have seen above that TM contributes to more than 50% of illicit capital flight from developing countries. Consistent with Asongu (2014d), most of the illicit capital flight in Africa is driven by resource-rich nations (EURODAD, 2008, p.7). Hence, interactions among resource-wealth, TM and illicit capital flight are fundamental to the poverty tragedy or the spirit of poverty in SSA (Asongu, 2015a). But in order to fully understand these nexuses, it is important to engage how illicit capital flight is linked to poverty.

Drawing from Asiedu et al. (2012) and Asongu (2015a), one of the justifications put forward for Africa's underdevelopment is the shortage of investment capital. In line with the Harrod-Domar model, three arguments have been advanced: (i) Africa is confronted with a 'financing gap' issue because invested capital is substantially lower than the capital required for sustainable growth investment; (ii) long-run development is achievable with the bridging of the 'financing gap' and (iii) for the 'financing gap' to be filled, the continent would need external finance in the forms of development assistance and debts. It is in this light that calls for more development assistance have been increasing after unsuccessful attempts at attracting foreign direct investment (FDI) through domestic financial markets and liberalisation policies (Asiedu, 2004; Asongu, 2012). According to the authors, the relevance of external finance in Africa's development has been encapsulated in the New Partnership for African Development (NEPAD) and the Millennium Development Goals (MDGs).

In line with Asiedu et al. (2012), dependence on external finance by African countries to fight poverty is problematic for a threefold reason. First, development assistance and FDI are extremely volatile and such volatility has substantial adverse consequences on recipient economies, especially during global financial meltdowns (see Kangoye, 2013; Quartey & Afful-Mensah, 2014). Second, a bulk of recent literature has also shown that the impact of development assistance on economic growth is ambiguous. These includes, provocative narratives like 'foreign aid follies' (Rogoff, 2014), sceptical surveys from more than four decades of development assistance (Doucouliagos & Paldam, 2008, 2009), radical positions (Asongu, 2014c) and clarifications on the questionable economics of development assistance in Africa (Asongu, 2015b), and inter alia, the need to reinvent foreign aid for inclusive and sustainable development in light of Piketty's (2014) celebrated literature (Asongu, 2015c). Third, efforts at attracting FDI to the SSA sub-region have not been very successful (Asiedu & Lien, 2011; Anyanwu, 2012). This narrative is consistent with the bulk of African business literature (Rolfe & Woodward, 2004; Bartels et al., 2009; Asongu, 2013ab).

The current of literature above provides evidence to the fact that, the use of foreign aid to compensate for TM and/or illicit capital in SSA has several shortcomings. In essence, given that previous attempts at attracting other forms of external financial flows like FDI have not been successful and with the tendency unlikely to change in the near future, it would be unrealistic to suppose that overly reliance on development assistance would in the short- and medium-runs compensate for Africa's investment needs. While solutions to the issue have varied from self-reliance (Fofack, 2014) to the recommendation '*that sub-Saharan African nations establish effective strategies toward mitigating illicit capital flight within the framework of a broader agenda of resource mobilization for economic development*' (Asongu, 2015, p.19), the conjectures of Fosu presented in Section 3 clearly emphasise the need to improve inequality structures before the growth benefits in poverty eradication can be fully reaped. Hence, TM is as important to existing inequality structures in policy priority. Therefore, the two policy syndromes should be tackled simultaneously, with greater emphasis on structural inequality. We illustrate narratives in the last-four sections with the case study of Zambia.

6. CASE STUDY: ZAMBIA, TRANSFER MISPRICING, GLENCORE, THE COPPER INDUSTRY, AND POVERTY

TM represents a rational asymmetric development issue of how much profit is fair? In other words how much should be rationally stolen from Africa by MNEs operating in resource-rich countries? As far as we have reviewed, a case study that can objectively illustrate the line of inquiry addressed by this chapter is Zambia, Glencore and the Copper industry. Glencore Plc is an Anglo-Swiss MNE, specialized in mining and commodity trading, headquartered in Baar-Switzerland, ranked 10th of the Fortune Global 500 of the world's largest corporations and third largest family business of the world (Why Poverty, 2013). Zambia as a nation has been blessed with abundant natural resources, especially in copper. However, the paradox is that the country is ranked among the bottom 20 in terms of poverty. Hence, the country is rich and at the same time poor, which translates the issues of inequality and asymmetric development (Why Poverty, 2013).

The overarching issue is why Zambia with its abundant natural resources is one of the world's poorest countries? In other words, why have booming copper prices not reduced her poverty? This has been widely debated in political and academic circles. In the former, some parliamentarians have even threatened to walk to the copper mines and request them to pay their taxes. On the latter, there is an evolving stream of literature on TP in the Zambian copper industry (Ping, 2007; Azémar & Corcos, 2009; Adam & Simpasa, 2010; Why Poverty, 2013). While copper represents averagely more than 70% of exports, the 'copper share of fiscal revenue' and 'copper revenue/GDP' have revolved respectively between 0.1% and 12.9% and between 0.0% and 2.8% for the period 1994-2008 (Meller & Simpasa, 2011, p.20). Despite the fact that the price of copper nearly quadrupled between 2001 and 2008, the shares of copper in fiscal revenue and 'revenue as a % of GDP' remained averagely unchanged. For instance in 2006, while Copper exports from Zambia stood approximately at 3 billion USD, corresponding tax revenue was just 50 million USD. And given that the Zambian government has an underlying contract of furnishing electricity, which stood at 150 million USD for that year, it was a loss to the Zambian economy (Why Poverty, 2013). The fact that tax revenues paid by mining industries to Zambia did not increase correspondingly with the burgeoning of world copper prices eloquently translates the concept of TM. In 2008, '*if Zambia had received for its copper exports the same price that Switzerland declared for its copper exports, in the same quite detailed commodity categories, Zambia's GDP would have nearly doubled that year*' (Why Poverty, 2013, 40:00mins to 40:15mins).

An audit of Mopani Copper Mines, initiated by the Zambian government has established evidence of TM. When the report was made public, the European Investment Bank suspended further loans to Glencore. The case has been reported to the OECD by one Zambian charity on charges that Glencore has been violating tax-related guidelines. Unfortunately, failure by Glencore to cooperate has led the OECD to admit it can do nothing about the case if one party refuses to cooperate (Why Poverty, 2013).

Glencore is the world's largest integrated commodity trader, with a yearly turnover of approximately 180 billion USD which is more than 8 times the GDP of Zambia. It controls Mopani Copper Mines in

Zambia, with a 73% stake and all copper produced by Mopani is sold to Glencore. The copper from Zambia is sold among subsidiaries of Glencore such that the highest margins are obtained from those located in countries with low or no tax requirements (Why Poverty, 2013).

Environmental issues have also been raised, with some of Glencore's activities suspended because of diluted acids drifting from production plants to homes. There have been incidences in 2005 and 2008 in which contaminated water has sent hundreds of people in townships near the Mopani Copper Mines to hospitals. Sulfur dioxide emitted by the mines is causing severe respiratory problems. Some accounts even sustain that the emissions of impurities by the mines is about 1000 times higher than the limits tolerated by the World Health Organization (WHO) (Why Poverty, 2013). We resist the itch of engaging this dimension further because it may derail us from the TM focus of the study.

Today, with the copper boom, unemployment is not decreasing and about 64% of Zambians still live below the poverty line (Why Poverty, 2013). Moreover, it is the fourth country with the highest inequality rate in the world (Veselinovic, 2015). A logical implication here is that even in the absence of TM, the elite of the country would still exercise rational asymmetric development practices by preventing the juice of economic prosperity from trickling down to the poor. Hence, it is fundamental to deal with the inequality structures in the country, so that, if and when fair taxes are paid by MNEs, their externalities are broad-based and not captured by a few.

We now devote some space to engaging how financial reporting standards in Zambia are being improved to address discussed TM issues. According to Curtis & Todorova (2011, p.23), the following general and specific and considerations elucidate Zambia's response to TM. First, on the general consideration, the country has fully adopted OECD guidelines on the issue. But while, the Zambia Revenue Authority (ZRA) requires documentation to be provided to justify TP, no specific guidance is provided concerning the quantity and quality of sufficient documentation. TP issues are tackled under general anti-avoidance provisions because there are no specific TP penalties. The authors further articulate that the ZRA does not possess its own TP database and areas reviewed by the underlying authority include: purchase of trading goods, royalties and management of fees. While the ZRA is improving its human resources through trainings abroad, there is yet no move to establish a unit within the organisation that specifically addresses TP issues.

Second, on the specific considerations, authors of the report caution that taxpayers should exercise caution when planning to enter the domestic market. Whereas subsidiaries and branches are objects of the same statutory rates, there are inherent disparities in the manner in which transfer of funds by related parties are treated. In essence, while funds may be repatriated to a related party 'free-of-withholding tax' by a branch, a subsidiary (absent a treaty) is obliged to declare a dividend. Therefore the latter fund is subjected to a 15% tax withhold. It follows that it is advisable to locate a holding company in a treaty country (Curtis & Todorova, 2011).

7. CONCLUDING IMPLICATIONS

A recent publication by the World Bank on Millennium Development Goals (MDGs) has established that extreme poverty has been decreasing in all regions of the world with the exception of sub-Saharan Africa (SSA), in spite of over two decades of growth resurgence. This chapter has explored the role of transfer pricing in SSA's extreme poverty tragedy. The analytical structure entails: (i) emphasis of rational asymmetric development as the dark side of transfer pricing; (ii) linkages between financial reporting, international financial reporting standards (IFRS), transfer pricing and poverty; (iii) evidence that the recent growth resurgence in African countries has been driven substantially by resource-rich countries which are experiencing high levels of exclusive growth and extreme poverty; (iv) the practice of transfer mispricing by multinationals operating in resource-rich countries of SSA and (v) a Zambian case study of extreme poverty and transfer mispricing by Glencore in the copper industry.

Two main policy implications are derived for the fight against extreme poverty. First, Africa needs to deal with its inequality structures, because the current tendency shows that even in the absence of transfer pricing, inequality is still worsening. Second, the concept of rational asymmetric development is not only limited to the relationship between developed nations and African countries by the bond of transfer mispricing or illicit capital flows. Such tax avoidance mechanisms also substantially exist between the rich and poor segments of African populations. Hence, the rich of poor countries also device all kinds of schemes to avoid declaring their full incomes and hence, limiting the tax paid for the ultimate delivery of collective or public commodities.

In essence, if the component of growth that survives transfer mispricing practices cannot trickle down to the poor, there is no guarantee that even with the absence of detrimental transfer pricing, the incremental growth would trickled-down to the poor. Dealing with the structures promoting inequality would entail, inter alia, understanding the role of inequality in poverty-growth transformations. Accordingly, inequality substantially affects the relationship of growth on poverty because the inequality elasticity of poverty is higher than the growth elasticity of poverty (Asongu & Kodila-Tedika, 2014). In more specific terms: "The study finds that the responsiveness of poverty to income is a decreasing function of inequality" (Fosu, 2010a, p. 818); "The responsiveness of poverty to income is a decreasing function of inequality, and the inequality elasticity of poverty is actually larger than the income elasticity of poverty" (Fosu, 2010b, p. 1432); and "In general, high initial levels of inequality limit the effectiveness of growth in reducing poverty while growing inequality increases poverty directly for a given level of growth" (Fosu, 2011, p. 11). This evidence is consistent with studies focusing on Africa (Fosu, 2010ac) and a broad sample of developing nations (Fosu, 2010b; Asongu et al., 2014).

ACKNOWLEDGMENT

The author is highly indebted to the editor and referee for constructive comments.

REFERENCES

Adam, C. S., & Simpasa, A. M. (2010). The Economics of the Copper Price Boom in Zambia. In A. Fraser & M. Larmer (Eds.), *Zambia, Mining, and Neoliberalism. Boom and Bust on the Globalized Copperbelt* (pp. 59–90). New York: Palgrave MacMillan.

Adewole, M. A., & Osabuohien, E. S. (2007). Analysis of Cost of Governance and Its Reduction Options in Nigeria. *The Nigerian Journal of Economic and Social Studies*, *49*(1), 137–159.

Alan, K., & Carlyn, R.-D. (2015). Is Africa Actually Developing? *World Development*, *66*(C), 598–613.

Amavilah, V. H. (2006). *Institutional change and economic performance: An off-the-cuff comment on Professors Daron Acemoglu, Simon Johnson, and James Robinson's three papers*. Glendale College.

Amavilah, V. H., (2014a). *Sir W. Arthur Lewis and the Africans: Overlooked economic growth lessons.* MPRA Paper No. 57126.

Amavilah, V. H., (2014b). *Knowledge= technology and human capital and the Lucas and Romer production functions.* MPRA Paper No. 58847.

Amavilah, V. H., (2015). *Social Obstacles to Technology, Technological Change, and the Economic Growth of African Countries: Some Anecdotal Evidence from Economic History.* MPRA Paper No. 63273.

Amavilah, V. H., Asongu, S. A., & Andrés, A. R. (2014). *Globalization, Peace & Stability, Governance, and Knowledge Economy.* African Governance and Development Institute Working Paper No. 14/012, Yaoundé.

America, R. (2013). Economic Development with Limited Supplies of Management. What to do about it – the case of Africa. *Challenge*, *56*(1), 61–71. doi:10.2753/0577-5132560103

Anderson, S., Cavanagh, J., & Lee, T. (2005). *Field guide to the global economy*. Washington, DC: Institute for Policy Studies.

Anyanwu, J. (2012). Why Does Foreign Direct Investment Go Where It Goes?: New Evidence From African Countries. *Annals of Economics and Finance*, *13*(2), 425–462.

Anyanwu, J. C. (2013). Characteristics and Macroeconomic Determinants of Youth Employment in Africa. *African Development Review*, *25*(2), 107–129. doi:10.1111/j.1467-8268.2013.12019.x

Anyanwu, J. C., & Augustine, D. (2013). Gender Equality in Employment in Africa: Empirical Analysis and Policy Implications. *African Development Review*, *25*(4), 400–420. doi:10.1111/1467-8268.12038

Asiedu, E. (2004). Policy Reform and Foreign Direct Investment to Africa: Absolute Progress but Relative Decline. *Development Policy Review*, *22*(1), 41–48. doi:10.1111/j.1467-8659.2004.00237.x

Asiedu, E., & Lien, D. (2011). Democracy, foreign direct investment and natural resources. *Journal of International Economics*, *84*(1), 99–111. doi:10.1016/j.jinteco.2010.12.001

Asiedu, E., Nana, F., & Nti-Addae, A. (2012). *The Paradox of Capital Flight from a Capital-Starved Continent*. Department of Economics, University of Kansas, Association of Concerned African Scholars, Bulletin No. 87, Fall, 2012. Retrieved from http://concernedafricascholars.org/wp-content/uploads/2012/11/caploss04-asiedu-14th.pdf

Asongu, S. A. (2012). Government quality determinants of stock market performance in African countries. *Journal of African Business*, *13*(2), 183–199. doi:10.1080/15228916.2012.727744

Asongu, S. A. (2013a). African Stock Market Performance Dynamics: A Multidimensional Convergence Assessment. *Journal of African Business*, *14*(3), 186–201. doi:10.1080/15228916.2013.844043

Asongu, S. A. (2013b). How Would Population Growth Affect Investment in the Future? Asymmetric Panel Causality Evidence for Africa. *African Development Review*, *25*(1), 14–29. doi:10.1111/j.1467-8268.2013.12010.x

Asongu, S. A. (2014a). *Knowledge Economy Gaps, Policy Syndromes and Catch-up Strategies: Fresh South Korean Lessons to Africa.* African Governance and Development Institute Working Paper No. 14/014, Yaoundé.

Asongu, S. A. (2014b). Knowledge Economy and Financial Sector Competition in African Countries. *African Development Review*, *26*(2), 333–346. doi:10.1111/1467-8268.12085

Asongu, S. A. (2014c). The Questionable Economics of Development Assistance in Africa: Hot-Fresh Evidence, 1996-2010. *The Review of Black Political Economy*, *41*(4), 455–480. doi:10.1007/s12114-014-9203-0

Asongu, S. A. (2014d). Fighting African Capital Flight: Empirics on Benchmarking Policy Harmonization. *The European Journal of Comparative Economics*, *11*(2), 93–122.

Asongu, S. A. (2015a). Rational Asymmetric Development, Piketty and the Spirit of Poverty in Africa. African Governance and Development Institute, No. 15/006, Yaoundé.

Asongu, S. A. (2015b). *A brief clarification to the questionable economics of foreign aid for inclusive human development.* African Governance and Development Institute Working Paper No. 14/028, Yaoundé.

Asongu, S. A. (2015c). Reinventing foreign aid for inclusive and sustainable development: Kuznets, Piketty and the great policy reversal. *Journal of Economic Surveys.* Retrieved from: http://onlinelibrary.wiley.com/doi/10.1111/joes.12109/abstract

Asongu, S. A., Amavilah, V. H., & Andrés, A. R. (2014a). *Economic Implications of Business Dynamics for KE-Associated Economic Growth and Inclusive Development in African Countries.* African Governance and Development Institute Working Paper No. 14/023, Yaoundé.

Asongu, S. A., Efobi, U., & Beecroft, I. (2014b). *Inclusive human development in pre-crisis times of globalisation-driven debts.* African Governance and Development Institute Working Paper No. 14/024, Yaoundé.

Asongu, S. A., & Kodila-Tedika, O. (2014). *Institutions and Poverty: A Critical Comment Based on Evolving Currents and Debates.* African Governance and Development Institute Working Paper No. 14/031, Yaoundé.

Asongu, S. A., & Kodila-Tedika, O. (2015). *Is Poverty in the African DNA (Gene)?.* African Governance and Development Institute Working Paper No. 15/011, Yaoundé.

Asongu, S. A., & Ssozi, J. (2016). (Forthcoming). Sino-African relations: Some Solutions and Strategies to the Policy Syndromes. *Journal of African Business.*

Azémar, C., & Corcos, G. (2009). Multinational Firms' Heterogeneity in Tax Responsiveness: The Role of Transfer Pricing. *World Economy*, *32*(9), 1291–1318. doi:10.1111/j.1467-9701.2009.01210.x

Baker, R. W. (2005). *Capitalism's Achilles heel.* John Wiley.

Bartels, F. L., Alladina, S. N., & Lederer, S. (2009). Foreign Direct Investment in Sub-SaharanAfrica: Motivating Factors and Policy Issues. *Journal of African Business*, *10*(2), 141–162. doi:10.1080/15228910903187791

Blas, J. (2014). Inequality mar Africa's rise. *Financial Times*. Retrieved October 18 2014 from: http://www.ft.com/intl/cms/s/0/9e74aa50-1e4d-11e4-ab52-00144feabdc0.html#axzz3GWsY4I91

Bond, P. (2010). Is Africa still being looted? World Bank dodges its own research. *LINKS International Journal of Socialist Renewal*. Retrieved August 21, 2015 from: http://links.org.au/node/1843

Borkowski, S. C. (1997). The transfer pricing concerns of developed and developing countries. *The International Journal of Accounting*, *32*(3), 321–336. doi:10.1016/S0020-7063(97)90014-5

Boyce, J. K., & Ndikumana, L. (2003). Public Debts and Private Assets: Explaining Capital Flight from Sub-Saharan African Countries. *World Development*, *31*(1), 107–130. doi:10.1016/S0305-750X(02)00181-X

Boyce, J. K., & Ndikumana, L. (2010). Measurement of Capital Flight: Methodology and Results for Sub-Saharan African Countries. *African Development Review*, *22*(4), 471–481. doi:10.1111/j.1467-8268.2010.00243.x

Boyce, J. K., & Ndikumana, L. (2012a). *Capital Flight from Sub-Saharan African Countries: Updated Estimate, 1970-2010*. Political Economy Research Institute, University of Massachusetts. Retrieved August 1, 2014 from: http://www.peri.umass.edu/fileadmin/pdf/ADP/SSAfrica_capitalflight_Oct23_2012.pdf

Boyce, J. K., & Ndikumana, L. (2012b). *Rich Presidents of Poor Nations: Capital Flight from Resource-Rich Countries in Africa*. Political Economy Research Institute, University of Massachusetts. Retrieved August 1, 2014 from: http://concernedafricascholars.org/wp-content/uploads/2012/11/caploss01-ndiku-14th.pdf

Brush, S. B., & Stabinsky, D. (1996). *Valuing Local Knowledge: Indigenous people and intellectual property rights*. Washington, DC: Island Press.

Caracciolo, F., & Santeramo, F. G. (2013). Price Trends and Income Inequalities: Will Sub-Saharan Africa Reduce the Gap? *African Development Review*, *25*(1), 42–54. doi:10.1111/j.1467-8268.2013.12012.x

Caulderwood, K. (2015). Sub-Saharan Africa Falls Behind In Fight Against Extreme Poverty: World Bank Report. *International Business Times*. Retrieved April 19, 2015 from: http://www.ibtimes.com/sub-saharan-africa-falls-behind-fight-against-extreme-poverty-world-bank-report-1881460

Chang, H-J., (2008). *Bad Samaritans: The Myth of Free Trade and the Secret History of Capitalism*. Bloomsbury Press.

Curtis, A., & Todorova, O. (2011). *Spotlight on Africa's transfer pricing landscape, Transfer pricing perspectives: Special edition. Taking a detailed look at transfer pricing in Africa*. Retrieved August 30, 2015 from: https://www.pwc.com/en_GX/gx/tax/transfer-pricing/management-strategy/assets/pwc-transfer-pricing-africa-pdf.pdf

Daouda, Y. H. (2013). La croissance économique est-elle pro-pauvres au Niger? *African Development Review*, *25*(2), 203–214. doi:10.1111/j.1467-8268.2013.12024.x

Deaton, A. (1999). Commodity Prices and Growth in Africa. *The Journal of Economic Perspectives*, *13*(3), 23–40.

Diak, D. (2014). A Look at Capital Flight from the Developing World. *GIVING what we can*. Retrieved from https://www.givingwhatwecan.org/blog/2014-10-16/look-capital-flight-developing-world

Donnelly, L. (2015, May). Illicit financial flows costing Africa billions. *Mail & Guardian*. Retrieved from http://mg.co.za/article/2015-05-25-illicit-financial-flows-costing-africa-billions/

Dorfman, J., & Johnson, E. A. J. (1939). Predecessors of Adam Smith: The Growth of British Economic Thought. *Political Science Quarterly*, *54*(1), 103–105. doi:10.2307/2143578

Doucougliagos, H., & Paldam, M. (2008). Aid effectiveness on growth: A meta study. *European Journal of Political Economy*, *24*(1), 1–24. doi:10.1016/j.ejpoleco.2007.06.002

Doucouliagos, H., & Paldam, M. (2009). The aid effectiveness literature: The sad results of 40 years of research. *Journal of Economic Surveys*, *23*(3), 433–461. doi:10.1111/j.1467-6419.2008.00568.x

Drine, I. (2013). 'Successful' Development Models: Lessons from the MENA Region. In *Achieving Development Success: Strategies and Lessons from the Developing World*. doi:10.1093/acprof:oso/9780199671557.003.0023

Efobi, U., Osabuohien, E., & Beecroft, I. (2013). The Macroeconomic Consequences of the Black Sunday in Nigeria. In J. Adibe (Ed.), *The Politics and Economics of Removing Subsidies on Petroleum Products in Nigeria*. London: Adonis & Abbey Publishers.

Elu, J., & Loubert, L. (2013). Earnings Inequality and the Intersectionality of Gender and Ethnicity In Sub-Saharan Africa: The Case of Tanzanian Manufacturing. *American Economic Review*, *103*(3), 289-292.

Englebert, P. (2002). Solving the mystery of the Africa dummy. *World Development*, *28*(10), 1821–1835. doi:10.1016/S0305-750X(00)00052-8

Ernst & Young. (2005). *Transfer pricing global reference guide*. Retrieved from http://www.ey.com/global/download.nsf/International/Global Transfer Pricing Guide August 2005/$file/GlobalTPGuide Aug05.pdf

Ernst & Young. (2006). *Global Transfer Pricing Surveys*. Retrieved from http://www.ey.com/Global/download.nsf/International/Tax - Global Transfer Pricing Survey Part 3/$file/EY GlobalTPSurvey3 Sep2006.pdf

EURODAD. (2008). *Addressing development's black hole: Regulating capital flight*. European Network on Debt on Development. Retrieved from http://www.taxjustice.net/cms/upload/pdf/Eurodad-WEED-CRBM-BWP_Capital_Flight.pdf

Fofack, H. (2014). *The Idea of Economic Development: Views from Africa*. WIDER Working Paper No. 2014/093.

Fofack, H., & Ndikumana, L. (2010). Capital Flight Repatriation: Investigation of its Potential Gains for Sub-Saharan African Countries. *African Development Review*, *22*(1), 4–22. doi:10.1111/j.1467-8268.2009.00226.x

Fosu, A. K. (2010a). Does Inequality Constrain Poverty Reduction Programs? Evidence from Africa. *Journal of Policy Modeling*, *32*(6), 818–827. doi:10.1016/j.jpolmod.2010.08.007

Fosu, A. K. (2010b). Inequality, Income and Poverty: Comparative Global Evidence. *Social Science Quarterly, 91*(5), 1432–1446. doi:10.1111/j.1540-6237.2010.00739.x PMID:21125764

Fosu, A. K. (2010c). The Effect of Income Distribution on the Ability of Growth to Reduce Poverty: Evidence from Rural and Urban African Economies. *American Journal of Economics and Sociology, 69*(3), 1034–1053. doi:10.1111/j.1536-7150.2010.00736.x

Fosu, A. K. (2011). *Growth, Inequality and Poverty Reduction in Developing Countries: Recent Global Evidence*. UNU WIDER Working Paper 2011/01.

Fosu, A. K. (2015a). Growth, Inequality and Poverty in Sub-Saharan Africa: Recent Progress in a Global Context. *Oxford Development Studies, 43*(1), 44–59. doi:10.1080/13600818.2014.964195

Fosu, A. K. (2015b). Growth and institutions in African Development. In A. K. Fosu (Ed.), *Growth and Institutions in African Development, First* (pp. 1–17). New York: Routledge Studies in Development Economics.

Fosu, A. K. (2015c). *Growth and Institutions in African Development, First* (A. K. Fosu, Ed.). New York: Routledge Studies in Development Economics.

Inekwe, J. N. (2013). FDI, Employment and Economic Growth in Nigeria. *African Development Review, 25*(4), 421–433. doi:10.1111/1467-8268.12039

Iwasaki, E., & El-Laithy, H. (2013). Estimation of Poverty in Greater Cairo: Case Study of Three 'Unplanned' Areas. *African Development Review, 25*(2), 173–188. doi:10.1111/j.1467-8268.2013.12022.x

Jerven, M. (2011). The quest for the African dummy: Explaining African post-colonial economic performance revisited. *Journal of International Development, 23*(2), 288–307. doi:10.1002/jid.1603

Kayizzi-Mugerwa, S. (2001). *Globalisation, Growth and Income Inequality: The African Experience*. Working Paper No. 186. OECD Development Centre.

Kayizzi-Mugerwa, S., Anyanwu, J. C., & Conceição, P. (2014). Regional Integration in Africa: An Introduction. *African Development Review, 26*(S1), 1–6. doi:10.1111/1467-8268.12102

Kodila-Tedika, O., & Agbor, A. J. (2014). Religious Diversity and Economic Development in Sub-Saharan Africa: So Far So Good. *Journal of African Development, 16*(1), 99–117.

Leautier, F. A. (2012). What Role for Africa After 50 Years of Independence: Provider of Natural Resources or a New Global Leader? *Journal of African Development, 14*(1), 127–151.

Lewis, A. (1955). *Theory of Economic Growth. Milton Park*. Routledge.

Lin, J. Y. (2015). The Washington Consensus Revisited A New Structural Economics Perspective. *Journal of Economic Policy Reform, 18*(2), 96–113. doi:10.1080/17487870.2014.936439

Looney, R. E. (2013). The Omani and the Bahraini Paths to Development: Rare and Contrasting Oil-Based Economic Success Stories. In A. FosuOxford University Press (Ed.), *Achieving Development Success: Strategies and Lessons from the Developing World*. doi:10.1093/acprof:oso/9780199671557.003.0020

Lucas, R. E. (1993). Making a miracle. *Econometrica, 61*(2), 251–272. doi:10.2307/2951551

Lwoga, E. T., Ngulube, P., & Stilwell, C. (2010). Managing indigenous knowledge for sustainable agricultural development in developing countries: Knowledge management approaches in the social context. *The International Information & Library Review*, *42*(3), 172–185. doi:10.1080/10572317.2010.10762862

Meller, P., & Simpasa, A. M. (2011). *Role of Copper in the Chilean & Zambian Economies: Main Economic and Policy Issues.* GDN Working Paper Series No. 43.

Mkondiwa, M., Jumbe, C. B. L., & Wiyo, K. A. (2013). Poverty–Lack of Access to Adequate Safe Water Nexus: Evidence from Rural Malawi. *African Development Review*, *25*(4), 537–550. doi:10.1111/1467-8268.12048

Mlachila, M., Tapsoba, R., & Tapsoba, S. J. A. (2014). *A Quality of Growth Index for Developing Countries: A Proposal.* IMF Working Paper No. 14/172.

Monga, C. (2014). The False Economics of Pre-Conditions: Policymaking in the The African Context. *Journal of African Development*, *16*(2), 121–140.

Moyo, D. (2009). *Dead Aid: Why Aid Is Not Working and How There is Another Way for Africa.* New York: Farrar, Straus and Giroux.

Mshomba, R. E. (2011). Africa and the World Trade Organization. Cambridge University Press.

Musila, J. W., & Sigué, S. P. (2010). Corruption and International Trade: An Empirical Investigation of African Countries. *World Economy*, *33*(1), 129–146. doi:10.1111/j.1467-9701.2009.01208.x

Ncube, M., Anyanwu, J. C., & Hausken, K. (2014). Inequality, Economic Growth and Poverty in the Middle East and North Africa (MENA). *African Development Review*, *26*(3), 435–453. doi:10.1111/1467-8268.12103

Ndlovu-Gatsheni, S. J. (2013). The Entrapment of African within the Global Colonial Matrices of Power: Eurocentrism, Coloniality and Deimperialieation in the Twenty-first century. *Journal of Developing Societies*, *29*(4), 331–353. doi:10.1177/0169796X13503195

Nkurunziza, J. D. (2012). Illicit Financial Flows: A Constraint on Poverty Reduction in Africa. Officer-in-charge, Africa Section, ALDCs Division of UNCTAD, Geneva.

Nunn, N. (2008). The Long-Term Effects of Africa's Slave Trades. *The Quarterly Journal of Economics*, *123*(1), 139–176. doi:10.1162/qjec.2008.123.1.139

Nunn, N. (2009). The importance of history for economic development. *Annual Review of Economics*, *1*(1), 65–92. doi:10.1146/annurev.economics.050708.143336

Nunn, N., & Puga, G. (2012). Ruggedness: The blessing of bad geography in Africa. *The Review of Economics and Statistics*, *94*(4), 20–36.

Obeng-Odoom, F. (2013). Africa's Failed Economic Development Trajectory: A Critique. *African Review of Economics and Finance*, *4*(2), 151–175.

Obeng-Odoom, F. (2014). *Africa: On the Rise, but to Where?* Forum for Social Economics; doi:10.1080/07360932.2014.955040

Osabuohien, E. S., Efobi, U. R., & Gitau, C. M. W. (2013). External intrusion, internal tragedy:environmental pollution and multinational corporations in Sub-Saharan Africa. In Principles and Strategies to Balance Ethical, Social and Environmental Concerns with Corporate Requirements (Advances in Sustainability and Environmental Justice, Vol. 12). Emerald Group Publishing Limited.

Osabuohien, E. S., Efobi, U. R., & Gitau, C. M. W. (2014). Beyond the environmental kuznets curvein Africa: Evidence from panel co-integration. *Journal of Environmental Policy and Planning*, *16*(4), 517–538. doi:10.1080/1523908X.2013.867802

Osabuohien, E. S., Efobi, U. R., & Gitau, C. M. W. (2015). Environment challenges in Africa: Further dimensions to the trade, MNCs and energy debate. *Management of Environmental Quality: An International Journal*, *26*(1), 118–137. doi:10.1108/MEQ-04-2014-0058

Piketty, T. (2014). *Capital in the Twenty First Century*. Harvard University Press. doi:10.4159/9780674369542

Ping, L. (2007). Transfer Pricing and Customs Valuation: Exploring Convergence. *Global Trade and Customs Journal*, *2*(3), 117–128.

Pinkivskiy, M., & Sala-i-Martin, X. (2014). Africa is on time. *Journal of Economic Growth*, *19*(3), 311–333. doi:10.1007/s10887-014-9103-y

Quartey, P., & Afful-Mensah, G. (2014), Foreign Aid to Africa: Flows, Patterns and Impact. In Oxford Handbook of Africa and Economics: Policies and Practices (vol. 2). Oxford University Press.

Raseroka, K. (2008). Information transformation Africa: Indigenous knowledge – Securing space in the knowledge society. *The International Information & Library Review*, *40*(4), 243–250. doi:10.1080/10572317.2008.10762789

Rogoff, K. (2014). *Foreign-Aid Follies*. Project Syndicate. Retrieved from https://www.projectsyndicate.org/commentary/kenneth-rogoff-urges-caution-in-helping-poor-countries-todevelop

Rolfe, R. J., & Woodward, D. P. (2004). Attracting foreign investment through privatization: The Zambian experience. *Journal of African Business*, *5*(1), 5–27. doi:10.1300/J156v05n01_02

Sikka, P., & Willmott, H. (2010). The dark side of transfer pricing: Its role in tax avoidance and wealth retentiveness. *Critical Perspectives on Accounting*, *21*(4), 342–356. doi:10.1016/j.cpa.2010.02.004

Stiglitz, J. E., (2007). *Making Globalization Work*. W. W. Norton & Company.

Tanzi, V. (2000). *Globalization, technological developments, and the work of fiscal termites*. IMF Working Paper No. 00/181. Washington, DC: IMF.

Tchamyou, S. V. (2014). *The Role of Knowledge Economy in African Business*. (Master Thesis). HEC-Management School, University of Liège.

UK Home Office. (1998). *Review of financial regulation in the crown dependencies*. London: The Stationery Office.

US Government Accountability Office. (2008). *Cayman islands: business and tax advantages attract U.S. persons and enforcement challenges exist. GAO Report to the Chairman and Ranking Member, Committee on Finance*. Washington, DC: U.S. Senate.

Veselinovic, M. (2015). Rich getting richer, poor getting poorer? Africa's inequality struggle. *CNN Africa View*. Retrieved from http://edition.cnn.com/2015/05/12/africa/africa-inequality/

Walsh, B. (2015, August). The International Tax System is 'Repulsive And Inequitable.' Here's A Way To Fix It. *Huffpost Politics*. Retrieved from http://www.huffingtonpost.com/entry/multinational-corporations-taxes_55d4baede4b055a6dab265d9

Why Poverty. (2013). *Stealing Africa-How much profit is fair?*. Retrieved from https://www.youtube.com/watch?v=WNYemuiAOfU&feature=iv&src_vid=HuBR2IaEkx0&annotation_id=annotation_725881

Word Bank. (2015). *World Development Indicators*. World Bank Publications.

Young, A. (2012). The African growth miracle. *Journal of Political Economy*, *120*(4), 696–739. doi:10.1086/668501

ENDNOTES

1. It is important to note that Mlachila et al. (2014) have presented a comparatively more holistic measurement of inclusive development, termed 'quality of growth'.
2. This is broadly consistent with recent African development literature that has been focusing on, inter alia: unemployment (Anyanwu, 2013; Inekwe, 2013), pro-poor growth (Daouda, 2013), income-inequality (Caracciolo & Santeramo, 2013: Ncube et al., 2014), gender-inequality (Anyanwu & Augustine, 2013; Elu & Loubert, 2013) and poverty (Iwasaki & El-Laithy, 2013; Mkondiwa et al., 2013).

Chapter 15
The Brazilian Case of IFRS Adoption
The Impacts and the New Perspectives

Marta Cristina Pelucio Grecco
Praesum Contabilidade Internacional, Brazil

Cecilia Moraes Santostaso Geron
Praesum Contabilidade Internacional, Brazil

ABSTRACT

This chapter contains a brief history of accounting practices in Brazil, the Brazilian convergence process that resulted in using the IFRS, and new perspectives about the IFRS after implementation. In order to highlight the issues, it includes some empirical evidence and cases. The USGAAP served as the major influence on Brazilian accounting from 1978 to 2007. In 2008, the process of the IFRS convergence started in Brazil, resulting in an important culture change. For the local standardization, the Brazilian Accounting Pronouncements Committee, known as the CPC, was created, issuing its norms in compliance with IFRS with no modifications. Brazil has a history of tax legislation influencing its accounting practices, but the process of Brazilian convergence to the IFRS has incurred a detachment of accounting from tax policies for corporate purposes. The chapter concludes with a description of the current activities associated with the IFRS and financial reports, such as the development of the XBRL (eXtensible Business Reporting Language) reporting standard.

INTRODUCTION

This chapter features a brief history of accounting practices in Brazil and describes the economic, legal, fiscal, and professional aspects of the adoption of the International Financial Reporting Standards (IFRS) and their respective impacts. The chapter is divided into three parts: (1) a brief history of accounting practices in Brazil, (2) a description of the Brazilian convergence process to the IFRS, and (3) a review of new perspectives on the IFRS postimplementation. In order to highlight the issues, some empirical evidences and particular cases are included.

DOI: 10.4018/978-1-4666-9876-5.ch015

A BRIEF HISTORY OF ACCOUNTING PRACTICES IN BRAZIL

The accounting law used in Brazil can be classified as code law (Lopes, 2002). According to the data published by the Brazilian Institute for Planning and Taxation (IBPT, 2013), the tax rules in force alone amount to 112 million book pages.

According to the IBPT, if those documents were printed on standard A4 pages, the book would cover the entire length of Brazil from north to south (Brazilian Institute for Planning and Taxation, 2013). Accounting in Brazil is defined by corporate law. Other types of corporations end up following the same rules as accounting due to a legal imposition of the federal tax authorities.

Figure 1 shows the major political and economic events that have taken place in Brazil since the 1940s along with the main corresponding legislation that has set the standards for the country's accounting standards.

Developmentalism in Brazil from Vargas Era to the Military Coup

Imposing a dictatorial regime known as the Vargas era, Getulio Vargas ruled Brazil continuously from 1930 to 1945. The period that followed, from 1946 to 1964, is known as the Second Brazilian Republic. During this time, the Brazilian economy was marked by developmentalism, industrial growth, an imbalance of public accounts, external debt, and inflation (Gremaud, 2002; Baer, 2002). Issued to regulate corporations, the Decree Law 2627 defined accounting standards. Because the capital market in Brazil was very small and restricted, the Brazilian corporate law of the period was quite simple.

In this paper, we highlight the creation of the CFC (Federal Accounting Council) in 1946 for the purpose of regulating the accounting profession in Brazil and issuing Brazilian accounting standards mandatory for all companies, whether they were public or not. The accounting standards adopted were

Figure 1. Evolution of Brazilian accounting and corresponding political and economic events

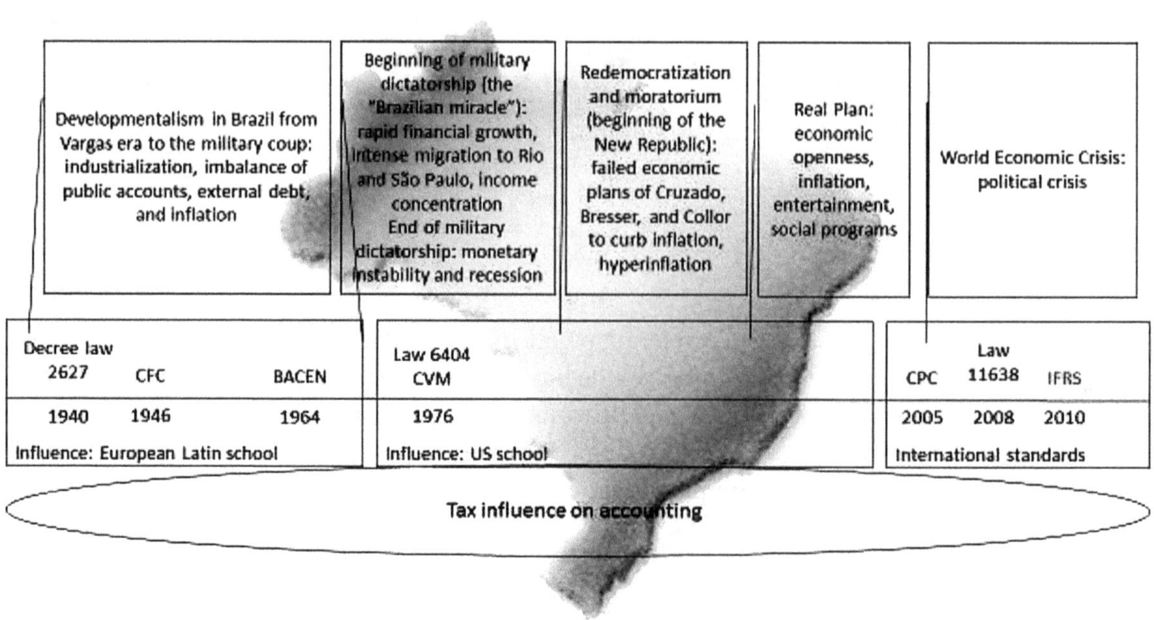

influenced by the accounting standards used in Latin Europe, particularly Italy and France. At the time, the main users of accounting were the internal (in general the stockholders are the managers), not the external (investors and creditors).

Military Dictatorship

The military coup that took power of Brazil on April 1, 1964, ruled the country until March 15, 1985. During the '70s, Brazil experienced strong economic growth, referred to as the "Brazilian miracle," and there was an intense migration of the population to Rio and São Paulo and a notable concentration of income. At the end of the military regime, Brazil faced monetary instability and a severe recession (Gremaud, 2002; Baer, 2002).

In the military period, the following two notable accounting institutions were created: the Central Bank of Brazil (BACEN) in 1964 and the Securities Commission (CVM) in 1976. Law 6404 was also issued in 1976, influenced by North American standards, which drastically altered the regulation of corporations and foreign accounting standards. It is important to note that CFC always issues Brazilian accounting standards according to corporate law.

Redemocratization and Moratorium

The current political period in Brazil, known as New Republic, began in 1985. The outset of this period marks the end of the military regime and the beginning of the Brazilian democratization process. As an effect of the cumulative economic policy that had taken place in the two previous periods, Brazil entered into a moratorium on its external debt, inflation soared, and the economic plans of Cruzado, Bresser, and Collor attempting to curb inflation failed (Gremaud, 2002; Baer, 2002).

Real Plan

The '90s were marked by economic openness, the effects of the world globalization process, and the Real Plan in 1994, designed by Fernando Henrique Cardoso to control the wave of hyperinflation. Several social programs were also created at that time in an attempt to implement better income distribution (Baer, 2002).

World Economic Crisis

The early 21st century has been marked by a succession of economic and political global crises (Krugman, 2010). In the sphere of accounting, the current millennium has seen a discussion about the international accounting harmonization and IFRS convergence around the world.

The Securities and Exchange Commission of Brazil (CVM) is a founding member of the International Organization of Securities Commissions (IOSCO) and actively participates in several committees and working groups, just as well the IOSCO Board. Among the IOSCO activities is the one that culminated in the agreement with the International Accounting Standards Committee (IASC) to create the International Accounting Standards Board (IASB) with the objective of issuing international accounting standards by means of the IFRS.

To enable the adoption of the IFRS in Brazil, the Accounting Pronouncements Committee (CPC) was created in 2005. In 2008 the Brazilian corporate law was amended by Law 11638. Full adoption of the IFRS in Brazil occurred in 2010. It is important to note that since 2008, the CFC has issued accounting standards exactly as they occur in CPC pronouncements. Thus, IFRS is indirectly mandatory for all companies in Brazil through the CPC. As highlighted by Carvalho and Salotti (2012, p. 235), "Brazil is a rare case of a complete adoption of IFRS, not only for consolidated financial statements, but also for the individual ones".

In addition to corporate law, specific boards regulate Brazilian companies and the accounting practices they adopt according to the type of activity they conduct. It is also noteworthy that historically there has been a strong tax influence on accounting.

The Influence of US Accounting Practices on Brazil's 1976 Corporate Law and Its Subsequent Manifestations

The adoption of the US teaching method by the University of São Paulo in 1964 changed the direction of accounting-education research in Brazil. Another great influence on this process was the arrival in Brazil of large Anglo American audit companies along with multinational corporations. The training offered by these companies influenced both the market and the legislators.

The consolidation of the US school in Brazil is a fait accompli given that the book *Introductory Accounting* (adopted in almost all Brazilian colleges) pays special tribute to the influence of Brazilian accounting on US accounting and also because of Brazil's promulgation of Law 6.404, known as the Corporation Law, in 1976, the accounting sections of which were inspired by the American doctrine.

Brazilian accounting underwent a significant change with the promulgation of the Corporation Law, created to attend to the Brazilian Stock Market demand and elaborated, initially, to establish rules for public companies. Law 6.404 was influenced by US-style accounting, which is the reason that the changes that have taken place since 1978 are very significant in that they signify a culture change.

Until the '60s, so-called real assets were Brazilians' main applications. The Law of Usury, which capped annual interest at 12 percent and inflation, contributed to this situation. Since 1964, the financial market has undergone restructuring: the Central Bank was created, established measures for its development.

In 1976, the Brazilian Capital Market included few companies, which is a reality that had to change. The market was encouraged by expanding the ways domestic companies could raise funds and enabling the development of the economy.

Although the corporate law came into force in 1978, with a legislative and regulatory framework that allowed investors to visualize an investment alternative in securities, the capital market did not have the expected growth.

Nevertheless, the corporate law introduced important new legal concepts for companies, adapting legal concepts that were already widely used in more developed economies to the Brazilian reality. Brazil's corporate law was hereby aligned with that of the United States and European countries, which had also reformed their laws concerning corporations.

A huge advance in Brazil's accounting sector was implemented. When they were faced with a new concept of the business relationship between their creditors, banks, and markets at the opening up of its capital, the needs of companies and businesses were met.

The new corporate law brought innovations both in relation to financial statements and their components and to establish accounting principles. The aim was to expand the amount as well as the quality of information that could be disclosed in order to strengthen the capital market in Brazil.

Since that time, the improvement of the quality and reliability of the information that would then be disclosed by the companies were emphasized. An Anglo-American model for the Brazilian accounting was adopted. This means that it was adopted a model facing the capital markets and for investors in this market.

The Brazilian capital market has specific characteristics that directly affect the quality and relevance of accounting information. These include share structure and institutional factors, sources of funding, and the government's significant participation in the economy.

The draft law was submitted to the examination of class institutions, experts in the field, and general public debate for over a year. It was intended to create the legal structure needed to strengthen the capital market in Brazil. There was a concern over creating a system that would ensure the minority shareholder the right to have defined rules without, however, constricting the businessperson. The objective was to allow entrepreneurs the freedom to choose the securities that would be best adapted to their enterprise (stocks, bonus, and debentures) as well as to guard the liability of managers and the modernization of the legal structure of large companies. In addition, the project emphasized the fact that the market institutions had increasing social importance and, consequently, more duties to the community.

An example of this concern was the demand for new financial statements. Before the corporate law went into effect, the only mandatory statements were the balance sheet and the profit-and-loss statement. After it was implemented, the presentation of the following statements became mandatory: a balance sheet, an income statement, and a statement of retained earnings, which could be replaced by a statement of changes in shareholders' equity, a statement of changes in financial position, and notes.

Over the years, market needs have changed and intensified, so that the corporate law, at first a breakthrough for businesses, has become a constraint.

The Importance of the Brazilian Securities Commission in Establishing Accounting Quality and in the Process of IFRS Adoption

The Securities and Exchange Commission of Brazil (CVM) has the power to discipline, regulate, and supervise the activities of members of the securities market in Brazil. Its role is to ensure the regularity and reliability of the information that companies make available to the market.

According to the CVM, with regard to the definition of policies and standards for the development of business with securities, CVM demand from market institutions, government or professional associations, prompt discussion of problems, promote the study of alternatives and adopt initiatives, so that any change in current practices is made with sufficient technical background and, institutionally, can be easily, assimilated as an expression of a common desire.

The financial statements of public companies should be generated not only to comply with the corporate law and CFC but also with all changes made by the CVM, through its instruction resolutions notes, guidance reports, and newsletters.

Except for the practices of public companies, Brazilian accounting practices remained almost static until 2007, when the CVM issued a series of rules for attending to the market necessities, with the accounting law having undergone few changes over those 30 years.

Many other boards regulating specific activities also started to issue accounting rules in Brazil. That has led us into the 21st century where the accounting standards in Brazil are composed of a series of rules promulgated by several regulating boards that, in many situations, present distortions and contradictions among their pronunciations.

In order to modernize the Brazilian accounting, which with the economic advancement had restrictions on the market, the CVM requested a change in corporate law, with the following objectives: (a) the emergence of a new economic reality in Brazil, quite different from that which existed when the law was enacted; and (b) the globalization of economies and opening of markets, with significant capital flows entering the country and with Brazilian companies raising funds abroad.

This request was answered with the enactment of Law 11.638 in 2007, which mainly changed the accounting provisions of the corporate law that were already in line with international accounting standards.

The Influence of Tax Law on Accounting

Although the corporate law was issued with a focus on public companies, the Brazilian government, one year after its promulgation, issued Decree Law 1.598 stretching its utilization to other types of enterprises for tax purposes. Although tax legislation determines only taxable profit, it has always had a strong influence on Brazilian accounting. Effectively, Brazilian accounting practices followed by different types of firms have been, since 1978, the American model adopted by the corporate law.

The corporate law states that accounting records must be made on the basis of generally accepted accounting principles and the calculation of the profit tax must be carried out separately, in a book called the Tax Calculation Book, or LALUR. In this book, the adjustments to net income are registered in order to get the taxable income, so that accounting can be conducted in accordance with its own rules and not tax rule standards. Even so, it is undeniable that, in practice, the adoption of this system does not have the extension that would be necessary for the accounting to be carried out without having an influence on tax rules.

Tax law defines the recognition and measurement of events differently from the accounting principles and corporate legislation. It controls these differences in its own books or, more recently, in digital files.

It can be said that micro- and small enterprises primarily follow the tax rules in the records of its economic events. The accounting professionals working in these companies devote most of their time to tax matters. In fact, if the company is not required by any specific legislation, regulatory board, or headquarters to present the accounts in accordance with what we call corporate law, then the priority will be the fulfillment of tax legislation.

THE BRAZILIAN CONVERGENCE PROCESS TO IFRS

We will now look at the Brazilian convergence process to IFRS and its consequences.

The New Structure for Developing Accounting Norms in Brazil

Besides the corporation law, Brazilian entities are also ruled by specific boards according to their activities; such boards even regulate their accounting practices. Among the most important boards are: the Central Bank of Brazil, or BACEN, which rules financial institutions; the Superintendence of Private

Insurance, or SUSEP, which rules insurance entities; the National Agency for Telecommunications, or ANATEL, which rules communication entities; and the National Agency of Energy Electricity, ANEEL, which rules energy entities.

In this scenario where various agents create various rules, it can be expected that the accounting practices in Brazil are different from the existing ones since the creation of the corporation law depends on the agency that issued them. It was necessary to have a single accounting-standard setting in our country that would converge with international accounting standards in order to diminish the business costs for having access to the most important capital markets in the world.

In order to centralize the process of accounting standardization, the CPC was created in Brazil in 2005 with the purpose of issuing accounting standards according to the IFRS. It is interesting to observe that besides promoting the IFRS adoption in Brazil, the CPC centralized the accounting standards that must be adopted by the CFC, CVM, and other regulatory boards.

According to the international convergence of accounting standards requirements, the CPC has joined the Brazilian Association of Listed Companies (ABRASCA); the Association of Investment Analysts and Professionals of the Capital Markets (APIMEC National); the Brazilian Securities, Commodities and Futures Exchange (BM&FBOVESPA), which is São Paulo's stock exchange; the Federal Accounting Council (CFC); the Foundation Institute of Accounting, Actuarial and Financial (FIPECAFI); and the Institute of Independent Auditors of Brazil (IBRACON). By joining, the issuance of such rules and the need for representation and democratic processes in the production of such statements are centralized. In fact, the board that regulates the accounting profession, public companies, academy, market analysts, and auditors were joined together to issue accounting standards.

Besides their members, BACEN, the CVM, the Brazilian Federal Revenue, and SUSEP are permanent guests of CPC representatives. In addition, other entities or experts may be invited and working groups on specific topics can be formed.

The CPC analyzes the internationally based IFRS and adapts the standards to the realities of Brazil. Thus, the issued pronouncements are not mere translations of the IFRS. The CPC can, for example, choose to only adopt one accounting policy for Brazil when there are two possible policies, in accordance with the IAS or IFRS. This is the case with the initial measurement of fixed assets, which is done according to the IFRS is the cost, where there is a choice between two ways for doing the subsequent measurement: The cost less depreciation and impairment losses might be calculated or such assets may be revalued. When the accounting pronouncement for fixed assets was considered in light of circumstances in Brazil, there was not the option of having revaluation, as it is at odds with the current Brazilian corporate law. It is fundamental to emphasize that the differences are actually just a few and it can be said that the Brazilian accounting practices are convergent to the IFRS in individual and consolidated financial statements.

Once the statements are issued by the CPC, they can be adopted by the various regulatory boards that determine the accounting of sectors (e.g., SUSEP for insurance companies, ANATEL for telecommunications companies, etc.); the CVM; and the CFC. In general, regulators except for the Central Bank have adopted the CPC pronouncements, which bring uniformity to accounting in the country. The financial institutions disclose their accounting statements directly to the IFRS for market capital purposes. For regulatory purposes, they follow Central Bank rules that are different from those of the CPC.

Since 2010, all listed companies and financial institutions in Brazil have been required to issue the IFRS. According to local standardization, all large-sized companies are required to submit the full IFRS (the full CPC is equivalent to the full IFRS). In Brazil, the determination of a large-sized company is done according to Law 11.638/07: To qualify, a company must be under common control and have presented assets over R$240 million or an annual gross revenue over R$300 million in the previous year. For Brazilian companies that are not considered to be large sized, an equivalent local norm named CPC PME (*pequenas e médias empresas*) requires the submission of the IFRS for SMEs (small- and medium-sized entities); the companies are also allowed to submit the full IFRS.

The IFRS for SME was adopted by the CFC, the organization that rules the accounting profession and is in charge of issuing Brazilian accounting norms. On December 10, 2009, the council named this board "NBC TG 1000" (Brazilian accounting norm general technic 1000), through CFC Resolution 1.255.

The bookkeeping of Brazilian companies considered microenterprises (with revenue up to R$3.6 million annually) is very simplified: It must be performed in compliance with ITG 1000, approved by resolution CFC 1.330/11, and named "simplified bookkeeping," which is not equivalent to IFRS. These companies can still opt for the IFRS for SME or the Full IFRS.

Table 1 shows the types of companies and their respective set of applicable accounting norms.

According to the research released by the IBPT, there were 16,002,903 companies in Brazil as of September 30, 2013. Table 2 shows the percentage of the total market that companies occupy by size.

According to the IBPT's size division in Table 2, there is not a distinction made between large-sized companies with revenue over R$300 million, according to Law 11.638/07. Among large-sized companies, a set of companies with revenue varying from R$48 and R$300 million should be included, but according to Law 11.638/07, they would all be considered SME.

Table 2 places a great part of Brazilian companies in the range that has the possibility of opting for the set of applicable accounting norms: Small-sized companies and microenterprises, which account for approximately 8.4 million companies and constitute 52.66 percent of the total, can opt for the Simplified Bookkeeping, IFRS for SME, or Full IFRS. Medium-sized companies, which comprise approximately

Table 1. Set of applicable accounting norms by company type and size

Type of Company	Size of Company	Norm to be Applied	Permitted Alternative
Corporations and large-sized companies	Total assets > R$240 million Total revenue > R$300 million	full IFRS	None
Small- and medium- sized companies	Total assets < R$240 million Total revenue from R$3.6 million to $300 million	IFRS for SME	full IFRS
Small-sized companies and microenterprises	Revenue < R$ 3.6 million	Simplified Bookkeeping (ITG 1000)	IFRS for SME or full IFRS

Table 2. Companies' percentage of market by size

Size	% of Total	Annual Revenue
Large	2.07%	Over R$48 million
Medium	14.79%	R$3.6 million to R$48 million
Small	10.78%	R$360,000 to R$3.6 million
Microenterprises	41.88%	Up to R$360,000
Individual entrepreneurs	21.47%	Up to R$60,000
Nonprofit and government entities	9.01%	Revenue not considered

Source: Brazilian Institute for Planning and Taxation (2013)

2.4 million entities and make up 14.79 percent of the total, can opt for the IFRS for SME or Full IFRS. Besides those, some large-sized companies can opt for this set of norms according to the IBPT.

The First Phase of IFRS Adoption in Brazil in 2008, Its Main Changes, and the Impacts on Public Companies

The Brazilian convergence process was divided into two phases. The first one took place in 2008 and the second one in 2010; the latter dealt with public and large entities that were already supposed to have complied with the new accounting practices. The main changes that occurred in this first phase and their consequences will be presented along with the viewpoints of several researchers.

Three different accounting periods of IFRS influence in Brazil can be classified: (1) *pre-IFRS period*: covers the accounting practices in effect until 2007; (2) *hybrid period*: applies to the accounting practices lasting from 2008 until 2009 that were partially convergent to the IFRS; and (3) *full IFRS period*: accounting practices that have been in effect since the complete adoption of the IFRS in 2010 and with balances represented in 2009 for comparative effect.

The first phase began with the enactment of Law 11638 and 14 accounting pronouncements issued by the CPC. Perhaps the biggest change brought about during this phase was a new accounting philosophy stressing the primacy of economic essence on the legal form, the primacy of a risk-and-benefits analysis on the legal property, and the adoption of standards-oriented principles and judgment.

The international accounting standards adopts the philosophy that accounting standards should be centered on principles rather than rules. This increases the responsibility of professionals in accounting, managers of companies, and auditors to exercise correct judgment in defining standards.

Brazilian accounting practices have also undergone various changes regarding the recognition, measurement, and disclosure of the financial position and performance of local companies. This first phase includes the following changes regarding the measurement among others:

1. Previously classified deferred assets were no longer recognized as preoperating expenses, and the new practices were recognized directly in the income. Expenditures for research and development that cause part of the change recognized as an asset, which were also classified as deferred assets, previously with lower restrictions than the ones defined by IFRS, were now considered as an expense.
2. Goods acquired through financial leasing were now recognized as assets rather than rental expenses. The concept of assets in corporate law had to be changed so that this practice could be adopted
3. The impairment of assets were adopted in accounting practices.
4. The relevant adjustment to the present value for the payable and receivable amounts in the long term as well as the payable and receivable amounts in the short term started to be adopted.
5. There was a ban on the revaluation of assets, enabled by the IFRS.
6. A new treatment of financial instruments was put in place, creating the possibility of accounting in regard to comprehensive income in some cases.
7. There were changes in the way inventories are measured, using the concept of net realizable value instead of market value, when compared to the cost.

It should be highlighted that the prohibition of asset revaluation meets the public's demand, because, according to common sense, several companies use this practice in order to manipulate their account numbers (Cardoso, Saravia, Tenório, & Silv, 2009). With regard to the disclosure, there were changes in the classification of the assets resulting in a compulsory set of financial statements and greater disclosure in the notes. As far as the classification of balance sheet items, there was a cessation of the fixed- and deferred- asset groups and a creation of groups of noncurrent assets and liabilities as well as the intangible assets subgroup and valuation adjustments equity, which belongs to the shareholders' equity. In the classification of revenue and expenditure items, extraordinary or nonoperating income were eliminated, creating a subtotal-of-income line before financial income and expenses. The continuing operations of the entity were also highlighted, after the net profit for income taxes, for the results of discontinued operations that previously did not exist.

As already discussed, Law 6.404/76 led to the view that accounting should provide useful information to the market; thus, creating a requirement for new financial statements.

In the process of convergence of Brazilian accounting practices to IFRS, the requirement for the cash flow statement was created, replacing the statement of sources and uses of funds and the comprehensive income statement. In this process of filling out the statement, public companies are required to also submit the statement of added value, which is not required in accordance with IFRS.

Table 3 presents a comparative summary of the financial statements required in Brazil before the Corporative Law, in the period when the Corporative Law was in effect, and the period after convergence to the IFRS.

Several researchers have analyzed the main changes that occurred in the first phase of the IFRS convergence process and the consequences of those changes. Alves-Oliveira and Lemes (2011) analyzed the Brazilian financial statements from the hybrid period in 2008 to evaluate the IFRS's adequation level concerning the information disclosed in the Brazilian and North American markets. A higher convergence level was detected between the US GAAP and the IFRS than between the Brazilian GAAP and IFRS, which suggests that the Brazilian financial statements tend to substantially modify, increasing the disclosure level.

Barbosa Neto, Dias, and Pinheiro (2009) compared the economic and financial indicators in the pre-IFRS and hybrid periods and found that they were not affected in a statistically significant way. In a similar study, Martins and Paulo (2010) found opposing results, suggesting that the partial adoption of the IFRS in the hybrid period reduced the divergences among the calculated indicators between the Brazilian and the international accounting standard in accordance with the Brazilian convergence process to the IFRS.

Table 3. Comparison of financial statements in different periods

Before Law 6.404/76	Since Law 6.404/76	Convergence to IFRS after 2008
Balance sheet	Balance sheet	Balance sheet
Statement of profit and loss	Income statement for the fiscal year	Income statement for the fiscal year
	Statement of retained earnings or Statement of changes in shareholders' equity	Statement of changes in shareholders' equity
	Statement of sources and uses of funds	Statement of cash flows
		Statement of added value
		Statement of comprehensive income
	Notes	Notes

Zonatto, Santos, Junior, and Bezerra (2011), in an analysis of the public and private companies electric in the energy sector, showed that size, financing needs, total indebtedness, fixed-asset ratio, and return on equity are the factors that explain the adherence to the international accounting standards.

Pelucio-Grecco, Formigoni, and Geron (2010) measured the impact of the changes on accounting practices of Brazilian public companies occurring in 2008. They observed an approximately 2 percent reduction in the equity due mostly to the reversal of the revaluation reserve, prohibited in Brazil since 2008. They also observed an approximately 5 percent reduction in the companies' profit or loss, due to the adoption of CPC 02, which equivalent to IAS 21 ("The Effects of Changes in Foreign Exchange Rates"). They additionally verified that the adoption of new accounting practices concerning measure, booking, and disclosure of financial instruments caused the most frequently identified adjustments.

According to Souza and Coutinho Filho (2007), the implementation of international accounting norms demands deep knowledge not only of local norms but also of international ones. The difficulties in the convergence process vary from the lack of qualified personnel to the fiscal influence on Brazilian culture.

Silva, Weffort, Peters, and Cia (2010) researched accounting professionals' perception that sanitation entities in Brazil had the greatest impacts on income and equity. Moreover, they analyzed the difficulties of implementing the changes to corporation laws in 2008. Regarding such changes, they observed the lack of knowledge in IFRSs, the difficulty with a foreign language, the lack of qualified professionals in the market, and the necessity of a higher support for information systems, causing an increase in the amount work and consequently the operational costs.

Reis, Shimamoto, and Barrios (2010) analyzed accounting professionals' perceptions, as registered at the CRC-PR, or the Regional Accounting Committee from Paraná, about the Brazilian convergence of accounting practices. According to their paper, the changes in accounting practices did not cause substantial changes in the performance of accounting professionals since small and medium entities are affected by those changes only after 2010. This work was performed during 2009.

According to Fernandes, Lima, Vieira, and Niyama (2010), professors in the field of accounting agree that using a public audience for analyzing the pronouncements issued by the CPC permits a more effective elaboration of accounting standards by the accounting class, which will give the accounting category more power and substantive authority.

Pelucio-Grecco, Geron, Formigoni, and Segura (2011) suggest that professionals' perceptions regarding the main difficulties in the implementation of the new Brazilian accounting practices are linked to the lack of recognition, measurement, and disclosure of the property, plant, and equipment and intangibles categories, in addition to the lack of qualified professionals and information technology support. It is interesting that despite the difficulties, the accounting and financial professionals think that the new accounting practices will bring positive impacts in terms of investments in Brazil.

The Second Phase of IFRS Adoption in 2010, the Main Changes, and the Impacts on Public Companies

In presenting the main changes that occurred in this second phase of convergence process, there is an emphasis on the necessity to make the scheme reflect Brazilian economic reality, especially concerning business combinations.

As the second phase came about, assets that were previously measured at historical cost value were now measured at fair value, with an emphasis on investment properties and biological assets. An important change also took place in the Brazilian accounting practice regarding tangible assets: Due to the tax influence on accounting, an accounting practice was adopted in which depreciation rates would be determined by tax legislation. In fact, the tax law determined that only effective depreciation expenses would be deductible up to the limit imposed by the legislation when using the linear method with no estimated residual value. With the adoption of IAS 16 in 2010, companies had to estimate the useful lives of their property and the residual values and analyze the application of the depreciation method that would best reflect the use of these assets.

Another important change that came about with the second phase is related to the recognition of revenue and inventory. In Brazil, again for tax influence, revenues were always recognized according to the tax documents issued. The inventory, in the same way, was recognized as an asset of the company based on the tax document. After 2010, the transfer of risks, benefits, and control started to be analyzed based on IAS 18 and IAS 2.

Also with regard to revenue, it should be noted that in Brazil there was always the primacy of gross revenues. Thus, the first line of the income statement for a year consisted of the gross income, which was followed by deductions of gross revenues, including taxes and other deductions, and only then came the net revenue. That is, Brazilians considered the revenue to be gross sales. With the emergence of IAS 18, the net income taxes and deductions were considered.

Prior to the convergence to IFRS, in a business combination, the net assets of the acquired company were kept to the existing cost of the acquiree on the balance sheet and the goodwill was measured by the difference between the amount paid and the cost value of these assets. IFRS 3 now measures the net assets of the acquired company at their fair values at the business combination date, and the goodwill is measured by the difference between the amount paid and the fair value of net assets, considering the participation of noncontrolling.

Another important change concerning the business combination was the nonamortization of goodwill, which must be tested for impairment annually. Prior to the IFRS, goodwill was amortized in Brazil over a period of five to ten years.

In order to highlight the consequences of Full IFRS adoption, some individual cases will be presented; for example, the Santander case in Brazil concerning the impacts on its equity and profit and loss. This Santander case was a very interesting one in that, in 2010, while the income was approximately US$3.5 billion, according to Brazilian GAAP, it was approximately US$1.8 billion according to the IFRS; the difference between the accounting norms was about US$ 1.7 billion. The empirical evidences will additionally be presented.

The following papers look at the economic consequences of full adoption of the IFRS in Brazil: Silva (2013) and Lima (2011) suggested that the IFRS adoption in Brazil improved the quality of accounting information and reduced the cost of capital. Pelucio-Grecco, Geron, Grecco, and Lima (2014) found that the IFRS had a restrictive effect on earnings management in Brazil and additionally found that the regulatory environment is the one with the most limiting effects.

The Changes in Tax Law

In order to meet the Brazilian Securities Commission's commitment to adopt the IFRS for public companies by 2010, the Brazilian government issued Law 11.638 in 2007, significantly altering the corporation law. Additionally, the government issued Law 11.941, determining that the changes in accounting law should not affect the taxable profit; the profit should be calculated as if there had been no change in the law.

In this way, since 2008, a convergence process to the IFRS has occurred in Brazil; however, besides the cultural changes in terms of accounting practices, unlike what took place in 1978, a detachment of accounting from tax purposes has been incurred. Consequently, between 2008 and 2014 companies followed the so-called transitional tax system, according to which those that had used the new accounting practices since 2008 were expected to adjust their financial statements to reflect the accounting practices they used on December 31, 2007 and send the adjustments to the tax authorities in a digital file. This requirement caused uncertainty for companies since it was not legally established which adjustments should be made. In addition, it was required that in declaring their income tax, companies should show their financial statements in accordance with the practices adopted since 2008 and make identical declarations aligned to the accounting practices in effect on December 31, 2007. From the remeasured profit following the 2007 calculation, the company should implement tax legislation and calculate the taxes due.

Recently, the Brazilian government issued Law 12.973/14, which defines the correct fiscal treatment of the new accounting practices adopted in the country. In this way, as set out in the decree law 1.598 issued in 1977, the fiscal law adopts the accounting practices and there is the expectation of a greater adhesion by small- and medium-sized companies due to fiscal demand.

In summary, the adjustments made to the accounting practices in effect at the time of IFRS convergence to reflect those in force on December 31, 2007, which were previously managed and revised in electronic file sent to the tax authorities, should, as of 2015, be managed in accounting subaccounts. Thus, the Federal Treasury will now receive information on companies' corporate accounting in separate electronic files showing the company's daily accounting log and depicting the accounting under tax rules. It is important to point out that the new tax law is not neutral regarding taxation as promised; for example, the new accounting practices have tax effects on income and on PIS (Social Integration Program) and COFINS (Contribution for the Financing of Social Security).

IFRS POSTIMPLEMENTATION: NEW PERSPECTIVES

In this final topic, the current work done by the CPC and other Brazilian boards, including the IASB, to maintain the quality of financial reports and their activity are discussed. Other endeavors associated with the IFRS and financial reports will also be highlighted: the development of the Brazilian XBRL (eXtensible Business Reporting Language) taxonomy, the implementation of integrated reporting in Brazil, and the approval of anticorruption law.

Brazil continues in its effort to change its existing accounting pronouncements using the CPC to ensure that these statements will be adopted by the regulatory boards. The country maintains ongoing efforts to make sure that its accounting standard complies with the international one.

In practical terms, the alignment of accounting to international standards will take place not only with public companies but also with those that are supervised or audited. Smaller companies that are not audited by any regulatory board inevitably follow tax rules in order to minimize possible tax risks, as the controls required by the tax authorities are too complicated and costly. However, for these companies, the trend is to follow the tax rules.

For each new change in accounting practices originating from a new standard of the IFRS or amendment to an existing pronouncement, the tax treatment will be defined by a change in the current tax law.

Although since 2010 it has been mandatory for companies listed in the Brazilian stock exchange (BM&FBOVESPA) to submit financial statements in accordance with the IFRS, it is not mandatory for them to submit financial information in XBRL.

Currently companies provide the financial statements to the Brazilian market in PDF (Portable Document Format), HTML (hypertext markup language), or Excel formats.

In the present global scenario, the corporate world needs to communicate and be understood clearly in order to gain market credibility. Considering the great advances in technology, wherein barriers such as distance have been diminished, the need to unify the language is found in relation to both accounting practices and strategic situations. A new image can thereby be transmitted within and outside of Brazilian society, for which the companies intend to prove modern, open, and transparent. XBRL optimizes the transmission of information over the Internet.

According to the IFRS Foundation, the IFRS and XBRL are intended to standardize reported financial statements in order to promote transparency and improve the quality and comparability of business information. The board emphasizes that the two entities form a perfect partnership. The IFRS Foundation's team mission in using XBRL is to create and provide a basic framework that will enable a consistent adoption of the standards featuring a high-quality taxonomy that uses the language of the IFRS.

The CFC and the CVM have been prepared to adopt the XBRL technology in the security market in Brazil.

In 2001, the Laboratory of Technology and Economics Faculty of Information Systems, Business Administration, and Accounting at the University of São Paulo (TECSI-FEA-USP) initiated research on XBRL under the direction of Prof. Edson Luiz Riccio. It is also from this research group that the first Brazilian XBRL taxonomy arose. The CFC established a commission to create a jurisdiction of XBRL, accrediting CFC as an entity along with XBRL International. The general Brazilian taxonomy for the financial statements of companies, such as commercial, industrial, and services, was approved by XBRL International on April 3, 2015.

Although the technology has not yet been adopted in Brazil for private companies, public entities have used the language for national consolidation of its financial data since 2014.

Concerning the advancement in the communication of information to the market, the Integrated Report also stands out, having emerged in response to the need to integrate financial and nonfinancial information.

Brazil has actively participated in the International Integrated Reporting Council (IIRC) since its creation in 2010. In addition, in order to keep the Brazilian market informed about the integrated reporting and to enable its implementation, the Brazilian Committee on Integrated Reporting was created. The committee has more than 200 participants representing more than 90 organizations. It is divided into five groups, each with a specific function: (1) WG 1: positions Brazil in the worldwide audience; (2) GT 2: communicates with the strategic public; (3) GT 3: pioneers companies; (4) GT 4: maintains relationships with investors; and (5) GT 5: performs road shows.

The participants of the pilot project include companies in the financial sector (Itaú Unibanco and BNDES), the energy sector (AES Brazil and CPFL), the oil and gas sector (Petrobras), the service sector (Via Gutenberg), the industrial sector (Votorantim Industrial), the transport sector (CCR), the insurance industry (BB and Mapfre), and the retail sector (Natura).

It should be pointed out that regarding nonfinancial information, in 2012 BM&FBOVESPA recommended that listed companies should indicate if they publish a sustainability report or a similar document and where it is available. If they don't, it suggested that they should explain why not. Several companies are already voluntarily preparing the annual sustainability report in accordance with the requirements of the Global Reporting Initiative, or GRI, which facilitates the implementation of the integrated report.

It is also noteworthy that in 2005 the Corporate Sustainability Index, or ISE, was created in the BM&FBOVESPA. After submitting a broad questionnaire that describes their social and environmental actions, 40 companies are annually stratified to make up the ISE.

Ultimately, the need for better corporate governance practices and the containment of corruption have been emphasized as a new perspective in Brazil. The scandals involving the energy giant Petrobras, in light of its importance as the largest Brazilian public company as well as being controlled by the government, led to a series of questions about corporate governance and the search for alternatives to contain corruption.

Iatridis (2012), in a comparative study looking at Brazil and South Africa, showed that the presence of effective mechanisms of corporative governance in South Africa reduce the agency cost, unlike what he observed in Brazil, where he found evidence of significant discretionary accruals.

It is worth remembering that the anticorruption law, Law 12.846, was approved in Brazil and has been in effect since 2014, just before scandals about corruption at Petrobras burst. It is expected that the law was approved in accordance with international commitments undertaken by Brazil acting as a signatory (with the Organization of American States, OAS; the Organization for Economic Co-operation and Development, or OECD; and the United Nations, or UN); actions are being taken to change this scenario.

It is expected that the inquiries about better corporate governance practices and fighting corruption will result in significant changes in the forms of internal control practiced, which will ensure investors, creditors, and society in general on the transparency and ethics of Brazilian companies.

REFERENCES

Alves-Oliveira, V. A., & Lemes, S. (2011). Nível de convergência dos princípios contábeis brasileiros e norte-americanos às normas do IASB: Uma contribuição para a adoção das IFRS por empresas brasileiras. *Revista Contabilidade & Finanças-USP*, *22*(56), 155–173. doi:10.1590/S1519-70772011000200003

Baer, W. (2002). *Economia brasileira*. NBL Editora.

Barbosa Neto, J. E., de Oliveira Dias, W., & Pinheiro, L. E. T. (2009). Impacto da convergência para as IFRS na análise financeira: Um estudo em empresas brasileiras de capital aberto. *Contabilidade Vista & Revista*, *20*(4), 131–153.

Cardoso, R. L., Saravia, E., Tenório, F. G., & Silva, M. A. (2009). Accounting regulation: Theories and analysis of the Brazilian accounting standards convergence to IFRS. *Revista de Administração Pública*, *43*(4), 773–799.

Carvalho, L. N., & Salotti, B. M. (2012). Adoption of IFRS in Brazil and the consequences to accounting education. *Issues in Accounting Education*, *28*(2), 235–242. doi:10.2308/iace-50373

Fernandes, B. V. R., Lima, D. H. S., Vieira, E. T., & Niyama, J. K. (2010). *Investigação empírica da percepção dos docentes dos cursos de graduação em ciências contábeis sobre a função e atuação do comitê de pronunciamentos contábeis*. 10º Congresso USP de Controladoria e Contabilidade.

Gremaud, A. P. (2002). *Economia brasileira*. São Paulo, Brazil: Atlas.

Iatridis, G. E. (2012). Audit quality in common-law and code-law emerging markets: Evidence on earnings conservatism, agency costs and cost of equity. *Emerging Markets Review*, *13*(2), 101–117. doi:10.1016/j.ememar.2012.01.001

IBPT. (2013). *Normas Tributárias em vigor equivalem a livro de 112 milhões de páginas*. Retrieved from https://www.ibpt.org.br/noticia/1266/Normas-tributarias-em-vigor-equivalem-a-livro-de-112-milhoes-de-paginas

Krugman, P. (2010). A crise de 2008 e a economia da depressão. *Revue d'Economie Politique*, *30*(1), 180.

Lima, V. S. D. (2011). *Incentivos no nível da firma e consequências econômicas da convergência ao IFRS no Brasil*. (Doctoral dissertation). University of São Paulo, São Paulo, Brazil.

Lopes, A. B. (2002). *Informação contábil e o mercado de capitais*. Cengage Learning Editores.

Martins, O. S., & Paulo, E. (2010). Reflexo da Adoção das IFRS na Análise de Desempenho das Companhias de Capital Aberto no Brasil (The Reflection of the Adoption of IFRS in the Performance Analysis of Publicly Traded Companies in Brazil). *Revista de Contabilidade e Organizações*, *4*(9), 30.

Pelucio-Grecco, M. C., Formigoni, H., & Geron, C. M. S. (2010). *The impact of the changes in the accounting practices in the conservatism level of the listed companies in Brazil*. 33rd EAA Annual Congress 2010, Istanbul, Turkey.

Pelucio-Grecco, M. C., Geron, C. M. S., Formigoni, H., & Segura, L. C. (2011). *Brazilian professionals' perception in relation to the accounting convergence process to IFRS*. 34th EAA Annual Congress 2011, Rome, Italy.

Pelucio-Grecco, M. C., Geron, C. M. S., Grecco, G. B., & Lima, J. P. C. (2014). The effect of IFRS on earnings management in Brazilian non-financial public companies. *Emerging Markets Review*, *21*, 42–66. doi:10.1016/j.ememar.2014.07.001

Reis, L. G., Shimamoto, L. S., & Barrios, R. A. (2010) *Convergência às normas internacionais de contabilidade: Uma análise sob a perspectiva dos profissionais contabilistas*. 15a Convenção Estadual dos Contabilistas.

Silva, P. C., Weffort, E. F. J., Peters, M. R. S., & Cia, J. N. S. (2010). *Impacto da adoção das IFRS nas empresas Brasileiras de saneamento: A percepção dos profissionais do setor*. Belo Horizonte, Brazil: Revista Contabilidade Vista & Revista, Universidade Federal de Minas Gerais.

Silva, R. L. M. D. (2013). *Adoção completa das IFRS no Brasil: Qualidade das demonstrações contábeis e o custo de capital próprio*. (Doctoral dissertation). University of São Paulo, São Paulo, Brazil.

Souza, A. A. S., & Coutinho Filho, F. B. (2007). *Harmonização Internacional: Um estudo sobre as dificuldades de convergência das normas contábeis brasileiras em relação às normas internacionais de contabilidade (IFRS)*. 7th Congresso USP de Controladoria e Contabilidade.

Chapter 16
The Determinants and Financial Statement Effects of IFRS Adoption in Nigeria

J. O. Odia
University of Benin, Nigeria

ABSTRACT

The chapter examines the determinants and financial statement effect s of IFRS adoption in Nigeria. It also investigate into the impact of effect of the adoption of IFRS on accounting figures and ratios in the financial statements of 50 companies quoted in the Nigerian Stock Exchange. The determinants considered include firm's characteristics (firm size, operating cash flow, leverage, turnover, growth in turnover, profitability, liquidity and earnings quality) and corporate governance variables (board size, board independence and audit type). The data were obtained from the annual reports of companies listed in the Nigerian Stock Exchange between 2011 and 2013 and was analyzed using the ordinary least square (OLS) and logistic regression which were used to test for determinants of IFRS adoption while the independent t-test was used to examine the financial statement effects. With regard to the determinants, the empirical result indicates only profitability and earnings quality have significant but negative association with IFRS adoption. Moreover, IFRS adoption has significant effect on the return on equity.

1. INTRODUCTION

In line with the adoption of IFRS by the European Union and many other countries, Nigeria adopted IFRS on 1st January 2012 under a three-year road map (between 2012 and 2014) for the adoption of IFRS by all companies. The Federal Executive Council in Nigeria approved 1st January 2012 as the effective date for convergence of Nigerian Accounting standards with IFRS by all Public interest entities and quoted companies in Nigeria. Actually, Nigeria started the IFRS adoption process in 2007 but the Financial Reporting Council (FRC) Bill was finally passed by the Senate on 18th May 2011 requiring all quoted companies to adopt IFRS as from 1st January 2012. The FRC Bill was signed into law on 20th July 2011 and replaced the Nigerian Accounting Standards Board (NASB) Act of 2003. The FRC Act

DOI: 10.4018/978-1-4666-9876-5.ch016

was to help the move the country towards the adoption of IFRS which would help align Nigeria with other countries, improve investors' confidence and help attract foreign direct investments in Nigeria. The first-time application of IFRS by adopting companies in Nigeria was in 2012.

The adoption of IFRS in Nigeria was predicated on the perceived benefits associated with a high quality accounting standard like the IFRS (Mike,2009, Okere,2009, Adegbie, 2010; Zakari,2010, Okaro, 2011, Adekoya, 2011, Iyoha & Jafaru, 2011 and Tanko,2012). However, as at 31st December, 2014, less than one-third of companies quoted on the Nigeria Stock Exchange are yet to prepare and present their financial reports using IFRS (Okpala,2012). From extant literature, there are various factors and implementation challenges of IFRS adoption by countries and firms documented by researchers from studies in both developed and developing countries (Abdelsalam & Weetman 2003, Zeghal & Mhedhbi,2006, Daske et al 2007a, Ayuba & Gugong, 2014, Masoud,2014) However, it is not clear the firm and corporate governance factors responsible for the differential and low-level adoption of IFRS by listed companies in Nigeria. Although a lot of empirical studies have been carried out on the benefits and challenges of implementation of IFRS in Nigeria (Madawaki,2012,Owolabi & Iyoha,2012,Donwa & Odia, 2013, Odia & Ogiedu, 2013, Odia,2015), there are limited researches on the determinants of IFRS adoption in Nigeria (Odia,2013).

Daske et al (2007) have argued that firms have considerable discretion in how they adopt IFRS. They posited that while some firms may simply adopt IFRS as a label, others may view the decision as a serious commitment to transparency. Using a large panel of IFRS (and IAS) adoptions from 1988 to 2004 across 24 countries, they argued this may be attributed to the reporting incentives or the economic consequences (cost of capital, bid-ask spreads and illiquidity) of IFRS adoption. Again, the level of compliance with IFRS has also been found to be related to company size, international visibility, and the quality of auditing, industry type, less reliance on debt leverage, dispersed ownership, high analyst following (Gassen & Sellhorn 2006, Daske et al,2007, Christensen, Lee & Walker 2007 & 2008, Albu & Albu 2012), institutional factors like nature of national accounting regulator (Albu & Albu 2012),effective company control systems and management dedication to quality reporting, oversight mechanism with expertise and power to achieve effective enforcement, and quality auditing (Brown &Tarca,2005), high analyst following. The differential compliance could also be linked to the cost of transition (ICAEW 2007, Fox et al, 2013)

Generally, most of the studies on the determinants of IFRS adoption are country specific with contradicting results on examining factors such as culture, economic growth, political system, educational level, capital and financial markets, privatization, foreign direct investment, legal environment, globalization and trade relationships. However, there are some studies examining the factors IFRS adoption at the company's level (Blanchette, Racicot & Sedzro, 2013). Ramanna and Sletten (2009) have argued that the firm-level studies are conditional on countries' decisions to allow or mandate IFRS. This suggests that that studies of IFRS adoption at the country-level can complement firms-level studies. Again, there are few researches based on small sample size and mixed evidences on how IFRS adoption has affected accounting figures and financial ratios of listed companies in Nigeria (Tanko,2012, Taiwo & Adejare,2014, Zayyad, Ahmad & Mubaraq,2014,Ibiamke & Ateboh-Briggs, 2014, Abata, 2015).Therefore, the chapter intends to consider first and foremost, the impact of some firm characteristics and corporate governance mechanisms on the IFRS adoption by listed companies in Nigeria. Second, the effects of IFRS adoption in Nigeria on some key financial statement items and financial ratios are considered. Using 50 non-financial companies quoted in the Nigerian Stock Exchange for the period 2011 to 2013, and basic statistical analyses like the regression analyses and parametric statistics, the chapter addresses both issues. It is believed that the findings will contribute positively to the IFRS adoption and capital market literature by revealing factors that determine IFRS adoption as well as the financial statement effects of IFRS adoption at the firm level from a developing country perspective.

The chapter is of vital significance as it contributes to the literature on the determinants and financial statement effects of IFRS adoption by listed companies and how key items in the financial statements of listed companies are affected by changes in new accounting information such as the IFRS based on the empirical evidence of a developing countries and emerging market like Nigeria.

The rest of the chapter is organized into four sections as follows: Section two provides background to the study by reviewing some of the relevant literature on the determinants and financial statement effects of IFRS adoption as well as the hypotheses development. Section three dwells on the methodology adopted. The data analysis and the discussion of the regression results are in Section four while the conclusion is the Section five.

2. BACKGROUND

2.1 General Background on IFRS Adoption

The globalization of the world's capital markets created the need for a single set of accounting standards around the world. It has argued that the global standard will enhance comparability and transparency of financial information for investors, result in greater willingness of investors to invest across borders, lower cost of capital and result in more efficient allocation of resources and higher economic growth (Barth, Landsman & Lang 2007,Daske, Hall, Leuz & Verdi 2008).In fact there recurring evidences that the adoption of IFRS improves the financial statement comparability and quality of financial information (Hung & Subramanyam, 2007, Armstrong *et al.*, 2010, Covrig, Defond & Hung, 2007.Daske *et al.*,2008; Gordon et al 2008, Bissessur & Hodgson, 2012).The perceived consistency of financial reporting across jurisdictions and sectors may also make it less costly for investors to compare economic positions of companies. This has the potential to reduce information asymmetry and enables capital markets to be more competitive, liquid and have lower cost of capital (Chambers & Penman,1984, Choi & Levich 1991,Covrig et al, 2007; Christensen, Lee & Walker, 2007).

Some studies have confirmed that adoption of IFRS at country level has increased direct foreign investment (Irvine & Lucas, 2006), resulted in high level of global market integration and improved quality accounting indicators (Chai, Tang, Jiang & Lin, 2010). Additionally, adoption of IFRS at the firm's level has enhanced accounting quality (Meeks & Swann,2009, Barth, 2008) and improve financial performance (Latridis, 2010).Taiwo and Adejare (2014) found a strong positive relationship between IFRS adoption and financial performance due to cost reduction of an organization as well as improvement in business efficiency and productivity.

Using the economic network theory, neo-institutional theory and isomorphic pressures as the theoretical framework, various factors such as culture, economic growth, political system, educational level, capital and financial markets, privatization, foreign direct investment, legal environment, globalization, trade relationships, company characteristics such as company size and leverage, and corporate governance mechanisms like big accounting firms have been found to determine the adoption of IFRS in developed and developing counties (Al-Akra et al., 2009; Nobes,1998, Irvine & Lucas,2006,Chamisa, 2000; Hove, 1986; Street, 2002; Zeghal & Mhedhbi, 2006,Zehri & Chouaibi,2013, Masoud,2014,DiMaggio &

Powell1983, Leuz & Wysocki,2008, Irvine 2008, Judge, Li & Pinsker 2010, Wysocki 2011). There are arguments in literature that financial reporting standards have co-developed with a country's economic, political, and cultural institutions (Ball, Kothari & Robin, 2000, Ball, Robin & Wu, 2003, Hail, Leuz & Wysocki, 2010).

More researchers have focused on examining the relationship between these factors and IFRS adoption. For instance, Zeghal and Mhedhbi (2006) examined the determinants of IAS/IFRS adoption by 32 developing countries. They concluded that developing countries with a capital market, advanced educational systems and high economic growth are more inclined to adopt IFRS. Choi and Meek (2008) framework suggested eight factors that determine the choice by countries to adopt IFRS which are: source of finance (equity and foreign debt financing); taxation; legal system; political and economic ties (colonialism and trade alliances), inflation; economic development, education and culture. Shima and Yang (2012:276) examined a comprehensive set of environmental characteristics based on Choi and Meek's (CM,2008) framework using 73 countries from 2000 to 2007.They found that CM's framework is fairly descriptive and factors relating to political and economic ties, reliance on foreign-sourced debt and common law legal systems create contracting incentives for IFRS adoption. Similarly, the need for capital investment, evidenced by greater economic growth and capital formation and higher literacy rates, creates signaling incentives for adoption. However, factors relating to size of capital markets, taxation and inflation produce disincentives for IFRS adoption.

Zehri and Chouaibi (2013) identified the determinants for the adoption of IAS/IFRS using a panel data of 74 developing countries (DCs) and found that DCs most likely to adopt IAS/IFRS have a high level of economic growth, along with a legal system of common law and an advanced educational level. Economic growth level constitutes a major determinant for adopting the international accounting standards (Al-Akra, Jahangir & Marashdeh, 2009; Larson, 1993,Zeghal & Mhedhbi, 2006, Masoud, 2014). Al-Akra et al. (2009) analyzed the impact of economic, political, legal and cultural factors on promoting the accounting practices in Jordan and concluded that political and economic factors are the most important contributor to the development. Government policy has significant influence on IFRS adoption (Chamisa, 2000, Joshi & Ramadhan, 2002, Xiao et al 2004, Mir & Rahaman 2005,). Ayuba & Gugong (2014) examined some factors influencing the adoption of IFRS among the various stakeholders in Nigeria and found that government policy has a positive significant relationship with the adoption of IFRS whereas company size was insignificantly related with IFRS adoption.

2.2. Firm Characteristics, Corporate Governance, and IFRS Adoption

There are numerous empirical evidences on the determinants of IFRS adoptions whether voluntary or mandatory IFRS adoption (e.g., Leuz & Verrecchia, 2000; Ashbaugh, 2001; Tarca, 2004) as well as studies examining the determinants and effects of mandatory IFRS adoption in certain countries (e.g. Comprix et al., 2003, Hope et al., 2006, Armstrong et al., 2010). Specifically, variables such as company size, leverage, profitability, liquidity, audit quality (Big 4), capital transparency and ownership structure have been re-occurring as a likely determinant.

The company size has been found to have mixed relationship with IFRS adoption. While some studies found insignificant relationship (Ahmad & Nicholls,1994, Street & Gray 2002, Glaum & Street 2003, Masoud,2014 and Ayuba & Gugong 2014), others studies such as: Dumontier and Raffournier (1998) Ashbaugh (2001); Bradshaw & Miller (2004), Tarca (2004), Affes and Callimaci (2007) and Hung and Subramanyam (2007) found that the company size affect the adoption of international standards.

Trembley (1989) found that adoption choice depends on company size and auditor's opinion in a study of 53 U.S. software specialized firms.

Masoud (2014) examined the factors affecting the decision to adopt IFRS standard by 78 emerging market economies between 2006 and 2014.The variables considered were: macro-economic variables (culture - Anglo-Saxon -, political system, educational system, legal environment, economic growth, privatization and foreign direct investment),firm characteristics (firm size, liquidity, and cost of equity capital) and corporate governance variables (audit quality (Big 4) and transparency).The results indicate that education system, legal environment, liquidity, privatization, audit quality and transparency had positive association with the decision to adoption IFRS whereas company size, foreign direct investment, political system and cost of equity capital has insignificant association. Irvine and Lucas (2006) identified big accounting firms to influence IFRS adoption in United Arab Emirate (UAE).

Since leverage is positively associated with the need for monitoring between shareholders and creditors, it can be argued that high leveraged firms are more eager to adopt IFRS in order to reduce borrowing costs compared to low leveraged firms (Masoud, 2014). Using a sample of 28 listed firms on the Swiss stock market (which apply local standards) and 51 companies that apply IAS/IFRS, Dumontier and Raffournier (1998) found the absence of a significant relationship between the voluntary adoption of IAS, the debt ratio and firm performance. Affes and Callimaci (2007) examined the motivations for an early adoption of IAS/IFRS by the German and Austrian listed companies and found that the relationship between debt and the anticipated adoption of IAS/IFRS appears to have little importance to highly indebted companies; their creditors might require compliance with debt covenants based on specific calculations. Moreover, Leuz and Verrechia (2000) examined the accounting choices of German companies listed on the DAX index for the year 1998. Using logistic regression analysis, they showed that firm size, financing needs and financial performance significantly explain the decision by German companies to adopt international standards.

The relationship between profitability and IFRS adoption are mixed. While Dumontier and Raffournier (1998), and Affes and Callimaci (2007) found no significant relationship, Marta Silva Guerreiro et al (2008) found positive relation between profitability and IFRS adoption.

Liquidity is defined as the ratio of current assets to current liabilities. The ratio shows the ability of the company to cover its short-term financial obligations. Prior studies found increase in liquidity after IFRS adoption (Daske et al., 2008, Platikanova & Perramon, 2009). In fact, Daske et al (2008) found that the liquidity benefits around IFRS adoption was absent in the European Union. Since good corporate governance like the engagement of Big 4 audit firm results in higher audit quality by reducing information asymmetry, a positive relationship has been found between some corporate governance variables and IFRS adoption. Masoud (2014) and Al-Basteki (1995) found that the decision to adopt IFRS was strongly influenced by the type of external auditor (Big 4) while Joshi and Ramadhan (2002) found that 86% of companies applying IFRS in Bahrain were audited by the Big 4.

2.3. The Financial Statement Effects of IFRS Adoption

Athanasios and Stergios (2010) examined whether the arithmetic mean of total assets, total liabilities, current assets, current liabilities, sales and earnings before taxes under Greek GAAP is statistically the same under IFRS of 90 randomly selected Greek companies listed in Athens Stock Exchange. They found that the differences in arithmetic means for all cases are not statistically different. Similarly, Stergios, Vazakidis and Dritsakis (2004) examined a sample of 40 Greek companies which voluntarily adopted the IFRS. The authors found that the arithmetic mean of total assets and total liabilities was statistically different. However the case was the same for earnings and sales. In both studies the arithmetic mean of the above is statistically the same. Nevertheless, the outcome for both studies is the same. Latridis (2010) concluded on the basis of data collected from listed firms on the London Stock Exchange that IFRS implementation has favorably affected the financial performance (measured by profitability and growth potentials). Jaruga, Fijalkowska, Jaruga-Baranowska and Frendzel (2007) examined the impact of the new standards on reported accounting numbers in Poland. Their study showed that IFRS caused increases in book value of equity by a factor of 10% and more in a third of the sample (up to 100% in one case), while few companies reported negative changes.

Callao, Jarne and Laínez (2007) examined whether the financial statements of Spanish firms are comparable when some companies apply IFRS and others continue to use existing Spanish standards. They also examined the effect of the adoption of IFRS on financial figures and ratios.The research sample included 35 firms listed on the Spanish stock market, with the exclusion of financial and insurance companies. The data was obtained from the half-yearly information reported by the firms to the Spanish National Securities Market Commission in the first half of 2004 and 2005. The results indicated that: (a) Comparability of the financial statements has worsened when applying the IFRS, which was explained as an effect from the application of both IFRS and local accounting standards. (b).There was no improvement in the relevance of financial reporting to local stock market because the gap between book and market values became wider when applying IFRS. (c) There are increases in cash and cash equivalents, long-term and total liabilities, cash ratio, indebtedness and return on equity but decreases in debtors, equity, operating income, solvency ratio and return on assets (measured in terms of the operating income).

Agca and Aktas (2007) investigated the extent of differences between the values of financial ratios gathered from financial statements prepared according to IAS/IFRS and in accordance with the Turkish accounting standards for 147 firms listed on Istanbul Stock Exchange. Significant differences are observed in both the whole sample and in some sectors. For the sectors, the significant differences are observed with the following ratios: cash ratio, inventory turnover ratio, asset turnover, return on equity and total liability ratio in sectors. While for the whole sample, the significant differences are observed for cash ratio and asset turnover.

Similarly, Lantto and Sahlström (2009) investigated the changes of key financial ratios of 91 firms after the conversion from Finnish Accounting Standards (FAS) to IFRS and to show whether the adoption of fair value accounting rules and stricter requirements on certain accounting issues caused the changes observed in accounting figures and financial ratios. The results of the study indicated that most of the FAS-based and IFRS-based balance sheets and income statements differ significantly (at 5% level), and that the adoption of IFRS changes the magnitude of the key accounting ratios of Finnish companies by considerably increasing the profitability ratios by 9-19% and gearing ratio moderately by 2.9%, and considerably decreasing the price- earning (PE) ratio by 11%, equity and quick ratios slightly by 0.2%. Silva, DoCouto and Cordeiro (2009) examined the impact of IFRS application and implementation on the financial information or consolidated accounts (balance sheet and profit and loss accounts) of Portuguese public listed companies, with the exception of financial and sporting institutions. The study found that all the items from the balance sheet and the profit and loss statements registered important and statistically significant variations,a depreciating price-earnings (PE) and earnings per share (EPS) ratios and an average decrease in the gearing ratios signaling a greater risk perception of investors in these firms.

Tsalavoutas and Evans (2010) examined 238 listed Greek firms. The objective of their study was to explore the impact of the transition to IFRS on the financial statements of Greek listed companies. Furthermore the study concentrated on the financial position, reported performance, gearing and liquidity ratios. The results showed that implementation of IFRS had a significant impact on companies' financial position and reported performance as well as on gearing and liquidity ratios. In fact, the impact on the shareholders' equity and net income was positive whereas there was a negative impact on gearing and liquidity ratios. Klimczak (2011) examined a sample of 159 firms in Poland and found that IFRS affected mostly balance sheet items, especially tangible fixed assets and investments; net earnings did not change by more than 12%. There was no evidence of an abnormal reaction or a surprise effect at the time of first IFRS statement publication. The author concluded that the average impact of IFRS adoption can be relatively small in a transition economy.

Blanchet, Raciciot and Girard (2011) examined the impact on financial ratios caused by the transition to International Financial Reporting Standards (IFRS) in Canada. T541The study revealed significantly higher volatility to most of the ratios under IFRS when compared to those derived under pre-change over Canadian GAAP. While the means and medians of IFRS ratios differed from the means and medians of the same ratios under pre-change over Canadian GAAP, the differences were not statistically significant. However, important individual discrepancies in some cases were observed. They discovered that ratios computed under IFRS are not directly comparable with those derived under pre-change over Canadian GAAP. Blanchette, Racicot and Sedzro (2013)

Lantto and Sahlström (2009),and Punda (2011) examined the effects of IFRS adoption on key financial ratios (KFRs) of UK listed firms; their results include that there exist a substantial change in the KFRs of firms in post IFRS adoption. The profitability ratios recorded significant increase i.e. (Operating Profit Margin increased by 10.8%, Return on Equity 27.0% and Return on Invested Capital increased by 11.4%).

Jindrichovska and Kubickova (2012) carried out a research with the objective of comparing differences in 16 financial ratios calculated with data according to IFRS and CAS (Czech accounting standards).The study discovered that there were no statistically important differences resulting from the two reporting formats (i.e. the traditional Czech accounting rules –CAS- and the IFRS provisions).The indicative results disclosed an important fact that the transition to IFRS could cause some deterioration of key indicators and thereby impact on the overall rating of Czech companies. A similarly study was by Nikolaos, Konstantinos and Dimitrios (2013) who examined the effect of the implementation of IFRS on the financial ratios of listed companies in Athens Stock Exchange (ASE) by emphasizing the differences between the Greek Accounting Standards (GAS) and IFRS as well as their impact on the financial ratios from financial statements prepared in accordance with the GAS or IFRS. The results showed significant differences between the two standards.

In Nigeria, Tanko (2012) reported that some selected companies in Nigeria tend to exhibit higher values on a number of profitability measures (such as EPS) under IFRS. Zayyad, Ahmad and Mubaraq (2014) examined the effect of IFRS adoption in Nigeria on the performance of an indigenous firm by comparing financial ratios computed from IFRS and Nigerian GAAP for 2010 and 2014.The financial ratios were: profitability, solvency and Investment. The result showed that there was no significant difference between the pair of ratios at 5% level of significance. The paper concluded that the disclosure of IFRS compliant set of financial statements was not attributable to higher performance evaluation. Rather the disclosure could have been motivated by the capital needs theory or signaling theory. Ibiamke and Ateboh-Briggs (2014) examined the impact of IFRS adoption by Nigerian listed firms on key financial ratios used by investors. They employed innovative design known as "same firm-year" research design to examine how IFRS adoption changes key financial ratios of Nigerian listed firms. They found that IFRS adoption has caused a negative but insignificant impact on the financial ratios of Nigerian listed firms. Therefore they recommended that analysts and other users of financial statement should be mindful of the new features of financial statement when making economic decisions.

Umoren and Enang (2015) examined whether the mandatory adoption of IFRS has improved the value relevance of financial information of 12 listed banks in Nigeria between 2010 and 2013.They found that the equity value and earnings of banks were relatively value relevant under IFRS than under the previous Nigerian SAS, and earnings per share was incrementally value relevant during post-IFRS period while book value of equity per share is incrementally less value relevant during the post-IFRS period. Abata (2015) examined the impact of IFRS on the financial reporting practices of 14 Nigerian banks by considering whether there were significant differences in the financial reports figures (total assets, total liabilities and equity) prepared under Nigerian GAAP and IFRS. The findings revealed statistically significant differences

3. RESEARCH METHOD

The sampling population comprises the entire quoted companies in the Nigerian Stock Exchange. However, listed companies providing financial services such as financial institutions and insurance companies were excluded due to their specialized financial statements, specific regulation (Callao et al,2007,Gaston et al,2012) and the adoption of IFRS by some banks before 2012.The sample consists of fifty non-financial companies that are listed in the NSE, and have applied IFRS in the preparation of their annual report since 2012. The sample was chosen based on convenient sampling. The data was collected from the annual reports of the sampled companies for the relevant period between 2011 and 2013.

Following the objective of the study, the financial statement effects of IFRS was investigated by comparing the items disclosed in the income statement and balance sheet as well as financial ratios before IFRS adoption (2011) and after IFRS adoption (2012- 2013).The panel ordinary least square (OLS) and logistic regression analyses were employed to determine whether there was association between the IFRS adoption and the determinants (Masoud,2014).In prior researches, the logistic regression has been employed to examine the possibility of non-linear relationships between the dependent and independent variables. Logistic regression is an appropriate approach where there is the occurrence of disproportionate sampling from two populations (Maddala, 1991). In logistic regression, the coefficients of the explanatory variables are unaffected by the unequal sampling rates from the two groups (Palepu,1986). Moreover, logistic regression has been applied to investigations of the determinants of IFRS adoption in emerging countries (see Zeghal & Mhedhbi, 2006, Zehri & Chouaibi, 2013, Masoud, 2014).

3.1. Model Specification

Following Masoud (2014), we specify the model for the relationship between IFRS adoption and the independent variables (firm characteristics and corporate government variables) as:

$$IFRS_{it} = f\,(BSIZE_{it}, BIND_{it}, AUD_{it}\ FSIZE_{it}, CFO_{it}, LEV_{it}, PROF_{it}, TURN_{it}, GROWTH_{it}, LIQ_{it}, EQ_{it}) \quad (1)$$

In econometric form, we can write the relationship as:

$$IFRS_{it} = \beta_0 + \beta_1 BSIZE_{it} + \beta_2 BIND_{it} + \beta_3 AUD + \beta_4 FSIZE_{it} + \beta 5CFO_{it} + \beta_6 LEV_{it} + \beta 7PROF_{it} + \beta_8 TURN_{it} + \beta_9 GROWTH_{it} + \beta_{10} LIQ_{it} + \beta_{11} EQ_{it} + U_t \quad (2)$$

The measurement of the dependent (IFRS adoption) and Independent variables is shown in Table 1.

To assess the existence of the multicollinearity we use the Variance Inflation Factor (VIF) and the correlation matrix. The VIF values were below 10 and the correlation was quite low suggest the absence of multicollinearity (see table 4). The confirmation or acceptance of each null hypothesis was based upon the result being not statistically significant for at least two of the methods. Therefore, if one method is statistically significant, the null hypothesis will be rejected.

3.2. Financial Statement Effects of IFRS Adoption

In this section, we examine the financial statement of IFRS adoption with regard to financial ratios and accounting figures in the balance sheet and income statement. The balance sheet items include: total assets, total liabilities, equity, current assets, current liabilities, fixed asset and long-term liabilities. The income statement items were turnover and net income while the financial ratios included current ratio, solvency ratio, indebtedness ratio and return on equity. The definition of each variable is shown in Table 2.

We test for significant differences in the values resulting from the application of IFRS for each variable in the balance sheet, income statement and the financial ratios for the same firms in the different periods under different conditions (pre and post IFRS adoption) in hypothesis 3a using the independent

Table 1. Measurement of variables

Dependent Variable		Proxy	Measurement of Variables	Expected sign
	IFRS adoption	IFRS	1 if a company adopt IFRS otherwise 0	
		$IFRS_i$	Probability of adopting IFRS	
Independent variables				
Corporate governance variables	Board size	BSIZE	Number of directors on the board	+
	Board independence	BIND	Proportion of non-executive directors on the board	+
	Audit firm type	AUD	1 if big 4 otherwise 0	+
Individual firm characteristics	Leverage	LEV	Proportion of total debts to total equity	+
	Profitability	PROF	Return on equity	+
	Company size	FSIZE	Logarithm of total assets	+
	Operating Cash flow	CFO	Operating cash flow scale down by total assets	+
	Revenues/earnings	TURN	Total sales scale down by total assets	+
	Revenues growth	GROWTH	Change in sales revenues/turnover	+
	Liquidity	LIQ	Current asset divided by current liabilities	+
	Earnings quality	EQ	Net income less cash flow from operations scale down by total assets	+

Table 2. Accounting figures and ratios

Accounting Figures	Definitions
Total assets	Fixed assets + Current assets
Total liabilities	Current liabilities + Long term liabilities
Equity	Funds contributed by shareholders + Retained earnings + Other reserves + Net income + Minority interest + Deferred income
Current assets	Stock + Debtors + Bank + Cash + Prepayment
Current liabilities	Short-term creditors + Short-term provisions
Fixed assets	Intangible assets + Property, plant and equipment + Long-term investments + Goodwill
Long term liabilities	Long-term creditors + Long-term provisions
Net income	Operating income + other Financial income – Financial expenses+ Extraordinary income – Extraordinary expenses – Taxes
Sales/turnover	Total earnings from sales
Financial Ratios	
Current ratio	Current assets/ Current liabilities
Solvency ratio	Total assets/Total liabilities
Indebtedness ratio	Total liabilities/Equity
Return on equity	Net income/Equity

Adapted from Callao et al (2007) and Gaston et al (2010)

t-test. This is because the one sample Kolmogorov- Smirnov test shows that the accounting figures and ratios values are normally distributed and the null hypothesis is rejected at 5% level of significance.

4. DATA ANALYSIS AND TEST OF HYPOTHESES

In this section, we first present the descriptive statistics of the determinants of IFRS adoption. This is followed by the correlation and regression analysis as well as the test of hypotheses.

4.1. Descriptive Statistics

Table 3 shows the descriptive statistics including the mean, standard deviation and the minimum and maximum values of all the variables. The average board size is about 9 members with a minimum of 5 and a maximum of 17 members. The board independence or average proportion of non-executive directors is 32.6%.About 68% of the companies are audited by the Big 4.The average company size is 7.69 billion naira with a minimum of 4.99 and a maximum of 8.45 billion.

The correlation matrix in Table 4 shows that turnover, profitability and earnings quality have significantly low and negative correlation with IFRS adoption. With regard to the test for multicollinearity, the correlation coefficients are low with the highest being 0.499.This indicates the absence of multicollinearity (see table 4).

Table 3. Descriptive statistics

Variables	Mean	Std. Dev.	Min	Max
BSIZE	9.13	2.39	5.00	17.00
BIND	0.326	0.32	0.00	0.89
AUD	0.68	0.47	0.00	1.00
FSIZE	7.69	0.762	4.99	8.45
CFO	5.22	2.68	0.00	9.32
LEV	2.09	6.51	2.33	76.24
TURN	4.05	36.53	0.08	449.85
GROWTH	0.21	1.12	-0.99	10.40
PROF	0.19	0.58	-2.24	5.68
LIQ	13.68	77.34	-4.082	543.00
EQ	0.69	15.46	-43.050	183.09

Table 4. Correlation matrix

	IFRS	BSIZE	BIND	AUD	FSIZE	CFO	LEV	TURN	GROWTH	PROF	LIQ	EQ
IFRS	1.000											
BSIZE	0.045	1.000										
BIND	-0.011	0.163	1.000									
AUD	0.390	0.158^{b}	-0.135^{b}	1.000								
FSIZE	0.073	0.499^{a}	-0.031	0.305^{a}	1.000							
CFO	0.014	0.264^{a}	-0.019	0.153^{b}	-0.018	1.000						
LEV	-0.099	-0.134^{c}	-0.096	0.083	0.007	0.007	1.000					
TURN	-0.119^{c}	-0.038	0.054	-0.115^{c}	0.018	0.117^{c}	-0.020	1.000				
GROWTH	-0.090	-0.048	-0.025	-0.030	0.066	0.104	-0.029	0.007	1.000			
PROF	-0.172^{b}	0.018	-0.005	0.224^{a}	0.125	0.205	0.239^{a}	-0.025	0.022	1.000		
LIQ	-0.004	0.061	-0.170	-0.257^{a}	-0.113	0.097	-0.031	-0.015	-0.010	0.003	1.000	
EQ	-0.134^{c}	0.016	-0.067	-0.102	0.003	-0.011	-0.013	-0.004	0.006	0.028	0.434^{a}	1.000

Note a,b,c are significant at 1%, 5% and 10% respectively

4.2. Regression Analysis

Table 5 shows the two statistical models for checking the effect of accounting ratios on IFRS adoption. Model 1 is a linear regression model that used OLS estimation: from the estimation we found that the model support that some accounting ratios have positive association with the tendencies for a company to comply with IFRS principles except for profitability and earnings quality which are negatively associated with IFRS adoption. Moreover, Model 2 is a logistic regression model and strongly supports that accounting ratios has positive impact on IFRS adoption. Again the R^2 values of 0.082 and 0.081 show that the independent variables explained only 8.2% and 8.1% respectively of the systemic variation in IFRS adoption.

Table 5. Regression results

Variables	Average Values		OLS Regression (Model 1)			Logistic Regression (Model 2)		
	IFRS= 0	IFRS=1	Coeff	T-value	Sign	Coeff	Z -value	Sign
Constant			0.633**	3.847	0.000	0.882	0.805	0.421
BSIZE	8.98	9.21	0.003	0.1619	0.872	0.038	0..441	0.659
BIND	2.92	2.85	-0.002	-0.175	0.862	-0.028	-0.427	0.669
AUD	0.68	0.68	0.009	0.096	0.924	0.148	0.333	0.739
FSIZE	7.09	7.21	0.076	1.189	0.237	0.339	1.113	0.266
CFO	2.21	2.62	0.011	0.707	0.481	0.047	0.628	0.530
LEV	3.01	1.66	-0.005	-0.759	0.449	-0.016	-0.409	0.683
TURN	10.21	1.00	-0.002	-1.548	0.124	-0.348	-1.335	0.182
GROWTH	0.35	0.14	-0.039	-1.118	0.266	-0.082	-0.454	0.649
PROF	**-0.33**	**0.11**	**-0.138***	-1.927	0.056	-0.845	-1.300	0.194
LIQ	14.25	13,53	0.000	0.509	0.611	0.003	0.678	0.498
EQ	-3.62	-0.77	**-0.004***	-1.664	0.098	-0.159	-0.692	0.489
R^2			0.081			0.082		
R^{-2}			0.015					

Note* implies significant at 10%

The results from both models show that FSIZE, CFO, LEV, TURN, GROWTH, LIQ, BSIZE, BIND and AUD do not have significant impact on compliance with IFRS adoption. The non-significance of these variables means that companies do not base their decisions to comply with IFRS considering these variables. However, profitability and earning quality have negative and significant association with IFRS adoption. The non-significance of FSIZE agrees with Ahmad and Nicholls(1994), Street and Gray (2002), Glaum and Street (2003), Masoud (2014) and, Ayuba and Gugong (2014) but disagrees with Dumontier and Raffournier (1998), Ashbaugh (2001), Bradshaw and Miller (2004), Tarca (2004), Affes and Callimaci (2007) and Hung and Subramanyam (2007). Again the non-significance that was found for liquidity support Daske et al (2008) but fail to agree with the significant positive association found by Platikanova & Perramon (2009) and Masoud (2014).The negative and significant association between profitability and IFRS adoption is inconsistent with the positive association found by Marta Silva Guerreiro et al (2008).

4.3. Financial Statement Effects of IFRS Adoption

We go further to compare the accounting ratios across firms that prepare their financial statement with the Nigerian GAAP and those that prepared with the IFRS regulations. The essence of this is to understand the differences that have existed in these accounting ratios and to find out if these differences are significant (figure 6).

Tables 6 shows the descriptive statistics and the mean, standard deviation, minimum and maximum values of the accounting values and ratios which is used to examine the financial effect in pre-IFRS (Nigerian GAAP) and post IFRS adoption period. Specifically, considering the mean in the pre and post IFRS adoption, there appears to be increase in the mean values of the balance sheet items like total assets, total liabilities, equity, current assets and liabilities and fixed assets. There is also increase in the current

Table 6. Descriptive statistics

	Variables	Minimum	Maximum	Mean	Standard Deviation
Under Nigerian GAAP	Total assets	98091 [a]	172248089	36966933.6	48026808,7
	Total liabilities	92,105	5565525466	127977167.9	785237870.5
	Equity	-1068343	7003598422	160306644.1	988896626.4
	Current asset	42487	6738651040	151796805.9	950771889.4
	Current liabilities	33209	62964090	13806630.76	174272382.99
	Fixed assets	400359	127781982	114829872.2	954630954.6
	Long term liabilities	8280	5560320319	1141705371	786242401.9
	Net income	-15619862	2304516057	52226844.62	325633040.3
	Sales or turnover	29430	4553064684	136695002.5	601808960.3
	Current ratio	-0.4734 [b]	12946130	37.457805	194.1182376
	Solvency ratio	-23.3396	122.9178	3.8691.36	18.4759263
	Indebtedness ratio	-2.3257	76.24448	3.018343	10.8584835
	Return on equity	-1.6612	5.6816	0.330403	0.8896396
Under IFRS	Total assets	115802	23258054	42710626.60	53078388.75
	Total liabilities	151,133	6602945454	157948872.4	93131610.4
	Equity	291702	7638709969	178230064.3	10785882215
	Current asset	195462	7738594389	173213669.8	109202971
	Current liabilities	37226	78516539	16357289.98	20234416.86
	Fixed assets	52074	135877631	130503043.2	1096425657
	Long term liabilities	15,200	6597639587	141591582.4	932508053.8
	Net income	-10147720	1196067395	29703419.48	169655281.5
	Sales or turnover	36133	258268251	44625471.82	62514003.78
	Current ratio	0.1551	1458.4976	38.862700	213.3725675
	Solvency ratio	-3.1201	27.0338	3.864084	6.6592088
	Indebtedness ratio	-1.9368	11.0839	1.593017	2.0752750
	Return on equity	-2.2440	0.7854	0.097192	0.3989948

Note: a the values of the accounting figures in the profit and loss accounts(ie sales and net income) and balance sheet items (total assets, total liabilities, fixed assets, long-term liabilities, current assets and current liabilities) which were taken from the annual reports of the sampled companies are in thousands (N'000). The percentage increases in the pre and post IFRS adoption period for the following items are: total assets (15.5%), total liabilities (23.4%), equity (11.2%), current assets (14.1%), current liabilities (18.5%), Fixed assets (13.6%);and the percentage decreases are long-term liabilities (87.5%),sales (67.4%) and net income (43.1%)

b. The accounting ratios are expressed as one accounting item over another. For instance, current ratio is current assets divided by the current liabilities. The mean values of the current ratio for pre-IFRS and post-IFRS are 37.46:1 and 38.86:1 respectively, representing an increase of 3.75%. The proportional change in the indebtedness ratio and return on equity represent a decrease of 47.2% and 70.6% respectively.

ratio. However, there are decreases in long-term liabilities, net income, sales, indebtedness ratio and return on equity. The solvency ratio remains unchanged given the mean value of 3.86 before and after IFRS adoption. It appears that IFRS adoption has more positive effect on the balance sheet items that the profit and loss items. However, the significant difference in the pre and post IFRS adoption period for these items is tested using the independent t-test.

The results in Table 7 indicate that for all the accounting figures and financial ratios, there were no significant difference in their values prior to, and after the adoption of IFRS. This is except for the significant difference in ROE. The result confirmed the findings of Ibiamke and Ateboh-Briggs (2014) that IFRS adoption has caused a negative and non-significant impact on the financial ratios of Nigerian listed firms. The result also supports Zayyad et al (2014) who found no significant difference between the pair of ratios computed from IFRS based financial statements and Nigerian GAAP based financial statements.

FUTURE RESEARCH DIRECTIONS

One limitation of this chapter is the non-consideration of macro-economic issues with regard to IFRS. Therefore, it is suggested that future researches should focus on:

1. Investigation of IFRS adoption in different sectors of emerging market economies using more firms with longer observation periods as well as inclusion both micro and macro-economic variables like culture, economic growth, political system, educational level, interest rate, capital and financial markets, privatization, foreign direct investment, legal environment, globalization and trade relationships, may yield more interesting results.

Table 7. Results of T-statistic

	Variable	T-Statistic	Sign.	Remark
Accounting Figures	Total assets	-0.921	0.359	No significant difference in pre and post IFRS adoption
	Total liabilities	-0.214	0.831	No significant difference in pre and post IFRS adoption
	Equity	0.006	0.995	No significant difference in pre and post IFRS adoption
	Current asset	-0.135	0.893	No significant difference in pre and post IFRS adoption
	Current liabilities	-1.112	0.268	No significant difference in pre and post IFRS adoption
	Fixed assets	0.775	0.442	No significant difference in pre and post IFRS adoption
	Long term liabilities	-0.187	0.852	No significant difference in pre and post IFRS adoption
	Net income	0.440	0.660	No significant difference in pre and post IFRS adoption
	Sales or turnover	1.482	0.148	No significant difference in pre and post IFRS adoption
Financial Ratios	Current ratio	0.208	0.836	No significant difference in pre and post IFRS adoption
	Solvency ratio	0.139	0.887	No significant difference in pre and post IFRS adoption
	Indebtedness ratio	1.206	0.230	No significant difference in pre and post IFRS adoption
	Return on equity	2.128*	0.035	Significant difference in pre and post IFRS adoption

Note* Significant at 5%

2. Investigation into the banking or financial sector and comparison with the non-financial sector may reveal additional results on IFRS adoption.
3. A survey study to examine the role of the board and other corporate governance agents on IFRS adoption in emerging economies.

CONCLUSION

The purpose of this chapter was to examine the determinants and financial statement effect of IFRS adoption in Nigeria. The results from the regression analyses show that firm characteristics and corporate governance variables have not played a dominant part in the mandatory adoption of IFRS in developing countries like Nigeria. Moreover, IFRS adoption has had insignificant impact on most accounting figures and ratios. The results may be useful for standards setting bodies in developing countries deciding to adopt the IFRS as it shows that the firm characteristic and corporate governance factors may not influence firms' decisions to comply with the regulations of the standard. It will also help academic researchers wanting to study the factors that determine IFRS adoption at the firm's level.

REFERENCES

Abata, M. A. (2015). The impact of international financial reporting standards (IFRS) adoption on financial reporting practice in the Nigerian banking sector. *Journal of Policy and Development Studies*, *9*(2), 169–184. doi:10.12816/0011215

Abdelsalam, O., & Weetman, P. (2003). Introducing international accounting standards to an emerging capital market: Relative familiarity and language effects in Egypt. *Journal of International Accounting, Auditing & Taxation*, *12*(1), 63–84. doi:10.1016/S1061-9518(03)00002-8

Adegbie, F. F. (2011). International financial reporting standards adoption, implications on management accounting and taxation in Nigerian economy. *International Journal of Research in Commerce Economics and Management*, *1*(2), 1–6.

Adegbie, S. Q. (2010). *IFRS adoption in Nigeria.* A paper presented at the World Bank Seminar on IFRS adoption in Nigeria.

Adekoya, O. (2011). Similarities and differences, IFRS and Nigerian GAAP. Lagos: Pricewater House Coopers International Limited (PWCIL).

Affes, H., & Callimaci, A. (2007). Les déterminants de l'adoption anticipée des norms comptables internationales: Choix financier ou opportunisme. *Comptabilité Contrôle Audit*, *13*(2), 149–166. doi:10.3917/cca.132.0149

Agca, A., & Aktas, R. (2007). First time application of IFRS and its impact on financial ratios: A study on Turkish listed firms. *Problems and Perspectives in Management*, *5*(2), 99–112.

Ahmed, K., & Nicholls, D. (1994). The impact of non - financial company characteristics on mandatory disclosure compliance in developing countries: The case of Bangladesh. *The International Journal of Accounting*, *29*, 62–77.

Al-Akra, M., Jahangir, A. M., & Marashdeh, O. (2009). Development of accounting regulation in Jordan. *The International Journal of Accounting*, *44*(2), 163–186. doi:10.1016/j.intacc.2009.03.003

Al-Basteki, H. (1995). The voluntary adoption of international accounting standards by Bahraini corporations. *Advances in International Accounting*, *8*, 47–64.

Albu, N., & Albu, C. N. (2012). IFRS in an emerging economy: Lessons from Romania. *Australian Accounting Review*, *22*(4), 341–352. doi:10.1111/j.1835-2561.2012.00196.x

Armstrong, C. S., Barth, M. E., Jagolinzer, A. D., & Riedl, E. J. (2010).Market reaction to the adoption of IFRS in Europe. *Accounting Review*. Retrieved from http://papers.ssrn.com/sol3papers.cfm?abstractid=903429

Ashbaugh, H. (2001). Non-US firms' accounting standard choices. *Journal of Accounting and Public Policy*, *20*(2), 129–153. doi:10.1016/S0278-4254(01)00025-4

Ashbaugh, H., & Pincus, M. (2001). Domestic accounting standards, international accounting standards and the predictability of earnings. *Journal of Accounting Research*, *39*(3), 417–434. doi:10.1111/1475-679X.00020

Athanasios, V., & Stergios, A. (2010). Measuring investors' reaction to the adoption of international financial reporting standards in Greece, using a market-based model. *American Journal of Economics and Business Administration*, *2*(1), 103–112. doi:10.3844/ajebasp.2010.103.112

Ayuba, A., & Gugong, B. K. (2014). Does government policy and company size influenced stakeholders perception on the adoption of international financial reporting standards (IFRS) in Nigeria. *International Journal of Economics. Finance and Management Sciences*, *2*(4), 257–262.

Ball, R., Kothari, S. P., & Robin, A. (2000). The effect of international institutional factors on properties of accounting earnings. *Journal of Accounting and Economics*, *29*(1), 1–51. doi:10.1016/S0165-4101(00)00012-4

Ball, R., Robin, A., & Wu, J. (2003). Incentives versus standards: Properties of accounting income in four East Asian countries. *Journal of Accounting and Economics*, *36*(1-3), 235–270. doi:10.1016/j.jacceco.2003.10.003

Barth, M. (2008). Global financial reporting: Implications for US academics. *Accounting Review*, *83*(5), 1159–1179. doi:10.2308/accr.2008.83.5.1159

Barth, M. E., Clinch, G., & Shibano, T. (1999). International accounting harmonization and global equity markets. *Journal of Accounting Research*, *46*, 467–498. doi:10.1111/j.1475-679X.2008.00287.x

Barth, M. E., Landsman, W. R., & Lang, M. (2008). International accounting standards and accounting quality. *Journal of Accounting Research*, *46*(3), 467–498. doi:10.1111/j.1475-679X.2008.00287.x

Barth, M.E., Landsman, W.R. & Lang, M.H. (2007). *International accounting standard and accounting quality*. Stanford University Graduate School of Business Research. Retrieved from http:ssrn.com/abstract=668041

Bartov, E., Goldberg, S., & Kim, M. (2005). Comparative value relevance among German, US and International accounting standards: A German stock market perspective. *Journal of Accounting, Auditing & Finance*, *20*, 95–119.

Beatty, A., Chamberlain, S., & Magliolo, J. (1996). An empirical analysis of the economic implications of fair value accounting for investment securities. *Journal of Accounting and Economics*, *22*(1-3), 43–77. doi:10.1016/S0165-4101(96)00429-6

Bissessur, S., & Hodgson, A. (2012). Stock market synchronicity- an alternative approach to assessing the information impact of Australian IFRS. *Accounting and Finance*, *52*(1), 187–212. doi:10.1111/j.1467-629X.2010.00388.x

Blanchette, M., Racicot, F. E., & Girard, J. Y. (2011). *The effects of IFRS on financial ratios: Early evidence in Canada*. Certified General Accountants Association of Canada.

Blanchette, M., Racicot, F. E., & Sedzro, K. (2013). *IFRS Adoption in Canada: An empirical analysis of the impact on financial statements*. Certified General Accountants Association of Canada.

Brown, P., & Tarca, A. (2005). A commentary on issues relating to the enforcement of international financial reporting standards in the EU. *European Accounting Review*, *14*(1), 181–212. doi:10.1080/0963818042000338997

Callao, S., Jarne, J. I., & Laínez, J. A. (2007). Adoption of IFRS in Spain: Effect on the comparability and relevance of financial reporting. *Journal of International Accounting, Auditing & Taxation*, *16*(2), 148–178. doi:10.1016/j.intaccaudtax.2007.06.002

Chamisa, E. E. (2000). The relevance and observance of IASC standards in developing countries and the particular case of Zimbabwe. *The International Journal of Accounting*, *35*(2), 267–286. doi:10.1016/S0020-7063(00)00049-2

Choi, F., & Levich, R. M. (1991). Behavioural effects of international accounting diversity. *Accounting Horizons*, (June): 1–13.

Choi, F., & Meek, G. (2008). *International Accounting* (6th ed.). Upper Saddle River, NJ: Pearson Education Inc.

Christensen, H. B., Lee, E., & Walker, M. (2007). Cross-section variation in the economic consequence of international accounting harmonization: The case of mandatory adoption in the U.K. *The International Journal of Accounting*, *42*(4), 341–379. doi:10.1016/j.intacc.2007.09.007

Christensen, H. B., Lee, E., & Walker, M. (2008). *Incentives or standards: what determines accounting quality changes around IFRS adoption?* Working Paper. University of Chicago and University of Manchester. Retrieved from http://papers.ssrn.com/sol3/papers.cfm?abstract_id=1013054

Covrig, V. M., Defond, L., & Hung, M. (2007). Home bias, foreign mutual fund holdings, and the voluntary adoption of international accounting standards. *Journal of Accounting Research*, *45*(1), 41–70. doi:10.1111/j.1475-679X.2007.00226.x

Daske, H., Hail, L., Leuz, C., & Verdi, R. (2008). Mandatory IFRS reporting around the world: Early evidence on the economic consequences. *Journal of Accounting Research*, *46*, 1085–1142.

Daske, H. C., Leuz, C., & Verdi, R. (2007). *Adopting a label: Heterogeneity in the economic consequence of IFRS adoption. Initiative on Global Markets*. The University of Chicago, Graduate School of Business. Working Paper No.5.

Deloitte and Touche. (2004). *First-Time Adoption: A Guide to IFRS*. Retrieved from www.iasplus.com/dttpubs/ifrs1guide.pdf

DiMaggio, P. J., & Powell, W. W. (1983). The iron cage revisited: Institutional isomorphism and collective rationality in organizational fields. *American Sociological Review*, *48*(2), 147–160. doi:10.2307/2095101

Ding, Y., Hope, O., Jeanjean, T., & Stolowy, H. (2006). Differences between domestic accounting standards and IAS: Measurement, determinants and implications. *Journal of Accounting and Public Policy*, *26*(1), 1–38. doi:10.1016/j.jaccpubpol.2006.11.001

Donwa, P. A., & Odia, J. O. (2012). Initial challenges of first-time adoption of International Financial Reporting Standards in Nigeria. *National Accountants*, *20*(1), 33–41.

Dumontier, P., & Raffournier, B. (1998). Why firms comply voluntarily with IAS; an empirical analysis with Swiss data. *Journal of International Financial Management and Accounting*, *9*(3), 216–245. doi:10.1111/1467-646X.00038

Fox, A., Helliar, C., Veneziani, M., & Hannah, G. (2013). The costs and benefits of IFRS implementation in the UK and Italy. *Journal of Applied Accounting Research*, *14*(1), 86–101. doi:10.1108/09675421311282568

Gassen, J., & Sellhorn, T. (2006). Applying IFRS in Germany - determinants and consequences. *Betriebswirtschaftliche Forschung und Praxis*, *58*(4), 365–386.

Gastón, S. C., García, C. F., Jarne, J. I. J., & Gadea, J. A. L. (2010). IFRS adoption in Spain and the United Kingdom: Effects on accounting numbers and relevance. *Advances in Accounting, incorporating. Advances in International Accounting*, *26*(2), 304–313. doi:10.1016/j.adiac.2010.08.003

Gordon, E., Jorgensen, B., & Linthicum, C. (2008). *Could IFRS replace US GAAP? A comparison of earnings attributes and informativeness in the US Market.* Working paper. Temple University, Columbia University, and University of Texas at San Antonio.

Hail, L., Leuz, C., & Wysocki, P. (2010). Global accounting convergence and the potential adoption of IFRS by the U.S. (Part I): Conceptual underpinnings and economics analysis. *Accounting Horizons*, *24*(3), 355–394. doi:10.2308/acch.2010.24.3.355

Hope, O., Jin, J., & Kang, T. (2006). Empirical evidence on jurisdictions that adopt FIRS. *Journal of International Accounting Research*, *5*(2), 1–20. doi:10.2308/jiar.2006.5.2.1

Hove, M. (1986). The Anglo-American influence on international accounting standards: The case of the disclosure standards of the international accounting standards committee. *Research in Third World Accounting*, *1*, 55–66.

Hung, M., & Subramanyam, K. R. (2007). Financial statement effects of adopting international accounting standards: The case of Germany. *Review of Accounting Studies*, *12*(4), 623–657. doi:10.1007/s11142-007-9049-9

Ibiamke, N. A., & Ateboh-Briggs, P. B. (2014). Financial ratios effect of international financial reporting standards (IFRS) adoption in Nigeria. *International Journal of Business and Management Invention*, *3*(3), 50–59.

ICAEW. (2007). *EU Implementation of IFRS and the fair value directive.* A report for the European Commission.

Irvine, H. J., & Lucas, N. (2006). The rationale and impact of the adoption of international financial reporting standards on developing nations: The case of the United Arab Emirates. In *Proceedings 18th Asian-Pacific Conference on International Accounting Issues*.

Irvine, H. (2008). The global institutionalization of financial reporting: The case of the United Arab Emirates. *Accounting Forum*, *32*(2), 125–142. doi:10.1016/j.accfor.2007.12.003

Jaruga, A., Fijalkowska, J., Jaruga-Baranowska, M., & Frendzel, M. (2007). The Impact of IAS/IFRS on Polish accounting regulations and their practical implementation in Poland. *Accounting in Europe*, *4*(1), 67–78. doi:10.1080/17449480701308675

Jindrichovska, I., & Kubickova, D, (2012). *Impact of IFRS adoption on key financial ratios: The case of the Czech Republic*. Paper accepted for EUFIN Conference, Prague, Czech Republic.

Joshi, P. L., & Ramadhan, S. (2002). The adoption of international accounting standards by small & closely held companies: Evidence from Bahrain. *The International Journal of Accounting*, *37*, 429–440.

Judge, W., Li, S., & Pinsker, R. (2010). National adoption of international accounting standards: An institutional perspective. *Corporate Governance: An International Review*, *18*(3), 161–174. doi:10.1111/j.1467-8683.2010.00798.x

Karamanou, I., & Nischiotis, G. (2005). *The valuation effects of firms voluntary adoption of international accounting standards*. Working Paper. University of Cyprus. Retrieved from http://papers.ssrn.com/so13/paper.com?abstractid=676323

Klimczak, K. M. (2011). Market reaction to mandatory IFRS adoption: Evidence from Poland. *Accounting and Management Information Systems*, *10*(2), 228–248.

Lantto, A., & Sahlström, P. (2007). Impact of international financial reporting standard adoption on key financial ratios. *Accounting and Finance*, *49*(2), 341–361. doi:10.1111/j.1467-629X.2008.00283.x

Latridis, G. (2010). IFRS adoption and financial statement effects: The UK case. *International Research Journal of Finance and Economics*, *38*, 165–172.

Leuz, C., & Wysocki, P.D. (2008). *Economic consequences of financial reporting and disclosure regulation: A review and suggestions for future research.* SSRN eLibrary.

lyoha, F. O., & Jafaru, J. (2011). *Institutional infrastructure and the adoption of international financial reporting standards in Nigeria*. Academic Press.

Madawaki, A. (2012). Adoption of international financial reporting standards in developing countries: The case of Nigeria. *International Journal of Business and Management*, *7*(3), 152–161. doi:10.5539/ijbm.v7n3p152

Maddala, G. S. (1991). A perspective on the use of limited-dependent variables models in accounting research. *Accounting Review*, *66*(4), 788–807.

Guerreiro, M. S., Rodrigues, L. L., & Craig, R. (2008). The preparedness of companies to adopt international financial reporting standards: Portuguese evidence. *Accounting Forum*, *32*(1), 75–88. doi:10.1016/j.accfor.2007.11.001

Masoud, N. (2014). Accounting, FRQ, emerging countries transition: How can a country implement an IFRS standard change successfully? *Global Journal of Management and Business Research: D Accounting and Auditing*, *14*(2/1), 36-55.

Meeks, G., & Swann, P. (2009). Accounting standards and the economics of standards. *Accounting and Business Review*, *39*(3), 191–210. doi:10.1080/00014788.2009.9663360

Mike, M. (2009). Seminar Understanding IFRS. National GAAP vs IFRS, Lagos, Nigeria.

Mir, M. Z., & Rahaman, A. S. (2005). The Adoption of international accounting standards in Bangladesh. *Accounting, Auditing & Accountability Journal*, *18*(6), 816–841. doi:10.1108/09513570510627720

Nikolaos, E., Konstantinos, P., & Dimitrios, V. (2013). *The impact of IFRS on ratios of listed and new listed companies of Athens Exchange*. Academic Press.

Nobes, C. (1998). Towards a general model of the reasons for international differences in financial reporting. *Abacus*, *34*(2), 162–187. doi:10.1111/1467-6281.00028

Odia, J. O. (2013). Factors affecting the Adoption of IFRS in Nigeria. Sokoto. *Journal of Social Sciences*.

Odia, J. O. (2015). *Perception of accounting academia and practitioners of IFRS adoption in Nigeria. ICAN Journal of Accounting and Finance, 4(1).*

Odia, J. O., & Ogiedu, K. O. (2013). IFRS Adoption: Issues, challenges and lessons for Nigeria and other adopters. *Mediterranean Journal of Social Sciences*, *4*(3), 389–399.

Okaro, S. C. (2011). *From SAS to IFRS- emerging issues and implications for Nigeria*. Retrieved from http://sscrn.com/abstract=1956027

Okere, E. O. (2009). *International financial reporting and accounting issues: Imperatives of attainment of economic development in Nigeria*. ICAN 39 Annual Accountants Conference.

Okpala, K. E. (2012). Adoption of IFRS and financial statements effects: The perceived implications on FDI and Nigeria Economy. *Australian Journal of Business and Management Research*, *2*(5), 76–83.

Owolabi, A., & Iyoha, F. (2012). Adopting International Financial Reporting Standards (IFRS) in Africa: Benefits, prospects and challenges. *African Journal of Accounting Auditing and Finance*, *1*(1), 77–86. doi:10.1504/AJAAF.2012.046127

Oyedele, T. (2011). *An overview of IFRS and challenges posed to professionals*. A paper presented at a seminar on IFRS adoption in Nigeria. The Chartered Institute of Taxation of Nigeria.

Palepu, K. G. (1986). Predicting takeover targets: A methodological and empirical analysis. *Journal of Accounting and Economics*, *8*(1), 3–35. doi:10.1016/0165-4101(86)90008-X

Platikanova, P., & Perramon, J. (2009). *Economic consequences of the first-time IFRS introduction in Europe*. Working Paper. Available at SSRN: http://ssrn.com/abstract=1005364

Punda, P. (2011). *The impact of international financial reporting standards (IFRS) adoption on key financial ratios – Evidence from the UK*. (Master's Thesis). Aarhus School of Business.

Ramanna, K., & Sletten, E. (2009). *Why do countries adopt international financial reporting standards?* Working Paper. Harvard Business School.

Shima, K. M., & Yang, D. C. (2012). Factors affecting IFRS adoption. *International Journal of Business*, *17*(3), 276–298.

Silva, F. J., DoCouto, G. M., & Cordeiro, R. M. (2009). Measuring the impact of international financial reporting standards (IFRS) to financial information of Portuguese companies RevistaUniversoContábil. *Blumenau*, *5*(1), 129–144.

Stergios, A., Vazakidis, A., & Dritsakis, N. (2004). *Financial statement effects of adopting international accounting standards*. Working Paper Series, University of Macedonia. Retrieved from http://users.uom.gr/~drits/publications/Financial_Statement_Effects.pdf

Street, D. L., & Gray, S. J. (2002). Factors influencing the extent of corporate compliance with international accounting standards: Summary of a research monograph. *Journal of International Accounting, Auditing & Taxation*, *11*(1), 51–76. doi:10.1016/S1061-9518(02)00054-X

Taiwo, F. H., & Adejare, A. T. (2014). Empirical analysis of the effect of international financial reporting standard (IFRS) adoption on accounting practices in Nigeria. *Archives of Business Research*, *2*(2), 1–14. doi:10.14738/abr.22.43

Tanko, M. (2012). The effect of international financial reporting standards (IFRS) adoption on the performance of firms in Nigeria. *Journal of Administration and Economic Sciences*, *5*(2), 133–157.

Tarca, A. (2004). International convergence of accounting practices: Choosing between IAS and US GAAP. *Journal of International Financial Management and Accounting*, *15*(1), 60–91. doi:10.1111/j.1467-646X.2004.00102.x

Tsalavoutas, I., & Evans, L. (2010). Transition to IFRS in Greece: Financial statement effects and auditor size. *Managerial Auditing Journal*, *25*(8), 814–842. doi:10.1108/02686901011069560

Umoren, A. O., & Enang, E. R. (2015). IFRS adoption and value relevance of financial statements of Nigerian listed banks. *International Journal of Finance and Accounting*, *4*(1), 1–7.

Wysocki, P. D. (2011). New institutional accounting and IFRS. *Accounting and Business Review*, *41*(3), 309–328. doi:10.1080/00014788.2011.575298

Xiao, J. Z., Weetman, P., & Sun, M. (2004). Political influence and coexistence of a uniform accounting system and accounting standards: Recent developments in China. *Abacus*, *40*(2), 194–218.

Zakari, M. I. (2010). *IFRS as a tool for cross-border financial reporting*. A paper presented at the Institute of Chartered Accountants of Nigeria (ICAN) conference on IFRS in Lagos.

Zayyad, A., Ahmad, U. B., & Mubaraq, S. (2014). Financial ratios as performance measure: A comparison of IFRS and Nigerian GAAP. *Accounting and Management Information Systems*, *13*(1), 82–97.

Zeghal, D., & Mhedhbi, K. (2006). An analysis of the factors affecting the adoption of international accounting standards by developing countries. *The International Journal of Accounting*, *41*(4), 373–386. doi:10.1016/j.intacc.2006.09.009

Zehri, F., & Chouaibi, J. (2013). Adoption determinants of the international accounting standards IAS/IFRS by the developing countries. *Journal of Economics. Finance and Administrative Science*, *18*(35), 56–62. doi:10.1016/S2077-1886(13)70030-1

APPENDIX

Table 8. Key differences between Nigeria-GAAP and IFRS

	NIGERIA GAAP	IFRS
Financial statement presentation	Income statement Balance sheet Cash flow statement Value added statement Accounting policies Notes	-Statement of comprehensive income (including income statement). - Statement of financial position (balance sheet) - Statement of changes in equity - Statement of cash flows - Accounting policies - Notes - Significant management estimates and judgments
Property plant and Equipment	Measured using cost model	Measured using cost model with detailed guidance regarding: - Componentization - Useful lives - Residual values -Impairment calculations and identifying cash generating units.
Related parties	Limited disclosure but expected	Detailed guidance on identification of related parties and detailed disclosure of related parties and transactions
Segment reporting	More on geography segment	- Operation segments based on management's view. - Threshold for reportable segments is results or assets of an individual segment should be 10% or more of all segments. - If the aggregate revenue of all reported segments on this basis less than75% of total, then more segments required until 75% threshold is reached.
IFRS 1- First time adoption of IFRS	Not applicable	Provides guidance and requirements on the transition to IFRS. Also provides relief for certain items in the preparation of the opening balance sheet.
Financial guarantees	Disclosed as contingent liabilities	Requires financial guarantees to be recognized at their fair value
Scope of consolidation	General principles investment under control are consolidated.	SPEs are potentially also consolidated
Employee benefits	General expense and disclosures on pensions	-Complex criteria of accounting -Recognize the undiscounted amount of short-term employee benefits
Risk management disclosures	Limited disclosure of foreign exchange and credit risk	Disclosure required for: - Credit risk and - Liquidity risk - Price risk - Capital risk management - Risk management
Leases	Based on general guidelines –operating and finance leases	-Currently similar but updates to IFRS e.g. IFRIC 4 will lead to only finance leases hence more items coming unto balance sheet. - Fair value and amortized costs used in valuations -Certain transactions/contracts containing hidden leases which needed to be accounted for
Impairments	No specific standard	- Carry out impairment test based on trigger vent - IFRS 36 – impairment on non – financial assets - IAS 39 – impairment on financial assets
Financial asset classification and valuation	Classification include: - Cost - Amortized cost	Classification include: -Amortized cost - Fair value This is driven by the business model and nature of the instrument.

Source: Oyedele, T. (2011)

Chapter 17
The Effect of International Financial Reporting Standards Adoption on Foreign Direct Investment and the Economy

Christopher Boachie
Central University College, Ghana

ABSTRACT

This chapter examines the effect of International Financial Reporting Standards (IFRS) adoption on Foreign Direct Investment (FDI) and Ghanaian economy. It is a cross sectional survey study, with the population consisting of both Preparers and Users of financial statements. Stratified Random sampling method was adopted to gather primary data. Findings showed that IFRS has been adopted in Ghana and it is perceived that IFRS implementation promotes FDI inflows and economic growth. This study recommends all stakeholders to have full implementation to reap benefits of the IFRS and principle - based standards. The implication is that preparers need to work on their skills and expertise gap through training and development and to ensure that these standards are included in the academic and professional curricula. Moreover, regulatory bodies should monitor and enforce these standards but where local content is needed, convergence should be the solution.

1. INTRODUCTION

The importance of international accounting practice studies has grown over the past few years in order to meet economic agent demands and to facilitate international business practices. It is essential to understand that international accounting convergence is an important topic for capital market regulators, investors, markets, governments and all others who deal with financial information of public companies. This brings out the importance of accounting as being an essential fiscal tool for various economic agents. The merit of international accounting convergence lies in its ability to minimize negative effects resulting from diversity of accounting practices in different countries (Cordeiro, Couto, & Silva, 2007). In such

DOI: 10.4018/978-1-4666-9876-5.ch017

a scenario, the introduction of International Financial Reporting Standards (IFRS) for listed companies in many countries around the world is viewed as one of the most significant regulatory changes in accounting history (Daske, Hail, Leuz, & Verdi, 2008).

This research constitutes an extension of the study conducted by Zeghal and Mhedhbi (2006) who concentrated on the major factors that influence the adoption of IAS by the developing countries. However seeing the considerable rising number of emerging countries intending to apply the IFRS and with the accelerated processes over the years ranging between 2008 and 2015 this chapters' contribution consists mainly of testing the effect of IFRS on two parameters: FDI and economic growth.

The adaptation of International Financial Reporting Standard has become a hot topic globally after a series of arguments. Although there are still different schools of thought endlessly arguing in favour of individual countries, why and how to adopt IFRS, the academic and business community begin to look further into IFRS empirically today. One of the hot topics is whether countries will benefit economically or not if they adopt IFRS. This problem is being expounded and discussed widely by scholars but failed to reach agreement globally. It is pity that there are few empirical literatures about the relationship between the adoption of IFRS and foreign direct investment and the economy. The aim of this chapter is to investigate the interaction between IFRS, foreign direct investment and the Ghanaian economy. This chapter contributes to the literature on IFRS by answering two questions: (i) is there any significant relationship between the adoption of IFRS and FDI? (ii) how does FDI inflow affect economic growth in Ghana? The remainder of this chapter proceeds as follows. The second section provides literature review and develop hypothesis. Third section describes the research design and the data. Fourth section reports the empirical results and fifth section concludes

2. LITERATURE REVIEW

2.1 Background

Internationalization of economic trade and globalization of businesses is on the ascendency. Consequently, financial statements prepared according to a nation's local accounting system may hardly meet the needs of investors, business partners, financiers and decision-makers who are conversant with international standards. Meanwhile, developing and emerging markets are the target of the world's leading industries that are operating in the saturated western countries. To better undertake their activities in developing countries; they must adopt international accounting standards that suit needs (Zeghal & Mhedhbi, 2006). Foreign investment is a major boost to the economies of developing countries. An investor may demand vivid and comprehensible financial information from a firm. This underscores the reason why developing countries must adopt International Accounting Standards (Zeghal & Mhedhbi, 2006).

To bridge the gap between accounting standards among countries, the International Accounting Standards Committee (IASC) was founded in 1973 by a group of professional accounting practitioners with an attempt to formulate a uniform and global accounting standards that would aim at reducing the discrepancies in international accounting principles and reporting practices. In this light, the International Accounting Standard (IAS) was proposed which has actively been championing the uniformity and standardization of accounting principles over two decades now. Meanwhile, in April 2001, the International Accounting Standards Board (IASB) took over the setting of International Accounting Standards from the International Accounting Standard (IASC). Henceforth, the IASB updated the already existing

International Accounting Standard (IAS) and referred to them as the International Financial Reporting Standards (IFRS). This study focuses on how Ghana as a typical case of a developing economy adopted the International Financial Reporting Standards and the possible effect on the economy.

In January, 2007, the Minister of Finance and Economic Planning - Ghana formally launched the adoption of IFRS. By December 2007, listed companies, government business enterprises, banks, insurance companies, securities brokers, pension and investment banks and public utilities have adopted IFRS and prepared their financial statements in accordance with the IFRS. In an address to the participants at the launching, the minister referred to a Report on Observance of Standards and Codes (ROSC) on Ghana that the world bank issued in March 2006, and noted that 'the adoption of IFRS would address certain weaknesses the ROSC of Ghana has identified' (UN, 2007).

There are proponents as well as opponents who have arguments for and against the global adoption of IFRS. According to Barth (2007), the adoption of a common body of international standards is expected to have the following benefits: lower the cost of financial information processing and auditing to capital market participants as users, familiarity with one common set of international accounting standards instead of various local accounting standards by Accountants and Auditors of financial reports, comparability and uniformity of financial statements among companies and countries making the work of investment analysts easy, attraction of foreign investors in addition to general capital market liberalization. Ball (2006) stated that many developing countries where the quality of local governance institutions is low, the decision to adopt IFRS will be beneficial. Lipsey and Chrystal (2003) noted that FDI often generates somewhat higher-paying jobs than might otherwise be available to local citizens, it generates investment that may not be possible with the local resources only, it links the recipient economy into the world economy in manners that would be hard to achieve by new firms of a purely local origin. According to Lipsey and Chrystal (2003) the FDI alters country's comparative advantages and improves its competitiveness through technology transfer and effects myriad externalities, domestic investment which can alter a country's volume and pattern of trade in many income enhancing directions. Countries that suffer from corruption, slow-moving, or ineffectual government are likely to resist the change (La Porta, Lopez-de-Silanes, Shleifer, &Vishny, 1999) but in such countries, the opportunity and switching costs are lower which makes the possibility of adopting IFRS advantageous. Kumar (2007) stated that the foreign capital has the potential to deliver enormous benefits to developing nations. In addition to helping bridge the gap between savings and investment in capital-scarce economies, capital often brings with it modern technology and encourages development of more mature financial sectors. Capital flows have proven effective in promoting growth and productivity in countries that have enough skilled workers and infrastructure. Some economists believe that capital flows also help discipline governments' macroeconomic policies.

Omneya, Abd-Elsalam and Weetman (2003) have examined the language effect on the first introduction of IFRS in Egypt. Through a sample of 72 locally listed companies, the authors have shown that Egyptian companies continue to encounter difficulties in implementing IFRS, given the disparities between the IFRS spirit and philosophy in respect of the local accounting traditions and cultures. This chapter reports evidence that adoption of IFRS has a positive effect on FDI and the economy. Chamisa (2000) has examined the international standards' role in improving the quality of financial information produced for a stock market in the developing countries. He noted that these standards are critically and crucially important for the developing countries with an active financial and capital market and are devoid of such importance regarding the other developing countries. Actually, this observation has been confirmed through the study conducted by Zeghal and Mhedhbi (2006) dealing with a sample examination composed of 32 developing countries having adopted the IAS and some other 32 countries which have not adopted them. They show that the developing countries enjoying capital markets, advanced education levels and high economic growth rates are most inclined to adopt the IFRS. Moreover, on examining the development of accounting regulations in Jordan, Al-Akra, Jahangir, and Marashdeh (2009) have analysed the impact of economic, political, legal and cultural factors on promoting the accounting practices. They concluded that the political and economic factors are the elements which contribute most to this development. From all that has been mentioned in the literature review, one can deduce that the research in the field of IFRS adoption determinants with respect with to the developing countries remains limited with somewhat mixed results. In fact, most of the reviewed studies have highlighted the importance of institutional criteria factors (economic growth, education level, capital markets) along with some specific features regarding these countries' operating companies (size, indebtedness levels, the quality of external audit) in deciding to adopt these standards.

2.2 Definition of Foreign Direct Investment

Foreign direct investment (FDI) in developing economies has grown rapidly following financial and political transformation. To increase their share of FDI inflows, most countries have eased restrictions on foreign direct investment, strengthened macro stability, privatized state-owned enterprises, instituted domestic financial reforms, capital account liberalization and granted tax incentives and subsidies. Ghana for instance through the Free Zones Act, 1995 and the Ghana Investment Promotion Act 1994 has granted certain tax incentives and investor protection policies to attract foreign investors and also make the environment conducive for their operations. This initiative and policy taken in Ghana have increased the number of foreign direct investment and helped in economic growth.

FDI has been defined by the International Monetary Fund as an investment that is made to acquire a lasting interest in an enterprise operating in an economy other than that of the investor, the investors' purpose being to have an effective voice in the management of the enterprise (IMF, 2012). Denisia (2010) also considers the definition of FDI from a macroeconomic view point, and indicates that FDI is a particular form of capital flows across borders, from countries of origin to host countries, which are found in the balance of payments. The variables of interest according to Denisia (2010, p. 54) are capital flows, stocks and revenues obtained from investments.

Foreign Direct Investment (FDI) in Ghana

The country of Ghana has the fastest growing economy in Africa with a GDP (US $) close to 42 billion (IMF, 2012). The 25 years of comparatively healthy management, competitive business environment, and sustained reductions in poverty levels has boosted Ghana's economy. Blessed with abundant natural resources, agricultural sector accounts for roughly one-quarter of GDP and employs more than half of the workforce, mainly small landholders. 2013 Index of Economic Freedom shows that Ghana's economic score is 61.3 and is ranked 7th out of 46 in the Sub-Saharan African region making its the overall score rise above the world's average. The Government of Ghana has been taking significant steps to draw FDI into the country, according to the 2013 Investment Climate Statement. To encourage foreign investment, the Government has replaced the previously unfriendly regulations with investor friendly laws. The Ghana Investment Promotion Center (GIPC) Act, 1994 (Act 478) governs investment in all sectors of the economy except minerals and mining, oil and gas and the Free Zones. Sector-specific laws further regulate banking, non-banking financial institutions, insurance, fishing, securities, telecommunications, energy, mining, and real estate.

2.3 Role and Nature of Foreign Direct Investment in Ghana

Foreign direct investment (FDI) plays an extraordinary and growing role in global business. It acts as agent of economic growth through generating and transplanting of technology, managerial skills and linkages to the world market. It provides Ghanaian firms with new marketing channels, cheaper production facilities, products, skills and financing. It provides an inflow of foreign capital and investment in addition to an increase in job opportunities in Ghana.

Companies who invest abroad are mainly looking to take advantage of cheaper wages, advanced infrastructure and skilled workforce and a less regulated business environment. As countries develop and approach industrialized nation status, inward FDI contributes to their further integration into the global economy by engendering and boosting foreign trade flows. Apparently, several factors come into play. They include the development and strengthening of international networks of related enterprises and an increasing importance of foreign subsidiaries in MNEs' strategies for distribution, sales and marketing (Andre-Pascal, 2002).

Trend of Foreign Direct Investment

When Rawlings first seized power in 1979, he adopted a radical and anti-business stance; growth fell to -3.2% and an FDI inflow of $2.8 million in 1981. The state of the economy witnessed a further negative growth rate of 3.5% in 1981 to 6.9% in 1982 in the year of his second advent; however, net inflow of FDI remained constant at $16.3 million (Tsikata, Asante, & Gyasi, 2004). In 1983, the Government of Ghana initiated the Economic Recovery Programme (ERP) and later Structural Adjustment Programme (SAP). These policies were adopted primarily to reverse the post-independence economic decline, reduce the impact of the 1980 debt crisis and, facilitate the attraction of value-added FDI inflows to Ghana. The ERP has been described as being generally successful at stimulating more FDI inflow through the lowering of inflation, the removal of tariff barrier which were greater impediments to FDI inflow and the abolishing of exchange rate controls. (Aryeetey, Barthel, Busse, Loehr, & Osei, 2000).

Since the advent of the Economic Recovery Programme (ERP) in 1983, three historical phases of FDI flows in Ghana can be distinguished (Tsikata *et al.*, 2000). The first period which spans from1983 to 1988 had a sluggish FDI net inflows, averaging US$4.2 million per annum, and the highest and lowest inflows during the period being US$5.6 million in 1984 and US $2.0 million in 1985 respectively. The high FDI inflow in 1985 was as a result of the establishment of a new investment code (PNDCL 116) that was to serve as the central Investment promotion Agency. Under this investment code were several incentives including tax holidays, exemption for import duties on capital and accelerated depreciation allowances. The second period which starts from 1989 to 1992 also recorded moderate inflows averaging US$18.1 million per annum with the highest and lowest inflows being US$22.5 million in 1992 and US$14.8 million in 1990, respectively. In addition, the period 1993 to 1996 witnessed significant (remaining in three digits) and oscillatory FDI net inflows, which reached a peak of US$233 million in 1994 (with the privatization of Ashanti Goldfields Company AGC), but dropped to US$106.5 million in 1995 before coming back to US$120 million in 1996. The peak inflow in 1944 was due to revision of the investment code which ultimately led to the passing of the GIPC Act, 1994 (Act 478). The government also established the Ghana Investment Promotion Council (GIPC) to not only encourage and promote investment in the country but also to coordinate investment in the country. The Gateway project was also initiated, along with all its incentives to make the country attractive to foreign investors. Furthermore, in 1994 the investment code was reviewed to improve the investment climate through:

1. The gradual but effective removal of administrative and some other bottlenecks that hindered the flow of private investment.
2. A review of the tax system to take into consideration the private sector investment by reducing the tax to 45% maximum by 1997 for some enterprises.
3. The establishment of retention accounts and foreign accounts for some companies in order to ensure that part of their profits are retained in the country to finance importation of essential spare parts, raw materials and machinery.
4. The enhancement of credit expansion in 1987 and 1988 to ensure that there was adequate finance to support the priority sectors of the economy.
5. The liberalization of the financial system.

1997-2003 saw flows oscillating, decreasing from US$81.8 million in 1997 to US$56 million in 1998 (the lowest over the 1993-2003 period), then peaking at US$267 million in 1999 before falling to US$115 million the following year. FDI dropped further to US$89 million and US$50 million, respectively, in 2001 and 2002 owing to the effect of the September 2001 attack on the United States and the consequent global FDI drop of 41% in 2001 and 21% in 2002 (UNCTAD, 2005). In 2003, the FDI recovery to US$137 million was due to a massive boost in FDI with the merger of Ashanti Goldfields and AngloGold and the beginning of a US$400 million gold mine investment by the US firm, Newmont. The period 2004 to 2011 also witnessed significant and increasing FDI net inflows, which reached a peak of US$3.2 billion in 2011 with the privatization of Ashanti Goldfields Company.

2.4 The Volume of Foreign Direct Investment Flows before and after IFRS Adoption

Ghana is one of the African countries that have attracted the most FDI targeted at the region. Consistently, FDI inflows to the country have been very high compared to most other African countries. In 2002, the country attracted a total FDI inflow amounting to $50.93 million. This increased steadily to $636.01 million in 2006. Ghana adopted IFRS in 2007. The FDI flows into Ghana have persistently increased from $1,383.18 million in 2007 to $3,227 million in 2013. There was a sharp increase of $747.17 million from 2006 to 2007. This can partly be attributed to the adoption of IFRS as foreign investors gain confidence in the Ghanaian market. This trend remained roughly stable until 2013 where FDI increased from $2527.35 million to $3,222.24 million in 2011 (see Table 1).

The economy of Ghana has depended on the following areas:

- **Manufacturing:** Ghana's industrial base is relatively advanced. Import–substitution industries include electronic manufacturing. RLG Communications is the first indigenous African company to assemble laptops, desktops, and mobile phones and is West Africa's biggest information and communications technology and mobile phone manufacturing company. As of 2012 there

Table 1. FDI profile in Ghana, 2002-2013

Year	Volume of FDI (US$'m)
2002	58.93
2003	136.75
2004	139.27
2005	144.97
2006	636.01
2007	1,383.18
2008	2,714.92
2009	2,372.54
2010	2,527.35
2011	3,222.24
2012	3,294.52
2013	3,227.00

Source: (GSS, 2015)

were four major companies in the textiles sector: Akosombo Textiles Limited, Tex Style Ghana Limited, Printex Ghana, and Ghana Textile Manufacturing Company.

- **Telecommunications:** Ghana's telecommunications statistics indicated that as of 2013 there are 26,336,000 cell-phone lines in operation. Competition among mobile-phone companies in Ghana is an important part of the telecommunications industry growth of Ghana, with companies obtaining more than 80 per 100 persons as mobile phone and fixed-line phone users. The mass media of Ghana is among the most liberal in Africa, with Ghana ranking as the 3rd freest in Africa and 30th most free in the world on the worldwide press freedom index.
- **Private Banking:** The financial services in Ghana have seen a lot of reforms in the past years. The Banking (Amendment) Act 2007 included the awarding of a general banking license to qualified banks, which allows offshore banks to operate in the country. Barclays Bank, Limited was the first to be awarded the general banking license in Ghana. It has therefore become possible for non-residence individuals and foreign companies to open offshore bank accounts in Ghana.
- **Hydrocarbon and Mining**: Ghana has 5 billion barrels (790×10^6 m^3) to 7 billion barrels (1.1×10^9 m^3) of petroleum in reserves. A large oilfield which contains up to 3 billion barrels (480×10^6 m^3) of sweet crude oil was discovered in 2007 (GSS, 2015). Oil exploration is on-going and the amount of oil continues to increase. Ghana produces crude oil, as of 15 December 2010, and until June 2011, Ghana exploited around 120,000 barrels per day and is expected to increase production up to 2.5 million barrels per day in 2014. Ghana has vast natural gas reserves, which is used by many foreign multinational companies operating in Ghana. The hydrocarbon industry has had major implications for regional and urban development in Ghana and these are likely to substantially increase in the years to come. Mining has gained importance in the Ghanaian economy since the turn of the 21st century, with a growth of around 30% in 2007. The main mining extractions are bauxite and gold.

- **Tourism:** The Ministry of Tourism has placed great emphasis upon further tourism support and development. Tourism contributed to 4.9% of GDP in 2009, attracting around 500,000 visitors (Ghana Investment Promotion Centre, 2015). Tourist destinations include Ghana's many castles and forts, national parks, beaches, natural reserves, landscapes and World Heritage buildings and sites.
- **Agriculture:** Ghana National Agricultural Export is the government arm that operates, maintains, and oversees the planting of cocoa, cashews, and other crops for export. Since its inception, it has drastically assisted the government in boosting agricultural sales. Agribusiness accounts for a small fraction of the gross domestic product. The main harvested crops are corn, plantain, rice, millet, sorghum, cassava and yam. Unlike the agricultural livestock, forestry, and fishing sectors, the crop sector is key to the Ghanaian agricultural industry.

3. RESEARCH HYPOTHESES

3.1. Economic Growth

Since the creation of IASB, countries have tried to improve their accounts by applying IAS criteria. Having been developed and prepared by an international standard setting accounting body, these standards are heavily dominated and inspired by certain facts held by the developed countries (Zehr & Abdelbaki, 2013). Indeed, on examining the IASB composition and structure, it clearly appears that the developed countries over predominates as compared to that of the developing countries. This geographical discrepancy manifested itself in terms of topics treated and covered by these elaborated standards. In fact, the latter are generally advanced and proposed by the developed countries' representatives and, thus, raise the problems that are most faced by firms operating in these countries. This confirms the fact that accounting development has never been dissociated from economic development. Arpen and Radebaugh (1985) have considered that economic development is indeed the fundamental variable that deeply influences the development of accounting seeing that it affects other functions in society. On the academic level, the results highlighting the IFRS relationship with economic growth are controversial. Indeed, while the study of Zeghal and Mhedhbi (2006) has demonstrated that the IFRS adoption is more tolerable by the developing countries with high economic growth. Woolley (1998) has observed that, in an Asian context, no significant differences could be noticed in terms of economic growth among IFRS adopting and those applying their local standards. In light of the IFRS literature on adoption (Hove, 1986; Chamisa, 2000; Streets, 2002; Standish, 2003; Zeghal and Mhedhbi, 2006; Al-Akra et al, 2009), a set of hypothesis have been derived that pertains to studying the effect of the developing countries' economy on the adoption of IFRS.

Hypothesis 1

Ho: There is no significant relation between IFRS adoption and FDI inflows in Ghana.
H_1: There is significant relation between IFRS adoption and FDI inflows in Ghana.

Hypothesis 2

H_0: The stock of FDI inflow does not lead to economic growth in Ghana.
H_1: The stock of FDI inflow leads to economic growth in Ghana.

3.2 Adoption and Implementation of IFRS in Ghana

In 2004, the World Bank and the Ministry of Finance and Economic Planning (MOFEP) commissioned a Report on the Observance of Standards and Codes (ROSC) in Ghana (World Bank, 2005). Reporting on the accounting and auditing practices in Ghana, ROSC observed that Ghana suffer from international weaknesses in regulation, compliance and enforcement of standards. Also, various weaknesses were identified in the laws and regulations governing financial reporting.

Although Ghana Accounting and Auditing Standards have been based on International Accounting Standards and International Standards on Auditing, respectively, they were out dated and significant gaps existed in comparison with the international equivalents. More so, full compliance with Ghana National Accounting Standards was not often achieved; some listed companies inappropriately claim compliance with International Accounting Standards. These were as a result of weak capacity and inadequate functioning of the Institute of Chartered Accountants. These also affected the monitoring and control of professional accountants' training and practice.

ROSC therefore recommended that the statutory framework, enforcement mechanisms, professional education and adoption of International Financial Reporting Standards (IFRSs) without any modifications, should replace the existing Ghana National Accounting Standards (World Bank, 2005).The Institute of Chartered Accountants Ghana, the country`s Accounting

Standard Setter joined the International Federation of Accountants (IFAC) in the year 2005. IFAC passed a directive by requesting its member countries to adopt IFRS. Consequently, Ghana put things in place and successfully launched the International Financial Reporting Standards (IFRS) on January 27, 2007. The conformity to the international accounting standards has been a major event championed by all to meet the ever increasing demands in the corporate reporting world. This mandated all public interest entity companies such as banks, listed companies, insurance companies, security brokers, pension funds just to mention but few to publish their financial statements for the periods covering or after 1 January 2007 in accordance with IFRS. But due to challenges of companies fully implementing the IFRS, 2008 was set as the reporting date. However, IFRS for Small and Medium Scale Enterprises (SMEs) were expected to be fully adopted in 2010. Though some opponents were of the view that the Institute of Chartered Accountants Ghana should not hasten the process but should do some consultations, whiles others believed it was a step in the right direction. The adoption was facilitated because, many believed it was not a matter of convenience but convergence and that if it delayed, the world will continue to move ahead (table 2).

Table 2 indicates absence of certain standards in GNAS in areas of accounting for government grants and disclosure of government assistance, borrowing cost, impairment of assets, intangible assets, financial reporting in hyperinflationary economies, first-time adoption of international financial reporting standards, non-current assets held for sale and discontinued operations, accounting and reporting by retirement benefit plan, share based payments, events after reporting date, related party disclosure and accounting for Agriculture. More so, there were differences in the treatments of the disclosure of

Table 2. Analysis of IFRS, Ghana National Accounting System (GNAS)

No	IFRS	Ghana (GNAS)
IAS 1	Detailed framework for the preparation of financial statements	Several aspects of the framework were omitted. Particularly, the qualitative characteristics of financial statements were not visible
IAS 1	Requirements to include statement of Changes in Equity	Not required under GNAS but the Companies code requires the disclosure of Capital Surplus and Income Surplus which could include some of the items to be included in the statement of changes in Equity
IAS 8	Changes in Accounting Policy	GNAS requires that the effect of certain changes in accounting policies should be included in the extraordinary items in the current period
IAS 27	Non-controlling interest is to be separately disclosed for both parent and subsidiary on the face of the income statement and the statement of financial position	GNAS omits the IAS disclosure of minority interest on face of income statement
IAS 12	Recognition of deferred tax assets and liabilities for all temporary differences	GNAS requires deferred tax assets and liabilities to be created only for timing differences relating to depreciation
IAS23	Full disclosure of borrowing costs	Disclosure for borrowing costs and the capitalization rate was absent
IAS41	Provides extensive guidance on account for agriculture and biological related assets.	GNAS does not have a substantive standard on accounting for Agriculture
IAS38	The recognition and measurement of intangible assets differs depending on whether they are purchased individually or acquired through a business combination, or whether they are internally generated	No substantive accounting standard dealing specifically with accounting for intangibles, example, measurement and recognition except goodwill in business combinations, but requires disclosure for Goodwill, patent, trademarks and similar assets
IFRS 5	Requires separate disclosures for discontinued operations	There is no substantive standard that provides detailed guidance on discontinued operations
IAS 40	Treats changes in value on investment property directly in the statement of comprehensive income	No substantive standard specifically for investment property, but accounting for investments in GNAS requires that investment property be accounted for as long term investments or as Property Plant and Equipment
	Requires that dividend liability should only be created when dividend is declared and not when it is proposed as these may or may not be ratified	GNAS allows dividend declared pending ratification at Annual General Meeting to be recognized as appropriation of retained earnings and forms a component of liabilities in the statement of financial position
IFRS 8	Leaves it up to management to decide on the definition of operating segment and the financial information provided but should reflect the way the business is managed	GNAS did not identifying primary or secondary segments but did required that industry segments and geographical segments be used as a basis for grouping the operations of an entity

Capital Surplus and Income Surplus, the effect of certain changes in accounting policies, deferred tax assets and liabilities, accounting for intangibles, dividend declared pending ratification and basis for segment accounting.

3.3 IFRS, FDI, and the Economy

The harmonization of financial reporting globally through the International Financial Reporting Standards is an accounting response to the integration of world capital markets. The IFRS is a global GAAP, setting principles–based and globally accepted standard published by the IASB to support those who adopted the preparation and presentation of a high quality, transparent and comparable financial statements that will aid easy interpretation. The presence of significant differences among various national accounting systems causes an information asymmetry of local investors at the expense of foreign ones, who do not possess detailed knowledge of local economic and political environment. Consequently, prohibitive informational obstacles to cross-country investments occur (Pagano, Röell, & Zechner, 2002); and foreign investors have to pay a 'penalty premium' in transactions with the local investors (Gordon & Bovenberg, 1996). Rossi and Volpin (2004) highlighted the importance of good accounting practice as an important factor for increasing the chance of cross-country investments. The gradual adoption of the IFRS worldwide reduces and eliminates the costs of gaining information for the decision-making, as companies use the same system of financial reporting standards regardless their domicile. In this way, the IFRS as high-quality accounting standards contribute to the smooth functioning of global capital markets and shall promote the flows of foreign capital to adopting countries. Despite this important feature, research analyses the benefits of IFRS implementation only from investors' and microeconomic, perspective.

There are economic consequences of the IFRS adoption and that forms the focus of this chapter. Research about the role of the IFRS adoption on foreign direct investments is relatively new. This chapter extends the literature on the IFRS and its effect on the economy. The first comprehensive analysis of the effects of IFRS on FDI was performed by Ramos (2008) on the sample of EU countries. The author used a gravity model. The results provide evidence that the IFRS adoption has positively influenced FDI. Ramos (2008) assumed that accounting harmonization is a workable strategy to attract foreign investors by reducing their risks for investing abroad. Different approach was adopted by Farooque *et al.* (2009) who studied the interdependence of corporate governance and FDI inflows on the sample of twelve year data of 173 countries. Their research also comprises of the evaluation of IFRS adoption and legal origin on FDI and governance. Their findings show that IFRS have stronger effect on the governance rather on FDI. However, through an increased quality of governance, the IFRS allows free movement of capital around the world. Beneish *et al.* (2010) found that the IFRS adoption in the European Union has significant impact on attracting foreign debt investment. The effect on foreign equity investments is relatively small. However, the results of the study are impaired because only four non- EU countries were used as control factors. Chen, Tang, Jiang, and Lin (2011) investigated the effect of widespread adoption of IFRS on bilateral FDI within the OECD countries. They found that the shift from local accounting standards to IFRS contributed positively to the FDI growth during the period between 2001 and 2005.

According to Kumar (2007) FDI which involves building long-term relationships with enterprises in foreign countries can be made in several ways. First, and most likely, it may involve parent enterprises injecting equity capital by purchasing shares in foreign affiliates. Second, it may take the form of reinvesting the affiliate's earnings. Third, it may entail short- or long-term lending between parents and affiliates. To be categorized as a multinational enterprise for inclusion in FDI data, the parent must hold a minimum equity stake of 10 percent in the affiliate (Kumar, 2007). Garkovic and Lavin (2002), noted that economic rationale for offering special incentive to attract FDI frequently is derives from the belief that foreign investment produces externalities in the form of technology transfer and spill overs. DeGregorio (2003), while contributing to the importance of FDI noted that it allows a country to bring in technologies and knowledge that are not readily available to domestic investors and increases productivity throughout the economy. Jeffrey and Spaulding (2005) also stated that FDI advantage includes; circumventing trade barriers, hidden and otherwise making the move from domestic export sales to a locally-based national sales office and capability to increase total production capacity, opportunities for co-production, joint ventures with local partners, and joint marketing arrangements.

According to Okoye and Akenbor (2012), there are perceived challenges to be presented by IFRS adoption and implementation. The intrinsic problems of aligning with IFRS pointed out that international accounting clearly has a language problem (Ukpai, 2002). Adams (2004) claimed that where an accounting standard conflicts with government policy, the standard is revised. For example the LIFO method of stock valuation is not allowable for tax purpose in Nigeria. Another problem inherent with the adoption of IFRS is the universal tendency to resist change. Gambari (2010) noted that the successful adoption of IFRS entails assessing technical accounting, tax implications, internal processes, and statutory reporting, technology infrastructure, and organizational issues.

4. METHODOLOGY

Data for the study were obtained from questionnaire on IFRS, foreign direct investment and economy. The population of this study consists of preparers and users of financial reports. The preparers are (31) active quoted companies in Ghana Stock Exchange between 2007 and 2014 represented by Directors / Finance Managers responsible for the preparation of financial statements who are selected as respondents due to their involvement and knowledge of IFRS. The users of financial reports are investors represented by (100) Investment analysts firms and institutional investors identified from the list of capital market operators compiled by the Ghana Stock Exchange. Investment Analyst are selected as respondents for the fact that they are principal users of financial reports (Clement & Tse, 2003; Mangena, 2004), they have good investment knowledge which aids analysis of financial reports and decision making (Baker, 1998). They also provide analytical information that meets the needs of their clients (Gebhardt, Reichadt &Wittenbrink, 2004). The Analyst's financial report usage rate is higher than that of all other users. A sample of 100 persons was selected at random, representing 76% of the total population. The survey questionnaire instrument consisted of seven question with a - 5 Likert scale response options divided into two sections. The options available Very Relevant (VR), Relevant (R), No Effect (NE) Irrelevant (I), and Very Irrelevant (VI). Various methods were employed to test the reliability and validity of the survey design. For structured problems described by Likert 5-scale table, Cronbach's alpha values was used to evaluate the internal consistency, reflecting the reliability of survey design. Pilot survey was adopted for the reliability test and it yielded correlation coefficient of 0.88. It was structured in line with the research questions and hypothesis of the study. To establish the relationship between IFRS and FDI Pearson Product Moment Correlation Coefficient was used. This is calculated as:

$$r = \frac{n\Sigma xy - \left(\Sigma x\right)\left(\Sigma y\right)}{\sqrt{[n\Sigma x^2 - (\Sigma x)^2][n\Sigma y^2 - (\Sigma y)^2]}}$$

5. EMPIRICAL RESULTS (TABLES 3-8)

Hypothesis 1

Ho: There is no significant relation between IFRS adoption and FDI inflows in Ghana.
H_1: There is a significant relation between IFRS adoption and FDI inflows in Ghana.

$$r = \frac{n\Sigma xy - \left(\Sigma x\right)\left(\Sigma y\right)}{\sqrt{[n\ \Sigma x^2 - \left(\Sigma x\right)^2][n\Sigma y^2 - \left(\Sigma y\right)^2]}}$$

Table 3. Responses on key issues relating to the relationship between IFRS adoption and FDI inflow into Ghana

S/N	Variables (Responses in %)	Preparers of Financial Statements (Finance Managers)					Users of Financial Statement (Investment Analyst)				
		VR	R	NE	I	VI	VR	R	NE	I	VI
1	IFRS improves the quality of Financial statements and increase access to global capital market	40.67	13.22	2.3	3.5	2.3	51.73	14.20	3.5	1.1	1.1
2	IFRS adoption ensures the use of one standard for parent and subsidiary companies	55.92	5.8	0.0	0.0	0.0	45.64	20.29	0.0	5.7	0.0
3	IFRS has positive effect on the information for control and decision making by investors	33.55	5.8	10.17	10.17	2.3	40.57	22.31	5.7	3.5	0.0
4	IFRS adoption has significant effect on FDI in flows	55.92	4.6	1.2	0.0	0.0	61.88	6.9	1.1	1.1	1.1

Source: Field survey, March 2015

Table 4. Calculation of correlation. Question 4 of questionnaire administered: IFRS adoption has significant effect on FDI inflows in Ghana.

Options	Preparers of Financial Reports (PFR)					Users of Financial Reports (UFR)			
	Point (x)	Response (y)	xy	x^2	y^2	Point (x)	Response (y)	x^2	y^2
VR	5	55	275	25	3025	5	61	25	3721
R	4	4	16	16	16	4	6	16	36
NE	3	1	3	9	1	3	1	9	1
I	2	0	0	4	0	2	1	4	1
VI	1	0	0	1	0	1	1	1	1
Σ	**15**	**60**	**294**	**55**	**3042**	**15**	**70**	**55**	**3760**

Source: Author's computation, March 2015

Table 5. Calculation of Correlation

Options	AA Point (x)	AA Response (y)	AA (xy)	AA (x^2)	AA (y^2)
VR	5	58	290	25	3364
R	4	5	20	16	25
NE	3	1	3	9	1
I	2	0.5	1	4	0.25
VI	1	0.5	0.5	1	0.25
Σ	15	65	314.5	55	3,390.5

Source: Author's Computation, March 2015 (Note: AA = Average aggregate)

Table 6. Response on key issues relating to the relationship between FDI inflows and economic growth the Ghana

S/N	Variables Responses (in %)	Preparers of Financial Statements (Finance Managers)					Users of Financial Statement (Investment Analyst)				
		VR	R	NR	I	VI	VR	R	NR	I	VI
1	FDI inflows ensures that technologies and funds are available to the local industry	40.67	13.22	2.4	3.3	2.4	52.75	12.17	4.6	1.1	1.1
2	FDI inflows lead to the mobilization of more input resources and improve GDP	55.92	5.8	0.0	0.0	0.0	44.63	20.29	1.1	5.7	0.0
3	Economic growth depend on FDI inflows	38.63	5.8	5.8	10.17	2.4	42.60	20.29	5.7	3.4	0.0

Table 7. Calculation of correlation

Options	Preparers of Financial Reports (PFR)					Users of Financial Reports (UFR)			
	Point (x)	Response (y)	xy	x^2	y^2	Point (x)	Response (y)	x^2	y^2
VR	5	38	190	25	1444	5	42	25	1764
R	4	5	20	16	25	4	20	16	400
NE	3	5	15	9	25	3	5	9	25
I	2	10	20	4	100	2	3	4	9
VI	1	2	2	1	4	1	0	1	0
Σ	**15**	**60**	**247**	**55**	**1598**		**70**	**55**	**2,198**

Table 8. Calculation of correlation

Options	AA Point (x)	AA Response (y)	AA (xy)	AA (x^2)	AA (y^2)
VR	5	40	200	25	1600
R	4	12.5	50	16	156.25
NE	3	5	15	9	25
I	2	6.5	13	4	42.25
VI	1	1	1	1	1
Σ	**15**	**65**	**279**	**55**	**1,824.50**

Source: Author's Computation, March 2015 (Note: AA = Average aggregate)

where

n = 5, Σx = 15, Σy = 65, Σxy = 314.50, Σx^2 = 55, Σy^2 = 3,390.5

$$r = \frac{5(275.5) - (15)(61.5)}{\sqrt{[5(55) - (15)^2][5(3,390.5) - (65)^2]}}$$

r = **0.57 (57%)**

Decision: The r calculated of 0.57 is greater than 0.5 level of significance. The alternate hypothesis is accepted. There is significant relation between IFRS adoption and implementation and FDI inflows in Ghana.

Hypothesis 2

H_0: The stock of FDI inflow does not lead to economic growth in Ghana.
H_1: The stock of FDI inflow leads to economic growth in Ghana.

$$r = \frac{n\Sigma xy - (\Sigma x)(\Sigma y)}{\sqrt{[n\ \Sigma x^2 - (\Sigma x)^2][n\Sigma y^2 - (\Sigma y)^2]}}$$

where:

n = 5, Σx = 15, Σy = 65, Σxy = 279, Σx^2 = 55, Σy^2 = 1,824.5

$$r = \frac{5(275.5) - (15)(61.5)}{\sqrt{[5(55) - (15)^2][5(1,824.5) - (65)^2]}}$$

r = **0.92 (82%)**

Decision: The r calculated of 0.92 is greater than 0.5 level of significance. The alternate hypothesis is accepted. The stock of FDI inflow leads to economic growth in Ghana

6. DISCUSSION OF RESULT

The research work centres on determining the relationship between IFRS adoption and foreign direct investment inflow as basis for economic growth in Ghana. The results of hypothesis tested revealed that there is a significant relationship between IFRS adoption and FDI in Ghana. This is in conformity with previous studies (Zeghal & Mhedhbi, 2006; Al-Akra et al., 2009). It is clearly discovered that the economic growth including FDI constitutes a major determinant for adopting the international accounting standards. Actually, this result confirms not only the hypothesis 1of this study but also the assertions of the strong association of economic growth and the accounting standards.

The rigorous process of conversion of existing records to IFRS involved training and employment of appropriate manpower. Government and policy makers have to put adequate infrastructure and regulatory framework in place to address those issues hindering its full implementation. The implication of IFRS on the economy is the fact that financial reporting among the countries that have adopted IFRS is uniform and comparability becomes easier as well as the ease of interpretation of financial statements. This will in many ways boost global investors' confidence and lead to cross border financial transaction. The IFRS adoption will definitely enhance international accounting as a sub discipline within the field of accountancy (Glautier & Underdown, 2001). The survey also revealed that the adoption of IFRS will promote companies' access to global capital markets thereby exposing them to cross-border investments. This agrees with Zeghal and Mhedhbi (2006) findings. However, the responses revealed that IFRS adoption has neither made much impact in making timely and accurate reports available nor has it made the financial statements more reliable. Quoted companies which have adopted IFRS are able to generate more funds from foreign sources through the capital market.

7. RECOMMENDATIONS

From the findings of this study, the researcher hereby recommends the following steps to ensure a successful adoption and implementation of IFRS in Ghana. Government and the regulators should ensure that there is availability of training facilities and materials for professional accountants on the concept of IFRS and issues relating to its implementation and conversion. Compliance with IFRS should be mandatory for both listed and unlisted companies and failure should be marched with appropriate sanctions. Government need to release more funds to educate all stakeholders with special reference to the academics, staff and accounting students who will uphold the future IFRS in the country and develop plan to help properly equip the company for upcoming changes (Lewis & Pendril, 1996). Professional accounting bodies in Ghana need to make IFRS training a part of their training programme at a reduce cost. While monitoring the IFRS implementation timetable, both government and regulators should ensure that ethical environment and corporate transparency are observed.

8. FUTURE RESEARCH

The findings of this research raise concerns on a number of important issues and may provide avenues for further research. For instance, one economic development indicator was employed in this chapter. One can construct other indices following the literature which may require more data or effort to be assembled. In cases of impact of IFRS, a dynamic analysis could be employed such as multiple regression and the extension of sample size to include other African countries.

9. CONCLUSION

In this study, attempts were made to assess the relationship between IFRS adoption and FDI and the effect on the Ghanaian economy. Based on the findings, it was concluded that the adoption of IFRS is a right step in the right direction. Although there are many issues and challenges facing the implementation, the benefits outweigh the challenge. With adoption, Ghana companies will produce a more credible financial statements that will not only be uniformed but also provide a basis for better interpretation. This invariably will boost investors' confidence and attract cross border financial transactions which is the basis for economic growth.

The empirical analysis results have shown that developing countries most favourable to the adoption of IFRS are those having a high economic growth rate, a high level of education and a common law based on a legal system. Available statistics about international flows in the form of investment in recent years have raised the interest of economic research. The traditional neoclassical model using the assumption of pure substitution effect between labour and capital has been replaced by models, which work with social networks. Therefore, FDI are supposed to flow to countries adopting IFRS in the long-term perspective. In addition, the adoption of the IFRS is only the first step. Because of cultural differences, the discrepancies in the actual quality of their implementation in financial statements of companies from different countries exist. The IFRS adoption is only one factor influencing the decision, where to allocate investments.

REFERENCES

Adams, P. (2004). *Resolving Conflicts in Accounting System - Issues and Arguments.* Lecture series, London, UK.

Al-Akra, M., Jahangir, A. M., & Marashdeh, O. (2009). Development of accounting regulation in Jordan. *The International Journal of Accounting, 44*(2), 163–186. doi:10.1016/j.intacc.2009.03.003

André-Pascal. (2002). *Foreign direct investment for development: maximizing benefit and minimizing cost.* OECD Publications.

Arpan, J. S., & Radebaugh, L. H. (1985). *International Accounting and Multinational Enterprising.* New York: Wiley.

Aryeetey, C., Barthel, F., Busse, M., Loehr, C., & Osei, R. (2008). *Empirical Study on the Determinants and Pro-Development Impacts of Foreign Direct Investment in Ghana.* Study Conducted on Behalf of German Ministry for Economic Cooperation and Development and the German Technical Cooperation.

Baker, R. G. (1998). The market for information evidence from finance directors, analysts and fund managers. *Accounting and Business Review, 29*(1), 3–20. doi:10.1080/00014788.1998.9729563

Ball, R. (2006). International Financial Reporting Standards (IFRS): Pros and cons for investors. *Accounting and Business Review, 36*(sup1), 5–27. doi:10.1080/00014788.2006.9730040

Barth, M. E. (2007). Research, Standard Setting, and Global Financial Reporting. *Foundations and Trends in Accounting, 1*(2), 71–165. DOI: 10.1561/1400000002

Chamisa, E. (2000). The relevance and observance of the IASC standards in developing countries and the particular case of Zimbabwe. *The International Journal of Accounting*, *35*(2), 267–286. doi:10.1016/S0020-7063(00)00049-2

Chen, H., Tang, Q., Jiang, Y., & Lin, Z. (2010). The Role of International Financial Reporting Standards in Accounting Quality:Evidence from the European Union. *Journal of International Financial Management and Accounting*, *21*(3), 220–278. doi:10.1111/j.1467-646X.2010.01041.x

Clement, M. B., & Tse, S. Y. (2003). Do investors respond to analysts' forecast revisions as if forecast accuracy is all that matters? *Accounting Review*, *78*(1), 227–249. doi:10.2308/accr.2003.78.1.227

Cordeiro, R., Couto, G., & Silva, F. (2007). *Measuring the Impact of International Financial Reporting Standards (IFRS) in Firm Reporting: The Case of Portugal*. Available at SSRN:http://ssrn.com/abstract=969972

Daske, H., Hail, L., Leuz, C., & Verdi, R. (2008). Mandatory IFRS reporting around the world: Early evidence on the economic consequences. *Journal of Accounting Research*, *46*, 1085–1142.

DeGregorio, J. (2003). *The role of FDI and Natural Recourses in Economic Development.* Working paper No. 196. Central Bank of Chile, Santiago.

Denisia, V. (2010). Foreign Direct Investment Theories: An Overview of the Main FDI Theories. *European Journal of Interdisciplinary Studies*, *3*, 53–59.

Gambari, Y. (2010). *Issues in the Implementation of IFRS, Accounting and Financial Reporting Issues.* Toronto: CICA.

Garkovi, M., & Levin, R. (2002). *Does FDI accelerate economic growth?* Working Paper. University of Minnesota.

Gebhardt, G., Reichadt, R., & Wittenbrink, C. (2004). Accounting for Financial Instruments in the Banking Industry: Conclusion from a Simulation Model. *European Accounting Review*, *13*(2), 341–371. doi:10.1080/0963818042000204733a

Ghana Investment Promotion Centre (GIPC). (2015). *The Ghana Investment Promotion Centre Quarterly report*. Retrieved from http://www.gipcghana.com/press-and- media/downloads.html

Ghana Statistical Service (GSS). (2015). *Foreign direct investment in Ghana*. Retrieved from http.www.statsghana.gov.gh

Glautier, M. W. E., & Underdown, B. (2001). *Accounting Theory and Practice* (7th ed.). Prentice Hall.

Graham, E. M. (1995). *Foreign Direct Investment in the World Economy.* IMF Working Papers 95/59. International Monetary Fund

Hove, M. (1986). The Anglo-American influence on international accounting standards: The case of the Disclosure standards of the international accounting standards committee. *Research in Third World Accounting*, *1*, 55–66.

Inernational Monetary Fund (IMF). (2012). *World Economic and Financial Surveys, Regional Economic Outlook, Sub Saharan Africa, Staying the course*. Retrieved from https://www.imf.org/external/pubs/ft/reo/2014/afr/eng/sreo1014.pdf

Jeffrey, P. G., & Spaulding, R. B. (2005). *Understanding Foreign Direct Investment (FDI) Going global, Citibank international business portal*. Retrieved: www.going-global.com/.../understanding_foreign_direct_inv

Kumar, A. (2007). *Does Foreign Direct Investment Help Emerging Economies? Economist's View*. Retrieved: http://economistsview.typepad.com/economistsview/2007/01/frb_dallas_does.html

La Porta, R., Lopez-de-Silanes, F., Shleifer, A., & Vishny, R. (1999). The quality of government. *Journal of Law Economics and Organization*, *15*(1), 222–279. doi:10.1093/jleo/15.1.222

Lipsey, R., & Chrystal, A. (2003). *Economics* (10th ed.). New Delhi: Oxford University Press.

Mangena, M. (2004). *On the perceived importance of disclosure items in UK interim financial reports: Evidence from the investment analysts*. Working paper series, Bradford University.

Okoye, P. V. C., & Akenbor, C. O. (2012). *Financial Reporting Framework in Nigeria and the Adoption of the International Financial Reporting Standards*. Retrieved from http://www.centerforpbbefr.rutgers.edu/2012PBFEAM/papers/008- Financial%20reporting.doc

Omneya, H. (2003). Introducing International Accounting Standards to an emerging capital market: Relative familiarity and language effect in Egypt. *Journal of International Accounting, Auditing & Taxation*, *12*(1), 63–84. doi:10.1016/S1061-9518(03)00002-8

Oyetayo, E. O., Arogundade, K. K., Adebisi, S. O., & Oluwakayode, E. F. (2011). FDI, Export and Economic Growth in Nigeria. *European Journal of Humanities and Social Sciences.*, *2*(1), 66–86.

Pagano, M., Röell, A., & Zechner, J. (2002). The Geography of Equity Listing: Why Do Companies List Abroad? *The Journal of Finance*, *57*(6), 2651–2694. doi:10.1111/1540-6261.00509

Standish, P. (2003). Evaluating capacity for direct participation in international accounting harmonisation: France as a test case. *Abacus*, *39*(2), 186–210. doi:10.1111/1467-6281.00126

Street, D. (2002). GAAP 2001 benchmarking national accounting standards against IAS: Summary of results. *Journal of International Accounting, Auditing & Taxation*, *11*(1), 77–90. doi:10.1016/S1061-9518(02)00055-1

Tsikata, G. K., Asante, Y., & Gyasi, E. M. (2000). *Determinants of Foreign Direct Investment in Ghana*. Overseas Development Institute.

Ukpai, N. A. (2002). The Snag in International Accounting Transactions. *Journal of Accountancy*, *3*(6), 214–222.

UNCTAD. (2005). *Economic Development In Africa: Rethinking The Role Of Foreign Direct Investment*. Retrieved from http://siteresources.worldbank.org/INTANNREP2K5/Resources/51563_English.pdf

Wooly, R. (1998). *International accounting standards and economic growth, an empirical investigation of their relationship in Asia*. Working Paper series Australia: School of Accounting and Law, RMIT.

Zeghal, D., & Mhedhbi, K. (2006). An analysis of the factors affecting the adoption of international accounting standards by developing countries. *The International Journal of Accounting*, *41*(4), 373–386. doi:10.1016/j.intacc.2006.09.009

Zehr, C., & Abdelbaki, A. (2013). Does adoption of international accounting standards promote economic growth in developing countries? *International Open Journal of Economics, 1*(1), 1-13. Available online at http://acascipub.com/Journals.php

KEY TERMS AND DEFINITIONS

Consolidated Financial Statements: The financial statements of a group in which the assets, liabilities, equity, income, expenses and cash flows of the parent and its subsidiaries are presented as those of a single economic entity.

Economic Growth: It is an increase in the capacity of an economy to produce goods and services, compared from one period of time to another. It can be measured in nominal terms, which include inflation, or in real terms, which are adjusted for inflation.

Financial Statement: It is a formal record of the financial activities of a business, person, or other entity. Relevant financial information is presented in a structured manner and in a form easy to understand.

Foreign Direct Investment (FDI): It is defined classically as a company from one country making a physical investment into building a factory in another country. The direct investment in buildings, machinery and equipment is in contrast with making a portfolio investment, which is considered an indirect investment. In recent years, given rapid growth and change in global investment patterns, the definition has been broadened to include the acquisition of a lasting management interest in a company or enterprise outside the investing firm's home country.

International Accounting Standards (IAS): These are accounting standards issued by the International Accounting Standards Board (IASB) and its predecessor, the International Accounting Standards Committee (IASC).

International Financial Reporting Standards (IFRS): It is a single set of accounting standards, developed and maintained by the IASB with the intention of those standards being capable of being applied on a globally consistent basis by developed, emerging and developing economies. This provides investors and other users of financial statements with the ability to compare the financial performance of publicly listed companies on a like-for-like basis with their international peers.

Pearson Product-Moment Correlation Coefficient (r): It is a measure of the strength of a linear association between two variables and is denoted by r. It represents a measure of the linear correlation (dependence) between two variables such as IFRS adoption and FDI or X and Y, giving a value between +1 and −1 inclusive, where 1 is total positive correlation, 0 is no correlation, and −1 is total negative correlation.

The International Accounting Standards Committee (IASC): It is an independent private-sector organization that in its own words is a 'body working to achieve uniformity in the accounting principles that are used by businesses and other organizations for financial reporting around the world.'

Compilation of References

A´lvarez, G., Sa´nchez, M., & Rodrı´guez, D. (2008). Voluntary and compulsory Information disclosed online. The effect of industry concentration and other explanatory factors. *Online Information Review, 32*(5), 601-616.

Abata, M. A. (2015). The impact of IFRS adoption on financial reporting practices in the Nigerian banking sector. *Journal of Policy and Development Studies*, *9*(2), 169–184. doi:10.12816/0011215

Abd-Elsalam, O. H., & Weetman, P. (2003). Introducing international accounting standards to an emerging capital market: Relative familiarity and language effect in Egypt. *Journal of International Accounting, Auditing & Taxation*, *12*(1), 63–84. doi:10.1016/S1061-9518(03)00002-8

Abdur Rouf, M., & Al Harun, A. (2011). Ownership structure and voluntary disclosure in annual reports of Bangladesh. *Pakistan Journal of Commerce and Social Sciences*, *5*(1), 129–139.

Ackah, C., Turkson, F., & Opoku, K. (2013). Trade Costs and Intra-Regional Trade Flows in ECOWAS. *Journal of West African Integration*, *1*(1), 1–43.

Adam, C. S., & Simpasa, A. M. (2010). The Economics of the Copper Price Boom in Zambia. In A. Fraser & M. Larmer (Eds.), *Zambia, Mining, and Neoliberalism. Boom and Bust on the Globalized Copperbelt* (pp. 59–90). New York: Palgrave MacMillan.

Adams, P. (2004). *Resolving Conflicts in Accounting System - Issues and Arguments.* Lecture series, London, UK.

Adegbie, S. Q. (2010). *IFRS adoption in Nigeria.* A paper presented at the World Bank Seminar on IFRS adoption in Nigeria.

Adegbie, F. F. (2011). International financial reporting standards adoption, implications on management accounting and taxation in Nigerian economy. *International Journal of Research in Commerce Economics and Management*, *1*(2), 1–6.

Adekoya, O. (2011). Similarities and differences, IFRS and Nigerian GAAP. Lagos: Pricewater House Coopers International Limited (PWCIL).

Adewole, M. A., & Osabuohien, E. S. (2007). Analysis of Cost of Governance and Its Reduction Options in Nigeria. *The Nigerian Journal of Economic and Social Studies*, *49*(1), 137–159.

Adhikari, A., & Tondkar, R. H. (1992). Environmental factors influencing accounting disclosure requirements of global stock exchanges. *Journal of International Financial Management and Accounting*, *4*(2), 75–105. doi:10.1111/j.1467-646X.1992.tb00024.x

Afego. (2011). *Stock price response to earnings announcement: evidence from the Nigeria stock market.* MPRA Paper No. 33931. University of Dundee.

Affes, H., & Callimaci, A. (2007). Les déterminants de l'adoption anticipée des norms comptables internationales: Choix financier ou opportunisme. *Comptabilité Contrôle Audit, 13*(2), 149–166. doi:10.3917/cca.132.0149

Agami, A. (2007). *Compliance of Companies Listed on Stock Exchanges in Emerging Markets With financial Reporting Standards: The case of Egypt*. Paper presented at the World Confederation of Accountants (WCA), Istanbul, Turkey.

Agca, A., & Aktas, R. (2007). First time application of IFRS and its impact on financial ratios: A study on Turkish listed firms. *Problems and Perspectives in Management, 5*(2), 99–112.

Aggarwal, R., & Goodell, J. W. (2010). Financial markets versus institutions in European countries: Influence of culture and other national characteristics. *International Business Review, 19*(5), 502–520. doi:10.1016/j.ibusrev.2009.07.010

Aggarwal, R., Klapper, L., & Wysocki, P. (2005). Portfolio preferences of foreign institutional investors. *Journal of Banking & Finance, 29*(12), 2919–2946. doi:10.1016/j.jbankfin.2004.09.008

Agostino, M. D., Drago, D., & Silipo, D. B. (2011). The value relevance of IFRS in the European banking industry. *Review of Quantitative Finance and Accounting, 36*(3), 437–457. doi:10.1007/s11156-010-0184-1

Agyei-Mensah, B. K. (2013). Adoption of International Financial Reporting Standard (IFRS) in Ghana and the Quality of Financial Statement Disclosures. *The International Journal of Accounting and Financial Reporting, 3*(2), 269–286. doi:10.5296/ijafr.v3i2.4489

Agyei-Mensah, B. K. (2015). The determinants of Financial Ratio Disclosures and Quality: Evidence from an Emerging Market. *International Journal of Accounting and Financial Reporting, 5*(1), 188–211. doi:10.5296/ijafr.v5i1.7267

Agyeman, O. S., Aboagye, E., & Ahali, A. Y. O. (2013). Prospect and Challenges of Corporate Governance in Ghana. *International Journal of Scientific and Research Publications, 3*(5), 1–9.

Ahmed, A. S., Neel, M., & Wang, D. (2013). Does Mandatory Adoption of IFRS Improve Accounting Quality? Preliminary Evidence. *Contemporary Accounting Research, 30*(4), 1344–1372. doi:10.1111/j.1911-3846.2012.01193.x

Ahmed, K., Chalmers, K., & Khlif, H. (2013). A meta-analysis of IFRS adoption Effects. *The International Journal of Accounting, 48*(2), 173–217. doi:10.1016/j.intacc.2013.04.002

Ahmed, K., & Courtis, J. K. (1999). Association Between Corporate Characteristics and Disclosure Levels in Annual Reports: A Meta-Analysis. *The British Accounting Review, 132*(1), 35–61. doi:10.1006/bare.1998.0082

Ahmed, K., & Nicholls, D. (1994). The impact of non - financial company characteristics on mandatory disclosure compliance in developing countries: The case of Bangladesh. *The International Journal of Accounting, 29*, 62–77.

AICPA. (2008). *Convergence with International Accounting Standards*. Retrieved from http://www.ifrs.com/updates/aicpa/Convergence_Accounting_Std.html

Ajao, M. G., & Wemambu, M. U. (2012). Volatility estimation and stock price prediction in the Nigerian stock market. *International Journal of Financial Research, 3*(1).

Ajinkya, Bhojraj, & Sengupta. (2005). The association between outside directors, institutional investors and the properties of management earnings forecast. *Journal of Accounting Research, 43*(3), 343-375.

Akdogan, N. (2007). Accounting in Turkey/Financial Reporting Standards Application Process: Problems, Solutions. *Journal of Financial Solutions, 80*, 101–117.

Akgün M., Pehlivanlı D., Gürünlü M. (2011). A Process Design for Auditing Fair Value. *International Journal of Economics and Finance, 3*(3).

Akhtaruddin, M., & Haron, H. (2010). Board composition, audit committees' effectiveness and corporate voluntary disclosure. *Asian Review of Accounting*, *18*(1), 68–82. doi:10.1108/13217341011046015

Al-Ajmi, J. (2008). The usefulness of corporate governance and financial ratios to credit and financial analysts: Evidence from Bahrain. European *Journal of Economics Finance and Administrative Sciences*, *11*(September), 107–125.

Al-Akra, M., Ali, M. J., & Marashdeh, O. (2009). Development of Accounting Regulation in Jordan. *The International Journal of Accounting*, *44*(2), 163–186. doi:10.1016/j.intacc.2009.03.003

Al-Akra, M., Eddie, I. A., & Ali, M. J. (2010). The influence of the introduction of accounting disclosure regulation on mandatory disclosure compliance: Evidence from Jordan. *The British Accounting Review*, *42*(3), 170–186. doi:10.1016/j.bar.2010.04.001

Alali, F. A., & Foote, P. S. (2012). The value relevance of international financial reporting standards: Empirical evidence in an emerging market. *The International Journal of Accounting*, *47*(1), 85–108. doi:10.1016/j.intacc.2011.12.005

Alan, K., & Carlyn, R.-D. (2015). Is Africa Actually Developing? *World Development*, *66*(C), 598–613.

Al-Basteki, H. (1995). The Voluntary Adoption of International Accounting Standards by Bahrain Corporations. *Advances in International Accounting*, *8*, 47–64.

Al-Basteki, H. (1995). The voluntary adoption of international accounting standards by Bahraini corporations. *Advances in International Accounting*, *8*, 47–64.

Albrecht, D. (2010). *Economic Consequences and the Political Nature of Accounting Standard Setting*. Retrieved from: https://profalbrecht.wordpress.com/2010/01/06/economic-consequences-and-the-political-nature-of-accounting-standard-setting/

Albu, N., Ca˘ta˘lin, N.A., Bunea, S., Calu, D.A., & Girbina, M.M. (2011). A story about IAS/IFRS implementation in Romania An institutional and structuration theory perspective. *Journal of Accounting in Emerging Economies, 1*(1), 76-100.

Albu, C. N., Alb, N., Pali-Pista, S. F., Gîrbină, M. M., Selimoglu, S. K., & Kovács, D. M. et al. (2013). Implementation of IFRS for SMEs in Emerging Economies: Stakeholder Perceptions in the Czech Republic, Hungary, Romania and Turkey. *Journal of International Financial Management & Accounting*, *24*(2), 140–175. doi:10.1111/jifm.12008

Albu, N., & Albu, C. N. (2012). International Financial Reporting Standards in an Emarging Economy: Lessons from Romania. *Australian Accounting Review*, *22*(63), 341–352. doi:10.1111/j.1835-2561.2012.00196.x

Albu, N., Albu, C. N., Bunea, S., St. Calu, D. A., & Girbina, M. M. (2011). A story about IAS/IFRS implementation in Romania. *Journal of Accounting in Emerging Economies*, *1*(1), 76–100. doi:10.1108/20421161111107868

Alhashim, D. D., & Arpan, J. S. (1992). International Dimension of Accounting (3rd ed). PWS-Kent Publishing Co.

AlHashim, D. D. (1994). International Dimensions in Accounting and Implications for Developing Nations. *Management International Review*, *34*, 28–35.

Aljifri, K., & Hussainey, K. (2007). The determinants of forward-looking information in annual reports of UAE companies. *Managerial Auditing Journal*, *22*(9), 881–894. doi:10.1108/02686900710829390

Aljifri, K., & Khasharmeh, H. (2006). An Investigation into the Suitability of the International Accounting Standards to the United Arab Emirates Environment. *International Business Review*, *15*(5), 505–526. doi:10.1016/j.ibusrev.2006.05.009

Al-Omari, A. M. (2010). The Institutional Framework of Financial Reporting in Jordan. *European Journal of Economics Finance And Administrative Sciences*, *1*(22), 32–50.

Alon, A. (2013). Complexity and Dual Institutionality: The Case of IFRS Adoption in Russia, *Corporate Governance. International Review (Steubenville, Ohio)*, *21*(1), 42–57.

Alp, A., & Ustundag, S. (2007). Financial reporting, transformation: Experience of Turkey. *Critical Perspectives on Accounting*, 2–17.

Al-Qahtani, A. K. (2005). The Development of Accounting Regulation in the GCC. *Managerial Auditing Journal*, *20*(3), 217–226. doi:10.1108/02686900510585564

Alrazeen, A., & Karbhari, Y. (2004). Users' perceptions of Corporate Information in Saudi Arabia: An Empirical Analysis. *International Journal of Commerce and Management*, *14*(3), 41–57. doi:10.1108/10569210480000183

Alsaeed, K. (2006). The association between firm-specific characteristics and disclosure. *Managerial Auditing Journal*, *21*(5), 476–496. doi:10.1108/02686900610667256

Al-Shammari, B., Brown, P. R., & Tarca, A. (2007). *Development of Enforcement Mechanisms Following Adoption of International Accounting Standards in the Gulf Co-Operation Council Member States*. Working Paper. Gulf Co-Operation Council Member States.

Alver, A., Alver, L., Mackevičius, J., Paupa, V., & Bailey, D. (1998). Baltic states. In D. Alexander & S. Archer (Eds.), *European accounting guide* (3rd ed.; pp. 1464–1475). Miller.

Alves, M., & Antunes, E. (2011). International Accounting Standards in Europe: A Comparative Study. *International Research Journal of Finance and Economics*, *61*, 64–73.

Alves-Oliveira, V. A., & Lemes, S. (2011). Nível de convergência dos princípios contábeis brasileiros e norte-americanos às normas do IASB: Uma contribuição para a adoção das IFRS por empresas brasileiras. *Revista Contabilidade & Finanças-USP*, *22*(56), 155–173. doi:10.1590/S1519-70772011000200003

Amavilah, V. H., (2014a). *Sir W. Arthur Lewis and the Africans: Overlooked economic growth lessons*. MPRA Paper No. 57126.

Amavilah, V. H., (2014b). *Knowledge= technology and human capital and the Lucas and Romer production functions*. MPRA Paper No. 58847.

Amavilah, V. H., (2015). *Social Obstacles to Technology, Technological Change, and the Economic Growth of African Countries: Some Anecdotal Evidence from Economic History*. MPRA Paper No. 63273.

Amavilah, V. H., Asongu, S. A., & Andrés, A. R. (2014). *Globalization, Peace & Stability, Governance, and Knowledge Economy*. African Governance and Development Institute Working Paper No. 14/012, Yaoundé.

Amavilah, V. H. (2006). *Institutional change and economic performance: An off-the-cuff comment on Professors Daron Acemoglu, Simon Johnson, and James Robinson's three papers*. Glendale College.

America, R. (2013). Economic Development with Limited Supplies of Management. What to do about it – the case of Africa. *Challenge*, *56*(1), 61–71. doi:10.2753/0577-5132560103

Ames, D. (2013). IFRS adoption and accounting quality: The case of South Africa. *Journal of Applied Economic and Business Research*, *3*(3), 154–165.

Ames, D. (2013). IFRS adoption and accounting quality: The case of South Africa. *Journal of Applied Economics and Business Research*, *3*(3), 154–165.

Ames, D. (2013). IFRS adoption and accounting quality: The case of South Africa. *Journal of Applied Economies and Business Research*, *3*(3), 154–165.

Amir, A., & Meeks, G. (2013). Bank failure, mark-to-market and the financial crisis. *Abacus*, *49*(3), 308–339. doi:10.1111/abac.12011

Amiram, D, (2009). Financial information globalization and foreign investment decisions. *Journal of International Accounting Research*, 41-70.

Amiram, D. (2012). Financial information globalization and foreign investment decisions. *Journal of International Accounting Research*, *11*(2), 57–81. doi:10.2308/jiar-50282

Anderson, N. (1993). *The Globalization GAAP* (Vol. 75). Management Accounting.

Anderson, S., Cavanagh, J., & Lee, T. (2005). *Field guide to the global economy*. Washington, DC: Institute for Policy Studies.

André-Pascal. (2002). *Foreign direct investment for development: maximizing benefit and minimizing cost*. OECD Publications.

Anyanwu, J. (2012). Why Does Foreign Direct Investment Go Where It Goes?: New Evidence From African Countries. *Annals of Economics and Finance*, *13*(2), 425–462.

Anyanwu, J. C. (2012). Why does Foreign Direct Investment Go Where It Goes? New Evidence from African Countries. *Annals of Economics and Finance*, *13*(2), 425–462.

Anyanwu, J. C. (2013). Characteristics and Macroeconomic Determinants of Youth Employment in Africa. *African Development Review*, *25*(2), 107–129. doi:10.1111/j.1467-8268.2013.12019.x

Anyanwu, J. C., & Augustine, D. (2013). Gender Equality in Employment in Africa: Empirical Analysis and Policy Implications. *African Development Review*, *25*(4), 400–420. doi:10.1111/1467-8268.12038

AOSSG. (2015). *Member Organisations.* Retrieved 18 Mar 2015 from: http://www.aossg.org/about-us/member-organisations

Archambault, J. J., & Archambault, M. E. (2009). An Analysis of Social Factors Influencing the Adoption of International Financial Reporting Standards. Journal for Global Business Advancement, 2(1-2).

Archambault, J. J., & Archambault, M. E. (2009). An analysis of social factors influencing the adoption of International Financial Reporting Standards. *Journal of Global Business Advancement*, *2*(1), 38–53. doi:10.1504/JGBA.2009.023093

Aripin, N., Tower, G., & Taylor, G. (2009). *Reporting financial ratios in annual reports: Voluntary disclosure perspective*. In Asian Academic Accounting Association (AAAA) Annual Conference, Istanbul, Turkey.

Armstrong, C. S., Barth, M. E., Jagolinzer, A. D., & Riedl, E. J. (2010).Market reaction to the adoption of IFRS in Europe. *Accounting Review.* Retrieved from http://papers.ssrn.com/sol3papers.cfm?abstractid=903429

Armstrong, C., Barth, M. E., Jagolizer, A. D., & Riedl, E. J. (2007). Market reaction to the adoption of IFRS in Europe. *Accounting Review*, *85*(1), 31–61. doi:10.2308/accr.2010.85.1.31

Arpan, J. S., & Radebaugh, L. H. (1985). *International Accounting and Multinational Enterprising*. New York: Wiley.

Aryeetey, C., Barthel, F., Busse, M., Loehr, C., & Osei, R. (2008). *Empirical Study on the Determinants and Pro-Development Impacts of Foreign Direct Investment in Ghana.* Study Conducted on Behalf of German Ministry for Economic Cooperation and Development and the German Technical Cooperation.

Ashbaugh, H. (2001). Non-US firms' accounting standard choices. *Journal of Accounting and Public Policy*, *20*(2), 129–153. doi:10.1016/S0278-4254(01)00025-4

Ashbaugh, H., Johnstone, K. M., & Warfield, T. D. (1999). Corporate reporting on the Internet. *Accounting Horizons*, *13*(3), 241–257. doi:10.2308/acch.1999.13.3.241

Ashbaugh, H., & Pincus, M. (2001). Domestic accounting standards, International Accounting Standards, and the predictability of earnings. *Journal of Accounting Research*, *39*(3), 417–434. doi:10.1111/1475-679X.00020

Ashbaugh-Skaife, H., Collins, D., Kinney, W., & Lanfond, R. (2008). The Effect of SOX internal control deficiencies on firm risk and cost of equity. *Journal of Accounting Research*, *47*(1), 1–43. doi:10.1111/j.1475-679X.2008.00315.x

Ashraf, J., & Ghani, W. I. (2005). Accounting Development in Pakistan. *The International Journal of Accounting, 40*, 175-201.

Ashraf, J., & Ghani, W. I. (2005). Accounting development in Pakistan. *The International Journal of Accounting*, *40*(2), 175–201. doi:10.1016/j.intacc.2005.01.010

Asiedu, E., Nana, F., & Nti-Addae, A. (2012). *The Paradox of Capital Flight from a Capital-Starved Continent*. Department of Economics, University of Kansas, Association of Concerned African Scholars, Bulletin No. 87, Fall, 2012. Retrieved from http://concernedafricascholars.org/wp-content/uploads/2012/11/caploss04-asiedu-14th.pdf

Asiedu, E. (2004). Policy Reform and Foreign Direct Investment in Africa: Absolute Progress but Relative Decline. *Development Policy Review*, *22*(1), 41–48. doi:10.1111/j.1467-8659.2004.00237.x

Asiedu, E. (2006). Foreign Direct Investment in Africa: The Role of Natural Resources, Market Size, Government Policy, Institutions and Political Instability. *World Economy*, *29*(1), 63–77. doi:10.1111/j.1467-9701.2006.00758.x

Asiedu, E., & Lien, D. (2011). Democracy, Foreign Direct Investment and Natural Resources. *Journal of International Economics*, *84*(1), 99–111. doi:10.1016/j.jinteco.2010.12.001

Askary, S. (2006). Accounting professionalism – a cultural perspective of developing countries. *Managerial Auditing Journal*, *21*(1), 102–111. doi:10.1108/02686900610634784

Askary, S., Pounder, J. S., & Yazdifar, H. (2008). Influence of Culture on Accounting Uniformity among Arabic Nations. *Education, Business and Society: Contemporary Middle Eastern Issues*, *1*(2), 145–154. doi:10.1108/17537980810890329

Asongu, S. (2011). *Law, Finance and Investment: Does Legal Origin Matter?* Retrieved from http://mpra.ub.uni-muenchen.de/34698/

Asongu, S. A. (2014a). *Knowledge Economy Gaps, Policy Syndromes and Catch-up Strategies: Fresh South Korean Lessons to Africa.* African Governance and Development Institute Working Paper No. 14/014, Yaoundé.

Asongu, S. A. (2015a). Rational Asymmetric Development, Piketty and the Spirit of Poverty in Africa. African Governance and Development Institute, No. 15/006, Yaoundé.

Asongu, S. A. (2015b). *A brief clarification to the questionable economics of foreign aid for inclusive human development.* African Governance and Development Institute Working Paper No. 14/028, Yaoundé.

Asongu, S. A. (2015c). Reinventing foreign aid for inclusive and sustainable development: Kuznets, Piketty and the great policy reversal. *Journal of Economic Surveys.* Retrieved from: http://onlinelibrary.wiley.com/doi/10.1111/joes.12109/abstract

Asongu, S. A., & Kodila-Tedika, O. (2014). *Institutions and Poverty: A Critical Comment Based on Evolving Currents and Debates.* African Governance and Development Institute Working Paper No. 14/031, Yaoundé.

Asongu, S. A., & Kodila-Tedika, O. (2015). *Is Poverty in the African DNA (Gene)?.* African Governance and Development Institute Working Paper No. 15/011, Yaoundé.

Asongu, S. A., Amavilah, V. H., & Andrés, A. R. (2014a). *Economic Implications of Business Dynamics for KE-Associated Economic Growth and Inclusive Development in African Countries.* African Governance and Development Institute Working Paper No. 14/023, Yaoundé.

Asongu, S. A., Efobi, U., & Beecroft, I. (2014b). *Inclusive human development in pre-crisis times of globalisation-driven debts.* African Governance and Development Institute Working Paper No. 14/024, Yaoundé.

Asongu, S. (2012). On the effect of foreign aid on corruption. *Economic Bulletin, 32*(3), 2174–2180.

Asongu, S. (2013). Fighting corruption when existing corruption-control levels matter. What do wealth-effects tell us in Africa? *Institutions, Etc., 5*(3), 53–74.

Asongu, S. (2014). Fighting African corruption when existing corruption-control levels matter in a dynamic cultural setting. *International Journal of Social Economics, 41*(10), 906–922. doi:10.1108/IJSE-05-2013-0117

Asongu, S. A. (2012). Government quality determinants of stock market performance in African countries. *Journal of African Business, 13*(2), 183–199. doi:10.1080/15228916.2012.727744

Asongu, S. A. (2013a). African Stock Market Performance Dynamics: A Multidimensional Convergence Assessment. *Journal of African Business, 14*(3), 186–201. doi:10.1080/15228916.2013.844043

Asongu, S. A. (2013b). How Would Population Growth Affect Investment in the Future? Asymmetric Panel Causality Evidence for Africa. *African Development Review, 25*(1), 14–29. doi:10.1111/j.1467-8268.2013.12010.x

Asongu, S. A. (2014b). Knowledge Economy and Financial Sector Competition in African Countries. *African Development Review, 26*(2), 333–346. doi:10.1111/1467-8268.12085

Asongu, S. A. (2014c). The Questionable Economics of Development Assistance in Africa: Hot-Fresh Evidence, 1996-2010. *The Review of Black Political Economy, 41*(4), 455–480. doi:10.1007/s12114-014-9203-0

Asongu, S. A. (2014d). Fighting African Capital Flight: Empirics on Benchmarking Policy Harmonization. *The European Journal of Comparative Economics, 11*(2), 93–122.

Asongu, S. A., & Ssozi, J. (2016). (Forthcoming). Sino-African relations: Some Solutions and Strategies to the Policy Syndromes. *Journal of African Business.*

Assenso-Okofo O., Ali J. M., & Ahmed K. (2009). The Development of Accounting and Reporting in Ghana. *The International Journal of Accounting, 46*(2011), 459-480.

Assenso-Okofo, O., Ali, M. J., & Ahmed, K. (2011). The development of accounting and reporting in Ghana. *The International Journal of Accounting, 46*(4), 459–480. doi:10.1016/j.intacc.2011.09.010

Atanassova, A. (2008). *IFRS adoption in Bulgarian banks: Non-numerical disclosure evidence*. Working Paper. University of Economics Varna.

Athanasios, V., & Stergios, A. (2010). Measuring investors' reaction to the adoption of international financial reporting standards in Greece, using a market-based model. *American Journal of Economics and Business Administration, 2*(1), 103–112. doi:10.3844/ajebasp.2010.103.112

Ayuba, A. (2012). A proposed rule-roadmap for the adoption of IFRS in Nigeria. Aresearch based perspective on FGN, NASB, & SEC. *American Journal of Economics*, 41–45. doi:10.5923/j.economics.20120001.10

Ayuba, A., & Gugong, B. K. (2014). Does government policy and company size influenced stakeholders perception on the adoption of international financial reporting standards (IFRS) in Nigeria. *International Journal of Economics. Finance and Management Sciences, 2*(4), 257–262.

Azémar, C., & Corcos, G. (2009). Multinational Firms' Heterogeneity in Tax Responsiveness: The Role of Transfer Pricing. *World Economy*, *32*(9), 1291–1318. doi:10.1111/j.1467-9701.2009.01210.x

Baer, W. (2002). *Economia brasileira*. NBL Editora.

Baker, R. C., & Barbu, E. M. (2009). *Institutions Involved in International Convergence of Accounting Standards: A Neo-Institutional and Historical Analysis*. CERAG.

Baker, R. G. (1998). The market for information evidence from finance directors, analysts and fund managers. *Accounting and Business Review*, *29*(1), 3–20. doi:10.1080/00014788.1998.9729563

Baker, R. W. (2005). *Capitalism's Achilles heel*. John Wiley.

Bala, M, (2013). Effects of IFRS adoption on financial reports of Nigerian listed entities: The case of oil and gas companies. *The Macrotheme Review: A Multidisciplinary Journal of Global Macro Trends, 2*(7), 9-26

Bala, M. (2013). Effects of IFRS adoption on the financial reports of Nigerian listed entities: The case of oil and gas companies. *The Macrotheme Review*, *2*(7), 9–26.

Ball R., Robin, A & Wu, J. S, (2000). Accounting standards, the institutional environment and issuer incentives: Effect on timely loss recognition in China. *Asia-Pacific Journal of Accounting and Economics, 17*(2), 71-96.

Ball, R. (2006). International Financial Reporting Standards (IFRS): pros and cons for investors. *Accounting and Business Research, 36*(sup1), 5-27.

Ball, R., Li, X., & Shivakumar, L. (2015). *Contractibility of Financial Statement Information Prepared Under IFRS: Evidence from Debt Contracts*. Retrieved from http://ssrn.com/abstract=2278946

Ball, R. (2006). *International Financial Reporting Standards (IFRS): Pros and Cons for Investors*. Accounting and Business Research.

Ball, R. (2006). International Financial Reporting Standards (IFRS): Pros and cons for investors. *Accounting and Business Review*, *36*(sup1), 5–27. doi:10.1080/00014788.2006.9730040

Ball, R., Kothari, S. P., & Robin, A. (2000). The effect of international institutional factors on properties of accounting earnings. *Journal of Accounting and Economics*, *29*(1), 1–51. doi:10.1016/S0165-4101(00)00012-4

Ball, R., Robin, A., & Wu, J. S. (2003). Incentives Versus Standards: Properties of Accounting Income in four East Asian Countries. *Journal of Accounting and Economics*, *36*(1-3), 235–270. doi:10.1016/j.jacceco.2003.10.003

Bandyopadhyay, S., Sandler, T., & Younas, J. (2014). Foreign Direct Investment, aid and terrorism. *Oxford Economic Papers*, *66*(1), 25–50. doi:10.1093/oep/gpt026

Bangho, J., & Plenborg, T. (2008). Value relevance of voluntary disclosure in the annual report. *Accounting and Finance*, *48*(2), 159–180. doi:10.1111/j.1467-629X.2007.00240.x

Barako, D. G. (2007). Determinants of voluntary disclosures in Kenyan companies annual reports. *African Journal of Business Management*, *1*(5), 113–128.

Barbosa Neto, J. E., de Oliveira Dias, W., & Pinheiro, L. E. T. (2009). Impacto da convergência para as IFRS na análise financeira: Um estudo em empresas brasileiras de capital aberto. *Contabilidade Vista & Revista*, *20*(4), 131–153.

Barbu, E. M., Dumontier, P., Feleaga, N., & Feleaga, L. (2014). Mandantory environment disclosures by companies complying with IASs/IFRSs: The cases of France, Germany and the UK. *The International Journal of Accounting*, *49*(2), 231–247. doi:10.1016/j.intacc.2014.04.003

Bartels, F. L., Alladina, S. N., & Lederer, S. (2009). Foreign Direct Investment in Sub-SaharanAfrica: Motivating Factors and Policy Issues. *Journal of African Business*, *10*(2), 141–162. doi:10.1080/15228910903187791

Barth, M. E. (2007). Research, Standard Setting, and Global Financial Reporting. *Foundations and Trends in Accounting*, *1*(2), 71–165. DOI: 10.1561/1400000002

Barth, M. E., Landsman, W. R., Lang, M. H., & Williams, C. D. (2013). *Effects on comparability and capital market benefits of voluntary adoption of IFRS by US firms: Insight from voluntary adoption of IFRS by non-US firms*. Working Paper No. 3074.

Barth, M. E., Landsman, W. R., Lang, M. H., & Williams, C. D. (2013). *Effects on Comparability and Capital Market Benefits of Voluntary Adoption of IFRS by US Firms: Insights from Voluntary Adoption of IFRS by Non-US Firms (January 3, 2013)*. Rock Center for Corporate Governance at Stanford University Working Paper No 133.

Barth, M.E., Landsman, W.R. & Lang, M.H. (2007). *International accounting standard and accounting quality*. Stanford University Graduate School of Business Research. Retrieved from http:ssrn.com/abstract=668041

Barth, E. M., Landsman, W. A., & Lang, M. H. (2008). International Accounting Standards and accounting quality. *Journal of Accounting Research*, *46*(3), 467–498. doi:10.1111/j.1475-679X.2008.00287.x

Barth, M. (2008). Global financial reporting: Implications for US academics. *Accounting Review*, *83*(5), 1159–1179. doi:10.2308/accr.2008.83.5.1159

Barth, M., Landsman, R., Young, D., & Zhuang, Z. (2011). *Relevance of Differences Between Net Income Based on IFRS and Domestic Standards for European firms*. International Accounting e-Journal.

Barth, M., & Landsman, W. (2010). How did financial reporting contribute to the financial crisis? *European Accounting Review*, *19*(3), 399–423. doi:10.1080/09638180.2010.498619

Barth, M., & Schipper, K. (2008). Financial Reporting Transparency. *Journal of Accounting, Auditing & Finance*, *23*, 173–190.

Bartov, E., Goldberg, S., & Kim, M. (2005). Comparative value relevance among German, U.S and International Accounting Standards: A German Stock Market perspective. *Journal of Accounting, Auditing & Finance*, *20*(2), 95–119.

Bartov, E., Goldberg, S., & Kim, M. (2005). Comparative value relevance among German, US and International accounting standards: A German stock market perspective. *Journal of Accounting, Auditing & Finance*, *20*, 95–119.

Beatty, A., Chamberlain, S., & Magliolo, J. (1996). An empirical analysis of the economic implications of fair value accounting for investment securities. *Journal of Accounting and Economics*, *22*(1-3), 43–77. doi:10.1016/S0165-4101(96)00429-6

Beest, F., Braam, G., & Boelens, S. (2009). *Quality of financial reporting: Measuring qualitative characteristics*. Nice Working Paper 09-108.

Belkaoui, A., & Kahl, A. (1978). *Corporate financial disclosure in Canada*. CCGAA Research Monograph.

Belsey, D. A., Kuhn, E., & Welsch, R. E. (1980). *Regression diagnostics, identifying influential data and sources of collinearity*. New York: John Wiley & Sons. doi:10.1002/0471725153

Beneish, M. D., Miller, B. P., & Yohn, T. L. (2010). *IFRS Adoption and Cross-Border Investment in Equity and Debt Markets*. Available at SSRN: http://ssrn.com/abstract=1403451

Beneish, M. D., Miller, B. P., & Yohn, T. L. (2012). The impact of financial reporting on equity versus debt markets: Macroeconomic evidence from mandatory IFRS adoption. *Journal of Accounting and Public Policy*, *34*(2015), 1–27.

Beneish, M. D., Miller, B. P., & Yohn, T. L. (2015). Macroeconomic evidence on the impact of mandatory IFRS adoption on equity and debt markets. *Journal of Accounting and Public Policy*, *34*(1), 1–27. doi:10.1016/j.jaccpubpol.2014.10.002

Beneish, M. D., & Yohn, T. L. (2008). Information friction and investor home bias: A perspective on the effect of global IFRS adoption on the extent of equity home bias. *Journal of Accounting and Public Policy*, *27*(6), 433–443. doi:10.1016/j.jaccpubpol.2008.09.001

Beuselinck, C., Joos, P., & Van der Meulen, S. (2007). *International earnings comparability*. Working Paper. Tilburg University.

Beuselinck, C., Joos, P., Khurana, I., & Van der Meulen, S. (2009). *Mandatory IFRS Reporting and Stock Price Informativeness*. SSRN eLibrary.

Bewaji, O. (2012). *The international financial reporting standards: Implication for the Nigerian accountants*. Paper presented at the 49th induction ceremony of the Institute of Chartered Accountants of Nigeria (ICAN).

Bhattacharjee, S., & Islam, M. Z. (2009). Problems of adoption and application of international financial reporting standards (IFRS) in Bangladesh. *International Journal of Business and Management*, *4*(12), 165–175. doi:10.5539/ijbm.v4n12p165

Bieniasz, A., Gołaś, Z., & Czerwińska-Kayzer, D. (2011). Klasyfikacja i prezentacja aktywów rolniczych w sprawozdaniu finansowym według polskich i międzynarodowych regulacji rachunkowości. *Zeszyty Teoretyczne Rachunkowości*, (64), 9-24.

Bissessur, S., & Hodgson, A. (2012). Stock market synchronicity- an alternative approach to assessing the information impact of Australian IFRS. *Accounting and Finance*, *52*(1), 187–212. doi:10.1111/j.1467-629X.2010.00388.x

Blanchette, M., Racicot, F. E., & Girard, J. Y. (2011). *The effects of IFRS on financial ratios: Early evidence in Canada*. Certified General Accountants Association of Canada.

Blanchette, M., Racicot, F. E., & Sedzro, K. (2013). *IFRS Adoption in Canada: An empirical analysis of the impact on financial statements*. Certified General Accountants Association of Canada.

Blas, J. (2014). Inequality mar Africa's rise. *Financial Times*. Retrieved October 18 2014 from: http://www.ft.com/intl/cms/s/0/9e74aa50-1e4d-11e4-ab52-00144feabdc0.html#axzz3GWsY4I91

Bogdan, D., Stefana, M., Marilen, D., & Gabriel, P. (2010). *National legislative systems and foreign standards and regulations: The case of International Financial Reporting Standards adoption*. Working Paper. University of Munich.

Bohusová, H. (2008). The empirical study of the SMEs position in the process of IFRS for SME application in the Czech Republic. *Economics and Management*, *1*, 157–162.

Bonaci, C. G., & Tudor, A. T. (2011). Fair Value Empirical Studies: An Overview on Accounting Research Literature. *Annales Universitatis Apulensis Series Oeconomica, 2*(13), 197 – 206.

Bond, P. (2010). Is Africa still being looted? World Bank dodges its own research. *LINKS International Journal of Socialist Renewal*. Retrieved August 21, 2015 from: http://links.org.au/node/1843

Boolaky, P. K. (2012). Accounting Development and International Financial Reporting Standards in Small Island Economies: The Case of Mauritius between 1960-2008. *Journal of Accounting in Emerging Economies*, *2*(1), 4–29. doi:10.1108/20421161211196102

Borkowski, S. C. (1997). The transfer pricing concerns of developed and developing countries. *The International Journal of Accounting*, *32*(3), 321–336. doi:10.1016/S0020-7063(97)90014-5

Boutchkova, M., & Meggison, W. (2000). Privatization and the rise of global capital market. *Financial Management*, *29*(4), 31–76. doi:10.2307/3666368

Boyatzis, R. E. (1998). *Transforming qualitative information: Thematic analysis and code development*. Thousand Oaks, CA: Sage Publications.

Boyce, J. K., & Ndikumana, L. (2012a). *Capital Flight from Sub-Saharan African Countries: Updated Estimate, 1970-2010*. Political Economy Research Institute, University of Massachusetts. Retrieved August 1, 2014 from: http://www.peri.umass.edu/fileadmin/pdf/ADP/SSAfrica_capitalflight_Oct23_2012.pdf

Boyce, J. K., & Ndikumana, L. (2012b). *Rich Presidents of Poor Nations: Capital Flight from Resource-Rich Countries in Africa*. Political Economy Research Institute, University of Massachusetts. Retrieved August 1, 2014 from: http://concernedafricascholars.org/wp-content/uploads/2012/11/caploss01-ndiku-14th.pdf

Boyce, J. K., & Ndikumana, L. (2003). Public Debts and Private Assets: Explaining Capital Flight from Sub-Saharan African Countries. *World Development*, *31*(1), 107–130. doi:10.1016/S0305-750X(02)00181-X

Boyce, J. K., & Ndikumana, L. (2010). Measurement of Capital Flight: Methodology and Results for Sub-Saharan African Countries. *African Development Review*, *22*(4), 471–481. doi:10.1111/j.1467-8268.2010.00243.x

Bradshaw, M., Bushee, B., & Miller, G. (2004). Accounting choice, home bias, and U.S. investment in Non-U.S. firms. *Journal of Accounting Research*, *42*(5), 795–841. doi:10.1111/j.1475-679X.2004.00157.x

Briston, R.J. (1978). The evolution of accounting in developing countries, *International Journal of Accounting: Education and Research*, (Fall), 105-120.

Brochet, F., Jagolinzer, A., & Riedl, E. (2011). *Mandatory IFRS Adoption and Financial Statement Comparability*. Harvard Business Review Working Paper 11-109.

Brochet, F., Jagolinzer, A., & Riedl, E. J. (2011). *Mandatory IFRS adoption and financial statement comparability*. Working Paper, 11-109.

Brochet, F., Jagolinzer, A. D., & Riedl, E. J. (2013). Mandatory IFRS Adoption and Financial Statement Comparability. *Contemporary Accounting Research*, *30*(4), 1373–1400. doi:10.1111/1911-3846.12002

Brown & Tarca. (2007). A Commentary on Issues Relating to the Enforcement of International Financial Reporting Standards in the EU. *European Accounting Review*, *14*(1), 181–212.

Brown, P. (2013). Some Observations on Research on the Benefits to Nations of Adopting IFRS. *Japanese Accounting Review*. Doi:10.11640/tjar.3.2013.01

Brown, P. (2011). International Financial Reporting: What are the benefits? *Accounting and Business Review*, *41*(3), 269–285. doi:10.1080/00014788.2011.569054

Brown, P., & Tarca, A. (2005). A commentary on issues relating to the enforcement of international financial reporting standards in the EU. *European Accounting Review*, *14*(1), 181–212. doi:10.1080/0963818042000338997

Bruggemann, U., Hitz, J. M., & Sellhon, T. (2013). Intended and unintended consequences of mandatory IFRS adoption: A review of extant evidence and suggestions for future research. *European Accounting Review*, *22*(1), 1–37. doi:10.1080/09638180.2012.718487

Brush, S. B., & Stabinsky, D. (1996). *Valuing Local Knowledge: Indigenous people and intellectual property rights*. Washington, DC: Island Press.

Bryman, A., & Cramer, D. (2007). *Quantitative data analysis with SPSS for windows*. London: Routledge.

Bui, T. M. V. (2011). *A study of the development of accounting in Vietnam.* (PhD thesis). RMIT University, Melbourne, Australia.

Bushee, B., & Leuz, C. (2005). Economic consequences of SEC disclosure regulation: Evidence from the OTC Bulletin Board. *Journal of Accounting and Economics*, *39*(2), 233–264. doi:10.1016/j.jacceco.2004.04.002

Bushman, R., Piotroski, J., & Smith, A. (2006). *Capital allocation and timely accounting recognition of economic losses.* Working Paper. University of North Carolina and University of Chicago.

Bushman, R., & Smith, A. (2001). Financial accounting information and corporate governance. *Journal of Accounting and Economics*, *32*(1-3), 237–333. doi:10.1016/S0165-4101(01)00027-1

Busse, M., & Hefeker, C. (2007). Political risk, institutions and foreign direct investment. *European Journal of Political Economy*, *23*(2), 397–415. doi:10.1016/j.ejpoleco.2006.02.003

Cafe, F. (2013). *Propose Vietnamese Accounting Standards for capital market (in Vietnamese).* Retrieved from http://cafef.vn/pageprintnews.aspx?news_id=201307160018200179

Cafe, F. (2013). *Propose Vietnamese Accounting Standards for capital market.* Retrieved from http://cafef.vn/pageprintnews.aspx?news_id=201307160018200179

Cai, F., & Wong, H. (2010). The effect of IFRS adoption on global market integration. *International Business and Economics Research Journal*, *9*(10), 25–34.

Cairns, D. (1990). Aid for the developing world. *Accountancy*, (March), 82-85.

Callao, S., & Jarne, J. I. (2010). Have IFRS affected earnings management in the European Union*? Accounting in Europe*, *7*(2), 159–189. doi:10.1080/17449480.2010.511896

Callao, S., Jarne, J., & Lainez, A. (2007). Adoption of IFRS in Spain: Effect on the comparability and relevance of financial reporting. *Journal of International Accounting, Auditing & Taxation*, *16*(2), 148–178. doi:10.1016/j.intaccaudtax.2007.06.002

Callen, J. L., Morel, M., & Richardson, G. (2011). Do culture and religion mitigate earings management? Evidence from a cross-country analysis. *International Journal of Disclosure and Governance*, *8*(2), 103–121. doi:10.1057/jdg.2010.31

Camfferman, K., & Zeff, S. (2007). *Financial Reporting and Global Capital Markets-A History of the International Accounting standards committee.* London: Oxford University Press. doi:10.1093/acprof:oso/9780199296293.001.0001

Capkun, V., Collins, D. W., & Jeanjean, T. (2013). *The Effect of IAS/IFRS Adoption on Earnings Management (Smoothing): A Closer Look at Competing Explanations.* Retrieved from: http://ssrncom/abstract=1850228 or http://dxdoiorg/102139/ssrn1850228

Caracciolo, F., & Santeramo, F. G. (2013). Price Trends and Income Inequalities: Will Sub-Saharan Africa Reduce the Gap? *African Development Review*, *25*(1), 42–54. doi:10.1111/j.1467-8268.2013.12012.x

Cardoso, R. L., Saravia, E., Tenório, F. G., & Silva, M. A. (2009). Accounting regulation: Theories and analysis of the Brazilian accounting standards convergence to IFRS. *Revista de Administração Pública*, *43*(4), 773–799.

Carmona, S., & Trombetta, M. (2008). On the global acceptance of IAS/IFRS accounting standards: The logic and implications of the principles-based system. *Journal of Accounting and Public Policy*, *27*(6), 455–461. doi:10.1016/j.jaccpubpol.2008.09.003

Carvalho, L. N., & Salotti, B. M. (2012). Adoption of IFRS in Brazil and the consequences to accounting education. *Issues in Accounting Education*, *28*(2), 235–242. doi:10.2308/iace-50373

Cascino, S & Gassen, J. (2010). *Mandatory IFRS adoption and accounting comparability.* SSRN eLibrary.

Cascino, S., & Gassen, J. (2012). *Comparability Effects of Mandatory IFRS Adoption.* SFB 649 Discussion Paper 2012-009. Retrieved 14 November 2014 from: http://sfb649.wiwi.hu-berlin.de/papers/pdf/SFB649DP2012-009.pdf

Caulderwood, K. (2015). Sub-Saharan Africa Falls Behind In Fight Against Extreme Poverty: World Bank Report. *International Business Times.* Retrieved April 19, 2015 from: http://www.ibtimes.com/sub-saharan-africa-falls-behind-fight-against-extreme-poverty-world-bank-report-1881460

CESR-The Committee of European Securities Regulations (2003). *Standard nº1 on Financial Information – Enforcement of Standards on Financial Information in Europe.* Author.

Chakroun, R. (2013). Family control, board of directors' independence and extent of voluntary disclosure in the annual reports: Case of Tunisian companies. *Journal of Business Studies Quarterly*, *5*(1), 22–42.

Chalmers, K. G., Godfrey, J. M., & Webster, J. C. (2011). Does a goodwill impairment regime better reflect the underlying economic attributes of goodwill? *Accounting and Finance*, *51*(3), 634–660. doi:10.1111/j.1467-629X.2010.00364.x

Chalmers, K., Clinch, G., & Godfrey, J. M. (2011). Changes in value relevance of accounting information upon IFRS Adoption: Evidence from Australia. *Australian Journal of Management.*, *36*(2), 151–173. doi:10.1177/0312896211404571

Chamisa, E. E. (2000). The Relevance and Observance of the IASC Standards in Developing Countries and the Particular Case of Zimbabwe. *The International Journal of Accounting, 35*(2), 267 – 286.

Chamisa. (2000). *The Relevance of and Observance of the IASC Standards in Developing Countries and the Particular Case of Zimbabwe.* University of Illinois.

Chamisa, E. E. (2000). The relevance and observance of the IASC Standards in developing countries and the particular case of Zimbabwe. *The International Journal of Accounting*, *35*(2), 267–286. doi:10.1016/S0020-7063(00)00049-2

Chand, P., Patel, C., & Patel, A. (2005). *Judgements of Professional Accountants in Fiji: Implications for Convergence of Accounting Standards.* Academic Press.

Chang, H-J., (2008). *Bad Samaritans: The Myth of Free Trade and the Secret History of Capitalism.* Bloomsbury Press.

Chan, S. Y. (2001). The use of graphs as decision aids in relation to information overload and managerial decision quality. *Journal of Information Science*, *27*(6), 417–425. doi:10.1177/016555150102700607

Chau, G. K., & Gray, S. J. (2002). Ownership structure and corporate voluntary disclosure in Hong Kong and Singapore. *The Journal of International Accounting*, *37*(2), 247–265. doi:10.1016/S0020-7063(02)00153-X

Chen, C.J., Ding, Y., & Xu, B. (2010). *Convergence of Accounting Standards and Foreign Direct Investment.* Finance and Corporate Governance Conference 2011 Paper.

Cheng, E., & Courtenay, S. (2006). Board composition, regulatory regime and voluntary disclosure. *The International Journal of Accounting*, *41*(3), 262–289. doi:10.1016/j.intacc.2006.07.001

Chen, H., Tang, Q., Jiang, Y., & Lin, Z. (2010). The role of International Financial Reporting Standards in accounting quality: Evidence from the European Union. *Journal of International Financial Management and Accounting*, *21*(3), 220–278. doi:10.1111/j.1467-646X.2010.01041.x

Chen, P., Yuan, D., & Bin, X. (2014). Convergence of accounting standards and foreign direct investment. *The International Journal of Accounting*, *49*(1), 53–86. doi:10.1016/j.intacc.2014.01.007

Chen, Y., & Rezaee, Z. (2012). The role of corporate governance in convergence with IFRS: Evidence from China. *International Journal of Accounting and Information Management, Vol, 20*(2), 171–188. doi:10.1108/18347641211218470

Chiha, H., Trabelsi, N. S., & Hamza, S. E. (2013). The effect of IFRS on earnings quality in a European stock market: Evidence from France. *Interdisciplinary Journal of Research in Business, 2*(12), 35–47.

Choi, F. D., & Levich, R. M. (1991). Behavioral Effects of International Accounting Diversity. *Accounting Horizons, 5*(2), 1–13.

Choi, F., & Levich, R. (1991). Behavioral effects of international accounting diversity. *Accounting Horizons, 5*(2), 1–13.

Choi, F., & Levich, R. M. (1991). Behavioural effects of international accounting diversity. *Accounting Horizons*, (June): 1–13.

Choi, F., & Meek, G. (2008). *International Accounting* (6th ed.). Upper Saddle River, NJ: Pearson Education Inc.

Chow, C. W., & Wong-Boren, A. (1987). Voluntary financial disclosure by Mexican corporations. *Accounting Review, 62*(3), 533–541.

Christensen, H. B., Lee, E., & Walker, M. (2008). *Incentives or standards: what determines accounting quality changes around IFRS adoption?* Working Paper. University of Chicago and University of Manchester. Retrieved from http://papers.ssrn.com/sol3/papers.cfm?abstract_id=1013054

Christensen, H. B., Lee, E., & Walker, M. (2008). *Incentives or Standards: What Determines Accounting Quality Changes Around IFRS Adoption?*. Available at: http://ssrn.com/abstract=1013054

Christensen, H., & Nikolaev, V. (2008). *Who uses fair value accounting for non-financial assets after IFRS adoption?* University of Chicago, Booth School of Business, working paper, No 09-12.

Christensen, H., Lee, E., & Walker, M. (2008). *Incentives or standards: What determines Accounting quality changes around IFRS adoption*? Presented at the annual meeting of the American Accounting Association, Anaheim, CA.

Christensen, H., Lee, E., & Walker, M. (2008). *Incentives or standards: What determines accounting quality changes around IFRS adoption?* Working Paper. Manchester Accounting and Finance Group and Manchester Business School.

Christensen, H. B., Lee, E., & Walker, M. (2007). Cross-sectional variation in the economic consequences of international accounting harmonization: The case of mandatory IFRS adoption in the UK. *The International Journal of Accounting, 42*(4), 341–379. doi:10.1016/j.intacc.2007.09.007

Chua, W. F., & Taylor, S. L. (2008). The rise and rise of IFRS: An examination of IFRS diffusion. *Journal of Accounting and Public Policy, 27*(6), 462–473. doi:10.1016/j.jaccpubpol.2008.09.004

Cinca, C. S., Molinero, C. M., & Larraz, J. L. G. (2005). Country and size effects in financial ratios: A European perspective. *Global Finance Journal, 16*(1), 26–47. doi:10.1016/j.gfj.2005.05.003

Clarkson, P., Hanna, J. D., Richardson, G. D., & Thompson, R. (2011). The impact of IFRS adoption on the value relevance of book value and earnings. *Journal of Contemporary Accounting and Economics, 7*(1), 1–17. doi:10.1016/j.jcae.2011.03.001

Clement, M. B., & Tse, S. Y. (2003). Do investors respond to analysts' forecast revisions as if forecast accuracy is all that matters? *Accounting Review, 78*(1), 227–249. doi:10.2308/accr.2003.78.1.227

Clements, C. E., Neill, J. D., & Stovall, O. (2010). Cultural Diversity, Country Size, And The IFRS Adoption Decision. *Journal of Applied Business Research, 26*(2), 115–126. doi:10.19030/jabr.v26i2.288

Clements, C. E., Neill, J. D., & Stovall, O. S. (2010). Cultural diversity, country size, and the IFRS adoption decision. *Journal of Applied Business Research*, *26*(2), 115–126.

Cohen, J. R., Pant, L. W., & Sharp, D. J. (1993). Culture-Based Ethical Conflicts Confronting Multinational Accounting Firms. *Accounting Horizons*, *7*(3), 1–13.

Collins, D. L., Pasewark, W. R., & Riley, M. E. (2012). Financial Reporting Outcomes under Rules-Based and Principles-Based Accounting Standards. *Accounting Horizons*, *26*(4), 681–705. doi:10.2308/acch-50266

Collins, S. (1989). The Move to Globalization: Is a Common International Accounting Language Feasible? *Journal of Accountancy*, *167*, 82–85.

Cooke, T. (1991). An assessment of voluntary disclosure in annual reports of Japanese corporations. *The International Journal of Accounting*, *26*(3), 174–189.

Cooke, T. E. (1989). Voluntary corporate disclosure by Swedish companies. *Journal of International Financial Management and Accounting*, *1*(2), 171–195. doi:10.1111/j.1467-646X.1989.tb00009.x

Cooke, T., & Wallace, R. (1990). Financial disclosure regulation and its environment: A review and further analysis. *Journal of Accounting and Public Policy*, *9*(2), 79–110. doi:10.1016/0278-4254(90)90013-P

Cooper, D. J., & Robson, K. (2006). Accounting, Profession and Regulation: Locating the Sites of Professionalization. *Accounting, Organizations and Society*, *31*(4-5), 415–444. doi:10.1016/j.aos.2006.03.003

Cordeiro, R., Couto, G., & Silva, F. (2007). *Measuring the Impact of International Financial Reporting Standards (IFRS) in Firm Reporting: The Case of Portugal*. Available at SSRN:http://ssrn.com/abstract=969972

Cormier, D. (2013). *The incidence of corporate governance and IFRS on information asymmetry and the value relevance of earnings: Some Canadian evidence*. Cahier de Recherche 2014-01.

Cormier, D. (2014). *The Incidence of Corporate Governance and IFRS on Information Asymmetry and the Value Relevance of Earnings: Some Canadian Evidence*. Retrieved from www.cifo.uqam.ca/publications/pdf/2014-01.pdf

Covrig, V., Defond, M. M., & Hung, M. (2007). Home bias, foreign mutual fund holdings and the voluntary adoption of International Accounting Standards. *Journal of Accounting Research*, *45*(1), 41–70. doi:10.1111/j.1475-679X.2007.00226.x

Cuijpers, R., & Buijink, W. (2005). Voluntary adoption of non local GAAP in the European Union: A study of determinants and consequences. *European Accounting Review*, *14*(3), 487–524. doi:10.1080/0963818042000337132

Curtis, A., & Todorova, O. (2011). *Spotlight on Africa's transfer pricing landscape, Transfer pricing perspectives: Special edition. Taking a detailed look at transfer pricing in Africa*. Retrieved August 30, 2015 from: https://www.pwc.com/en_GX/gx/tax/transfer-pricing/management-strategy/assets/pwc-transfer-pricing-africa-pdf.pdf

Daniel, P., Suranova, Z., & De Beelde, I. (2001). The development of accounting in Slovakia. *European Accounting Review*, *10*(2), 343–359. doi:10.1080/09638180126639

Danjou, P., & Walton, P. (2012, June1). The Legitimacy of the IASB. *Accounting in Europe*, *9*(1), 1–15. doi:10.1080/17449480.2012.664396

Daouda, Y. H. (2013). La croissance économique est-elle pro-pauvres au Niger? *African Development Review*, *25*(2), 203–214. doi:10.1111/j.1467-8268.2013.12024.x

Dargenidou, C., Mcleay, S. & Raonic, I. (2006). *Expected Earnings Growth and the Cost of Capital: An Analysis of Accounting Regime Change in the European Financial Market*. Academic Press.

Darrough, M. (1993). Disclosure policy and competition: Cournot vs. Bertrand. *Accounting Review*, *68*, 534–561.

Das, K. D., & Dutta, C. B. (2012). *Global Financial Crisis and Foreign Development Assistance Shocks in Least Developed Countries*. Retrieved from http://mpra.ub.uni-muenchen.de/id/eprint/40281

Daske, H. C., Leuz, C., & Verdi, R. (2007). *Adopting a label: Heterogeneity in the economic consequence of IFRS adoption. Initiative on Global Markets*. The University of Chicago, Graduate School of Business. Working Paper No.5.

Daske, H. (2006). Economic benefits of adopting IFRS or US-GAAP – have the expected cost of equity capital really decreased? *Journal of Business Finance & Accounting*, *33*(3), 329–373. doi:10.1111/j.1468-5957.2006.00611.x

Daske, H., & Gebhardt, G. (2006). International Financial Reporting Standards and Experts Perceptions of Disclosure Quality. *Abacus*, *42*(3).

Daske, H., Hail, L., Leuz, C., & Verdi, R. (2008). Mandatory IFRS reporting around the world: Early evidence on the economic consequences. *Journal of Accounting Research*, *46*(5), 1085–1142.

Daske, H., Hail, L., Leuz, C., & Verdi, R. (2008). Mandatory IFRS Reporting around the World: Early Evidence on the Economic Consequences. *Journal of Accounting Research*, *46*(5), 1085–1142.

Daske, H., Hail, L., Leuz, C., & Verdi, R. (2008). Mandatory IFRS reporting around the world: Early evidence on the economic consequences. *Journal of Accounting Research*, *46*(5), 1085–1142.

Daske, H., Hail, L., Leuz, C., & Verdi, R. (2013). Adopting a Label: Heterogeneity in the Economic Consequences Around IAS/IFRS Adoptions. *Journal of Accounting Research*, *51*(3), 495–547. doi:10.1111/1475-679X.12005

Daske, H., Hall, L., Leuz, C., & Verdi, R. (2008). Mandatory IFRS Reporting around the World: Early evidence on the Economic Consequences. *Journal of Accounting Research*, *46*, 1085–1142.

Daude, C., & Stein, E. (2007). The Quality of Institutions and Foreign Direct Investment. *Economics and Politics*, *19*(3), 317–344. doi:10.1111/j.1468-0343.2007.00318.x

Day, R. G. (2000). *UK Accounting Regulation: An Historical Perspective. Working Paper Series*. Bournemouth University, School of Finance & Law.

De Franco, G., Kothari, S., & Verdi, R. (2009). *The benefits of financial statement comparability*. Working Paper. MIT Sloan School of Management.

Deaton, A. (1999). Commodity Prices and Growth in Africa. *The Journal of Economic Perspectives*, *13*(3), 23–40.

DeFond, M., Hu, X., Hung, M., & Li, S. (2011). The impact of mandatory IFRS adoption on foreign mutual fund ownership: The role of comparability. *Journal of Accounting and Economics*, *51*(3), 240–258. doi:10.1016/j.jacceco.2011.02.001

DeGregorio, J. (2003). *The role of FDI and Natural Recourses in Economic Development*. Working paper No. 196. Central Bank of Chile, Santiago.

Deloitte and Touche. (2004). *First-Time Adoption: A Guide to IFRS*. Retrieved from www.iasplus.com/dttpubs/ifrs1guide.pdf

Deloitte. (2011). *Use of IFRSs by jurisdiction*. Available from: http://www.iasplus.com/country/useias.htm

Demaki, G. O. (2013). Prospects and challenges of International Financial Reporting Standards to economic development in Nigeria. *Global Journal of Management and Business Research*, *13*(1), 69–74.

Denisia, V. (2010). Foreign Direct Investment Theories: An Overview of the Main FDI Theories. *European Journal of Interdisciplinary Studies*, *3*, 53–59.

Devalle, A., Onali, E., & Magarini, R. (2010). Assessing the value relevance of accounting data after the introduction of IFRS in Europe. *Journal of International Financial Management and Accounting*, *21*(2), 85–119. doi:10.1111/j.1467-646X.2010.01037.x

Dhaliwal, D., Wen, H., Li, Y., & Pereira, R. (2013). *Does mandatory IFRS adoption facilitate financial market integration?* Paper presented at the American Accounting Association (AAA) Annual meeting and Conference, Consequences of IFRS Adoption, California.

Di Maggio, P. J., & Powell, W. W. (1983, April). The Iron Cage Revisited: Institutional Isomorphism and Collective Rationality in Organizational Fields. *American Sociological Review*, *48*(2), 147–160. doi:10.2307/2095101

Diak, D. (2014). A Look at Capital Flight from the Developing World. *GIVING what we can.* Retrieved from https://www.givingwhatwecan.org/blog/2014-10-16/look-capital-flight-developing-world

Diamond, D., & Verrecchia, R. (1991). Disclosure, liquidity, and the cost of capital. *The Journal of Finance*, *46*(4), 1325–1359. doi:10.1111/j.1540-6261.1991.tb04620.x

Ding, Y., Hope, O. K., Jeanjean, T., & Stolowy, H. (2007). Differences between domestic accounting standards and IAS: Measurement, determinants and implications. *Journal of Accounting and Public Policy*, *26*(1), 1–38. doi:10.1016/j.jaccpubpol.2006.11.001

Ding, Y., Jeanjean, T., & Stolowy, H. (2005). Why do national GAAP differ from IAS? *The International Journal of Accounting*, *40*(4), 325–350. doi:10.1016/j.intacc.2005.09.004

Djankov, S., La Porta, R., Florencio, L., & Andrei, S. (2003). Courts. *The Quarterly Journal of Economics*, *118*(2), 453–517. doi:10.1162/003355303321675437

Dobija, D. (2010). Dylematy standaryzacji sprawozdawczości finansowej, wyceny i pomiaru ryzyka. *Zeszyty Teoretyczne Rachunkowości*, (57), 5-14.

Dobija, D., & Klimczak, K. K. (2010). Development of accounting in Poland: Market efficiency and the value relevance of reported earnings. *The International Journal of Accounting*, *45*(3), 356–374. doi:10.1016/j.intacc.2010.06.010

Donnelly, L. (2015, May). Illicit financial flows costing Africa billions. *Mail & Guardian.* Retrieved from http://mg.co.za/article/2015-05-25-illicit-financial-flows-costing-africa-billions/

Donwa, P. A., & Odia, J. O. (2012). Initial challenges of first-time adoption of International Financial Reporting Standards in Nigeria. *National Accountants*, *20*(1), 33–41.

Dorfman, J., & Johnson, E. A. J. (1939). Predecessors of Adam Smith: The Growth of British Economic Thought. *Political Science Quarterly*, *54*(1), 103–105. doi:10.2307/2143578

Doucougliagos, H., & Paldam, M. (2008). Aid effectiveness on growth: A meta study. *European Journal of Political Economy*, *24*(1), 1–24. doi:10.1016/j.ejpoleco.2007.06.002

Doucouliagos, H., & Paldam, M. (2009). The aid effectiveness literature: The sad results of 40 years of research. *Journal of Economic Surveys*, *23*(3), 433–461. doi:10.1111/j.1467-6419.2008.00568.x

Drine, I. (2013). 'Successful' Development Models: Lessons from the MENA Region. In *Achieving Development Success: Strategies and Lessons from the Developing World.* doi:10.1093/acprof:oso/9780199671557.003.0023

Drury, C. (2007). *Management and Cost Accounting* (6th ed.). London: Thomson Learning.

Dumontier, P., & Raffournier, B. (1998). Why firms comply voluntarily with IAS: An empirical analysis with Swiss data. *Journal of International Financial Management & Accounting*, *9*(3), 216–245. doi:10.1111/1467-646X.00038

Durocher, S., Fortin, A., & Cote, L. (2007). Users' participation in the Accounting Standard-setting Process: A Theory-building Study. *Accounting, Organizations and Society*, *32*(1-2), 29–59. doi:10.1016/j.aos.2006.03.004

Easley, D., & O'Hara, M. (2004). Information and the cost of capital. *The Journal of Finance*, *59*(4), 1553–1583. doi:10.1111/j.1540-6261.2004.00672.x

Easterly, W. (2008). Introduction. In W. Easterl (Ed.), *Reinventing Foreign Aid.* Cambridge, MA: The MIT Press.

ECOVIS SV. (2013, January). *The Ministry of Finance shall amend the 37 Vietnamese Standards on Auditing (VSA) and 26 Vietnamese Accounting Standards (VAS) in 2013.* Newsletter.

Efobi, U. (2014). *IFRS Adoption and the Environment: Is Africa closing her Eyes to Something?* Working paper available at SSRN.

Efobi, U. R. (2015b). IFRS Adoption and the Environment: Is Africa Closing Her Eyes to Something? In Beyond the UN Global Compact: Institutions and Regulations (pp. 169-195). doi:10.1108/S2051-503020150000017016

Efobi, U., Iyoha, F., & Mukoro, D. (2014). *IFRS Adoption and Foreign Investment in Africa: Institutions also Matter.* Working paper available at SSRN.

Efobi, U. R. (2015a). Politicians' Attributes and Institutional Quality in Africa: A Focus on Corruption. *Journal of Economic Issues*, *49*(3), 787–813. doi:10.1080/00213624.2015.1072393

Efobi, U., Osabuohien, E., & Beecroft, I. (2013). The Macroeconomic Consequences of the Black Sunday in Nigeria. In J. Adibe (Ed.), *The Politics and Economics of Removing Subsidies on Petroleum Products in Nigeria.* London: Adonis & Abbey Publishers.

Eichhorst, P., Steens, B. Van der Tas, L. & Smits, M. (2002). *IAS 2005. preparing your enterprise for new International Financial Reporting Standards* (E&Y cap gemini).

Elad, C. (2015). The development of accounting in Franc Zone countries in Africa. *The International Journal of Accounting*, *50*(1), 75–100. doi:10.1016/j.intacc.2014.12.006

Elbannan, M. A. (2011). Accounting and stock market effects of international accounting standards adoption in an emerging economy. *Review of Quantitative Finance and Accounting*, *36*(2), 207–245. doi:10.1007/s11156-010-0176-1

El-Firjani, E., & Faraj, S. (2014). *An Empirical Investigation into the Motives for the Adoption of International Accounting Standards (IASs) Within Developing Countries: The Case of Libya.* Paper presented at the British Accounting & Finance Association 50th Annual Conference, London, UK.

El-Gazzar, S. M., Finn, P. M., & Jacob, R. (1999). An empirical investigation of multinational firms' compliance with International Accounting Standards. *The International Journal of Accounting*, *34*(2), 239–248. doi:10.1016/S0020-7063(99)00005-9

Elliott, B., & Elliott, J. (2007). Financial Accounting and Reporting (11th ed). Prentice Hall.

Elu, J., & Loubert, L. (2013). Earnings Inequality and the Intersectionality of Gender and Ethnicity In Sub-Saharan Africa: The Case of Tanzanian Manufacturing. *American Economic Review*, *103*(3), 289-292.

Emenyonu, E. N., & Gray, S. J. (1992). EC accounting harmonisation: An empirical study of measurement practices in France, Germany and the UK. *Accounting and Business Review*, *23*(89), 49–58. doi:10.1080/00014788.1992.9729860

Eng, L. L., & Mak, Y. T. (2003). Corporate governance and voluntary disclosure. *Journal of Accounting and Public Policy*, *22*(4), 325–345. doi:10.1016/S0278-4254(03)00037-1

Englebert, P. (2002). Solving the mystery of the Africa dummy. *World Development*, *28*(10), 1821–1835. doi:10.1016/S0305-750X(00)00052-8

Ernest, J. (2014). Český průmysl je náš jen z poloviny [Czech industry is our only half]. *Statistika & My*, *4*(10), 8-19. Retrieved June 7 2015 from: http://www.statistikaamy.cz/wp-content/uploads/2014/12/18041410.pdf

Ernst & Young. (2005). *Transfer pricing global reference guide*. Retrieved from http://www.ey.com/global/download.nsf/International/Global Transfer Pricing Guide August 2005/$file/GlobalTPGuide Aug05.pdf

Ernst & Young. (2006). *Global Transfer Pricing Surveys*. Retrieved from http://www.ey.com/Global/download.nsf/International/Tax - Global Transfer Pricing Survey Part 3/$file/EY GlobalTPSurvey3 Sep2006.pdf

Ernst & Young. (2013). Kenya firms post false company results. Ernst & Young's 2013 Europe, Middle East, India and Africa Fraud Survey. *Navigating Today's Complex Business Risks*. Retrieved from http://www.theeastafrican.co.ke/news/Kenya-firms-post-false-company-results-/-/2558/1862740/-/ji0al/-/index.html

EURODAD. (2008). *Addressing development's black hole: Regulating capital flight*. European Network on Debt on Development. Retrieved from http://www.taxjustice.net/cms/upload/pdf/Eurodad-WEED-CRBM-BWP_Capital_Flight.pdf

European Commission. (2015). *Country Report Czech Republic 2015*. Retrieved from: http://ec.europa.eu/europe2020/pdf/csr2015/cr2015_czech_en.pdf

Faraj, S., & El-Firjani, E. (2014). Challenges Facing IASs/IFRS Implementation by Libyan Listed Companies. *Universal Journal of Accounting and Finance*, *2*, 57–63.

FASB. (2012). *International Convergence of Accounting Standards*. Retrieved from http://www.fasb.org/jsp/FASB/Page/SectionPage&cid=1176156245663

Fearnley, S., Gillies, A., Hines, T., & Willett, C. (2006). *Bewildered but Better Informed: A Qualitative, Interview-based Study into the Attitudes of some UK Accountants and Regulators to the EU IFRS Conversion Project Prior to its Implementation in the UK*. Working Paper. University of Portsmouth, Business School.

Fernandes, B. V. R., Lima, D. H. S., Vieira, E. T., & Niyama, J. K. (2010). *Investigação empírica da percepção dos docentes dos cursos de graduação em ciências contábeis sobre a função e atuação do comitê de pronunciamentos contábeis*. 10º Congresso USP de Controladoria e Contabilidade.

Field, T., Lys, T., & Vincent, L. (2001). Empirical research on accounting choice. *Journal of Accounting and Economics*, *31*(1-3), 255–307. doi:10.1016/S0165-4101(01)00028-3

Fijałkowska J., Jaruga-Baranowska M. (2007). The Impact of IAS/IFRS Adoption on the Presentation of the Financial Position and Performance of Polish Listed Companies. *Theoretical Journal of Accounting*, (41), 97-114.

Florou, A., & Pope, P. (2012). Mandatory IFRS adoption and institutional investment decisions. *Accounting Review*, *87*(6), 1993–2025. doi:10.2308/accr-50225

Fofack, H. (2014). *The Idea of Economic Development: Views from Africa*. WIDER Working Paper No. 2014/093.

Fofack, H., & Ndikumana, L. (2010). Capital Flight Repatriation: Investigation of its Potential Gains for Sub-Saharan African Countries. *African Development Review*, *22*(1), 4–22. doi:10.1111/j.1467-8268.2009.00226.x

Fogarty, T. J., Hussein, M. E. A., & Ketz, J. E. (1994). Political Aspects of Financial Accounting Standard Setting in the USA. *Accounting, Auditing & Accountability Journal*, *7*(4), 24–46. doi:10.1108/09513579410069830

Fosu, A. K. (2011). *Growth, Inequality and Poverty Reduction in Developing Countries: Recent Global Evidence*. UNU WIDER Working Paper 2011/01.

Fosu, A. K. (2011). *Terms of trade and growth of resource economies: A tale of two countries.* UNU-WIDER Working Paper No.2011/28

Fosu, A. K. (2010a). Does Inequality Constrain Poverty Reduction Programs? Evidence from Africa. *Journal of Policy Modeling, 32*(6), 818–827. doi:10.1016/j.jpolmod.2010.08.007

Fosu, A. K. (2010b). Inequality, Income and Poverty: Comparative Global Evidence. *Social Science Quarterly, 91*(5), 1432–1446. doi:10.1111/j.1540-6237.2010.00739.x PMID:21125764

Fosu, A. K. (2010c). The Effect of Income Distribution on the Ability of Growth to Reduce Poverty: Evidence from Rural and Urban African Economies. *American Journal of Economics and Sociology, 69*(3), 1034–1053. doi:10.1111/j.1536-7150.2010.00736.x

Fosu, A. K. (2015a). Growth, Inequality and Poverty in Sub-Saharan Africa: Recent Progress in a Global Context. *Oxford Development Studies, 43*(1), 44–59. doi:10.1080/13600818.2014.964195

Fosu, A. K. (2015b). Growth and institutions in African Development. In A. K. Fosu (Ed.), *Growth and Institutions in African Development, First* (pp. 1–17). New York: Routledge Studies in Development Economics.

Fosu, A. K. (2015c). *Growth and Institutions in African Development, First* (A. K. Fosu, Ed.). New York: Routledge Studies in Development Economics.

Fowokan, T. (2011). *IFRS adoption in Nigeria-tax implications.* Paper presented at CITN Seminar on IFRS adoption in Nigeria. Retrieved July 30, 2012 from http://www.docstoc.com/docs/89676635/IFRS-Adoption-in-Nigeria-Tax-Implications-Paper-presented-by-Mrs-Titilayo-Fowokan-ACA-ACTI-CITN-Seminar-on-IFRS-Adoption-in-Nigeria-Overview-%EF%82%97-Introdu

Fox, A, Helliar, C, Veneziani, M and Hannah, G. (2013). The Costs and Benefits of IFRS Implementation in the UK and Italy. *Journal of Applied Accounting Research, 14*(1).

Fox, A., Hannah, G., Helliar, C., & Veneziani, M. (2013). The costs and benefits of IFRS implementation in the UK and Italy. *Journal of Applied Accounting Research, 14*(1), 86–101. doi:10.1108/09675421311282568

Francis, J., Lafond, R., Olsson, P., & Schipper, K. (2004). Costs of Equity and Earning Attributes. *Accounting Review, 79*(4), 967–1010. doi:10.2308/accr.2004.79.4.967

Frost, C.A., Gordon, E.A., & Pownall, G. (2008). *Financial Reporting and Disclosure Quality, and Emerging Market Companies Access to Capital in Global Markets.* SSRN eLibrary.

Gaffikin, M. (2006). *Regulation: Standardising Accounting Practice. Working Papers Series.* School of Accounting & Finance, University of Wollongong.

Gambari, Y. (2010). *Issues in the Implementation of IFRS, Accounting and Financial Reporting Issues.* Toronto: CICA.

Garkovi, M., & Levin, R. (2002). *Does FDI accelerate economic growth?* Working Paper. University of Minnesota.

Gassen, J., & Sellhorn, T. (2006). Applying IFRS in Germany - determinants and consequences. *Betriebswirtschaftliche Forschung und Praxis, 58*(4), 365–386.

Gastón, S. C., García, C. F., Jarne, J. I. J., & Gadea, J. A. L. (2010). IFRS adoption in Spain and the United Kingdom: Effects on accounting numbers and relevance. *Advances in Accounting, incorporating. Advances in International Accounting, 26*(2), 304–313. doi:10.1016/j.adiac.2010.08.003

Gatti, D. D., Gallegati, M., Greenwald, B. C., Russo, A., & Stiglitz, J. E. (2012). Mobility constraints, productivity trends, and extended crises. *Journal of Economic Behavior & Organization, 83*(3), 375–393. doi:10.1016/j.jebo.2012.03.011

Gavana, G, Guggiola, G & Marenzi, A, (2013). Evolving connection between tax and financial reporting in Italy. *Accounting in Europe, 10*(1), 43-70.

Gebhardt, G., Reichadt, R., & Wittenbrink, C. (2004). Accounting for Financial Instruments in the Banking Industry: Conclusion from a Simulation Model. *European Accounting Review, 13*(2), 341–371. doi:10.1080/0963818042000204733a

Gee, M, Haller, A & Nobes, C, (2010). The influence of tax on IFRS consolidated statements: The convergence of Germany and the UK. *Accounting in Europe, 7*(1), 97.

Gee, M., Haller, A., & Nobes, C. (2010). The influence of tax on IFRS consolidated statements: The convergence of Germany and the UK. *Accounting in Europe, 7*(1), 97–122. doi:10.1080/17449480.2010.485382

Gelb, D., Holtzman, M. P., & Mest, D. (2008, December). International operations and voluntary disclosures by U.S.-based multinational corporations. *Advances in Accounting, 24*(2), 243–249. doi:10.1016/j.adiac.2008.09.002

Georgiou, G. (2004). Corporate Lobbying on Accounting Standards: Methods, Timing and Perceived Effectiveness. *Abacus, 40*(2), 219–237. doi:10.1111/j.1467-6281.2004.00152.x

Georgiou, G. (2010). The IASB Standard-setting Process: Participation and Perceptions of Financial Statement Users. *The British Accounting Review, 42*(2), 103–118. doi:10.1016/j.bar.2010.02.003

Gernon, H., Meek, G., & Mueller, G. (1987). Accounting: an international perspective. Homewood, IL: Irwin.

Ghana Investment Promotion Centre (GIPC). (2015). *The Ghana Investment Promotion Centre Quarterly report*. Retrieved from http://www.gipcghana.com/press-and- media/downloads.html

Ghana Statistical Service (GSS). (2015). *Foreign direct investment in Ghana*. Retrieved from http.www.statsghana.gov.gh

Gibbins, M., Richardson, A., & Waterhouse, J. (1990). The Management of Corporate Financial Disclosures: Opportunism, Ritualism, Policies and Processes. *Journal of Accounting Research, 28*(1), 121–143. doi:10.2307/2491219

Gillis, P. L. (2011). *The Big Four in China: Hegemony and Counter- hegemony in the Development of the Accounting Profession in China*. (PhD thesis). Macquarie Graduate School of Management, Macquarie University, Sydney, Australia.

Glaeser, E., La Porta, R., Lopez-De-Silanes, F., & Shleifer, A. (2004). Do institutions cause growth? *Journal of Economic Growth, 9*(3), 271–303. doi:10.1023/B:JOEG.0000038933.16398.ed

Glautier, M. W. E., & Underdown, B. (2001). *Accounting Theory and Practice* (7th ed.). Prentice Hall.

Glautier, M. W. E., & Underdown, B. (2001). *Accounting Theory and Practice (7th ed.)* London: Prentice Hall.

Gmytrasiewicz, M. (2009). Dyskusyjne metody ustalania i prezentacji wartości według Międzynarodowych Standardów Sprawozdawczości Finansowej. *Zeszyty Teoretyczne Rachunkowości*, (53), 63-70.

Goldstein, M. (2009). *Drive for Accounting Convergence Slows, G20 key*. Retrieved from http://www.reuters.com/article/reuters

Gonen, S., & Ugurluel, G. (2007). Turkey, International Financial Reporting Standards (IFRS) Transition Challenges Facing Applications and Solutions. *Journal of World Tax, 316*, 229–236.

Gordon, E., Jorgensen, B., & Linthicum, C. (2008). *Could IFRS replace US GAAP? A comparison of earnings attributes and informativeness in the US Market.* Working paper. Temple University, Columbia University, and University of Texas at San Antonio.

Gordon, L. A., Loeb, M. P., & Zhu, W. (2012). The Impact of IFRS Adoption on Foreign Direct Investment. *Journal of Accounting and Public Policy, 31*(4), 374–398. doi:10.1016/j.jaccpubpol.2012.06.001

Grabiński, K., & Kędzior, M. (2007b). Bilanse według ustawy o rachunkowości i Międzynarodowych Standardów Rachunkowości. *Rachunkowość, 11*, 7-21.

Grabiński, K., & Kędzior, M. (2007a). An empirical evidence on convergence of Polish Accounting Rules and International Financial Reporting Standards on the basis of Polish PLC listed on the Warsaw Stock Exchange. *30th Annual Congress*, European Accounting Association, Lisbon.

Grabiński, K., & Kędzior, M. (2007c). *Wpływ zastosowania Międzynarodowych Standardów Rachunkowości na wartość analityczną sprawozdań finansowych spółek notowanych na Giełdzie Papierów Wartościowych w Warszawie. In Rachunkowość w teorii i praktyce*. Poznań: Wydawnictwo Akademii Ekonomicznej w Poznaniu.

Grabiński, K., Kędzior, M., & Krasodomska, J. (2014). The Polish accounting system and IFRS implementation process in the view of empirical research. *Accounting and Management Information Systems*, *13*(2), 281–310.

Graham, E. M. (1995). *Foreign Direct Investment in the World Economy.* IMF Working Papers 95/59. International Monetary Fund

Gray, S. G., McSwenney, L. B., & Shaw, J. C. (1984). *Information disclosure and the multinational corporation*. London: John Wiley and Sons.

Gray, S. J. (1988). Towards a Theory of Cultural Influence Internationally on the Development of Accounting Systems Internationally. *Abacus*, *24*(I), 1–15. doi:10.1111/j.1467-6281.1988.tb00200.x

Gray, S. J., & Roberts, C. B. (1991). East-West Accounting Issues: A New Agenda. *Accounting Horizons*, *5*(March), 42–50.

Greenberg, M. D., Helland, E., Clancy, N., & Dertouzes, J. N. (2013). *Fair value accounting, historical cost accounting, and systemic risk: Policy issues and options for strengthening valuation and reducing risk.* RAND Centre for Corporate Ethics and Governance. Retrieved December 28, 2014 from: www.rand.org

Gresilova, I. (2013). *Chicken Or Egg? The Relationship Between IFRS Adoption And FDI.* A Thesis submitted in partial fulfillment of the requirements for the degree of MA in Financial Economics. Kyiv School of Economics. Retrieved from www.kse.org.ua/download.php?downloadid=299

Guenther, D., & Young, D. (2000). The association between financial accounting measures and real economic activity: A multinational study. *Journal of Accounting and Economics*, *29*(1), 53–72. doi:10.1016/S0165-4101(00)00013-6

Guerreiro, M. S., Rodrigues, L. L., & Craig, R. (2008). The preparedness of companies to adopt international financial reporting standards: Portuguese evidence. *Accounting Forum*, *32*(1), 75–88. doi:10.1016/j.accfor.2007.11.001

Gul, F. A., & Leung, S. (2004). Board leadership, outside directors' expertise and voluntary disclosures. *Journal of Accounting and Public Policy*, *23*(5), 351–379. doi:10.1016/j.jaccpubpol.2004.07.001

Habib, A., & Azim, I. (2008). Corporate governance and the value relevance of accounting information: Evidence from Australia. *Accounting Research Journal*, *21*(2), 167–194. doi:10.1108/10309610810905944

Habib, A., & Jiang, H. (2015). Corporate governance and financial reporting quality in China: A survey of recent evidence. *Journal of International Accounting, Auditing & Taxation*, *24*, 29–45. doi:10.1016/j.intaccaudtax.2014.12.002

Hail, L. (2002). The impact of voluntary corporate disclosures on the ex-ante cost of capital for Swiss firms. *European Accounting Review*, *11*(4), 741–773. doi:10.1080/0963818022000001109

Hail, L., & Leuz, C. (2006). International differences in the cost of equity capital: Do legal institutions and securities regulation matter? *Journal of Accounting Research*, *44*(3), 485–531. doi:10.1111/j.1475-679X.2006.00209.x

Hail, L., & Leuz, C. (2009). Cost of capital effects and changes in growth expectations around U.S. cross-listings. *Journal of Financial Economics*, *93*(3), 428–454. doi:10.1016/j.jfineco.2008.09.006

Hail, L., Leuz, C., & Wysocki, P. (2010). Global accounting convergence and the potential adoption of IFRS by the U.S. (part 1): Conceptual underpinnings and economic analysis. *Accounting Horizons*, *24*(3), 355–394. doi:10.2308/acch.2010.24.3.355

Hail, L., Leuz, C., & Wysocki, P. (2010). Global accounting convergence and the potential adoption of IFRS by the U.S. (part 11): Political factors and future scenarios for U.S. accounting standards. *Accounting Horizons*, *24*(4), 567–588. doi:10.2308/acch.2010.24.4.567

Haller, A. (2002). Financial Accounting Developments in the European Union: Past Events and Future Prospects. *The European Accounting Review*, *11*, 1-153.

Haniffa, R. M., & Cooke, T. E. (2002). Culture, corporate governance and disclosure in Malaysian Corporations. *Abacus*, *38*(3), 317–349. doi:10.1111/1467-6281.00112

Harris, T., & Muller, K. III. (1999). The market valuation of IAS versus US-GAAP accounting measures using Form 20-F reconciliations. *Journal of Accounting and Economics*, *26*(3), 285–312. doi:10.1016/S0165-4101(99)00003-8

HassabElnaby, H. R., Epps, R. W., & Said, A. A. (2003). The Impact of Environmental Factors on Accounting Development: An Egyptian Longitudinal Study. *Critical Perspectives on Accounting*, *14*(3), 273–292. doi:10.1006/cpac.2002.0530

Hassan, M. K. (2008). The development of accounting regulations in Egypt: Legitimating the International Accounting Standards. *Managerial Auditing Journal*, *23*(5), 467–484. doi:10.1108/02686900810875299

Haverals, J. (2005). IAS/IFRS. In *Belgium: Quantitative Analysis Of The Impact On The Tax Burden Of Companies. '1 Université Libre de Bruxelles – Centre Emile Bernheim*. SBS.

He, X., Wong, T., & Young, D. (2009). *Challenges for implementation of fair value accounting in emerging markets: Evidence from IFRS adoption in China*. Retrieved December 28, 2014 from https://tippie.uiowa.edu/accounting/mcgladrey/pdf/wong_tj.pdf

Hegarty, J., Gielen, F., & Barros, A. C. H. (2004). *Implementation of International Accounting and Auditing Standards: lessons learned from the World Bank's Accounting and Auditing ROSC Program*. Washington, DC: World Bank. Retrieved 1 December 2012 from: http://www.worldbank.org/ifa/LessonsLearned_ROSC_AA.pdf

Hegarty, J., Gielen, F., & Barros, A.C.H. (2004). *Implementation of International Accounting and Auditing Standards: Lessons learned from the World Bank's Accounting and Auditing ROSC Program*. Academic Press.

Helin, A. (2006). Sprawozdanie finansowe według MSSF. Zasady sporządzania i prezentacji. C.H.Beck.

Herbert, W. & Tsegba, N. (2013). Economic Consequences of International Financial Reporting Standards (IFRS) Adoption: Evidence from a Developing Country. *European Journal of Business and Management*, *5*(28).

Hibbard, R. L., II. (2012). *Global Implementation of IFRS*. University of Tennessee Honors Thesis Projects. Retrieved June 26, 2015 from: http://trace.tennessee.edu/utk_chanhonoproj/1485

Higson, A. (2003). *Corporate Financial Reporting: Theory and Practice*. London: SAGE Publications.

Hill, N. T., Shelton, S. W., & Stevens, K. T. (2002). Corporate Lobbying Behaviour on Accounting for Stock-Based Compensation: Venue and Format Choices. *Abacus*, *38*(1), 78–90. doi:10.1111/1467-6281.00098

Hofstede Center. (2015). *Poland*. Retrieved from: http://geert-hofstede.com/poland.html

Hofstede, G. (1980). *Culture's Consequences: International Differences in Work Related Values*. Beverly Hills, CA: Sage Publications.

Hofstede, G. (1984). *Culture's Consequences: International Differences in Work-Related Values*. Beverly Hills, CA: Sage Oublications.

Hofstede, G. (1997). *Cultures and Organisations: Software of Mind*. New York: McGraw-Hill.

Holsti, O.R. (1969). *Content analysis for the social sciences and humanities*. Reading, MA: Addison-Wesley.

Hoogendoorn, M. N. (1996). Accounting and taxation in Europe-A comparative overview. *European Accounting Review*, *5*(sup1), 783–794. doi:10.1080/09638189600000050

Hope, O.-K., Jin, J., & Kang, T. (2006). Empirical Evidence on Jurisdictions that Adopt IFRS. *Journal of International Accounting Research*, *5*(2), 1–20. doi:10.2308/jiar.2006.5.2.1

Hopwood, A. G. (1994). Some reflections on 'The harmonization of accounting within the EU'. *European Accounting Review*, *3*(2), 241–254.

Horton, J., Serafeim, G., & Serafeim, I. (2013). Does Mandatory IFRS Adoption Improve the Information Environment? *Contemporary Accounting Research*, *30*(1), 388–423. doi:10.1111/j.1911-3846.2012.01159.x

Ho, S. M. S., & Wong, K. R. (2001). A study of the relationship between corporate governance structures and the extent of voluntary disclosure. *Journal of International Accounting, Auditing & Taxation*, *10*(2), 139–156. doi:10.1016/S1061-9518(01)00041-6

Hossain, M., Perera, M. H. B., & Rahmam, A. R. (1995). Voluntary disclosure in the annual reports of New Zealand companies. *Journal of International Financial Management and Accounting*, *6*(1), 69–85. doi:10.1111/j.1467-646X.1995.tb00050.x

Houqe, M., & Easton, S. (2013). *Does Mandatory IFRS Adoption improve Information Quality in Low Investor Protection Countries? Evidence from France, Sweden and Switzerland*. Available at: http://ssrn.com/abstract=2224278

Hove, M. R. (1986). Accounting practices in developing countries: Colonialism's legacy of inappropriate technologies. In Readings in International Accounting (pp. 81-100). London: International Thomson Business Press.

Hove, M. (1986). The Anglo-American influence on international accounting standards: The case of the disclosure standards of the international accounting standards committee. *Research in Third World Accounting*, *1*, 55–66.

Hove, M. (1986). The Anglo-American influence on international accounting standards: The case of the Disclosure standards of the international accounting standards committee. *Research in Third World Accounting*, *1*, 55–66.

Hsieh, H., & Shannon, S. E. (2005). Three approaches to qualitative content analysis. *Qualitative Health Research*, (Nov): 15, 1277–1288. PMID:16204405

Huerta, E., & Zaidi, S. (2014). IFRS Adoption and Enforcement as Antecedents of Economic Growth. *International Journal of Accounting and Financial Reporting*, *4*(1). DOI: 10.5296/ijafr.v4i1.5410

Hung, M., & Subramanyam, K. R. (2007). Financial statement effects of adopting International Accounting Standards: The case of Germany. *Review of Accounting Studies*, *12*(4), 623–657. doi:10.1007/s11142-007-9049-9

IASB. (2008). Exposure draft on an improved conceptual framework for financial reporting: The objective of financial reporting and qualitative characteristics of decision-useful financial reporting information. London: IASB.

IASB. (2008). *IASB and FASB to Hold First Round Table on Global Financial Crisis in London on 14 November*. Press Release. Retrieved from www.iasb.org

IASB. (2010). *The Conceptual Framework for Financial Reporting*. London: IASB.

IASC. (1995). The full text of all International Standards extant at 1 January 1995 and current Exposure Drafts. London, UK: IASC.

Iatridis, G., & Dalla, K. (2011). The impact of IFRS implementation on Greek listed companies: An industrial sector and stock market index analysis. *International Journal of Managerial Finance, 7*(3), 284-303.

Iatridis, G. E. (2012). Audit quality in common-law and code-law emerging markets: Evidence on earnings conservatism, agency costs and cost of equity. *Emerging Markets Review, 13*(2), 101–117. doi:10.1016/j.ememar.2012.01.001

Ibiamke, N. A., & Ateboh-Briggs, P. B. (2014). Financial ratios effect of international financial reporting standards (IFRS) adoption in Nigeria. *International Journal of Business and Management Invention, 3*(3), 50–59.

IBPT. (2013). *Normas Tributárias em vigor equivalem a livro de 112 milhões de páginas*. Retrieved from https://www.ibpt.org.br/noticia/1266/Normas-tributarias-em-vigor-equivalem-a-livro-de-112-milhoes-de-paginas

ICAEW. (2007). *EU Implementation of IFRS and the fair value directive.* A report for the European Commission.

ICAEW. (2007). *EU Implementation of IFRS and the fair value directive.* A report for the European Commission. Available from http://ec.europa.eu/internal_market/accounting/docs/studies/2007-eu_implementation_of_ifrs.pdf

ICAEW . (2014). The Effects of Mandatory IFRS Adoption in the EU: A Review of Empirical Research. ICAEW. Available from http://www.icaew.com/~/media/Files/Technical/Financial-reporting/Information for better markets/IFBM/effects-of-mandatory-ifrs-adoption-oct2014-

Ignatowski, R. (2008). Instytucjonalne działania na rzecz spójności w stosowaniu MSR. *Zeszyty Teoretyczne Rachunkowości*, (44), 91-100.

Ignatowski, R. (2008). Reakcja rynków kapitałowych na stosowanie MSR. Przegląd badań empirycznych. *Zeszyty Teoretyczne Rachunkowości*, (43), 5-24.

Ignatowski, R. (2012). Światowa harmonizacja rachunkowości w perspektywie teoretycznej. *Zeszyty Teoretyczne Rachunkowości, 67*, 33–53.

Ikpefan, O. A., & Akande, A. O. (2012). International financial reporting standard (IFRS): Benefits, obstacles and intrigues for implementation. *Research Journal of Finance and Accounting, 3*(10), 143–151.

IMF. (2009). *London Summit – Leaders' Statement*. Retrieved from https://www.imf.org/external/np/sec/pr/2009/pdf/g20_040209.pdf

Inchausti, B. (1997). The influence of company characteristics and accounting regulations on information disclosure by Spanish firms. *European Accounting Review, 6*(1), 45–68. doi:10.1080/096381897336863

Inekwe, J. N. (2013). FDI, Employment and Economic Growth in Nigeria. *African Development Review, 25*(4), 421–433. doi:10.1111/1467-8268.12039

Inernational Monetary Fund (IMF). (2012). *World Economic and Financial Surveys, Regional Economic Outlook, Sub Saharan Africa, Staying the course*. Retrieved from https://www.imf.org/external/pubs/ft/reo/2014/afr/eng/sreo1014.pdf

Inglehart, E., & Baker, W. E. (2001). Modernization's Challenge to Traditional Values: Who's Afraid of Ronald McDonald? *The Futurist, 2001*, 16–21.

Irvine, H. (2008). The global institutionalization of financial reporting: The case of the United Arab Emirates. *Accounting Forum, 32*(2), 125–142. doi:10.1016/j.accfor.2007.12.003

Irvine, H. J., & Lucas, N. (2006). The rationale and impact of the adoption of international financial reporting standards on developing nations: The case of the United Arab Emirates. In *Proceedings 18th Asian-Pacific Conference on International Accounting Issues.*

Ismail, W. A., Van Zijl, T., & Dunstan, K. (2010). *Earnings quality and the adoption of IFRS-based accounting standards: Evidence from an emerging market.* Working Paper. University of Wellington and Bond University.

Ismail, W.A.W., Kamarudin, K.A., Zijl, T., & Dunstan, K. (2013). Earnings quality and the adoption of IFRS-based accounting standards: Evidence from an emerging market. *Asian Review of Accounting, 21*(1), 53-73.

Istvánfyová, J., Mejzlik, L., & Pelak, J. (2010). Progression of Financial Reporting in Czech Republic and its Regulation. *European Financial and Accounting Journal, 5*(1), 64–77.

Iwasaki, E., & El-Laithy, H. (2013). Estimation of Poverty in Greater Cairo: Case Study of Three 'Unplanned' Areas. *African Development Review, 25*(2), 173–188. doi:10.1111/j.1467-8268.2013.12022.x

Iyoha, F. O. (2012). Company attributes and the timeliness of financial reporting in Nigeria. *Business Intelligence Journal, 5*(1), 41–49.

Iyoha, F. O., & Jimoh, J. (2011). *Institutional infrastructure and the adoption of International Financial Reporting Standards (IFRS) in Nigeria. School of doctoral studies (European Union).* Journal.

Jackling, B., Howieson, B., & Natoli, R. (2012). Some Implications of IFRS Adoption for Accounting Education. *Australian Accounting Review, 22*(4), 331–340. doi:10.1111/j.1835-2561.2012.00197.x

Jacob, R. A., & Madu, C. N. (2009). International Financial Reporting Standards: An indicator of high quality. *International Journal of Quality & Reliability Management, 25*(7), 712–722. doi:10.1108/02656710910975778

Jahmani, O. (2013). Ownership structure and corporate voluntary disclosure: Evidence from Bahrain. *International Journal of Accounting and Financial Reporting, 3*(2), 133–148. doi:10.5296/ijafr.v3i2.4088

Jain, P. (2011, March). IFRS implementation in India: Opportunities and challenges. *World Journal of Social Sciences, 1*(1), 125–136.

Jaruga, A. (2004). *Polish capital market and earnings management: evidence from Warsaw Stock Exchange.* Paper presented at the 27th European Accounting Association Congress, Prague, Czech Republic.

Jaruga, A. (2005). Adoption of IAS/IFRS in Poland: Challenges and problems. In M. Dobija (Ed.), *General Theory of Accounting.* Krakow: Academy of Economics.

Jaruga, A. (Ed.). (2002). *Międzynarodowe regulacje rachunkowości. Wpływ na rozwiązania krajowe.* Warszawa: C. H. Beck.

Jaruga, A., Fijalkowska, J., Jaruga-Baranowska, M., & Frendzel, M. (2007). The Impact of IAS/IFRS on Polish Accounting Regulations and their Practical Implementation in Poland. *Accounting in Europe, 4*(1), 67–78. doi:10.1080/17449480701308675

Jaruga, A., Walinska, E., & Bankiewich, A. (1996). The relationship between accounting and taxation in Poland. *European Accounting Review, 5*(sup1), 883–897. doi:10.1080/09638189600000057

Jeanjean, T., & Stolowy, H. (2008). Do accounting standards matter? An exploratory analysis of earnings management: Before and after IFRS adoption. *Journal of Accounting and Public Policy, 27*(6), 480–494. doi:10.1016/j.jaccpubpol.2008.09.008

Jeffrey, P. G., & Spaulding, R. B. (2005). *Understanding Foreign Direct Investment (FDI) Going global, Citibank international business portal.* Retrieved: www.going-global.com/.../understanding_foreign_direct_inv

Jemakowicz, E. K., & Gornik, T. S. (2004). Implementing IFRS from the perspective of EU publicly traded companies. *Journal of International Accounting, Auditing & Taxation, 15*(2), 170–192. doi:10.1016/j.intaccaudtax.2006.08.003

Jensen, M., & Meckling, W. H. (1976). Theory of the firm: Managerial behavior, agency costs, and ownership structure. *Journal of Financial Economics, 11*(4), 305–360. doi:10.1016/0304-405X(76)90026-X

Jermakowicz, E. K. (2004). Effects of adoption of International Financial Reporting Standards in Belgium: The evidence from BEL-20 companies. *Accounting in Europe, 1*(1), 51–70. doi:10.1080/0963818042000270811

Jermakowicz, E. K., Prather-Kinsey, J., & Wulf, I. (2007). The value relevance of accounting income reported by DAX-30 German companies. *Journal of International Financial Management and Accounting, 18*(3), 151–191. doi:10.1111/j.1467-646X.2007.01011.x

Jerven, M. (2011). The quest for the African dummy: Explaining African post-colonial economic performance revisited. *Journal of International Development, 23*(2), 288–307. doi:10.1002/jid.1603

Jindrichovska, I., & Kubickova, D, (2012). *Impact of IFRS adoption on key financial ratios: The case of the Czech Republic.* Paper accepted for EUFIN Conference, Prague, Czech Republic.

Jindrichovska, I., Kubickova, D., & Kocmanova, S. (2014). The development of accounting and application of IFRS in the Czech Republic. *Accounting and Management Information Systems, 13*(2), 198–235.

Johnson, S., & Leone, M. (2009). *CFO's on IFRS: Forget about It.* Retrieved from http://www.cfo.com/article.cfm/13517383?f=home_featured

Johnson, D. C. (2011). *Political Systems, Lobbying, and the Adoption of International Financial Reporting Standards.* doi:10.2139/ssrn.1753225

Jones, S., & Higgins, A. D. (2006). Australia's Switch to International Financial Trporting Standards: A Perspective from Account Preparers. *Accounting and Finance, 46*(4), 629–652. doi:10.1111/j.1467-629X.2006.00186.x

Jones, S., & Higgins, D. (2006). Australia's Switch to International Financial Reporting Standards: A perspective from Account Preparers. *Journal of Accounting, Auditing & Finance, 20*, 95–119.

Joshi, P. L., & Ramadhan, S. (2002). The Adoption of International Accounting Standards by Small and Closely Held Companies: Evidence from Bahrain. *The International Journal of Accounting, 37*, 429 – 440.

Joshi, P. L., & Ramadhan, S. (2002). The adoption of international accounting standards by small & closely held companies: Evidence from Bahrain. *The International Journal of Accounting, 37*, 429–440.

Judge, W., Li, S., & Pinsker, R. (2010). National adoption of International Accounting Standards: An institutional perspective. *Corporate Governance International Review (Steubenville, Ohio), 18*(3), 161–174.

Judge, W., Li, S., & Pinsker, R. (2010). National Adoption of International Accounting Standards: An Institutional Perspective. *Corporate Governance International Review (Steubenville, Ohio), 18*(3), 161–174.

Judge, W., Li, S., & Pinsker, R. (2010). National adoption of international accounting standards: An institutional perspective. *Corporate Governance: An International Review, 18*(3), 161–174. doi:10.1111/j.1467-8683.2010.00798.x

Judkowiak, A. (2014). Informacja o instrumentach finansowych w sprawozdaniach finansowych sporządzanych zgodnie z MSSF i polskimi zasadami rachunkowości. *Zeszyty Teoretyczne Rachunkowości, 77*, 91–105.

Kabalski, P. (2007). Dylematy ujmowania kosztów finansowania zewnętrznego w kontekście nowelizacji MSR 23. *Zeszyty Teoretyczne Rachunkowości*, (41), 131-141.

Kaboyo, O., & Wamwea, G. (2014). *Motivation Factors For Earning Management Practice In Public Listed Companies in Kenya.* A Research Paper Presented at the 5th African International Business and Management (AIBUMA) Conference. Retrieved from business.uonbi.ac.ke/.../MotivationFactorsForEarning

Kager, B., Schanz, D., & Niemann, R. (2011). Estimation of tax values based on IFRS information: An analysis of German DAX30 and Austrian ATX listed companies. *Accounting in Europe.*, *8*(1), 89–123. doi:10.1080/17449480.2011.574362

Kalinowski, J. (2011). Porównywalność sprawozdań finansowych firm deweloperskich na tle krajowych i międzynarodowych regulacji rachunkowości. *Zeszyty Teoretyczne Rachunkowości*, *60*, 145–168.

Kamieniecka, M. (2009). Odroczony podatek dochodowy w międzynarodowych i krajowych uregulowaniach rachunkowości – podobieństwa i różnice. *Zeszyty Teoretyczne Rachunkowości*, *51*, 35–45.

Kangarlouei, S. J., Agababa, M., & Motavassel, M. (2013). Assessment of Social, Economic and Political Impact of Adopting International Accounting Standards in Iran. *World Applied Sciences Journal*, *21*(2), 214–220.

Kanthapanit, C., Sofocleous, S., & Clark, C. (2011). Adoption of international financial reporting standards in Thailand: Influence on decision making of individual shareholder. *Global Review of Accounting and Finance*, *2*(1), 18–28.

Kapoor, B., & Ruhela, J. (2013). IFRS Implementation – Issues and Challenges for India. *International Journal of Business and Management Research*, *3*(2), 103–106.

Karamanou, I., & Nischiotis, G. (2005). *The valuation effects of firms voluntary adoption of international accounting standards*. Working Paper. University of Cyprus. Retrieved from http://papers.ssrn.com/so13/paper.com?abstractid=676323

Karamanou, I., & Nishiotis, G. P. (2009). Disclosure and the Cost of Capital: Evidence from the Market's Reaction to Firm Voluntary Adoption of IAS. *Journal of Business Finance & Accounting*, *36*(7-8), 793–821. doi:10.1111/j.1468-5957.2009.02154.x

Karampinis, N. I., & Hevas, D. L. (2013). Effects of IFRS adoption on tax-induced incentives for financial earnings management: Evidence from Greece. *The International Journal of Accounting*, *48*(2), 218–247. doi:10.1016/j.intacc.2013.04.003

Katz, M. L., & Shapiro, C. (1985). Network externalities, competition, and compatibility. *The American Economic Review*, *75*, 424–440.

Kaufmann, D., Kraay, A., & Mastruzzi, M. (2010). *The World Governance Indicators: Methodology and Analytical Issues.* World Bank Policy Research Working Paper, No. 5430. Retrieved from: SSRN: http://ssrn.com/abstract=1682130

Kayizzi-Mugerwa, S. (2001). *Globalisation, Growth and Income Inequality: The African Experience.* Working Paper No. 186. OECD Development Centre.

Kayizzi-Mugerwa, S., Anyanwu, J. C., & Conceição, P. (2014). Regional Integration in Africa: An Introduction. *African Development Review*, *26*(S1), 1–6. doi:10.1111/1467-8268.12102

Kędzior, M., & Grabiński, K. (2011). Ocena opracowywanego przez IASB i FASB projektu założeń koncepcyjnych sprawozdawczości finansowej. *Zeszyty Teoretyczne Rachunkowości*, *61*, 55–88.

Kesti, J. (2005) Germany in European Tax Handbook. Amsterdam: International Bureau of Fiscal Documentation. Part A.1.3.4.

Kettunen, J. (2011). *Translation of IFRS standards into local languages: understanding problematics of translation.* Retrieved 1 April 2015 from: http://www.lse.ac.uk/accounting/pdf/Kettunen.pdf

Kinnunen, J., Niskanen, J., & Kasanen, E. (2000). To whom are IAS earnings informative? Domestic versus foreign shareholders' perspectives. *European Accounting Review*, *9*(4), 499–517. doi:10.1080/09638180020025330

Kiziukiewicz, T. (2009). Zasady ujawniania aktywów biologicznych w sprawozdaniach finansowych jednostek rolniczych według Międzynarodowych Standardów Sprawozdawczości Finansowej. *Zeszyty Teoretyczne Rachunkowości*, *49*, 99–108.

Klimczak, K. M. (2011). Market Reaction to Mandatory IFRS Adoption: Evidence from Poland. *Accounting and Management Information Systems*, *10*(2), 228–248.

Klimczak, K. M. (2011). Market reaction to mandatory IFRS adoption: Evidence from Poland. *Accounting and Management Information Systems*, *10*(2), 228–248.

Knack, S. (2006). *Measuring Corruption in Eastern Europe and Central Asia: A Critique of the Cross Country Indicators*. Washington, DC: World Bank. doi:10.1596/1813-9450-3968

Kodila-Tedika, O., & Agbor, A. J. (2014). Religious Diversity and Economic Development in Sub-Saharan Africa: So Far So Good. *Journal of African Development*, *16*(1), 99–117.

Komlos, J. (2015). How Natural Is the Natural Rate of Unemployment? *Challenge*, *8*(2), 160–167. doi:10.1080/05775132.2015.998151

Kosonboon, L. D. (2004). *The Relevance of International Accounting Standards for Developing Countries: The Case of IAS 41 in Thailand.* (Ph.D Thesis). University of Strathclyde, Glasgow, UK.

Krippendorff, K. (1980). *Content analysis: an introduction to its methodology*. Beverly Hills, CA: Sage Publications.

Krugman, P. (2010). A crise de 2008 e a economia da depressão. *Revue d'Economie Politique*, *30*(1), 180.

Kucharczyk, B. (2009). Wartość godziwa w wycenie aktywów finansowych – praktyka banków polskich. *Zeszyty Teoretyczne Rachunkowości*, *52*, 89–103.

Kumar, A. (2007). *Does Foreign Direct Investment Help Emerging Economies? Economist's View*. Retrieved: http://economistsview.typepad.com/economistsview/2007/01/frb_dallas_does.html

Kumar, G., Wilder, M., & Stocks, M. (2008). Voluntary Accounting Disclosures by U.S.-Listed Asian Companies. *Journal of International Accounting Research*, *7*(1), 25–50. doi:10.2308/jiar.2008.7.1.25

Kvaal, E., & Nobes, C. (2010). International differences in IFRS policy choice: A research note. *Accounting and Business Review*, *40*(2), 173–187. doi:10.1080/00014788.2010.9663390

Kwok, W. C. C., & Sharp, D. (2005). Power and International Accounting Standard Setting Evidence from Segment Reporting and Intangible Assets Projects. *Accounting AedIting & Accotftability Journal*, *18*(1), 74–99. doi:10.1108/09513570510584665

La Porta, R., Florencio, L., & Andrei, S. (2008). The Economic Consequences of Legal Origins. *Journal of Economic Literature*, *46*(2), 285–332. doi:10.1257/jel.46.2.285

La Porta, R., Florencio, L., Andrei, S., & Robert, W. V. (1997). Legal Determinants of External Finance. *The Journal of Finance*, *52*(3), 1131–1150. doi:10.1111/j.1540-6261.1997.tb02727.x

La Porta, R., Florencio, L., Andrei, S., & Robert, W. V. (1998). Law and Finance. *Journal of Political Economy*, *106*(6), 1113–1155. doi:10.1086/250042

La Porta, R., Florencio, L., Cristian, P., & Andrei, S. (2004). Judicial Checks and Balances. *Journal of Political Economy*, *112*(2), 445–470. doi:10.1086/381480

La Porta, R., Florenico, L., Shleifer, A., & Vishny, R. W. (2000). Agency problems and dividend policies around the world. *The Journal of Finance*, *55*(1), 1–33. doi:10.1111/0022-1082.00199

La Porta, R., Lopez-de-Silanes, F., Shleifer, A., & Vishny, R. (1999). The quality of government. *Journal of Law Economics and Organization*, *15*(1), 222–279. doi:10.1093/jleo/15.1.222

Lakhal, F. (2007). Ownership structure and voluntary disclosures: the case of French-listed firms. *Corporate Ownership and Control, 5*(1), 131-138.

Lambert, R., Leuz, C., & Verrecchia, R. (2007). Accounting information, disclosure, and the cost of capital. *Journal of Accounting Research*, *45*(2), 385–420. doi:10.1111/j.1475-679X.2007.00238.x

Lambert, R., Leuz, C., & Verrecchia, R. E. (2012). Information Asymmetry, Information Precision, and the Cost of Capital. *Review of Finance*, *16*(1), 1–29. doi:10.1093/rof/rfr014

Lang, M., Raedy, J., & Yetman, M. (2003). How Representative are Firms that are Cross Listed In the United States? An analysis of Accounting Quality. *Accountability in Research*, *41*, 363–386.

Lantto, A., & Sahlström, P. (2007). Impact of international financial reporting standard adoption on key financial ratios. *Accounting and Finance*, *49*(2), 341–361. doi:10.1111/j.1467-629X.2008.00283.x

Larson, R. K. (1993). International Accounting Standards and Economic Growth: An Empirical Investigation of their Relationship in Africa. In R. S. O. Wallace (Ed.), *Research in Third World Accounting* (Vol. 2, pp. 27–43). JAI Press Ltd.

Larson, R. K., & Street, D. L. (2004). Convergence with IFRS in an expanding Europe: Progress and obstacles identified by large accounting firms' survey. *Journal of International Accounting, Auditing & Taxation*, *13*(2), 89–119. doi:10.1016/j.intaccaudtax.2004.09.002

Larson, R., & Kenny, S. (1995). An empirical analysis of international accounting standards, equity markets and economic growth in developing countries. *Journal of International Financial Management and Accounting*, *6*(2), 130–157. doi:10.1111/j.1467-646X.1995.tb00054.x

Lasmin. (2011). An institutional perspective on International Financial Reporting Standards adoption in developing countries. *Academy of Accounting & Financial Studies Journal*, 61-71.

Lasmin, R. (2011). The unwanted effects of the International Financial Reporting Standards (IFRS) adoption: evidence from developing countries. *Proceedings of the Allied Academies Internet Conference*, *13*(1).

Latridis, G. (2010). IFRS adoption and financial statement effects: The UK case. *International Research Journal of Finance and Economics*, *38*, 165–172.

Latridis, G. (2010). International Financial Reporting Standards and the quality of financial statements information. *International Review of Financial Analysis*, *19*(3), 193–204. doi:10.1016/j.irfa.2010.02.004

Laux, C., & Leuz, C. (2010). Did fair-value accounting contribute to the financial Crisis?. *The Journal of Economic Perspectives*, *24*(1), 93–118. doi:10.1257/jep.24.1.93

Leautier, F. A. (2012). What Role for Africa After 50 Years of Independence: Provider of Natural Resources or a New Global Leader? *Journal of African Development*, *14*(1), 127–151.

Lee, E., Walker, M., & Christensen, H. (2008). Mandating IFRS: its Impact on the Cost of Equity Capital in Europe. *ACCA Research Report, 105*(1).

Lee, E., Walker, M., & Zeng, C. (2013). *Does IFRS Convergence Affect Financial Reporting Quality in China? Research report 131. The Association of Certified* Public Accountants.

Lee, E., Walker, M., & Zeng, C. (2013). *Does IFRS Convergence Affect Financial Reporting Quality in China?. Research report 131. The Association of Certified* Public Accountants.

Leftwich, R. W. (1983). Accounting information in private markets: Evidence from private lending agreements. *Accounting Review, 58*(1), 23–42.

Leung, R., & Ilsever, J. (2013). Review of Evidence between Corporate Governance and Mandatory IFRS Adoption from the Perspective of Agency Theory and Information Asymmetry. *Universal Journal of Accounting and Finance, 1*(3), 85–94.

Leuz, C., & Wysocki, P. D. (2008). *Economic Consequences of Financial Reporting and Disclosure Regulation: A Review and Suggestions for Future Research.* SSRN eLibrary.

Leuz, C., & Wysocki, P.D. (2008). *Economic consequences of financial reporting and disclosure regulation: A review and suggestions for future research.* SSRN eLibrary.

Leuz, C. (2003). IAS versus US GAAP: Information-asymmetry based evidence from Germany's new market. *Journal of Accounting Research, 41*(3), 445–472. doi:10.1111/j.1475-679X.2003.00111.x

Leuz, C. (2004). Proprietary versus non-proprietary disclosures: Evidence from Germany. In C. Leuz, D. Pfaff, & A. Hopwood (Eds.), *The Economics and Politics of Accounting* (pp. 164–197). Oxford, UK: Oxford University Press. doi:10.1093/0199260621.003.0007

Leuz, C., Nanda, D., & Wysocki, P. (2003). Earnings Management and Investor Protection: An International Comparison. *Financial Economics, 69*(3), 505–527. doi:10.1016/S0304-405X(03)00121-1

Leuz, C., & Verrecchia, R. (2000). The Economic consequences of increased disclosure. *Journal of Accounting Research, 38*(Supplement), 91–124. doi:10.2307/2672910

Leventis, S., Dimitropoulos, P., & Anandarajan, A. (2011). Loan loss provisions, earnings management and capital management under IFRS: The case of EU Commercial banks. *Journal of Financial Services Research, 40*(1-2), 103–122. doi:10.1007/s10693-010-0096-1

Lewis, A. (1955). *Theory of Economic Growth. Milton Park.* Routledge.

Li, S. (2009, September). Does mandatory adoption of international financial reporting standards in the European union reduce the cost of equity capital? *The Accounting Review.*

Liebowitz, S. J., & Margolis, S. E. (1994). Network externality: An uncommon tragedy. *The Journal of Economic Perspectives, 8*(2), 133–150. doi:10.1257/jep.8.2.133

Lima, V. S. D. (2011). *Incentivos no nível da firma e consequências econômicas da convergência ao IFRS no Brasil.* (Doctoral dissertation). University of São Paulo, São Paulo, Brazil.

Lin, J. Y. (2015). The Washington Consensus Revisited A New Structural Economics Perspective. *Journal of Economic Policy Reform, 18*(2), 96–113. doi:10.1080/17487870.2014.936439

Lin, S., Riccardi, W., & Wang, C. (2012). Does accounting quality change following a switch from US GAAP to IFRS? Evidence from Germany. *Journal of Accounting and Public Policy, 31*(6), 641–657. doi:10.1016/j.jaccpubpol.2012.10.006

Lipsey, R., & Chrystal, A. (2003). *Economics* (10th ed.). New Delhi: Oxford University Press.

Li, Q., & Resnick, A. (2003). Reversal of Fortunes: Democratic Institutions and Foreign Direct Investment Inflows to Developing Countries. *International Organization, 57*(1), 175–211. doi:10.1017/S0020818303571077

Liu, C., Yao, L. J., Hu, N., & Liu, L. (2011). The impact of IFRS on accounting quality in a regulated market: An empirical study of China. *Journal of Accounting, Auditing & Finance*.

Looney, R. E. (2013). The Omani and the Bahraini Paths to Development: Rare and Contrasting Oil-Based Economic Success Stories. In A. FosuOxford University Press (Ed.), *Achieving Development Success: Strategies and Lessons from the Developing World*. doi:10.1093/acprof:oso/9780199671557.003.0020

Lopes, A. B. (2002). *Informação contábil e o mercado de capitais*. Cengage Learning Editores.

Louis, H., & Urcan, O. (2012). *The Effect of IFRS on Foreign Direct Investment: Evidence from Cross-Border Acquisitions*. Paper presented at Singapore Management University.

Louis, H., & Urcan, O. (2013). *The Effect of IFRS on Foreign Direct Investments: Evidence from Cross-Border Acquisitions*. Available at SSRN: http://ssrn.com/abstract=2164995 or10.2139/ssrn.2164995

Lucas, R. E. (1993). Making a miracle. *Econometrica*, *61*(2), 251–272. doi:10.2307/2951551

Lundholm, R., & Winkle, M. V. (2006). Motives for disclosure and non-disclosure: A framework and review of the evidence. *Accounting and Business Review*, *36*(Special issue), 43–48. doi:10.1080/00014788.2006.9730044

Lwoga, E. T., Ngulube, P., & Stilwell, C. (2010). Managing indigenous knowledge for sustainable agricultural development in developing countries: Knowledge management approaches in the social context. *The International Information & Library Review*, *42*(3), 172–185. doi:10.1080/10572317.2010.10762862

lyoha, F. O., & Jafaru, J. (2011). *Institutional infrastructure and the adoption of international financial reporting standards in Nigeria*. Academic Press.

Mackenzie, B., Coetsee, D., Njikizana, T., Selbst, E., Chamboko, R., Colyvas, B., & Hanekom, B. (2013). Interpretation and Application of International Financial Reporting Standards. John Wiley & Sons, Inc.

Madawaki, A. (2012). Adoption International Financial Reporting Standards in developing countries: The case of Nigeria. *International Journal of Business and Management*, *7*(3), 152–161. doi:10.5539/ijbm.v7n3p152

Madawaki, A. (2014). Impact of regulatory framework and environmental factors on accounting practices by firms in Nigeria. *Procedia: Social and Behavioral Sciences*, *164*, 282–290. doi:10.1016/j.sbspro.2014.11.078

Maddala, G. S. (1991). A perspective on the use of limited-dependent variables models in accounting research. *Accounting Review*, *66*(4), 788–807.

Malone, D., Fries, C., & Jones, T. (1993). An Empirical investigation of the extent of corporate financial disclosure in the oil and gas industry. *Journal of Accounting, Auditing & Finance*, *8*(3), 249–273.

Mangena, M. (2004). *On the perceived importance of disclosure items in UK interim financial reports: Evidence from the investment analysts*. Working paper series, Bradford University.

Markiewicz-Rudnicka, D., & Piotrowska, K. (2009). Sprawozdanie finansowe a zmiany w Międzynarodowych Standardach Sprawozdawczości Finansowej. *Zeszyty Teoretyczne Rachunkowości*, *51*, 119–128.

Márquez-Ramos, L. (2011). European accounting harmonization: consequences of IFRS adoption on trade in goods and foreign direct investments. *Emerging Markets Finance and Trade, 47*(sup4), 42-57.

Martins, O. S., & Paulo, E. (2010). Reflexo da Adoção das IFRS na Análise de Desempenho das Companhias de Capital Aberto no Brasil (The Reflection of the Adoption of IFRS in the Performance Analysis of Publicly Traded Companies in Brazil). *Revista de Contabilidade e Organizações*, *4*(9), 30.

Mary, J., Okoye, A. E., & Samson, A. O. (2013). Accounting standards in Nigeria: The journey so far. *Research Journal of Business and Accounting, 2*(1), 1-10.

Mashayekhi, B., & Mashayekhi, S. (2008). Development of Accounting in Iran. *The International Journal of Accounting, 43*(1), 66–86. doi:10.1016/j.intacc.2008.01.004

Masoud, N. (2014). Accounting, FRQ, emerging countries transition: How can a country implement an IFRS standard change successfully? *Global Journal of Management and Business Research: D Accounting and Auditing, 14*(2/1), 36-55.

Masztalerz, M. (2012). O standardach rachunkowości - zasady czy reguły. *Zeszyty Teoretyczne Rachunkowości, 66*, 123–131.

McCombie. K., & Deo, H. (2005). The International Harmonization of Accounting Standards: Making progress in Accounting Practice or an Endless Struggle?. *Journal of American Academy of Business, 7.*

McGregor, W. (2012). *In defence of IFRS financial statements.* CPA Australia Ltd.

McKinnon, J. L., & Dalimunthe, L. (1993). Voluntary disclosure of segment information by Australian diversified companies. *Accounting and Finance, 33*(1), 33–50. doi:10.1111/j.1467-629X.1993.tb00192.x

Mcleay, S., Neal, D., & Ajd Tollington, T. (1999). International Standardisation and Harmonisation: A New Measurement Technique. *Journal of International Financial Management and Accounting, 10*(1), 42–70. doi:10.1111/1467-646X.00042

Mcleay, S., Ordelheide, D., & Young, S. (2000). Constituent Lobbying and its Impact oj the Development of Financial Reporting Regulations: Evidence from Eermani. *Journal of Accounting, Organizations and Society, 25*(1), 79–98. doi:10.1016/S0361-3682(99)00028-8

Meek, G. K., Roberts, C. B., & Gray, S. J. (2005). Factors Influencing Voluntary Annual Report Disclosures by U.S., U.K. and Continental European Multinational Corporations. *Journal of International Business Studies, 26*(3), 555–572. doi:10.1057/palgrave.jibs.8490186

Meeks, G., & Swann, P. (2009). Accounting standards and the economics of standards. *Accounting and Business Review, 39*(3), 191–210. doi:10.1080/00014788.2009.9663360

Meller, P., & Simpasa, A. M. (2011). *Role of Copper in the Chilean & Zambian Economies: Main Economic and Policy Issues.* GDN Working Paper Series No. 43.

Messner, Z. (2002). Komitet Standardów Rachunkowości. *Rachunkowość*, (10).

Mike, M. (2009). Seminar understanding IFRS. National GAAP vs IFRS, Lagos, Nigeria.

Mike, M. (2009). Seminar Understanding IFRS. National GAAP vs IFRS, Lagos, Nigeria.

Mir, M. Z., & Rahaman, A. S. (2005). The Adoption of International Accounting Standards in Bangladesh. *Accounting, Auditing & Accountability Journal, 18*(6), 816–841. doi:10.1108/09513570510627720

Mir, M. Z., & Rahaman, A. S. (2005). The adoption of international accounting standards in Bangladesh: An exploration of rationale and process. *Accounting, Auditing & Accountability Journal, 18*(6), 816–841.

Mitchell, J. (2006). Selective reporting of financial ratios in Australian annual reports: Evidence from a voluntary reporting environment. *Accounting Research Journal, 19*(1), 5–30.

Mkondiwa, M., Jumbe, C. B. L., & Wiyo, K. A. (2013). Poverty–Lack of Access to Adequate Safe Water Nexus: Evidence from Rural Malawi. *African Development Review, 25*(4), 537–550. doi:10.1111/1467-8268.12048

Mlachila, M., Tapsoba, R., & Tapsoba, S. J. A. (2014). *A Quality of Growth Index for Developing Countries: A Proposal.* IMF Working Paper No. 14/172.

MoF. (2013). *Proposed Draft for the Circular of amendment 8 VAS in Stage 1*. Retrieved from http://www.mof.gov.vn/portal/page/portal/mof_vn/Suggestion_Legal?p_detail=1&p_topic_id=7378

Monga, C. (2014). The False Economics of Pre-Conditions: Policymaking in the The African Context. *Journal of African Development*, *16*(2), 121–140.

Morais, A. I., & Curto, J. D. (2008). Accounting quality and the adoption of IASB standards: *Portuguese evidence. Revista Contabilidade and Financas*, *19*(48), 103–111. doi:10.1590/S1519-70772008000300009

Morrisset, J. (2000). Foreign Direct Investment in Africa: Policies also Matter. *Transnational Corporation*, *9*(2), 107–125.

Morunga, M., & Bradbury, M. E. (2010). *Has IFRS resulted in information overload?* Discussion Paper Series 221.

Morunga, M., & Bradbury, M. E. (2012). The impact of IFRS on annual report length. *Australasian Accounting. Business and Finance Journal*, *6*(5), 47–62.

Moyo, D. (2009). *Dead Aid: Why Aid Is Not Working and How There is Another Way for Africa*. New York: Farrar, Straus and Giroux.

Mshomba, R. E. (2011). Africa and the World Trade Organization. Cambridge University Press.

Mueller, G. G., Gernon, H., & Meek, G. (1987). *Accounting: An International Perspective*. IRWIN.

Mueller, G., Gernon, H., & Meek, G. (1994). *Accounting: an international perspective*. Burr Ridge, IL: Irwin.

Mullerova, L., Pasekova, M., & Kubickova, D. (2010). Analysis of Differences in Reporting According to IFRS in SMEs in the Czech Republic and its influence on Performance. *ACTA VŠFS*, (2), 106-125.

Mulyadi, M. S., Soepriyanto, G., & Anwar, Y. (2012). IFRS adoption and taxation issue. *International Journal of Arts and Commerce*, *1*(7), 159–165.

Musila, J. W., & Sigué, S. P. (2010). Corruption and International Trade: An Empirical Investigation of African Countries. *World Economy*, *33*(1), 129–146. doi:10.1111/j.1467-9701.2009.01208.x

Myers, R. (1990). *Classical and modern regression with applications*. Boston, MA: Duxbury.

Myers, S., & Majluf, N. (1984). Corporate financing and investment decisions when firms have information that investors do not have. *Journal of Financial Economics*, *13*(2), 187–221. doi:10.1016/0304-405X(84)90023-0

Naser, K., & Nuseibeh, R. (2003). Quality of Financial Reporting: Evidence from the Listed Saudi nonfinancial Companies. *The International Journal of Accounting, 38*, 41-69.

Ncube, M., Anyanwu, J. C., & Hausken, K. (2014). Inequality, Economic Growth and Poverty in the Middle East and North Africa (MENA). *African Development Review*, *26*(3), 435–453. doi:10.1111/1467-8268.12103

Ndirangu, E. (2014). *The Effect of Cross Listing on the Accounting Quality Of Firms Cross Listed in East African Markets*. Master's thesis at the University of Nairobi. Retrieved from erepository.uonbi.ac.ke/handle/11295/77882

Ndlovu-Gatsheni, S. J. (2013). The Entrapment of African within the Global Colonial Matrices of Power: Eurocentrism, Coloniality and Deimperialieation in the Twenty-first century. *Journal of Developing Societies*, *29*(4), 331–353. doi:10.1177/0169796X13503195

Negash, M. (2012). IFRS and environmental accounting. *Management Research Review*, *35*(Iss: 7), 577–601. doi:10.1108/01409171211238811

Nguyen, L., Hooper, K., & Sinclair, R. (2013). Conservatism versus Change in the Vietnamese Accounting Field. *Corporate Ownership & Control*, *11*(1), 471–482.

Nikolaos, E., Konstantinos, P., & Dimitrios, V. (2013). *The impact of IFRS on ratios of listed and new listed companies of Athens Exchange*. Academic Press.

Nkurunziza, J. D. (2012). Illicit Financial Flows: A Constraint on Poverty Reduction in Africa. Officer-in-charge, Africa Section, ALDCs Division of UNCTAD, Geneva.

Nobes, C., & Parker, R. (2012). *Comparative International Accounting* (12th ed.). Pearson Education Limited. Retrieved from: https://www.kpmg.com/CZ/cs/IssuesAndInsights/ArticlesPublications/Factsheets/Documents/KPMG-Investment-in-the-Czech-Republic-2014.pdf

Nobes, C. (1998). Towards a general model of the reasons for international differences in financial reporting. *Abacus*, *34*(2), 162–187. doi:10.1111/1467-6281.00028

Nobes, C. (2006). The survival of international differences under IFRS: Towards a research agenda. *Accounting and Business Review*, *36*(3), 233–245. doi:10.1080/00014788.2006.9730023

Nobes, C., & Parker, R. (2010). *Comparative international accounting* (11th ed.). London: Prentice-Hall.

Nobes, C., & Parker, R. (2010). *Comparative International Accounting*. Pearson Education Limited.

North, D. C. (1991). Institutions. *The Journal of Economic Perspectives*, *5*(1), 97–112. doi:10.1257/jep.5.1.97

Nunn, N. (2008). The Long-Term Effects of Africa's Slave Trades. *The Quarterly Journal of Economics*, *123*(1), 139–176. doi:10.1162/qjec.2008.123.1.139

Nunn, N. (2009). The importance of history for economic development. *Annual Review of Economics*, *1*(1), 65–92. doi:10.1146/annurev.economics.050708.143336

Nunn, N., & Puga, G. (2012). Ruggedness: The blessing of bad geography in Africa. *The Review of Economics and Statistics*, *94*(4), 20–36.

Obazee, J. O. (2009). Practical challenges in implementing IFRS. *ABWA Journal*, *1*(3), 7–17.

Obeng-Odoom, F. (2013). Africa's Failed Economic Development Trajectory: A Critique. *African Review of Economics and Finance*, *4*(2), 151–175.

Obeng-Odoom, F. (2014). *Africa: On the Rise, but to Where?* Forum for Social Economics; doi:10.1080/07360932.2014.955040

Obloj, K., & Kostera, M. (1993). Polish privatisation, action, symbolism and cultural barriers. *Industrial and Environmental Crisis Quarterly*, *7*(3), 7–21.

Ocansey, E. O. N. D., & Enahorol, J. A. (2014). Comparative study of the international financial reporting standard implementation in Ghana and Nigeria. *European Scientific Journal*, *10*(13), 529–546.

Odia, J. O. (2013). Factors affecting the Adoption of IFRS in Nigeria. Sokoto. *Journal of Social Sciences*.

Odia, J. O. (2015). *Perception of accounting academia and practitioners of IFRS adoption in Nigeria. ICAN Journal of Accounting and Finance, 4(1).*

Odia, J. O., & Ogiedu, K. O. (2013). IFRS adoption: Issues, challenges and lessons for Nigeria and other adopters. *Mediterranean Journal of Social Sciences*, *4*(3), 389–399.

Odia, J. O., & Ogiedu, K. O. (2013). IFRS Adoption: Issues, challenges and lessons for Nigeria and other adopters. *Mediterranean Journal of Social Sciences*, *4*(3), 389–399.

Oduware, U. (2012). *Comparability of IFRS Financial Statements*. Retrieved from https://www.deloitte.com/assets/Dcom-

Oduware, U. (2012). *IFRS adoption in Nigeria & optimising the gains of global investment climate*. Retrieved December 28 2014 from https://www.wecadeloitte.com/extranet/data/ifrsacademy/content/_1355906750_30C8SXR170.pdf Accessed.

Okafor, C., & Ogiedu, K. O. (2011). Potential effects of the adoption and implementation of international financial accounting standards (IFRS) in Nigeria. *JORIND*, *9*(2), 345–358.

Okaro, S. C. (2011). *From SAS to IFRS- emerging issues and implications for Nigeria*. Retrieved from http://sscrn.com/abstract=1956027

Okere, E. O. (2009). *International financial reporting and accounting issues: Imperatives of attainment of economic development in Nigeria*. ICAN 39 Annual Accountants Conference.

Okoye, P. V. C., & Akenbor, C. O. (2012). *Financial Reporting Framework in Nigeria and the Adoption of the International Financial Reporting Standards*. Retrieved from http://www.centerforpbbefr.rutgers.edu/2012PBFEAM/papers/008- Financial%20reporting.doc

Okoye, P. V. C., Okoye, J. F. N., & Ezejiofor, R. A. (2014). Impact of IFRS adoption on stock market movement in Nigerian corporate organization. *International Journal of Academic Research in Business and Social Sciences.*, *4*(9), 202–218. doi:10.6007/IJARBSS/v4-i9/1150

Okpala, K.E. (2012). Adoption of IFRS and Financial Statement effects: The Perceived Implications on FDI and Nigeria Economy. *Australian Journal of Business and Management Research, 2*(5), 76-83.

Okpala, K. E. (2012). Adoption of IFRS and financial statements effects: The perceived implications on FDI and Nigeria Economy. *Australian Journal of Business and Management Research*, *2*(5), 76–83.

Okpala, K. E. (2012). Adoption of IFRS and financial statements effects: The perceived implications on FDI and Nigerian economy. *Australian Journal of Business and Management Research*, *2*(5), 76–83.

Olowo-Okere, E. (2009). *The International Financial Reporting and accounting issues: Imperatives of attainment of economic development of Nigeria*. Paper presented at 39th annual conference of the Institute of Chartered Accountants of Nigeria.

Ormrod, P., & Taylor, P. (2004). The Impact of the Change to International Accounting Standards on Loan Covenants in the UK. *Accounting in Europe*, *1*, 71–94. doi:10.1080/0963818042000262775

Osabuohien, E. (2011). *Analysis of International Trade Performance in SSA: Impact of Institutional Framework*. (Unpublished Thesis). Covenant University.

Osabuohien, E. S., Efobi, U. R., & Gitau, C. M. W. (2013). External intrusion, internal tragedy:environmental pollution and multinational corporations in Sub-Saharan Africa. In Principles and Strategies to Balance Ethical, Social and Environmental Concerns with Corporate Requirements (Advances in Sustainability and Environmental Justice, Vol. 12). Emerald Group Publishing Limited.

Osabuohien, E. S. (2014). Large-Scale Agricultural Land Investments and Local Institutions in Africa: The Nigerian Case. *Land Use Policy*, *39*, 155–165. doi:10.1016/j.landusepol.2014.02.019

Osabuohien, E. S., Efobi, U. R., & Gitau, C. M. W. (2014). Beyond the environmental kuznets curvein Africa: Evidence from panel co-integration. *Journal of Environmental Policy and Planning*, *16*(4), 517–538. doi:10.1080/1523908X.2013.867802

Osabuohien, E. S., Efobi, U. R., & Gitau, C. M. W. (2015). Environment challenges in Africa: Further dimensions to the trade, MNCs and energy debate. *Management of Environmental Quality: An International Journal*, *26*(1), 118–137. doi:10.1108/MEQ-04-2014-0058

Osabuohien, E., & Efobi, U. (2013). Africa's Money in Africa. *The South African Journal of Economics*, *81*(2), 291–306. doi:10.1111/saje.12012

Osabuohien, E., & Efobi, U. (2014). Assessment of Trade Performance of OIC African Members in the Face of Global Economic Crisis. *Journal of Economic Cooperation and Development*, *35*(1), 1–22.

Osiński, Ł. (2015). *Minister gospodarki Niemiec: Nasz handel z Polską jest większy od wymiany handlowej z Rosją*. Gazeta Wyborcza. Retrieved from: http://wyborcza.biz/biznes/1,100896,17883053,Minister_gospodarki_Niemiec__Nasz_handel_z_Polska.html

Outa, E. (2011). The Impact of IFRS adoption on the accounting quality of Companies listed in Kenya. *The International Journal of Accounting and Financial Reporting*, *1*(1). Retrieved from http://www.macrothink.org/journal/index.php/ijafr/article/view/1096/905

Outa, E. (2011). *The Impact of International Financial Reporting Standards (IFRS) Adoption on the Accounting Quality of Listed Companies in Kenya*. Available at http://ssrn.com/abstract=1976146

Outa, E. (in press). Earnings Management & Corporate governance Disclosures: Empirical evidence from East Africa. *Journal of Accounting in Emerging Economies*.

Outa, E. R. (2011). The impact of (IFRS) adoption on the accounting quality of listed companies in Kenya. *International Journal of Accounting and Financial Reporting*, *1*(1), 212–241. doi:10.5296/ijafr.v1i1.1096

Owolabi, A., & Iyoha, F. (2012). Adopting International Financial Reporting Standards (IFRS) in Africa: Benefits, prospects and challenges. *African Journal of Accounting Auditing and Finance*, *1*(1), 77–86. doi:10.1504/AJAAF.2012.046127

Owusu-Ansah, S. (1998). The impact of corporate attributes on the extent of mandatory disclosure and reporting by listed companies in Zimbabwe. *The International Journal of Accounting*, *33*(5), 605–631. doi:10.1016/S0020-7063(98)90015-2

Oyedele, T. (2011). *An overview of IFRS and challenges posed to professionals*. A paper presented at a seminar on IFRS adoption in Nigeria. The Chartered Institute of Taxation of Nigeria.

Oyedele, T. (2011). *An overview of IFRS and challenges posed to professionals*. Paper presented at a seminar on IFRS adoption in Nigeria.

Oyetayo, E. O., Arogundade, K. K., Adebisi, S. O., & Oluwakayode, E. F. (2011). FDI, Export and Economic Growth in Nigeria. *European Journal of Humanities and Social Sciences.*, *2*(1), 66–86.

Paananen, M. (2008). *The IFRS adoption's effect on accounting quality in Sweden*. Working Paper. University of Hertfordshire.

Paananen, M., & Lin, C. (2008). *The Development of Accounting Quality of IAS and IFRS Over time: The case of Germany*. Presented at the annual meeting of the American Accounting Association, Anaheim, CA.

Pagano, M., Röell, A., & Zechner, J. (2002). The Geography of Equity Listing: Why Do Companies List Abroad? *The Journal of Finance*, *57*(6), 2651–2694. doi:10.1111/1540-6261.00509

Palepu, K. G. (1986). Predicting takeover targets: A methodological and empirical analysis. *Journal of Accounting and Economics*, *8*(1), 3–35. doi:10.1016/0165-4101(86)90008-X

Parker, R. H. (1996). Harmonising the notes in the UK and France: A case study in de jure harmonisation. *European Accounting Review*, *5*(2), 317–337. doi:10.1080/09638189600000019

Pasekova, M., Bialic-Davendra, M., Müllerová, L., Hvastová, J., Manova, E., Sowa, B., & Cizevska, L. (2010). IFRS for SMES: Current issues in reporting of SMES in the Czech Republic, Slovak Republic, Poland and Ukraine. In *Proceedings of the 5th International Conference, Accounting and Management Information Systems (AMIS 2010)*. Editura Ase.

Pasekova, M. (2012). *Implementace IFRS do malých a středních podniků* [Implementation of IFRS in small and medium enterprices]. Prague: Wolters Kluwer.

Pawan, J. (2011). IFRS implementation in India: Opportunities and Challenges. *World Journal of Social Sciences*, *1*(1), 125–136.

Pelucio-Grecco, M. C., Formigoni, H., & Geron, C. M. S. (2010). *The impact of the changes in the accounting practices in the conservatism level of the listed companies in Brazil*. 33rd EAA Annual Congress 2010, Istanbul, Turkey.

Pelucio-Grecco, M. C., Geron, C. M. S., Formigoni, H., & Segura, L. C. (2011). *Brazilian professionals' perception in relation to the accounting convergence process to IFRS*. 34th EAA Annual Congress 2011, Rome, Italy.

Pelucio-Grecco, M. C., Geron, C. M. S., Grecco, G. B., & Lima, J. P. C. (2014). The effect of IFRS on earnings management in Brazilian non-financial public companies. *Emerging Markets Review*, *21*, 42–66. doi:10.1016/j.ememar.2014.07.001

Peng, S., & van der Laan Smith, J. (2010). Chinese GAAP and IFRS: An analysis of the convergence process. *Journal of International Accounting, Auditing & Taxation*, *19*(1), 16–34. doi:10.1016/j.intaccaudtax.2009.12.002

Perera, M. H. B. (1985). *The relevance of International Accounting Standards to developing countries*. Working Paper. University of Glasgow.

Perera, H., & Baydoun, N. (2007). Convergence with International Financial Reporting Standards: The Case of Indonesia. *Advances in International Accounting*, *20*(1), 201–224. doi:10.1016/S0897-3660(07)20007-8

Perera, M. H. B. (1989). Accounting in developing countries: A case for localized uniformity. *The British Accounting Review*, *21*(2), 141–158. doi:10.1016/0890-8389(89)90193-5

Pham, H. H. (2012). *A Comparative Study of Vietnamese and International Accounting Standards*. (PhD Thesis). School of Accounting, Curtin University.

Pham, T. (2010). *International Financial Reporting Standards effects on banks in Vietnam*. (Bachelor thesis). International Business, JAMK University of Applied Sciences, Finland.

Phan, D. (2010). *The Relevance of International Financial Reporting Standards in Vietnam*. Paper presented at the 2nd Engaging with Vietnam Conference by Monash University and Vietnam National University, Hanoi, Vietnam.

Phan, D. (2014). What Factors are Perceived to Influence Consideration of IFRS Adoption by Vietnamese Policymakers?. *Journal of Contemporary Issues in Business and Government, 20*(1), 27-40.

Phan, D., & Mascitelli, B. (2014a). Optimal approach and timeline for IFRS adoption in Vietnam: Perceptions of accounting professionals. *Research in Accounting Regulation Journal, 26*(2), 222-229.

Phan, D., & Mascitelli, B. (2014b). IFRS adoption in Vietnam: If, When and How?. *Corporate Ownership & Control, 11*(4), 428-436.

Phan, D., Mascitelli, B., & Barut, M. (2013). *Perceptions of Accounting Professionals towards International Financial Reporting Standards (IFRS) in Developing Country: Evidence from Vietnam.* Paper presented at the 3rd Global Accounting, Finance and Economics Conference, Rydges Melbourne, Australia.

Phan, D., Mascitelli, B., & Barut, M. (2014). Perceptions Toward International Financial Reporting Standards (IFRS): The Case of Vietnam. *The Global Review of Accounting and Finance, 5*(1), 132-152.

Phan, D., Mascitelli, B., & Barut, M. (2014, March). Perceptions Towards International Financial Reporting Standards (IFRS): The Case of Vietnam. *Global Review of Accounting and Finance.*, *5*(1), 132–152.

Pielichaty, E. (2008). Skutki przekwalifikowania instrumentów finansowych w wyniku zmiany intencji inwestora w świetle Międzynarodowych Standardów Rachunkowości. *Zeszyty Teoretyczne Rachunkowości*, *44*, 173–183.

Piketty, T. (2014). *Capital in the Twenty First Century.* Harvard University Press. doi:10.4159/9780674369542

Ping, L. (2007). Transfer Pricing and Customs Valuation: Exploring Convergence. *Global Trade and Customs Journal*, *2*(3), 117–128.

Pinkivskiy, M., & Sala-i-Martin, X. (2014). Africa is on time. *Journal of Economic Growth*, *19*(3), 311–333. doi:10.1007/s10887-014-9103-y

Platikanova, P., & Perramon, J. (2009). *Economic consequences of the first-time IFRS introduction in Europe.* Working Paper. Available at SSRN: http://ssrn.com/abstract=1005364

Pope, P., & McLeay, S. (2011). The European IFRS Experiment: Objectives, Research, Challenges and some early Evidence. *Accounting and Business Review*, *41*(3), 233–266. doi:10.1080/00014788.2011.575002

Portes, R., & Rey, H. (2005). The determinants of cross-border equity flows. *Journal of International Economics*, *65*(2), 269–296. doi:10.1016/j.jinteco.2004.05.002

Prather-Kinsey, J., Jermakowicz, E., & Vongphanith, T. (2008). *Capital Market Consequences of European Firms Mandatory Adoption of IFRS.* Presented at the annual Meeting of the American Accounting Association, Anaheim, CA.

Princeton. (2007). *Panel Data Analysis Fixed and Random Effects using Stata* (v. 4.2). Retrieved from http://www.princeton.edu/~otorres/Panel101.pdf

Private Securities Litigation Reform Act of 1995. (n.d.). Retrieved from www.cga.ct.gov/2002.rpt.2002-R-0695.htm

Prochazka, D. & Ilinitchi, C. P. (2011). The Theoretical Relationships among Foreign Direct Investments, Migration and IFRS Adoption. *European Financial and Accounting Journal, 2011*(4), 85-100.

Prochazka, D., & Pelak, J. (2015). Impact of IFRS Adoption on Capital Markets of the New EU Countries. In *Finance and Performance of Firms in Science, Education and Practice.* Zlín: T. Bata University, FAME. Retrieved from: http://ufu.utb.cz/konference/sbornik2015.pdf)

Prochazka, D. (2014). The IFRS as Tax Base: Potential Impact on a Small Open Economy. *European Financial and Accounting Journal*, *9*(4), 59–75.

Prochazka, D., & Ilinitchi, C. P. (2011). The Theoretical Relationships among Foreign Direct Investments, Migration and IFRS Adoption. *European Financial and Accounting Journal*, *4*, 85–100.

Prochazka, D., & Ilinitchi, C. P. (2012). Is any connection between the IFRS adoption and foreign direct investments/migration? *AMIS*, *2012*, 903–917.

Punda, P. (2011). *The impact of international financial reporting standards (IFRS) adoption on key financial ratios – Evidence from the UK.* (Master's Thesis). Aarhus School of Business.

Purvis, S. E. C., Gernon, H., & Diamond, M. A. (1991). The IASC and its Comparability Project Prerequisites for Success. *Accounting Horizons*, *5*(2), 25–44.

Quartey, P., & Afful-Mensah, G. (2014), Foreign Aid to Africa: Flows, Patterns and Impact. In Oxford Handbook of Africa and Economics: Policies and Practices (vol. 2). Oxford University Press.

Qu, X., & Zhang, G. (2010). Measuring the Convergence of National Accounting Standards with International Financial Reporting Standards: The Application of Fuzzy Clustering Analysis. *The International Journal of Accounting*, *45*(3), 334–355. doi:10.1016/j.intacc.2010.06.008

Radebaugh, L. H., & Gray, S. J. (2002). International Accounting & Multinational Enterprises (5th ed.). Hermitage Publishing Services.

Rahman, M. Z. (2000). *Accounting Standards in the East Asia Region*. Paper presented to the Second Asian Roundtable on Corporate Governance "The Role of Disclosure in Strengthening Corporate Governance and Accountability", Hong Kong.

Rahman, A. R., Ng, L. W., & Tower, G. D. (1994). Public Choice and Accounting Standard Setting in New Zealand: An Exploratory Study. *Abacus*, *30*(1), 98–117. doi:10.1111/j.1467-6281.1994.tb00345.x

Rahman, A., Perera, H., & Ganesh, S. (2002). Accounting Practice Harmony, Accounting Regulation and Firm Characteristics. *Abacus*, *38*(1), 46–77. doi:10.1111/1467-6281.00097

Rajan, R., & Zingales, L. (1998). Financial dependence and growth. *The American Economic Review*, 559–586.

Ramanna, K., & Sletten, E. (2009). Why do countries adopt International Financial Reporting Standards? Harvard Business School 09-102.

Ramanna, K., & Sletten, E. (2009). *Why do countries adopt International Financial Reporting Standards?* Harvard Business School Working Paper 09(10).

Ramanna, K., & Sletten, E. (2009). *Why do countries adopt International Financial Reporting Standards?* Harvard Business School Working Paper, 9-102.

Ramanna, K., & Sletten, E. (2009). *Why do countries adopt international financial reporting standards?* Working Paper. Harvard Business School.

Ramanna, K., & Sletten, E. (2009). *Why do countries adopt international financial reporting standards?*. Harvard Business School Accounting and Management Unit Working Paper No. 09-102.

Ramos, L. M. (2008). *The Effect of IFRS Adoption on Trade and Foreign Direct Investments.* International Trade and Finance Association Working Paper No. 19.

Ramos, L. M. (2010). *European Accounting Harmonization: Consequences of IFRS Adoption on Trade in Goods and Foreign Direct Investments.* Retrieved from: www.alde.es/encuentros/anteriores/xiiieea/trabajos/pdf/046.pdf

Raseroka, K. (2008). Information transformation Africa: Indigenous knowledge – Securing space in the knowledge society. *The International Information & Library Review*, *40*(4), 243–250. doi:10.1080/10572317.2008.10762789

Rawashdeh, M. (2003). Effects of Introducing International Accounting Standards on Amman Stock Exchange. *Journal of American Academy of Business*, *3*(1-2), 361–366.

Reinhart, C., & Rogoff, K. (2009). *The Aftermath of Financial Crises.* National Bureau of Economic Research Working Paper 14656.

Reis, L. G., Shimamoto, L. S., & Barrios, R. A. (2010) *Convergência às normas internacionais de contabilidade: Uma análise sob a perspectiva dos profissionais contabilistas.* 15a Convenção Estadual dos Contabilistas.

Riahi-Belkaoui, A. (2000). Accounting Theory (4th ed.). London: Business Press.

Riro, G., Waweru, N., & Uliana, E. O. (in press). Quality of financial reporting: Case Studies from an emerging market. *Afro Asian Journal of Finance and Accounting.*

Robert, C. (2011). *The Financial Crisis Report- US government.* Retrieved from www.gpo.gov/fdsys/pkg/GPO-FCIC/pdf/GPO-FCIC.pd

Rodrigues, L. L., & Craig, R. (2007). Assessing international accounting harmonization using Hegelian dialectic, isomorphism and Foucault. *Critical Perspectives on Accounting, 18*(6), 739–757.

Roe, J. (2014). Transition from US GAAP to IFRS: Analysis of impact on income tax administration in USA. *European Financial and Accounting Journal, 9*(4), 86–109.

Rogoff, K. (2014). *Foreign-Aid Follies.* Project Syndicate. Retrieved from https://www.projectsyndicate.org/commentary/kenneth-rogoff-urges-caution-in-helping-poor-countries-todevelop

Rohwer, A. (2009). *Measuring Corruption: A Comparison between the Transparency International's Corruption Perception Index and the World Bank's Worldwide Governance Indicators.* CESifo DICE Research Report 3/2009. Retrieved September 6 2014 from: https://www.cesifo-group.de/portal/pls/portal/docs/1/1192926.PDF

Rolfe, R. J., & Woodward, D. P. (2004). Attracting foreign investment through privatization: The Zambian experience. *Journal of African Business, 5*(1), 5–27. doi:10.1300/J156v05n01_02

ROSC. (2010). *Report on the Observance of Standards and Codes (ROSC) on Kenya Accounting and Auditing Standards.* Washington, DC: World Bank.

ROSC. (2011). *Report on the observance of standard and codes (Nigeria), accounting and auditing.* World Bank.

ROSC. (2014). *Report on the Observance of Standards and Codes (ROSC) on Uganda Accounting and Auditing Standards.* Washington, DC: World Bank.

Ross, S. A. (1977). The determination of financial structure: The incentive signaling approach. *The Bell Journal of Economics, 8*(Spring), 23–40. doi:10.2307/3003485

Ryba, A. (2011). Zmiana metody wyceny środków trwałych zgodnie z Międzynarodowymi Standardami Sprawozdawczości Finansowej a porównywalność sprawozdań finansowych. *Zeszyty Teoretyczne Rachunkowości, 60*, 251–264.

Saidi, F. (2013). Accounting Developments in Algeria: The Road to IFRS. *International Research Journal of Applied Finance, 4*, 124–142.

Salter, B. S., & Niswander, F. (1995). Cultural Influence on the Development of Accounting Systems Internationally: A Test of Gray's (1998) Theory. *Journal of International Business Studies, 26*(2), 379 – 397.

Salter, S. (1998). Corporate financial disclosure in emerging markets: Does economic development matter? *The International Journal of Accounting, 33*(2), 211–234. doi:10.1016/S0020-7063(98)90027-9

Samra, R., Bottle, A., & Aylin, P. (2015). Monitoring patient safety in primary care: An exploratory study using in-depth semistructured interviews. *BMJ Open, 5*(9), e008128. doi:10.1136/bmjopen-2015-008128 PMID:26362663

Samuels, J.M., & Oliga, J.C. (1982). Accounting standards in developing countries. *International Journal of Accounting Education and Research*, (Fall), 69-88.

Sanada, M. (2012). *Legitimacy of Global Accounting Standards: A New Analytical Framework*. Academic Press.

Sartawi, I. S. M., Hindawi, R. M., Bsoul, R., & Jamil Ali, A. (2014). Board Composition, Firm characteristics, and voluntary disclosure: The case of Jordanian firms listed on the Amman stock exchange. *International Business Research*, *7*(6), 67–82. doi:10.5539/ibr.v7n6p67

Saudagaran, S. M. (2004). *International Accounting: A user perspective*. USA Globus Printing Inc.

Sawani, A. (2009). The Changing Accounting Environment: International Accounting Standards and US implementation. *Journal of Finance and Accountancy*, *1*(August), 1–9.

Schipper, K. (2005). The Introduction of International Accounting Standards in Europe: Implications for International Convergence. *European Accounting Review*, *14*(1), 101–126. doi:10.1080/0963818042000338013

Schroll, R. (1995). The new accounting system in the Czech Republic. *European Accounting Review*, *4*(4), 827–832. doi:10.1080/09638189500000052

Shima, K. M., & Yang, D. C. (2012). Factors affecting IFRS adoption. *International Journal of Business*, *17*(3), 276–298.

Shima, K. M., & Yang, D. C. (2012). Factors affecting the adoption of IFRS. *International Journal of Business*, *17*(3), 276–298.

Sikka, P., & Willmott, H. (2010). The dark side of transfer pricing: Its role in tax avoidance and wealth retentiveness. *Critical Perspectives on Accounting*, *21*(4), 342–356. doi:10.1016/j.cpa.2010.02.004

Silva, R. L. M. D. (2013). *Adoção completa das IFRS no Brasil: Qualidade das demonstrações contábeis e o custo de capital próprio*. (Doctoral dissertation). University of São Paulo, São Paulo, Brazil.

Silva, F. J., DoCouto, G. M., & Cordeiro, R. M. (2009). Measuring the impact of international financial reporting standards (IFRS) to financial information of Portuguese companies RevistaUniversoContábil. *Blumenau*, *5*(1), 129–144.

Silva, P. C., Weffort, E. F. J., Peters, M. R. S., & Cia, J. N. S. (2010). *Impacto da adoção das IFRS nas empresas Brasileiras de saneamento: A percepção dos profissionais do setor*. Belo Horizonte, Brazil: Revista Contabilidade Vista & Revista, Universidade Federal de Minas Gerais.

Singhvi, S. S., & Desai, H. B. (1971). An empirical analysis of the quality of corporate financial disclosure. *Accounting Review*, *46*(1), 129–138.

Sobańska, I., & Michalak, M. (2009). Wykorzystanie informacji prospektywnych w sprawozdawczości finansowej zorientowanej na wartość na przykładzie MSR 36 Utrata wartości aktywów. *Zeszyty Teoretyczne Rachunkowości*, (53), 219-237.

Soderstrom, N. S., & Sun, K. J. (2007, December1). IFRS Adoption and Accounting Quality: A Review. *European Accounting Review*, *16*(4), 675–702. doi:10.1080/09638180701706732

Song, J., & Windram, B. (2004). Benchmarking audit committee effectiveness in financial reporting. *International Journal of Auditing*, *8*(3), 195–205. doi:10.1111/j.1099-1123.2004.00090.x

Souza, A. A. S., & Coutinho Filho, F. B. (2007). *Harmonização Internacional: Um estudo sobre as dificuldades de convergência das normas contábeis brasileiras em relação às normas internacionais de contabilidade (IFRS)*. 7th Congresso USP de Controladoria e Contabilidade.

Srijunpetch, S. (2004). *The Implementation of International Accounting Standards in Thailand.* (Unpublished PhD Thesis). The University of Manchester, Manchester, UK.

Stainbank, L. J. (2014). Factors influencing the adoption of International Financial Reporting Standards by African countries. *SA Journal of Accounting Research, 28*(1), 79–95.

Standish, P. (2003). Evaluating capacity for direct participation in international accounting harmonisation: France as a test case. *Abacus, 39*(2), 186–210. doi:10.1111/1467-6281.00126

Stenka, R., Ormrod, P., & Chan, A. (2008) *Accounting for business combinations – the consequences of IFRS adoption for UK listed entities.* Working paper, SSRN.

Stergios, A., Vazakidis, A., & Dritsakis, N. (2004). *Financial statement effects of adopting international accounting standards.* Working Paper Series, University of Macedonia. Retrieved from http://users.uom.gr/~drits/publications/Financial_Statement_Effects.pdf

Stiglitz, J. E., (2007). *Making Globalization Work.* W. W. Norton & Company.

Stiglitz, J. E. (2002). *Globalization and its Discontents.* New York.

Stiglitz, J. E. (2010). *Freefall: America, free markets, and the sinking of the world economy.* WW Norton & Company.

Street, D. L., & Gray, S. J. (1999). How Wide Is the Gap Between IASC and U.S. GAAP? Impact of IASC Comparability Project and Recent International Developments. *Journal of International Accounting, Auditing & Taxation, 8*(1).

Street, D. L. (2002). GAAP 2001: Benchmarking national accounting standards against IAS: Summary of results. *Journal of International Accounting, Auditing & Taxation, 11*(1), 77–90. doi:10.1016/S1061-9518(02)00055-1

Street, D. L., & Gray, S. J. (2002). Factors Influencing the Extent of Corporate Compliance with International Accounting Standards: Summary of a Research Monograph. *Journal of International Accounting, Auditing & Taxation, 11*(1), 51–76. doi:10.1016/S1061-9518(02)00054-X

Strouhal, J. (2011). *Harmonization of SME's Financial Reporting in Emerging CEE Countries* (1st ed.). Wisconsin: WSEAS.

Sucher, P., & Jindrichovska, I. (2004). Implementing IFRS: a case study of the Czech Republic. *Accounting in Europe, 1*, 109–141.

Suchman, M. C. (1995). Managing Legitimacy: Strategic and Insititutional Approaches. *Academy of Management Review, 20*(3), 571–610.

Sun, K. (2006). *Financial reporting quality, capital allocation efficiency, and financing structure: An international study.* Working Paper. University of Hawaii at Manoa.

Swenson, C., & Lee, N. (2009). How Will IFRS Affect Accounting for Income Taxes? *Corporate Taxation Insider.* Available from: http://www.cpa2biz.com/Content/media/PRODUCER_CONTENT/Newsletters/

Tabachnick, B. G., & Fidell, L. S. (1996). *Using multivariate statistics.* New York: HarperCollins.

Taiwo, F. H., & Adejare, A. T. (2014). Empirical analysis of the effect of international financial reporting standard (IFRS) adoption on accounting practices in Nigeria. *Archives of Business Research, 2*(2), 1–14. doi:10.14738/abr.22.43

Tan, H., Wang, S., & Welker, M. (2009). *Foreign Analyst Following and Forecast Accuracy around Mandated IFRS Adoptions.* Working Paper. Available at: http://www.bus.wisc.edu/accounting/faculty/documents/PaperMikeWelker17-09.pdf

Tandy, P. R., & Wilburn, N. L. (1992). Constituent Participation in Standard setting: The FASB's first 100 Statements. *Accounting Horizons*, (June): 47–58.

Tang, L., & Koveos, P. E. (2008). A Framework to Update Hofstede's Cultural Value Indices: Economic Dynamics and Institutional Stability. *Journal of International Business Studies*, *39*(6), 1045–1063. doi:10.1057/palgrave.jibs.8400399

Tanko, M. (2012). The effect of international financial reporting standards (IFRS) adoption on the performance of firms in Nigeria. *Journal of Administration and Economic Sciences*, *5*(2), 133–157.

Tanzi, V. (2000). *Globalization, technological developments, and the work of fiscal termites.* IMF Working Paper No. 00/181. Washington, DC: IMF.

Tarca, A. (2012). *The Case for Global Accounting Standards - Arguments and Evidence.* Academic Press.

Tarca, A. (2012). *The Case for Global Accounting Standards: Arguments and Evidence.* Available at SSRN: http://ssrn.com/abstract=2204889

Tarca, A. (2004). International convergence of accounting practices: Choosing between IAS and US GAAP. *Journal of International Financial Management and Accounting*, *15*(1), 60–91. doi:10.1111/j.1467-646X.2004.00102.x

Tasios, S., & Bekiaris, M. (2012). Auditor's perceptions of financial reporting quality: The case of Greece. *International Journal of Accounting and Financial Reporting*, *2*(1), 57–74. doi:10.5296/ijafr.v2i1.1286

Taylor Zarzeski, M. (1996). Spontaneous harmonization effects of culture and market forces on accounting disclosures practices. *Accounting Horizons*, *10*(1).

Taylor, G., Tower, G., Van Der Zahn, M., & Neilson, J. (2008). Corporate governance determinants on Australian resource companies' financial instrument disclosure practices. *Asian Review of Accounting*, *16*(1), 56–73. doi:10.1108/13217340810872472

Taylor, P., & Turley, S. (1986). *The Regulation of Accounting.* New York: Blackwell Inc.

Tchamyou, S. V. (2014). *The Role of Knowledge Economy in African Business.* (Master Thesis). HEC-Management School, University of Liège.

Terzi, S., Oktem, R., & Sen, I. K. (2013). Impact of adopting international financial reporting standards: Empirical evidence from Turkey. *International Business Research*, *6*(4), 55–66. doi:10.5539/ibr.v6n4p55

Thomas, M. A. (2010). What do the World Governance Indicators Measure? *European Journal of Development Research*, *22*(1), 31–54. doi:10.1057/ejdr.2009.32

Thorell, P., & Whittington, G. (1994). The harmonization of accounting within the EU: Problems, perspectives and strategies. *European Accounting Review*, *3*(2), 215–240. doi:10.1080/09638189400000019

Toborek-Mazur, J. (2014). Wpływ koncepcji konsolidacji sprawozdań finansowych na zmiany w międzynarodowych standardach rachunkowości. *Zeszyty Teoretyczne Rachunkowości*, *76*(76(132)), 89–114. doi:10.5604/16414381.1108293

Tower, G. (1993). A Public Accountability Model of Accounting Regulation. *The British Accounting Review*, *25*(1), 61–85. doi:10.1006/bare.1993.1006

Tsakumis, G. T. (2007). The Influence of Culture on Accountants' Application of Financial Reporting Rules. *Abacus*, *43*(1), 27–48. doi:10.1111/j.1467-6281.2007.00216.x

Tsalavoutas, I., & Evans, L. (2010). Transition to IFRS in Greece: Financial statement effects and auditor size. *Managerial Auditing Journal*, *25*(8), 814–842. doi:10.1108/02686901011069560

Tsikata, G. K., Asante, Y., & Gyasi, E. M. (2000). *Determinants of Foreign Direct Investment in Ghana*. Overseas Development Institute.

Tweedie, D. (2009). Sir David Tweedie Takes On IFRS. *AICPA Corporate Finance Insider*. Retrieved from http://www.ifrs.com/overview/general_listing.html

Tweedie, D., & Seidensttein, T. (2005). Setting a global standard: The case for Accounting Convergence. *Northwestern Journal of International Law and Business*, *25*(3), 589.

Tyrrall, D., Woodward, D., & Rakhimbekova, A. (2007). The relevance of International Financial Reporting Standards to a developing country: Evidence from Kazakhstan. *The International Journal of Accounting*, *42*(1), 82–110. doi:10.1016/j.intacc.2006.12.004

Uddin, S., & Tsamenyi, M. (2010). *Research in Accounting in Emerging Economies*. Emerald Group Publishing Limited.

UK Home Office. (1998). *Review of financial regulation in the crown dependencies*. London: The Stationery Office.

Ukpai, N. A. (2002). The Snag in International Accounting Transactions. *Journal of Accountancy*, *3*(6), 214–222.

Umoren, A. O., & Enang, E. R. (2015). IFRS adoption and value relevance of financial statements of Nigerian listed banks. *International Journal of Finance and Accounting*, *4*(1), 1–7.

Umoren, A. O., & Enang, E. R. (2015). IFRS adoption and value relevance of financial statements of Nigerian listed banks. *International Journal of Finance and Accounting.*, *4*(1), 1–7.

UNCTAD. (2005). *Economic Development In Africa: Rethinking The Role Of Foreign Direct Investment*. Retrieved from http://siteresources.worldbank.org/INTANNREP2K5/Resources/51563_English.pdf

UNCTAD. (2006). *Review of Practical Implementation Issues Of International Financial Reporting Standards - Case Study In Kenya*. Washington, DC: UNCTAD. Retrieved from www.unctad.org/en/docs/c2isard37_en.pdf

UNCTAD. (2009). *Nigerian investment policy*. Author.

UNCTAD. (2009). World Investment Report 2009. Geneva, Switzerland: UNCTAD.

UNCTAD. (2014). *Report on human capacity development in accounting and corporate reporting*. Retrieved from http://www.iasplus.com/en/news/2014/05/unctad

United Nation Conference on Trade and Development (UNCTAD). (2008). *Conference proceedings held in New York and Geneva*. Author.

US Government Accountability Office. (2008). *Cayman islands: business and tax advantages attract U.S. persons and enforcement challenges exist. GAO Report to the Chairman and Ranking Member, Committee on Finance*. Washington, DC: U.S. Senate.

Utomi, P. (1998). *Managing uncertainty. Competition and strategy in emerging economies*. Ibadan, Nigeria: Spectrum Books LTD.

VACPA & CAPA. (2012). The Vital Role of Professional Accountancy Organisations. *The Vital Role of Professional Accountancy Organisations*. Vietnam Association of Certified Public Accountants (VACPA) and Confederation of Asian and Pacific Accountants (CAPA).

Van Lent, L. (1997). Pressure and Politics in Financial Accounting Regulation: The Case of the Financial Conglomerates in the Netherlands. *Abacus*, *33*(1), 88–114. doi:10.1111/1467-6281.00005

Van Tendeloo, B., & Vanstraelen, A. (2005). Earnings management under German GAAP versus IFRS. *European Accounting Review*, *14*(1), 155–180. doi:10.1080/0963818042000338988

VCCI. (2011). *ACCA - A Strategic Partner of Vietnam in Developing Local Accounting and Audit Profession to Global Standards*. Vietnam Business Forum.

Velayutham, S. (1996). Corporatization and the Regulation of Accounting Services. *The British Accounting Review*, *28*(4), 351–368. doi:10.1006/bare.1996.0023

Vellam, I. (2012). *The adoption of IFRS in Poland: an institutional approach*. (PhD Thesis). University of Greenwich.

Vellam, I. (2004). Implementation of International Accounting Standards in Poland: Can True Convergence be achieved in Practice? *Accounting in Europe*, *1*(1), 143–167. doi:10.1080/0963818042000262784

Veron, N. (2007). *The Global Accounting Experiment*. Brussels: Bruegel Blue Print Series.

Verrecchia, R. (1983). Discretionary disclosure. *Journal of Accounting and Economics*, *5*, 179–194. doi:10.1016/0165-4101(83)90011-3

Veselinovic, M. (2015). Rich getting richer, poor getting poorer? Africa's inequality struggle. *CNN Africa View*. Retrieved from http://edition.cnn.com/2015/05/12/africa/africa-inequality/

Vo, V. T. H. (2014). *Follow-up on the Accounting Development Tool (ADT) - Enhancing Vietnam's capacity for producing high-quality corporate reports*. Paper presented at the Intergovernmental Working Group of Experts on International Standards of Accounting and Reporting (ISAR), Palais des Nations, Geneva.

Vo, V. T. H. (2014). *Follow-up on the Accounting Development Tool (ADT) - Enhancing Vietnam's capacity for producing high-quality corporate reports*. Geneva: ISAR.

Wallace, R. S. (1993). Development of Accounting Standards for Developing and Newly Industrialized Countries. *Research in Third World Accounting, 2*, 121-165.

Wallace, R. S. O., Naser, K., & Mora, A. (1995). The relationship between the comprehensiveness of corporate annual reports and firm characteristics in Spain. *Accounting and Business Review*, *25*(97), 41–53. doi:10.1080/00014788.1994.9729927

Walsh, B. (2015, August). The International Tax System is 'Repulsive And Inequitable.' Here's A Way To Fix It. *Huffpost Politics*. Retrieved from http://www.huffingtonpost.com/entry/multinational-corporations-taxes_55d4baede4b055a6dab265d9

Wang, K., Sewon, O., & Claiborne, C. (2008). Determinants and consequences of voluntary disclosure in an emerging market: Evidence from China. *Journal of International Accounting, Auditing & Taxation*, *17*(1), 14–30. doi:10.1016/j.intaccaudtax.2008.01.001

Wang, Y., & Campbell, M. (2012). Corporate governance, earnings management, and IFRS: Empirical evidence from Chinese domestically listed companies. *Advances in Accounting, Incorporating. Advances in International Accounting*, *28*(1), 189–192. doi:10.1016/j.adiac.2012.03.007

Waniak-Michalak, H., Czajor, P., & Michalak, J. (2012). *Impact of mandatory IFRS implementation on earnings quality. Evidence from the Warsaw Stock Exchange*. World Value Survey. Retrieved from http://www.worldvaluessurvey.org/

Watson, A., Shrives, P., & Marston, C. (2002). Voluntary disclosure of accounting ratios in the UK. *The British Accounting Review*, *34*(4), 289–313. doi:10.1006/bare.2002.0213

Watts, J. (1993). *Accounting in the Business Environment*. London: Pitman Publishing.

Weber, R. P. (1986). *Basic content analysis, quantitative applications in the social sciences* (Vol. 49). Sage Publications.

Weetman, P., Davie, E. S., & Collins, W. (1996). Lobbying on Accounting Issues Preparer/user Imbalance in the Case of the Operating and Financial Review. *Accounting, Auditing & Accountability Journal, 9*(1), 59–76. doi:10.1108/09513579610109978

Wei, Y., Liu, X., Song, H., & Romilly, P. (2001). Endogenous innovation growth theory and regional income convergence in China. *Journal of International Development, 13*(2), 153–170. doi:10.1002/jid.721

Welbenberger, B. E., Stahl, A. B., & Vorstius, S. (2004). Changing from German GAAP to IFRS or US GAAP: A Survey of German Companies. *Accounting in Europe, 1*(1), 169–189. doi:10.1080/0963818042000262748

Whittington, G. (2005). The Adoption of International Accounting Standards in the European Union. *European Accounting Review, 14*(1), 127–153. doi:10.1080/0963818042000338022

Why Poverty. (2013). *Stealing Africa-How much profit is fair?*. Retrieved from https://www.youtube.com/watch?v=WNYemuiAOfU&feature=iv&src_vid=HuBR2IaEkx0&annotation_id=annotation_725881

Williamson, O. E. (2000). The new institutional economics: Taking stock, looking ahead. *Journal of Economic Literature, 38*(3), 595–613. doi:10.1257/jel.38.3.595

Winney, K., Marshall, D., Bender, B., & Swiger, J. (2010). Accounting globalization: Roadblocks to IFRS adoption in the United States. *Global Review of Accounting and Finance, 1*(1), 167–178.

Wong, P. (2004). *Challenges and Successes in Implementing International: Standards Achieving Convergence to IFRSs and IASs*. IFAC -International Federation of Accountants.

Wooly, R. (1998). *International accounting standards and economic growth, an empirical investigation of their relationship in Asia*. Working Paper series Australia: School of Accounting and Law, RMIT.

Word Bank. (2015). *World Development Indicators*. World Bank Publications.

World Bank. (2005). Report on Observance of Standards and Codes. Ghana: World Bank.

World Bank. (2012). *Market economy for a middle-income Vietnam*. Joint Donor Report to the Vietnam Consultative Group Meeting.

World Bank. (2015). *Reports on the Observance of Standards & Codes. Topics: Accounting and auditing*. Retrieved 1 April 2015 from: http://www.worldbank.org/ifa/rosc_aa.html

Wyatt, A., & Yospe, J. (1993). Wake-up Call to American Business: International Accounting Standards are on the Way. *Journal of Accountancy*, 80–85.

Wysocki, P. (2011). New Institutional Accounting and IFRS. *Accounting and Business Review, 41*(3), 309–328. doi:10.1080/00014788.2011.575298

Xiao, J. Z., Weetman, P., & Sun, M. (2004). Political influence and coexistence of a uniform accounting system and accounting standards: Recent developments in China. *Abacus, 40*(2), 194–218.

Yanesari, A., Gerayli, M., Ma'atoofi, A., & Abadi, A. (2012). Board characteristics and corporate voluntary disclosure: An Iranian perspective. *Archives des Sciences, 64*(5), 478–484.

Yip, R. W., & Young, D. (2012). Does mandatory IFRS adoption improve information comparability? *Accounting Review, 87*(5), 1767–1789. doi:10.2308/accr-50192

Young, A. (2012). The African growth miracle. *Journal of Political Economy, 120*(4), 696–739. doi:10.1086/668501

Young, D., & Guenther, D. (2002). Financial reporting environments and international capital mobility. *Journal of Accounting Research, 41*(3), 553–579. doi:10.1111/1475-679X.00116

Zakari, M. I. (2010). *IFRS as a tool for cross-border financial reporting*. A paper presented at the Institute of Chartered Accountants of Nigeria (ICAN) conference on IFRS in Lagos.

Zarova, M., & Mejzlik, L. (2009). Have IFRS Positive Impact on the Regulatory Accounting Systems in Continental European Countries? *European Financial and Accounting Journal, 2009*(1), 5-24.

Zarova, M. (2008). Accounting Reform in the Czech Republic. In R. W. McGee (Ed.), *Accounting Reform in Transition and Developing Economies* (pp. 89–100). Miami, FL: Springer.

Zarova, M., Prochazka, D., & Roe, J. (2010). *Financial reporting and management in Central and Eastern Europe*. Praha: Nakladatelství Oeconomica.

Zayyad, A., Ahmad, U. B., & Mubaraq, S. (2014). Financial ratios as performance measure: A comparison of IFRS and Nigerian GAAP. *Accounting and Management Information Systems, 13*(1), 82–97.

Zeff, S. (2007). Some obstacles to global financial reporting comparability and Convergence at a high Level of quality. *The British Accounting Review, 39*(4), 290–302. doi:10.1016/j.bar.2007.08.001

Zeff, S. A. (1978). The rise of economic consequences. *Journal of Accountancy*, 56–63.

Zeff, S. A. (2002). Political Lobbying on Proposed Standards: A Challenge to the IASB. *Accounting Horizons, 16*(1), 43–54. doi:10.2308/acch.2002.16.1.43

Zeghal, D., & Mhedhbi, K. (2006). *An analysis of the factors affecting the adoption of international accounting standards by developing countries*. University of Illinois.

Zeghal, D., & Mhedhbi, K. (2006). An analysis of the factors affecting the adoption of international accounting standards by developing countries. *The International Journal of Accounting, 41*(4), 373–386. doi:10.1016/j.intacc.2006.09.009

Zehr, C., & Abdelbaki, A. (2013). Does adoption of international accounting standards promote economic growth in developing countries? *International Open Journal of Economics, 1*(1), 1-13. Available online at http://acascipub.com/Journals.php

Zehri, F., & Chouaibi, J. (2013). Adoption determinants of the international accounting standards IAS/IFRS by the developing countries. *Journal of Economics. Finance and Administrative Science, 18*(35), 56–62. doi:10.1016/S2077-1886(13)70030-1

Zhou, H., Xiong, Y., & Ganguli, G. (2009). Does The Adoption Of International Financial Reporting Standards Restrain Earnings Management? Evidence from an Emerging Market. *Academy of Accounting and Financial Studies Journal, 13*, 43–56.

Zikmund, W. G. (2010). *Business Research Methods* (6th ed.). Fort Worth, TX: Harcourt College Publisher.

Zimnicki, T., & Sojak, S. (2008). Wartość dodana sprawozdań finansowych wynikająca z ujawnienia segmentów działalności według MSR 14. *Zeszyty Teoretyczne Rachunkowości, 46*, 135–163.

About the Contributors

Matthias Nnadi is a lecturer at Cranfield University School of Management.

Sailesh Tanna is Principal Lecturer at Coventry University.

* * *

Ben Kwame Agyei-Mensah is a Chartered Management Accountant and a member of the Chartered Institute of Management Accountants, (CIMA), U.K. and also holds a doctorate degree in business administration (DBA) from SMC university of Switzerland. His MBA is from Paris Graduate School of Management, France. He has 9 years university teaching experience covering both undergraduate and post graduate levels. He is currently an associate professor in Accounting and Finance at Solbridge international School of Business, in Korea. He teaches accounting and finance at both undergraduate and Master's level. Prior to moving to Korea, he held faculty positions in several universities in Ghana. He also has experience in supervising student theses at undergraduate, masters, and PhD levels. He has several years' industrial experience as an accountant with several companies in Ghana. His research interest covers management accounting, financial reporting and financial management. As a prolific researcher he has research papers published in international journals such as; Social Science Research Network (SSRN), African Journal of Business Management, International Journal of Academic Research in Business and Social Sciences, Journal of Applied Finance and Banking, International Journal of Accounting and Financial Reporting.

Christopher Boachie is a lecturer of Central Business School, Central University College in Ghana, an academic and a practising Chartered Accountant (ACCA-UK) with specialization in corporate finance, international trade, auditing, financial statement fraud and financial risk management. He was educated in Kwame Nkrumah University of Science and Technology in Kumasi Ghana, Technical University of Freiberg in Germany and the London School of Accountancy (UK). He is currently reading his PhD at Open University of Malaysia. He has considerable, teaching, consulting and practise experience in the application of accountancy and finance theory and risk management.

Phan Thi Hong Duc, PhD, is a Certified Practicing Accountant and a Lecturer/Course Coordinator at RMIT University Vietnam. Prior to RMIT, Duc taught and conducted research at different universities in Vietnam and Australia, including Swinburne University of Technology (SUT), University of Economics and Law (UEL), Vietnam-German University (VGU), International Education Institute (IEI), Vietnam National University (VNU). Before joining academia, Duc had over 15 years of working experiences in accounting, finance, banking, consulting areas for KPMG, National Australia Bank, World Bank Group and many other public and private enterprises. Duc holds a PhD on the topic of international accounting standards from Swinburne University, Melbourne, Australia. Her research works have been published in reputable international accounting journals including Research in Accounting Regulation, Contemporary Issues in Business and Government, Global Review of Accounting and Finance. Duc has been a recipient of several research grants. She is also a peer-reviewer of some reputable academic journal specialised in accounting issues in Asian region.

Essa R. El-Firjani is a Senior lecturer at Tripoli University.

Shamsaddeen M. Faraj is a Senior lecturer at the AL-Gabal AL-Garbi University Accounting Faculty in Libya. Dr. Faraj graduated from the University of Liverpool in the UK and has publications in national and international Journals. He is a member of the British Accounting and Finance Association BAFA. He also has participated in international accounting conferences.

Cecilia Moraes Santostaso Geron is PhD student in Accounting by São Paulo University. Obtained the Accounting Master in 2008 and graduated in Accounting in 1989 by São Paulo University. She is director in ANEFAC - National Association of Executives in Finance, Administration and Accounting in Brazil at Board International Accounting Standards. She is professor of Professional Masters in Accounting and researcher in Mackenzie Presbyterian University since 2014. She has expertise in international accounting, which is her main teaching and research interests. She has published articles in periodicals and conference proceedings She is partner of the Praesum International Accounting since February 1995, working in accounting advice of multinational companies like Rhodia, Monsanto, Microsoft, Rolls-Royce and APC.

Marta Cristina Pelucio Grecco is PhD in Business Administration by Mackenzie Presbyterian University. Obtained the Accounting Master in 2002 and graduated in Accounting in 1989 by São Paulo University. She is certified in IFRS by ACCA in 2010. She is attended the course: International Management Program by EUROMED in Marseille – France in 2006. She is executive director in ANEFAC - National Association of Executives in Finance, Administration and Accounting in Brazil at Board International Accounting Standards. She is professor of Professional Masters in Accounting and researcher in Mackenzie Presbyterian University since 2008. She has expertise in international accounting, which is her main teaching and research interests. She has published articles in periodicals and conference proceedings She is partner of the Praesum International Accounting since February 1995, working in accounting advice of multinational companies like Rhodia, Monsanto, Microsoft, Rolls-Royce and APC.

Irena Jindrichovska received her MSc and PhD in Economics from the University of Economics in Prague. She was a researcher in the Social and Economics Institute of the Czech Academy of Science. She worked as an internal auditor at Société Générale bank Prague. Subsequently she lectured finance and accounting at Charles University in Prague. After moving to Great Britain, she worked at the University of Wales, Aberytszwyth and at the University of Buckingham. She is now involved with teaching at the Institute of Hospitality Management in and the Anglo-American University in Prague. She works with the Association of Accountants, ACCA and CFA. Apart from lecturing she devotes her academic capacity to research in accounting and economics.

Mahesh Joshi is Senior Lecturer in Accounting in the School of Accounting at RMIT University in Melbourne, Australia. He has around 25 years of teaching experience in Australia and India. Before joining RMIT University, he has worked in different capacities at Central Queensland University and Swinburne University in Australia, and constituents of Punjab University and Punjabi University in India. His major teaching and research interests are in the areas of international Financial Reporting Standards, Intellectual Capital Reporting and Valuation and Accounting Education. His work has been published in high quality international journals, conference proceedings and book chapters.

Marcin Kędzior, PhD, Education 1996 - 2002 Cracow University of Economics, Faculty of Management, specializing in accounting 2000 - 2001 Fachhochschule Pforzheim / Germany, semester in English 2000 - 2000 series of lectures in English / Cracow University of Economics 1999 Exchange Students / Wirtschaftsuniversität Wien, Austria Achievements. Marcin Kędzior has publications on the Philadelphia list as well as in magazines with international indexation, numerous Rector's Awards, Cracow University of Economics for scientific, organizational and teaching achievements, Gold, Silver Awards /Polish Accounting Association /PAA Main Board in Warsaw, as well as awards and prizes at scientific conferences. Experience includes 2009 - 2015 Official Delegate of PAA in EFAA (the European Federation of Accountants and Auditors for SMEs), Education Expert Group and Accounting Expert Group, Brussels 2011 - 2015 Member of the Committee responsible for Cooperation with Foreign Countries, Polish Accounting Association /PAA Main Board in Warsaw 2007 - 2015 Polish Accounting Association, a member of the Board of the Regional Branch in Cracow, Chairman of the Committee responsible for Organization and Development and Chairman of the Committee responsible for Accounting 2003 X - 2015 Cracow University of Economics, Department of Financial Accounting 2003 Airline Accounting Centre / Deutsche Lufthansa A.G. - Accountant 2002 Plus Discount/ Tengelmann A.G./ Controlling Specialist Additional skills Certificates: International Management Certificate, Fachhochschule Pforzheim ZentraleMittelstufenprüfung, the Goethe Institut Languages English – advanced; German - intermediate Interests International accounting and international finance, managerial accounting, sports, travel, movie.

Dana Kubickova is a Graduate of University of Economy, Prague – 1978; PhD - University of Economy, Prague - 1985 (specialisation: Theory of economic education); 1985 - 1992 - University of Economy, Prague - senior lecturer; 1992 - 1997 - Business Academy; 1997 - till now - University of Finance and Administration - senior lecturer, specialisation: Accountancy, International Accounting Standards; 2006-2012 Deputy head of Department of Business Economy; research projects in the area of IFRS and its implementation issues; author of articles, textbooks, professional publications.

Abdulkadir Madawaki, Bsc. Accounting at Usmanu Danfodiyo University, Sokoto, Msc. International Accounting at University Utara, Malaysia, Phd Research Fellow at University Malaya, Malaysia, Lecturer 1 Department of Accounting, Katsina University, Katsina, Nigeria.

Bruno Mascitelli prior to joining academic worked for the Australian Trade Commission (Austrade) based in Milan Italy for almost 18 years. He also worked for the US Commercial Service in Melbourne for a further 2 years. In 2000 he joined Swinburne University of Technology where he teaches and researches in the area of International Business, international migration and European Political economy. His latest book is entitled "the Austrade Story".

J. O. Odia (PhD) is a Senior Lecturer in the Department of Accounting, University of Benin Nigeria. His current research interests include: Adoption of IFRS by developing countries, management accounting change and corporate sustainability.

Koholga Ormin holds BSc, MSc and PhD in Accounting. He is a lecturer with the Department of Accounting, Adamawa State University, Mubi, Nigeria. And currently the Acting Head of Department of Accounting. His research areas of interest include corporate sector financial reporting, accounting theory and thoughts. He has attended conferences and published in several local and international journals. Dr. Koholga Ormin is a pioneer member of the Accounting and Finance Research Association (AFRA).

Erick Outa is adjunct faculty at Strathmore University, researcher and higher education consultant and has been adjunct faculty USIU in Kenya. He has been Deputy Vice Chancellor Finance and Administration, USIU, Chair of Business at Riara University and CFO/Director Sara Lee H& BC Africa among others. He is a member of the Institute of Certified Public Accountants of Kenya, member of the Institute of Directors, member Academy of International Business –Sub Sahara Africa and a member of the Global Corporate Governance Forum. He has published in the areas of IFRS, corporate governance and higher education development. He holds a Doctorate degree in Business Leadership from the University of South Africa and an MBA from the University of Cape Town.

Duc Hong Thi Phan, PhD, is a Certified Practicing Accountant and a Lecturer/Course Coordinator at RMIT University Vietnam. Prior to RMIT, Duc taught and conducted research at different universities in Vietnam and Australia, including Swinburne University of Technology (SUT), University of Economics and Law (UEL), Vietnam-German University (VGU), International Education Institute (IEI), Vietnam National University (VNU). Before joining academia, Duc had over 15 years of working experiences in accounting, finance, banking, consulting areas for KPMG, National Australia Bank, World Bank Group and many other public and private enterprises. Duc holds a PhD on the topic of international accounting standards from Swinburne University, Melbourne, Australia. Her research works have been published in reputable international accounting journals. Duc has been a recipient of several research grants. She is also a peer-reviewer reputable academic journal specialized in accounting issues in Asian region.

Lesley Stainbank is an Emeritus Professor at the University of KwaZulu-Natal. She is currently based at the Durban University of Technology where her focus is on research and supervision of masters and doctoral students. She has a masters degree in financial accounting (M. Com) from the University of Natal and a doctoral degree (D. Com) from the University of South Africa. She is also a Chartered Accountant (South Africa). She has over 30 years experience in teaching financial accounting at all levels, including the masters level, and is a co-author of the textbook A Student's Guide to International Financial Reporting which is widely prescribed in South Africa. Her research interests include differential reporting, corporate governance, and accounting education. She has published in a number of journals including the South African Journal of Accounting Research, Meditari Accountancy Research, Journal of Accounting in Emerging Economies, South African Journal of Economics and Management, and Accounting Education: An International Journal.

Venancio (Ven) Tauringana is a Professor of Accounting and Head of Research and Professional Practice for the Department of Accounting, Finance and Economics in the Faculty of Management, Bournemouth University. He received a Masters' Degree (M.Acc) in International Accounting and Financial Management from the University of Glasgow and a PhD in Accounting from Edinburgh Napier University, Scotland. He is an associate member of the Institute of Environment Management and Assessment (IEMA), Institute of Chartered Secretaries and Administrators (ICSA) and Fellow of the Higher Education Academy (FHEA). His research interests are concentrated in the areas of corporate governance, voluntary disclosures and their consequences, working capital management and environmental reporting. His research has been published in a variety of journals including the British Journal of Management, European Accounting Review, Journal of Accounting, Auditing and Finance, British Accounting Review. He is currently the Vice President of the African Accounting and Finance Association (AAFA). His main teaching expertise is in the areas of Financial Reporting and Environmental reporting.

Nelson Waweru received his PhD in management accounting at the University of Cape Town and is a Professor of Accounting to the School of Administrative Studies, Faculty of Liberal arts and Professional Studies, at York University. Professor Waweru was a lecturer at the University of Nairobi, and a Professor of Accounting and Finance for the United States International University, Africa. He is the author of several published papers. Professor Waweru is a member of the American Accounting Association (AAA), the Institute of Certified Management Accountants of Ontario (CMA), and Chartered Professional Accountants of Ontario (CPA).

Index

S

T

V

W

www.ingramcontent.com/pod-product-compliance
Lightning Source LLC
LaVergne TN
LVHW081250011026
849162LV00006BA/1323
* 9 7 8 1 4 6 6 6 9 8 7 6 5 *